The Rag Street Journal

The Rag Street Journal

The Ultimate Guide to Shopping Thrift and Consignment Stores Throughout the U.S. and Canada

Elizabeth Mason

a.k.a. "The Paper Bag Princess"

AN OWL BOOK

Henry Holt and Company • New York

Photo, page iv: **Nina Ricci Haute Boutique Paris** black silk gown, $125, Concern's Closet, Los Angeles; original cost estimated at $1,800 at Neiman-Marcus. Black over-the-elbow satin gloves, $5, Salvation Army's secret drawer, Toronto. Starburst black rhinestone earrings, $3, Laguna Beach Women's Club rummage sale.

Henry Holt and Company, Inc.
Publishers since 1866
115 West 18th Street
New York, New York 10011

Henry Holt® is a registered
trademark of Henry Holt and Company, Inc.

Published in Canada by Fitzhenry & Whiteside Ltd.,
195 Allstate Parkway, Markham, Ontario L3R 4T8.

Library of Congress Cataloging-in-Publication Data
Mason, Elizabeth.
The rag street journal: the ultimate guide to shopping thrift and
consignment stores throughout the U.S. and Canada/Elizabeth Mason.
—1st Owl ed.
p. cm.
Includes bibliographical references.
"An Owl book."
1. Thrift shops—United States.   2. Thrift shops—Canada.
3. Consignment sale shops—United States.   4. Consignment sale
shops—Canada.   I. Title.
HF5482.4.M37   1995   95-13329
381'.19—dc20   CIP

ISBN 0-8050-3728-4

Henry Holt books are available for special
promotions and premiums. For details contact:
Director, Special Markets.

First Edition—1995

Designed by Paula R. Szafranski

Printed in the United States of America
All first editions are printed on acid-free paper. ∞

1 3 5 7 9 10 8 6 4 2

All photographs copyright © 1995 by Pam Springsteen, except photograph on page 91 by
Struan Campbell-Smith.

The author is in no way associated with or endorsed by Robert Munsch, author of *The Paper Bag Princess*, or Annick Press Ltd., publisher of *The Paper Bag Princess*.

To my dear grandmother,
Agnes Boyd Meiker Purdy

Contents

Acknowledgments

Some people come into our lives, and quickly go.
Some stray for a while, leave footprints
on our hearts, and we are never ever the same.
~Flavia Weedn

This book represents a culmination of a lifetime spent pursuing, pestering, probing, searching, scouting, scrutinizing, elbowing, examining, and emphatically questioning every aspect of secondhand shopping; it is therefore the result of insights, information, and inspiration drawn from many different people. I have sought every possible authoritative source in an effort to make this a truly complete and accurate book, useful in every phase of collecting and selling clothing and accessories.

I'd like to start by thanking all the many thrift store clerks who recognized my gentle "haggling" as my passion for getting the best possible price. And, a warm thanks to the clerk who rang up my very first pair of Chanel shoes for just four dollars!

Now, to the following friends and family I send my love and deepest appreciation with these thoughts:

My brilliant literary manager, mentor, and friend, Dr. Kenneth Atchity, as well as his partner, my inspired New York agent, Jeff Herman, for enduring my tortuous taxi tale.

My faithful editor at Henry Holt, Theresa Burns, for her enthusiasm in unleashing me and my ideas on the world.

To Richard, for finally finding me, and to Michael, for showing him the way.

My devoted and loving family for suffering my interminable tales of thrift store bargains. My mother for passing to me her passion for collecting, and my father for teaching me how to stretch the wrapping paper and a dollar. My grandmother Agnes Mason for blessing this world with her gentleness for ninety-two years and counting. My sister Katherine for lightening my load and my overflowing closets by helping herself to my fabulous castoffs. My twin brother, Derek, for all his support and for allowing me to turn him into a model for the day, and my brothers Ian and Grant for supplying me with a niece and nephews to shower with all of my amusing treasures.

Michael Levine deserves great thanks for rousing me to start a "Thrifting Revolution." Shirley K. Stalker was of inestimable help in proofing the first manuscript and making suggestions for its improvement. Jeff McManus for his help and art direction with photographs. Lisa Prudomme for her holistic care over my mind, body, and soul. Ann Marie Adriansen for appreciating and bolstering my sense of humor and style. Don Nevile-Smith and his son Kevin for their selfless hospitality in Toronto. Margaret McNair and Chinook for their enduring friendship.

My business associates who lent heart, soul, and all their computer equipment, especially Doug Rewers and John Bermel of CI Communications. To Peyman Rashtchi of Supercolor in Laguna Beach, California, my endless gratitude for processing all my film.

Finally, to *all* out there in the vast thrift frontier who selflessly gave of their time and knowledge, without whose help this book would not have been possible. It is delicate business soliciting information from these non-profit heroes. Most prefer to go quietly undisturbed as the "silent angels" of our society. Their philanthropic efforts are truly the spirit behind this book.

Introduction

I would like to start this book by dedicating it to my dear grandma Agnes Mason. She was the one who first convinced me that a precious sunny afternoon of my summer vacation should be spent in Montebello Park in St. Catharines, Ontario, at what they used to call a penny sale. I was only seven years old, and there I was, forgoing the playground for dreams of all that I could acquire for just a penny. And let me tell you: back then, you could truly get some *great stuff* for a penny. In fact, I spent most of the rest of that summer with Grandma tracking down every sale we could get our little hands on. I have yet to stop.

As you might have guessed by my surname, I am Scottish through and through—on both sides of the family! Not that I would ever call myself cheap. I prefer thrifty or, as some may have it, frugal. As Grandma always said, "Mind the pennies and the pounds will take care of themselves."

I have often told friends, "If I had to choose between having great sex or exploring an uncharted thrift store, I am sorry, my love, I would simply have to choose the latter." Okay, it's my addiction of choice. It's my muse. It makes me feel special. After all, anyone can buy retail, but it takes a truly creative spirit to buy secondhand. In fact, on any given day about the only thing on my body that isn't secondhand are my knickers.

In my many years as a thrifter I have acquired a designer wardrobe to rival any celebrity on Mr. Blackwell's Best Dressed list. My closets are simply bursting at the seams with contemporary designs from the likes of Donna Karan to the more outlandish Dolce & Gabbana, as well as a fabulous collection of vintage designers such as Pucci, Traina-Norell, and Rudi Gernreich.

I'll give you an example of what is possible by describing an outfit I threw on one day to attend a business meeting. It consisted of the following:

Item	My Cost		Original Cost
Dusty rose Alaia knit skirt	flea market	$10.00	$ 450.00
Black matte jersey Rick Beach top	thrift store	$18.00	$ 150.00
Black Donna Karan belt	rummage	$15.00	$ 325.00
Black Edouard Rambauo purse	thrift store	$ 7.00	$ 225.00
Black suede Omari shoes	thrift store	$20.00	$ 195.00
Gucci watch	garage sale	$25.00	$ 325.00
DKNY pantyhose	new on sale	$ 2.95	$ 8.00
Totals		**$97.95**	**$1,628.00**

This represents a whopping savings of $1,531.

Over the years, I have found I'm not the only one attracted to the hunt. I had the good fortune to be working with the actress Faye Dunaway on the ABC miniseries *Casanova* while living in Madrid, Spain. One afternoon at lunch, Faye mentioned her desire to attend the Rastro, Madrid's famed flea market. I perked up and gave her all the specs on the Rastro, as well as the scoop on all the consignment stores around town. (Thrifters are somewhat like those collectors of vintage automobiles who thrill to the sight of a fellow enthusiast—pulling to the side of the road, they'll chat endlessly about their shared passion, often with complete strangers!) Faye and I scoured the Rastro, several antique shows, and a handful of consignment shops together for days, leaving us one day left of Faye's time in Madrid to do my favorite consignment shop, Contraste. Sadly, Faye was shooting her last scene that day, and the shop was scheduled to close at 3:00 P.M. After our pleading, the ladies who owned the shop finally agreed to stay open late for us. We had a terrific time and bought up a storm. Out of respect to my fellow thrifter, I will not disclose what Faye bought, but I can tell you her taste is as eclectic and eccentric as mine, so we did battle over a few fabulous finds!

I really started to get into shopping thrift, consignment, and resale shops when I was in my early teens and living in Toronto. All the girls I knew in high school would spend their hard-earned baby-sitting dollars in the department stores and retail boutiques. Not me! I discovered the garment (or fashion) district first. While working as a fit model for a number of local clothing manufacturers, I learned that they were willing to sell me their merchandise at wholesale prices. Not only was I getting great fashion for at least 50 to 60 percent below retail cost, but I was also buying it direct, before the merchandise had hit the department stores. As a result, I became the trendsetter in my high school.

At the same time, many manufacturers started opening up small storefronts to their manufacturing plants to cash in on this new shopping trend and to move out their overruns, leftover orders that have been either returned or canceled by the retailers. It wasn't long before they realized they didn't have to offer their merchandise at the true wholesale price. They kept edging their prices upward until they were just slightly below retail. Now, for some, that is still a saving. But I started looking for the bigger and better deal. For an aspiring model and actress, the demands of an extensive and fashionable wardrobe were great, but I had very limited funds. I needed new alternatives.

As it turned out, I stumbled across a very large Salvation Army store in the garment district in Toronto. This was my very first experience with thrift store shopping. I still have wonderful dreams about shopping in this particular store: three floors of never-ending possibilities. Most of the original staff are still there, and it has been nearly *twenty* years since I first dared to venture inside their doors. It is still the first place I search out every time I return to Toronto. I know of a few special drawers where they stash away their more delectable goodies—for customers like you and me to discover!

It has been a long and joyous journey since that first experience. I have been fortunate, working in the film and television industry, to have had the opportunity to travel to many parts of the world, and I'm here to say that not one item has been left unturned. I have shopped every thrift store, resale or consignment shop, flea market, rummage sale, garage sale, and antique market that lay in my path!

There was a time when I would make most of my own clothing from scratch. I was even so bold as to create my own label and design for many of my model friends. But once I discovered thrift shopping, sewing simply no longer made sense. I could buy a designer outfit in a thrift store for a fraction of the cost of the material to make it from scratch and save myself all that time and effort. I now channel my design instincts into re-creating something unique out of the garments I buy.

I have chosen to write this book for two reasons. First, to share with all my friends and customers who continually ask me, Where are the best thrift stores and how can I find such fabulous stuff as you find? I suppose I got tired of photocopying my secret lists and jotting addresses down on all those little scraps of paper. I have decided to expose it all here: my twenty years as a thrifter, my entire "little black book" of favorite thrift stores. I also hope to share with you the knowledge I acquired about the resale industry while owning and operating a consignment store.

Armed with all the suggestions I offer you here as to how to get the most out of secondhand shopping and the listings of many of the best shops across the country, you will be able to hunt down some of the best shops in the cities and towns where you reside or visit. Even if you are on a short trip and all you have is a couple of hours, this book will help you locate that store and get you in and out with an armload of treasures, long before your traveling companions even notice you are missing!

To be truthful, I need this book myself. I can't tell you how many times I've been shopping in a certain area and have completely forgotten a great store just around the corner because I did not have my up-to-date list with me in the car. It is understandable that this book could not possibly list every store across the country due to space constraints. For this reason I have chosen to list what I consider to be the best of the top thrift organizations' shops as well as a selected number of independent thrift shops. My choice was based primarily on the overall reputation of the organization that owns and operates a particular store or chain, as well as the consis-

Garment compliments of National Assistance League
Ralph Lauren khaki safari coat, $7, original cost approximately $125.
SK&Co. rust skirt, $6, original cost approximately $65. (*Accessories from author's private collection.*)

tency in the quality of merchandise that I have found to be available through these particular organizations.

My second reason for writing this book is because our waste production is truly of growing concern to me and others like myself. According to the Environmental Protection Agency, the United States leads the world in waste production, generating approximately 200 million tons a year, enough to fill a convoy of garbage trucks stretching eight times around the globe. Discarded clothing makes up 4 percent of the solid waste stream each year. By encouraging my readers to shop resale, thrift, and consignment stores, I hope to take a bite out of that percentage and keep some of this clothing and merchandise out of our ever dwindling landfill space.

My goal is to encourage the reader to think like a thrifter, rather than simply plod along in a connect-the-dots fashion. This book is divided into two parts. Part I will give you some helpful information on what to look for and how to find it, sell it, or preserve it. Part II presents a listing of the shops where you will find all these wonderful treasures. The type of shopping that I will be describing is full of adventure and satisfaction. I am truly hard-pressed to think of a more exciting way to spend my leisure time. I hope that after you finish reading this book, you'll share my enthusiasm. Happy hunting!

The Rag Street Journal

PART I

The Basics of Secondhand Shopping and Selling

1

Thrift Stores

Who Is a Thrifter?

Thrift stores are very peculiar places. You might expect to find the disadvantaged person shopping them, nobody else. Yet the customers are as varied as the merchandise. In these tough economic times, practically everyone is out looking for an alternative way to shop and save money.

Years ago, in our parents' day, some people may have been ashamed to be seen in a thrift shop or to admit that they were wearing secondhand clothing; it simply wasn't done. I still have friends today who say that they feel uncomfortable shopping in thrift stores because they believe the shops are really there to serve only the financially struggling. But this is not so. It is the smart shoppers who can afford to buy retail who are out to make their dollars stretch even further. The junior executive who is eager for promotion understands that she needs to dress two levels above her present position in order to appear promotable. Employers tend to recognize wise and savvy shoppers, for perhaps this quality will influence their business decisions as well.

Today you will find celebrities, doctors, lawyers, business executives, students, young mothers, costume designers, and people of all ages and nationalities shopping in thrift stores. They all have two things in common: One, they are looking for an alternative to shopping retail because they demand a better return on their consumer dollar. Two, they are treasure hunters and collectors at heart. They don't mind rolling up their sleeves and digging in to find that diamond in a bed of coal.

I recall walking into a Salvation Army store a few years ago and seeing a large pile of the ugliest 1970s clothing one could imagine stacked high on the sales counter. I could not believe that a person today could have such terrible taste, or that they could afford to buy such a vast quantity of clothing. Upon further inquiry, I discovered that the customer was actually a costume designer I knew from a film I had recently worked on, buying clothing for a movie to be set in the seventies. She and I then spent the better part of that afternoon searching through the store for more wild seventies clothing. We had a blast rediscovering everything from Sergio Valente jeans to patch-pocket elephant pants!

If I had a penny for every time I overheard someone in a thrift store say "Look at this—I once had one of these!" I'd be a millionaire. It's my fond belief that many of us are attempting to recapture our childhoods through our collecting. I am sure this is one of the reasons why 1960s cartoons and toy collectibles are currently so sought after—they can bring back a flood of memories that tickle us all over. You simply cannot put a price on that.

Thrift stores are a tremendous resource for all sorts of reasons. Young mothers are wise to scope out thrift shops for children's clothes. Kids grow so fast, it's ridiculous to pay retail for something they will wear for only one or two seasons. Unfortunately, after the age of five kids are so hard on their clothing that it is often difficult to find much in really good condition.

If you are still a little uneasy about buying and wearing secondhand clothing, try this on for size. You know that Donna Karan dress you just bought for $850? Chances are, someone else bought that same dress last week. She tucked the price tag up in her sleeve, danced the night away, and then returned it the next day to the department store claiming that she had changed her mind. That same dress had probably been tried on dozens of times by other shoppers who weren't as bold.

I also know for a fact that many boutiques have their sales staff wear the clothing from the shop while they are selling on the floor. At the end of their shift, they simply steam the garments and place them back on the sales racks for the unsuspecting consumers to purchase.

Then there are the fashion shows and photo shoots where the models wear either a manufacturer's or boutique's merchandise. They even go so far as to use masking tape on the soles of the models' shoes so they do not show any wear. After the shoot, the merchandise can go straight back to the sales floor or be sent to a discounted sample sale. So once again I ask, What's the big deal with buying secondhand? You may have been doing it all along.

Whether you are on a budget, need dress-up costumes at bargain prices, make your living in the resale businesses, or just love the hunt, nowhere else will you find such an assortment of merchandise spanning the hands of time. That is what sets thrift store shopping apart from retail.

Types of Thrift Stores

There are many different types of thrift, charity, and nonprofit stores. Most thrift stores are affiliated with a specific charity or nonprofit organization and must indicate in writing above the sales desk exactly what that charity is. You will discover many interesting things about some of these organizations in the chapter on the top ten thrift organizations, which describes some of their philanthropic work.

If you are unclear as to which organization a particular store funds and are concerned with where your consumer dollars are headed, you may ask whether it is an IRS (or Revenue Canada) qualified organization, and most stores should tell you. Or you may check IRS Publication 78, *Cumulative List of Organizations*, which lists most qualified organizations. You can find this list at your local library or call your local IRS office. You may also ask to see the store's business license (typically located with their charity affiliation documents).

Personally, I like to know up front where the money from my purchase is going, as well as what percentages of the gross sales are dispersed to that charity or nonprofit organization. There are many businesses out there that claim to be charity thrift stores, but they may not be allied with any charity other than their own. They may be using the term *thrift store* to entice you with the hopes of getting especially good bargains. This type of store is fairly easy to identify. Often it has a personal name for the business incorporating the word *thrift*, e.g., Elizabeth's Thrift Shop. Usually it is staffed by a sole proprietor and may be slightly higher priced than the others.

You should understand that in order to qualify as a nonprofit organization, only a very small percentage of the shop's profits, after costs, must find its way to the designated charity. Certain shrewd entrepreneurs exploit the system by attaching themselves to a nonprofit organization in order to take advantage of the tax breaks and the unsuspecting consumer donations. It is the donations they are really after, allowing them to put money in their pockets by selling the goods you have donated to them. They may legitimize themselves in your eyes by supplying you with a tax receipt for those donated goods; if you are truly concerned, you may request a copy of their charity's annual report and ask what percentage of their profits are actually going to that charity.

You can also identify a privately owned store by its more complex tagging and inventory system. Most of the larger chain thrift stores price all merchandise the same: all jackets are one price, dresses another. The privately owned thrift stores, however, tend to price everything separately, taking into consideration just how much they can get for that particular item. (Some of the larger chains, such as Salvation Army, Goodwill, and the American Cancer Society, to name a few, are now taking their cue from the privately owned stores by selecting certain merchandise for individual and higher pricing.)

For most of us, the goal is getting the best merchandise at the lowest possible price. It is almost a given that you will find it easier to barter with the privately owned businesses than with the large chains, since the former do not have the large organization behind them and need to pay the rent each month. That sale you are haggling over may be more important to them than you think.

How to Locate a Thrift Shop

If a thrift shop is not listed in *The Rag Street Journal*, then the best way to locate it is to start with your local telephone directory. You will probably find it listed in the Yellow Pages under the headings "Thrift Stores," "Resale," "Used Clothing," or "Furniture." Keep in mind, though, that an ad in the Yellow Pages can be very costly, starting at $100 a month. Most nonprofit organizations simply do not have the money to consider this option. You can call your local chamber of commerce and request a listing of the nonprofit shops in your vicinity. Some towns have formed resale associations to promote shopping resale and encourage recycling.

If you're adventurous, simply get in your car and drive. I always keep a notepad in my car for those important sightings. If I spot a thrift store

A Garment's Circle of Life

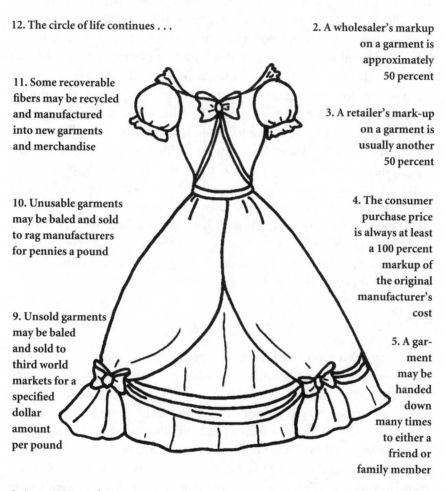

1. Garment designers and manufacturers

12. The circle of life continues . . .

11. Some recoverable fibers may be recycled and manufactured into new garments and merchandise

10. Unusable garments may be baled and sold to rag manufacturers for pennies a pound

9. Unsold garments may be baled and sold to third world markets for a specified dollar amount per pound

2. A wholesaler's markup on a garment is approximately 50 percent

3. A retailer's mark-up on a garment is usually another 50 percent

4. The consumer purchase price is always at least a 100 percent markup of the original manufacturer's cost

5. A garment may be handed down many times to either a friend or family member

8. A garment may be donated to a thrift store and sold at 5 to 10 percent of the original retail selling price

6. A garment may be placed "on consignment" and sold for 40 to 70 percent of the original retail selling price

7. A garment may be sold at a garage sale or flea market at 10 to 20 percent of the original retail selling price

(usually from a block away) and am unable to stop at that moment, I write down the name and address for future investigation.

A sure way to distinguish a thrift or consignment shop from a retail shop is to look at their window display. Thrift or consignment shops' window displays are usually eclectic, indicating a wide variety of mixed merchandise. They rarely have any continuity to their merchandise on display because they rely on the donations or consignments of their patrons, whereas a retail shop will usually display a line of merchandise with numerous articles that will mix and match. Often, the thrift or consignment shop will try to create a display for special occasions, perhaps choosing all green clothing if it's St. Patrick's Day, or spring colors if Easter is coming up. They also do not subscribe to the idea that less is more, but tend to cram as much as they possibly can into the windows. One clue to selecting a good thrift shop is a window display that has an exciting selection of their better merchandise, including some collectibles and antiques.

Many of the independent and smaller thrift shops' signs are easily identified because they are hand-painted. Soon you will become very familiar with the larger chains' signs and logos, and your heart will begin to pound like mine when you turn that corner and see that bright red Salvation Army shield or that blue smiling Goodwill face.

Hours of Operation

A thrift store's hours of operation vary from business to business. Most are open Monday through Saturday from 10:00 A.M. until 4:00 P.M., though some stay open until 5:00 or 6:00 P.M. Some Jewish nonprofit thrift shops will close Saturday in recognition of their Sabbath and open again on Sunday. Other stores have varied days and hours that are normally posted on their windows or door. If the hours of operation are not stated on their business card, I'm always careful to jot them down on the back. Many privately owned stores will often be open seven days a week and for much longer hours. Because most of the nonprofit stores are staffed by volunteers, it is possible that the shop may not adhere to the posted hours. It is always advisable to call ahead if you are not familiar with a particular shop's routine. I have found that some of the thrift stores that are open only two or three days a week can have some of the best merchandise. This is because the resale dealers and pickers find it much more difficult to coordinate their shopping time in them, therefore they may not be as picked-over.

How Often Should You Frequent a Shop?

Most shops have a consistent turnover of goods, so if you are looking for a particular item you may find it advantageous to pop in frequently with the hope of lucking out. Organizations like the Salvation Army and Goodwill advertise that they put out fresh merchandise on a daily basis. I am not shy about following an employee who is wheeling a rack of clothing out on the floor in the hopes of getting a first look. I have even known shoppers to run brief daily sorties through shops simply as a form of entertainment. I can tell you, when I return home to Toronto and drop by the Salvation Army on Richmond Street, the same woman is shopping there every time. The only thing that changes is the hat she's wearing! I might add that this has been going on for more than fifteen years.

It's a good idea to make your presence known when you arrive. Introduce yourself to the staff. Establish yourself as a regular customer who spends money and the staff will usually be more inclined to indicate better items to you and to let you know when certain things might be coming in or made available.

Shopping "Equipment"

Most thrift stores have shopping bags available for your purchases, but it is always a good idea to carry your own just in case. A light nylon bag with a zipper is best. Many stores will ask you to check all of your bags as you enter the store. If you can lock up your bag, do so. I had the misfortune of checking a Balducci's shopping bag at the counter of a Greenwich Village thrift store in New York. It was filled with a hundred dollars' worth of food I had just bought to prepare a Valentine's dinner. When I went to pick it up after shopping, my great big bag had been replaced by a smaller Balducci's shopping bag that contained exactly two packages of Scottish caramels and a jar of matzoh balls! The employee behind the sales desk had given away my bag.

But there's a happy ending to this story. As luck would have it, the thrift store was part of the Goodwill Industries chain. The management assured me they would give me the cash value of my lost bag if it was not returned by the end of the day. Be advised that this is really an exception to the rule, so don't rely on it. Fortunately for me, when I called back to the thrift store just before closing, someone had indeed returned my bag. Who says New Yorkers don't have a heart? I guess they just really love their matzoh balls!

The thing to keep in mind is that *most stores are not responsible for your belongings*, despite the fact that they require you to check them. Many of them have a card or numbering system in the same way a coat-check in a restaurant will. Always make sure you are given a number for your bag, and inspect the contents of your bag before you leave the shop. Never expect the sales staff to remember your face or your bag.

I often suggest to people that they carry an old pair of gloves with them when they shop. Clothing racks can be very crammed, and gloves help save your hands and nails from hanger damage. Not all the clothing has been cleaned prior to being put on display, and you will come in contact with many other people's germs as you sort through their previously owned garments. I always keep a package of wash-up towelettes in my car, preferably the antibacterial type. It is a good idea to wash your hands after shopping.

Most shops use recycled bags brought in by donors, and they are not always in the best condition. It would be great if we all got in the habit of using a reusable shopping bag every time we shop.

Lastly, carrying plenty of change for the parking meters is a good tip on any trip.

Choosing Your Shopping Partner

Believe it or not, this is a very sensitive issue for most people. I myself have had bad luck in this department and shopped with some *very* competitive acquaintances. It can start from the moment you get out of the car. It's that look in your lifelong friends' eyes that gives them away as they race ahead, leaving you digging for a quarter to put in the parking meter. They proclaim over their shoulder as they dash hell-bent for the shop door, "Oh, sorry, silly me, I haven't got any change." Once in the store, he or she always tries to stay one step ahead of you, crisscrossing in front as you attempt to go through the racks. Now, I don't know about you, but a rack that has already been picked over by someone (especially someone I feel is as talented as myself!) is just not worth continuing to look through. That's why I always try to work a separate rack from my companions. This tends to keep the treasure hunt fair. I have actually been about to pick up a lovely piece of costume jewelry when a person I was shopping with snatched it right out from under me.

Things don't have to be this way. A good rule of thumb is to shop with someone who has different taste from you, and preferably one who wears a different size. You can never go wrong if you choose a good, trusted friend—the kind who will turn over to you that fabulous Thierry Mugler dress if it doesn't fit her! It is delightful to discover an item you know your companion collects and to see the expression on his face as you approach him with the words, "Look what I found for you—a beautiful hickory wood–shafted mashie golf club with its original leather grip in mint condition!"

As in most areas of life, good shopping etiquette is based on the golden rule: "Do unto others as you would have them do unto you." Walk calmly from the car, and try to enjoy the experience. There are always plenty of finds to go around—if not in this store, then in the very next one down the street. Don't be greedy. If you already have one of a particular item, or it's not right for you, pass it on to your acquaintance. You will find that this kind of shopping has a certain karma; they will likely do the same for you later. Remember: A good shopping partner is hard to come by, but a great friend is even harder to find.

What Type of Merchandise Can You Expect to Find?

You will find a direct correlation between the patrons, or members of the charity the store services, and the type of merchandise you will find in it. This is because many of the patrons who volunteer their services either to the thrift store operations or to other areas of service within the charity, also donate their belongings to the thrift store. The more affluent the patrons, the better the quality of the donations and merchandise in the shop.

The location of the store will also determine the merchandise. If a store is located in a more affluent neighborhood, it stands to reason people from that community will also be donating to that particular store. I have also found that the more transient a city is, the more abundant the good merchandise in the thrift stores. It is also true that the more affluent the city is, the better the merchandise. This is the major reason that California and New York have perhaps the best thrift stores in all of North America. There

Yves Saint Laurent '60s black velvet Nehru jacket with embroidered spiders, $40, Stuyvesant Goodwill, Manhattan.

Atlast Studio white cotton ruffled blouse, $5, Salvation Army, Santa Monica, Calif., original cost approximately $35.

GEM antique sterling silver pocket watch, fob, and chain, worn here as a necklace, author's private collection.

Walter Steiger stainless steel and patent leather '70s platform shoes as seen in the film *Forrest Gump*, $25, a Hollywood garage sale.

Donna Karan deco style panty hose, resurrected from her 1990 collection, $12.

is so much money, and so many people coming and going, that folks seem to donate their possessions rather than taking things with them. That's not to say that a fabulous find can't be discovered in a quiet rural area.

Often, the larger thrift chains will have a main store or warehouse where things are sorted and then distributed to the appropriate locations. After all, it doesn't make sense to send designer outfits into an area where the consumer is looking for wash-and-wear work clothing. The better neighborhoods will therefore often have better merchandise. This is especially true with the larger chains, such as Goodwill Industries, the American Cancer Society Discovery Shops, and the Salvation Army.

Thrift stores sell everything and anything: clothing, household items, computer equipment, tools, jewelry, toys, furniture, antiques, and all manner of collectibles. Certain chains specialize in certain items. Whenever that information is available, I have indicated it in Part II of this book; however, you may wish to call ahead if you are looking for a particular item, because the inventory is dependent on donations.

Many of the larger chains, such as Goodwill Industries and the Salvation Army, will launder or sterilize some of their merchandise, but don't count on it. It is advisable to launder your items yourself once you have purchased them. (Any store selling mattresses must by law have a special license and use a sterilizing system on all mattresses and linens.)

Where Does the Merchandise Come From?

The merchandise in a thrift store comes from many different sources. It is often donated by individuals who are patrons of the particular charity, or people who believe in their cause. Some simply donate out of kindness of heart; others may be more interested in the tax deduction they get; and then there are those who simply wish to dispose of unwanted items. Many major department stores and boutiques will donate merchandise that has been left over after their sales. I was told an amusing story once by a lovely young woman whose father was an affluent politician with a compulsion to snatch up everything he thought was "such a deal." One day this gentleman sent his daughter fifteen pairs of shoes that originally sold for more than $200 each. He, of course, paid only $35 a pair at a department store clearance sale. I'm sure he bought them for her with the best of intentions, except that they were all too small. Bought on sale at a retail store—"no refunds no returns"—off to the Goodwill Industries shop they all went.

Lucky were those folks who then bought those $200 shoes for $4.50 a pair. "Such a deal!"

Who Works at a Thrift Store?

Until recently, most of the staff in a charity or thrift store were volunteers. But this is changing rapidly. Many of the more upscale thrift stores, such as the American Cancer Society Discovery Shops, are recruiting employees from the mainstream retail industry. It is not uncommon to discover that a manager in a thrift store was once a salesperson or manager at a major department store. This trend is giving the more upscale thrift stores a competitive edge over higher-priced retail shops. You will find that there are more and more paid employees in the thrift industry, who have been selectively recruited to manage a thrift store. It's always a good idea to inquire who the manager is. He or she can tell you when new merchandise is coming in, as well as negotiate a markdown for you. After all, getting the best merchandise at the best possible price is what this is all about, isn't it?

If a shop is a church-run organization, the staff will usually be volunteer members (with the proceeds going to the church). Other volunteers are patrons of the particular charity. All volunteers have their own reasons for donating their time and energy and should be treated dearly for their efforts and kindness of spirit. Many are simply giving back to a charity that was there in their time of need, or are helping to raise funds for a cause they truly believe in.

Choosing Your Merchandise

Most savvy antique and collectibles dealers know exactly when the new merchandise is scheduled to arrive. Many are said to have special arrangements with the management to have first pick before the merchandise is even unloaded from the delivery trucks. You will often see them hanging around the stockroom doors talking to employees and managers in the hope of snagging the best deals before they hit the sales floor.

Some people complain to me that they are overwhelmed by the sheer amount of merchandise packed into a thrift store. Because everything is donated, these businesses do not have to worry about cash flow, hence they are usually bulging at the seams. This makes it difficult for the novice shopper to find something suitable without a great deal of digging and hunting.

For some, this could take hours and hours, and even then they may come up exhausted, frustrated, dirty, and empty-handed.

I like to think that I can "fleece" (pull the best merchandise) an uncharted thrift store in twenty minutes, depending on the size of the shop. In others, it may take just a few moments to decide that the type of merchandise being offered is not what I am looking for. I do this by "scanning," which I'll discuss in the next section.

If time is at a premium (as it is with most of us), don't waste it looking at things you don't need. The first thing I do is check out the window displays for unique items selected to attract shoppers. If there is something in the window I like, I go immediately to the salesperson or cashier and ask if I can see it. Always be sure to ask for *all* the items you wish to see out of the window simultaneously; you don't want to make things difficult by sending the salesperson back to the window.

The window display items are often sold only on certain dates. Many will have a sign indicating on what day the display items will become available. If not, you can always ask. You also may be able to put your name on that item; however, that may not firmly hold the piece for you. It's better if they allow you to pay for the item, which ensures that it is yours, then have you come back to pick it up on the day they redo their window display. If you really want a certain item, and they won't let you reserve it, the best bet is to come back when the store is scheduled to open on the day the display items are to be made available for purchase. You may find you have some competition, so *be on time!*

Once you are inside the store, deciding where to start can be a challenge. Sometimes I start with the sales desk. This is usually a good place to find jewelry and small collectible items. Any eye-catching pieces, or things that could easily be lost or stolen are usually kept under lock and key in the display cabinets by the sales desk. Always check this first. If you see something you like, don't hesitate to get the salesperson's attention. If you wait until you have finished shopping the rest of the store, the item may be gone. Believe me—it's happened to me many times!

If you decide you would like to buy a certain item from the display cabinet, ask if they mind putting it aside for you while you shop the rest of the store. However, it's probably wise to pay for it right away. There may be a change of shift behind the sales desk, and the next staff person may not know this particular item was being saved for you. They may unknowingly sell it to someone else—or worse, buy it themselves. I've seen it happen! In fact, some shops have a policy set up for employee purchases. The employee is not entitled to purchase an item until it has been out on the sales floor for a minimum of three hours. This ensures the customer a fair shot at purchasing it first.

Where you go next is really a personal preference. Some may like to go straight for the clothing, whereas I find that the clothing is the most time-consuming, so I will do the furniture, accessories, shoes, and bric-a-brac next. Then, I move into the clothing areas last.

Scanning

Scanning is a very important skill for thrifters to learn, and can be improved upon only with patience and practice. When scanning any area, I like to stand a few feet back and let my eyes travel down the length of the shelves or racks, rather than moving myself. Your eye will become so well trained in time that things will just pop out at you, with little or no conscious thought on your part. There are many variables in your individual scanning technique, depending on what you are scanning and how well organized the store is. For example, if you're looking for shoes, and all the shelves are organized according to size, that will obviously save you some time right there. If not, you may scan for size, style, color, and general condition of the shoes. After a while you will become so good at scanning that you will virtually pick up only a pair that is your size and one you would consider buying. This will save your spending wasted moments picking up dozens of pairs to see if they suit your needs.

Scanning clothing is slightly more complicated, because racks are so jam-packed and there are many more variables. What I look for first is fabric. A gorgeous fabric usually denotes a great designer piece. Couple that with a detail—tailor hand-picked lapels, fabulous jet (petrified coal) or black glass buttons—and you've probably hit the jackpot. The other thing to scan for is color. There is no point pulling out a red dress if you look like a dead fish in red. Some better thrift stores will try to separate things into color groups, but don't count on this. It is best if you train yourself right from the start to pull an appropriate item from a combined rack.

What stores typically do is separate different *types* of garments. They place blouses with blouses and skirts with skirts, etc. If there are racks on either side, in long rows, I start with one section on one side of the row first. I scan that, then turn around and do the same on the other row. I then move down the rows and start all over with another section. This is a great time-saver, and you will not have to walk the whole row twice.

Designer or "Back" Room

Before you leave, always ask if a store has a designer or "back" room. This is a boutique section that is not open to the general public without an appointment. It is also where they keep their better merchandise. It is often open only on certain days and for a limited number of hours, depending on the availability of staff. Once again, jot down the hours of operation and the name of the manager on the back of the store's business card. If I know I am planning to be in that area on a particular day, I will call and make an appointment ahead of time.

Sometimes you can be lucky enough to catch the manager as soon as you arrive at the store. This may give him or her enough time (while you shop the rest of the store) to free up a staff member to take you into the boutique. You will almost never be allowed to shop in the back room or boutique alone, so don't be offended when you see that you are being chaperoned. These types of businesses have a tremendous amount of shoplifting. The reason they try to separate out some of the better merchandise is so that they can police it more efficiently. I find it terribly unfortunate that people feel it is okay to steal from these charities, since most all of their profits are usually going to an important cause.

Locating a boutique room is truly a thrill. The staff has cut your work in half by sorting through all the store's merchandise and selecting the better labels and designer merchandise to put here. You will, however, find that things will be slightly higher in price in these back rooms, but never as high as retail and certainly *always* worth your consideration.

When space for a back or private room is not available, many shops will keep a rack of selected better clothing behind the counter. It's not often the management will allow the customer behind the sales desk to look through the rack, but you will usually find a salesperson willing to assist you.

You may also find that some stores keep their better jewelry in a locked cabinet out of sight or in a private back room. It's a good bet, if you do not see any jewelry or nice odd buttons out in the main part of the store, that this is the case. Don't be shy. Go and ask someone to show you the "hidden" merchandise—under their watchful gaze, of course. Sometimes a staff person is designated to bring the jewelry out for sale only on a certain day. A little investigating is well worth it, I assure you.

Inspecting Your Goods
Prior to Purchasing

Once you have selected your treasures, take them closer to the doorway of the store, where you will have ample natural light. You will find that many thrift stores have terrible lighting, and you may miss subtle stains if you don't take the item into bright light. You should also look for any moth holes in your wool or cashmere items. Hold the garment outstretched to the light. This should make noticeable even the smallest hole as the light shines through it. A small flashlight also works well to spot moth holes— just shine it down a sleeve or pant leg. Pay close attention to the cuffs, as they seem to be the areas that show the greatest wear.

Linen and silk garments have their own special folly. What you truly need to look for here is perspiration stains, both under the arms and around the collar or waist, where the garment was tucked in. I also like to check all seams. Often a garment has been donated because the person had gained weight. This does not ensure they didn't try to wear it through the weight gain, which usually results in strained and damaged seams. However, some things are certainly salvageable. This is especially true if the item is a little large for you. You can always take it in, thereby hiding the damaged seams.

Be aware that oftentimes a garment has been altered to either a larger or smaller size; therefore, the original size tag may be deceiving. Always check for any telltale signs of alterations. They are usually in the waistbands, cuffs, or side seams. Remember, a bad alteration can ruin the fit of a garment and is often the reason the person has disposed of an item.

Can a Damaged Item
Save You Money?

Finding a flaw in a garment can work to your advantage. Items are usually prepriced. If the tag does not indicate "as is" on it, then you can often negotiate a discount based on the damage. This is especially true if buttons are missing or a zipper is broken, which may have occurred after the item was placed on the sales floor. These are things that you will need to repair and that will cost money, so the sales staff will occasionally take that into consideration. Some stores do not discount their prices at the counter. They will send the item back to their stockroom for mending or repricing. This system is designed to discourage you from asking for that discount. It will probably result in your losing the opportunity to purchase that item, because the person who does the pricing will not be in that day.

You may wish to weigh the difference between the desirability of that item and the cost to you to repair it. If I truly like the piece, I will purchase it "as is," at the ticketed price. But as I always say, it never hurts to ask for the discount. Be warned, I must admit I have a fairly substantial collection of garments that I thought I would fix—we all know about that road that was paved with good intentions. With all the wonderful merchandise available to you, why settle for anything that may hang around waiting to be mended?

Labels to Look For

My feeling is that you must first love a garment before you look inside to find the label. Don't be seduced by the label alone. If you'll never wear it, there's no point in owning it, unless it is simply to add to your collection, and even then I like to limit my collection to things that I will wear. That said, the last thing I look at before I make a purchase is the label. If you have done your homework, by the time you have pulled the garment, you will already have a lovely designer piece in your hand. Beware—caveat emptor—there are imposters. With the abundance of fine designer clothing available to you through thrift stores, you may as well get the best. Better merchandise always lasts longer and requires replacement less frequently. It simply gives you more *value* for your money.

Many people have asked me how I can identify certain designers at a glance, and how I know the value of a particular piece of merchandise. My answer is simple—I do not spend all my time in thrift stores! I do a great deal of window shopping in retail stores. I will browse through the boutique and designer sections in the high-end department stores. I will read many of the leading fashion magazines to stay abreast of the changing trends and new designers. I like to look at labels and price tags and take a mental inventory. This will be very important to you if you are interested in reselling any of your fabulous finds later.

A Designer Salute (author's creation)

Originala black vintage '50s jacket, $5.

Black wool crepe shawl worn as a skirt: fabric from a Beverly Hills estate sale, $10; silk tassels from a Hollywood garage sale, $5.

Vintage designer labels from author's private collection.

Pearl and rhinestone earrings, $4, Junior League rummage sale.

Friend Pawprint in her pearl and crystal necklace, $5, Hollywood garage sale.

There are virtually hundreds of designers old and new who are worth considering for their classic and timeless style that transcends present trends. The following list represents a sampling of my personal favorites.

Joseph Abboud

Adrian* (ca. 1941–1952)

Azzedine Alaia*

Jean Allen*

Elizabeth Arden*

Giorgio Armani (ca. 1974–present)

Balenciaga* (ca. 1937–1968)

Balmard*

Pierre Balman (ca. 1945–1982)

Barnes

Bartlett

Geoffrey Beene (ca. 1950–present)

Mr. Blackwell*

Bill Blass* (ca. 1959–present)

Marcel Boucher*

Donald Brooks

Byblos

Callot Soeurs*

Robert Capucci (ca. 1950–present)

Capucine*

Yvonne Carette

Bonnie Cashin* (ca. 1949–present)

Celine

Chanel* (ca. 1908–1971)†

Ceil Chapman*

Chloé

Ossi Clark*

Sybil Connolly*

Jo Copeland*

Andre Courreges* (ca. 1961–present)

Lilly Dache*

Oscar De La Renta* (ca. 1965–present)

Ann Demeulemeester

Pamela Denis

Comme des Garçons

Jean Desses

Christian Dior* (1947–present)

Dolce & Gabbana

Doucet* (1871–1932)

Vito Emanuele

Escada

Jacques Faith* (ca. 1937–1957)

Louis Féraud

Gianfranco Ferre

Alberta Ferretti

Fortuny* (1906–1949)

Gallenga*

John Galliano* (ca. 1951–present)

Jean-Paul Gaultier

Genny

Rudi Gernreich*

Romeo Gigli

Hubert de Givenchy* (1952–present)

Gres* (ca. 1934–present)

Jacques Griffe*

Halston* (ca. 1958–1990)

Katharine Hamnett

Hermés*

Mark Jacobs

Jacqmar*

Charles James* (1924–1978)

Gemma Kahng

Norma Kamali* (ca. 1968–present)

Donna Karan

Patrick Kelly*

---

*Indicates that these designers are very collectible as antique and vintage pieces.

†It's also important to note that in some cases the designer has passed on, yet the descendants of their design house have continued to design in their name.

Krizia
Karl Lagerfeld
  (ca. 1964–present)
Lanvin* (ca. 1890–
  present)†
Ted Lapidus
Homer Layne*
Hervé Leger*
Lucien Lelong*
Leonard
Tina Leser*
Lilli Ann*
Loewe
Bob Mackie
Claire McCardell*
  (ca. 1949–1958)
Mary McFadden
Mainbocher*
Badgley Mischka
Issey Miyake (ca. 1970–
  present)
Missoni
Isaac Mizrahi

Molyneaux*
Claude Montana
Moschino
Thierry Mugler*
Jean Muir
Todd Oldham
Paul Parnes*
Jean Patou* (ca. 1910–
  present)
Pattullo
Poiret*
Prada
Pucci*
Paquin*
Lola Prusa*
Lilly Pulitzer*
Mary Quant*
Pedro Rodriguez*
Helene Rose*
Christian Francis Roth*
Maggy Rouff*
Jil Sanders

Arnold Scaasi*
Schiaparelli* (ca. 1927–
  1971)
Franklin Simon*
Adele Simpson*
Steven Sprouse*
St. Johns Knits
Anna Sui
Traina-Norell*
Pauline Trigere*
Richard Tyler
Emanuel Ungaro
Valentino (ca. 1959–
  present)
Van Noten
Gianni Versace
Vera Wang
Vivienne Westwood
Charles Frederick
  Worth* (ca. 1858–
  1956)
Yves Saint Laurent*
  (ca. 1957–present)

At recent couture, antique clothing, and accessories auctions held at the William Doyle Galleries in New York, creations by some of the designers I have listed went for thousands of dollars. The following is a selection of some of the prices that were realized at that auction:

Maggy Rouff crinoline ball gown, ca. 1957	Sold for $ 5,500
YSL for Christian Dior trapeze dress, ca. 1958	Sold for $ 3,800
Schiaparelli evening dress and jacket, ca. 1937–38	Sold for $ 5,500

Jean Patou chemise evening dress, ca. 1925	Sold for $ 1,150
Fortuny Delphos long-sleeve tea gown	Sold for $ 5,462
Adrian cocktail dress, ca. 1950	Sold for $ 1,035
Jacques Fath late-day dress, ca. 1950s	Sold for $ 4,312
Charles James ball gown, ca. 1951	Sold for $29,900
Rudi Gernreich kite dress, ca. 1967	Sold for $ 747
Yves Saint Laurent beaded mini dress, ca. 1967	Sold for $ 3,910
Hermés Kelly bag, wine red	Sold for $ 1,035
Cecil Beaton drawing of Coco Chanel, ca. 1970	Sold for $ 9,775

Trying Things On

Common sense says it truly is best to try things on before you purchase them. Unfortunately, not all thrift stores provide a dressing room. This may be because of lack of space or the high rate of theft that occurs in most dressing rooms. Be prepared to try things on out in the open, wherever you can grab some floor space and a mirror. I always like to wear something form-fitting when I shop, like leggings, so that garments can be tried on over my clothes. Often, both men and women share the mirrors when dressing rooms are not provided. I have occasionally shopped in stores where the women seem to control the larger mirror on one side of the room and the men are left with a smaller one clear across the store.

Try to wear shoes that can easily be slipped off and on. There is nothing worse than a pair of high-top sneakers or boots that you must keep unlacing and relacing. In addition to the added effort, they never seem to flatter an outfit and can be a little discouraging when you are attempting to make up your mind about a potential purchase. You also want to wear a garment that does not require a lot of buttoning and unbuttoning.

Many people suffer what's referred to as thrift store burn-out. That's why I like to scan the whole store first before I start trying anything on. Many times we get fed up too soon because things don't fit. This happens when you are constantly jumping in and out of a dressing room, taking your clothes off and throwing them back on.

You may want to find a shopping cart or basket to make it easier to carry all your treasures around the store. I always carry a purse that I can strap across my body, out of harm's way. (It is important to note that pickpockets are everywhere, and thrift stores are no exception.) This also enables you to have both hands free to shop.

If the store does not have a cart or basket available for your shopping convenience, you may request that they put your selections behind the sales desk until you are ready to try them on or purchase them. Again, I caution you to make sure that the sales staff clearly understand that they are to save these items for you, as you intend to purchase them should they fit. It doesn't hurt to keep an eye on them yourself, and check in with the salesperson every so often so they know you're still in the store. The staff can get very busy and lose you in the crowd, or the staff may have a shift changeover.

Sales and Fashion Shows

Often a thrift store will hold back much of its better merchandise a few months before Christmas. This is because they are preparing for a big pre-Christmas blowout sale to raise a great deal of money for their Christmas fund. Ask your favorite shops if they do this, and get the dates and times of the sale. Be at least one hour early—I guarantee you will still not be the first in line.

It is also a good idea to look into the thrift stores after their semiannual or Christmas sales for any items that did not sell at the sale. Often the manager overprices an item. If it does not sell, it will be reduced and returned to the store for regular sales. The rule of thumb is that the items will usually be marked down by about 50 percent after a special sale.

Charity and thrift stores are known to hold annual fashion shows in which the clothing is available for purchase after the show. You will find that they have selected the best merchandise, and it may have a tendency to be higher priced than it would be in the store. This is often a closed event for the patrons of the charity, but it can't hurt to ask for an invitation. It is also important to note when the items that were in the fashion show will be back in the store and available for purchase. You may also wish to become a member of a specific charity in order to gain an invitation to their events or pre-sales.

Cash, Check, or Credit Card?

You should be aware that *"All* Sales Are Final." In my travels, *I have never known a store* ever to give a refund. When purchasing your items, you will find that the policy of these stores varies greatly. All will accept cash. Some of the national chains, like Goodwill Industries and the Salvation Army, will take most major credit cards. However, very few of the smaller shops will accept a check, unless they know and trust you, and never without a driver's license as identification. This is where establishing a rapport with the management comes in handy. You may find a few stores are a little more flexible on their rules than others. But never count on it.

Are Thrift Stores Really a Bargain?

Most thrift stores are still the best bargain going, although I have found that more and more are competing with the consignment businesses. Some, such as the National Assistance League, have even stated to take merchandise in on consignment, thus blurring the line between thrift and consignment (nonprofit and profit) businesses. They will offer the consignee (you) the going percentage rate (usually 50 percent) and take their portion of their profit and apply it to their charity. In this way, they are still able to attract the better merchandise that may otherwise have found its way to the regular consignment businesses.

Because resale and consignment businesses are fast becoming a mainstream shopping alternative, it seems that everyone, including thrift stores, is jumping on the price-hike bandwagon. Many of the thrift stores in the larger urban areas such as Manhattan's Upper East Side are beginning to price themselves right out of the thrift store category. That is not to say that you can no longer find a bargain, just that you have to dig a little deeper.

2

Rummage Sales

Rummage sales are my favorite type of sale, bar none! Unfortunately, the old-fashioned rummage sales where you could buy a great pair of vintage earrings for a dime are becoming as rare as a white elephant in today's market. Yet they are still the cheapest sales going. Rummage sales are held by individual churches or charity organizations, such as the Junior League, about twice a year—once in the spring to raise money for their summer projects, then again in October or November to raise money for the less fortunate at Christmas. Rummage sales go by many different names, including penny sale, church bazaar, and of course, white elephant sale.

Patrons of the specific charity holding the sale donate everything, therefore the variety of merchandise you'll find at a rummage sale is endless, and I have yet to see anyone ever come out empty-handed! There are usually plenty of electronic gizmos and tools in addition to clothing, jewelry, bric-a-brac, and more than enough toys to keep the kids out of your hair for a few hours.

How to Locate a Rummage Sale

You may find notices about rummage sales listed in your local newspaper or your local chamber of commerce's community events calendar, or tacked up in grocery stores and dry cleaners in the neighborhood. Sales are almost always advertised with a large sign outside the church prior to the event. They are normally open free to the public, but at times a presale is held, requiring a paid admission, on either the day or evening prior to the sale. (The presale may not be indicated in the advertisement, so you will want to call well in advance and get whatever information you can.) The admission is usually very modest and well worth it for a "first-look" advantage; however, the price of the merchandise offered is often twice what it will be at the public sale. The presale is usually when most of the dealers in town snap up all the best items, especially any jewelry, antiques, or collectibles. The presale is also a good opportunity to introduce yourself and establish a relationship with the sales organizing committee in order to acquire any firsthand news that will assist your advantage over other buyers.

Getting the Most Out of the Sale

On the morning of the actual sale, you will want to arrive at least one hour ahead of time. Bring a folding chair, if you can, because you may have a long wait in line. Remember, too, that there is a certain etiquette involved in saving places in line. People who have waited in line for hours will tolerate your saving a place for *one* other person who's been sent for the coffee and doughnuts. *Do not* try to get your whole family or a mass of friends inserted before you, or you will be, as the saying goes, cruising for a bruising! People take this very seriously.

I always like to suggest that you bring plenty of cash to a sale. Because this is a church function, they are rarely set up to take checks or credit cards. If they do accept a check, they will still require a driver's license with a current address as identification. They will rarely if ever accept credit cards, even on larger items such as their collectibles or antiques, because they do not have a business set up with the bank that enables them to process those charges.

The Silent Auction

A silent auction is held for some of the better items at a rummage sale, especially the antiques and collectibles. Always be sure to check with an attendant, because the auction is often held in a back room and can easily be overlooked. At a silent auction items are placed out on display with a piece of paper next to them. At the top of the page will be printed a minimum starting bid. Below are spaces for you to fill in your name and the amount you wish to bid on that item. Note that your bid must be higher than the minimum indicated, and bids are expected to escalate in increments of five or ten dollars per bid. Other bidders are free to up your bid at any time, so you must stay on top of your bid if you wish to be awarded the merchandise. There is a cutoff time for all bids and once the bell has been rung, the person with the last and highest bid will be able to purchase that item.

The Bake Sale

Be on the lookout for the bake sale section. No doubt, you were up so early that morning to get to the sale that you missed breakfast. You can usually find some delicious banana bread, brownies, fudge, pies, and plenty of jams and jellies. All cost far less than what you would pay in the grocery store, and are much better because they have been homemade with fine ingredients and lots of tender loving care! The items are usually made by the ladies of the charity, and often the children will try their hand at baking as well. For both young and old, this is their opportunity to do something substantial for the cause. For this reason, I would encourage everyone to stop by and purchase a cookie or two.

Rummage Sale Shopping "Equipment"

When I go to a rummage sale, I always carry a purse with a shoulder strap that can be safely strapped across my body. Men are advised to keep their wallets in either their front trousers pocket or breast pocket. With so many people crammed in together, rummage sales can also be a pickpocket's dream. *Be careful!*

The ultimate piece of equipment, of course, is a bundle buggy or luggage cart. You may want to check with the organizers of the sale before you bring one, though, because often these items are not allowed in the building. The advantage of these, of course, is that you do not have to lug things around, and they are fairly maneuverable. My second choice is a very large shopping bag strong enough to hold plenty of stuff. Boxes are often made available for you, but I find them very difficult to carry around the sale, especially in the overcrowded halls of the church. A small nylon suitcase or a nylon shopping bag with a shoulder strap is preferable to a box; it should be strong but light. You will really need these items if you're going to do any real "combat shopping," as I like to call it! At a crowded sale, you simply do not have time to examine every item individually. Pick up items that are of particular interest, stuff them in your bag or cart, and once you have covered the entire sale, find some quiet corner to call your own and go through everything. The faster you are, the better your chances of snagging the best bargains. Remember, this is no time for sleeping on your feet, this is a marathon! May the best shopper win! Some buyers put their name and telephone number on large Post-it notes reading SOLD so they can hold items too large to carry prior to paying for them.

Dress comfortably, in something form-fitting that you can pull garments on over and shoes that you can easily slip on and off, as I have suggested for thrift store shopping. This will save you a great deal of time when trying things on. If they have a dressing room, you can be sure it will be a communal one set up for the women with a separate one for the men.

You may also want to wear a pair of old gloves at a rummage sale, because you will be doing a great deal of digging. Most importantly, you should wear running shoes because you really need to fly.

"Casing the Joint"

A rummage sale is a great place to employ the scanning technique I described on page 16. You truly want to know where everything is immediately. There is one little trick I will share with you that can put you ahead of the crowds: *Bring some items to donate yourself.* It is best if you do this the evening before the sale, which is often when the volunteers are there setting up. When they invite you in for a moment you can, as I like to refer to it, "case the joint"!

While there, find out in what area they will be setting up the jewelry and/or the antiques and collectibles. The designer clothing may also be in a separate area or back room. This way, when you do make it through those doors in the morning, you can make a beeline straight for the section you want. Otherwise, by the time you locate the jewelry table, all the truly good items may be bought and paid for! A rummage sale jewelry table can be one of the most frenzied affairs in your rummage shopping experience, so be prepared to fight for that piece of Kenneth J. Lane, or that beautiful rhinestone Weiss brooch. Be forewarned, too, that the staff at the jewelry table usually requires that you pay for everything right there. So make your transaction a speedy one and move on.

Always Go Back for a Second Look

After I have "done" the whole sale, I usually go back for a last look. By this time many people have tried things on, found they don't fit, and discarded them. The dressing room is an especially good source for this. Most people don't take the time to put things back out on the floor after they have tried them on, so you can truly find some treasures strewn on the dressing room floor. Don't be shy about being the first one in the dressing room to speak up and request an item from someone else when you see they are about to discard it. But at the same time don't be unnecessarily aggressive. You may also find discarded items at the sales desk. Oftentimes people change their minds once they reach the cashier, perhaps deciding that an item is too expensive or discovering that they haven't brought enough money. This could be your good fortune. I have also witnessed many dealers offering a novice collector additional money for an item that the beginner has just purchased. A good rummage sale can be an absolute wonderland of fun and excitement. Expect the unexpected and you won't be disappointed!

3

Garage Sales, Estate Sales, Flea Markets, Auctions, and Antique Shows

Garage sales, estate sales, flea markets, and auctions are important sources for purchasing items and developing a feel for pricing and the value of merchandise. The more sales you attend, the more you will become acquainted with the trends in the merchandise being offered, as well as the prices that the market will bear. If you plan to grow from a weekend shopper to a full-time dealer you will need to develop a deep passion for all of the various buying venues and be prepared to make attending them a way of life.

Whichever of these sales you attend, that old adage still stands fast and true: "The early bird catches the worm." That means you must be out the door and on your way to that sale long before the morning mist has had an opportunity to evaporate from the rose, or all that will be left will be the thorns!

Garage Sales

When preparing to go to a garage or estate sale, you must do your homework. Since most garage sales are held on either Saturday or Sunday, most serious garage salers start to scour their local papers by the Thursday prior to the sale or, at the very least, the night before. Familiarize yourself with the style of ads that attract you and upon attendance have proven to be fruitful. Learn to spot a winner by knowing what you're looking for. Aggressive shoppers call around to any of the ads that have telephone numbers listed, or even go so far as to drive over to the address days ahead of time in the hopes of getting a jump on other buyers. The very least they do is map out where they will go the morning of the sale. This can be as simple as taking a highlighter pen to your classified section. Always check the garage sale, estate sale, and antique auction sections.

Most sales start at 8:00 A.M., and I would say that the good merchandise is scooped up within the first half hour of a sale. There are some who believe there may still be a few undiscovered treasures to be had once the morning rolls on. My feeling is that by 11:00 A.M., most sales have been picked over. There may be exceptions, such as when someone sleeps in and starts their sale later than planned, or if it rains in the morning and clears up later in the day. But I don't like pot luck. My time is valuable, as I am sure yours is, too, and I appreciate a sure thing.

Garage sales can be your best source of all for fabulous merchandise. As with thrift stores or rummage sales, you will find anything and everything at a garage sale. Most people who hold a sale are nonprofessionals who simply want to clear out their closets at any price. Some may be doing some spring cleaning; others may be moving clear across the country and don't wish to incur the cost of shipping things they have decided they just don't need anymore. This means you will be able to pick things up for a fraction of their original cost. Rarely will anyone ever want to have to carry an item back into their house once they have made the commitment to sell it, so the buyer really has the advantage over the seller.

Estate Sales

Estate sales are usually much more professional than your average garage sale. In general they have better merchandise, especially in the antiques and collectibles. The term *estate sale* originally referred to the selling of items from the estate of someone who is deceased; however this is not always the case, and in truth it has become a term widely used to attract a higher-end buyer. Many estate sales are held by a company that specializes in this type of sale. They will have any antiques or collectibles appraised prior to the sale, and you can be sure their pricing structure will reflect these appraisals. You may also find that if it is a professionally run estate sale, the company will also *pad* the sale with items from other estate sales that may not have sold the first time around. The company may also have an antique store and will use merchandise from their store to fill out an estate sale. This can often be detected by an inconsistency in the style of items being offered.

You will undoubtedly find some lovely purchases at an estate sale, but because of the level of professionalism it may be more difficult to find an exceptional bargain.

Flea Markets

Of all the resale categories, flea markets start the earliest. Most dealers begin setting up at 4:00 A.M. It is common knowledge that a lot of money exchanges hands long before the public is admitted to the sale, mostly dealers buying from each other. They will in turn sell those items at a substantial markup later that day. Some markets have a special policy for "early bird shoppers" who are undaunted by dark and cold mornings. These hardy types show up around 6:00 A.M., flashlights in hands, and pay an inflated admission fee, which can be as much as $15, instead of the usual $5. Apparently, there are even charter flights that bring shoppers to the Rose Bowl flea market in Pasadena, California, once a month. As with all sales, it is important to get there early.

Cash is absolutely the operative word in this venue. Unless you are Elizabeth Taylor or the Queen of England, most dealers won't take your check, as they have all, at times, been "burned."

It's usually a good idea to bring your own strong shopping bags to a flea market. Most dealers seem always to have the same excuse: "We've sold so much today, we've run out of bags." As with rummage sale shopping, a smart shopper will bring a bundle buggy or luggage cart to the flea market. I have seen many people purchase large items and then leave them with the dealers to pick up on their way out. This may work at a smaller flea market, but in many of the markets I have shopped at, it's an absolute nightmare to find that dealer again in the labyrinth of tables and stalls. It is best to take your smaller purchases with you when you buy them.

Some buyers, especially dealers, travel in teams in order to cover more ground in a shorter period of time. I have even witnessed many of them using walkie-talkies to communicate with each other! This allows them to help each other make decisions about certain purchases from anywhere in the market. Dealers who are both selling and buying at a venue will use walkie-talkies as well so that they can move away from their booth to shop, allowing their partner to negotiate a sale with them while they're away from their table. These flea markets can be very large and if you are serious about your business and have a partner, you may want to consider investing in a set.

Once you have covered the flea market and you still have time to spare, go through it again, this time in the opposite direction. You will be amazed at what you missed your first time through.

Auctions

There are many different types of auctions. You may find listed in your local classified section or telephone directories names of the larger auction houses: Christie's, Butterfield & Butterfield, and Sotheby's. Then there are police auctions, charity (Salvation Army and Goodwill Industries) auctions, and moving and storage company auctions; government, county, and military base auctions; the private auction houses; and just about any company that may be going out of business. You can write for a listing of government auctions to: Federal Government Sales, Pueblo, CO 81009.

To be honest, auctions are not my favorite type of sale, because of the competition factor. I prefer to walk into a shop, pick something up, and either choose to buy it or not. At an auction, you must compete for that item. If you're not on your toes, you can lose. Oh, I hate when that happens! In addition, it always seems that the very item you are interested in—perhaps the *only* item you are interested in—can take the entire day or evening to come before the gavel. Furthermore, it is the person who is willing to pay the highest price for an item that will walk away with it. Since I am always trying to pay the lowest price, this process doesn't really appeal to me. However, there are plenty of exceptions at auctions. You can definitely walk away with fabulous merchandise at great prices if you can stand having your heart palpitate every time someone ups your bid! In all fairness, I do rather enjoy the entertainment value of a good auction. They usually draw quite a crew of both spectators and buyers. It is always fascinating to see what other people buy at auction, too!

Most auctions will have a printed program that you would be wise to study prior to the sale. The larger auctions houses will usually have a fancy glossy one with photo illustrations that they will sell for approximately $25. Programs are well worth the price as a reference tool after the auction for putting a value on items you may acquire in the future. Be sure to request that they send you the realized price list for the items that were sold. You can usually arrange this by putting your name on an envelope and leaving it with their administrative office.

All auctions require that you register with their office with a valid driver's license if you intend to bid. You will then be given what is referred to as a paddle, which is usually your number on a large card that you will hold up every time you bid. If you do not have a number, they will not accept your bid. Many auction houses will also require you to place a deposit of cash or a credit card with them, which will establish you as a serious buyer. Be assured they will always apply that deposit to any purchases you make or return it when you hand in your paddle and choose to leave the auction. Don't think you can decide to borrow another dealer's paddle and number at the last minute when you see an item come up for auction, or you may find that dealer requesting a fee to use their number.

There is also a more practical reason for attending an auction, and that is to see what other dealers are buying and what they are willing to pay for those items. This can be a great indication of what is popular at the moment and what's not. Be sure to distinguish the private collector from the dealers when you are considering what they are willing to pay for certain items. Most private collectors will stop at nothing to get what they want and will often overbid for an item simply because they want it and can't stand the idea of anyone else getting it!

A word of caution here: Arrive early enough to view anything you intend to bid on. There are plenty of reproductions and fakes out there. If it sounds too good to be true, it probably is, as the saying goes. You can almost always bet that if they don't show you the back of that beautiful Victorian cabinet when the stage hands are holding it up for display, they have something to hide. You may find that it turns out to have a pressed wood back and staple gun joints!

If you are planning on bidding on an expensive piece, you may be wise to search out an expert's opinion first. Have a good look around—all the way around! Take note of other people's responses to the particular item you are interested in. It is often wise not to let on that you are extremely interested in a particular item until the bidding starts, since you do not want to encourage your competition to consider that item. Let them assume no one else is actively interested, and you will have the upper hand. Once you have decided to bid on a particular item, set your limit and stick to it. Remember, many auction houses attach an additional 10 percent buyer's premium to the final gavel price.

You would be wise to become familiar with other dealers and their merchandise. If dealers have a piece of merchandise in an auction and it is not commanding the price they were expecting, they may bid on the item themselves. This is done to drive up the price. Most reputable auction houses will discourage this. Dealers will sometime work around the house rules by having a friend bid on the item for them. Always be sure you know the value of a piece, so you don't overbid for it. Adhering to your self-imposed spending limit on an item prior to its going up for sale will help to keep you from getting carried away in a competitive bidding war.

Police Auctions

Most cities' police departments hold auctions periodically, depending on the amount of stolen and unclaimed merchandise they have accumulated. The money raised through the sale of these goods usually goes to fund internal programs such as youth programs or to offset the cost of operations.

You may find some pretty reasonable buys at these auctions. There is always plenty of stereo equipment and cameras. You will also find a good selection of bicycles. Their pricing is usually very fair; however, for the most part the people who attend police auctions are buying for their own use and therefore are willing to pay slightly higher prices than a dealer who intends to resell an item. Many of the police departments hold annual gun auctions, which are apparently their most popular auctions and can raise a substantial amount of money.

Contact your local police department to find out where and when they will be holding their next sale.

Antique Shows

Antique shows are professionally run businesses where many independent dealers pay for an allotted space at the show and offer their merchandise for sale to the general public. Many of these shows travel around the country and are offered up in a particular location either monthly, quarterly, or annually. Antique shows, like flea markets, can be great places for you to do some very serious window shopping and price comparisons. This is another venue where you will get a feel for what the market will bear as well as collectible trends. This is where you will do most of your research. When you find a dealer willing to talk, ask as many questions as you can on everything you have an interest in. If you see similar items at different dealers' tables, always compare pricing and attempt to establish a reason as to why one item may be priced higher than another by asking for an explanation. If you are at all serious about becoming a dealer, frequent as many shows as you can.

Antique shows normally start a little later than flea markets and rummage or garage sales, usually around 10:00 A.M. As with all sales, it's best to get there when they open the doors; however, many times you can do more aggressive negotiating a little later in the day. Many antique dealers become concerned when they have not sold a particular item by a certain point in the day and are dreading packing it up and hauling it back to some distant place.

Most good antique shows charge an admission fee, normally about $5. Be sure to put your name down on their mailing list for their next show. Many send out a card that will not only remind you of their upcoming show but also give you a considerable discount on the admission price.

All antique dealers love to do business with cash, and you can usually cut your best deal that way. Few are equipped to take credit cards unless they are very high-end dealers and have established business with a banking institution. Most will take personal checks as long as you have ample identification.

What to Buy at a Flea Market, Auction, or Antique Show

If you are buying at a flea market for your own use and not for resale, then simply cut your best deal and enjoy your purchase. However, if you are buying an item for resale, keep in mind that the dealers at these sales have already put their best markup on the items. It is not often that you can buy something at *their* price and then turn around and make a handsome profit on the item at *your* sale next week, unless you have stumbled across a novice dealer who is less experienced at the pricing game. Unless you have found this type of seller you will probably not be able to realize a sizable markup. However, if you have a high-end antique shop where you can move that item at a higher price, you may be lucky. The beginners (or first-timers) are out there, so it is still worthwhile shopping these markets for re-sale items. Always keep in mind that unless you arrive at the crack of dawn it doesn't matter how savvy you are—all the best buys will be gone.

Auctions are generally a good place to buy if you are planning to resell. You can get some exceptional deals on box-lot items. Box lots are just that, large boxes of mixed items. It is wise to arrive early enough to view the general contents so the box you purchase is more than a surprise package. You can usually find a few interesting pieces and turn a tidy profit on the items. Auctions are where many antique and flea market dealers get the bulk of their merchandise, because they can buy a lot all at once rather than searching many separate venues.

4

The Art of
Persuasive Bartering

If you are ever to succeed in the resale or antique business, one of the most important things you need to learn is the fine art of negotiating. You will need to ply your skill at both buying and selling. Understanding how to cut the best deal on an item will also help you to counter someone's offer when they attempt to purchase your merchandise. Having a well-honed bartering banter will quickly establish you as a professional dealer, and you will find it commands respect from other dealers and ultimately gets you the best possible price on any merchandise you wish to buy.

The Object of the Game

Remember that for many, bartering and bargaining are forms of mutual entertainment. In some cultures sellers are offended if you *don't* attempt to bargain with them. You will be buying from dealers as your business grows, so it is wise to hone your skills early. The object of the game is to get the best possible price. Many people are tremendously apprehensive or shy about asking for a better price or discount. I have already touched on various circumstances that may justify your asking for a discount, for instance, when an item is flawed or damaged. Yet there is absolutely no reason why you should not ask for a reduced price simply because you would like to pay less for that item. It may be that you feel the item is slightly overpriced, or you may be inclined to believe, as I do, that you're not worth your salt unless you get something knocked off!

How do you do this? As suggested in Chapter 1 on thrift store shopping, it is always best to go straight to the top and find the dealer, owner, or manager. They will ultimately be the one that the sales staff turns to get the authorization anyway. *Be direct.* Know what you're willing to pay for that item, and be willing to buy it if they do give you their best price. There is nothing worse for a future relationship with a particular seller than if you ask for their best price; they give it to you; and then you choose not to buy it!

I have had it suggested to me that it is wise to dress down when shopping at flea markets or thrift stores, so that the dealers won't size you up and allow their price to reflect what they think you can afford to pay. In fact, I once had an amusing conversation with a dealer whom I had bought from on several occasions. He remarked that the reason he did not recognize me from the other times was that I had been in disguise, hoping to get a better deal. My response to him was, "I could approach you dripping in diamonds and I would still walk away paying the price I want to pay for an item. It's not what you wear or who you are, *it's how you crack the deal!*"

Industry, Dealers, or Members of the Trade

If you are a professional dealer you may request a dealer price or industry discount when making a purchase from other dealers or professional businesses. Most will give you a standard 10 percent off the listed price. Some may give you as much as 40 percent off. The discount may also be contingent on how desirable an item is. Obviously, if the dealer has had it for a long time or it has been hanging around a shop collecting dust, they may be more inclined to let it go for a more substantial discount. Most antique dealers welcome art directors, interior decorators, and set decorators by also offering them similar discounts.

If you are a dealer or a member of the trade and are in possession of a valid resale license, you may request that you not pay sales tax on a particular item. The reason for this is that you are not the end user. You will be selling that item to the ultimate end user and charging *them* the sales tax at the time of their purchase. People have been known to abuse this system to avoid paying the sales tax on their personal purchases. It is not, however, a wise decision, since the government is really cracking down on this. If the IRS finds an item reported by the seller that did not have sales tax recorded, and that item does *not* show up on your books that year (as being sold with a sales tax charge), then you may face some rather grave charges (e.g., tax fraud, sales tax evasion) and a tax audit to boot!

The Approach That Works for Me

Never tell the seller up front what you are willing to pay for an item. Once you have told them, you may feel obligated to buy that item and pay more for it than what the seller may be willing to take. I like to ask, as I browse, what the dealer is willing to sell an item for. I may even ask for the price of an item I am not seriously interested in. By doing this you create a type of buying power. If the dealer senses that you are considering buying a number of items, he or she may quote you a more favorable price on each item in the hopes that you will purchase them all.

When I am at the cash desk, I make sure I ask for a price on each item separately. Once I have been given the best price on each item individually, I will then ask for the best price if I was to take all of it. In this way you indicate that there is potential for you to buy it all, but only if the seller gives you a further reduction.

Some dealers may give you both the discount on the individual item and an additional amount off the total—but don't count on it. They are at least as sharp as we are and, after all, they are in the business to maximize their profit. You will gain bargaining leverage by having a large amount to purchase when attempting your best price. By the same token, if you are shopping with someone else, consolidate your purchases at the counter and have one of you negotiate the deal as one purchase. The more you buy, the better the discount.

Remember to be courteous and respectful. You want the seller on your side. If something is truly priced fairly, don't ask for the discount (unless you really need it). This philosophy will always play in your favor with future transactions. It is inevitable that you will pass that way again, and you do not want the proprietor thinking, "Here comes that stingy cheapskate again!" Don't kid yourself: they remember a "cheapskate" just as clearly as a "big spender"! They know if you were willing to pay an honest price for things, or if they wanted to throw you out of the shop for pleading for a discount. No one likes a pushy person.

Find the approach that works best for you. Be straight, fair, and honest. Both parties will walk away feeling satisfied that they have made a good deal. A win-win situation is best for both the buyer and the seller!

The Direct Approach:
Just Ask!

The following are some phrases that I have found work well and are accepted by most professional dealers across the country. These will help you to open the floor to negotiation and also to receive a discount or better price. You may wish to use a combination of these phrases or find the one that best suits your personal style and approach to bargaining.

"What is your best price?"
"What is the best you can do on this?"
"Will you come down any on this?"
"Why don't we split the difference?" (between what you want to
    pay and the seller hopes to get)
"Would you take (*quote a price*) for this?"
"What if I take *all* of it?"
"Do you offer an *industry* (or *to the trade*) discount?"
"I have a resale license (or vendor's permit) and don't wish to pay
    sales tax."

5

Consignment Stores

Consignment or resale stores are a growing industry, with private-venture stores cropping up across the country. Many people are turning to the idea of opening a consignment shop as opposed to a retail shop because of the lower start-up cost and overhead in merchandise. Most of their merchandise is placed in the shop at no cost on consignment, and to many that makes good business sense.

There is really no difference between a resale shop and a consignment shop, although some may say that a resale shop will only buy secondhand merchandise outright, whereas a consignment shop takes the merchandise on consignment. Consigning your possessions can be a simple and convenient way of disposing of unwanted or unused belongings. It's also an excellent opportunity for new designers to test their creations on the market, because the shops are more open to trying merchandise if they don't have to pay for it upfront. Consignment is also another way to manage our resources through recycling, thus keeping discarded clothing out of the solid waste stream.

Consignment shops are as varied as the merchandise they sell. Some consignment shops sell only clothing and accessories, while others may specialize in furniture or antiques. They all work more or less on the same basis of *shared profits*. The store will attempt to sell your merchandise over a designated period of time and share the profits of the sale with you—it's that simple.

How to Choose a Consignment Store
That's Right for You

You'll need to do a little investigating beforehand to select the best consignment shop for your specific needs. After all, you will be entrusting a stranger with merchandise that you invested cold hard cash in. Wholesalers would not dream of supplying merchandise to an unfamiliar retail shop until they receive a satisfactory credit check and have established a solid relationship, so why should you?

If you do not find a consignment shop in your area, then try your local telephone directory. Look under "Resale Clothing," "Consignment," and "Used Clothing or Merchandise." You should begin with an anonymous telephone query about their consignment policy. Ask what their consignment percentage split is. (How much of the selling price goes to you, the *consignor*, and how much does the store, the *consignee*, keep?) Most will offer somewhere between 40 percent and 60 percent of the selling price to the consignor. Depending on their policy, that percentage may change after a certain date, if the merchandise has not sold. Always try to get at least 50 percent, and never take less than 40 percent.

Some stores will specify a *list price* for your merchandise on your inventory contract. They will then mark up a higher selling price on the ticket, the *floor price*. Your percentage is calculated on the listed price indicated on your contract, not on the floor price of your merchandise as indicated on the garment ticket. The difference is usually to cover miscellaneous costs for processing your merchandise through their system, including repairs, ironing or steaming, tagging, computer entry of inventory, stamps and mailing of store promotions, advertising, and flyers. These are all hard, out-of-pocket costs, and often the management of some businesses will try to recover these through a direct fee to you or through the consumer by way of an increased floor price. Others may charge you only for pressing and/or repairs. You should be aware, though, that this cost will be charged back to you for each item, whether it sells or not.

Choose a store that suits your type of merchandise. Always shop the store first. If the racks are overcrowded and badly maintained, perhaps this is not the store for you. Be discriminating. You don't want to consign your Chanel suit to a store that seems to specialize in ready-to-wear sports clothes that favor polyester. Chances are, the customer who would appreciate your gently worn Chanel is not going to frequent that particular shop. You may want to locate one in a more affluent neighborhood, to increase your chances of selling at a higher price. It's all about supply and demand.

Do They Have a Markdown Policy?

You will also want to know if they have a markdown system. Some businesses mark merchandise down on a monthly basis to keep merchandise moving (*turnover*). It is important to know this, because if you expect an item to sell for your listed price, but it has remained in the store over a period of time and is now in the markdown system, you may be very disappointed by the final selling price. You always have the right to pick up your merchandise prior to markdowns if you do not wish to have it sold at a discount. (I have been told of occasions when an owner or store employee who coveted a piece of merchandise had placed it in the stockroom so that the days would tick by and they could purchase it at the reduced price based on the store's markdown policy. In these cases the merchandise never got an honest chance to sell to a regular customer at the full list price.)

If the store has a markdown policy, be sure to keep your eye on the dates. That is *your* responsibility. The store may also have the right to reduce the price of your merchandise if it becomes damaged, which does happen. You will want to go over your merchandise carefully when you bring it in and periodically afterward to take any damages into account. If buttons need replacing, replace them. If something else is in need of repair, repair it, or allow it to be discounted and humbly take your loss.

Your Consignment Contract

One of the most important things to be aware of is your contract. Read the fine print before you sign it. Your contract should have an expiration date on it, list the percentage you will receive as the consignor, and describe the terms by which you receive your payment for sold merchandise. Most businesses pay their consignors bimonthly. Ask if their inventory system is on

Garment and accessories compliments of Goodwill Toronto
Jaeger mauve two-piece suit, $10, original cost approximately $800.
Gucci watch, $30, original cost approximately $325.
Birks black crocodile purse, $5, original cost approximately $2,000.
Chanel cream sling-back shoes, $4, original cost approximately $500.

computer. Be very wary of any business that still operates on a manual system, since it is difficult for them to track your merchandise accurately and extremely time-consuming to prepare your checks. This often results in longer waits for your consignment check, as well as the chance for human error.

I am always skeptical of the shops that claim you can drop by anytime to pick up any money accumulated in your account. Often, the owner is not in and the sales staff is not authorized to give a cash or check disbursement.

And what if they have already made their bank deposits and do not have enough money in the till, or *float*, to pay out to your account when you just happen to drop by? It is much more professional to issue checks on a given day each month.

Your contract should have a place to inventory every item you bring in. Do not leave the store until you are sure every item has been listed on your contract, and that you have a true copy of that document. Never leave your merchandise to be inventoried at a later time (unless you know and trust the proprietor personally). Some businesses may claim that they are too busy to do the inventory at that moment and that they will send a copy of the inventory to you in the mail. If they are too busy, then they should not have scheduled an appointment with you at that time. Simply say you will return with your merchandise at a more convenient time, or some of your items may be unaccounted for and missing.

Pricing Your Merchandise

When inventorying your merchandise, work with the management to establish a selling price. Try to be as accurate as possible in recalling the original price you paid for each item. When defining an appropriate selling price, you must take into consideration what condition the item is in and how old it is. You must also consider that it would also have gone on sale at the retail level. With all of this in mind, consignment items are normally priced at roughly half the original purchase price. It is important to realize that most businesses are deft at pricing your merchandise, and they too want the highest possible price for your merchandise. So don't take it personally if they suggest a lower selling price than what you expected. Bear in mind, if it is overpriced, it will sit in the store longer and run a greater risk of being damaged, lost, or stolen. It will eventually go through the markdown process anyway.

Lost or Stolen Merchandise

Most contracts will state that "The management is *not* responsible for lost, stolen, or damaged merchandise." Always ask if the store has a security system. If it does, ask how it works and have the management give you a demonstration. Some businesses may offer their consignors the opportunity to use their electronic security tagging system for a nominal fee of approximately 50 cents per tag. Some may tag merchandise selling for over $50 at no cost to the consignor. Ask about their policy on security, and get it in writing on your contract whenever possible.

Don't Fall Prey to
Unscrupulous Business Practices

Remember that unscrupulous behavior is truly the exception and not the rule, and yet it pays to be aware of the pitfalls in dealing with some consignment business owners and their employees. The most important thing to do right from the start is to make sure you're dealing with a reputable company. You may wish to check with the Better Business Bureau or look for member status with the National Association of Resale and Thrift Shops (NARTS). Recognized shops must display their membership decal. You may call or write to NARTS to verify a shop's standing at any time: 157 Halsted, Chicago Heights, IL 60411 (fax: 708-755-0403, phone: 800-544-0751). NARTS has a professional code of ethics that all members are bound to follow in order to remain in good standing.

If you are already doing business with a shop and have any doubts, the best thing to do is to frequent the store yourself. Just drop by now and again to check the status of your merchandise. If is important to realize, though, that most stores will *not* go over your inventory with you item by item unless you have an appointment. Many will do so only if you are completely removing your merchandise from the store, and that is almost always done by appointment only. It is very time-consuming and the least loved job of all, so don't look for a tremendous amount of cooperation. *You really need to service your own account.*

Make sure you note the expiration date on your contract and follow the instructions in the fine print. If it says you must pick up your merchandise in person on or before the expiration date, do it. Failure to do so could mean that your merchandise will become the property of the store, or they may have the right to dispose of your merchandise as they see fit. Often this is referred to as a donation to their selected charity, and occasionally it may mean that they will receive the tax writeoff themselves. In the worst-case scenario they may in fact sell the merchandise and not be obligated to pay you anything, because your contract has expired.

If they do donate your merchandise, you may request a copy of the donation slips they should have received from the charity. You may request that they donate your things on your behalf, and that you would like the tax donation form to be filled out in your name and returned to you. Or alternatively, you could pick up your merchandise when your contract expires and donate it yourself, then receive the tax deduction directly from the charity of your choice.

Checklist for Choosing a Consignment Shop

- The store's location
- Type of merchandise it specializes in
- Your original purchase price
- Hours of operation
- Contract
- Percentage of sale to you (40%–50%+)
- Expiration date of contract
- Markdown date
- Markdown policy for damages or time lapsed
- Inventory system on computer
- Payment schedule
- Do they have a security system?
- What do they do with their donations?
- Is there a different floor price?
- Are there any charges for inventory, or steaming or pressing of your garments?

Buying at a Consignment Store

A consignment store can be a great place to buy. If they have a considerable markdown system, you can find some terrific bargains. Always ask about their pricing system when you enter the store. You may find that the Yves Saint Laurent suit that was originally priced at $250 has now been reduced to half price or even less.

Buying things out of season is another smart way to get a good deal. If you choose classic and timeless merchandise, you can easily put the garment away until next year. You will find that a consignment store will reduce its out-of-season merchandise quite substantially to move it out. Consignment stores also tend to sell clothing that is no more than a season or two old. You will therefore find that you can get a wider selection of contemporary clothing in them than in, say, a thrift store. Although you will not find the tremendous bargains that you would at a thrift store, rummage sale, garage sale, or flea market, it is my belief that you will pay at least 50 percent to 70 percent less than you would retail.

If You're Planning to Open (or Buy)
Your Own Consignment Shop

Owning and operating a consignment business is a wonderful alternative if you have ever considered opening a retail boutique. Many of the points to follow will apply to either a retail or consignment business. The most important difference between retail and consignment is the amount of paperwork involved in consignments and the time involved in managing your consignors. Your store will be only as good as its merchandise, and the merchandise will be only as good as the consignors you attract.

This is really a people business, and you will need to have a tremendous amount of patience. You can't expect to simply open the doors and have the business run itself. Your daily tasks and responsibilities will include sorting through mounds of clothing, as well as staying on top of fashion trends and being able to spot a garment that has selling potential a second or third time around. Most important, you need to be sure that this is truly a business you feel passionate about. If you do decide that you would like to open a shop of your own. there are a few good books available on the subject, in particular *Too Good to Be Threw*, by Kate Holmes, that give advice to consignment store operators. In the meantime, consider these important issues before making any serious steps:

- Location, location, location
- Number of years in business
- Why are they selling the shop?
- Why do *you* want to buy it?
- Are they members of NARTS?
- Gross & net income of the store
- Have they owned the shop from its inception?
- Why have they *not* opened another shop?
- Will they open another shop? (If so, where?)
- Will they be taking their consignors with them?
- Number of pieces of merchandise in the store?

- How many of those pieces does the store own?
- Value of the merchandise owned by the store?
- Times per year they "turn over" their inventory
- Average daily sales (weekends)
- Amount of an average sale?
- Average ticket price of an individual item?
- When do most of the sales occur?
- Do sales fluctuate with seasonal change?
- What are their store hours?
- A typical amount paid to an individual consignor
- The number of *current* consignors
- What is their consignment split?
- When do they issue consignment checks?
- Is the store set up on computer?
- Do they have a bar code inventory system?
- Do they have a book-keeper?
- Will they show you their consignor books?
- What demographics do they cater to?
- New-to-used ratio of merchandise sold
- Merchandise the store specializes in?
- Is parking available?
- What type of insurance is required?
- Number of employees at present?
- What type of advertising budget do they have?
- What type of advertising do they do?
- Do they have a *current* mailing list?
- Amount of walk-by traffic the store gets
- Is there a security system for the merchandise?
- What kind of shrinkage have they had?
- Is there an alarm system for the store?
- What type of register do they have?
- Is the shop in need of repairs?
- Is the landlord willing to do upgrades?
- What type of fixtures does the store have?
- What is the rent?
- Who pays utilities?
- What type of lease can you expect to get?
- Is there a washroom on the premises?
- Is the washroom up to standards?

- Are there dressing rooms? How many?
- Is there an office area to process the merchandise?
- Is there available space for expansion?
- Have the store's policies changed?

6

Holding Your Own Sale

In this high-tech, speed-driven, economic environment we seem to be taking jobs away from ourselves with our own technology. It is no small wonder that everyone is scrambling to unearth new and more innovative ways to make or save a buck. What I am seeing more and more of is the idea of reselling for profit, or what many refer to as "the underground economy." Tens of millions of dollars are made every week in this country from the profits derived from antique sales, swap meets, flea markets, and garage sales. Some 45,000 people attend the Rose Bowl Flea Market, held once a month in Pasadena, California. In previous chapters I taught you how to buy for your own personal use. Here I hope to lead you through an enjoyable hobby, into what just might reward you a fair profit.

Resale License
(Seller's or Vendor's Permit)

The first thing you want to do is acquire a resale license, also referred to as a vendor's permit or seller's permit. You can acquire one in the United

States by applying to your local office of the State Board of Equalization or in Canada to the Ministry of Revenue. You will need to acquire a separate license for every location (event) or state you intend to sell in. In most states your permanent residence must appear on your original license as your principal location. In the state of California, a separate form known as a BT-530-B must be attached with the address of any temporary location (flea market, etc.) where you plan to sell in the state; check with your local offices for the appropriate form in your state. Temporary location permits are often made available at the events office of the flea market where you will be selling, but do not depend on it. It is advisable that you acquire the proper permit from your local State Board of Equalization prior to the event. If you do intend to acquire one at the event on the day of the sale, be sure to have your valid *principal location* seller's permit with you at that time. The venue operators are required by law to ask to see your permit; they are often subjected to state inspection and can face up to a $1,000 penalty for each unverified rental. It is advisable to have your permit with you at all times.

There are no fees for these permits as long as you are in good standing. If you have had a problem in the past with a permit or with taxes owed, you may be required to post a bond to ensure that your taxes will be paid in the future. This amount could be substantial, so try to remain in good standing and file your taxes appropriately. All you need to do is keep your books up-to-date and send in the sales tax you have collected on any of the merchandise sold in that quarter. It is that simple.

In many states you will also be required to complete a Swap Meet Sellers Information Report when you sell at any swap meet or flea market. The main reason for this is, according to Business and Profession codes, you are required to report on these forms all property offered or displayed for sale or exchange, to assist in tracing and recovering stolen property and detecting sales tax evasion.

Choosing the Right Venue

There are many different venues through which to sell. The most common are yard sales, garage sales, estate sales, flea markets, swap meets, or professional antique markets held monthly, quarterly, or annually. Many people have asked me what the difference is between a flea market and a swap meet. It has been my experience that many swap meets will sell predominantly new merchandise—more specifically, a large percentage of knockoff or fake merchandise from the Orient—whereas a *true* flea market will sell mainly collectibles and antiques. The terms are certainly interchangeable, though, and can vary from state to state.

There is really no difference between a garage sale and a yard sale, expect that one is often held in a garage and the other is held in the front or backyard. Estate sales may be a good source for furniture and antiques, though of course the items offered for sale will undoubtedly be as varied as the person who originally owned them.

There are also some interesting variations on the garage sale theme such as *moving sale* or *divorce sale*. I have always found that divorce sales are well worth attending. The divorcée or divorcé is almost always willing to sell her or his gifts from the other at ridiculously low prices. If you yourself are holding a divorce sale, *never let your emotions get in the way*. You may well come out of the sale with more than just bad memories. Ladies, go for the gusto—get as much as you can for that tacky little cocktail dress your ex-husband bought for his mistress and you found in the back of *your* closet!

Choosing the right venue is usually a trial-and-error game. A market that may work for someone selling country antiques may be the wrong market for someone selling vintage clothing. It's always wise to shop the venue prior to laying out money for rent on a space there. This way you can assess for yourself what type of merchandise is being sold and gauge its price points and the type of consumers that are shopping there.

Even when choosing to hold your own yard or garage sale, you may wind up with some unfortunate surprises, such as a very poor turnout. Some neighborhoods simply do not get the type of drive-by shoppers that others do. I have found that taking a friend up on an offer to have the sale at their house can prove to be very profitable. You should always take into consideration the income level of the neighborhood. You might think you could make an absolute killing by holding your sale in Beverly Hills, but beware! Most people who live in such an area are not your early Saturday morning garage salers. You may sell better in a working class to upper middle class neighborhood. This is where the economy has driven consumers to the streets, in search of a serious bargain. You may also think, "If I build it, they will come." This is not necessarily so. If you have a large front driveway, hold your sale there. A front lawn will work too, but you may find that you have quite a bit of damage to your expensive lawn from people trampling it all day.

Garage Sale Regulations in Your Neighborhood

You may find that you can get away with the occasional garage sale on your own property without acquiring a resale license (seller's or vendor's permit). You should check the regulations on holding garage sales in your residential area with your city hall or State Board of Equalization (or Ministry of Revenue in Canada). Some local governments allow you to hold a private sale of personal belongings only two to four times a year and require you to acquire the necessary permits to do so. If you do not have the necessary permits and licenses, you may find your local police department enforcing those regulations and closing your sale down. Many local retail businesses are opposed to the independent vendor and feel that garage sales and flea markets cut into their retail profits.

Thinking of Opening a Shop?

You may not be ready to jump straight into the full-time responsibility of owning and operating a shop. Holding private sales or renting space at a particular venue is a great way to get your feet wet without a high financial risk. You can feel out the industry gradually and take your time deciding if this line of work is really for you. While you are deciding, you can be building your inventory, honing your bartering skills, and developing an eye for buying.

Choosing a Partner for Your Sale

It is to everyone's advantage that you have a partner (or more than one). There is something to be said about safety in numbers, not to mention the moral support you can receive from a good partner. In addition, it is very difficult to set up a sale all on your own. It is nearly impossible to patrol your merchandise if you are running in and out of your home or vehicle to retrieve things. The setup time is when some people will practice sleight of hand on your things, so you truly need a second or third set of eyes. Also, with a partner or two, you can share your advertising and participation fees.

It is important for your partner to know the price of every item if you have chosen not to put price tags on your merchandise. They also need to know what leeway they have in negotiating the final selling price with the buyer. You don't want to return from your washroom break to discover that they have decided to sell something for a quarter of what you'd planned.

The most important thing to consider when choosing a business partner is their passion. Do they love this business as much as you do? Whether you decide to hold a garage sale at home or venture out to one of the many flea markets or antique shows, it is a tremendous amount of work. Unless your partner is willing to go the distance with and for you, you may find yourselves with irreconcilable differences. There are all those 5:00 A.M. mornings when you would just as soon roll over and go back to sleep, but your signs have to be put up in the neighborhood. Then there is the setup, all the lifting and schlepping of your great stuff, and the long fourteen-hour days when nothing sells! Then, there's striking the set—taking the signs down from the neighborhood.

You should also factor in all the work you need to do ahead of the sale: putting your mailer out, making up your signs—the list goes on and on! What you need is a partner who is truly willing to put in as much as you are. You should decide up front how you are dividing the labor and assign tasks. If you are an artist and they are better at selling, then you make the signs and do the setup; let them work the tables. Try to distribute the workload evenly; in this way, no one will be looking over anyone's shoulder judging their participation. These sales can be terrific fun if you choose your partner carefully. There is nothing like having a great team. The day races by, and you usually make much more money.

Promoting Your Sale

Advertising is *always* a good idea, and word-of-mouth promotion can be especially valuable. A helpful book to teach you a few tricks of the promotional trade is *Guerrilla P.R.: How You Can Wage an Effective Publicity Campaign . . . Without Going Broke*, by Michael Levine (HarperBusiness; also available on Dove Audio cassette). A well-executed publicity stunt or "magnet event" adds to the success of any business.

You will, of course, cover your neighborhood with tasteful signs. They should be the same color as the flyers you sent out. This will separate your sale from the others on your block. It's also wise to put a larger sign or banner on your property a few days ahead of the sale, indicating the date and time. Remember to take advantage of the many free listings available to you in your community newspaper's classified sections and recycler-type magazines. If you can get access to a fax machine you may find that you will get faster results with placing your ad.

The last resort is to pay for an ad. Choose your words wisely, because every one costs you money. My budget for an ad in a major newspaper is $50, or approximately four lines. Look for the buzzwords that attract you to other people's ads. Words like "Collectibles," "Antiques," "Great Finds," "Model/Actress Selling Wardrobe," "Lots of Jewelry," and "Dealers Welcome." Inviting dealers is always a good idea, because it indicates to others that you believe your merchandise is good enough that dealers would be interested in buying it for resale. This also means you are selling at prices at which dealers would be interested in buying.

Your Mailing List

It makes sense to keep a mailing list with your customers' phone numbers and addresses so you can invite customers who bought from you in the past to your next sale. The simplest way to acquire your own mailing list is to use a receipt book to record sales. Choose the type that has a place for the customer's name and address at the top of the page. This way, you not only will have a permanent record of their address, but you also will remember what they purchased, along with the most important information—*how much* they spent. It's also a good idea to go back over past receipts, to review the things that sold well, so you can consider buying similar items again.

I transfer my list to my computer, thus giving me easy access to it when sending out my flyer for the next sale. It is very handy to have a database program that will print out labels. If you do not have a computer, you can take your list to a typing service, which will put it on floppy disk for you and update it as your business expands. They may also print out your labels for you. Another handy tool is a postage stamp affixer, which you can buy at any good office supply store or your local post office. You may also find that the new self-adhering stamps (available in the United States in books of eighteen) save a tremendous amount of time and energy.

Having a mailing list can save you money on advertising. Newspaper ads can be expensive, and many larger newspapers charge you a higher rate when they see you running ads every other week, because they assume you are a professional business and should be paying commercial rates. Running ads in the newspapers is a broad, shotgun approach that's good for reaching new potential customers. Granted, your mailer will cost you money, too, but the people you are targeting have already bought from you and will likely buy again. This is especially true when you offer them the incentive of a discount (e.g., get 10 percent off when they present the flyer at the time of purchase). Take note to always indicate that you are offering a 10 percent discount off your list price. I have had customers bargain me down first, then present their flyer and ask for an additional discount. Sending out a personal flyer as an invitation to attend your sale makes your customer feel valued, and they are. Whenever possible, I like to write a personal note on my preprinted flyer.

If you are like me, with a hectic schedule, it is sometimes hard to plan your sales more than a week or so in advance. I like my flyers to arrive a few days prior to my sale. I mail them on a Monday, or at the very latest, Tuesday if my sale is on Saturday. Mailing a week earlier is even better. You will have to use a first-class stamp, unless you are a registered charity or have a bulk mailing rate.

Be sure to put your return address on the flyers you mail out. This is easy if you have an automatic address stamp pad made up for you or print out your return address on labels you can attach. This way you can keep your mailing list up-to-date with change of addresses and delete the names of those people whose flyers are returned to you because they have left no forwarding address. (On an average mailing, I get approximately 10 percent of the flyers I send out returned to me.)

Along with directions to your sale, it is also a good idea to include a contact telephone number. I have had many customers call me days prior to my sale to tell me they are coming or to ask me to save them certain items. The number is also handy if your customers get lost. It is wise to indicate an alternative sale date on your flyer in the event of bad weather.

You may wish to print up a few hundred extra flyers and spend the time distributing them to mailboxes and on the windshields of the cars parked in your neighborhood the night before your sale or early in the morning of the day of the sale. You must use your own judgment in deciding how your neighbors will respond to this. You should always gather up any flyers that may have been discarded on the street. Another good idea is to post your flyers on any local bulletin boards in your neighborhood, especially in grocery stores and laundromats.

Posting Signs

You may wonder, when you have gone to all the trouble of posting big beautiful signs to lure your potential customers, why they have been torn down virtually moments after you put them up. Some cities with a high concentration of yard and garage sales have patrols that will remove your signs and fine you as much as $300 for illegally placing the signs on public property. I find it is best to put the signs up at about 6:00 A.M. the day of the sale and take them down immediately afterward. Be considerate: don't go stapling them to a neighbor's beautiful tree just because it's growing curbside. The last thing you want is an irate neighbor. Concrete and metal lamp posts have always been my best bet. Fluorescent paper is a good eye-catching material to use for your signs. You have but seconds to get your message across, so do ensure that your lettering is large and legible from a distance. If you use a computer to create your sign, choose a simple font in bold, like Palatino, Times, or New York. It is always good to place another sign just beyond the first one. The first one will attract the attention, the second one is usually the one they will read. Arrows with the address on them work really well when leading a driver to your sale.

I have had it suggested to me that the more attractive or professional looking a sign is, the more expensive the merchandise being sold. In my experience I have not found this to be true. I am, however, more excited by an attractive, well-executed sign and will race to its destination in the hopes of discovering equally attractive merchandise.

At the sale, it is advisable to post your refund or return policy in a prominent place for buyers to see so that they know up front whether you are willing to give a refund or exchange. As a rule, most resellers *do not*; however, if you personally guarantee that an item is in working order when you sell it, you should return their money promptly if it is not.

Holding a Sale in Your Home

If you live in an apartment, particularly in a large city, you may not have access to a driveway or front lawn. In this case, you might consider the local flea and antique markets as places to sell your merchandise. Holding a sale in your home does pose some risks, mostly involving theft and damage, but following a few basic safety precautions heads off most problems. Rope off areas you do not want customers to enter, and hold the sale in the main area of the home, as close to the front doors as possible. Never attempt to hold the sale on your own. Always make sure you have a few hefty guys on hand for security. It is advisable to put expensive stereo and television equipment that is not for sale away and out of sight. Be extra careful when locking afterward, especially if you are vacating the home or apartment.

Monitor the people coming into your sale. Never let too many in at once and, if you can, set up a system to check their large bags at the door. This is always a good policy. Even just mentioning "Please, check your bags," makes people aware that *you* are aware.

How Often Should You Hold a Sale?

Never send a mailer to your existing customer base more than once every two months. If you do plan to hold a sale more frequently, run an ad in the newspapers to attract new customers or simply put signs up in your neighborhood. The reason for this is you don't want your repeat customers to get bored with your sale or your merchandise (you may not have had an opportunity to replenish your inventory since your last sale). What you can do though is *move your sale around* to different locations. Make sure you travel far enough out of your general area—it is surprising how far your customers will travel. They always seem a little perturbed when they stumble across your sale just down the street from your previous location. Another good reason to move around is that you attract new buyers.

Some dealers do not like to hold a sale on a long weekend, because of the low turnout with people leaving town, but others will tell you that they find long weekends and holidays their best selling times. It stands to reason that you should not hold a sale the weekend after Christmas—however, the weekends leading up to Christmas are very profitable. Follow the retail trends and you won't go too far wrong.

Most sales are held on Saturday and Sunday, but there are some towns and cities where folks hold their sales on a Friday. Some believe that it is primarily housewives who shop at garage sales. The reason they feel that Friday is a fruitful day to hold a sale is because children are in school (unless it's summer) and the mothers have the better part of the day available to them to shop, whereas Saturdays are usually reserved for the kids and doing the grocery shopping. It really boils down to your neighborhood, and trial and error. You will know soon enough what the best days for your sale are.

The spring and fall seem to be the best times of year to hold a sale. As with retail, this is the time when most people tend to spruce up their homes and wardrobes.

Hiring a Professional Estate Sale Service

If you are selling the entire contents of your home or apartment, you may want to consider hiring a professional estate sale company. This is particularly wise if you have a house full of valuable antiques and fine furniture. Of course, you have to pay them a fee. If you follow the advice in this book, you should be able to operate your own sale with equal success. The one advantage a professional service has over you is that they have an established mailing list to draw upon when advertising a sale. Get appraisals on any items you are unsure of whenever possible. Never sell anything if you don't know the value. It can be a truly heartbreaking experience when you discover that you just sold Grandma's wedding rings for a third of their resale value. Some of the larger auction houses, such as Butterfield & Butterfield, hold a free clinic once a month where they will appraise a maximum of four items free of charge. They offer this service as a promotional incentive for dealers and individuals to put their items into Butterfield auctions.

Setting Up

Take the time necessary to set up right. Presentation and packaging are 90 percent of the game. The more attractive the presentation, the higher the price you can demand for your merchandise. If it means getting out of bed an hour early, then do it. Remember, 70 percent of your sales for the day will happen in the first two hours, so be prepared. You can purchase long folding card tables at most major hardware stores. They are lightweight and portable and sell for about $35. I find that it is much more attractive to cover all of my display tables to the ground with some type of decorative covering. Using the same colored tablecloths on *all* your tables at a large flea market can help to set you apart from the crowd and establish which tables belong to you and whom customers should pay for the merchandise they have selected. It also allows you ample hiding places to stow away all the unsightly boxes and bags you carried all that lovely stuff in. There are companies that make fitted table coverings, and if you plan to do this type of sale on a regular basis or intend to go into this full-time, it's an investment worth considering.

My setup is always contingent on the environment, taking security into consideration first and aesthetics second. Set your sale up so that the hot sun is not blazing down on your merchandise. Not only will it fade the clothing you have on your racks, but it can also dry out your fine leather goods in a hurry, causing them to crack beyond repair. The sun can also make metal goods and jewelry too hot to handle, and cause stones to pop out of their settings once the glue holding them heats up. A portable sun shield canopy or large patio umbrella will cost approximately $100. This is a worthwhile purchase, if you consider you're protecting your investment.

I like to set up tables in such a way that people can shop them from only *one* side, while I man the inside. It's all about controlling the crowd. If you plan to sell clothing, it would be wise to invest in a garment rack of some sort. Always do up all buttons and zippers on garments so they look their best on the racks. If I have garment racks, I like to secure them up against a wall where, once again, the shopper can approach them from only one side, thus making it easier to monitor them. I secure all of my small valuables and jewelry in wooden or aluminum display cases with glass lids with locks. These cases can be purchased from dealers at most major flea markets or swap meets for about $25. They should be placed on your display tables in such a way that they can be opened only from the *inside* of the table, where you should be standing. You may wish to construct a small sign that says, "I would be happy to show you anything, so please ask for assistance." After all, you want your customers to feel free to experience the merchandise. That may be all they need to encourage them to purchase it!

Many dealers who sell very expensive pieces of jewelry don't want to hand the pieces to a potential buyer over the counter, preferring instead to invite them to the inside of their table to view these pieces. If you are selling rings and have a multihole ring display, it is advisable to place a specific marker in any empty slot. Some dealers will simply place a small SOLD tag or coin in an empty slot to keep track of what has been sold.

If you have chosen to sell shoes or boots, take my advice! *Never* put the complete pair out on display. Leave the mate in a box under your table, out of sight. When both shoes are available, they somehow have a habit of "walking" away without being paid for. It's also more attractive to get shoes up off the ground, if you can. A tall bookshelf works well for this. You may wish to put the right shoe out, because most people have a larger right foot.

If possible, always put out a full-length mirror for people who want to try things on. A freestanding (but well anchored) table mirror is also handy for selling jewelry. You will want to secure any objects that have the potential to topple and harm a toddler when their curious little hands start to tug at items or your table covering.

You may also want to make an area available as a dressing room. It is best to make it a communal dressing room for the women. It is rare that a man will ask to try something on, so it is not necessary to supply a separate dressing room for them. A good way to discourage shoplifting is to periodically (and unexpectedly) knock on the dressing room door and pop your head in, to see if they need any help. Chatting customers up in the dressing room can also encourage sales. Don't be shy—offer them your selection. Besides, who knows your merchandise better than you?

If you wish to attract customers who appreciate quality merchandise and in turn are willing to pay a decent price for it, you should appear to appreciate the same, and dress accordingly. You need to establish yourself as an expert in your field. If you're selling antique and costume jewelry, then select a few of your best pieces to adorn yourself with. Many dealers will wear some of their more expensive pieces of jewelry with the price tags exposed to attract the buyers. A dealer will often wear his or her expensive merchandise for security reasons as well, preferring to keep the higher ticket items closer at hand.

The Psychology of "The Sell"

Your sale is no different from a boutique. You just don't have a roof over your head. By the way, this is also what I say to those customers who occasionally tell me that they think my prices are too high for a garage sale. In my mind it's not where or how you are selling the merchandise; it is the *quality* of the merchandise that determines the price. I have even had shop owners come to my sales and say that they cannot believe the prices I am getting for much of my merchandise. It is close to, or as much as, what they are asking for the same merchandise in their shops. At a garage sale, everyone thinks they are always getting a pretty good deal and even if they are not sure, they always snatch up those items, for fear that the next person behind them is going to grab them. This produces tremendous competition, which helps to drive up prices.

A point that I have heard debated by many dealers is whether or not to price all your merchandise. Some claim that it is best not to price your items, thus forcing your buyers to inquire, which enables you to engage them in conversation and bargaining. My personal feeling is that pricing your merchandise establishes you as a fair player. Often, a customer feels they are being assessed by their appearance as to what price you will offer an item to them for, and they suspect the price may be different for the next person who strolls along. I have also found that pricing your merchandise will distinguish the "lookie-lookers" from the serious buyers. You have given them an opportunity to make an immediate decision as to whether or not they can afford the item and that it has a fair value placed on it. (Though this doesn't mean they are not going to ask for a discount on that item.) Another good reason for pricing all your merchandise is so that your partner or friend does not have to keep tracking you down every time a potential buyer wants to know a price.

A good rule of thumb to follow when determining a price to place on an item is the 1-to-4 rule. If you paid $1 for it then you should sell it for $4. This is also called a "four-time mark-up." There are certainly going to be exceptions, especially if you have bought right. There will be those items that you will have paid very little for as a result of your savvy shopping that you will be able to price at a very handsome profit. Shop around, ask what other dealers are selling similar items for. Attend as many sales as you can and ask other dealers for prices of items you're not even interested in. Create a mental inventory of items and their price ranges. You may not have a particular item in your inventory today, but one might come your way soon, and you need to know its value or you may end up selling it to a more knowledgeable dealer and have them turn a tidy profit on your item later on down the line. At the same time, be prepared to allow a dealer to purchase some items at a price that they can then mark up and turn a profit on. That is the nature of the game. It is really a matter of where you wish to position yourself.

Keeping Track of Your Money

The simplest and safest place to keep your money is in a fanny pack, a little pouch that buckles around your waist. Always make sure you have plenty of change when you start your day, as it could mean the difference between making or losing a sale.

As for making change, learn from the experts. I always keep a paperweight of some sort on my table. If someone hands me a twenty dollar bill for a three-dollar purchase, I place the twenty dollar bill under the weight with plenty of the bill still exposed for the customer to see. I then get them their change from my fanny pack. Once I have satisfied them with the correct change, I then place their twenty dollar bill in my pack. All the while, I explain to them what change I am giving *them*, on the basis of what dollar amount they have given *me*. This practice will head off any uncertainty on either the buyer's or the seller's part as to how much money was originally handed off.

Go with your instincts when deciding whether to take someone's check or not. If you are unsure about someone, then it's probably best if you don't take their check. Most people understand that this is up to your discretion, so they are rarely offended when you decline to take their checks. If you do decide to accept them it is best to get at least *two different* types of identification, the first being a driver's license with a current address that matches the address on the check, and the second, a Social Security card (or in Canada, Social Insurance card). Both are very advantageous in tracking down someone who has passed you a bad check.

If a check is for a small amount, say ten or twenty dollars, I usually feel comfortable accepting it. After all, their bank will charge them almost the same amount in service fees if the check is sent back for insufficient funds, and it doesn't make much sense for someone to bounce a check for a small amount on an *active* account. The other argument for taking a check for a small amount is that most people have some overdraft protection.

If you do get a bad check, there are ways in which you can recover the funds. You must go to your local district attorney's office, bureau of investigations, and file a bad check report with their bad check enforcement program. Follow the instructions and you may be pleasantly surprised when the district attorney's office sends you a recovery in the mail sometime later. (You are more likely to receive a recovery if you were able to obtain the Social Security number of the person who wrote the check.) The district attorney's office will then be able to run a search through bank and employment records to locate this person. It is a crime to knowingly write a bad check, and a warrant will be issued for their arrest. Most people come forward with a restitution (reimbursement) rather than risk going to jail.

What to Sell

I should start by saying that there are certain items that you are forbidden by law to sell in any state: guns and firearms, tear gas, mace, drug paraphernalia, counterfeit merchandise, fireworks, alcohol, and non-domestic animals. You may find that there are regulations about other items in your particular location, so it's best to check with your local government or police department.

Apart from these items, what you sell is entirely a personal decision. You may find that you gravitate to a specific type of collectible, such as fifties kitchen stuff, or perhaps have developed a feel for vintage and designer clothing. You should be passionate about any merchandise you decide to sell, because you may have it for awhile. You want to sell it with the same passion you had when you first acquired it. *Know your market.* If you find things aren't being picked up and looked at, then avoid featuring them in the front of your sale, or don't buy them for resale again. I have found from personal experience, for example, that used shoes do not fare well. By contrast, cowboy boots fly off the tables. If you do decide to sell shoes or boots at your sales, make sure that you buy only full leather footwear. I prefer leather-lined uppers and soles. Sure bets on cowboy boots are Lucchese, Justin, and Dan Post. Remember, the better the quality, the higher the resale price.

It's always better to have a good variety of merchandise, so that you can capture a wider customer range. I find that I can never go too far wrong if there is a continuity and consistency of quality and style to my merchandise. When it comes to clothing, it's best to stick with the very high-end designer pieces. Your merchandise should always be a combination of unique, eclectic, and classic. Never sell anything mediocre. It is not worth trying to get a decent price on a garment that was only moderately priced when it originally sold at the retail level. Look for those beautiful Claude Montana pants for $8 at Salvation Army and sell them for $45–$50 at your sale. That's a healthy markup and absolutely attainable.

When you are buying items for resale and you find that you really have to think long and hard about an item before you buy it, *don't buy it*! If you do buy, be sure that you, in turn, have a buyer for that item. Picture that buyer in your mind. See them using it. The best sellers are things that people can use, things that are functional. People are much less frivolous with their money these days. They are buying basic items to round out their wardrobes or functional necessities for their home. Now, if you can offer them something that is also fun, attractive, or collectible at the same time, then you have a winner on your hands. You know you have a good piece of merchandise in your possession when *you* do not want to part with it.

Hot Sellers

You can pick up numerous trade publications that will keep you abreast of the latest trends in the collectible market. However, you truly need to develop your own following. You may choose to deal mainly in small collectibles and high-end designer women's clothing, often incorporating a few good vintage pieces. I have listed many of my favorite designers, as well as the ones that are highly desirable and collectible, in Chapter 1.

Hot sellers are usually *separates*. Jackets and blazers sell really well, and black seems to be the color of choice. If a jacket's original price was $250–$300, it is highly conceivable that you can get $45 or more for it at your sale.

As far as what sizes you should buy, I have found it best to stay away from the very small sizes, 2 through 4, or the very large sizes, 14 and up. The best are the average sizes, such as 7/8, 9/10, and occasionally 11/12. Smaller women tend to have fewer problems with fit or the need to disguise certain figure problems. Frankly, smaller women are an easier sell.

Men are another question altogether. Most don't like to shop, let alone buy *used* clothing. This feeling may be ego driven. Perhaps they don't want anyone to think they *have* to buy secondhand clothing. But trends are changing, and men are becoming more open to alternative ways to dress stylishly for less.

Sure bets for men are stylish sports jackets and cowboy boots. Medium to extra-large sizes are always the ones in demand. For some reason, it is very hard to get a guy to try something on—they simply do not have the patience women do. For this reason, jackets seem to please. If you really want to attract the men to your sale, be sure to feature a large assortment of sports (particularly golf), electronic, and camera equipment!

Hot Sellers in Leather Goods

Other hot sellers include handbags, suitcases, and unique leather goods in exotic skins. (A tip on identifying crocodile vs. alligator: crocodile has a tiny little dot in the center of each scale that is referred to as a sensory pit; alligator doesn't.) Generally speaking, there is no difference in the quality or value of crocodile versus alligator. The leather goods that you buy for re-sale should all be high-end designer and/or vintage items. Anything by Bally, Bottega Veneta, Dooney & Bourke, Chanel, Robert Clergerie, Coach, Mark Cromer (MCM), Mark Cross, Fendi, Maud Frizon, Ghurka, Gucci, Cole-Haan, Hartman, Hermés, Judith Lieber, Prada, or Louis Vuitton will always be snatched up as soon as it is put out on your table.

Your leather goods should always be in the best possible condition, and should be carefully cleaned and polished prior to being put out on display. Almost anything in exotic skins, such as lizard, alligator, crocodile, and snake, will command a high ticket. Moisturizing your leather is important too. A day in the sun for a vintage alligator purse could spell disaster if you have not applied a generous coat of leather conditioner, mink oil, or saddle soap. Showing care for your merchandise will instill confidence in your customers, who are always more willing to buy something from you if they realize that you place value on it. Your customer may also be hesitant to buy a particular item if *they* are unsure how to care for it, so be ready with some good advice.

It always looks better if you stuff your leather bags to their fullest. I normally use old cleaning bags or grocery bags, which also help them to sit upright on your display tables. You may think that this seems a little extreme for a garage sale, but it could mean the difference between getting $5 for that bag or $30. It's absolutely worth the effort!

Recognizing a Fake

Since the late seventies, it has become increasingly popular to manufacture counterfeit versions of expensive brand-name items. You may recall the thousands of fake Rolex watches that were imported from the Orient and later confiscated and destroyed by the Rolex company. Manufacturers vowed to wage an all-out war against counterfeiters; judging by the amount of fake merchandise out there today, it would appear to be a futile battle.

There are numerous ways to identify a fake item, but it takes time and practice to do it quickly. The following are some characteristics to consider when examining the most commonly manufactured fake, Louis Vuitton.

- The metal studs that hold handles and straps in place should have a raised-surface *L.V.* on them.
- Most handbags and luggage are leather lined.
- All have the name *Louis Vuitton* embossed *inside* the item.
- The initials *L.V.* on the edges of the item should never appear to be cut off. Only the flowerlike emblem should appear at the edge.
- The color and quality of the accenting leather details should be in keeping with Louis Vuitton high standards.
- The stitch detail on the leather, as well as the color of the stitching, should always be subtle and blend well with the item, not bright yellow as I have seen on some fakes.
- The style of the item. You should become familiar with the various styles that Louis Vuitton manufactures. For example, they do not make a zip-up bomber jacket.
- The shoulder straps are always double-sided stitched leather and sealed along the edges (many fakes have a black or burnt red edging made with a marker).

Jewelry

Jewelry always sells well and is favored by collectors, young and old. Many of the larger department store chains now have an estate jewelry or vintage jewelry section in order to capture the trend in the market. However, I have found that they are not offering value on these older pieces, and for the most part their prices are almost double what you should pay at a flea market or antique store, for that matter.

Because many vintage jewelry pieces are so desirable, reproductions are often being made and sold as originals. It requires a well-trained eye to spot a reproduction, so it is advisable, if you are planning on purchasing an expensive piece, to buy from a reputable dealer and whenever possible get a valued opinion first.

You may find that a good third or perhaps even half of your profits will come from the sale of jewelry. You can almost never go wrong with good gold pieces that have a charm of their own. As with furniture, jewelry must be one hundred or more years old before it can be considered antique. Most of what I will be referring to is from the Art Deco period (1920s) to present-day. There are absolutely gorgeous pieces from the Georgian (1714–1837), Early to Late Victorian (1837–1901), Art Nouveau (1880–1914), Arts and Crafts (1890–1914), and Edwardian (1901–1910) periods. Most of those pieces, however, are extremely expensive. You may find it wiser to start with more affordable pieces. Begin by educating yourself extensively in the field. There are many good books available that cover antique and collectible jewelry. One that I have found particularly helpful is *The Buyer's Guide to Affordable Antique Jewelry*, by Anna M. Miller (Carol Publishing).

Many books promote the idea that antique jewelry is an excellent investment—one that will weather inflation better than many other assets. This can be true if you know where and how to sell these lovely treasures. You may find yourself hard pressed to find a buyer who is willing to give you a generous increase on your purchase price, especially if you have only a few pieces to sell. Remember, most dealers need to buy items at a price that they can realize a profit from. Unless you have a large client base and are well connected to the antique and collectible jewelry trade, you may be doing a tremendous amount of leg work to resell the few pieces of jewelry you once thought were a good investment. If you do choose to specialize in jewelry with your own sales, you may wish to start off with the less expensive pieces and work your way up as your profits increase along with your knowledge.

Whenever possible, try to buy pieces that are a full parure (all the matching pieces: earrings, bracelet, brooch, ring, and necklace) or demi-parure (with only a few matching pieces). Also, the value of any piece of jewelry will increase with the presence of its original box.

Bejeweled and Bedazzled

Kenneth Lane twisted ribbon bracelet, $5, Malibu garage sale. An assortment of Victorian to present-day gold and gold-filled engraved bangles and bracelets, prices from $1 to $25, from various flea markets and thrift sales.

Pauline Rader chain belt with lion-head and pink pearl, seen worn as a necklace, $25, Manhattan Pier antique show.

Gerry's lion-head pendant with emerald-colored eyes, $10, Santa Monica, Calif., flea market.

Kenneth Lane multicolored jewels and pearl necklace, $10, Discovery Shop, Los Angeles.

Kenneth Lane Lucite chandelier pendant, $10, Laguna Beach, Calif., estate sale.

S.A.L. cross with multicolored stones and pearls, $6, Kansas City, Mo., flea market. Poseidon and sea nymphs pendant, $18, 2nds Limited, Laguna Beach, Calif. Waist chains with a selection of '60s icons and zodiac signs as well as one with enameled coats of arms, both creations of the author.

It is best to look for heavy, cast metal pieces. Weight always seems to add to the attractiveness of a piece, as well as the perceived quality. A sure-fire way to identify the difference between a semiprecious, precious, or paste (glass) is that paste will show more wear on the surface and around the edges. If the piece has rhinestones or paste, it is much more attractive if the stones are faceted in place. This means that there are tiny little prongs holding the stones in place, much in the way a precious or semiprecious stone is set in fine jewelry. This is by far more desirable than a piece that has had the stones merely glued in place. Over time, the glue becomes tired and the stones may discolor or fall out altogether.

Timeless charm is what you must search for. Revisionist trends in present fashions can also enhance the sale of old costume jewelry. Everything returns in time.

Most good pieces have a designer's name somewhere on them, either on the clasp, edges, or back of the item. You will, however, find some exceptions to this rule. Some tags have been removed by the original owner, who did not feel it was necessary to leave them in place, especially if they were uncomfortable to the wearer or hung obtrusively. Carry a strong magnifying glass or jeweler's loupe (Triplet 10X is all you need; about $20 at most fine jewelers) when buying or selling. Even if your eyes are good, your customer's may not be. Showing the name of a designer, the karat, or the hallmark of a piece could mean the difference between making a sale and losing it.

Repairing Costume Jewelry

Most repairs are really quite simple, requiring only a little Krazy Glue and a pair of small needle-nose pliers. You can purchase replacement pieces (*findings*) at any bead and craft store. Earring backs, loose stones, brooch pins, or loops for reattaching broken pieces are easily found. You should attempt to repair any broken pieces yourself, rather than suggesting that your buyer may find it easy to repair. A restored piece will demand a much higher price than a piece with stones missing. Take the time to match and replace rhinestones that have yellowed with age.

Gold Jewelry

Gold jewelry can be sold according to its karat, weight, and market value. It may also be sold according to its aesthetic beauty. It stands to reason that platinum, 14K, 18K, white, yellow, and rose color, and 22–24K will be more valuable, although you may find some lovely old pieces that have been made out of only 9K. Unfortunately, 10K items sit very low on the totem pole and are rarely sought after in the resale market because of the amount of gold in them. American-made gold jewelry is marked with the word *karat*, abbreviated as K or k, English gold by the word *carat* (C or c), and European by the numbers *585* (which represents 14K or 14C) and *750* (the same as 18K or 18C). (Unmarked gold from Asian countries, India, and other foreign countries should be tested for authenticity and karat grade.)

It is advisable to have a piece appraised by a reputable company. Never have it appraised by the same establishment that you are attempting to sell to, unless you have done business with them in the past. Even some of the most reputable auction houses in the country have been known to under-value an item. If you can, get at least two opinions, especially if you are intending to sell the "family jewels." Remember that independent dealers are just like you; they want to buy at the lowest possible price so they can sell for the highest possible return.

Bakelite Jewelry

Bakelite jewelry has long been favored by ardent collectors, and prices continue to climb today. Bakelite is a plastic that was invented in 1901 by Dr. Leo Baekeland while he was experimenting with various substances in his quest for a new type of rubber electrical insulation. Early Bakelite pieces were usually in muddy colors such as yellow, brown, black, and green as designers attempted to reproduce the look of jade and amber with Bakelite. A good source for information on Bakelite is the bimonthly newsletter by the Society of Decorative Plastics, P. O. Box 199, Guerneville, CA 95446.

As far as identifying the differences between Lucite, plastic, and Bakelite, I believe your ability will come only with experience. Lucite is made from petroleum and therefore has a slippery texture. Plastics are much lighter in weight than Bakelite. Color is one of the key factors that dealers go by when identifying true Bakelite and its time period. Bakelite is a heat-resistant substance; therefore it is warm to the touch and never cold, as plastic tends to be. It also has a very solid sound when you tap it, whereas most plastics sound hollow. Some say Bakelite sounds similar to bamboo when you tap two pieces together.

Another sure-fire way to test Bakelite is to give it a vigorous rub with your finger, and then smell the area you have just rubbed. There should be a prominent odor similar to phenolic resin. Some dealers like to test Bakelite with a hot needle—because it is heat resistant it can be difficult to pierce. If a hot needle slides easily into the item, you can assume that it is not Bakelite, but rather a type of plastic that may even have been manufactured to look like Bakelite. I would, however, dissuade anyone from using this method, as it will damage the piece. Most dealers will attempt to pin-prick the piece in an inconspicuous place, but in my mind, I know there's a pinhole in the item that was *not* necessary.

I heard a fascinating story recently from a Bakelite dealer in New York. He said, "You must be very careful *not* to get bitten by the Bakelite bug, because if you do, watch out—it could take your whole leg off!" Apparently, Bakelite collectors are absolutely *mad*, and will stop at nothing to acquire a piece. One woman's husband threatened to cut up all her credit cards if she did not stop buying Bakelite jewelry—but even that didn't stop her. This woman ended up with several thousand dollars' worth of Bakelite jewelry on layaway. As with all form of collecting, this can truly become a compulsive addiction. So watch out that the "Bakelite bug" doesn't bite you!

Often, a piece of Bakelite will become dull and scratched over time, losing much of its original luster. There is a wonderful product on the market that has been designed for restoring plastics for the automotive industry. It is called Novus Plastic Polish, and it removes fine scratches, haziness, and abrasions from most plastic surfaces. In the case of Bakelite jewelry, this can greatly increase its value. You can find this product in most auto parts and accessories stores, or call directly at 1-800-548-6872 for a distributor near you.

You may find, as I have, that when you clean and restore your Bakelite your cloth becomes mustard yellow. Don't be alarmed—you are not removing any natural pigment. What you are removing is years of nicotine stains from those items whose owners smoked.

Jewelry Designers to Look For

If it is your desire to focus on selling primarily vintage jewelry, then it would be wise to familiarize yourself with the most sought after costume and fine jewelry designer names. You may wish to list these names on little cue cards that you can refer to when out on a buying expedition.

Accesse Craft

Bijoux Cascio

Boucher

Marcel
  Boucheron*
  (M.B.)

Butler and
  Wilson (B&W)

Carlyle

Hattie Carnegie

Cartier

Castillo

Castlecliff

Alice Caviness

Chanel*

Ciner

Coppola &
  Toppo

Coro

Ugo Correani

Delillo

D'Orlan

Christian Dior

Dunay

Eisenberg
  Original and Ice

Fabergé*

Flato

Florenza

Fouquet*

Gorham

Gripoix for
  Chanel

Har

Miriam Haskell*

Hobe

Hollycraft

Jean-Pierre
  Barrette Jeanne

George Jensen

Jomaz

Joseff of
  Hollywood*

Donna Karan

Kramer

Christian Lacroix

Laguna

Rene Lalique*

Claude Lalanne
  for YSL

K.J.L., Kenneth
  Jay Lane*

Les Bernard, Inc.

Marcus

Marvella

Matisse

Mauboussin

Jo Maz

Joseph Mazer

Mimi

Napier

Nardi

Pauline Rader

Regency

Reja

Renoir

Nina Ricci

Roger

Nettie Rosenstein

Sandor

Sautoir

Scaasi

Marina Schiano
  (at YSL)

Schiaparelli

Schiebler

Schlumberger*

Schreiner

Simmons

Adele Simpson

Starett

Sterle

Swarovski Daniel
  & Co.

Swatch watches

Tiffany*

Tomaz

Trabert & Hoeffer

Triffary (Royal
  Sterling
  Crowns and
  Jelly Bellies*)

Pauline Trigere

Tussco (sterling
  silver)

Valentino

Van Cleef and
  Arpels*

Vendrome

Vogue

Wander

Warner

David Webb*

Weiss

Whiting and
  Davis Co.

Yves Saint
  Laurent, YSL*

Anything gold, 14K (585), 18K (750), 24K

Anything Bakelite* (especially true black carved pieces, polka dot, and red)

---

*Particularly desirable in the present market. Their value can range anywhere from a few hundred to many thousands of dollars.

Pricing Your Merchandise

What should you sell an item for? This is a question I get asked all the time. Once again, the answer is very subjective and based on many variables, such as market value, desirability, supply and demand, and rarity. The geographical area of your sale and customer demographics will also affect the pricing of your merchandise. You may find that you can get a greater markup on jewelry than on clothing. Buyers are not hesitant to spend larger dollar amounts on jewelry, feeling it will only appreciate in value. The trick here is to always buy low, so you can sell high. There are some items you may not be able to mark up as much as others; however, having them in your sale may help establish you as a serious "player" and enhance the sales of the rest of your merchandise.

As mentioned earlier in this chapter, if you buy something for $10, you should get at least $40 for it when you resell it, or a four-to-one markup. This takes into consideration all the time and effort you have invested in finding that item, as well as your gas and travel time (not to mention the wear and tear on your vehicle). You must also consider the money you have invested in advertising, plus the risk you are taking by tying up your money with the purchase of these items. Add to that the hours it takes you to price, set up, and sell your merchandise. It's hard work! By the time you factor in your shopping for the merchandise, hard out-of-pocket costs, and time spent preparing and selling, you have a full-time business on your hands. You should be bringing in enough money to support the time and effort exerted. How much should that be? If you can walk away with a clear profit of $1,000 after a two-day sale, then you have a business worth keeping. Keep up the good work! Of course, don't look for great profits right away; it takes time—and money—to make money.

There are many antique and collectible price guides on the market that are good for general pricing guidelines. However, you should bear in mind that those prices are what someone wishes to sell an item for, not what they are willing to pay. A very useful book and one of my favorites is *Wanted to Buy*, published by Collector Books. In it you will find a listing of serious buyers who are willing to pay cash for the desired antiques or collectibles listed in the book. This is a pretty decent gauge for what the market is willing to bear, if you consider those dealers are willing to put their offers in writing. The book may not list everything you have to sell, but it is definitely a starting point, and well worth its price.

Striking the Set

Striking the set is by far the least enjoyed job, especially if you are dealing with a great number of small, breakable items. Start gradually, about half an hour before you are scheduled to close the sale. This is a good signal to your customers that they now have only a limited amount of time to make their decisions, and it encourages them to speed up that process. It stands to reason that you should start by packing up the least desirable items first, leaving the items with more sale potential until last. Be sure to return your unsold merchandise to the same containers you removed them from. If you have indicated the general contents on the containers, you will find that returning your items to their proper containers will save you a tremendous amount of time in setting up your next sale. Keep only one shoe of each pair in each storage box. That way, you need open only one box, the one marked *right shoe*, when selecting one from the pair to put out, as I described in the section on setting up your sale.

Turning Other People's Closets
into Cash for You

There is an opportunity here for you to increase your profits by selling other people's merchandise. The advantage to this is the fact that the merchandise doesn't cost you anything. You will also find, as you become really good at this, that your friends will be forever indebted to you. You cannot begin to imagine how happy you will make them when you start to peel away all the clutter in their closets and replace it with cash in their pockets . . . so they can start all over again.

There is no reason why you cannot operate your sale in the same way that consignment shops operate, by taking merchandise from your friends and acquaintances and selling it on consignment at your sale. Together you establish a fair selling price, and when it sells, you take your percentage. What that percentage is, is entirely up to both of you. On average, most dealers take a minimum of 25 percent. They may go as high as 50 percent or 60 percent, depending on the money they have invested in their sale (including participation fees, or advertising through newspapers and direct mail) and the effort it requires to sell those items.

Now that you are wearing the dealer's hat, remember you are doing all the work for your consignors. If they have only a few items, they would not be able to attract the buyers you have if they attempted to hold a sale on their own. Your diverse array of merchandise will help to sell theirs, and that is definitely worth a good percentage of the selling price of their items. However, I recommend that you be choosy. Don't simply take in all the merchandise you can to make a buck. Bad merchandise can sometimes bring down the value of your good merchandise. So tell your friends to take those rusty old pots and dirty old sneakers and donate them to their favorite charity. You don't want them at *your* sale!

Inviting other people to sell at your sale can also be to your advantage. You can have them participate in financing the advertising to help reduce your out-of-pocket expenses. You may choose to charge them a participation fee (say, $40 to $50), if you have a strongly established client base. If you have an extensive mailing list and draw a substantial crowd, then it is only fair that they pay to participate in your sale. After all, you have spent a good deal of money and time to develop those clients. You have a draw factor, much like the professional flea markets and antique shows and shops.

Another good reason for inviting others to sell at your sale is to add some variety to your merchandise. You will want to invite only those who have merchandise that differs from yours; there's no sense in setting up a competitive environment. Your customers will look forward to finding new dealers at your sales.

The Last Resort:
Selling on Consignment

Once you have exhausted all the possible venues where you can sell directly to the public, your last resort is selecting the best of your remaining merchandise and taking it to a consignment store. By following my advice on Consignment Stores in Chapter 5, you should not have much difficulty selecting a shop that is both honest and appropriate for your merchandise. I like to refer to this as "the last resort," because you will have to share your profits with someone else. Always attempt to sell direct first in order to make the highest possible return on your money. Often, a consignment shop for furniture and antiques may have a better chance of selling a very expensive piece for you, because they have a more sophisticated environment in which to enhance the sale. If you bought that item at a good price to begin with, both of you may be able to realize a generous shared profit.

Selling to a Vintage Store

You may choose to sell some of your better vintage or antique clothing and accessories to a vintage shop. Most vintage or antique clothing shops do not take merchandise on consignment, preferring to buy outright. Some consignment stores are cashing in on the vintage clothing trend and may have a small department dedicated to selling vintage. However, you would be wise to check the story policy first. Not all of them will be interested in buying directly from you. Most of them like to "pick" at thrift stores and flea markets themselves. Call around first. Keep in mind that they will want to buy your items from you at just a fraction above what you paid for them. Snoop at vintage boutiques to get a good idea of trends and the retail prices of your vintage merchandise before offering it for sale.

7

Donating to Charity and Nonprofit Shops

Once you have attempted to sell your goods through consignment and re-sale shops, as well as your own private garage sale, you can still receive a tax deduction for your leftover items. It's always best to check with the charity of your choice first, to ensure that they will issue a receipt for tax purposes. Always do this prior to bringing your things in. Most of the larger charities are set up to issue such receipts, but policies may vary from shop to shop. Some will issue a form to make a comprehensive listing of your donated items as well as a dollar amount for the *fair market value* (see the chart on IRS allowable deductions later in this chapter) for those items. The IRS calls this supplementary documentation; it will help to avoid any red flags come tax time!

It is always best to check with your tax adviser or accountant for the maximum allowable to deduct each year. The charity will normally ask you for an estimate of the value of your donations, so be prepared to give them a fairly accurate and honest dollar amount. Remember, they are always happy to receive your things, so don't be timid about requesting a tax form. Even many major department stores and retail boutiques will donate leftover stock at the end of a sale or at year-end to take advantage of a tax break. That is why there tends to be an abundance of new merchandise in the thrift stores as we approach the end of the year.

Remember our motto, "Reduce, Reuse, Repair, and Recycle!" Never throw anything away. You will be surprised at what a charity thrift store is willing to accept as a donation, from children's toys to household fixtures and appliances. First, check with the charity to which you intend to donate your things to ensure that they accept certain items. Some will not take large appliances or furniture that requires any repair. Most will not take mattresses and bedding, because of health regulations.

There is always someone less fortunate than ourselves who can make very good use of our discarded things. If the items are not fit to resell, the store may donate them to homeless shelters. A friend of mine once shot a television commercial that required a grocery store set. At the end of the shoot, he was left with a truckload of perfectly good groceries. I suggested that we drive them to downtown Los Angeles and donate them to one of the hostels for the homeless. You can't imagine the reception we received as we pulled into their parking lot at the hostel and started unloading all that food!

IRS Definitions of
Charitable Contributions

A charitable contribution, as described in Publication 526 from the Internal Revenue Service, is a contribution or gift to, or for the use of, a *qualified organization*. The contribution is voluntary and is made without getting, or expecting to get, anything of value in return.

Qualified organizations include nonprofit groups that are religious, charitable, educational, scientific, or literary in purpose, or that work to prevent cruelty to children or animals. You can deduct your contributions only if you make them to a qualified organization. To become qualified, organizations (other than churches, which are exempted) must apply to the IRS (or Revenue Canada).

Examples of qualified organizations as stated in Publication 526 are:

- Churches, synagogues, temples, mosques, and other religious organizations
- Federal, state, and local governments (your contribution must be solely for public purpose)

- Nonprofit schools and hospitals
- Public parks and recreation facilities
- Salvation Army, Red Cross, CARE, Goodwill Industries, United Way, Boy Scouts, Girl Scouts, Boys and Girls Clubs of America, etc.
- War veterans' groups

Eligible contributions include the costs you pay for a student living with you, sponsored by a qualified organization, and out-of-pocket expenses when you serve a qualified organization as a volunteer. If you give property (durable goods) to a qualified organization, you generally can deduct the fair market value of the property at the time of the contribution. Your deduction for charitable contributions is generally limited to 50 percent of your adjusted gross income, but in some cases 20 percent and 30 percent limits may apply.

Fair market value is defined as the price at which property would change hands between a willing buyer and a willing seller, neither being required to buy or sell, and both having reasonable knowledge of all the relevant facts. The fair market value of used clothing and other personal items is usually far less than the price you paid for them. There are no fixed formulas or methods for finding the value of items of clothing. You should claim the price that the buyers of used items actually pay in used clothing stores, such as consignment or thrift shops: approximately 25 to 30 percent of the original cost.

The fair market value of used household goods, such as furniture, appliances, and linens, is also much lower than the price paid when new. These items may have little or no market value because they are in worn condition, out of style, or no longer useful. For this reason, formulas (such as using a percentage of the cost to buy a new replacement item) are not acceptable in determining value.

You should support your valuation with photographs, canceled checks, receipts from your purchase of the items, or other evidence. Magazine or newspaper articles and photographs that describe the items, and statements by the recipients of the items, are also useful. Do not include any of this evidence with your tax return; retain it in case you are asked to produce it as evidence. (*Source:* IRS Publication 526)

Revenue Canada Charity Taxation

Revenue Canada Taxation, Customs and Excise Charity Division says you may deduct 17 percent of the value of an item if the value is less than $250. You may deduct 29 percent if the value is above $250. Your total charitable deduction is limited to 20 percent of your *net* income. Anything above that amount may be carried forward for up to five years.

The following is an excerpt from Revenue Canada Taxation, Interpretation Bulletin, Income Tax Act, Deductible Gifts and Official Donations Receipts, Form #IT-110R2:

> The Canadian tax system encourages taxpayers to support the activities of registered charities by allowing the deduction of gifts made to such charities in computing a donor's taxable income.
>
> The gift must be a voluntary transfer of property without valuable consideration, such as: property—usually cash—that is transferred by a donor to a registered charity. The transfer is voluntary. Any legal obligation on the payor would cause the transfer to lose status as a gift. The transfer is made without expectation of return. No valuable consideration—no benefit of any kind—to the donor or to anyone designated by the donor may result from the payment or gift.

Note that most thrift stores in Canada do not issue tax-deductible donation receipts for any donation valued under $50. Some will issue a receipt only for items that are *new* and not used, especially clothing.

Estimated IRS Allowable Deductions

The following chart indicates the range of reasonable fair market values (approximately 25 to 30 percent of the original cost) that the IRS will allow as deductible donations for clothing, furniture, appliances, and dry goods. This chart is based on present resale prices for similar merchandise found in thrift and consignment stores.

Women's Clothing		Men's Clothing		Children's Clothing	
Dress	$5–$50	Suit	$5–$100	Coat	$4–$20
Suit	$5–$100	Coat	$15–$90	Dress	$5–$10
Purse	$5–$20	Briefcase	$5–$40	Suit	$5–$25
Hat	$4–$15	Hat	$5–$15	Pants	$3–$9
Coat	$15–$100	Jacket	$5–$50	Sweaters	$3–$10
Shoes	$5–$25	Shoes	$5–$25	Shoes	$3–$10
Jewelry	$5–$45	Jewelry	$5–$45	Boots	$3–$15
Sweaters	$5–$30	Sweaters	$5–$30	Shirt	$3–$10
Pants	$5–$25	Pants	$5–$25	Toys	$2–$10

Dry Goods		Furniture		Appliances	
Rugs	$5–$25	Love seat	$40–$200	Washer	$40–$100
Blanket	$5–$15	Sofa	$40–$300	Dryer	$40–$100
Curtains	$2–$7	Sofa bed	$40–$200	Refrigerator	$40–$180
Bed linens	$2–$20	Dresser	$30–$150	Color TV	$75–$200
Pillows	$2–$10	Lamp	$15–$30	Computer	$20–$150
Towels	$2–$5	Table	$10–$100	Stove	$50–$150
Bedspread	$2–$20	Chairs (4)	$10–$85	Radio	$10–$50
Broadloom	$8–$50	Armchair	$15–$85	Vacuum	$10–$60

8

Tips on Cleaning, Storage, and Alterations

Not everything you find at the various venues you shop will be in perfect condition. After all, the reason it was donated or sold in the first place might be some type of damage or imperfection. It is often up to you to bring it back to life. Happily there are many tips, which I will share with you, to make your job of transforming your purchases much easier.

Reconditioning Leather Goods

Restoring leather goods such as luggage, purses, and shoes may be as simple as applying a healthy coat of leather conditioner. You may have to mix up a few different colors of shoe cream to get just the right color to bring an article back to its original state. Meltonian cream is by far the best on the market for bringing back the luster to leather. Read the instructions on the product before you apply it, and test a small area first. Keep in mind that if you are restoring a handbag, you do not want to leave any residue on the bag that can rub off on your clothing when you use it. You can be a little more generous when working with luggage. Exotic skins often come out better if you use a product that is designed specifically for them, although Meltonian cream is also fine.

Be very careful with lighter-colored leather. If you use mink oil or saddle soap, you will likely leave the item a few shades darker than the original. If you are working on a light tan–colored item, it may be best to start with a cream that is a few shades lighter than the item itself and continue to apply coats of the polish until the desired color is reached. Treat any leather item as if it were a pair of shoes you are polishing. Give it a substantial coat of leather conditioner first: this will make it easier to apply your color, and you will not have to use as much. Then apply the desired color of cream polish and let it stand for a time. Once it has dried, brush vigorously with a large medium-bristle shoe brush. Never use the same brush for dark leather and lighter leather, as it may transfer color residue to the latter.

A wire suede brush is quite good for reviving the nap on suede. Be careful not to brush so hard that you strip the nap, and always brush in the same direction as the nap. There are a few products on the market for reviving the color of suede, such as Angelus suede dye and dressing and Trendi suede renew. You can find these products in better shoe repair stores. Often, if a dark-colored suede item is badly discolored or stained, I will dye it black.

Small scuffs and marks can be removed from soft leather with a pencil eraser. Clean the eraser first by rubbing it on a clean piece of white paper. Gently rub the eraser on the scuff. (Spot-check the item before you attack a large area.) Brush off the residue left by the eraser with a soft clean cloth. There are cleaning stones on the market that are very good at removing soil from suede and Nubuck leather. They are used in much the same way as an eraser.

Angelus makes a leather cleaning solvent for removing small stains. If it is a recent stain you are working on, the sooner you attack that stain, the luckier you will be at removing it.

Cotton swabs work well when applying leather conditioner to small crevices, edges, and shoulder straps. Once again, keep in mind that you do not want to leave any residue on a shoulder strap lest it ends up staining your clothes.

Patent leather is easily brought back to life with a generous application of petroleum jelly. Once it is applied, let the item stand for a time, then buff it with a lint-free, soft cloth.

Leather Dyeing

Leather dyeing is very intimidating to people, which may be why shoe repair shops can charge *so* much for this service. If you buy a good product and follow the directions correctly, you should not encounter any serious setbacks. The most important thing is to treat the item first with the preparing solution. The preparer strips off the outside protective coat that the manufacturer applied to protect the original color, so that your new color will penetrate the leather. Obviously, it doesn't make sense to attempt to dye a pair of black shoes white, because of the amount of dye it would take. The surface will support only so much dye before it starts to crack and flake off. Be sure to select a color that can easily cover the original color. Another tip is to throw away those ridiculous brushes the manufacturers include with their dye. Instead try using a medium-sized artist's paintbrush. A cotton swab will work well in a pinch. After your item has dried completely, brush it with your shoe brush. You may also choose to give it a coat of Meltonian cream and polish it, as you would any other item. This will give the item a high-gloss finish and bring it back as close as you can expect to its original condition. Be sure to wash your brushes out well, with plenty of soap and water—otherwise, they may harden and become damaged.

Garment Dyeing

You can often revive a garment by dipping it in a bath of Rit fabric dye. You may find that stripping the original color first with Rit color remover will make the new color adhere better to the fabric. I have found that wool and cashmere sweaters are a dream to dye, and that natural fabrics will take the dye much better than synthetics. You will also find that even if the garment is made out of a natural fiber, it may have been constructed with synthetic thread. Unfortunately, most synthetic thread will not take the new color you are attempting to add.

Dissolve the dye in a small amount of hot water first, then add cold water. The instructions on the package will tell you to use hot water when dyeing a garment, but many of the fabrics you will be dyeing will shrink if placed in hot water. I have found that the dye works equally well in cold water.

Some people soak the dyed item in a bath of salt water (a solution of regular table salt and tap water) after they have dyed it. This apparently helps the dye to set into the garment.

Call me frugal, but I always save the dye solution by pouring it through a funnel back into a large bottle for future dyeing. If you choose to do this as well, it is advisable that you do your dyeing in a large container rather than a sink or washing machine.

Cleaning Garments

Although 100 percent natural fibers are usually more expensive and desirable, an 80 percent natural and 20 percent synthetic blend will hold its shape better and longer. Many of the top designers are moving toward these blends to increase the lifespans of their creations. There are also many fashion firms that are manufacturing environmentally responsible clothing with organically grown fibers, genetically colored cotton, and other undyed and unbleached materials. Some of these environmental trendsetters are Roots, Levi Strauss & Co., J. Crew, Esprit, and Robin Kay Knits of Canada. They are now using genetically colored, unbleached and undyed cotton, as well as cottons dyed with natural vegetable dyes. You will find that they are also choosing to use buttons of natural shell, wood, carved nuts, and recycled glass. One of the nice things about these new "eco-fashions" is that you can say good-bye to those expensive dry cleaning bills, because they are all either machine or hand washable.

Whatever the fiber content, when it comes to cleaning there are plenty of tricks out there to go around. There is a wonderful book on the market, *Clean and Green*, by Annie Berthold-Bond, that you can order by calling (914) 679-5573. In it you will find a tremendous amount of information on common household alternatives that can be used as cleansing products, as well as many environmentally friendly commercially manufactured products too numerous to mention here.

- Creases can be removed from hems by rubbing them with a solution of white vinegar and water, then pressing.
- Makeup stains can be removed by rubbing with a slice of white bread.
- A sticky zipper can run smoothly again after running a bar of soap or a pencil lead over it.
- White chalk will absorb oils from a soiled collar.
- Rub in a small amount of shampoo to remove "ring around the collar."

- Make a paste out of either baking soda or table salt and water and rub into a perspiration stain.
- Cream of tartar will work well on various stains when applied as a paste mixed with water.
- Add ¼ cup of table salt to a final rinse to keep clothes from freezing if you are line-drying in the winter.
- Hair spray is said to remove ink from washable fabrics.
- Ice works well at removing chewing gum.
- *Never* apply water without detergent to a grease stain, as this will only cause the grease stain to set.
- A few tablespoons of Epsom salts work well as a fabric brightener.
- Lemon juice works well as a bleaching agent in conjunction with exposing the rinsed garment to direct sunlight to dry.

There are various spot removing products on the market. The best ones are sold in the notions departments of fabric stores: Rit fabric whitener and rust remover, Zout, Whink, Bleach Stick, white vinegar, lemon juice, baby shampoo, toothpaste, salt, packaged dry cleaning solvent, diluted hydrogen peroxide, diluted ammonia, and glycerin. It is advisable to spot-check any garment for colorfastness, especially if the product you are using has any bleach in it.

I have not had a great deal of success with using vinegar and/or salt. What does work well on protein or blood stains is toothpaste! This is a good trick if you are traveling and do not have your regular cleaning supplies with you. Use a paste rather than a gel, and one without all the fancy colors or additives. Although the environmentally safe detergents and bleaches may not be as tough on dirt and stains as some of the leading brands, I encourage you to use them whenever possible.

Linen

Linen has a character all its own and is extremely durable. Check to see that the garment is preshrunk, otherwise you may find a slight shrinkage. Also check the label for its colorfastness. Linen seems to have a tough time holding its color during hand washing. What makes it even more difficult to clean these days is that manufacturers are blending linen with so many

Garments compliments of the Salvation Army Metro Toronto Recycling Center.
Twin brother Derek Mason's blue wool crepe Italian sports jacket, $7.99.
Nephew Colin Mason's jacket, trousers, and shoes, total cost $9.00.
My outfit: **Ports** black wool pleated skirt, $4.99; **Cassidy** black wool bolero jacket,
$5.99; **Anne Klein** black wool sweater, $2.99; **Prada** black leather purse, $40.00;
Miriam Haskell pin, $5.00.

other fibers. Be assured it is almost impossible to remove those horrible yellow stains that mysteriously appear under the arms. Most stains are actually caused by the chemicals in our deodorant mixed with our natural perspiration as well as the chemicals the manufacturer may have treated the fabric with. The best deodorant causing the least amount of damage is the rock crystal type, now readily available in most health food stores and larger drugstores.

When it comes to cleaning *unlined* linen, hand washing is by far the best. Dry cleaners use a cleaning solution that, over time (especially if they are not changing the solution frequently enough), will yellow your linen. (This yellowing will also occur if you dry-clean white cotton shirts, rather than having them laundered.) Hand washing does present much more work because of the pressing you have to do afterward, but there is no reason you cannot take that item to the dry cleaners for "*steam* pressing only." Granted, dry cleaners hate this because they can't charge as much, but you will be much happier with the results. Take care that you don't overpress linen or it will become shiny. Steam wrinkles out first, then gently press while the item is still moist, using plenty of steam, or a spritzer bottle of water. If you don't have a professional steamer, your shower will work as well. Hang the garment in the bathroom, turn the shower all the way to hot, and close the door for fifteen to twenty minutes. Then lightly press the item while it's still damp.

Silk

Silk can be cleaned in much the same way you clean linen. It is the strongest of all natural fibers and is extremely resilient and absorbent. Most manufacturers' labels will indicate that the garment should be dry-cleaned, but this is mainly to protect them from liability for damage if the garment is not properly hand-washed. If the silk has a print on it, the colors will run if you attempt to hand-wash it; in that case, you really should only dry-clean it. You will find that even when using cold water, hand washing will remove some of the sizing that the makers have applied to the garment, and you may lose some of its shape as well as color. Never wring or rub silk while washing—gently squeeze excess water and hang to dry on a plastic-coated hanger. You will get the best results from ironing if it is done while the garment is still slightly damp.

Wool

I never like to send any kind of sweater to a dry cleaner. This applies to cashmere, wool, and synthetic blends. Over time, the pressing that they do always removes the shape. Instead, I will hand-wash sweaters. Products such as Woolite are overpriced in my opinion, and never seem to do a better job than ordinary machine wash soap used sparingly.

Never hang your sweaters to dry. Find a large glass table if you can, and lay them out. If you must place them on a wooden table, put a large towel underneath the sweater. Keep in mind that if the towel is a dark color, some of the dye from it may run into your sweater, especially if the sweater is lighter. A white towel is always best. There are drying racks on the market that I swear by. They are made of nylon net suspended on plastic-covered wire legs. They can be stretched across a table or a bathtub for drying. If you are in a hurry, you can place an oscillating fan in front to speed up the drying process. These racks can be found in many notions departments. A blow dryer set on cool works well to bring the fluff back to angora or cashmere.

When placing the item out flat to dry, push together the ridges in the cuffs and waistbands to recapture their original form. Squeeze the ridges until they almost meet each other. The waistband and cuffs may appear to be smaller than normal. This helps to put the shape and elasticity back into the sweater. If the sweater has become pilled, you can remove the tiny fuzz balls with a little gizmo known as a Defuzz It, available in most notions departments; I prefer it to the electric sweater shavers.

Synthetics

All synthetics such as rayon, nylon, polyester, orlon, and Lycra spandex should be washed as you would all other fine washables—by hand.

Tips for Dry Cleaning

I would like to start by encouraging you *not* to dry-clean your garments, because the chemicals used in the process are indoor air pollutants, suspected carcinogens, and highly toxic to both humans and the environment. If you must dry-clean, I should point out that a large percentage of dry cleaners never pre-spot anything. They simply toss everyone's garments into one big communal drum where they are left to tumble around. That is why you often get your garment back with that piece of chocolate you sat on at the movie theater still stuck to the seat of your trousers! When dropping your cleaning off, always point out to the attendant the stain(s) you want removed. Often, they will have little stickers you can indicate the spot with. Oh, they *hate* me! I will stand there and place stickers everywhere, so they have no choice but to pre-spot. Also, you should check your garments when you pick them up. If it's not done right, have them do it again. After all, you are paying for it. While you're at it, if you are running many of your garments through their service, it's not a bad idea to ask for a special deal. They are usually quite accommodating and may have membership or discount cards.

Preservation of Your Vintage Treasures

If you are truly serious about developing an antique and vintage clothing collection, I would suggest that you look into becoming a member of the National Costume Society of America, 55 Edgewater Drive, P.O. Box 73, Earleville, MD 21919, (410) 275-2329; or the Canadian Conservation Institute, 1030 Innes Road, Ottawa, Ontario, Canada K1A 0C8, (613) 998-3721. The information they have available for their members is extremely beneficial and a tremendous resource. You may also wish to contact your local museums, as many have a department for the preservation of costumes and textiles.

I could not possibly teach you everything you will need to know about preserving your antique and vintage fashions in this short section, but I will attempt to give you some very helpful tips: Wood contains *lignins* (a polymer that functions as a natural binder and support for the cellulose fibers of woody plants). Lignins break down and form an acid that will drastically damage your vintage clothing over time. Therefore all the expensive cedar closets and blocks that are on the market should be considered a hazard to your valuable antique and vintage clothing. You can avoid damage from these lignins by sealing the wood with an acrylic emulsion or by using acid-free paper.

- Never use wooden hangers unless you have covered them, for the reasons above. Wooden hangers, if used properly, are your best choice because they can easily be cut to fit a garment. This is especially true when hanging a child's garment.

· *All* hangers should be covered with *needle-punched polyester batting,* surrounded by *unbleached cotton muslin.* You can use this batting to cover the tips of a clip hanger to avoid clip-pinch damage. The batting can also be used to stuff a hat, shape a collar, or fill out a sleeve.

· Do up all buttons, zippers, and snaps. This will ensure that the garment hangs properly and will help to avoid unwanted creases.

· Store your beaded garments folded and wrapped in acid-free tissue paper or *lens tissue,* available at a photographic supply store. A hanging beaded garment can tear under its own weight.

· Be careful when washing old sequined garments. The old sequins were made of a gelatin substance, which may dissolve in water and most certainly will lose its color.

· Vintage silks should never be folded, because they will eventually break on the fold lines. They should be rolled and stored in acid-free tissue.

· Avoid prolonged exposure to direct sunlight as well as artificial light, as it will bleach the color and destroy the fabric over time. You may wish to cover lights with UV filters or place black felt over windows and skylights where you are storing your garments.

· Natural bleach is safer than chlorine bleach.

· Use clean white cotton gloves (available at a photographic supply store) when handling your delicate fabrics. Gloves will keep the oils on your hands from being transferred to your garments. The oils will eventually stain and damage the fabric.

· Wash or dry clean as infrequently as possible. Washing will expand and contract fibers, which will eventually weaken them.

· Vacuuming your garment is a more advisable method of removing superficial dirt. Place a light nylon screen over the garment and use the soft brush adaptation of your vacuum.

· Always remove dry-cleaning bags immediately. Do not store your garments in plastic garment bags, because they have the potential to trap moisture and thus damage your garment. Use clean old cotton sheets draped over the garment. You can snip a hole in the center to slip a hanger through. If you must use a plastic garment bag, always leave it open so that moisture can escape. You may wish to tag the outside of the garment bag for quick identification.

• Do not store anything in a damp basement. Even the best storage closet will eventually grow mold and mildew, which can soil and destroy fabric as well as leaving an odor that is next to impossible to remove. Keep the *silica gel* packages from your vitamin bottles and toss them into your storage area. The more the merrier. This will help to dissipate moisture.

• Your storage temperature should be moderated to approximately 65°F.

• Moth balls are extremely toxic to both moths and humans. There are herbal alternatives (such as Richards Moth-Away, P.O. Box 92019, Long Beach, CA 90809) available at local health food stores that work equally well. You can also place boric acid in all the cracks and crevices of your closets and drawers, which is where the moths like to lay their eggs. These hatch into the larvae that perpetrate the damage on your garments. The sticky moth traps are an added ally in the battle against moths.

Alterations

Many items I buy require some type of alteration. Many were donated because they became damaged, outdated, or too small. The work could be as simple as altering a hemline. It always baffles me when I come across a perfectly good skirt that simply needs a few inches taken off the bottom. Normally I try to do all alterations myself. But if I'm feeling lazy, I drop a big load of alterations off at a good tailor and have them do it all. Then I simply incorporate the cost into the resale price of that garment. You should never pay more than $10 per skirt hem, and that should include a lining alteration as well. This can apply to dresses or even trousers. Trousers from the seventies are cut very long because of the high platforms we wore back then. They too can easily be hemmed and/or tapered.

Re-creations

What I truly like to get my hands on are the "re-creations." Because of their uniqueness and desirability, they also command the most money. "Re-creations" require a very active imagination. If you ever played dress-up, I think you will understand. Throw caution to the wind, for this is the *new* fashion. I cannot describe here all that is required in re-creating something, because every garment is different. But I can help expand your imagination with the possibilities.

To start with, you need a fabulous garment. I work mainly with exciting vintage or antique pieces. The present trend is to find something from the sixties or seventies and bring it forward to the nineties. However, I have been known to hack up a contemporary designer's nightmare to get at the heart of things and salvage something wearable out of their bad intentions. If you come across a garment that has something wonderful about it, but something else just doesn't cut it—then do just that, *cut* it away! You would be surprised how lovely the beaded bodice on a dress can look when it has been liberated and converted into a blouse.

A "re-creation" could be as simple as removing antiquated buttons and replacing them with something contemporary, or vice versa. Or it can be as elaborate as something I created by cutting the bottom away from an ankle-length vintage party dress and bringing it up to the waistline with a gathering elastic to create a full-layered look. I am never opposed to cutting off outdated sleeves or tapering A-lines on dresses and skirts. Another favorite of mine is to remove short straps from outdated handbags and replace them with a nice heavyweight chain strap that is timeless yet fashionable.

I realize that some of the alterations I'm describing here may seem too difficult for some of you who do not sew. And yet the definition of a brilliant businessperson is someone who knows how to delegate! That is when having a good, affordable tailor is definitely a plus.

9

The Top Ten Thrift
Organizations Across the
United States and Canada

For me, one of the greatest pleasures of thrift store shopping is knowing that my money and merchandise are going to one of the many worthwhile causes. This chapter is *not* about which cause is better than the next. In this chapter I have selected and profiled what I consider to be ten of the best charity organizations that operate thrift stores as a way of funding their causes. There are approximately twenty-two national charity organizations that operate thrift stores, so it was tremendously difficult to narrow the number to just ten. Some of these you will recognize at a glance. A few have been with us since the early 1900s. Most relentlessly fight a silent crusade, raising money through the sale of your donated goods in the hopes of finding cures, giving aid, helping to educate, and filling in the gaping holes where government funding leaves off. We may not have time in our busy lives to volunteer our personal services to these organizations. However, shopping in these nonprofit stores can be our small way of keeping this giant ball rolling forward!

Association for Retarded Citizens
SOUTHEAST LOS ANGELES COUNTY

The Association for Retarded Citizens (ARC)
Value Village Thrift Store

The Association for Retarded Citizens of Southeast Los Angeles County (ARC-SELAC) was founded in 1955 in Lynnwood, California, by a small group of extraordinary parents of children with mental retardation. ARC-SELAC serves an ever-increasing number of individuals in a wide variety of programs that include:

- Adult special programs to develop living, communication, social, and survival skills for people with severe and profound retardation.
- Southeast Industries (ARC-SELAC's packaging and assembly plant), one of California's largest work training centers. Here, 250 people learn job skills while earning a salary and building self-esteem and social skills. They are supported by counseling and family support services to encourage self-determination and self-advocacy and to address the broad range of their needs.
- Southeast Employment Center, which recruits, trains, places, and supports individuals in community jobs as well as in Value Village thrift shops.
- Basic education, which maintains and upgrades cognitive skills. Classes include math, reading, money management, and community awareness.
- Independent living, which teaches housekeeping and personal health skills.
- Parent support groups, a resource center run by and for parents and family members.

By establishing Southeast Employment Center, ARC-SELAC has made a major commitment to developing their supported employment program and placing as many qualified individuals as possible in regular jobs in the community at large.

Current funding comes primarily from the California Departments of Rehabilitation and Developmental Services, contracts serviced by Southeast Industries, corporate contributions, and Value Village thrift stores. (ARC Value Village thrift stores should not be mistaken for TVI Inc. Value Village thrift stores). Value Village thrift stores are a booming venture for many ARC Chapters.

Most of their shops are cheery and brimming with possibilities. While they are undoubtedly in the business of making money for their organization, their pricing policy is still somewhat moderate. They seem to prefer to deal in volume—"Move it out" is their battle cry!

What does the future hold for ARC-SELAC? They are dedicated to providing innovative services that promote independence and integration for all individuals with mental retardation. They are looking to expand their present resources, and to ensure the effective implementation of their aggressive programs and farsighted vision, as they maintain a commitment to providing a caring and supportive environment for all people associated with ARC-SELAC, in whatever capacity. This can only mean that their Value Village stores are going to get better and better!

The Salvation Army
Salvation Army Thrift Stores

Just think back to any world disaster and who do you recall being on the front lines? The Salvation Army. They come to disaster areas, hospitals, nursing homes, and institutions, bringing love to the less fortunate, even to those whose situations are less than hopeful. They provide hundreds of services, great and small, offering comfort and care, sympathy and solace. Their tireless work and far-reaching programs include a hot cup of coffee from their mobile canteens; adult rehabilitation centers for alcohol and drug addiction; day care centers; residences for homeless veterans, men, women, children, senior citizens, and those persons suffering from HIV and AIDS; and last, world relief efforts.

The Salvation Army's motto sums up their programs: "It isn't easy. It's not quick. But it's possible. Because it's worth it."

The thrift stores are just one way that the Salvation Army raises funds for their campaign. These thrift stores may not be quite as posh as all the rest, but never underestimate them; there is wonderful merchandise to be found. It is true that with the current economic climate and the greater and greater demand for antiques and collectibles, you are not likely to find a Tiffany lamp lurking about in the dust. But you can find high-quality designer clothing if you are willing to do some digging! The pricing staff is usually good at spotting the vintage clothing when it comes through and pricing it accordingly. They tend to overlook much of the higher-end designer clothing, which ends up priced in with all the rest. We will keep that as our little secret!

A large portion of the clothing that is collected by the Salvation Army is also used in relief efforts. In Los Angeles in January 1994, they distributed clothing and blankets to many of the earthquake victims. As long as there is a battleground of social needs, there will always be a place for the Salvation Army! Being part of the top ten is a medal this army should wear proudly.

National Assistance League
Assistance League Thrift Shops

The National Assistance League was originally established in Los Angeles in 1919 as the Assistance League of Southern California. As the Assistance League philosophy of service spread to surrounding communities, additional chapters were formed. The National Assistance League was founded in 1935 and incorporated in 1949. There are presently 95 chapters, with over 25,000 members in 24 states.

The purpose of this organization is to serve individual communities through the chapters' philanthropic projects. After researching and identifying community needs, local chapters develop projects to meet those needs. The projects are ongoing—once adopted, they continue as long as the need exists. Their projects include Operation School Bell (providing clothing for needy schoolchildren), day care centers, bookmobiles, seniors' group activities, family counseling, scholarships/camperships, summer schools, youth clubs, and a children's theater.

In 1993, National Assistance League raised in excess of $15.4 million, 76 percent of which was returned directly to the local community through individual projects. Over $3 million of the money was raised through their sixty-six thrift stores. Their thrift stores come in all shapes and sizes, as well as names! Many are called Bargain Box, some Bargain Bin or Bargain Basket. Some have really cute names like Nifty Assistance Shoppe, Turnstyle, or Thriftique. All can be easily identified in Part 9 under National Assistance League.

The Turnabout Thrift Shop of Laguna Beach, California, is one of my all-time favorites. It is small by comparison to most shops, but big on charm and warm, friendly smiles. The biggest attraction is the wonderful merchandise that passes through those doors! There is usually an abundance of designer clothing and interesting collectibles. Some of my favorite possessions have come from that shop. Perhaps it is the eclectic nature of the artistic community in Laguna Beach. Then there are always the flamboyant Laguna locals to consider!

I will tell you a little secret: the Turnabout Thrift Shop closes during the summer months, but when it opens its doors again that first week in September, you had better be first in line. It's better than front-row seats at the Pageant of the Masters! (Laguna's celebrated experience of the arts is also not to be missed.) Whether you shop in California, Texas, or Kansas, the National Assistance League thrift shops are always worth saying, "Hey, let's stop!"

AMERICAN CANCER SOCIETY®

THERE'S NOTHING MIGHTIER THAN THE SWORD

American Cancer Society
Discovery Thrift Shops

The American Cancer Society, founded in 1913, is composed of more than 85,000 dedicated volunteers who represent nearly every occupation and walk of life, and 540 staff members. It is led by a volunteer board of directors made up of community leaders, physicians, and other health professionals and concerned citizens.

The American Cancer Society is the only voluntary cancer control organization that fights cancer nationally. Their programs of research, education, and patient services are funded entirely by public contributions. They receive *no* government funding. Their life-saving information and caring goes out to residents of communities throughout the United States.

The American Cancer Society is quick to point out that there are lookalike organizations out there. Unfortunately, many organizations with similar-sounding names have been created out of self-interest rather than public interest. Some of these lookalike cancer organizations use sweepstakes, surveys, free prizes, and other gimmicks to get your attention *and* your money. Often as little as one cent of your dollar is spent by these organizations in supporting community programs.

The American Cancer Society opened its first resale shop in 1965 in response to donations of merchandise from private estates, individuals, and retailers. There are now more than a hundred shops throughout the United States. All proceeds from merchandise sales are used to provide the necessary funding for research, education, and family services programs provided by the American Cancer Society. California alone raises over $7 million annually through their special events and thrift stores.

The Discovery Thrift Shops are located in most major communities and are a delight to shop in. The shops are clean and bright, and the volunteer staff is always cheery and eager to please! Their upscale appearance is not reflected in the pricing of their designer clothing and collectibles. They have established a pricing formula that they apply to all of their stores across the country, so you can expect a high degree of consistency from one store to the next. Their pricing staff is encouraged to be up on current fashion and its prices, so there are those items that they will price slightly higher than the rest.

Discovery shops will place an item for sale only if approximately 75 percent of the wear life remains in it. Their pricers will estimate the original retail price of that item and then discount the store's selling price by one fourth (if the item is used) or one third (if the item is new). For example: a fashionable used dress in good condition that originally sold for $100 would be priced at $25. You will find that they also have a generous markdown formula, applied every two months. Savvy shoppers would be wise to familiarize themselves with this.

One out of every five deaths in this country is caused by cancer. The American Cancer Society's Discovery Thrift Shops contribute funds to battling the various forms of this deadly disease. The money they raise *is* making a difference!

HOUSING WORKS
THRIFT SHOPS

Housing Works Thrift Shops

Housing Works provides advocacy, housing, and supportive services for homeless men, women, and children living with AIDS and HIV in New

York City. The goal of this community-based organization is to enable homeless persons living with AIDS and HIV to re-establish control and dignity in their lives. Several hundred individuals and families are currently enrolled in Housing Works programs such as Intake and Advocacy, Scattered Site Housing, and Independent Living.

Housing Works Thrift Shop, Inc., is a subsidiary of Housing Works organized to provide ongoing financial support and visibility for the programs of Housing Works through the sale of donated goods. The stores, staffed with friendly, knowledgeable professionals, also provide occupational training for clients of Housing Works. Although Housing Works has only two thrift stores, both located in Manhattan, the combination of the merchandise available there and the work that they do in the community more than qualifies them as a top thrift store organization, equal to those chains with hundreds of stores.

Housing Works has recently introduced a new thrift store to their organization, and I had the good fortune to attend its opening day! The new store is much more upscale than their original store. It was apparent that much time and careful planning went into the opening of this store, for the fine merchandise is presented with eye-catching and stylish displays. The layout is spacious and convenient, with numerous dressing rooms as well as floor-to-ceiling mirrors. It would be difficult to distinguish the *new* Housing Works Thrift Shop from that of a posh boutique. This is especially true when you enter their designer room, where I found fabulous items from Chanel, Prada, and Donna Karan at a fraction of their original price! This is not the type of store where you might expect to spot an overlooked highly collectible stuffed Stieff toy for a dollar, but you can expect to pay a fair and reasonable price for great merchandise.

The National Council of Jewish Women
Council Thrift Shops

The National Council of Jewish Women (NCJW), based in Los Angeles, was founded over a century ago as a nonprofit, nonsectarian social service agency focusing on the needs of women and children. Currently, its largest and most important outreach program is Women Helping Women services, which was created in 1983 in response to the needs of the women of our community. Women Helping Children grew out of this program. The proceeds from the Council thrift shops are what keep the NCJW/LA in the business of helping people help themselves. This money provides the major source of funding for their community service, social action, and educational programs. Both women and children from a network of homeless and battered women's shelters receive vouchers for free clothing and blankets at any of their thrift stores. Los Angeles' first Council thrift shop was established in 1923. Not only do they now operate six wonderful thrift stores, but they also host a fabulous flea market three times a year, and it has proved to be a tremendous fund raiser. They rent spaces in their parking lot to outside antique and collectible dealers selling both new and used merchandise. Inside the building they have their designer resale boutique, jewelry showcases, and estate and collectible sale room.

Most of the larger and higher-value donations are sent to auction in order to derive the highest possible amount for these items, and ultimately the largest dollar amount to be put to good use. But don't be upset, there are still plenty of wonderful things for sale at both the stores and the flea market. This event not only has expanded with each flea market, but has become a community event for savvy shoppers—people call and ask when the next one is going to be and are virtually lined up at the door (of course, I am *first* in line when they open at 9:00 A.M.)!

NCJW/LA has just announced that it will soon hold "Thrift Shop Chic

Fashion Shows," for various organizations. This sounds like fun, and I suggest that you call them to get on their invitation list!

One of the advantages to donating your saleable items to the NCJW is that they will give you a written evaluation of the fair market value of the donation. You may also self-appraise. This can make a great difference at tax time. Either appraisal is considered "supporting documentation" by the IRS, and is acceptable as proof of the worth of the donation. This, along with all the wonderful things they do, is a very good incentive to donate to the NCJW.

The Council thrift shops have been top ten contenders since long before I was even a glint in my father's eye!

MOTION
PICTURE &
TELEVISION
FUND

SCREEN SMART SET AUXILIARY

The Motion Picture & Television Fund
Screen Smart Set Cinema Glamour Shop

The Cinema Glamour Shop that supports the Motion Picture & Television Fund has been in business for more than twenty years. The Screen Smart Set, a Fund auxiliary organization that operates the Cinema Glamour Shop, is extremely proud to boast that they have raised over $3 million in those twenty-plus years. The money they raise, as part of the MPTF Foundation, goes to provide health and child care as well as residential and charitable services.

June Van Dyke, the store manager, was assistant to the Oscar-winning costume designer Edith Head for twenty-five years. Ms. Van Dyke's flare for style pervades the store. There is a delightful theatrical ambiance, and many of the volunteers who work there are themselves from the entertainment industry. You can be sure that much of the clothing has come from

Hollywood actresses and studio wardrobe departments. Your purchases almost always guarantee a delightful anecdote from one of the volunteers as to who may have donated that item or what film it was featured in.

There is always a wide array of beautiful designer clothing. I once bought an incredible Thierry Mugler dress there for $35 and an Anne Klein matte jersey jumpsuit for $25! They also have a small collectibles section and occasionally some interesting costume jewelry.

I had the pleasure of attending the annual Screen Smart Set Auxiliary Celebrity Fashion Show and Luncheon recently. It was a wonderfully entertaining and delightful event. The sale of the designer fashions featured in the show raised approximately $6,443. I wanted so desperately to purchase a sapphire-blue silk cut-velvet evening dress donated by Elizabeth Taylor. I missed by just a moment. Not to worry, I was more than satisfied by my purchase of a gorgeous Hermés scarf for $15 and Givenchy chain belt for $20. And of course, there is always next year!

There is also a Celebrity Auction every October at the Regent Beverly Wilshire Hotel that's not to be missed! Call the store for further details.

I expect that the Cinema Glamour Shop will remain on *The Rag Street Journal*'s top ten list for at least the next twenty years!

Goodwill Industries
Goodwill Thrift Shops

The first Goodwill Industries was founded in Boston in 1902. A wholly nonprofit organization, the Goodwill Industries provides services to thousands of people who face employment difficulties.

In the beginning, Goodwill's focus was on new immigrants who were barred from employment because they did not speak English when they arrived in Boston back in the early 1900s. Over time, Goodwill's focus shifted to people with *visible* physical disabilities. However, advances in medical technology, legislation, and public awareness meant that these people were now leading much fuller lives, including work. Today, Goodwill increasingly serves people with *invisible* disabilities, which may be developmental, educational, social, psychological, or cultural.

Goodwill's job training programs have changed too. No longer limited to providing employment only within Goodwill, the agency now offers job training programs that lead to competitive employment. Although the training programs vary from one member organization to the next, some of them include computer training, data processing, food services and hospitality, banking industry training, retail and customer service, as well as health care occupations.

There are more than 1,400 Goodwill retail stores, which are operated by some 183 separate Goodwill organizations across North America. There are also some 52 associate member organizations in 36 countries across the globe. Their international headquarters is located in Bethesda, Maryland.

Although some Goodwills do receive some government funding or support from the United Way, for many, the retail stores generate a large percentage of Goodwill Industries' revenues, so they do not rely heavily on tax dollars or government grants. Their retail stores earn the much-needed funds necessary to keep their job training programs running.

Through the sale of reusable items, Goodwill recycles millions of pounds of clothing and household goods per year, thus saving our ever-dwindling landfill space. Clothing that does not sell in the stores is sold off to textile recyclers for pennies a pound.

My all-time favorite Goodwill store stands at the corner of Jarvis Street and Adelaide in Toronto. I have been shopping there for more than fifteen years. I never miss an opportunity to pay it a visit every time I am in Toronto. Unfortunately, I usually have to purchase a new suitcase to carry home all the wonderful things I have bought there! One thing is consistent—I have never come away empty-handed.

This Toronto store has recently added a Collector's Corner, which is an absolute must for antique and collectible enthusiasts. Because it is a volunteer operation, it is open only on Tuesday. Collector's Corner is tucked way in the back, on the second floor.

Most of Goodwill's retail stores have a kind of blanket pricing policy. Some shops have a printed price list or sign at the cash counter. All are incredibly reasonable. Some shops have caught on to the trend in the thrift store industry, of offering a boutique section. Goodwill does this by displaying racks of merchandise that is "individually priced." Still, their prices are some of the best in town.

Many Goodwill Industries have been closing their smaller outlets in order to upgrade and consolidate them into larger stores. These can also be a good source for antique and collectible furniture, some of which has been refinished through Goodwill's own programs.

When you support Goodwill Industries with a donation or purchase, you support not only consumer value and environmentally sound reuse, but also a very successful self-funding job training program. No Band-Aid solution, Goodwill's programs provide people with the tools they need to change the direction of their lives.

No one could have doubted that Goodwill would be a celebrated member of *The Rag Street Journal*'s top ten!

Ventura County Rescue Mission
The Mission Bargain Center

It is estimated that there are more than five thousand homeless and needy people living on the streets in Ventura County, California. Most lack warm, safe shelter, and approximately 40 percent of them are women and children. The faces of these less fortunate people have changed over the years. While there are greater and greater numbers of people with substance abuse, many of today's homeless are more likely to be physically and mentally challenged, or those with low incomes, the elderly, veterans, or those who lack English language skills. The average age of most who are homeless is just thirty-one.

In 1972 the Ventura County Rescue Mission opened its doors to all the broken, lonely lost men and women in need. Today it serves in excess of 350 hot meals a day and puts up more than 27,000 men, women, and children each year.

The question here is, Where does one begin the rehabilitation of a person who's been battered by the streets, who didn't get his fair share of breaks, and who feels ashamed, abandoned, and alone? After a hot shower and a good meal at the Rescue Mission, newcomers are interviewed and tested in order to assess their needs and deficiencies.

The Rescue Mission's philosophy is founded on the need for prevention as well as cure. While they are grateful to help *all* in need, the "heartbeat" of the mission is their drug and alcohol recovery program. In their one-year Christian residence program, they teach about the dangers of substance abuse and offer ongoing counseling as well as active support groups.

The mission recognizes that education and knowledge is the way up and out for most of the less fortunate who have come to their doors. For this reason, courses in math, language, typing, computer skills, and vocational studies are taught daily. They also offer help to those in the program who need guidance with tax and legal problems, driver's licenses and VA forms, and anything else that may distract them from their primary goal: recovery.

The mission has recently developed a new program for children that has met with tremendous success. It's called "Camp Good News," and for the past three years they have made it possible for twenty-five children to attend this Christian camp located in the beautiful mountains east of San Luis Obispo. It's a week packed full of fun and adventure, coupled with Bible studies, nature walks, games, swimming, hiking, and crafts. Those of us who were fortunate enough to attend camp in our youth know that those endless summer days are intrinsic to our gleeful childhood memories. I personally wouldn't trade those memories for the world.

Whether the mission is supplying summer camp, food, shelter, clothing, training, or counseling to those in need, it is all available at no charge. In the past this has been made possible solely by the generous donations and gifts from the caring individuals, churches, and businesses in Ventura County.

Despite the overwhelming generosity of their patrons, there is always a need for more and more funding, so last fall the mission bought an old warehouse, rallied the support of many of the men in their recovery program as well as hiring locals, and opened their first retail thrift store, the Ventura County Rescue Mission Bargain Center.

They started big, with over 26,000 square feet of space for sales, a work-room, and a warehouse. Jerry Roberg, the director of the mission, studied the marketplace. He dug in and really learned what he was doing prior to opening the doors to their first thrift store. It would seem that his home-work has really paid off, for the Bargain Center Thrift Store now nets ap-proximately 35 percent of the mission's operating budget.

Jerry understands the value of advertising and the nature of the con-sumer. He created a pleasant and attractive atmosphere that encourages shoppers to buy. The store is bright and cheerful with racks and racks of well-merchandised clothing and accessories as well as household goods, all at bargain prices.

I had the pleasure of touring the entire operation from the storefront to the giant clothing balers in the warehouse. A dozen people work on the flood of clothing in a nonstop ballet, moving the garments from inspection tables, placing items unsuitable for sale into bins for the balers and ulti-mately recycling, and putting saleable items on hangers and racks—all of it moving in its endless journey through the "Circle of Life," creating funding to hope and recovery.

TVI Inc. Value Village and
Super Savers Thrift Stores

The Value Village legacy dates back to the late 1920s with Benjamin and Orlo Ellison. These two brothers purportedly helped build the Salvation Army's sprawling thrift store chain. By the late 1940s, the two brothers had become disenchanted with the Salvation Army and struck out on their own. Could it be possible that they perceived the tremendous potential of the entrepreneurial side of the thrift store industry, in a for-profit world?

Benjamin opened a thrift store under a management contract with the Purple Hearts Veteran's Charity in Sacramento, California, and taught the thrift store business to his son William. William, in turn, passed on the family's thrift store know-how to his son Thomas.

William Ellison began a management company with another veterans' store in 1954, on Mission Street in San Francisco. William opened his first Value Village thrift store in 1966, in Renton, Washington. Over the last ten years, his youngest son, Chief Executive Officer Thomas Ellison, has built TVI Inc. into a $97 million (1992 sales) outfit with over 100 Value Village thrift stores (and sister stores called Savers and Village des Valeurs) across the United States and Canada. William and Thomas Ellison, along with Thomas's brother-in-law, John Bacon, own 100 percent of TVI and sister company Value Village Stores Ltd.

Unlike other thrift stores that I have profiled, Value Village is a *for*-profit organization. However, they do help to fund the worthy causes of more than thirty-six charities across North America, including Big Brothers, Big Sisters, Canadian Diabetes Association, Association for Retarded Citizens, the National Multiple Sclerosis Society, and Save the Children Federation. Each of the Value Village/Savers stores has a buy/sell relationship with a local charity. The charities pay for telephone teams to call and solicit donations. Trucks sent by the charities pick up donated clothes and household goods and deliver them to nearby TVI stores.

This is apparently a good deal for the charities. In 1993, Seattle-based Northwest Center for the Retarded, TVI's largest supplier in the Northwest, grossed nearly $3 million from its deliveries to TVI. After covering the cost of telephone solicitors and truck drivers, its net profit was approximately $1.2 million! Value Village stores have allowed charity organizations to get into the resale business without a large investment of money and with minimal resources. With the present state of the economy, it has become harder and harder for charitable organizations to receive as much money in donations as they have during more favorable times. Also, more and more non-profit organizations are cropping up across the country, and all are frantically competing for the ever-dwindling charity dollar.

The marked difference between Value Village/Savers thrift stores and many other large chain thrift stores is their size and merchandising. The stores look more like Wal-Mart than a typical thrift store. Most of the stores are over 20,000 square feet and have earned a reputation as the department store of thrift! They are brightly lit with rows and rows of color-coordinated and sized clothing. Unlike many other thrift stores, they offer comfortable, spacious dressing rooms. A section in many U.S. stores, called Labels, features new goods purchased in bulk from national and regional department stores that are unable to clear these items from their inventory.

This is perfectly good merchandise that may simply be out of season or has passed through a department store's sales and markdowns, yet did not sell. This is a great way for department stores and boutiques to dispose of un-sold merchandise, and for Value Village/Savers to pass incredible savings on to the consumer.

In contrast to the traditional thrift shop, TVI has a seven-day return policy. As long as goods still have their tag in place, they can be exchanged for a store credit. Thomas Ellison says he got the idea from Nordstrom de-partment stores. Apparently Nordstrom claims that for every dollar they refund, they sell back three. Value Village has found that the same equation holds true for them.

Now, you might think that because Value Village/Savers is a *for*-profit thrift store, their pricing would be higher than those of *non*profit thrift op-erations. Quite the contrary! Their pricing is as low as or lower than most of their major competitors. A secondhand blouse that would have retailed for $40 new would sell at Value Village for $3.99. In their Labels depart-ment, a $55 polo shirt, with the department store price tag still hanging off the sleeve, retails for $11.99.

From its increasingly aggressive marketing efforts, including an adver-tising campaign in excess of $2 million annually, to its attention to mer-chandising, TVI Inc. and Value Village Stores Ltd. have applied traditional retailing techniques in an industry that is more often run like a bake sale!

TVI and Value Village may be for-profit operations, but in their quest for financial success they have generated millions of dollars for many wor-thy nonprofit organizations—monies that they would otherwise not have been capable of raising on their own. It is for this reason I have chosen to rank them among the top ten thrift organizations in North America.

PART II

My Favorite Thrift Stores

A Note About the Thrift Store Listings

The following thrift store listings throughout the United States and Canada are by no means intended to be comprehensive. Such a listing would have filled a book three times this size! From a master database of more than 10,000 shops, I have—not without pain—chosen approximately 3,000 to represent the major charity organizations that I feel offer the best and most consistent quality of merchandise. You will also find a few organizations here that may have only one store, such as the Cinema Glamour Shop in Los Angeles. These have been included because they are truly exceptional stores, ones I personally love to shop in, that offer an outstanding range of merchandise, from top designer clothing to antiques and fine jewelry.

In Chapter 10, the stores are listed alphabetically by U.S. state, then by city within each state. In Chapter 11, they are listed alphabetically by Canadian province. All listings include an address, the type of merchandise to be found there, and when possible, a phone number, hours of operation, and the store manager's name. (In many cases, stores are reluctant to give out numbers and names, since staff hours and personnel change frequently, and there is not always someone available to take calls. If you see a store listed in your area, try your local telephone directory for a current number.)

10

U.S. Thrift Stores, by State

Alabama

Salvation Army Thrift Store
430 Noble St.
Anniston, AL 36201
TYPE OF MERCHANDISE: Clothing, housewares, furniture
DONATION TAX RECEIPT: Receipt given upon request

Salvation Army Thrift Store
1907 Second Ave.
Bessemer, AL 35020
CONTACT: Tracy Dow
HOURS: Mon.–Sat. 9–5
TYPE OF MERCHANDISE: Clothing, housewares, furniture
DONATION TAX RECEIPT: Receipt given upon request

Salvation Army Thrift Store
1401 F.L. Shuttlesworth Dr.
Birmingham, AL 35234
CONTACT: Randa Richardson
PHONE: 205-252-8151

HOURS: Mon.–Sat. 9–5
TYPE OF MERCHANDISE: Specializes in 99-cent clothing sales
DONATION TAX RECEIPT: No donations at this store
COMMENTS: Periodic senior citizens discount sales

Salvation Army Thrift Store
1849B Center Point Pkwy.
Birmingham, AL 35215
HOURS: Mon.–Sat. 9–5
TYPE OF MERCHANDISE: Clothing, housewares, furniture
DONATION TAX RECEIPT: Receipt given upon request

Goodwill Industries Thrift Store
2350 Green Springs Hwy. S
Birmingham, AL 35205
TYPE OF MERCHANDISE: Clothing, housewares, furniture
DONATION TAX RECEIPT: Receipt given upon request

Salvation Army Thrift Store
2373 First St. NE
CROSS STREET: Center Point Plaza
Shopping Center
Birmingham, AL 35215
CONTACT: Geraldine Earnest
PHONE: 205-854-1921
HOURS: Mon.–Sat. 9–5
TYPE OF MERCHANDISE: Clothing, bric-a-brac, and costumes
DONATION TAX RECEIPT: Receipt given upon request

Goodwill Industries Thrift Store
7627 First Ave. N
Birmingham, AL 35206
TYPE OF MERCHANDISE: Clothing, housewares, furniture
DONATION TAX RECEIPT: Receipt given upon request

Goodwill Industries Thrift Store
1706 Douglas Ave.
Brewton, AL 36427
PHONE: 205-867-2254, 867-5723
HOURS: Mon.–Fri. 9–8, Sun. 10–6
TYPE OF MERCHANDISE: Clothing, housewares, furniture
DONATION TAX RECEIPT: Receipt given upon request
YEARS IN BUSINESS: 38

Goodwill Industries Thrift Store
124 Fourth St. SW
Cullman, AL 35055
TYPE OF MERCHANDISE: Clothing, housewares, furniture
DONATION TAX RECEIPT: Receipt given upon request
COMMENTS: Bargain center

Goodwill Industries Thrift Store
125 S. Eufaula Ave.
Eufaula, AL 36027
TYPE OF MERCHANDISE: Clothing, housewares, furniture
DONATION TAX RECEIPT: Receipt given upon request

Goodwill Industries Thrift Store
110 N. Green Rd.
Fairhope, AL 36532
PHONE: 205-928-8087, 928-8195

HOURS: Mon.–Fri. 9–8, Sun. 10–6
TYPE OF MERCHANDISE: Clothing, housewares, furniture
DONATION TAX RECEIPT: Receipt given upon request
YEARS IN BUSINESS: 38

Salvation Army Thrift Store
525 Broad St.
Gadsden, AL 35901
TYPE OF MERCHANDISE: Clothing, housewares, furniture
DONATION TAX RECEIPT: Receipt given upon request

Salvation Army Thrift Store
2112 Oakwood Ave. NW
Huntsville, AL 35810
TYPE OF MERCHANDISE: Clothing, housewares, furniture
DONATION TAX RECEIPT: Receipt given upon request

Goodwill Industries Thrift Store
301 Washington St. NW
Huntsville, AL 35801
TYPE OF MERCHANDISE: Clothing, housewares, furniture
DONATION TAX RECEIPT: Receipt given upon request

Salvation Army Thrift Store
305 Seminole Dr. SW
Huntsville, AL 35805
TYPE OF MERCHANDISE: Clothing, housewares, furniture
DONATION TAX RECEIPT: Receipt given upon request

Goodwill Industries Thrift Store
1814 Fourth Ave.
Jasper, AL 35501
TYPE OF MERCHANDISE: Clothing, housewares, furniture
DONATION TAX RECEIPT: Receipt given upon request

Disabled American Vets Thrift Store
1004 Dauphin Island Pkwy.
Mobile, AL 36605
TYPE OF MERCHANDISE: Clothing, housewares
DONATION TAX RECEIPT: Receipt given upon request
COMMENTS: Pickup service

Salvation Army Thrift Store
1023 Dauphin St.
Mobile, AL 36604
TYPE OF MERCHANDISE: Clothing,
housewares, furniture
DONATION TAX RECEIPT: Receipt given
upon request
Goodwill Industries Thrift Store
266-C Azalea Rd.
Mobile, AL 36609
PHONE: 205-342-1967, 342-9360
HOURS: Mon.–Fri. 9–8, Sun. 10–6
TYPE OF MERCHANDISE: Clothing,
housewares, furniture
DONATION TAX RECEIPT: Receipt given
upon request
YEARS IN BUSINESS: 38
Goodwill Industries Thrift Store
3926 Airport Blvd.
Mobile, AL 36608
TYPE OF MERCHANDISE: Clothing,
housewares, furniture
DONATION TAX RECEIPT: Receipt given
upon request
Saint Vincent De Paul Thrift Store
411 S. Broad St.
Mobile, AL 36603
TYPE OF MERCHANDISE: Clothing,
housewares, furniture
DONATION TAX RECEIPT: Receipt given
upon request
COMMENTS: Monthly markdowns
Salvation Army Thrift Store
45 Belt Shopping Center
Mobile, AL 36610
TYPE OF MERCHANDISE: Clothing,
housewares, furniture
DONATION TAX RECEIPT: Receipt given
upon request
Salvation Army Thrift Store
1369 Federal Dr.
Montgomery, AL 36107
TYPE OF MERCHANDISE: Clothing,
housewares, furniture
DONATION TAX RECEIPT: Receipt given
upon request
Disabled American Vets Thrift Store
32 Perry Ct.
Montgomery, AL 36105

TYPE OF MERCHANDISE: Clothing,
housewares
DONATION TAX RECEIPT: Receipt given
upon request
Salvation Army Thrift Store
3863 S. Court St.
Montgomery, AL 36105
TYPE OF MERCHANDISE: Clothing,
housewares, furniture
DONATION TAX RECEIPT: Receipt given
upon request
Disabled American Vets Thrift Store
521 W. Fairview Ave.
Montgomery, AL 36105
TYPE OF MERCHANDISE: Clothing,
housewares
DONATION TAX RECEIPT: Receipt given
upon request
Goodwill Industries Thrift Store
900 Air Base Blvd.
Montgomery, AL 36108
TYPE OF MERCHANDISE: Clothing,
housewares, furniture
DONATION TAX RECEIPT: Receipt given
upon request
Salvation Army Thrift Store
1412 Third Ave.
Phenix City, AL 36867
TYPE OF MERCHANDISE: Clothing,
housewares, furniture
DONATION TAX RECEIPT: Receipt given
upon request
Goodwill Industries Thrift Store
935 Highway 43 N
Saraland, AL 36571
PHONE: 205-679-1880, 679-1676
HOURS: Mon.–Sat. 9–8, Sun. 10–6
TYPE OF MERCHANDISE: Clothing,
housewares, furniture
DONATION TAX RECEIPT: Receipt given
upon request
YEARS IN BUSINESS: 38
Salvation Army Thrift Store
237 Broad St.
Selma, AL 36701
TYPE OF MERCHANDISE: Clothing,
housewares, furniture
DONATION TAX RECEIPT: Receipt given
upon request

Salvation Army Thrift Store
2044 Springdale Ln.
CROSS STREET: Tarrant Shopping Center
Tarrant, AL 35217
CONTACT: Mary Boswell
PHONE: 205-849-6161
HOURS: Mon.–Sat. 9–5
TYPE OF MERCHANDISE: Clothing, bric-a-brac, antiques
DONATION TAX RECEIPT: Receipt given upon request
COMMENTS: Fix-it-yourself collectible furniture

Goodwill Industries Thrift Store
2309 Sixth St.
Tuscaloosa, AL 35401
TYPE OF MERCHANDISE: Clothing, housewares, furniture
DONATION TAX RECEIPT: Receipt given upon request

Salvation Army Thrift Store
514 14th St.
CROSS STREET: Near the University of Alabama
Tuscaloosa, AL 35401
CONTACT: Essie Colvin
PHONE: 205-758-9108
HOURS: Mon.–Sat. 9–5
TYPE OF MERCHANDISE: Clothing, housewares, furniture
DONATION TAX RECEIPT: Receipt given upon request

Alaska

Salvation Army Thrift Store
171 Muldoon Rd.
Anchorage, AK 99504
TYPE OF MERCHANDISE: Clothing, housewares, furniture
DONATION TAX RECEIPT: Receipt given upon request

Salvation Army Thrift Store
3920 Mountain View Dr.
Anchorage, AK 99508
TYPE OF MERCHANDISE: Clothing, housewares, furniture
DONATION TAX RECEIPT: Receipt given upon request

TVI Value Village Thrift Store
5437 E. Northern Lights Blvd., Suite #4
Anchorage, AK 99504
CONTACT: Bret Wright
PHONE: 907-337-2184
HOURS: Mon.–Sat. 9–9, Sun. 10–6
TYPE OF MERCHANDISE: Clothing, housewares, furniture
DONATION TAX RECEIPT: No

Salvation Army Thrift Store
2222 S. Cushman St.
Fairbanks, AK 99701
TYPE OF MERCHANDISE: Clothing, housewares, furniture
DONATION TAX RECEIPT: Receipt given upon request

TVI Value Village Thrift Store
3027 Airport Way
Fairbanks, AK 99701
CONTACT: Lynda Fenton
PHONE: 907-474-4828
HOURS: Mon.–Sat. 9–9, Sun. 10–6
TYPE OF MERCHANDISE: Clothing, housewares, furniture
DONATION TAX RECEIPT: No

Salvation Army Thrift Store
527 E. Fifth Ave.
Fairbanks, AK 99705
TYPE OF MERCHANDISE: Clothing, housewares, furniture
DONATION TAX RECEIPT: Receipt given upon request

Salvation Army Thrift Store
517 Main St.
Kenai, AK 99611
TYPE OF MERCHANDISE: Clothing, housewares, furniture
DONATION TAX RECEIPT: Receipt given upon request

Salvation Army Thrift Store
1010 Water St.
Ketchikan, AK 99901
TYPE OF MERCHANDISE: Clothing, housewares, furniture
DONATION TAX RECEIPT: Receipt given upon request

Arizona

Disabled American Vets Thrift Store
49 N. Mesa Dr.
Apache Junction, AZ 85220
Saint Vincent De Paul Thrift Store
11518 E. Apache Trail
Apache Junction, AZ 85220
TYPE OF MERCHANDISE: Clothing,
housewares, furniture
DONATION TAX RECEIPT: Receipt given
upon request
COMMENTS: Monthly markdowns
Salvation Army Thrift Store
201 N. Eighth St.
Avondale, AZ 85323
TYPE OF MERCHANDISE: Clothing,
housewares, furniture
Salvation Army Thrift Store
403 N. Florence
Casa Grande, AZ 85222
TYPE OF MERCHANDISE: Clothing,
housewares, furniture
DONATION TAX RECEIPT: Receipt given
upon request
TVI Savers Thrift Store
1106 N. Arizona Ave.
Chandler, AZ 85224
CONTACT: Jackie Halleen
PHONE: 602-899-7776
HOURS: Mon.–Sat. 9–9, Sun. 10–6
TYPE OF MERCHANDISE: Clothing,
housewares, furniture
DONATION TAX RECEIPT: No
Salvation Army Thrift Store
81 W. Boston
Chandler, AZ 85224
TYPE OF MERCHANDISE: Clothing,
housewares, furniture
DONATION TAX RECEIPT: Receipt given
upon request
National Assistance League Cedar Closet
2912 N. West St.
Flagstaff, AZ 86004
PHONE: 602-779-3029
TYPE OF MERCHANDISE: Clothing,
housewares, furniture
DONATION TAX RECEIPT: Receipt given
upon request
COMMENTS: Monthly markdowns

American Cancer Society Discovery Shop
6611 W. Peroria #3 and 4
Glendale, AZ 85302
PHONE: 602-486-3392
TYPE OF MERCHANDISE: Clothing, bric-a-
brac
DONATION TAX RECEIPT: Receipt given
upon request
COMMENTS: Monthly markdowns
Saint Vincent De Paul Thrift Store
7018 N. 57th Ave.
Glendale, AZ 85301
TYPE OF MERCHANDISE: Clothing,
housewares, furniture
DONATION TAX RECEIPT: Receipt given
upon request
COMMENTS: Monthly markdowns
Salvation Army Thrift Store
161 E. Cedar St.
Globe, AZ 85501
TYPE OF MERCHANDISE: Clothing,
housewares, furniture
DONATION TAX RECEIPT: Receipt given
upon request
Salvation Army Thrift Store
240 N. Broad St.
Globe, AZ 85501
TYPE OF MERCHANDISE: Clothing,
housewares, furniture
DONATION TAX RECEIPT: Receipt given
upon request
ARC Thrift Store
2032 E. Andy Devine Ave.
Kingman, AZ 86401
TYPE OF MERCHANDISE: Clothing,
housewares, furniture
DONATION TAX RECEIPT: Receipt given
upon request
Saint Vincent De Paul Thrift Store
3361 Kiowa Blvd.
Lake Havasu City, AZ 86403
TYPE OF MERCHANDISE: Clothing,
housewares, furniture
DONATION TAX RECEIPT: Receipt given
upon request
COMMENTS: Monthly markdowns

Salvation Army Thrift Store
1260 W. University
Mesa, AZ 85202
TYPE OF MERCHANDISE: Clothing,
housewares, furniture
DONATION TAX RECEIPT: Receipt given
upon request
TVI Savers Thrift Store
2049 W. Broadway Rd.
Mesa, AZ 85202
CONTACT: Chad Tatum
PHONE: 602-962-1552
HOURS: Mon.–Sat. 9–9, Sun. 10–6
TYPE OF MERCHANDISE: Clothing,
housewares, furniture
DONATION TAX RECEIPT: No
Saint Vincent De Paul Thrift Store
2352 W. Main St.
Mesa, AZ 85201
TYPE OF MERCHANDISE: Clothing,
housewares, furniture
DONATION TAX RECEIPT: Receipt given
upon request
COMMENTS: Monthly markdowns
Salvation Army Thrift Store
416 Live Oak St.
Miami, AZ 85539
TYPE OF MERCHANDISE: Clothing,
housewares, furniture
DONATION TAX RECEIPT: Receipt given
upon request
Goodwill Industries Thrift Store
12608 N. Black Canyon Hwy.
Phoenix, AZ 85029-1345
TYPE OF MERCHANDISE: Clothing,
housewares, furniture
DONATION TAX RECEIPT: Receipt given
upon request
TVI Savers Thrift Store
13621 N. 32nd St.
Phoenix, AZ 85032
CONTACT: Tim O'Neal
PHONE: 602-971-7704
HOURS: Mon.–Sat. 9–9, Sun. 10–6
TYPE OF MERCHANDISE: Clothing,
housewares, furniture
DONATION TAX RECEIPT: No

Saint Vincent De Paul Thrift Store
1414 E. Van Buren
Phoenix, AZ 85006
TYPE OF MERCHANDISE: Clothing,
housewares, furniture
DONATION TAX RECEIPT: Receipt given
upon request
COMMENTS: Monthly markdowns
Salvation Army Thrift Store
1625 S. Central
Phoenix, AZ 85040
TYPE OF MERCHANDISE: Clothing,
housewares, furniture
DONATION TAX RECEIPT: Receipt given
upon request
Salvation Army Thrift Store
1727 E. McDowell Rd.
Phoenix, AZ 85040
TYPE OF MERCHANDISE: Clothing,
housewares, furniture
DONATION TAX RECEIPT: Receipt given
upon request
Salvation Army Thrift Store
203 N. Eighth St.
Phoenix, AZ 85034
TYPE OF MERCHANDISE: Clothing,
housewares, furniture
DONATION TAX RECEIPT: Receipt given
upon request
Salvation Army Thrift Store
24 E. Mohave St.
Phoenix, AZ 85004
TYPE OF MERCHANDISE: Clothing,
housewares, furniture
DONATION TAX RECEIPT: Receipt given
upon request
COMMENTS: Main store
Disabled American Vets Thrift Store
2610 W. Bethany Home Rd.
Phoenix, AZ 85017
TYPE OF MERCHANDISE: Clothing,
housewares, furniture
TVI Savers Thrift Store
2625 W. Bethany Home Rd.
Phoenix, AZ 85017
CONTACT: Robert Hasty
PHONE: 602-242-4288
HOURS: Mon.–Sat. 9–9, Sun. 10–6

TYPE OF MERCHANDISE: Clothing, housewares, furniture
DONATION TAX RECEIPT: No
Saint Vincent De Paul Thrift Store
2945 E. Bell Rd.
Phoenix, AZ 85032
TYPE OF MERCHANDISE: Clothing, housewares, furniture
DONATION TAX RECEIPT: Receipt given upon request
COMMENTS: Monthly markdowns
Disabled American Vets Thrift Store
3038 W. Van Buren St.
Phoenix, AZ 85009
TYPE OF MERCHANDISE: Clothing, housewares, furniture
DONATION TAX RECEIPT: Receipt given upon request
Goodwill Industries Thrift Store
3144 Grand Ave.
Phoenix, AZ 85017
TYPE OF MERCHANDISE: Clothing, housewares, furniture
DONATION TAX RECEIPT: Receipt given upon request
Salvation Army Thrift Store
336 E. Dunlap Ave.
Phoenix, AZ 85020
TYPE OF MERCHANDISE: Clothing, housewares, furniture
DONATION TAX RECEIPT: Receipt given upon request
TVI Savers Thrift Store
3517 W. Bell Rd.
Phoenix, AZ 85023
CONTACT: Dave Bareno
PHONE: 602-938-1616
HOURS: Mon.–Sat. 9–9, Sun. 10–6
TYPE OF MERCHANDISE: Clothing, housewares, furniture
DONATION TAX RECEIPT: No
Salvation Army Thrift Store
4022 N. 67th Ave.
Phoenix, AZ 85033
TYPE OF MERCHANDISE: Clothing, housewares, furniture
DONATION TAX RECEIPT: Receipt given upon request

Goodwill Industries Thrift Store
417 N. 16th St.
Phoenix, AZ 85006
TYPE OF MERCHANDISE: Clothing, housewares, furniture
DONATION TAX RECEIPT: Receipt given upon request
Salvation Army Thrift Store
4208 S. Central Ave.
Phoenix, AZ 85040
TYPE OF MERCHANDISE: Clothing, housewares, furniture
DONATION TAX RECEIPT: Receipt given upon request
Disabled American Vets Thrift Store
4810 S. Central Ave.
Phoenix, AZ 85040
TYPE OF MERCHANDISE: Clothing, housewares, furniture
DONATION TAX RECEIPT: Receipt given upon request
National Assistance League Thrift Shop
7044 N. Seventh St.
Phoenix, AZ 85020
PHONE: 602-944-9845
TYPE OF MERCHANDISE: Clothing, housewares, furniture
DONATION TAX RECEIPT: Receipt given upon request
COMMENTS: Monthly markdowns
Salvation Army Thrift Store
2324 N. Scottsdale Rd.
Scottsdale, AZ 85257
TYPE OF MERCHANDISE: Clothing, housewares, furniture
DONATION TAX RECEIPT: Receipt given upon request
Saint Vincent De Paul Thrift Store
220 Meyer Dr.
Sierra Vista, AZ 85635
TYPE OF MERCHANDISE: Clothing, housewares, furniture
DONATION TAX RECEIPT: Receipt given upon request
COMMENTS: Monthly markdowns
Salvation Army Thrift Store
280 E. Wilcox Dr.
Sierra Vista, AZ 85705

TYPE OF MERCHANDISE: Clothing, housewares, furniture
DONATION TAX RECEIPT: Receipt given upon request

Salvation Army Thrift Store
598 Meyer Dr.
Sierra Vista, AZ 85635
TYPE OF MERCHANDISE: Clothing, housewares, furniture
DONATION TAX RECEIPT: Receipt given upon request

Salvation Army Thrift Store
336 E. Dunlop
Sunnyslope, AZ 85020
TYPE OF MERCHANDISE: Clothing, housewares, furniture
DONATION TAX RECEIPT: Receipt given upon request

Salvation Army Thrift Store
2324 N. Scottsdale
Tempe, AZ 85251
TYPE OF MERCHANDISE: Clothing, housewares, furniture
DONATION TAX RECEIPT: Receipt given upon request

National Assistance League Thriftique
1309 N. Alvernon Way
Tucson, AZ 85712
PHONE: 602-326-1585
TYPE OF MERCHANDISE: Clothing, housewares, furniture
DONATION TAX RECEIPT: Receipt given upon request
COMMENTS: Monthly markdowns

Salvation Army Thrift Store
2719 S. Sixth Ave.
Tucson, AZ 85713
TYPE OF MERCHANDISE: Clothing, housewares, furniture
DONATION TAX RECEIPT: Receipt given upon request

Salvation Army Thrift Store
2900 W. Valencia Rd.
Tucson, AZ 85706
TYPE OF MERCHANDISE: Clothing, housewares, furniture
DONATION TAX RECEIPT: Receipt given upon request

Goodwill Industries Thrift Store
2907 N. First Ave.
Tucson, AZ 85719
TYPE OF MERCHANDISE: Clothing, housewares, furniture
DONATION TAX RECEIPT: Receipt given upon request

Salvation Army Thrift Store
411 N. Fourth Ave.
Tucson, AZ 85706
TYPE OF MERCHANDISE: Clothing, housewares, furniture
DONATION TAX RECEIPT: Receipt given upon request

American Cancer Society Discovery Shop
4605 E. Speedway Blvd.
Tucson, AZ 85712
PHONE: 602-323-9001
TYPE OF MERCHANDISE: Clothing, bric-a-brac
DONATION TAX RECEIPT: Receipt given upon request
COMMENTS: Monthly markdowns

Salvation Army Thrift Store
5501 E. Pima Ave.
Tucson, AZ 85712
TYPE OF MERCHANDISE: Clothing, housewares, furniture
DONATION TAX RECEIPT: Receipt given upon request

TVI Savers Thrift Store
5845 E. Broadway Blvd.
Tucson, AZ 85711
CONTACT: Debbie Hendricks
PHONE: 602-571-2001
HOURS: Mon.–Sat. 9–9, Sun. 10–6
TYPE OF MERCHANDISE: Clothing, housewares, furniture
DONATION TAX RECEIPT: No

Salvation Army Thrift Store
Fifth Ave. & 38th St.
Tucson, AZ 85713
TYPE OF MERCHANDISE: Clothing, housewares, furniture
DONATION TAX RECEIPT: Receipt given upon request

Salvation Army Thrift Store
  701 E. Ft. Lowell
  Tucson, AZ 85716
  TYPE OF MERCHANDISE: Clothing,
  housewares, furniture
  DONATION TAX RECEIPT: Receipt given
  upon request
Goodwill Industries Thrift Store
  7044 E. Golf Links Rd.
  Tucson, AZ 85730
  TYPE OF MERCHANDISE: Clothing,
  housewares, furniture
  DONATION TAX RECEIPT: Receipt given
  upon request
Salvation Army Thrift Store
  7109 Golf Links Rd.
  Tucson, AZ 85710
  TYPE OF MERCHANDISE: Clothing,
  housewares, furniture
  DONATION TAX RECEIPT: Receipt given
  upon request
Salvation Army Thrift Store
  8054–8060 E. 22nd St.
  Tucson, AZ 85710
  TYPE OF MERCHANDISE: Clothing,
  housewares, furniture
  DONATION TAX RECEIPT: Receipt given
  upon request
Saint Vincent De Paul Thrift Store
  829 S. Sixth Ave.
  Tucson, AZ 85701
  TYPE OF MERCHANDISE: Clothing,
  housewares, furniture
  DONATION TAX RECEIPT: Receipt given
  upon request
  COMMENTS: Monthly markdowns
Salvation Army Thrift Store
  104 S. Fourth Ave.
  Yuma, AZ 85364
  TYPE OF MERCHANDISE: Clothing,
  housewares, furniture
  DONATION TAX RECEIPT: Receipt given
  upon request
National Assistance League Thrift Shop
  1054 S. Fourth Ave.
  Yuma, AZ 85366
  PHONE: 602-782-9314
  TYPE OF MERCHANDISE: Clothing,
  housewares, furniture

DONATION TAX RECEIPT: Receipt given
  upon request
  COMMENTS: Monthly markdowns

Arkansas

Goodwill Industries Thrift Store
  504 Oak St.
  Conway, AR 72032
  TYPE OF MERCHANDISE: Clothing,
  housewares, furniture
  DONATION TAX RECEIPT: Receipt given
  upon request
Salvation Army Thrift Store
  219 W. 15th St.
  Fayetteville, AR 72701
  TYPE OF MERCHANDISE: Clothing,
  housewares, furniture
  DONATION TAX RECEIPT: Receipt given
  upon request
Junior League Bargain Box
  311 Garrison Ave.
  Fort Smith, AR 72901
  TYPE OF MERCHANDISE: Clothing,
  housewares, furniture
  DONATION TAX RECEIPT: Receipt given
  upon request
Goodwill Industries Thrift Store
  422 Garrison Ave.
  Fort Smith, AR 72901
  TYPE OF MERCHANDISE: Clothing,
  housewares, furniture
  DONATION TAX RECEIPT: Receipt given
  upon request
Salvation Army Thrift Store
  512 N. "B" St.
  Fort Smith, AR 72901
  TYPE OF MERCHANDISE: Clothing,
  housewares, furniture
  DONATION TAX RECEIPT: Receipt given
  upon request
Salvation Army Thrift Store
  109 Crescent St.
  Hot Springs Nat. Park, AR 71901
  TYPE OF MERCHANDISE: Clothing,
  housewares, furniture
  DONATION TAX RECEIPT: Receipt given
  upon request

Salvation Army Thrift Store
107 S. Fisher St.
Jonesboro, AR 72401
TYPE OF MERCHANDISE: Clothing,
housewares, furniture
DONATION TAX RECEIPT: Receipt given
upon request

Salvation Army Thrift Store
3718 W. Roosevelt Rd.
Little Rock, AR 72204
CONTACT: Capt. James Lane
TYPE OF MERCHANDISE: Clothing,
housewares, furniture
DONATION TAX RECEIPT: Receipt given
upon request

Salvation Army Thrift Store
316 S. Main St.
Pine Bluff, AR 71601
TYPE OF MERCHANDISE: Clothing,
housewares, furniture
DONATION TAX RECEIPT: Receipt given
upon request

California

Salvation Army Thrift Store
28859 Roadside Dr.
Agoura, CA 91301
TYPE OF MERCHANDISE: Clothing,
housewares, furniture
DONATION TAX RECEIPT: Receipt given
upon request

Saint Vincent De Paul Thrift Store
2315 Lincoln Ave.
Alameda, CA 94501
TYPE OF MERCHANDISE: Clothing,
housewares, furniture
DONATION TAX RECEIPT: Receipt given
upon request
COMMENTS: Monthly markdowns

Rescue Mission Thrift Store
4056 Sebastopol Rd.
Alameda, CA 94501
TYPE OF MERCHANDISE: Clothing,
housewares, furniture
DONATION TAX RECEIPT: Receipt given
upon request

Salvation Army Thrift Store
1382 Solano
Albany, CA 94706
TYPE OF MERCHANDISE: Clothing,
housewares, furniture
DONATION TAX RECEIPT: Receipt given
upon request

Salvation Army Thrift Store
1010 E. Main
Alhambra, CA 91801
TYPE OF MERCHANDISE: Clothing,
housewares, furniture
DONATION TAX RECEIPT: Receipt given
upon request

Salvation Army Thrift Store
1100 N. Anaheim Blvd.
Anaheim, CA 92805
TYPE OF MERCHANDISE: Clothing,
housewares, furniture
DONATION TAX RECEIPT: Receipt given
upon request

City of Hope Thrift Shop
1269 E. Lincoln Ave.
Anaheim, CA 92805
TYPE OF MERCHANDISE: Clothing,
housewares, furniture
DONATION TAX RECEIPT: Receipt given
upon request

Salvation Army Thrift Store
1300 S. Lewis St.
Anaheim, CA 92805
TYPE OF MERCHANDISE: Clothing,
housewares, furniture
DONATION TAX RECEIPT: Receipt given
upon request

Salvation Army Thrift Store
1900 "A" St.
Antioch, CA 94509
TYPE OF MERCHANDISE: Clothing,
housewares, furniture
DONATION TAX RECEIPT: Receipt given
upon request

Goodwill Industries Thrift Store
2701 W. Tenth St.
Antioch, CA 94509
PHONE: 510-779-9214
HOURS: 7 days a week, 10–7

TYPE OF MERCHANDISE: Clothing,
housewares, furniture
DONATION TAX RECEIPT: Receipt given
upon request
City of Hope Thrift Shop
4275 E. Live Oak Ave.
Arcadia, CA 91006
TYPE OF MERCHANDISE: Clothing,
housewares, furniture
DONATION TAX RECEIPT: Receipt given
upon request
Salvation Army Thrift Store
1183 "K" St.
Arcata, Ca 95521
TYPE OF MERCHANDISE: Clothing,
housewares, furniture
DONATION TAX RECEIPT: Receipt given
upon request
Salvation Army Thrift Store
510 High St.
Auburn, CA 95603
TYPE OF MERCHANDISE: Clothing,
housewares, furniture
DONATION TAX RECEIPT: Receipt given
upon request
American Cancer Society Discovery Shop
948 Lincoln Way, Suite C
Auburn, CA 95603
PHONE: 916-888-7434
TYPE OF MERCHANDISE: Clothing, bric-a-
brac
DONATION TAX RECEIPT: Receipt given
upon request
COMMENTS: Monthly markdowns
Salvation Army Thrift Store
200 19th St.
Bakersfield, CA 93301
TYPE OF MERCHANDISE: Clothing,
housewares, furniture
DONATION TAX RECEIPT: Receipt given
upon request
Salvation Army Thrift Store
2621 River Blvd.
Bakersfield, CA 93306
TYPE OF MERCHANDISE: Clothing,
housewares, furniture
DONATION TAX RECEIPT: Receipt given
upon request

American Cancer Society Discovery Shop
5616 Stockdale Highway
Bakersfield, CA 93309
CONTACT: Barbara Louden
PHONE: 805-324-1359
TYPE OF MERCHANDISE: Clothing, bric-a-
brac
DONATION TAX RECEIPT: Receipt given
upon request
COMMENTS: Monthly markdowns
Goodwill Industries Thrift Store
805 19th St.
Bakersfield, CA 93301
TYPE OF MERCHANDISE: Clothing,
housewares, furniture
DONATION TAX RECEIPT: Receipt given
upon request
National Assistance League Bargain Box
916 California Ave.
Bakersfield, CA 93301
PHONE: 805-323-1317
TYPE OF MERCHANDISE: Clothing,
housewares, furniture
DONATION TAX RECEIPT: Receipt given
upon request
COMMENTS: Monthly markdowns
Disabled American Vets Thrift Store
13550 Ramona Blvd.
Baldwin Park, CA 91706
CONTACT: Karl Cade
TYPE OF MERCHANDISE: Clothing,
housewares, furniture
DONATION TAX RECEIPT: Receipt given
upon request
Salvation Army Thrift Store
9535 Artesia Blvd.
Bellflower, CA 90706
TYPE OF MERCHANDISE: Clothing,
housewares, furniture
DONATION TAX RECEIPT: Receipt given
upon request
Salvation Army Thrift Store
600 El Camino Real
Belmont, Ca 94002
TYPE OF MERCHANDISE: Clothing,
housewares, furniture
DONATION TAX RECEIPT: Receipt given
upon request

Goodwill Industries Thrift Store
40 Solano Sq.
Benicia, CA 94510
PHONE: 707-746-8621
HOURS: Seven days a week, 10–7
TYPE OF MERCHANDISE: Clothing,
housewares, furniture
DONATION TAX RECEIPT: Receipt given
upon request
Saint Vincent De Paul Thrift Store
2009 San Pablo Ave.
Berkeley, CA 94702
TYPE OF MERCHANDISE: Clothing,
housewares, furniture
DONATION TAX RECEIPT: Receipt given
upon request
COMMENTS: Monthly markdowns
Goodwill Industries Thrift Store
2058 University Ave.
Berkeley, Ca 94704
PHONE: 510-649-1287
HOURS: Seven days a week, 10–7
TYPE OF MERCHANDISE: Clothing,
housewares, furniture
DONATION TAX RECEIPT: Receipt given
upon request
American Cancer Society Discovery Shop
9314 W. Pico
Beverly Hills, CA 90035
CONTACT: Lisa Temple
PHONE: 310-276-6812
TYPE OF MERCHANDISE: Clothing,
housewares, furniture
DONATION TAX RECEIPT: Receipt given
upon request
COMMENTS: Great designer clothing and
jewelry
Saint Vincent De Paul Thrift Store
12860 Highway 9
Boulder Creek, CA 95006
TYPE OF MERCHANDISE: Clothing,
housewares, furniture
DONATION TAX RECEIPT: Receipt given
upon request
COMMENTS: Monthly markdowns
Saint Vincent De Paul Thrift Store
Highway 4 & Sunrise
Brentwood, CA 94513

TYPE OF MERCHANDISE: Clothing,
housewares, furniture
DONATION TAX RECEIPT: Receipt given
upon request
COMMENTS: Monthly markdowns
Saint Vincent De Paul Thrift Store
6277 Manchester Blvd.
Buena Park, CA 90621
TYPE OF MERCHANDISE: Clothing,
housewares, furniture
DONATION TAX RECEIPT: Receipt given
upon request
COMMENTS: Monthly markdowns
Salvation Army Thrift Store
7035–37 Stanton Ave.
Buena Park, Ca 90620
TYPE OF MERCHANDISE: Clothing,
housewares, furniture
DONATION TAX RECEIPT: Receipt given
upon request
Goodwill Industries Thrift Store
8888 Knott Ave.
Buena Park, Ca 90620
TYPE OF MERCHANDISE: Clothing,
housewares, furniture
DONATION TAX RECEIPT: Receipt given
upon request
American Cancer Society Discovery Shop
1410 Broadway
Burlingame, CA 94010
CONTACT: Marge Humphrey
PHONE: 415-343-9100
TYPE OF MERCHANDISE: Clothing, bric-a-
brac, housewares
DONATION TAX RECEIPT: Receipt given
upon request
COMMENTS: Monthly markdowns
Goodwill Industries Thrift Store
40 W. Fifth St.
Calexico, CA 92231
CONTACT: Carmelita Peterson
PHONE: 619-225-2200
HOURS: Mon.–Tues. 9:30–5:30, Wed. 7–5:30,
Thurs.–Fri. 9:30–5:30, Sat.–Sun. 9:30–5
TYPE OF MERCHANDISE: Clothing,
housewares, furniture
DONATION TAX RECEIPT: Receipt given
upon request

COMMENTS: Sidewalk sale on Wednesday and Saturday

Salvation Army Thrift Store
2440 B Las Dosas
Camarillo, CA 93010
TYPE OF MERCHANDISE: Clothing, housewares, furniture
DONATION TAX RECEIPT: Receipt given upon request

Salvation Army Thrift Store
146 San Tomas Aquino
Campbell, CA 95008
TYPE OF MERCHANDISE: Clothing, housewares, furniture
DONATION TAX RECEIPT: Receipt given upon request

Goodwill Industries Thrift Store
60 S. San Tomas Aquino Rd.
CROSS STREET: Campbell Ave.
Campbell, CA 95008
CONTACT: Bonnie Marcil
PHONE: 408-374-0682
HOURS: Mon.–Th. 9–7, Fri. 9–8, Sat. 9–6, Sun. 11–5
TYPE OF MERCHANDISE: Clothing, housewares, furniture
DONATION TAX RECEIPT: Receipt given upon request

Salvation Army Thrift Store
21371 Roscoe Blvd.
Canoga Park, CA 91304
TYPE OF MERCHANDISE: Clothing, housewares, furniture
DONATION TAX RECEIPT: Receipt given upon request

Council Thrift Shop
21616 Sherman Way
Canoga Park, CA 91303
PHONE: 818-348-2681
TYPE OF MERCHANDISE: Clothing, housewares, furniture
DONATION TAX RECEIPT: Receipt given upon request
COMMENTS: Excellent merchandise, annual sales

City of Hope Thrift Shop
21819 Sherman Way
Canoga Park, CA 91303

TYPE OF MERCHANDISE: Clothing, housewares
DONATION TAX RECEIPT: Receipt given upon request

Salvation Army Thrift Store
17657 Sierra Highway
Canyon Country, CA 91351
TYPE OF MERCHANDISE: Clothing, housewares, furniture
DONATION TAX RECEIPT: Receipt given upon request

Goodwill Industries Thrift Store
11264 Merritt St.
Castroville, CA 95012
TYPE OF MERCHANDISE: Clothing, housewares, furniture
DONATION TAX RECEIPT: Receipt given upon request

Saint Vincent De Paul Thrift Store
1044 Nord Ave.
Chico, CA 95926
TYPE OF MERCHANDISE: Clothing, housewares, furniture
DONATION TAX RECEIPT: Receipt given upon request
COMMENTS: Monthly markdowns

American Cancer Society Discovery Shop
2201 Pillsbury Rd. #C-4
Chico, CA 95926
CONTACT: Angie Dalton
PHONE: 916-343-6178
TYPE OF MERCHANDISE: Clothing, bric-a-brac
DONATION TAX RECEIPT: Receipt given upon request
COMMENTS: Monthly markdowns

Salvation Army Thrift Store
12524 Central Ave.
Chino, CA 91710
TYPE OF MERCHANDISE: Clothing, housewares, furniture
DONATION TAX RECEIPT: Receipt given upon request

Salvation Army Thrift Store
1655 Broadway
Chula Vista, CA 92010
TYPE OF MERCHANDISE: Clothing, housewares, furniture

DONATION TAX RECEIPT: Receipt given upon request

Salvation Army Thrift Store
15407–17 E. Valley
City of Industry, CA
TYPE OF MERCHANDISE: Clothing, housewares, furniture
DONATION TAX RECEIPT: Receipt given upon request

Goodwill Industries Thrift Store
1830 Clovis Ave.
Clovis, CA 93612
PHONE: 209-298-7125
HOURS: Seven days a week
TYPE OF MERCHANDISE: Clothing, housewares, furniture
DONATION TAX RECEIPT: Receipt given upon request

Salvation Army Thrift Store
234 Clovis Ave.
Clovis, CA 93612
TYPE OF MERCHANDISE: Clothing, housewares, furniture
DONATION TAX RECEIPT: Receipt given upon request

Salvation Army Thrift Store
1209 E. Compton Blvd.
Compton, CA 90221
TYPE OF MERCHANDISE: Clothing, housewares, furniture
DONATION TAX RECEIPT: Receipt given upon request

Saint Vincent De Paul Thrift Store
3325 N. Main St.
Concord, CA 94523
TYPE OF MERCHANDISE: Clothing, housewares, furniture
DONATION TAX RECEIPT: Receipt given upon request
COMMENTS: Monthly markdowns

Goodwill Industries Thrift Store
3495 Clayton Rd.
Concord, CA 94519
PHONE: 510-676-8140
HOURS: Seven days, 10–7
TYPE OF MERCHANDISE: Clothing, housewares, furniture
DONATION TAX RECEIPT: Receipt given upon request

American Cancer Society Discovery Shop
2600 E. Coast Hwy. Suite H
Corona del Mar, CA 92625
CONTACT: Sheila Farmer
PHONE: 714-640-4777
TYPE OF MERCHANDISE: Clothing, housewares
DONATION TAX RECEIPT: Receipt given upon request
COMMENTS: Good designer finds, higher priced

Salvation Army Thrift Store
506 E. Second St.
Corona, CA 91720
TYPE OF MERCHANDISE: Clothing, housewares, furniture
DONATION TAX RECEIPT: Receipt given upon request

Salvation Army Thrift Store
2126 Harbor Blvd.
Costa Mesa, CA 92627
TYPE OF MERCHANDISE: Clothing, housewares, furniture
DONATION TAX RECEIPT: Receipt given upon request

Goodwill Industries Thrift Store
620 W. 19th St.
Costa Mesa, CA 92627
TYPE OF MERCHANDISE: Clothing, housewares, furniture
DONATION TAX RECEIPT: Receipt given upon request

Salvation Army Thrift Store
1444 N. Citrus Ave.
Covina, CA 91722
TYPE OF MERCHANDISE: Clothing, housewares, furniture
DONATION TAX RECEIPT: Receipt given upon request

Salvation Army Thrift Store
11160 W. Washington Blvd.
Culver City, CA 90230
PHONE: 213-836-8344
TYPE OF MERCHANDISE: Clothing, housewares, furniture
DONATION TAX RECEIPT: Receipt given upon request

City of Hope Thrift Shop
3835 Main St.
Culver City, CA 90232-2619
CONTACT: Dorothy Polansky
PHONE: 310-839-7179
TYPE OF MERCHANDISE: Clothing and housewares
DONATION TAX RECEIPT: Receipt given upon request

Salvation Army Thrift Store
330 A-D "G" St.
Davis, CA 95616
TYPE OF MERCHANDISE: Clothing, housewares, furniture
DONATION TAX RECEIPT: Receipt given upon request

Goodwill Industries Thrift Store
902 Main St.
Delano, CA 93215
TYPE OF MERCHANDISE: Clothing, housewares, furniture
DONATION TAX RECEIPT: Receipt given upon request

Salvation Army Thrift Store
913 Main St.
Delano, CA 93215
TYPE OF MERCHANDISE: Clothing, housewares, furniture
DONATION TAX RECEIPT: Receipt given upon request

Goodwill Industries Thrift Store
1025 N. Adams
Dixon, CA 95620
PHONE: 916-678-3840
HOURS: Seven days, 10–7
TYPE OF MERCHANDISE: Clothing, housewares, furniture
DONATION TAX RECEIPT: Receipt given upon request

Salvation Army Thrift Store
9444 E. Firestone
Downey, CA 90241
TYPE OF MERCHANDISE: Clothing, housewares, furniture
DONATION TAX RECEIPT: Receipt given upon request

Goodwill Industries Thrift Store
1420 Huntington Dr.
Duarte, CA 91010

TYPE OF MERCHANDISE: Clothing, housewares, furniture
DONATION TAX RECEIPT: Receipt given upon request

Goodwill Industries Thrift Store
7745 Amador Valley Blvd.
Dublin, CA 94568
PHONE: 510-833-9610
HOURS: Seven days, 10–7
TYPE OF MERCHANDISE: Clothing, housewares, furniture
DONATION TAX RECEIPT: Receipt given upon request

Salvation Army Thrift Store
101 E. Main St.
El Cajon, CA 92020
TYPE OF MERCHANDISE: Clothing, housewares, furniture
DONATION TAX RECEIPT: Receipt given upon request

Goodwill Industries Thrift Store
131 Rea Ave.
El Cajon, CA 92020
CONTACT: Linda Fennell
PHONE: 619-225-2200, 225-1934
HOURS: Mon.–Fri. 9:30–6, Sat. 10–6, Sun. 10–5
TYPE OF MERCHANDISE: Clothing, housewares, furniture
DONATION TAX RECEIPT: Receipt given upon request

Saint Vincent De Paul Thrift Store
2325 Fletcher Pkwy.
El Cajon, Ca 92020
TYPE OF MERCHANDISE: Clothing, housewares, furniture
DONATION TAX RECEIPT: Receipt given upon request
COMMENTS: Monthly markdowns

American Cancer Society Discovery Shop
10313 San Pablo Blvd.
El Cerrito, CA 94530
CONTACT: Anna Breslan
PHONE: 415-527-1469
TYPE OF MERCHANDISE: Clothing, bric-a-brac
DONATION TAX RECEIPT: Receipt given upon request
COMMENTS: Monthly markdowns

Salvation Army Thrift Store
10721 E. Valley Blvd.
El Monte, CA 91731
TYPE OF MERCHANDISE: Clothing,
housewares, furniture
DONATION TAX RECEIPT: Receipt given
upon request
Goodwill Industries Thrift Store
3730 San Pablo Dam Rd.
El Sobrante, CA 94803
PHONE: 510-758-4968
HOURS: Seven days, 10–7
TYPE OF MERCHANDISE: Clothing,
housewares, furniture
DONATION TAX RECEIPT: Receipt given
upon request
Salvation Army Thrift Store
183 E. Washington St.
Escondido, CA 92025
TYPE OF MERCHANDISE: Clothing,
housewares, furniture
DONATION TAX RECEIPT: Receipt given
upon request
Goodwill Industries Thrift Store
329 W. Grand Ave.
Escondido, CA 92025
CONTACT: Bob Kruse
PHONE: 619-225-2200, 225-1934
HOURS: Mon.–Fri. 9–8, Sat. 10–6,
Sun. 10–5
TYPE OF MERCHANDISE: Clothing,
housewares, furniture
DONATION TAX RECEIPT: Receipt given
upon request
COMMENTS: Fresh stock throughout
each day
Saint Vincent De Paul Thrift Store
608 N. Escondido Blvd.
Escondido, CA 92025
TYPE OF MERCHANDISE: Clothing,
housewares, furniture
DONATION TAX RECEIPT: Receipt given
upon request
COMMENTS: Monthly markdowns
Saint Vincent De Paul Thrift Store
212 "G" St.
Eureka, CA 95501
TYPE OF MERCHANDISE: Clothing,
housewares, furniture

DONATION TAX RECEIPT: Receipt given
upon request
COMMENTS: Monthly markdowns
American Cancer Society Discovery Shop
2942 "F" St.
Eureka, CA 95501
CONTACT: Pam McKnight
PHONE: 707-443-2155
TYPE OF MERCHANDISE: Clothing, bric-a-
brac
DONATION TAX RECEIPT: Receipt given
upon request
COMMENTS: Monthly markdowns
Saint Vincent De Paul Thrift Store
763 Center St.
Fairfax, CA
TYPE OF MERCHANDISE: Clothing,
housewares, furniture
DONATION TAX RECEIPT: Receipt given
upon request
COMMENTS: Monthly markdowns
Salvation Army Thrift Store
1001 Texas St.
Fairfield, CA 94533
TYPE OF MERCHANDISE: Clothing,
housewares, furniture
DONATION TAX RECEIPT: Receipt given
upon request
Goodwill Industries Thrift Store
180 Grobric Ct.
Fairfield, CA 94535
PHONE: 707-864-5440
HOURS: Seven days, 10–7
TYPE OF MERCHANDISE: Clothing,
housewares, furniture
DONATION TAX RECEIPT: Receipt given
upon request
Goodwill Industries Thrift Store
821 Texas St.
Fairfield, Ca 94533
PHONE: 707-429-2338
HOURS: Seven days, 10–7
TYPE OF MERCHANDISE: Clothing,
housewares, furniture
DONATION TAX RECEIPT: Receipt given
upon request

Salvation Army Thrift Store
8644 Sierra Ave.
Fontana, CA 92335
TYPE OF MERCHANDISE: Clothing,
housewares, furniture
DONATION TAX RECEIPT: Receipt given
upon request

Salvation Army Thrift Store
40733 Chapel Way
Fremont, CA 94538
PHONE: 510-659-0637
HOURS: Mon.–Fri. 9–5
TYPE OF MERCHANDISE: Clothing,
housewares, furniture
DONATION TAX RECEIPT: Receipt given
upon request

Saint Vincent De Paul Thrift Store
8177 Decoto Rd.
Fremont, CA 94536
TYPE OF MERCHANDISE: Clothing,
housewares, furniture
DONATION TAX RECEIPT: Receipt given
upon request
COMMENTS: Monthly markdowns

LARC Bargain Store
1476 N. Van Ness Ave.
Fresno, CA 93728
TYPE OF MERCHANDISE: Clothing,
housewares, toys
DONATION TAX RECEIPT: Receipt given
upon request

Goodwill Industries Thrift Store
2611 E. Hammond
Fresno, CA 93703
PHONE: 209-266-0532
HOURS: Seven days a week
TYPE OF MERCHANDISE: Clothing,
housewares, furniture
DONATION TAX RECEIPT: Receipt given
upon request

American Cancer Society Discovery Shop
3071 W. Shaw #101
Fresno, CA 93711
CONTACT: Darcy Fuller
PHONE: 209-226-1600
TYPE OF MERCHANDISE: Clothing, bric-a-
brac

DONATION TAX RECEIPT: Receipt given
upon request
COMMENTS: Monthly markdowns

Salvation Army Thrift Store
4507 E. Tulare
Fresno, CA 93702
TYPE OF MERCHANDISE: Clothing,
housewares, furniture
DONATION TAX RECEIPT: Receipt given
upon request

Salvation Army Thrift Store
6574 N. Blackstone Ave.
Fresno, CA 93710
TYPE OF MERCHANDISE: Clothing,
housewares, furniture
DONATION TAX RECEIPT: Receipt given
upon request

Disabled American Vets Thrift Store
701 Van Ness Ave.
Fresno, Ca 93721
TYPE OF MERCHANDISE: Clothing,
housewares
DONATION TAX RECEIPT: Receipt given
upon request

Salvation Army Thrift Store
710 S. Parallel St.
Fresno, CA 93721
TYPE OF MERCHANDISE: Clothing,
housewares, furniture
DONATION TAX RECEIPT: Receipt given
upon request

Salvation Army Thrift Store
804 S. Parallel St.
Fresno, CA 93721
TYPE OF MERCHANDISE: Clothing,
housewares, furniture
DONATION TAX RECEIPT: Receipt given
upon request

Salvation Army Thrift Store
205–7 N. Harbor Blvd.
Fullerton, CA 92632
TYPE OF MERCHANDISE: Clothing,
housewares, furniture
DONATION TAX RECEIPT: Receipt given
upon request

Salvation Army Thrift Store
316 N. Raymond
Fullerton, CA 92631

TYPE OF MERCHANDISE: Clothing,
housewares, furniture
DONATION TAX RECEIPT: Receipt given
upon request
Goodwill Industries Thrift Store
333 S. Brookhurst Rd.
Fullerton, CA 92633
TYPE OF MERCHANDISE: Clothing,
housewares, furniture
DONATION TAX RECEIPT: Receipt given
upon request
Salvation Army Thrift Store
12962 Main St.
Garden Grove, CA 92640
TYPE OF MERCHANDISE: Clothing,
housewares, furniture
DONATION TAX RECEIPT: Receipt given
upon request
Salvation Army Thrift Store
9866 Garden Grove Blvd.
Garden Grove, CA 92640
TYPE OF MERCHANDISE: Clothing,
housewares, furniture
DONATION TAX RECEIPT: Receipt given
upon request
Goodwill Industries Thrift Store
16220 S. Western Ave.
Gardena, CA 90247
TYPE OF MERCHANDISE: Clothing,
housewares, furniture
DONATION TAX RECEIPT: Receipt given
upon request
Salvation Army Thrift Store
7341 Monterey St.
Gilroy, CA 95920
TYPE OF MERCHANDISE: Clothing,
housewares, furniture
DONATION TAX RECEIPT: Receipt given
upon request
Saint Vincent De Paul Thrift Store
7680 Monterey
Gilroy, CA 95020
TYPE OF MERCHANDISE: Clothing,
housewares, furniture
DONATION TAX RECEIPT: Receipt given
upon request
COMMENTS: Monthly markdowns

Salvation Army Thrift Store
114 S. Brand Blvd.
Glendale, CA 91204
TYPE OF MERCHANDISE: Clothing,
housewares, furniture
DONATION TAX RECEIPT: Receipt given
upon request
Salvation Army Thrift Store
214 N. Brand Blvd.
Glendale, CA 91203
PHONE: 818-242-6557
TYPE OF MERCHANDISE: Clothing,
housewares, furniture
DONATION TAX RECEIPT: Receipt given
upon request
Out of the Closet Thrift Store
3160 Glendale Blvd.
CROSS STREET: Atwater Village
Los Angeles, CA 90039
PHONE: 213-664-4394
HOURS: Mon.–Sat. 10–6, Sun. 12–6
TYPE OF MERCHANDISE: Clothing, bric-a-
brac
DONATION TAX RECEIPT: Receipt given
upon request
Salvation Army Thrift Store
109 S. Fairview
Goleta, CA
TYPE OF MERCHANDISE: Clothing,
housewares, furniture
DONATION TAX RECEIPT: Receipt given
upon request
Salvation Army Thrift Store
117 Neal St.
Grass Valley, CA 95945
TYPE OF MERCHANDISE: Clothing,
housewares, furniture
DONATION TAX RECEIPT: Receipt given
upon request
Goodwill Industries Thrift Store
1400 Grand Ave.
Grover City, CA 93433
PHONE: 805-481-8500
HOURS: Mon.–Sat. 10–6, Sun. 12–5
TYPE OF MERCHANDISE: Clothing,
housewares, furniture
DONATION TAX RECEIPT: Receipt given
upon request

Salvation Army Thrift Store
1628 Grand Ave.
Grover City, CA 93433
TYPE OF MERCHANDISE: Clothing,
housewares, furniture
DONATION TAX RECEIPT: Receipt given
upon request

Salvation Army Thrift Store
202 E. Eighth St.
Hanford, CA 93230
TYPE OF MERCHANDISE: Clothing,
housewares, furniture
DONATION TAX RECEIPT: Receipt given
upon request

Saint Vincent De Paul Thrift Store
22331 Mission Blvd.
Hayward, CA 94541
TYPE OF MERCHANDISE: Clothing,
housewares, furniture
DONATION TAX RECEIPT: Receipt given
upon request
COMMENTS: Monthly markdowns

Salvation Army Thrift Store
22500 Foothill Blvd.
Hayward, CA 94541
TYPE OF MERCHANDISE: Clothing,
housewares, furniture
DONATION TAX RECEIPT: Receipt given
upon request

LARC Thrift Store
22801 Mission Blvd.
Hayward, CA 94541
TYPE OF MERCHANDISE: Clothing,
housewares
DONATION TAX RECEIPT: Receipt given
upon request

Goodwill Industries Thrift Store
25200 Mission Blvd.
Hayward, CA 94544
PHONE: 510-889-8524
HOURS: Seven days, 10–7
TYPE OF MERCHANDISE: Clothing,
housewares, furniture
DONATION TAX RECEIPT: Receipt given
upon request

Goodwill Industries Thrift Store
889–893 W. "A" St.
Hayward, CA 94541

PHONE: 510-785-3967
HOURS: Seven days, 10–7
TYPE OF MERCHANDISE: Clothing,
housewares, furniture
DONATION TAX RECEIPT: Receipt given
upon request

Salvation Army Thrift Store
200 Lytton Spring Rd.
Healdsburg, CA 95448
TYPE OF MERCHANDISE: Clothing,
housewares, furniture
DONATION TAX RECEIPT: Receipt given
upon request

Salvation Army Thrift Store
137 S. Harvard
Hemet, CA 92343
TYPE OF MERCHANDISE: Clothing,
housewares, furniture
DONATION TAX RECEIPT: Receipt given
upon request

Salvation Army Thrift Store
16261 Main St.
Hesperia, CA 92345
TYPE OF MERCHANDISE: Clothing,
housewares, furniture
DONATION TAX RECEIPT: Receipt given
upon request

Goodwill Industries Thrift Store
9891 Yorktown Ave.
Huntington Beach, CA 92646
TYPE OF MERCHANDISE: Clothing,
housewares, furniture
DONATION TAX RECEIPT: Receipt given
upon request

Salvation Army Thrift Store
2726 E. Gage Ave.
Huntington Park, CA 90255
TYPE OF MERCHANDISE: Clothing,
housewares, furniture
DONATION TAX RECEIPT: Receipt given
upon request

American Cancer Society Discovery Shop
201 N. La Brea
Inglewood, CA 90301
CONTACT: Desiree Williams
PHONE: 310-677-2555
TYPE OF MERCHANDISE: Clothing,
housewares, furniture

DONATION TAX RECEIPT: Receipt given upon request

Saint Vincent De Paul Thrift Store
23595 Moulton Pkwy.
Laguna Hills, CA 92653
TYPE OF MERCHANDISE: Clothing, housewares, furniture
DONATION TAX RECEIPT: Receipt given upon request
COMMENTS: Monthly markdowns

Saint Vincent De Paul Thrift Store
570 W. La Habra Blvd.
La Habra, CA 90631
TYPE OF MERCHANDISE: Clothing, housewares, furniture
DONATION TAX RECEIPT: Receipt given upon request
COMMENTS: Monthly markdowns

Salvation Army Thrift Store
23820 Mercury Rd.
Lake Forest, CA 92630
TYPE OF MERCHANDISE: Clothing, housewares, furniture
DONATION TAX RECEIPT: Receipt given upon request

American Cancer Society Discovery Shop
3957 Hardwick St.
Lakewood, CA 90712
CONTACT: Cheri Fulbright
PHONE: 213-633-7059
TYPE OF MERCHANDISE: Clothing, bric-a-brac
DONATION TAX RECEIPT: Receipt given upon request
COMMENTS: Monthly markdowns

Salvation Army Thrift Store
10912 Main St.
Lamont, CA 93307
TYPE OF MERCHANDISE: Clothing, housewares, furniture
DONATION TAX RECEIPT: Receipt given upon request

Salvation Army Thrift Store
340 E. Avenue I
Lancaster, CA 93534
TYPE OF MERCHANDISE: Clothing, housewares, furniture
DONATION TAX RECEIPT: Receipt given upon request

Salvation Army Thrift Store
45025 Yucca Ave.
Lancaster, CA 93534
TYPE OF MERCHANDISE: Clothing, housewares, furniture
DONATION TAX RECEIPT: Receipt given upon request

Salvation Army Thrift Store
15617 S. Hawthorne
Lawndale, CA 90260
TYPE OF MERCHANDISE: Clothing, housewares, furniture
DONATION TAX RECEIPT: Receipt given upon request

Goodwill Industries Thrift Store
1374 Railroad Ave.
Livermore, CA 94550
PHONE: 510-373-7990
HOURS: Seven days, 10–7
TYPE OF MERCHANDISE: Clothing, housewares, furniture
DONATION TAX RECEIPT: Receipt given upon request

Saint Vincent De Paul Thrift Store
1817 W. Second St.
Livermore, CA 94550
TYPE OF MERCHANDISE: Clothing, housewares, furniture
DONATION TAX RECEIPT: Receipt given upon request
COMMENTS: Monthly markdowns

Salvation Army Thrift Store
2491 First St.
Livermore, CA 94550
TYPE OF MERCHANDISE: Clothing, housewares, furniture
DONATION TAX RECEIPT: Receipt given upon request

Salvation Army Thrift Store
121 S. Cherokee Ln.
Lodi, CA 95240
TYPE OF MERCHANDISE: Clothing, housewares, furniture
DONATION TAX RECEIPT: Receipt given upon request

Goodwill Industries Thrift Store
200 E. Oak St.
Lodi, Ca 95240

PHONE: 209-368-6938
HOURS: Seven days
TYPE OF MERCHANDISE: Clothing,
housewares, furniture
DONATION TAX RECEIPT: Receipt given
upon request

Goodwill Industries Thrift Store
2300 Pacific Coast Hwy.
Lomita, CA 90717
TYPE OF MERCHANDISE: Clothing,
housewares, furniture
DONATION TAX RECEIPT: Receipt given
upon request

Salvation Army Thrift Store
1370 Alamitos Ave.
Long Beach, CA 90813
TYPE OF MERCHANDISE: Clothing,
housewares, furniture
DONATION TAX RECEIPT: Receipt given
upon request

Volunteers of America
1505 Alamitos Ave.
Long Beach, CA 90813
TYPE OF MERCHANDISE: Clothing,
housewares, furniture
DONATION TAX RECEIPT: Receipt given
upon request

Council Thrift Shop
244 E. Third St.
Long Beach, CA 90802
TYPE OF MERCHANDISE: Clothing,
housewares, furniture
DONATION TAX RECEIPT: Receipt given
upon request

Salvation Army Thrift Store
6190 Atlantic Blvd.
Long Beach, CA 90805-2923
TYPE OF MERCHANDISE: Clothing,
housewares, furniture
DONATION TAX RECEIPT: Receipt given
upon request

Goodwill Industries Thrift Store
800 Pacific Ave.
Long Beach, CA 90813-4282
TYPE OF MERCHANDISE: Clothing,
housewares, furniture
DONATION TAX RECEIPT: Receipt given
upon request

American Cancer Society Discovery Shop
142 Main St.
Los Altos, CA 94022
CONTACT: Judy Vajata
PHONE: 415-949-0505
TYPE OF MERCHANDISE: Clothing, bric-a-
brac
DONATION TAX RECEIPT: Receipt given
upon request
COMMENTS: Monthly markdowns

City of Hope Thrift Shop
1035 S. Fairfax Ave.
Los Angeles, CA 90019
CONTACT: City of Hope AIDS Hospice
PHONE: 213-935-2032
HOURS: Mon.–Sat. 10–4
TYPE OF MERCHANDISE: Clothing,
housewares, furniture
DONATION TAX RECEIPT: Receipt given
upon request

Council Thrift Shop
1052 S. Fairfax Blvd.
Los Angeles, CA 90019
PHONE: 213-938-8122
HOURS: Open daily, call for annual sale
dates
TYPE OF MERCHANDISE: Clothing,
housewares, furniture
DONATION TAX RECEIPT: Receipt given
upon request
COMMENTS: Excellent merchandise,
annual sales

Council Thrift Shop
11571 Santa Monica Blvd.
Los Angeles, CA 90025
CONTACT: National Council of Jewish
Women
PHONE: 310-477-9613
TYPE OF MERCHANDISE: Clothing,
housewares, furniture
DONATION TAX RECEIPT: Receipt given
upon request
COMMENTS: Excellent merchandise,
annual sales

Council Thrift Shop
12204 Venice Blvd.
Los Angeles, CA 90066-3814

TYPE OF MERCHANDISE: Clothing, housewares, furniture
DONATION TAX RECEIPT: Receipt given upon request

City of Hope Thrift Shop
155 S. Western Ave.
Los Angeles, CA 90004
TYPE OF MERCHANDISE: Clothing, housewares, furniture
DONATION TAX RECEIPT: Receipt given upon request

Goodwill Industries Thrift Store
1608 Sawtelle Blvd.
Los Angeles, CA 90025
PHONE: 213-473-9844
TYPE OF MERCHANDISE: Clothing, housewares, furniture
DONATION TAX RECEIPT: Receipt given upon request

Salvation Army Thrift Store
1940 W. Pico Blvd.
Los Angeles, CA 90006
PHONE: 213-389-6774
TYPE OF MERCHANDISE: Clothing, housewares, furniture
DONATION TAX RECEIPT: Receipt given upon request
COMMENTS: Large store, collectible section

Saint Vincent De Paul Thrift Store
210 N. Avenue 21
Los Angeles, CA 90031
TYPE OF MERCHANDISE: Clothing, housewares, furniture
DONATION TAX RECEIPT: Receipt given upon request
COMMENTS: Monthly markdowns

Goodwill Industries Thrift Store
235 S. Broadway
Los Angeles, CA 90012
TYPE OF MERCHANDISE: Clothing, housewares, furniture
DONATION TAX RECEIPT: Receipt given upon request

American Cancer Society Discovery Shop
318 S. Robertson Blvd.
Los Angeles, CA 90048
PHONE: 310-274-7568

TYPE OF MERCHANDISE: Clothing, housewares, furniture
DONATION TAX RECEIPT: Receipt given upon request
COMMENTS: Celebrity donations, great stuff!

Goodwill Industries Thrift Store
342 San Fernando Rd.
Los Angeles, Ca 90031
PHONE: 213-226-0153
TYPE OF MERCHANDISE: Clothing, housewares, furniture
DONATION TAX RECEIPT: Receipt given upon request
COMMENTS: Annual estate sale: call for details

American Cancer Society Discovery Shop
3421 W. Sixth St.
Los Angeles, CA 90005
TYPE OF MERCHANDISE: Clothing, bric-a-brac
DONATION TAX RECEIPT: Receipt given upon request
COMMENTS: Monthly markdowns

Cinema Glamour Shop, Screen Smart Set
343 N. La Brea Ave.
CROSS STREET: Third St.
Los Angeles, CA 90036
CONTACT: June Van Dyke
PHONE: 213-933-5289
HOURS: Mon.–Fri. 10–4
TYPE OF MERCHANDISE: Designer clothing, bric-a-brac
DONATION TAX RECEIPT: Receipt given upon request
COMMENTS: Celebrity donations

Out of the Closet Thrift Store
360 N. Fairfax Ave.
CROSS STREET: Fairfax District
Los Angeles, CA 90036
PHONE: 213-934-1956
HOURS: Mon.–Sat. 10–6, Sun. 12–6
TYPE OF MERCHANDISE: Clothing, housewares, furniture
DONATION TAX RECEIPT: Receipt given upon request

City of Hope Thrift Shop
3804 W. Pico Blvd.
Los Angeles, Ca 90019
TYPE OF MERCHANDISE: Clothing,
housewares, furniture
DONATION TAX RECEIPT: Receipt given
upon request
Council Thrift Shop
455 N. Fairfax Ave.
Los Angeles, CA 90036
CONTACT: National Council of Jewish
Women
PHONE: 213-651-2080
HOURS: Open daily, call for annual sale
dates
TYPE OF MERCHANDISE: Clothing,
housewares, furniture
DONATION TAX RECEIPT: Receipt given
upon request
COMMENTS: Excellent merchandise,
annual sales
Children's Hospital Thrift
4551 W. Sunset Blvd.
Los Angeles, CA 90027
PHONE: 213-663-1975
HOURS: Tues.–Sat. 10–4
TYPE OF MERCHANDISE: Clothing,
housewares, furniture
DONATION TAX RECEIPT: Receipt given
upon request
Goodwill Industries Thrift Store
4801 Whittier Blvd.
Los Angeles, CA 90022
PHONE: 213-266-1440
TYPE OF MERCHANDISE: Clothing,
housewares, furniture
DONATION TAX RECEIPT: Receipt given
upon request
Salvation Army Thrift Store
4931 Whittier Blvd.
Los Angeles, CA 90022
PHONE: 213-693-9727
TYPE OF MERCHANDISE: Clothing,
housewares, furniture
DONATION TAX RECEIPT: Receipt given
upon request
Out of the Closet Thrift Store
1408 N. Vine St.

Los Angeles, CA 90038
PHONE: 213-466-7601
HOURS: Mon.–Sat. 10–6, Sun. 12–6
TYPE OF MERCHANDISE: Clothing, bric-a-
brac
DONATION TAX RECEIPT: Receipt given
upon request
Salvation Army Thrift Store
655–59 Stanford Ave.
Los Angeles, CA 90021
TYPE OF MERCHANDISE: Clothing,
housewares, furniture
DONATION TAX RECEIPT: Receipt given
upon request
Salvation Army Thrift Store
801 E. Seventh St.
Los Angeles, CA 90021
PHONE: 213-620-1270
TYPE OF MERCHANDISE: Clothing,
housewares, furniture
DONATION TAX RECEIPT: Receipt given
upon request
COMMENTS: Large selection of furniture
and clothing
Salvation Army Thrift Store
8601–15 S. Vermont St.
Los Angeles, CA 90047
PHONE: 213-759-7681
TYPE OF MERCHANDISE: Clothing,
housewares, furniture
DONATION TAX RECEIPT: Receipt given
upon request
American Cancer Society Discovery Shop
9327 W. Pico Blvd.
Los Angeles, CA 90035
CONTACT: Lisa Temple
PHONE: 310-276-6812
TYPE OF MERCHANDISE: Clothing,
housewares, bric-a-brac
DONATION TAX RECEIPT: Receipt given
upon request
COMMENTS: Great clothing, some
collectibles
WCIL Couture & Not So Couture
10641 W. Pico Blvd.
Los Angeles, CA 90064
PHONE: 310-470-8077
HOURS: Wed. 10-2, periodic Sat. sales

TYPE OF MERCHANDISE: Clothing, accessories
DONATION TAX RECEIPT: Receipt given upon request
COMMENTS: Fabulous designer clothing

UCLA Medical Auxiliary Thrift Shop
11271 Massachusetts Ave.
Los Angeles, CA 90025
PHONE: 310-478-1793
HOURS: Tues.–Fri. 10–4, Sat. 10–1
TYPE OF MERCHANDISE: Clothing, collectibles, furniture
DONATION TAX RECEIPT: Receipt given upon request

Goodwill Industries Thrift Store
213 S. "C" St.
Madera, CA 93638
PHONE: 209-674-0278
HOURS: Seven days
TYPE OF MERCHANDISE: Clothing, housewares, furniture
DONATION TAX RECEIPT: Receipt given upon request

Salvation Army Thrift Store
231 S. "C" St.
Madera, CA 93637
TYPE OF MERCHANDISE: Clothing, housewares, furniture
DONATION TAX RECEIPT: Receipt given upon request

Salvation Army Thrift Store
128 N. Garfield
Manteca, CA 95336
TYPE OF MERCHANDISE: Clothing, housewares, furniture
DONATION TAX RECEIPT: Receipt given upon request

Goodwill Industries Thrift Store
223 E. Yosemite Ave.
Manteca, CA 95336
PHONE: 209-522-1576
HOURS: Seven days
TYPE OF MERCHANDISE: Clothing, housewares, furniture
DONATION TAX RECEIPT: Receipt given upon request

Goodwill Industries Thrift Store
649 Main St.
Martinez, CA 94553

TYPE OF MERCHANDISE: Clothing, housewares, furniture
DONATION TAX RECEIPT: Receipt given upon request

Salvation Army Thrift Store
900 "F" St.
Marysville, CA 95901
TYPE OF MERCHANDISE: Clothing, housewares, furniture
DONATION TAX RECEIPT: Receipt given upon request

American Cancer Society Discovery Shop
746 Santa Cruz Ave.
Menlo Park, CA 94025
CONTACT: Chrissy Haas
PHONE: 415-325-8939
TYPE OF MERCHANDISE: Clothing, bric-a-brac
DONATION TAX RECEIPT: Receipt given upon request
COMMENTS: Monthly markdowns

Saint Vincent De Paul Thrift Store
131 W. Main St.
Merced, CA 95340
TYPE OF MERCHANDISE: Clothing, housewares, furniture
DONATION TAX RECEIPT: Receipt given upon request
COMMENTS: Monthly markdowns

Salvation Army Thrift Store
227 W. Main St.
Merced, CA 95340
TYPE OF MERCHANDISE: Clothing, housewares, furniture
DONATION TAX RECEIPT: Receipt given upon request

Goodwill Industries Thrift Store
435 W. Main St.
Merced, CA 95340
PHONE: 209-723-1217
HOURS: Seven days
TYPE OF MERCHANDISE: Clothing, housewares, furniture
DONATION TAX RECEIPT: Receipt given upon request

American Cancer Society Discovery Shop
777 E. Blythedale
Mill Valley, CA 94941
CONTACT: Donna Kahn

PHONE: 415-389-1164
TYPE OF MERCHANDISE: Clothing, bric-a-brac
DONATION TAX RECEIPT: Receipt given upon request
COMMENTS: Monthly markdowns

Goodwill Industries Thrift Store
91 S. Abbott Ave.
CROSS STREET: Calaveras Blvd.
Milpitas, CA 95035
CONTACTS: Shirley Castillo, Dolores Martinez
PHONE: 408-262-4131
HOURS: Mon.–Thurs. 9–7, Fri. 9–8, Sat. 9–6, Sun. 11–5
TYPE OF MERCHANDISE: Clothing, housewares, furniture
DONATION TAX RECEIPT: Receipt given upon request

Goodwill Industries Thrift Store
102 S. Santa Cruz
Modesto, CA 95354
PHONE: 209-522-1576
HOURS: Seven days
TYPE OF MERCHANDISE: Clothing, housewares, furniture
DONATION TAX RECEIPT: Receipt given upon request

Salvation Army Thrift Store
1101 Seventh St.
Modesto, CA 95354
TYPE OF MERCHANDISE: Clothing, housewares, furniture
DONATION TAX RECEIPT: Receipt given upon request

Goodwill Industries Thrift Store
1238 Crows Landing Rd.
Modesto, CA 95351
TYPE OF MERCHANDISE: Clothing, housewares, furniture
DONATION TAX RECEIPT: Receipt given upon request

American Cancer Society Discovery Shop
1801 "H" St. #B-2
Modesto, CA 95354
CONTACT: Judy Scabia
PHONE: 209-524-7241
TYPE OF MERCHANDISE: Clothing, bric-a-brac

DONATION TAX RECEIPT: Receipt given upon request
COMMENTS: Monthly markdowns

Goodwill Industries Thrift Store
571 Lighthouse Ave.
Monterey, CA 93940
PHONE: 408-649-6056
HOURS: Mon.–Sat. 10–6, Sun. 12–5
TYPE OF MERCHANDISE: Clothing, housewares, furniture
DONATION TAX RECEIPT: Receipt given upon request

Goodwill Industries Thrift Store
17630 Monterey Hwy.
CROSS STREET: Main St.
Morgan Hill, Ca 95037
PHONE: 408-778-3253
HOURS: Mon.–Thurs. 9–7, Fri. 9–8, Sat. 9–6, Sun. 11–5
TYPE OF MERCHANDISE: Clothing, housewares, furniture
DONATION TAX RECEIPT: Receipt given upon request

Goodwill Industries Thrift Store
855 E. El Camino Real
CROSS STREET: Sunnyvale Ave.
Mountain View, CA 94040
CONTACT: Linda Cervantez
PHONE: 408-736-8558
HOURS: Mon.–Th. 9–7, Fri. 9–8, Sat. 9–6, Sun. 11–5
TYPE OF MERCHANDISE: Clothing, housewares, furniture
DONATION TAX RECEIPT: Receipt given upon request

Salvation Army Thrift Store
1234 Third St.
Napa, CA 94559
TYPE OF MERCHANDISE: Clothing, housewares, furniture
DONATION TAX RECEIPT: Receipt given upon request

Goodwill Industries Thrift Store
1683 Imola Ave.
CROSS STREET: (In River Park)
Napa, CA 94559
PHONE: 707-257-6610
HOURS: Mon.–Sat. 10–6, Sun. 12–5

TYPE OF MERCHANDISE: Clothing, housewares, furniture
DONATION TAX RECEIPT: Receipt given upon request
COMMENTS: Sunday super sales every week

American Cancer Society Discovery Shop
3940 Bel Aire Plaza
Napa, CA 94558
CONTACT: Gerdina Herring
PHONE: 707-224-4398
TYPE OF MERCHANDISE: Clothing, bric-a-brac
DONATION TAX RECEIPT: Receipt given upon request
COMMENTS: Monthly markdowns

Salvation Army Thrift Store
921–925 National Blvd.
National City, CA 92050
TYPE OF MERCHANDISE: Clothing, housewares, furniture
DONATION TAX RECEIPT: Receipt given upon request

Salvation Army Thrift Store
35201 Neward Blvd.
Newark, CA 94560
PHONE: 510-791-9198
HOURS: Mon.–Fri. 9–5
TYPE OF MERCHANDISE: Clothing, housewares, furniture
DONATION TAX RECEIPT: Receipt given upon request

Council Thrift Shop
6110 Lankershim Blvd.
North Hollywood, CA 91606
PHONE: 818-985-5020
TYPE OF MERCHANDISE: Clothing, housewares, furniture
DONATION TAX RECEIPT: Receipt given upon request
COMMENTS: Excellent merchandise, annual sales

Salvation Army Thrift Store
6120 N. Lankershim Blvd.
North Hollywood, CA 91606
PHONE: 818-985-8105
TYPE OF MERCHANDISE: Clothing, housewares, furniture

DONATION TAX RECEIPT: Receipt given upon request
COMMENTS: Great furniture and antiques

Goodwill Industries Thrift Store
6241 Laurel Canyon Blvd.
North Hollywood, CA 91606
PHONE: 818-980-4777
TYPE OF MERCHANDISE: Clothing, housewares, furniture
DONATION TAX RECEIPT: Receipt given upon request

Out of the Closet Thrift Store
6247 Laurel Canyon Blvd.
North Hollywood, CA 91606
PHONE: 818-769-0503
HOURS: Mon.–Sat. 10–6, Sun. 12–6
TYPE OF MERCHANDISE: Clothing, housewares
DONATION TAX RECEIPT: Receipt given upon request

American Cancer Society Discovery Shop
9719 Reseda Blvd.
Northridge, CA 91324
CONTACT: Jill Angel
PHONE: 818-772-0194
TYPE OF MERCHANDISE: Clothing, bric-a-brac
DONATION TAX RECEIPT: Receipt given upon request
COMMENTS: Monthly markdowns

Salvation Army Thrift Store
11773 E. Firestone
Norwalk, CA 90650
TYPE OF MERCHANDISE: Clothing, housewares, furniture
DONATION TAX RECEIPT: Receipt given upon request

Saint Vincent De Paul Thrift Store
881 Grant Ave.
Novato, CA 94945
TYPE OF MERCHANDISE: Clothing, housewares, furniture
DONATION TAX RECEIPT: Receipt given upon request
COMMENTS: Monthly markdowns

American Cancer Society Discovery Shop
928 Grant Ave.
Novato, CA 94947-3220

PHONE: 415-898-1149
TYPE OF MERCHANDISE: Clothing, bric-a-brac
DONATION TAX RECEIPT: Receipt given upon request
COMMENTS: Monthly markdowns

Salvation Army Thrift Store
120 S. "F" St.
Oakdale, CA 95360
TYPE OF MERCHANDISE: Clothing, housewares, furniture
DONATION TAX RECEIPT: Receipt given upon request

Goodwill Industries Thrift Store
1220 Broadway
Oakland, CA 94612
PHONE: 510-834-6123
HOURS: Seven days, 10–7
TYPE OF MERCHANDISE: Clothing, housewares, furniture
DONATION TAX RECEIPT: Receipt given upon request

Goodwill Industries Thrift Store
212 Ninth St.
Oakland, CA 94607
TYPE OF MERCHANDISE: Clothing, housewares, furniture
DONATION TAX RECEIPT: Receipt given upon request

Goodwill Industries Thrift Store
2601 Telegraph Ave.
Oakland, CA 94612
TYPE OF MERCHANDISE: Clothing, housewares, furniture
DONATION TAX RECEIPT: Receipt given upon request

Goodwill Industries Thrift Store
2925 E. 14th St.
Oakland, CA 94601
PHONE: 510-534-3037
HOURS: Seven days, 10–7
TYPE OF MERCHANDISE: Clothing, housewares, furniture
DONATION TAX RECEIPT: Receipt given upon request

American Cancer Society Discovery Shop
3241 Grand Ave.
Oakland, CA 94610

CONTACT: Hency Clark
PHONE: 415-452-2201
TYPE OF MERCHANDISE: Clothing, bric-a-brac
DONATION TAX RECEIPT: Receipt given upon request
COMMENTS: Monthly markdowns

Salvation Army Thrift Store
601 Webster St.
Oakland, CA 94607
TYPE OF MERCHANDISE: Clothing, housewares, furniture
DONATION TAX RECEIPT: Receipt given upon request

Goodwill Industries Thrift Store
6624 San Pablo Ave.
Oakland, CA 94601
HOURS: Seven days, 10–7
TYPE OF MERCHANDISE: Clothing, housewares, furniture
DONATION TAX RECEIPT: Receipt given upon request

Saint Vincent De Paul Thrift Store
9235 San Leandro St.
Oakland, CA 94603
TYPE OF MERCHANDISE: Clothing, housewares, furniture
DONATION TAX RECEIPT: Receipt given upon request
COMMENTS: Monthly markdowns

Goodwill Industries Thrift Store
414 N. Hill St.
Oceanside, CA 93054
CONTACT: Bob Kruse
PHONE: 619-225-2200, 225-1934
HOURS: Mon.–Fri. 9–8, Sat. 10–6, Sun. 10–5
TYPE OF MERCHANDISE: Clothing, housewares, furniture
DONATION TAX RECEIPT: Receipt given upon request

Goodwill Industries Thrift Store
125 S. Mountain Ave.
Ontario, CA 91762
TYPE OF MERCHANDISE: Clothing, housewares, furniture
DONATION TAX RECEIPT: Receipt given upon request

Salvation Army Thrift Store
207 West St.
Ontario, CA 91761
TYPE OF MERCHANDISE: Clothing,
housewares, furniture
DONATION TAX RECEIPT: Receipt given
upon request
Saint Vincent De Paul Thrift Store
180 S. Cypress
Orange, CA 92666
TYPE OF MERCHANDISE: Clothing,
housewares, furniture
DONATION TAX RECEIPT: Receipt given
upon request
COMMENTS: Monthly markdowns
Goodwill Industries Thrift Store
1828 E. Collins Ave.
Orange, CA 92667
TYPE OF MERCHANDISE: Clothing,
housewares, furniture
DONATION TAX RECEIPT: Receipt given
upon request
Salvation Army Thrift Store
686 N. Tustin Ave.
Orange, CA 92667
TYPE OF MERCHANDISE: Clothing,
housewares, furniture
DONATION TAX RECEIPT: Receipt given
upon request
Rescue Mission Ventura Bargain Center
125 Harrison St. N.
CROSS STREETS: Oxnard Blvd. & Cooper
Oxnard, CA 93030
CONTACT: Jerry Roberg
PHONE: 805-487-1234
TYPE OF MERCHANDISE: Clothing,
housewares, furniture
DONATION TAX RECEIPT: Receipt given
upon request
COMMENTS: Large, well merchandised,
and good finds
Salvation Army Thrift Store
545 S. Oxnard Blvd.
Oxnard, CA 93030
TYPE OF MERCHANDISE: Clothing,
housewares, furniture
DONATION TAX RECEIPT: Receipt given
upon request

American Cancer Society Discovery Shop
184 County Club Gate
Pacific Grove, CA 93950
CONTACT: Joey Cobley
PHONE: 408-372-0866
TYPE OF MERCHANDISE: Clothing,
housewares, bric-a-brac
DONATION TAX RECEIPT: Receipt given
upon request
COMMENTS: Monthly markdowns
Goodwill Industries Thrift Store
4085 El Camino Way
CROSS STREET: W. Meadow
Palo Alto, Ca 94306
CONTACTS: Ellen Salas, Ludmilla
Tallmadge
PHONE: 415-494-1416
HOURS: Mon.–Thurs. 9–7, Fri. 9–8, Sat.
9–6, Sun. 11–5
TYPE OF MERCHANDISE: Clothing,
housewares, furniture
DONATION TAX RECEIPT: Receipt given
upon request
Junior League: The Clothesline
1230 E. Colorado Blvd.
CROSS STREET: Hill St.
Pasadena, CA 91106
PHONE: 818-793-2383
HOURS: Tue.–Sat. 10–4
TYPE OF MERCHANDISE: Clothing,
housewares, furniture
DONATION TAX RECEIPT: Receipt given
upon request
COMMENTS: Back-to-school sale, Sept.;
Toy sale, Dec.
Salvation Army Thrift Store
35 Waverly
Pasadena, CA 91105
TYPE OF MERCHANDISE: Clothing,
housewares, furniture
DONATION TAX RECEIPT: Receipt given
upon request
COMMENTS: Antique store
Salvation Army Thrift Store
56 W. Del Mar Blvd.
Pasadena, CA 91105
TYPE OF MERCHANDISE: Clothing,
housewares, furniture

DONATION TAX RECEIPT: Receipt given upon request
American Cancer Society Discovery Shop
77 N. Raymond Ave.
Pasadena, CA 91103
CONTACT: Bebe Prizant
PHONE: 818-793-3004
TYPE OF MERCHANDISE: Clothing, bric-a-brac
DONATION TAX RECEIPT: Receipt given upon request
COMMENTS: Monthly markdowns
Salvation Army Thrift Store
136 Petaluma Blvd.
Petaluma, CA 94952
TYPE OF MERCHANDISE: Clothing, housewares, furniture
DONATION TAX RECEIPT: Receipt given upon request
Goodwill Industries Thrift Store
172 Petaluma Blvd.
Petaluma, CA 94952
PHONE: 707-778-7485
HOURS: Mon.–Sat. 9:30–6, Sun. 12–5
TYPE OF MERCHANDISE: Clothing, housewares, furniture
DONATION TAX RECEIPT: Receipt given upon request
COMMENTS: Sunday super sales every week
Goodwill Industries Thrift Store
620-G San Pablo Ave.
Pinole, CA 94564
PHONE: 510-724-0408
HOURS: Seven days, 10–7
TYPE OF MERCHANDISE: Clothing, housewares, furniture
DONATION TAX RECEIPT: Receipt given upon request
Goodwill Industries Thrift Store
3725 Railroad Ave.
Pittsburg, CA 94565
PHONE: 510-432-4776
HOURS: Seven days, 10–7
TYPE OF MERCHANDISE: Clothing, housewares, furniture
DONATION TAX RECEIPT: Receipt given upon request

Saint Vincent De Paul Thrift Store
390 Central Ave.
Pittsburg, CA 94565
TYPE OF MERCHANDISE: Clothing, housewares, furniture
DONATION TAX RECEIPT: Receipt given upon request
COMMENTS: Monthly markdowns
American Cancer Society Discovery Shop
681 Main St.
Placerville, CA 95667
CONTACT: Joan Maxwell
PHONE: 916-626-6071
TYPE OF MERCHANDISE: Clothing, bric-a-brac
DONATION TAX RECEIPT: Receipt given upon request
COMMENTS: Monthly markdowns
Goodwill Industries Thrift Store
1699 Contra Costa Blvd.
Pleasant Hill, CA 94523
PHONE: 510-676-7217
HOURS: Seven days, 10–7
TYPE OF MERCHANDISE: Clothing, housewares, furniture
DONATION TAX RECEIPT: Receipt given upon request
Salvation Army Thrift Store
1806 Linda Dr.
Pleasant Hill, CA 94523
TYPE OF MERCHANDISE: Clothing, housewares, furniture
DONATION TAX RECEIPT: Receipt given upon request
Saint Vincent De Paul Thrift Store
3325 N. Main St.
Pleasant Hill, CA 94523
TYPE OF MERCHANDISE: Clothing, housewares, furniture
DONATION TAX RECEIPT: Receipt given upon request
COMMENTS: Monthly markdowns
American Cancer Society Discovery Shop
1987-D Santa Rita
Pleasanton, CA 94566
CONTACT: Temia Demalopoulos
PHONE: 415-462-7374

TYPE OF MERCHANDISE: Clothing, bric-a-brac
DONATION TAX RECEIPT: Receipt given upon request
COMMENTS: Monthly markdowns
Saint Vincent De Paul Thrift Store
807 Main St.
Pleasanton, CA 94566
TYPE OF MERCHANDISE: Clothing, housewares, furniture
DONATION TAX RECEIPT: Receipt given upon request
COMMENTS: Monthly markdowns
Goodwill Industries Thrift Store
587 E. Pomona Mall
Pomona, CA 91766
TYPE OF MERCHANDISE: Clothing, housewares, furniture
DONATION TAX RECEIPT: Receipt given upon request
Salvation Army Thrift Store
454–456 E. Holt Ave.
Pomona, CA 91767
TYPE OF MERCHANDISE: Clothing, housewares, furniture
DONATION TAX RECEIPT: Receipt given upon request
Salvation Army Thrift Store
162 W. Olive St.
Porterville, CA 93257
TYPE OF MERCHANDISE: Clothing, housewares, furniture
DONATION TAX RECEIPT: Receipt given upon request
Salvation Army Thrift Store
339 S. Main St.
Porterville, CA 93257
TYPE OF MERCHANDISE: Clothing, housewares, furniture
DONATION TAX RECEIPT: Receipt given upon request
American Cancer Society Discovery Shop
2625 Park Marina Dr.
Redding, CA 96001
CONTACT: Kathy Savard
PHONE: 916-224-3032
TYPE OF MERCHANDISE: Clothing, bric-a-brac

DONATION TAX RECEIPT: Receipt given upon request
COMMENTS: Monthly markdowns
Salvation Army Thrift Store
835 Industrial St.
Redding, CA 96002
TYPE OF MERCHANDISE: Clothing, housewares, furniture
DONATION TAX RECEIPT: Receipt given upon request
Salvation Army Thrift Store
801 W. Colton
Redlands, CA 92373
TYPE OF MERCHANDISE: Clothing, housewares, furniture
DONATION TAX RECEIPT: Receipt given upon request
Salvation Army Thrift Store
2406 Artesia
Redondo Beach, CA 90278
TYPE OF MERCHANDISE: Clothing, housewares, furniture
DONATION TAX RECEIPT: Receipt given upon request
Goodwill Industries Thrift Store
317 Torrance Blvd.
Redondo Beach, CA 90277
TYPE OF MERCHANDISE: Clothing, housewares, furniture
DONATION TAX RECEIPT: Receipt given upon request
Salvation Army Thrift Store
660 Veterans Blvd.
Redwood City, CA 94063
TYPE OF MERCHANDISE: Clothing, housewares, furniture
DONATION TAX RECEIPT: Receipt given upon request
Saint Vincent De Paul Thrift Store
831 Main St.
Redwood City, CA 94063
TYPE OF MERCHANDISE: Clothing, housewares, furniture
DONATION TAX RECEIPT: Receipt given upon request
COMMENTS: Monthly markdowns
MCC Nearly New
1012 "G" St.
Reedley, Ca 93654

PHONE: 209-638-3560
TYPE OF MERCHANDISE: Clothing,
housewares, furniture
DONATION TAX RECEIPT: Receipt given
upon request
Salvation Army Thrift Store
1602 Tenth St.
Reedley, CA 93654
TYPE OF MERCHANDISE: Clothing,
housewares, furniture
DONATION TAX RECEIPT: Receipt given
upon request
Salvation Army Thrift Store
422 S. Third
Renton, CA 98055
TYPE OF MERCHANDISE: Clothing,
housewares, furniture
DONATION TAX RECEIPT: Receipt given
upon request
Saint Vincent De Paul Thrift Store
1025 13th St.
Richmond, CA 94801
TYPE OF MERCHANDISE: Clothing,
housewares, furniture
DONATION TAX RECEIPT: Receipt given
upon request
COMMENTS: Monthly markdowns
Goodwill Industries Thrift Store
1221 Macdonal Ave.
Richmond, CA 94801
PHONE: 510-236-5913
HOURS: Seven days, 10–7
TYPE OF MERCHANDISE: Clothing,
housewares, furniture
DONATION TAX RECEIPT: Receipt given
upon request
Salvation Army Thrift Store
1430 Cutting Blvd.
Richmond, CA 94804
TYPE OF MERCHANDISE: Clothing,
housewares, furniture
DONATION TAX RECEIPT: Receipt given
upon request
Salvation Army Thrift Store
10020/30 Magnolia Ave.
Riverside, CA 92503
TYPE OF MERCHANDISE: Clothing,
housewares, furniture

DONATION TAX RECEIPT: Receipt given
upon request
Salvation Army Thrift Store
4281 N. Main St.
Riverside, CA 92501
TYPE OF MERCHANDISE: Clothing,
housewares, furniture
DONATION TAX RECEIPT: Receipt given
upon request
Goodwill Industries Thrift Store
6086 Magnolia Ave.
Riverside, CA 92506
TYPE OF MERCHANDISE: Clothing,
housewares, furniture
DONATION TAX RECEIPT: Receipt given
upon request
Saint Vincent De Paul Thrift Store
8989 Mission Blvd.
Riverside, CA 92509
TYPE OF MERCHANDISE: Clothing,
housewares, furniture
DONATION TAX RECEIPT: Receipt given
upon request
COMMENTS: Monthly markdowns
Saint Vincent De Paul Thrift Store
141 Riverside Ave.
Roseville, CA 95678
TYPE OF MERCHANDISE: Clothing,
housewares, furniture
DONATION TAX RECEIPT: Receipt given
upon request
COMMENTS: Monthly markdowns
Salvation Army Thrift Store
10 Pesce Way
Sonora, CA 95370
TYPE OF MERCHANDISE: Clothing,
housewares, furniture
DONATION TAX RECEIPT: Receipt given
upon request
Saint Vincent De Paul Thrift Store
1511 Del Paso Blvd.
Sacramento, CA 95815
TYPE OF MERCHANDISE: Clothing,
housewares, furniture
DONATION TAX RECEIPT: Receipt given
upon request
COMMENTS: Monthly markdowns

American Cancer Society Discovery Shop
2744 Marconi Ave.
Sacramento, CA 95821
CONTACT: Tami Steelman
PHONE: 916-484-0227
TYPE OF MERCHANDISE: Clothing, bric-a-brac
DONATION TAX RECEIPT: Receipt given upon request
COMMENTS: Monthly markdowns

Salvation Army Thrift Store
315 16th St.
Sacramento, CA 95814
TYPE OF MERCHANDISE: Clothing, housewares, furniture
DONATION TAX RECEIPT: Receipt given upon request

American Cancer Society Discovery Shop
8535 Elk Grove Blvd.
Sacramento, CA 95831
CONTACT: Vera Maldonado
PHONE: 916-427-6741
TYPE OF MERCHANDISE: Clothing, bric-a-brac
DONATION TAX RECEIPT: Receipt given upon request
COMMENTS: Monthly markdowns

Goodwill Industries Thrift Store
1258 N. Main St.
Salinas, CA 93906
PHONE: 408-449-6361
HOURS: Mon.–Sat. 10–6, Sun. 12–5
TYPE OF MERCHANDISE: Clothing, housewares, furniture
DONATION TAX RECEIPT: Receipt given upon request

American Cancer Society Discovery Shop
229 Main St.
Salinas, CA 93901
CONTACT: Linda Rangel
PHONE: 408-758-1382
TYPE OF MERCHANDISE: Clothing, bric-a-brac
DONATION TAX RECEIPT: Receipt given upon request
COMMENTS: Monthly markdowns

Salvation Army Thrift Store
232 Monterey St.
Salinas, CA 93901

TYPE OF MERCHANDISE: Clothing, housewares, furniture
DONATION TAX RECEIPT: Receipt given upon request

Saint Vincent De Paul Thrift Store
251 E. Market St.
Salinas, CA 93901
TYPE OF MERCHANDISE: Clothing, housewares, furniture
DONATION TAX RECEIPT: Receipt given upon request
COMMENTS: Monthly markdowns

Salvation Army Thrift Store
320 N. Main St.
Salinas, CA 93906
TYPE OF MERCHANDISE: Clothing, housewares, furniture
DONATION TAX RECEIPT: Receipt given upon request

Goodwill Industries Thrift Store
350 Encinal
Salinas, Ca 93908
TYPE OF MERCHANDISE: Clothing, housewares, furniture
DONATION TAX RECEIPT: Receipt given upon request

Goodwill Industries Thrift Store
708 E. Alisal St.
Salinas, CA 93905
PHONE: 408-424-5346
HOURS: Mon.–Sat. 10–6, Sun. 12–5
TYPE OF MERCHANDISE: Clothing, housewares, furniture
DONATION TAX RECEIPT: Receipt given upon request

Salvation Army Thrift Store
824 W. Mill St.
San Bernardino, CA 92401
TYPE OF MERCHANDISE: Clothing, housewares, furniture
DONATION TAX RECEIPT: Receipt given upon request
COMMENTS: As-is store

Salvation Army Thrift Store
925 W. Tenth St.
San Bernardino, CA 92410
TYPE OF MERCHANDISE: Clothing, housewares, furniture

DONATION TAX RECEIPT: Receipt given upon request
COMMENTS: As-is store
Goodwill Industries Thrift Store
899 W. Third St.
San Bernardino, CA 92410
TYPE OF MERCHANDISE: Clothing, housewares, furniture
DONATION TAX RECEIPT: Receipt given upon request
Salvation Army Thrift Store
300 El Camino Real
San Bruno, CA 94066
TYPE OF MERCHANDISE: Clothing, housewares, furniture
DONATION TAX RECEIPT: Receipt given upon request
Amvets Thrift Store
3441 Sutherland St.
San Diego, CA 92110
PHONE: 619-297-4200
TYPE OF MERCHANDISE: Clothing, housewares, furniture
DONATION TAX RECEIPT: Receipt give upon request
Goodwill Industries Thrift Store
1281 N. Santa Fe St.
San Diego, CA 92109
CONTACT: Bob Kruse
PHONE: 619-225-2200, 225-1934
HOURS: Mon.–Fri. 9–8, Sat. 10–6, Sun. 10–5
TYPE OF MERCHANDISE: Clothing, housewares, furniture
DONATION TAX RECEIPT: Receipt given upon request
COMMENTS: Fresh stock throughout each day
Salvation Army Thrift Store
1335 Broadway
San Diego, CA 92101
TYPE OF MERCHANDISE: Clothing, housewares, furniture
DONATION TAX RECEIPT: Receipt given upon request
Goodwill Industries Thrift Store
1430 Garnet Ave.
San Diego, CA 92109
CONTACT: Bob Kruse

PHONE: 619-225-2200, 225-1934
HOURS: Mon.–Fri. 9–8, Sat. 10–6, Sun. 10–5
TYPE OF MERCHANDISE: Clothing, housewares, furniture
DONATION TAX RECEIPT: Receipt given upon request
COMMENTS: Fresh stock throughout each day
Saint Vincent De Paul Thrift Store
1550 Market
San Diego, CA 92101
PHONE: 619-233-1800
TYPE OF MERCHANDISE: Clothing, housewares, furniture
DONATION TAX RECEIPT: Receipt given upon request
COMMENTS: Monthly markdowns
Salvation Army Thrift Store
2920 University Ave.
San Diego, CA 92104
TYPE OF MERCHANDISE: Clothing, housewares, furniture
DONATION TAX RECEIPT: Receipt given upon request
Goodwill Industries Thrift Store
3270 Grayling Dr.
San Diego, CA 92123
CONTACT: Bob Kruse
PHONE: 619-225-2200, 225-1934
HOURS: Mon.–Fri. 9–8, Sat. 9–6, Sun. 9–5
TYPE OF MERCHANDISE: Clothing, housewares, furniture
DONATION TAX RECEIPT: Receipt given upon request
COMMENTS: Fresh stock throughout each day
Saint Vincent De Paul Thrift Store
3350 "E" St.
San Diego, CA 92102
CONTACT: Keith Mackay
TYPE OF MERCHANDISE: Clothing, housewares, furniture
DONATION TAX RECEIPT: Receipt given upon request
COMMENTS: Monthly markdowns
Saint Vincent De Paul Thrift Store
342 W. San Ysidro Blvd.
San Diego, CA 92173

TYPE OF MERCHANDISE: Clothing, housewares, furniture
DONATION TAX RECEIPT: Receipt given upon request
COMMENTS: Monthly markdowns

American Cancer Society Discovery Shop
3639B Midway Dr.
San Diego, CA 92110
CONTACT: Gretchen Hope
PHONE: 619-224-4336
TYPE OF MERCHANDISE: Clothing, bric-a-brac
DONATION TAX RECEIPT: Receipt given upon request
COMMENTS: Monthly markdowns

Goodwill Industries Thrift Store
3663 Rosecrans St.
San Diego, CA 92110
CONTACT: Linda Fennell
PHONE: 619-225-2200, 225-1934
HOURS: Mon.–Fri. 9–5, Sat. 10–6, Sun. 10–5
TYPE OF MERCHANDISE: Clothing, housewares, furniture
DONATION TAX RECEIPT: Receipt given upon request

Goodwill Industries Thrift Store
402 Fifth Ave.
San Diego, CA 92101
PHONE: 619-225-2200, 225-1934
HOURS: Mon.–Fri. 8:30–6, Sat. 10–6, Sun. 10–5
TYPE OF MERCHANDISE: Clothing, housewares, furniture
DONATION TAX RECEIPT: Receipt given upon request

Goodwill Industries Thrift Store
4359 Home Ave.
San Diego, CA 92105
CONTACT: Linda Fennell
PHONE: 619-225-2200, 225-1934
HOURS: Mon.–Fri. 8:30–8, Sat. 10–6, Sun. 10–5
TYPE OF MERCHANDISE: Clothing, housewares, furniture
DONATION TAX RECEIPT: Receipt given upon request

Goodwill Industries Thrift Store
444 Fifth Ave.

San Diego, CA 92101
CONTACT: Linda Fennell
PHONE: 619-225-2200, 225-1934
HOURS: Mon.–Fri. 10–6, Sun. 10–5
TYPE OF MERCHANDISE: Clothing, housewares, furniture
DONATION TAX RECEIPT: Receipt given upon request

Goodwill Industries Thrift Store
453 Fourth Ave.
San Diego, CA 92101
CONTACT: Carmelita Peterson
PHONE: 619-225-2200, 225-1934
HOURS: Mon.–Fri. 8–4:30
TYPE OF MERCHANDISE: Clothing, housewares, furniture
DONATION TAX RECEIPT: Receipt given upon request

Saint Vincent De Paul Thrift Store
4574 Park Blvd.
San Diego, CA 92116
TYPE OF MERCHANDISE: Clothing, housewares, furniture
DONATION TAX RECEIPT: Receipt given upon request
COMMENTS: Monthly markdowns

Salvation Army Thrift Store
4606 Mission Bay Dr.
San Diego, CA 92109
TYPE OF MERCHANDISE: Clothing, housewares, furniture
DONATION TAX RECEIPT: Receipt given upon request

Salvation Army Thrift Store
6331 University Ave.
San Diego, CA 92115
TYPE OF MERCHANDISE: Clothing, housewares, furniture
DONATION TAX RECEIPT: Receipt given upon request

Salvation Army Thrift Store
6875 El Cajon Blvd.
San Diego, CA 92115
TYPE OF MERCHANDISE: Clothing, housewares, furniture
DONATION TAX RECEIPT: Receipt given upon request

Salvation Army Thrift Store
901 12th St.
San Diego, CA 92101
TYPE OF MERCHANDISE: Clothing,
housewares, furniture
DONATION TAX RECEIPT: Receipt given
upon request

Salvation Army Thrift Store
110 N. Maclay St.
San Fernando, CA 91340
TYPE OF MERCHANDISE: Clothing,
housewares, furniture
DONATION TAX RECEIPT: Receipt given
upon request

Goodwill Industries Thrift Store
1132 Pico St.
San Fernando, CA 91340
TYPE OF MERCHANDISE: Clothing,
housewares, furniture
DONATION TAX RECEIPT: Receipt given
upon request

Salvation Army Thrift Store
1173 Sutter St.
San Francisco, CA 94109
TYPE OF MERCHANDISE: Clothing,
housewares, furniture
DONATION TAX RECEIPT: Receipt given
upon request

Salvation Army Thrift Store
1185 Sutter St.
San Francisco, CA 94109
TYPE OF MERCHANDISE: Clothing,
housewares, furniture
DONATION TAX RECEIPT: Receipt given
upon request

Salvation Army Thrift Store
1509–39 Valencia St.
San Francisco, CA 94110
TYPE OF MERCHANDISE: Clothing,
housewares, furniture
DONATION TAX RECEIPT: Receipt given
upon request

Saint Vincent De Paul Thrift Store
1519 Haight St.
San Francisco, CA 94117
TYPE OF MERCHANDISE: Clothing,
housewares, furniture

DONATION TAX RECEIPT: Receipt given
upon request
COMMENTS: Monthly markdowns

City of Hope Nifty Thrifty Shop
1619 Ocean Ave.
San Francisco, CA 94112
TYPE OF MERCHANDISE: Clothing,
housewares, furniture
DONATION TAX RECEIPT: Receipt given
upon request

Goodwill Industries Thrift Store
1700 Fillmore St.
CROSS STREET: Post
San Francisco, CA 94115
CONTACT: Allen Carter
PHONE: 415-441-2159
HOURS: Mon.–Sat. 10–6, Sun. 10:30–5:30
TYPE OF MERCHANDISE: Clothing,
housewares, furniture
DONATION TAX RECEIPT: Receipt given
upon request

Goodwill Industries Thrift Store
1700 Haight St.
CROSS STREET: Cole
San Francisco, CA 94117
CONTACT: Amy Mathers, Valerie Morris
PHONE: 415-387-1192
HOURS: Sun–Fri. 11–7, Sat. 10–7
TYPE OF MERCHANDISE: Clothing,
housewares, furniture
DONATION TAX RECEIPT: Receipt given
upon request
COMMENTS: Large shop, clean, great
prices.

Saint Vincent De Paul Thrift Store
1745 Folsom St.
San Francisco, CA 94103
TYPE OF MERCHANDISE: Clothing,
housewares, furniture
DONATION TAX RECEIPT: Receipt given
upon request
COMMENTS: Monthly markdowns

Junior League Next to New Shop
2226 Fillmore St.
San Francisco, CA 94115-2222
TYPE OF MERCHANDISE: Clothing,
housewares, toys
DONATION TAX RECEIPT: Receipt given
upon request

Goodwill Industries Thrift Store
2279 Mission St.
CROSS STREET: 19th
San Francisco, CA 94110
CONTACT: Cris Timboy, Gaspara Holiday
PHONE: 415-826-5759
HOURS: Mon.–Sat. 10–6, Sun. 10–5
TYPE OF MERCHANDISE: Clothing,
housewares, furniture
DONATION TAX RECEIPT: Receipt given
upon request

Goodwill Industries Thrift Store
241 Tenth St.
CROSS STREET: Howard & Folsom
San Francisco, CA 94103
CONTACT: John Bennett, Mario Burrion-
Rosales
PHONE: 415-252-1677
HOURS: Mon.–Sat. 10–6, Sun. 10:30–
5:30
TYPE OF MERCHANDISE: Clothing,
housewares, furniture
DONATION TAX RECEIPT: Receipt given
upon request

Salvation Army Thrift Store
3550 Army St.
San Francisco, CA 94110
TYPE OF MERCHANDISE: Clothing,
housewares, furniture
DONATION TAX RECEIPT: Receipt given
upon request

Goodwill Industries Thrift Store
3801 Third St. Suite 330
San Francisco, CA 94124
CONTACT: Nadine Durretti, Josefina
Dayao
PHONE: 415-641-4470
HOURS: Mon.–Sat. 10–6, Sun. 12–6
TYPE OF MERCHANDISE: Clothing,
housewares, furniture
DONATION TAX RECEIPT: Receipt given
upon request

Goodwill Industries Thrift Store
820 Clement St.
CROSS STREET: 9th Ave.
San Francisco, CA 94118
PHONE: 415-668-3635
TYPE OF MERCHANDISE: Clothing,
housewares, furniture

DONATION TAX RECEIPT: Receipt given
upon request

Goodwill Industries Thrift Store
822 Geary St.
CROSS STREET: Hyde
San Francisco, CA 94109
PHONE: 415-922-0405
HOURS: Mon.–Sat. 10–6, Sun. 11– 5:30
TYPE OF MERCHANDISE: Clothing,
housewares, furniture
DONATION TAX RECEIPT: Receipt given
upon request

American Cancer Society Discovery Shop
1451A Foxworthy Ave.
San Jose, CA 95118
CONTACT: Peggy Miller
PHONE: 408-265-5535
TYPE OF MERCHANDISE: Clothing, bric-a-
brac
DONATION TAX RECEIPT: Receipt given
upon request
COMMENTS: Monthly markdowns

Goodwill Industries Thrift Store
1579 Meridian Ave.
CROSS STREET: Bollinger
San Jose, CA 95125
CONTACTS: Faye Marcil, Barbara Miller
PHONE: 408-266-7151
HOURS: Mon.–Th. 9–7, Fri. 9–8, Sat. 9–6,
Sun. 11–5
TYPE OF MERCHANDISE: Clothing,
housewares, furniture
DONATION TAX RECEIPT: Receipt given
upon request

Saint Vincent De Paul Thrift Store
2040 S. Seventh St.
San Jose, CA 95112
TYPE OF MERCHANDISE: Clothing,
housewares, furniture
DONATION TAX RECEIPT: Receipt given
upon request
COMMENTS: Monthly markdowns

Salvation Army Thrift Store
4114 Monterey Hwy.
San Jose, CA 95115-3626
TYPE OF MERCHANDISE: Clothing,
housewares, furniture

DONATION TAX RECEIPT: Receipt given upon request

Salvation Army Thrift Store
702 W. Taylor St.
San Jose, CA 95109
TYPE OF MERCHANDISE: Clothing, housewares, furniture
DONATION TAX RECEIPT: Receipt given upon request

Saint Vincent De Paul Thrift Store
32252 Camino Capistrano
San Juan Capistrano, CA 92675-3715
TYPE OF MERCHANDISE: Clothing, housewares, furniture
DONATION TAX RECEIPT: Receipt given upon request
COMMENTS: Monthly markdowns

Goodwill Industries Thrift Store
14410 Washington Ave. #110
San Leandro, CA 94578
PHONE: 510-614-9658
HOURS: Seven days, 10–7
TYPE OF MERCHANDISE: Clothing, housewares, furniture
DONATION TAX RECEIPT: Receipt given upon request

Goodwill Industries Thrift Store
14750 E. 14th St.
San Leandro, CA 94577-2819
PHONE: 510-352-6966
HOURS: Seven days , 10–7
TYPE OF MERCHANDISE: Clothing, housewares, furniture
DONATION TAX RECEIPT: Receipt given upon request

Salvation Army Thrift Store
2179 E. 14th St.
San Leandro, CA 94577
TYPE OF MERCHANDISE: Clothing, housewares, furniture
DONATION TAX RECEIPT: Receipt given upon request

Goodwill Industries Thrift Store
712 Marsh St.
San Luis Obispo, CA 93401
PHONE: 805-544-4965
HOURS: Mon.–Sat. 10–6, Sun. 12–5
TYPE OF MERCHANDISE: Clothing, housewares, furniture

DONATION TAX RECEIPT: Receipt given upon request

American Cancer Society Discovery Shop
767A Foothill Blvd.
San Luis Obispo, CA 93405
CONTACT: Barbara Lee
PHONE: 805-543-1524
TYPE OF MERCHANDISE: Clothing, bric-a-brac
DONATION TAX RECEIPT: Receipt given upon request
COMMENTS: Monthly markdowns

Goodwill Industries Thrift Store
870 Industrial Way #E
San Luis Obispo, CA 93401
HOURS: Mon.–Sat. 10–4
TYPE OF MERCHANDISE: Clothing, housewares, furniture
DONATION TAX RECEIPT: Receipt given upon request

Saint Vincent De Paul Thrift Store
113 S. "B" St.
San Mateo, CA 94401
TYPE OF MERCHANDISE: Clothing, housewares, furniture
DONATION TAX RECEIPT: Receipt given upon request
COMMENTS: Monthly markdowns

Goodwill Industries Thrift Store
28 W. 25th Ave.
San Mateo, CA 94403
CONTACTS: Delilah Batac, Eileen Wieland
PHONE: 415-525-2780
HOURS: Mon., Wed. 10–6, Thurs., Fri. 10–7, Sat. 10–6, Sun. 11–6
TYPE OF MERCHANDISE: Clothing, housewares, furniture
DONATION TAX RECEIPT: Receipt given upon request

Saint Vincent De Paul Thrift Store
650 Elportal Center
San Pablo, CA 94806
TYPE OF MERCHANDISE: Clothing, housewares, furniture
DONATION TAX RECEIPT: Receipt given upon request
COMMENTS: Monthly markdowns

Salvation Army Thrift Store
13577 San Pablo Ave.
San Pablo, CA 94806
TYPE OF MERCHANDISE: Clothing,
housewares, furniture
DONATION TAX RECEIPT: Receipt given
upon request
Salvation Army Thrift Store
387 W. Sixth St.
San Pedro, CA 90731-3317
TYPE OF MERCHANDISE: Clothing,
housewares, furniture
DONATION TAX RECEIPT: Receipt given
upon request
Salvation Army Thrift Store
544 S. Pacific Ave.
San Pedro, CA 90731
TYPE OF MERCHANDISE: Clothing,
housewares, furniture
DONATION TAX RECEIPT: Receipt given
upon request
Goodwill Industries Thrift Store
1920 Fourth St.
San Rafael, CA 94901-2671
TYPE OF MERCHANDISE: Clothing,
housewares, furniture
DONATION TAX RECEIPT: Receipt given
upon request
American Cancer Society Discovery Shop
266 Northgate One
San Rafael, CA 94903
CONTACT: Ann Albee
PHONE: 415-456-0340
TYPE OF MERCHANDISE: Clothing, bric-a-
brac
DONATION TAX RECEIPT: Receipt given
upon request
COMMENTS: Monthly markdowns
Salvation Army Thrift Store
350 Fourth St.
San Rafael, CA 94901
TYPE OF MERCHANDISE: Clothing,
housewares, furniture
DONATION TAX RECEIPT: Receipt given
upon request
Saint Vincent De Paul Thrift Store
508 Irwin Ave.
San Rafael, CA 94901

TYPE OF MERCHANDISE: Clothing,
housewares, furniture
DONATION TAX RECEIPT: Receipt given
upon request
COMMENTS: Monthly markdowns
Goodwill Industries Thrift Store
809 Lincoln
CROSS STREET: Third
San Rafael, CA 94901
CONTACT: Ann Zwetzig, Charlene Lilley
PHONE: 415-456-5273
HOURS: Mon.–Fri. 10–7, Sat. 10–6,
Sun. 11–5:30
TYPE OF MERCHANDISE: Clothing,
housewares, furniture
DONATION TAX RECEIPT: Receipt given
upon request
Salvation Army Thrift Store
910 Lincoln Ave.
San Rafael, CA 94901
TYPE OF MERCHANDISE: Clothing,
housewares, furniture
DONATION TAX RECEIPT: Receipt given
upon request
Goodwill Industries Thrift Store
1306 S. Main St.
Santa Ana, CA 92707
TYPE OF MERCHANDISE: Clothing,
housewares, furniture
DONATION TAX RECEIPT: Receipt given
upon request
Disabled American Vets Thrift Store
201 S. Sullivan St.
Santa Ana, CA 92704
TYPE OF MERCHANDISE: Clothing,
housewares, furniture
DONATION TAX RECEIPT: Receipt given
upon request
Saint Vincent De Paul Thrift Store
2017 S. Main St.
Santa Ana, CA 92707
TYPE OF MERCHANDISE: Clothing,
housewares, furniture
DONATION TAX RECEIPT: Receipt given
upon request
COMMENTS: Monthly markdowns
Salvation Army Thrift Store
2519–2603 W. First St.

Santa Ana, CA 92703
TYPE OF MERCHANDISE: Clothing,
housewares, furniture
DONATION TAX RECEIPT: Receipt given
upon request
Goodwill Industries Thrift Store
2702 W. Fifth St.
Santa Ana, CA 92703
TYPE OF MERCHANDISE: Clothing,
housewares, furniture
DONATION TAX RECEIPT: Receipt given
upon request
Goodwill Industries Thrift Store
410 N. Fairview St.
Santa Ana, CA 92703
CONTACT: Gail Rentz
TYPE OF MERCHANDISE: Clothing,
housewares, furniture
DONATION TAX RECEIPT: Receipt given
upon request
Salvation Army Thrift Store
710 S. Main St.
Santa Ana, CA 92701
TYPE OF MERCHANDISE: Clothing,
housewares, furniture
DONATION TAX RECEIPT: Receipt given
upon request
Salvation Army Thrift Store
610 State St.
Santa Barbara, CA
TYPE OF MERCHANDISE: Clothing,
housewares, furniture
DONATION TAX RECEIPT: Receipt given
upon request
Salvation Army Thrift Store
700 N. Milpas St.
Santa Barbara, CA 93103
TYPE OF MERCHANDISE: Clothing,
housewares, furniture
DONATION TAX RECEIPT: Receipt given
upon request
Salvation Army Thrift Store
1494 Halford
Santa Clara, CA 95051
TYPE OF MERCHANDISE: Clothing,
housewares, furniture
DONATION TAX RECEIPT: Receipt given
upon request

Goodwill Industries Thrift Store
2800 El Camino Real
CROSS STREET: Kiely
Santa Clara, CA 95051
CONTACT: Dale Rice, Darnell Miller
PHONE: 408-247-2800
HOURS: Mon.–Th. 9–7, Fri. 9–8, Sat. 9–6,
Sun 11–5
TYPE OF MERCHANDISE: Clothing,
housewares, furniture
DONATION TAX RECEIPT: Receipt given
upon request
American Cancer Society Discovery Shop
23132 Valencia Blvd.
Santa Clarita, CA 91355
CONTACT: Lisa Cohen
PHONE: 805-287-9088
TYPE OF MERCHANDISE: Clothing,
housewares, bric-a-brac
DONATION TAX RECEIPT: Receipt given
upon request
COMMENTS: Monthly markdowns
Salvation Army Thrift Store
161 Seabright Ave.
Santa Cruz, CA 95062
TYPE OF MERCHANDISE: Clothing,
housewares, furniture
DONATION TAX RECEIPT: Receipt given
upon request
Goodwill Industries Thrift Store
204 Union St.
Santa Cruz, CA 95060
PHONE: 408-423-1078
HOURS: Mon.–Sat. 10–6, Sun. 12–5
TYPE OF MERCHANDISE: Clothing,
housewares, furniture
DONATION TAX RECEIPT: Receipt given
upon request
Goodwill Industries Thrift Store
2525 Soquel Dr.
Santa Cruz, CA 95065
PHONE: 408-462-1300
HOURS: Mon.–Sat. 10–6, Sun. 12–5
TYPE OF MERCHANDISE: Clothing,
housewares, furniture
DONATION TAX RECEIPT: Receipt given
upon request

Salvation Army Thrift Store
322 E. Front St.
Santa Cruz, CA 95060
TYPE OF MERCHANDISE: Clothing,
housewares, furniture
DONATION TAX RECEIPT: Receipt given
upon request

Goodwill Industries Thrift Store
350 Encinal St.
Santa Cruz, CA 95060
HOURS: Mon.–Sat. 9–12, 1–4, Sun. 11–4
TYPE OF MERCHANDISE: Clothing,
housewares, furniture
DONATION TAX RECEIPT: Receipt given
upon request

Salvation Army Thrift Store
825 41st Ave.
Santa Cruz, CA 95061
TYPE OF MERCHANDISE: Clothing,
housewares, furniture
DONATION TAX RECEIPT: Receipt given
upon request

Salvation Army Thrift Store
1447 S. Broadway
Santa Maria, CA 93013
TYPE OF MERCHANDISE: Clothing,
housewares, furniture
DONATION TAX RECEIPT: Receipt given
upon request

Goodwill Industries Thrift Store
1539 Stowell Center Plaza
Santa Maria, CA 93454-7121
TYPE OF MERCHANDISE: Clothing,
housewares, furniture
DONATION TAX RECEIPT: Receipt given
upon request

Salvation Army Thrift Store
919 N. Broadway
Santa Maria, CA 93454
TYPE OF MERCHANDISE: Clothing,
housewares, furniture
DONATION TAX RECEIPT: Receipt given
upon request

Salvation Army Thrift Store
1021 Olympic Blvd.
Santa Monica, CA 90404
TYPE OF MERCHANDISE: Clothing,
housewares, furniture

DONATION TAX RECEIPT: Receipt given
upon request
COMMENTS: As-is/auction

Salvation Army Thrift Store
1658 11th St.
Santa Monica, CA 90404
PHONE: 310-450-7235
TYPE OF MERCHANDISE: Clothing,
housewares, furniture
DONATION TAX RECEIPT: Receipt given
upon request
COMMENTS: Large collectibles and
furniture section

Salvation Army Thrift Store
1290A Sebastopol Rd.
Santa Rosa, CA 95407
TYPE OF MERCHANDISE: Clothing,
housewares, furniture
DONATION TAX RECEIPT: Receipt given
upon request

Goodwill Industries Thrift Store
11 W. Barham Ave.
CROSS STREET: Dutton Ave.
Santa Rosa, CA 95407
PHONE: 707-523-0550
HOURS: Mon.–Sat. 10–6, Sun. 12–5
TYPE OF MERCHANDISE: Clothing,
housewares, furniture
DONATION TAX RECEIPT: Receipt given
upon request
COMMENTS: Sunday super sales

American Cancer Society Discovery Shop
2300 Mendocino Ave.
Santa Rosa, CA 95401-3171
CONTACT: Goldie Salada
PHONE: 707-526-3349
TYPE OF MERCHANDISE: Clothing, bric-a-
brac
DONATION TAX RECEIPT: Receipt given
upon request
COMMENTS: Monthly markdowns

Goodwill Industries Thrift Store
3535 Industrial Dr.
CROSS STREET: behind Kmart
Santa Rosa, CA 95403
PHONE: 707-545-2492
HOURS: Mon.–Sat. 9:30–5:30, Sun. 11–5
TYPE OF MERCHANDISE: Clothing,
housewares, furniture

DONATION TAX RECEIPT: Receipt given upon request
COMMENTS: Sunday super sales

American Cancer Society Discovery Shop
9660 Mission Gorge Rd. "F"
Santee, CA 92071
CONTACT: Kym Wright
PHONE: 619-562-7290
TYPE OF MERCHANDISE: Clothing, bric-a-brac
DONATION TAX RECEIPT: Receipt given upon request
COMMENTS: Monthly markdowns

Goodwill Industries Thrift Store
670 E. San Ysidro Blvd.
San Ysidro, CA 92173
CONTACT: Carmelita Peterson
PHONE: 619-225-2200, 225-1934
HOURS: Mon.–Sat. 9:30–5:30, Sun. 10–5
TYPE OF MERCHANDISE: Clothing, housewares, furniture
DONATION TAX RECEIPT: Receipt given upon request
COMMENTS: Ask about parking lot sales

Saint Vincent De Paul Thrift Store
1269 Fremont Blvd.
Seaside, CA 93955
TYPE OF MERCHANDISE: Clothing, housewares, furniture
DONATION TAX RECEIPT: Receipt given upon request
COMMENTS: Monthly markdowns

Salvation Army Thrift Store
1850 Fremont St.
Seaside, CA 95955
TYPE OF MERCHANDISE: Clothing, housewares, furniture
DONATION TAX RECEIPT: Receipt given upon request

Goodwill Industries Thrift Store
729 Broadway Avenue
Seaside, CA 93955
PHONE: 408-394-1212
HOURS: Mon.–Sat. 10–6, Sun. 12–5
TYPE OF MERCHANDISE: Clothing, housewares, furniture
DONATION TAX RECEIPT: Receipt given upon request

Salvation Army Thrift Store
205 Central
Shafter, CA
TYPE OF MERCHANDISE: Clothing, housewares, furniture
DONATION TAX RECEIPT: Receipt given upon request

American Cancer Society Discovery Shop
4454 Van Nuys Blvd. Suite 101
Sherman Oaks, CA 91403
CONTACT: Jeanne Burr
PHONE: 818-905-9141
TYPE OF MERCHANDISE: Clothing, bric-a-brac
DONATION TAX RECEIPT: Receipt given upon request
COMMENTS: Monthly markdowns

Salvation Army Thrift Store
1492 Los Angeles Ave.
Simi Valley, CA 93030
TYPE OF MERCHANDISE: Clothing, housewares, furniture
DONATION TAX RECEIPT: Receipt given upon request

Goodwill Industries Thrift Store
225 Kenwood Way
So. San Francisco, CA 94080
CONTACT: Sam Rodriguez, Josefina Espiritu
PHONE: 415-737-9827
HOURS: Mon.–Sat. 10–6, Sun. 11–6
TYPE OF MERCHANDISE: Clothing, housewares, furniture
DONATION TAX RECEIPT: Receipt given upon request
COMMENTS: Occasional good finds

Saint Vincent De Paul Thrift Store
344 Grand Ave.
So. San Francisco, CA 94080
TYPE OF MERCHANDISE: Clothing, housewares, furniture
DONATION TAX RECEIPT: Receipt given upon request
COMMENTS: Monthly markdowns

Salvation Army Thrift Store
9805 Campo Rd.
Spring Valley, CA 91977
TYPE OF MERCHANDISE: Clothing, housewares, furniture

DONATION TAX RECEIPT: Receipt given upon request

American Cancer Society Discovery Shop
207 E. Alpine Ave.
Stockton, CA 95204
CONTACT: Pat Wogen
PHONE: 209-941-2737
TYPE OF MERCHANDISE: Clothing, bric-a-brac
DONATION TAX RECEIPT: Receipt given upon request
COMMENTS: Monthly markdowns

Goodwill Industries Thrift Store
66 S. Wilson Way
Stockton, CA 95205
PHONE: 209-466-3252
HOURS: Seven days
TYPE OF MERCHANDISE: Clothing, housewares, furniture
DONATION TAX RECEIPT: Receipt given upon request

Goodwill Industries Thrift Store
730 E. Market St.
Stockton, CA 95202
TYPE OF MERCHANDISE: Clothing, housewares, furniture
DONATION TAX RECEIPT: Receipt given upon request

Goodwill Industries Thrift Store
Stanislaus at Crosstown Freeway
Stockton, CA 95202
PHONE: 209-466-2311
HOURS: Mon.–Fri. 7:30–3
TYPE OF MERCHANDISE: Clothing, housewares, furniture
DONATION TAX RECEIPT: Receipt given upon request
COMMENTS: As-is sales

Salvation Army Thrift Store
1247 S. Wilson Way
Stockton, CA 95205
TYPE OF MERCHANDISE: Clothing, housewares, furniture
DONATION TAX RECEIPT: Receipt given upon request

Salvation Army Thrift Store
812 El Camino Real
Sunnyvale, CA 94087

PHONE: 408-749-0451
TYPE OF MERCHANDISE: Clothing, housewares, furniture
DONATION TAX RECEIPT: Receipt given upon request

Salvation Army Thrift Store
8226–8232 Sunland Blvd.
Sun Valley, CA 91352
TYPE OF MERCHANDISE: Clothing, housewares, furniture
DONATION TAX RECEIPT: Receipt given upon request

Salvation Army Thrift Store
506 Center St.
Taft, CA 93262
TYPE OF MERCHANDISE: Clothing, housewares, furniture
DONATION TAX RECEIPT: Receipt given upon request

Salvation Army Thrift Store
2103 W. Torrance Blvd.
Torrance, CA 90501
TYPE OF MERCHANDISE: Clothing, housewares, furniture
DONATION TAX RECEIPT: Receipt given upon request

Goodwill Industries Thrift Store
22725 S. Western Ave.
Torrance, CA 90501
TYPE OF MERCHANDISE: Clothing, housewares, furniture
DONATION TAX RECEIPT: Receipt given upon request

Salvation Army Thrift Store
4310 Pacific Coast Hwy.
Torrance, CA 90505
TYPE OF MERCHANDISE: Clothing, housewares, furniture
DONATION TAX RECEIPT: Receipt given upon request

Salvation Army Thrift Store
3 East 11th St.
Tracy, CA 95376
PHONE: 209-832-0346
TYPE OF MERCHANDISE: Clothing, housewares, furniture
DONATION TAX RECEIPT: Receipt given upon request

Salvation Army Thrift Store
7235 Foothill Blvd.
Tujunga, CA 91042
TYPE OF MERCHANDISE: Clothing,
housewares, furniture
DONATION TAX RECEIPT: Receipt given
upon request

Salvation Army Thrift Store
216 S. "K" St.
Tulare, CA 93724
TYPE OF MERCHANDISE: Clothing,
housewares, furniture
DONATION TAX RECEIPT: Receipt given
upon request

Salvation Army Thrift Store
223–233 E. Main St.
Turlock, CA 95380
TYPE OF MERCHANDISE: Clothing,
housewares, furniture
DONATION TAX RECEIPT: Receipt given
upon request

Goodwill Industries Thrift Store
300 E. Main St.
Turlock, CA 95380
PHONE: 209-669-65335
HOURS: Seven days
TYPE OF MERCHANDISE: Clothing,
housewares, furniture
DONATION TAX RECEIPT: Receipt given
upon request

Goodwill Industries Thrift Store
1005 N. State St.
Ukiah, CA 95482
PHONE: 707-462-9660
HOURS: Mon.–Sat. 10–6, Sun. 12–5
TYPE OF MERCHANDISE: Clothing,
housewares, furniture
DONATION TAX RECEIPT: Receipt given
upon request
COMMENTS: Sunday super sales every week

Salvation Army Thrift Store
289 N. Main St.
Ukiah, CA 95482
TYPE OF MERCHANDISE: Clothing,
housewares, furniture
DONATION TAX RECEIPT: Receipt given
upon request

MCC Serendipity
116 N. Second Ave.
Upland, CA 91786
PHONE: 909-981-4633
TYPE OF MERCHANDISE: Clothing,
housewares
DONATION TAX RECEIPT: Receipt given
upon request

American Cancer Society Discovery Shop
1236 Foothill Blvd.
Upland, CA 91786
CONTACT: Doris Story
PHONE: 714-981-7466
TYPE OF MERCHANDISE: Clothing, bric-a-
brac
DONATION TAX RECEIPT: Receipt given
upon request
COMMENTS: Monthly markdowns

Goodwill Industries Thrift Store
1317 E. Monte Vista Ave.
Vacaville, CA 95685
PHONE: 707-864-5440
HOURS: Seven days, 10–7
TYPE OF MERCHANDISE: Clothing,
housewares, furniture
DONATION TAX RECEIPT: Receipt given
upon request

Goodwill Industries Thrift Store
1039 Tennessee St.
Vallejo, CA 94590
PHONE: 707-643-3624
HOURS: Seven days, 10–7
TYPE OF MERCHANDISE: Clothing,
housewares, furniture
DONATION TAX RECEIPT: Receipt given
upon request

Salvation Army Thrift Store
2136 Sacramento St.
Vallejo, CA 94590
TYPE OF MERCHANDISE: Clothing,
housewares, furniture
DONATION TAX RECEIPT: Receipt given
upon request

American Cancer Society Discovery Shop
3712 Sonoma Blvd.
Vallejo, CA 94589
CONTACT: Irene Buck
PHONE: 707-643-6606

TYPE OF MERCHANDISE: Clothing, bric-a-brac
DONATION TAX RECEIPT: Receipt given upon request
COMMENTS: Monthly markdowns

Salvation Army Thrift Store
539 Tennessee St.
Vallejo, CA 94548
TYPE OF MERCHANDISE: Clothing, housewares, furniture
DONATION TAX RECEIPT: Receipt given upon request

Goodwill Industries Thrift Store
14565 Lanark St.
Van Nuys, CA 91402
TYPE OF MERCHANDISE: Clothing, housewares, furniture
DONATION TAX RECEIPT: Receipt given upon request

Salvation Army Thrift Store
6059 Van Nuys Blvd.
Van Nuys, CA 91401
TYPE OF MERCHANDISE: Clothing, housewares, furniture
DONATION TAX RECEIPT: Receipt given upon request

Salvation Army Thrift Store
4100L Telegraph Rd.
Ventura, CA 93002
TYPE OF MERCHANDISE: Clothing, housewares, furniture
DONATION TAX RECEIPT: Receipt given upon request

American Cancer Society Discovery Shop
434 E. Main St.
Ventura, CA 93001
CONTACT: Val Bowman
TYPE OF MERCHANDISE: Clothing, bric-a-brac
DONATION TAX RECEIPT: Receipt given upon request
COMMENTS: Monthly markdowns

Goodwill Industries Thrift Store
76 S. Oak St.
Ventura, CA 93001
TYPE OF MERCHANDISE: Clothing, housewares, furniture
DONATION TAX RECEIPT: Receipt given upon request

Salvation Army Thrift Store
14716 Seventh St.
Victorville, CA 92392
TYPE OF MERCHANDISE: Clothing, housewares, furniture
DONATION TAX RECEIPT: Receipt given upon request

Goodwill Industries Thrift Store
15421 Village Dr.
Victorville, CA 92392
TYPE OF MERCHANDISE: Clothing, housewares, furniture
DONATION TAX RECEIPT: Receipt given upon request

Goodwill Industries Thrift Store
3237 Mooney Blvd.
Visalia, CA 93277
PHONE: 209-732-7922
HOURS: Seven days
TYPE OF MERCHANDISE: Clothing, housewares, furniture
DONATION TAX RECEIPT: Receipt given upon request

American Cancer Society Discovery Shop
3336 S. Mooney Blvd.
Visalia, CA 93277
CONTACT: Harlene Hanson
PHONE: 209-627-1955
TYPE OF MERCHANDISE: Clothing, bric-a-brac
DONATION TAX RECEIPT: Receipt given upon request
COMMENTS: Monthly markdowns

Salvation Army Thrift Store
339 N.W. Third St.
Visalia, CA 93277
TYPE OF MERCHANDISE: Clothing, housewares, furniture
DONATION TAX RECEIPT: Receipt given upon request

Salvation Army Thrift Store
1056 E. Vista Way
Vista, CA 92084
TYPE OF MERCHANDISE: Clothing, housewares, furniture
DONATION TAX RECEIPT: Receipt given upon request

American Cancer Society Discovery Shop
800 Escondido Ave. "E"
Vista, CA 92083
CONTACT: Joyce D. Velluntini
PHONE: 619-724-9222
TYPE OF MERCHANDISE: Clothing, bric-a-brac
DONATION TAX RECEIPT: Receipt given upon request
COMMENTS: Monthly markdowns

American Cancer Society Discovery Shop
1538 Locust
Walnut Creek, CA 94596
CONTACT: Nora Jamond
PHONE: 415-944-1991
TYPE OF MERCHANDISE: Clothing, bric-a-brac
DONATION TAX RECEIPT: Receipt given upon request
COMMENTS: Monthly markdowns

Salvation Army Thrift Store
23 E. Lake St.
Watsonville, CA 95076
TYPE OF MERCHANDISE: Clothing, housewares, furniture
DONATION TAX RECEIPT: Receipt given upon request

Saint Vincent De Paul Thrift Store
135 E. Lake Ave.
Watsonville, CA 95076
TYPE OF MERCHANDISE: Clothing, housewares, furniture
DONATION TAX RECEIPT: Receipt given upon request
COMMENTS: Monthly markdowns

Goodwill Industries Thrift Store
470 Main St.
Watsonville, CA 95076
PHONE: 408-722-2376
HOURS: Mon.–Sat. 10–6, Sun. 12–5
TYPE OF MERCHANDISE: Clothing, housewares, furniture
DONATION TAX RECEIPT: Receipt given upon request

American Cancer Society Discovery Shop
995 S. Glendora Ave.
West Covina, CA 91790
CONTACT: Leslie Evans
PHONE: 818-814-2212
TYPE OF MERCHANDISE: Clothing, bric-a-brac
DONATION TAX RECEIPT: Receipt given upon request
COMMENTS: Monthly markdowns

Council Thrift Shop
7818 Santa Monica Blvd.
West Hollywood, CA 90046
PHONE: 213-654-8516
TYPE OF MERCHANDISE: Clothing, housewares, furniture
DONATION TAX RECEIPT: Receipt given upon request
COMMENTS: Great designer clothing, annual sales

Goodwill Industries Thrift Store
5948 Westminster Blvd.
Westminster, CA 92683
TYPE OF MERCHANDISE: Clothing, housewares, furniture
DONATION TAX RECEIPT: Receipt given upon request

Salvation Army Thrift Store
7138 Westminster Ave.
Westminster, CA 92683
TYPE OF MERCHANDISE: Clothing, housewares, furniture
DONATION TAX RECEIPT: Receipt given upon request

Salvation Army Thrift Store
12908 E. Bailey
Whittier, CA 90601
TYPE OF MERCHANDISE: Clothing, housewares, furniture
DONATION TAX RECEIPT: Receipt given upon request

Rescue Mission Thrift Store
371 Windsor River Rd.
Windsor, CA 95492
TYPE OF MERCHANDISE: Clothing, housewares, furniture
DONATION TAX RECEIPT: Receipt given upon request

Salvation Army Thrift Store
438 College St.
Woodland, CA 95695
TYPE OF MERCHANDISE: Clothing, housewares, furniture
DONATION TAX RECEIPT: Receipt given upon request

American Cancer Society Discovery Shop
720A Onstott Rd.
Yuba City, CA 95993
CONTACT: Lois Aldridge
PHONE: 916-755-3112
TYPE OF MERCHANDISE: Clothing, bric-a-brac
DONATION TAX RECEIPT: Receipt given upon request
COMMENTS: Monthly markdowns

Colorado

Salvation Army Thrift Store
9771 W. 55th Ave.
Arvada, CO 80003
TYPE OF MERCHANDISE: Clothing, housewares, furniture
DONATION TAX RECEIPT: Receipt given upon request

Salvation Army Thrift Store
15575 E. Colfax Ave.
Aurora, CO 80011
TYPE OF MERCHANDISE: Clothing, housewares, furniture
DONATION TAX RECEIPT: Receipt given upon request

Salvation Army Thrift Store
3280 28th St.
Boulder, CO 80301
TYPE OF MERCHANDISE: Clothing, housewares, furniture
DONATION TAX RECEIPT: Receipt given upon request

Goodwill Industries Thrift Store
149 N. Main St.
Brighton, CO 80601
TYPE OF MERCHANDISE: Clothing, housewares, furniture
DONATION TAX RECEIPT: Receipt given upon request

Salvation Army Thrift Store
30–50 N. Main St.
Brighton, CO 80601
TYPE OF MERCHANDISE: Clothing, housewares, furniture
DONATION TAX RECEIPT: Receipt given upon request

Salvation Army Thrift Store
310 Main St.
Canon City, CO 80911
TYPE OF MERCHANDISE: Clothing, housewares, furniture
DONATION TAX RECEIPT: Receipt given upon request

Salvation Army Thrift Store
103 N. Circle Dr.
Colorado Springs, CO 80909
TYPE OF MERCHANDISE: Clothing, housewares, furniture
DONATION TAX RECEIPT: Receipt given upon request

ARC Thrift Store Value Village
1119 N. Circle Dr.
Colorado Springs, CO 80909
TYPE OF MERCHANDISE: Clothing, housewares, furniture
DONATION TAX RECEIPT: Receipt given upon request

Goodwill Industries Thrift Store
2304 W. Colorado Ave.
Colorado Springs, CO 80904
TYPE OF MERCHANDISE: Clothing, housewares, furniture
DONATION TAX RECEIPT: Receipt given upon request

American Cancer Society Discovery Shop
2308 Wasatch Ave.
Colorado Springs, CO 8007
TYPE OF MERCHANDISE: Clothing, bric-a-brac
DONATION TAX RECEIPT: Receipt given upon request
COMMENTS: Monthly markdowns

Saint Vincent De Paul Thrift Store
2328 E. Platte Ave.
Colorado Springs, CO 80909
TYPE OF MERCHANDISE: Clothing, housewares, furniture
DONATION TAX RECEIPT: Receipt given upon request
COMMENTS: Monthly markdowns

Goodwill Industries Thrift Store
2501 E. Platte Ave.
Colorado Springs, CO 80909
TYPE OF MERCHANDISE: Clothing, housewares, furniture

DONATION TAX RECEIPT: Receipt given upon request

Goodwill Industries Thrift Store
324 E. Pikes Peak Ave.
Colorado Springs, CO 80903
TYPE OF MERCHANDISE: Clothing, housewares, furniture
DONATION TAX RECEIPT: Receipt given upon request

Goodwill Industries Thrift Store
326 Main St.
Colorado Springs, CO 80911
TYPE OF MERCHANDISE: Clothing, housewares, furniture
DONATION TAX RECEIPT: Receipt given upon request

Salvation Army Thrift Store
2222 W. Colorado Ave.
Colorado Springs, CO 80907
TYPE OF MERCHANDISE: Clothing, housewares, furniture
DONATION TAX RECEIPT: Receipt given upon request

Salvation Army Thrift Store
505 S. Weber St.
Colorado Springs, CO 80903
TYPE OF MERCHANDISE: Clothing, housewares, furniture
DONATION TAX RECEIPT: Receipt given upon request

Salvation Army Thrift Store
5620 S. Hwy. 85/87
Colorado Springs, CO 80911
TYPE OF MERCHANDISE: Clothing, housewares, furniture
DONATION TAX RECEIPT: Receipt given upon request

Disabled American Vets Thrift Store
7400 Hwy. 2
Commerce City, CO 80022
TYPE OF MERCHANDISE: Clothing, housewares, furniture
DONATION TAX RECEIPT: Receipt given upon request

Salvation Army Thrift Store
2205 E. Colfax
Denver, CO 80206
TYPE OF MERCHANDISE: Clothing, housewares, furniture

DONATION TAX RECEIPT: Receipt given upon request

Goodwill Industries Thrift Store
3181 W. Alameda Ave.
Denver, CO 80219
TYPE OF MERCHANDISE: Clothing, housewares, furniture
DONATION TAX RECEIPT: Receipt given upon request

Salvation Army Thrift Store
421 S. Federal Blvd.
Denver, CO 80223
TYPE OF MERCHANDISE: Clothing, housewares, furniture
DONATION TAX RECEIPT: Receipt given upon request

Salvation Army Thrift Store
4751 Broadway
Denver, CO 80216
PHONE: 303-294-0580
TYPE OF MERCHANDISE: Clothing, housewares, furniture
DONATION TAX RECEIPT: Receipt given upon request

Salvation Army Thrift Store
4845 Broadway
Denver, CO 80216
PHONE: 303-293-8574
TYPE OF MERCHANDISE: Clothing, housewares, furniture
DONATION TAX RECEIPT: Receipt given upon request

Junior League of Denver Inc.
6300 E. Yale Ave.
Denver, CO 80222
TYPE OF MERCHANDISE: Clothing, housewares, furniture
DONATION TAX RECEIPT: Receipt given upon request
COMMENTS: Toy sales

Disabled American Vets Thrift Store
8755 Washington St.
Denver, CO 80229
TYPE OF MERCHANDISE: Clothing, housewares, furniture
DONATION TAX RECEIPT: Receipt given upon request

Salvation Army Thrift Store
101 W. Floyd Ave.
Englewood, CO 80110
TYPE OF MERCHANDISE: Clothing,
housewares, furniture
DONATION TAX RECEIPT: Receipt given
upon request

Goodwill Industries Thrift Store
4011 S. Broadway
Englewood, CO 80110
TYPE OF MERCHANDISE: Clothing,
housewares, furniture
DONATION TAX RECEIPT: Receipt given
upon request

Goodwill Industries Thrift Store
320 Walnut St.
Fort Collins, CO 80524
TYPE OF MERCHANDISE: Clothing,
housewares, furniture
DONATION TAX RECEIPT: Receipt given
upon request

TVI Savers Thrift Store
4106 S. College Ave. Unit 100
Fort Collins, CO 80525
PHONE: 303-282-9446
TYPE OF MERCHANDISE: Clothing,
housewares, furniture
DONATION TAX RECEIPT: No

Salvation Army Thrift Store
5620 S. Hwy. 85–87
Fountain, CO 80817
TYPE OF MERCHANDISE: Clothing,
housewares, furniture
DONATION TAX RECEIPT: Receipt given
upon request

Rescue Mission Thrift Shop
1059 Main St.
Grand Junction, CO 81501
TYPE OF MERCHANDISE: Clothing,
housewares, furniture
DONATION TAX RECEIPT: Receipt given
upon request

Goodwill Industries Thrift Store
1012 11th St.
Greeley, CO 80631
TYPE OF MERCHANDISE: Clothing,
housewares, furniture
DONATION TAX RECEIPT: Receipt given
upon request

Salvation Army Thrift Store
1215 Eighth Ave.
Greeley, CO 80631
TYPE OF MERCHANDISE: Clothing,
housewares, furniture
DONATION TAX RECEIPT: Receipt given
upon request

MCC Crossroads Gift and Thrift
203 Colorado
La Junta, CO 81050
PHONE: 719-384-7551
TYPE OF MERCHANDISE: Clothing,
housewares, furniture
DONATION TAX RECEIPT: Receipt given
upon request

MCC More for Less
270 S. Pierce
Lakewood, CO 80226
TYPE OF MERCHANDISE: Clothing,
housewares, furniture
DONATION TAX RECEIPT: Receipt given
upon request

Salvation Army Thrift Store
516 Main St.
Longmont, CO 80501
TYPE OF MERCHANDISE: Clothing,
housewares, furniture
DONATION TAX RECEIPT: Receipt given
upon request

Salvation Army Thrift Store
421 E. 4th St.
Loveland, CO 80537
PHONE: 970-667-5042
TYPE OF MERCHANDISE: Clothing,
housewares, furniture
DONATION TAX RECEIPT: Receipt given
upon request

Goodwill Industries Thrift Store
111 Lincoln St.
Pueblo, CO 81004
PHONE: 719-542-1922
HOURS: Mon.–Sat. 10–5
TYPE OF MERCHANDISE: Clothing,
housewares, furniture
DONATION TAX RECEIPT: Receipt given
upon request

Salvation Army Thrift Store
1625 Prairie Ave.
Pueblo, CO 81003
TYPE OF MERCHANDISE: Clothing,
housewares, furniture
DONATION TAX RECEIPT: Receipt given
upon request

Goodwill Industries Thrift Store
250 S. Santa Fe Ave.
Pueblo, CO 81003
PHONE: 719-543-4483
HOURS: Mon.–Sat. 10–5
TYPE OF MERCHANDISE: Clothing,
housewares, furniture
DONATION TAX RECEIPT: Receipt given
upon request

Salvation Army Thrift Store
2639 Elizabeth St.
Pueblo, CO 81003
TYPE OF MERCHANDISE: Clothing,
housewares, furniture
DONATION TAX RECEIPT: Receipt given
upon request

Salvation Army Thrift Store
880 E. 88th Ave.
Thornton, CO
TYPE OF MERCHANDISE: Clothing,
housewares, furniture
DONATION TAX RECEIPT: Receipt given
upon request

Connecticut

Salvation Army Thrift Store
1174 E. Main St.
Bridgeport, CT 06608
TYPE OF MERCHANDISE: Clothing,
housewares, furniture
DONATION TAX RECEIPT: Receipt given
upon request

Salvation Army Thrift Store
1313 Connecticut Ave.
Bridgeport, CT 06607
TYPE OF MERCHANDISE: Clothing,
housewares, furniture
DONATION TAX RECEIPT: Receipt given
upon request

Salvation Army Thrift Store
30 Fairfield Ave.
Bridgeport, CT 06604
TYPE OF MERCHANDISE: Clothing,
housewares, furniture
DONATION TAX RECEIPT: Receipt given
upon request

Salvation Army Thrift Store
25 Collins Rd.
Bristol, CT 06010
TYPE OF MERCHANDISE: Clothing,
housewares, furniture
DONATION TAX RECEIPT: Receipt given
upon request

Salvation Army Thrift Store
129 Main St.
Danbury, CT 06810
TYPE OF MERCHANDISE: Clothing,
housewares, furniture
DONATION TAX RECEIPT: Receipt given
upon request

Salvation Army Thrift Store
465B Main St.
East Hartford, CT 06118
TYPE OF MERCHANDISE: Clothing,
housewares, furniture
DONATION TAX RECEIPT: Receipt given
upon request

Salvation Army Thrift Store
565 Enfield St.
Enfield, CT 06082
TYPE OF MERCHANDISE: Clothing,
housewares, furniture
DONATION TAX RECEIPT: Receipt given
upon request

Salvation Army Thrift Store
2834 Fairfield Ave.
Fairfield, CT 06430
TYPE OF MERCHANDISE: Clothing,
housewares, furniture
DONATION TAX RECEIPT: Receipt given
upon request

Salvation Army Thrift Store
1359 Dixwell Ave.
Hamden, CT 06514
TYPE OF MERCHANDISE: Clothing,
housewares, furniture

DONATION TAX RECEIPT: Receipt given
upon request

Goodwill Industries Thrift Store
163 Washington St.
Hartford, CT 06106
HOURS: Mon.–Sat. 9–5
TYPE OF MERCHANDISE: Clothing,
housewares, furniture
DONATION TAX RECEIPT: Receipt given
upon request

Salvation Army Thrift Store
333 Homestead Ave.
Hartford, CT 06112
TYPE OF MERCHANDISE: Clothing,
housewares, furniture
DONATION TAX RECEIPT: Receipt given
upon request

Salvation Army Thrift Store
385 Broad St.
Manchester, CT 06040
TYPE OF MERCHANDISE: Clothing,
housewares, furniture
DONATION TAX RECEIPT: Receipt given
upon request

Salvation Army Thrift Store
Rte. 195/College Mart
Mansfield, CT 06250
TYPE OF MERCHANDISE: Clothing,
housewares, furniture
DONATION TAX RECEIPT: Receipt given
upon request

Salvation Army Thrift Store
537 Washington St.
Middletown, CT 06457
TYPE OF MERCHANDISE: Clothing,
housewares, furniture
DONATION TAX RECEIPT: Receipt given
upon request

Goodwill Industries Thrift Store
82 New Haven Ave.
Milford, CT 06460
TYPE OF MERCHANDISE: Clothing,
housewares, furniture
DONATION TAX RECEIPT: Receipt given
upon request

Goodwill Industries Thrift Store
148 E. Main St.
New Britain, CT 06051

TYPE OF MERCHANDISE: Clothing,
housewares, furniture
DONATION TAX RECEIPT: Receipt given
upon request

Salvation Army Thrift Store
165 Arch St.
New Britain, CT 06050
TYPE OF MERCHANDISE: Clothing,
housewares, furniture
DONATION TAX RECEIPT: Receipt given
upon request

Salvation Army Thrift Store
240 Grand Ave.
New Haven, CT 06513
TYPE OF MERCHANDISE: Clothing,
housewares, furniture
DONATION TAX RECEIPT: Receipt given
upon request

Salvation Army Thrift Store
274 Crown St.
New Haven, CT 06511
TYPE OF MERCHANDISE: Clothing,
housewares, furniture
DONATION TAX RECEIPT: Receipt given
upon request

Goodwill Industries Thrift Store
887 Grand Ave.
New Haven, CT 06511
TYPE OF MERCHANDISE: Clothing,
housewares, furniture
DONATION TAX RECEIPT: Receipt given
upon request

Salvation Army Thrift Store
170 Bank St.
New London, CT 06320
TYPE OF MERCHANDISE: Clothing,
housewares, furniture
DONATION TAX RECEIPT: Receipt given
upon request

Salvation Army Thrift Store
3261 Berlin Turnpike
Newington, CT 06111
TYPE OF MERCHANDISE: Clothing,
housewares, furniture
DONATION TAX RECEIPT: Receipt given
upon request

Goodwill Industries Thrift Store
515 Wall Ave.
Norwalk, CT 06850
TYPE OF MERCHANDISE: Clothing,
housewares, furniture
DONATION TAX RECEIPT: Receipt given
upon request
Goodwill Industries Thrift Store
688 Boston Post Rd.
Old Saybrook, CT 06475
TYPE OF MERCHANDISE: Clothing,
housewares, furniture
DONATION TAX RECEIPT: Receipt given
upon request
Salvation Army Thrift Store
212 Boston Post Rd.
Orange, CT
TYPE OF MERCHANDISE: Clothing,
housewares, furniture
DONATION TAX RECEIPT: Receipt given
upon request
Salvation Army Thrift Store
166 Union St.
Rockville, CT 06066
TYPE OF MERCHANDISE: Clothing,
housewares, furniture
DONATION TAX RECEIPT: Receipt given
upon request
Salvation Army Thrift Store
896 Washington Blvd.
Stamford, CT 06904
TYPE OF MERCHANDISE: Clothing,
housewares, furniture
DONATION TAX RECEIPT: Receipt given
upon request
Salvation Army Thrift Store
57 Main St.
Torrington, CT 06790
TYPE OF MERCHANDISE: Clothing,
housewares, furniture
DONATION TAX RECEIPT: Receipt given
upon request
Salvation Army Thrift Store
284 S. Colony Rd.
Wallingford, CT 06492
TYPE OF MERCHANDISE: Clothing,
housewares, furniture

DONATION TAX RECEIPT: Receipt given
upon request
Salvation Army Thrift Store
96 Grove St.
Waterbury, CT 06710
TYPE OF MERCHANDISE: Clothing,
housewares, furniture
DONATION TAX RECEIPT: Receipt given
upon request
Salvation Army Thrift Store
160 Shield St.
West Hartford, CT 06110
TYPE OF MERCHANDISE: Clothing,
housewares, furniture
DONATION TAX RECEIPT: Receipt given
upon request
Salvation Army Thrift Store
530 Windsor Ave.
Windsor, CT 06095
TYPE OF MERCHANDISE: Clothing,
housewares, furniture
DONATION TAX RECEIPT: Receipt given
upon request

Delaware

Salvation Army Thrift Store
1056 S. Dupont Hwy.
Dover, DE 19901
TYPE OF MERCHANDISE: Clothing,
housewares, furniture
DONATION TAX RECEIPT: Receipt given
upon request
Salvation Army Thrift Store
21 Commerce St.
Harrington, DE 19952
TYPE OF MERCHANDISE: Clothing,
housewares, furniture
DONATION TAX RECEIPT: Receipt given
upon request
Salvation Army Thrift Store
117 S.E. Front St.
Milford, DE 19963
TYPE OF MERCHANDISE: Clothing,
housewares, furniture
DONATION TAX RECEIPT: Receipt given
upon request

Goodwill Industries Thrift Store
200 New Castle Ave.
New Castle, DE 19720
TYPE OF MERCHANDISE: Clothing,
housewares, furniture
DONATION TAX RECEIPT: Receipt given
upon request

Goodwill Industries Thrift Store
136 E. Main St.
Newark, DE 19711
TYPE OF MERCHANDISE: Clothing,
housewares, furniture
DONATION TAX RECEIPT: Receipt given
upon request

Salvation Army Thrift Store
245 Elkton Rd.
Newark, DE 19711
TYPE OF MERCHANDISE: Clothing,
housewares, furniture
DONATION TAX RECEIPT: Receipt given
upon request

Salvation Army Thrift Store
16 W. Mt. Vernon St.
Smyrna, DE 19977
TYPE OF MERCHANDISE: Clothing,
housewares, furniture
DONATION TAX RECEIPT: Receipt given
upon request

Goodwill Industries Thrift Store
1015 W. Fourth St.
Wilmington, DE 19805
TYPE OF MERCHANDISE: Clothing,
housewares, furniture
DONATION TAX RECEIPT: Receipt given
upon request

Salvation Army Thrift Store
107 S. Market St.
Wilmington, DE 19801
TYPE OF MERCHANDISE: Clothing,
housewares, furniture
DONATION TAX RECEIPT: Receipt given
upon request

Goodwill Industries Thrift Store
301 S. Maryland Ave.
Wilmington, DE 19804
TYPE OF MERCHANDISE: Clothing,
housewares, furniture

DONATION TAX RECEIPT: Receipt given
upon request

Salvation Army Thrift Store
604 Market St.
Wilmington, DE 19801
TYPE OF MERCHANDISE: Clothing,
housewares, furniture
DONATION TAX RECEIPT: Receipt given
upon request

District of Columbia

American Rescue Workers Thrift Shop
1019 H St. NE
Washington, DC 20002
PHONE: 202-396-9823
HOURS: Mon.–Sat. 9–4:45
DONATION TAX RECEIPT: Check with store
policy
COMMENTS: Donations during shop hours

Goodwill Industries Thrift Store
2200 S. Dakota Ave. NE
Washington, DC 20018
PHONE: 202-636-4225
HOURS: Mon.–Sat. 10–6, Sun. 12–6
TYPE OF MERCHANDISE: Clothing,
housewares, furniture
DONATION TAX RECEIPT: Receipt given
upon request

Junior League Shop
3066 M St. NW
Washington, DC 20007
PHONE: 202-337-6120
HOURS: Mon.–Sat. 10–5, Sun. 12–5
TYPE OF MERCHANDISE: Clothing for men,
women, and children
DONATION TAX RECEIPT: Receipt given
upon request

Amvets Thrift Store
6101 Georgia Ave. NW
Washington, DC 20011
TYPE OF MERCHANDISE: Clothing, bric-a-
brac
DONATION TAX RECEIPT: Receipt given
upon request

American Rescue Workers Thrift Shop
745 Eighth St. SE
Washington, DC 20002

PHONE: 202-547-9701
HOURS: Mon.–Sat. 9–4:45
TYPE OF MERCHANDISE: Clothing, housewares
DONATION TAX RECEIPT: Check with store policy

Florida

Goodwill Industries Thrift Store
1350 W. Church St.
Bartow, FL 33830
CONTACT: Della Bumjardner
PHONE: 813-533-5961
HOURS: Mon.–Sat. 9–7, Sun. 1–5
TYPE OF MERCHANDISE: Clothing, housewares, furniture
DONATION TAX RECEIPT: Receipt given upon request
COMMENTS: Holiday and special sales
Goodwill Industries Thrift Store
241 S. Main St.
Belle Glade, FL 33430
TYPE OF MERCHANDISE: Clothing, housewares, furniture
DONATION TAX RECEIPT: Receipt given upon request
Salvation Army Thrift Store
518 E. Ocean Ave.
Boynton Beach, FL 33435
TYPE OF MERCHANDISE: Clothing, housewares, furniture
DONATION TAX RECEIPT: Receipt given upon request
Saint Vincent De Paul Thrift Store
1426 14th St.
Bradenton, FL 33505
TYPE OF MERCHANDISE: Clothing, housewares, furniture
DONATION TAX RECEIPT: Receipt given upon request
COMMENTS: Monthly markdowns
Salvation Army Thrift Store
2415 14th Street W
Bradenton, FL 34205
PHONE: 813-746-8157
HOURS: Mon.–Sat. 9–5
TYPE OF MERCHANDISE: Clothing, housewares, furniture

DONATION TAX RECEIPT: Receipt given upon request
COMMENTS: Half-price sales
Goodwill Industries Thrift Store
5138 Cortez Rd. W
Bradenton, FL 34210
TYPE OF MERCHANDISE: Clothing, housewares, furniture
DONATION TAX RECEIPT: Receipt given upon request
Junior League Thrift Shop
20 E. Liberty St.
Brooksville, FL 34601
TYPE OF MERCHANDISE: Clothing for men, women, and children
DONATION TAX RECEIPT: Receipt given upon request
Goodwill Industries Thrift Store
34 Brook Plaza
Brooksville, FL 34601
TYPE OF MERCHANDISE: Clothing, housewares, furniture
DONATION TAX RECEIPT: Receipt given upon request
Saint Vincent De Paul Thrift Store
101 N. Fort Harrison Ave.
Clearwater, FL 34615
TYPE OF MERCHANDISE: Clothing, housewares, furniture
DONATION TAX RECEIPT: Receipt given upon request
COMMENTS: Monthly markdowns
Salvation Army Thrift Store
1446 S. Missouri Ave.
Clearwater, FL 34616
PHONE: 813-447-1913
HOURS: Mon.–Sat. 9–5
TYPE OF MERCHANDISE: Clothing, housewares, furniture
DONATION TAX RECEIPT: Receipt given upon request
COMMENTS: Half-price sales
Goodwill Industries Thrift Store
108 E. Sugarland Hwy.
Clewiston, FL 33440
TYPE OF MERCHANDISE: Clothing, housewares, furniture
DONATION TAX RECEIPT: Receipt given upon request

Goodwill Industries Thrift Store
109 Maryland Ave.
Cocoa, FL 32922
TYPE OF MERCHANDISE: Clothing,
housewares, furniture
DONATION TAX RECEIPT: Receipt given
upon request

Junior League Encore Shop
2325 Salzedo St.
Coral Gables, FL 33134
CONTACT: Mildred Helms
PHONE: 305-444-2660
HOURS: Mon.–Sat. 10–4
TYPE OF MERCHANDISE: Clothing,
housewares, toys
DONATION TAX RECEIPT: Receipt given
upon request
COMMENTS: Annual rummage sale in
November

Goodwill Industries Thrift Store
650 N. Suncoast Blvd.
Crystal River, FL 34429
TYPE OF MERCHANDISE: Clothing,
housewares, furniture
DONATION TAX RECEIPT: Receipt given
upon request

Junior League Thrift Shop
122 S. Palmetto Ave.
Daytona Beach, FL 32114
TYPE OF MERCHANDISE: Clothing for men,
women, and children
DONATION TAX RECEIPT: Receipt given
upon request

Junior League Thrift Shop
200 Orange Ave.
Daytona Beach, FL 32114
HOURS: Mon.–Sat. 9:30–4
TYPE OF MERCHANDISE: Clothing,
housewares, furniture
DONATION TAX RECEIPT: Receipt given
upon request

Junior League Service Village
233 N. Amelia Ave.
Deland, FL 32724
TYPE OF MERCHANDISE: Clothing for men,
women, and children
DONATION TAX RECEIPT: Receipt given
upon request

Junior League Thrift Shop
1428 N.E. 26th St.
Fort Lauderdale, FL 33305
TYPE OF MERCHANDISE: Clothing for men,
women, and children
DONATION TAX RECEIPT: Receipt given
upon request

Saint Vincent De Paul Thrift Store
513 W. Broward Blvd.
Fort Lauderdale, FL 33312
TYPE OF MERCHANDISE: Clothing,
housewares, furniture
DONATION TAX RECEIPT: Receipt given
upon request
COMMENTS: Monthly markdowns

Salvation Army Thrift Store
1801 W. Broward Blvd.
Fort Lauderdale, FL 33312
HOURS: Mon.–Sat. 9–8
TYPE OF MERCHANDISE: Clothing,
housewares, furniture
DONATION TAX RECEIPT: Receipt given
upon request

Goodwill Industries Thrift Store
1919 N. Tamiami
Fort Myers, FL 33903
TYPE OF MERCHANDISE: Clothing,
housewares, furniture
DONATION TAX RECEIPT: Receipt given
upon request

Saint Vincent De Paul Thrift Store
2200 First St.
Fort Myers, FL 33901
TYPE OF MERCHANDISE: Clothing,
housewares, furniture
DONATION TAX RECEIPT: Receipt given
upon request
COMMENTS: Monthly markdowns

Salvation Army Thrift Store
3051 Fowler St.
Fort Myers, FL 33901
TYPE OF MERCHANDISE: Clothing,
housewares, furniture
DONATION TAX RECEIPT: Receipt given
upon request

Goodwill Industries Thrift Store
3738 Palm Beach Blvd.
Fort Myers, FL 33916

TYPE OF MERCHANDISE: Clothing, housewares, furniture
DONATION TAX RECEIPT: Receipt given upon request

Goodwill Industries Thrift Store
4525 Del Prado Blvd. S
Fort Myers, FL 33904
TYPE OF MERCHANDISE: Clothing, housewares, furniture
DONATION TAX RECEIPT: Receipt given upon request

LARC Thrift Store
905 Pondella Rd.
Fort Myers, FL 33903
TYPE OF MERCHANDISE: Clothing, housewares, furniture
DONATION TAX RECEIPT: Receipt given upon request

Goodwill Industries Thrift Store
3130 S. Federal Hwy.
Fort Pierce, FL 34982
TYPE OF MERCHANDISE: Clothing, housewares, furniture
DONATION TAX RECEIPT: Receipt given upon request

Salvation Army Thrift Store
701 Orange Ave.
Fort Pierce, FL 34950
TYPE OF MERCHANDISE: Clothing, housewares, furniture
DONATION TAX RECEIPT: Receipt given upon request

Salvation Army Thrift Store
86 Eglin Pkwy. NE
Fort Walton Beach, FL 32548
TYPE OF MERCHANDISE: Clothing, housewares, furniture
DONATION TAX RECEIPT: Receipt given upon request

Junior League Thrift Shop
430 N. Main St.
Gainesville, FL 32601
TYPE OF MERCHANDISE: Clothing for men, women, and children
DONATION TAX RECEIPT: Receipt given upon request

Goodwill Industries Thrift Store
716 N. Main St.
Gainesville, FL 32601
TYPE OF MERCHANDISE: Clothing, housewares, furniture
DONATION TAX RECEIPT: Receipt given upon request

Goodwill Industries Thrift Store
107 Sixth St.
Haines City, FL 33844
CONTACT: Erma Sams
PHONE: 813-422-3397
HOURS: Mon.–Sat. 9–5, Sun. 1–5 except summer
TYPE OF MERCHANDISE: Clothing, housewares, furniture
DONATION TAX RECEIPT: Receipt given upon request
COMMENTS: Holiday and special sales

Goodwill Industries Thrift Store
461 Palm Ave.
Hialeah, FL 33010
TYPE OF MERCHANDISE: Clothing, housewares, furniture
DONATION TAX RECEIPT: Receipt given upon request

Salvation Army Thrift Store
7802 N.W. 103rd
CROSS STREET: Palmetto X Way
Hialeah Gardens, FL 33016
PHONE: 305-819-4146
HOURS: Mon.–Sat. 9–5
TYPE OF MERCHANDISE: Clothing, housewares, furniture
DONATION TAX RECEIPT: Receipt given upon request

Salvation Army Thrift Store
2225 US 19
Holiday, FL 34691
PHONE: 813-937-7841
HOURS: Mon.–Sat. 9–5
TYPE OF MERCHANDISE: Clothing, housewares, furniture
DONATION TAX RECEIPT: Receipt given upon request
COMMENTS: Half-price sales

Goodwill Industries Thrift Store
1577 Nova Rd.
Hollyhill, FL 32117
PHONE: 904-257-3247
HOURS: Mon.–Sat. 9–8, Sun. 12–5
TYPE OF MERCHANDISE: Clothing,
housewares, furniture
DONATION TAX RECEIPT: Receipt given
upon request

Saint Vincent De Paul Thrift Store
1090 S.W. 56th Ave.
Hollywood, FL 33023
TYPE OF MERCHANDISE: Clothing,
housewares, furniture
DONATION TAX RECEIPT: Receipt given
upon request
COMMENTS: Monthly markdowns

Saint Vincent De Paul Thrift Store
3037 Johnson St.
Hollywood, FL 33020
TYPE OF MERCHANDISE: Clothing,
housewares, furniture
DONATION TAX RECEIPT: Receipt given
upon request
COMMENTS: Monthly markdowns

Salvation Army Thrift Store
28610 S.W. 157th Ave.
Homestead, FL 33033
TYPE OF MERCHANDISE: Clothing,
housewares, furniture
DONATION TAX RECEIPT: Receipt given
upon request

Goodwill Industries Thrift Store
32 S. Krome Ave.
Homestead, FL 33030
TYPE OF MERCHANDISE: Clothing,
housewares, furniture
DONATION TAX RECEIPT: Receipt given
upon request

Goodwill Industries Thrift Store
206 N. Third St.
Immokalee, FL 33934
TYPE OF MERCHANDISE: Clothing,
housewares, furniture
DONATION TAX RECEIPT: Receipt given
upon request

Salvation Army Thrift Store
10900 Beach Blvd.
Jacksonville, FL 32246
CONTACT: Bill Keskey
PHONE: 904-645-3919
FAX: 904-645-5815
HOURS: Mon.–Sat. 9–6
TYPE OF MERCHANDISE: Clothing,
housewares, furniture
DONATION TAX RECEIPT: Receipt given
upon request

Goodwill Industries Thrift Store
130 Sixth Ave. N
Jacksonville, FL 32250
TYPE OF MERCHANDISE: Clothing,
housewares, furniture
DONATION TAX RECEIPT: Receipt given
upon request

Rescue Mission Thrift Store
1714 N. Main St.
Jacksonville, FL 32206
TYPE OF MERCHANDISE: Clothing,
housewares, furniture
DONATION TAX RECEIPT: Receipt given
upon request

Rescue Mission City
234 W. State St.
Jacksonville, FL 32202
CONTACTS: Rev. Billy Fox, Virginia
Crawford
TYPE OF MERCHANDISE: Clothing,
housewares, furniture
DONATION TAX RECEIPT: Receipt given
upon request

Rescue Mission City Thrift
910 Edgewood Ave. N
Jacksonville, FL 32254
TYPE OF MERCHANDISE: Clothing,
housewares, furniture
DONATION TAX RECEIPT: Receipt given
upon request

Goodwill Industries Thrift Store
1363 E. Vine St.
Kissimmee, FL 34744
PHONE: 407-933-0002
HOURS: Mon.–Sat. 9–8, Sun. 12–5
TYPE OF MERCHANDISE: Clothing,
housewares, furniture

DONATION TAX RECEIPT: Receipt given upon request

Goodwill Industries Thrift Store
901 N. Marion St.
Lake City, FL 32055
TYPE OF MERCHANDISE: Clothing, housewares, furniture
DONATION TAX RECEIPT: Receipt given upon request

Goodwill Industries Thrift Store
204 E. Interlake Blvd.
Lake Placid, FL 33852
CONTACT: Ray Roberts
PHONE: 813-465-6566
HOURS: Mon.–Sat. 9–6
TYPE OF MERCHANDISE: Clothing, housewares, furniture
DONATION TAX RECEIPT: Receipt given upon request
COMMENTS: Holiday and special sales

Junior League Thrift Shop
2884 S. Military Trl.
Lake Worth, FL 33463
TYPE OF MERCHANDISE: Clothing for men, women, and children
DONATION TAX RECEIPT: Receipt given upon request

Goodwill Industries Thrift Store
3199 US 98 N
Lakeland, FL 33805
TYPE OF MERCHANDISE: Clothing, housewares, furniture
DONATION TAX RECEIPT: Receipt given upon request

Goodwill Industries Thrift Store
4125 US 98 N
Lakeland, FL 33809
CONTACT: Sandy Fairless
PHONE: 813-858-6999
HOURS: Mon.–Sat. 9–9, Sun. 1–5
TYPE OF MERCHANDISE: Clothing, housewares, furniture
DONATION TAX RECEIPT: Receipt given upon request
COMMENTS: Holiday and special sales

Goodwill Industries Thrift Store
4620 S. Florida Ave.
Lakeland, FL 33813

CONTACT: Jean Duncan
PHONE: 813-644-7036
HOURS: Mon.–Sat. 9–7, Sun. 1–5
TYPE OF MERCHANDISE: Clothing, housewares, furniture
DONATION TAX RECEIPT: Receipt given upon request
COMMENTS: Daily special sales and holiday sales

Salvation Army Thrift Store
717 N. Florida Ave.
Lakeland, FL 33801
TYPE OF MERCHANDISE: Clothing, housewares, furniture
DONATION TAX RECEIPT: Receipt given upon request

American Cancer Society Discovery Shop
12551 Indiana Rocks Rd. Suite #14
Largo, FL 34644
CONTACT: Pamela Roper
PHONE: 813-593-2606
TYPE OF MERCHANDISE: Clothing, bric-a-brac
DONATION TAX RECEIPT: Receipt given upon request
COMMENTS: Monthly markdowns

Goodwill Industries Thrift Store
10601 C-113 US Hwy. 441
Leesburg, FL 34788
PHONE: 904-728-3488
HOURS: Mon.–Sat. 9–8, Sun. 12–5
TYPE OF MERCHANDISE: Clothing, housewares, furniture
DONATION TAX RECEIPT: Receipt given upon request

Goodwill Industries Thrift Store
821 S. Highway 17-92 Suite 101
Longwood, FL 32750
PHONE: 407-695-3800
HOURS: Mon.–Sat. 9–8, Sun. 12–5
TYPE OF MERCHANDISE: Clothing, housewares, furniture
DONATION TAX RECEIPT: Receipt given upon request

Goodwill Industries Thrift Store
821 US 17-92
Maitland, FL 32751

TYPE OF MERCHANDISE: Clothing, housewares, furniture
DONATION TAX RECEIPT: Receipt given upon request

Salvation Army Thrift Store
1757 Overseas Hwy.
Marathon, FL 33050
TYPE OF MERCHANDISE: Clothing, housewares, furniture
DONATION TAX RECEIPT: Receipt given upon request

Salvation Army Thrift Store
320 S. State Rd.
Margate, FL
PHONE: 305-979-6999
HOURS: Mon.–Sat. 9–4
TYPE OF MERCHANDISE: Clothing, housewares, furniture
DONATION TAX RECEIPT: Receipt given upon request

Goodwill Industries Thrift Store
104 N. Jefferson St.
Marianna, FL 32446
TYPE OF MERCHANDISE: Clothing, housewares, furniture
DONATION TAX RECEIPT: Receipt given upon request

Salvation Army Thrift Store
1080 Hickory St.
Melbourne, FL 32901-1958
TYPE OF MERCHANDISE: Clothing, housewares, furniture
DONATION TAX RECEIPT: Receipt given upon request

Goodwill Industries Thrift Store
1894 N. Wickham Rd.
Melbourne, FL 32909
PHONE: 407-259-1875
HOURS: Mon.–Sat. 9–8, Sun. 12–5
TYPE OF MERCHANDISE: Clothing, housewares, furniture
DONATION TAX RECEIPT: Receipt given upon request

Saint Vincent De Paul Thrift Store
12003 N.W. Seventh Ave.
Miami, FL 33168
TYPE OF MERCHANDISE: Clothing, housewares, furniture

DONATION TAX RECEIPT: Receipt given upon request
COMMENTS: Monthly markdowns

Salvation Army Thrift Store
28610 S.W. 15th Ave.
CROSS STREET: S. Dixie Hwy. (US 1)
Miami, FL 33033
PHONE: 305-247-5477
HOURS: Mon.–Sat. 9–8
TYPE OF MERCHANDISE: Clothing, housewares, furniture
DONATION TAX RECEIPT: Receipt given upon request

Salvation Army Thrift Store
5600 N.W. 7th Ave.
CROSS STREET: 56th St.
Miami, FL 33127
PHONE: 305-757-1316
HOURS: Mon.–Sat. 9–5
TYPE OF MERCHANDISE: Clothing, housewares, furniture
DONATION TAX RECEIPT: Receipt given upon request

Salvation Army Thrift Store
8001 N.W. 27th Ave.
CROSS STREET: N.W. 79th St.
Miami, FL 33147
PHONE: 305-836-8088
HOURS: Mon.–Sat. 9–8
TYPE OF MERCHANDISE: Clothing, housewares, furniture
DONATION TAX RECEIPT: Receipt given upon request

Salvation Army Thrift Store
90 N.W. 23rd St.
CROSS STREET: N. Miami Ave.
Miami, FL 33127
PHONE: 305-573-4200
FAX: 305-573-4208
HOURS: Mon.–Sat. 9–5
TYPE OF MERCHANDISE: Clothing, housewares, furniture
DONATION TAX RECEIPT: Receipt given upon request

Salvation Army Thrift Store
9790 S.W. Bird Rd.
CROSS STREETS: Bird Rd. (S.W. 40th and 97th Ave.)

Miami, FL 33165
PHONE: 305-554-9669
HOURS: Mon.–Sat. 9–8:30
TYPE OF MERCHANDISE: Clothing,
housewares, furniture
DONATION TAX RECEIPT: Receipt given
upon request
Salvation Army Thrift Store
104 Willing St.
Milton, FL 32570
TYPE OF MERCHANDISE: Clothing,
housewares, furniture
DONATION TAX RECEIPT: Receipt given
upon request
NCJW Thrift Shop
12900 W. Dixie Hwy.
N. Miami, FL 33161
PHONE: 305-891-6872
FAX: 305-893-0621
HOURS: Tues.–Sat. 10–5
TYPE OF MERCHANDISE: Clothing,
housewares, furniture
DONATION TAX RECEIPT: Receipt given
upon request
COMMENTS: Profits go toward helping the
disadvantaged
Goodwill Industries Thrift Store
2795 Davis Blvd.
Naples, FL 33942
TYPE OF MERCHANDISE: Clothing,
housewares, furniture
DONATION TAX RECEIPT: Receipt given
upon request
Saint Vincent De Paul Thrift Store
3196 Davis Blvd.
Naples, FL 33942
TYPE OF MERCHANDISE: Clothing,
housewares, furniture
DONATION TAX RECEIPT: Receipt given
upon request
COMMENTS: Monthly markdowns
Salvation Army Thrift Store
40 12th St. S
Naples, FL 33940
TYPE OF MERCHANDISE: Clothing,
housewares, furniture
DONATION TAX RECEIPT: Receipt given
upon request

Goodwill Industries Thrift Store
2920 W. Silver Springs Blvd.
Ocala, FL 34475
TYPE OF MERCHANDISE: Clothing,
housewares, furniture
DONATION TAX RECEIPT: Receipt given
upon request
Goodwill Industries Thrift Store
11636 E. Colonial Drive
Orlando, FL 32817
PHONE: 407-277-4999
HOURS: Mon.–Sat. 9–8, Sun. 12–5
TYPE OF MERCHANDISE: Clothing,
housewares, furniture
DONATION TAX RECEIPT: Receipt given
upon request
Goodwill Industries Thrift Store
2806 N. Hiawassee Rd.
Orlando, FL 32818
PHONE: 407-578-8826
HOURS: Mon.–Sat. 9–8, Sun. 12–5
TYPE OF MERCHANDISE: Clothing,
housewares, furniture
DONATION TAX RECEIPT: Receipt given
upon request
Salvation Army Thrift Store
3955 W. Colonial Dr.
Orlando, FL 32808
CONTACT: Delmar Taylor
TYPE OF MERCHANDISE: Clothing,
housewares, furniture
DONATION TAX RECEIPT: Receipt given
upon request
Goodwill Industries Thrift Store
6400 S. Orange Ave.
Orlando, FL 32809
PHONE: 407-859-4750
HOURS: Mon.–Sat. 8:30–5, Sun. 12–5
TYPE OF MERCHANDISE: Clothing,
housewares, furniture
DONATION TAX RECEIPT: Receipt given
upon request
Saint Vincent De Paul Thrift Store
7339 E. Colonial Dr.
Orlando, FL 32807
TYPE OF MERCHANDISE: Clothing,
housewares, furniture

DONATION TAX RECEIPT: Receipt given
upon request
COMMENTS: Monthly markdowns
American Cancer Society Discovery Shop
107 S. County Rd.
Palm Beach, FL 33480
TYPE OF MERCHANDISE: Clothing, bric-a-
brac
DONATION TAX RECEIPT: Receipt given
upon request
COMMENTS: Monthly markdowns
Goodwill Industries Thrift Store
1210 US 301
Palmetto, FL 34221
TYPE OF MERCHANDISE: Clothing,
housewares, furniture
DONATION TAX RECEIPT: Receipt given
upon request
Salvation Army Thrift Store
401 E. Sixth St.
Panama City, FL 32401
TYPE OF MERCHANDISE: Clothing,
housewares, furniture
DONATION TAX RECEIPT: Receipt given
upon request
Goodwill Industries Thrift Store
5306 US 98 E
Panama City, FL 32404
TYPE OF MERCHANDISE: Clothing,
housewares, furniture
DONATION TAX RECEIPT: Receipt given
upon request
Saint Vincent De Paul Thrift Store
2200 W. Desoto St.
Pensacola, FL 32505
TYPE OF MERCHANDISE: Clothing,
housewares, furniture
DONATION TAX RECEIPT: Receipt given
upon request
COMMENTS: Monthly markdowns
Goodwill Industries Thrift Store
7601 Park Blvd.
Pinellas Park, FL 34665
TYPE OF MERCHANDISE: Clothing,
housewares, furniture
DONATION TAX RECEIPT: Receipt given
upon request

Goodwill Industries Thrift Store
901 State 60 W
Plant City, FL 33567
TYPE OF MERCHANDISE: Clothing,
housewares, furniture
DONATION TAX RECEIPT: Receipt given
upon request
Saint Vincent De Paul Thrift Store
2323 N. Dixie Hwy.
Pompano Beach, FL 33060
TYPE OF MERCHANDISE: Clothing,
housewares, furniture
DONATION TAX RECEIPT: Receipt given
upon request
COMMENTS: Monthly markdowns
Salvation Army Thrift Store
451 Copans Rd.
Pompano Beach, FL 33064
PHONE: 305-782-3925
HOURS: Mon.–Sat. 9–6
TYPE OF MERCHANDISE: Clothing,
housewares, furniture
DONATION TAX RECEIPT: Receipt given
upon request
COMMENTS: Yard sales held every other
Saturday
Salvation Army Thrift Store
6009 Ridge Rd.
Port Richey, FL 34668
PHONE: 813-847-0264
HOURS: Mon.–Sat. 9–5
TYPE OF MERCHANDISE: Furniture,
clothing, collectibles
DONATION TAX RECEIPT: Receipt given
upon request
COMMENTS: Half-price sales
Saint Vincent De Paul Thrift Store
7944 Grand Blvd.
Port Richey, FL 34668
TYPE OF MERCHANDISE: Clothing,
housewares, furniture
DONATION TAX RECEIPT: Receipt given
upon request
COMMENTS: Monthly markdowns
Goodwill Industries Thrift Store
1117 W. Jefferson St.
Quincy, FL 32351

TYPE OF MERCHANDISE: Clothing, housewares, furniture
DONATION TAX RECEIPT: Receipt given upon request
Saint Vincent De Paul Thrift Store
2647 Old Dixie Hwy.
Riviera Beach, FL 33404
TYPE OF MERCHANDISE: Clothing, housewares, furniture
DONATION TAX RECEIPT: Receipt given upon request
COMMENTS: Monthly markdowns
Goodwill Industries Thrift Store
11 Seventh Ave. NE
Ruskin, FL 33570
TYPE OF MERCHANDISE: Clothing, housewares, furniture
DONATION TAX RECEIPT: Receipt given upon request
Junior League Thrift Shop
670 Central Ave.
St. Petersburg, FL 33701
TYPE OF MERCHANDISE: Clothing for men, women, and children
DONATION TAX RECEIPT: Receipt given upon request
Salvation Army Thrift Store
4311 34th St.
St. Petersburg, FL 33711
PHONE: 813-866-7619
HOURS: Mon.–Sat. 9–6
TYPE OF MERCHANDISE: Clothing, furniture, collectibles
DONATION TAX RECEIPT: Receipt given upon request
COMMENTS: Half-price sales
Salvation Army Thrift Store
5885 66th St. N
St. Petersburg, FL 33709
CONTACT: Maj. Glen R. Winters
TYPE OF MERCHANDISE: Clothing, housewares, furniture
DONATION TAX RECEIPT: Receipt given upon request
Salvation Army Thrift Store
5321 Fourth St. N
St. Petersburg, FL 33702
PHONE: 813-521-4208

HOURS: Mon.–Sat. 9–6
TYPE OF MERCHANDISE: Furniture, clothing, collectibles
DONATION TAX RECEIPT: Receipt given upon request
COMMENTS: Half-price sales
Saint Vincent De Paul Thrift Store
535 Ninth St. N
St. Petersburg, FL 33701
TYPE OF MERCHANDISE: Clothing, housewares, furniture
DONATION TAX RECEIPT: Receipt given upon request
COMMENTS: Monthly markdowns
Salvation Army Thrift Store
5885 66th St. N
St. Petersburg, FL 33709
PHONE: 813-541-7434
HOURS: Mon.–Fri. 9–6, Sat. 9–9
TYPE OF MERCHANDISE: Furniture, clothing, collectibles
DONATION TAX RECEIPT: Receipt given upon request
COMMENTS: Half-price sales
Goodwill Industries Thrift Store
300 E. Third St.
Sanford, FL 32771
PHONE: 407-323-2272
HOURS: Mon.–Sat. 9–5:30, Sun. 12–5
TYPE OF MERCHANDISE: Clothing, housewares, furniture
DONATION TAX RECEIPT: Receipt given upon request
Salvation Army Thrift Store
2280 17th St.
Sarasota, FL 34237
PHONE: 813-954-4549
HOURS: Mon.–Sat. 9–5
TYPE OF MERCHANDISE: Clothing, furniture, collectibles
DONATION TAX RECEIPT: Receipt given upon request
COMMENTS: Half-price sales
Saint Vincent De Paul Thrift Store
512 S. Orange Ave.
Sarasota, FL 34236
TYPE OF MERCHANDISE: Clothing, housewares, furniture

DONATION TAX RECEIPT: Receipt given upon request
COMMENTS: Monthly markdowns

Goodwill Industries Thrift Store
7501 Fifteenth St. E
Sarasota, FL 34243
TYPE OF MERCHANDISE: Clothing, housewares, furniture
DONATION TAX RECEIPT: Receipt given upon request

Saint Vincent De Paul Thrift Store
906 Canal Circle
Sebastian, FL 32958
TYPE OF MERCHANDISE: Clothing, housewares, furniture
DONATION TAX RECEIPT: Receipt given upon request
COMMENTS: Monthly markdowns

Goodwill Industries Thrift Store
6838 US Hwy. 27 N
Sebring, FL 33872
CONTACT: Juanita Evans
PHONE: 813-471-6160
HOURS: Mon.–Sat. 9–7, Sun. 1–5
TYPE OF MERCHANDISE: Clothing, housewares, furniture
DONATION TAX RECEIPT: Receipt given upon request
COMMENTS: Holiday and special sales

Goodwill Industries Thrift Store
419 N. Ridgewood Dr.
Sebring, FL 33870
TYPE OF MERCHANDISE: Clothing, housewares, furniture
DONATION TAX RECEIPT: Receipt given upon request

Saint Vincent De Paul Thrift Store
3060 N.W. 60th Ave.
Sunrise, FL 33313
TYPE OF MERCHANDISE: Clothing, housewares, furniture
DONATION TAX RECEIPT: Receipt given upon request
COMMENTS: Monthly markdowns

Saint Vincent De Paul Thrift Store
15406 Capital Cir. SW
Tallahassee, FL 32310

TYPE OF MERCHANDISE: Clothing, housewares, furniture
DONATION TAX RECEIPT: Receipt given upon request
COMMENTS: Monthly markdowns

Goodwill Industries Thrift Store
2475 Apalachee Pkwy.
Tallahassee, FL 32301
TYPE OF MERCHANDISE: Clothing, housewares, furniture
DONATION TAX RECEIPT: Receipt given upon request

Goodwill Industries Thrift Store
300 Mabry St.
Tallahassee, FL 32304
TYPE OF MERCHANDISE: Clothing, housewares, furniture
DONATION TAX RECEIPT: Receipt given upon request

Salvation Army Thrift Store
803 Railroad Ave.
Tallahassee, FL 32310
TYPE OF MERCHANDISE: Clothing, housewares, furniture
DONATION TAX RECEIPT: Receipt given upon request

Saint Vincent de Paul Thrift Store
12310 N. Nebraska Ave.
Tampa, FL 33603
TYPE OF MERCHANDISE: Clothing, housewares, furniture
DONATION TAX RECEIPT: Receipt given upon request
COMMENTS: Monthly markdowns

Salvation Army Thrift Store
2815 S. Macdill Ave.
Tampa, FL 33629
TYPE OF MERCHANDISE: Clothing, housewares, furniture
DONATION TAX RECEIPT: Receipt given upon request

Saint Vincent De Paul Thrift Store
3501 N. Florida Ave.
Tampa, FL 33603
TYPE OF MERCHANDISE: Clothing, housewares, furniture
DONATION TAX RECEIPT: Receipt given upon request
COMMENTS: Monthly markdowns

Goodwill Industries Thrift Store
4829 E. Broadway Ave.
Tampa, FL 33605
TYPE OF MERCHANDISE: Clothing,
housewares, furniture
DONATION TAX RECEIPT: Receipt given
upon request

Salvation Army Thrift Store
5100 N. Florida Ave.
Tampa, FL 33603
TYPE OF MERCHANDISE: Clothing,
housewares, furniture
DONATION TAX RECEIPT: Receipt given
upon request

Goodwill Industries Thrift Store
6924 N. Armenia Ave.
Tampa, FL 33604
TYPE OF MERCHANDISE: Clothing,
housewares, furniture
DONATION TAX RECEIPT: Receipt given
upon request

Salvation Army Thrift Store
8217 N. Nebraska Ave.
Tampa, FL 33604
TYPE OF MERCHANDISE: Clothing,
housewares, furniture
DONATION TAX RECEIPT: Receipt given
upon request

Salvation Army Thrift Store
609 Main St.
Titusville, FL 32796
TYPE OF MERCHANDISE: Clothing,
housewares, furniture
DONATION TAX RECEIPT: Receipt given
upon request

Salvation Army Thrift Store
1879 S. Tamiami Trail
Venice, FL 34293
PHONE: 813-493-1496
HOURS: Mon.–Sat. 9–4:30
TYPE OF MERCHANDISE: Furniture,
clothing, collectibles
DONATION TAX RECEIPT: Receipt given
upon request
COMMENTS: Half-price sales

Saint Vincent De Paul Thrift Store
515 Cervina Dr.
Venice, FL 33595

TYPE OF MERCHANDISE: Clothing,
housewares, furniture
DONATION TAX RECEIPT: Receipt given
upon request
COMMENTS: Monthly markdowns

Saint Vincent De Paul Thrift Store
1745 14th Ave.
Vero Beach, FL 32960
TYPE OF MERCHANDISE: Clothing,
housewares, furniture
DONATION TAX RECEIPT: Receipt given
upon request
COMMENTS: Monthly markdowns

Saint Vincent De Paul Thrift Store
5480 85th St.
Vero Beach, FL 32967
TYPE OF MERCHANDISE: Clothing,
housewares, furniture
DONATION TAX RECEIPT: Receipt given
upon request
COMMENTS: Monthly markdowns

Salvation Army Thrift Store
2300 S.W. 56th Ave.
West Hollywood, FL 33023
PHONE: 305-961-7523
HOURS: Mon.–Sat. 10–6
TYPE OF MERCHANDISE: Clothing,
housewares, furniture
DONATION TAX RECEIPT: Receipt given
upon request
COMMENTS: Semi-annual and annual
auto and boat auctions

Saint Vincent De Paul Thrift Store
2500 N. Dixie Hwy.
West Palm Beach, FL 33407
TYPE OF MERCHANDISE: Clothing,
housewares, furniture
DONATION TAX RECEIPT: Receipt given
upon request
COMMENTS: Monthly markdowns

Saint Vincent De Paul Thrift Store
2560 Westgate Ave.
West Palm Beach, FL 33409
TYPE OF MERCHANDISE: Clothing,
housewares, furniture
DONATION TAX RECEIPT: Receipt given
upon request
COMMENTS: Monthly markdowns

Saint Vincent De Paul Thrift Store
2647 Old Dixie Hwy.
West Palm Beach, FL 33404
TYPE OF MERCHANDISE: Clothing,
housewares, furniture
DONATION TAX RECEIPT: Receipt given
upon request
COMMENTS: Monthly markdowns

Junior League Thrift Boutique
2884 S. Military Trail
West Palm Beach, FL 33415
CONTACT: Pat Winters
PHONE: 407-433-4089
HOURS: Mon.–Sat. 9–6, closed Mon.
summer hours
TYPE OF MERCHANDISE: Clothing,
housewares, furniture
DONATION TAX RECEIPT: Receipt given
upon request
COMMENTS: Boutique "Patch" section

Rescue Mission Gospel Thrift Shop
524 Northwood Rd.
West Palm Beach, FL 33407
TYPE OF MERCHANDISE: Clothing,
housewares
DONATION TAX RECEIPT: Receipt given
upon request

Goodwill Industries Thrift Store
800 Tenth St.
West Palm Beach, FL 33403
TYPE OF MERCHANDISE: Clothing,
housewares, furniture
DONATION TAX RECEIPT: Receipt given
upon request

Goodwill Industries Thrift Store
600 Sixth St. NW
Winter Haven, FL 33880
CONTACT: Peggy Ledford
PHONE: 813-299-1486
HOURS: Mon.–Sat. 9–7, Sun. 1–5
TYPE OF MERCHANDISE: Clothing,
housewares, furniture
DONATION TAX RECEIPT: Receipt given
upon request
COMMENTS: Holiday and special sales

Junior League Bargain Box
505–507 Virginia Ave.
Winter Park, FL 32789
PHONE: 407-644-4043
HOURS: Mon.–Sat. 9–4
TYPE OF MERCHANDISE: Clothing for the
entire family
DONATION TAX RECEIPT: Receipt given
upon request

Goodwill Industries Thrift Store
750 Orange Ave.
Winter Park, FL 32789
PHONE: 407-628-5553
HOURS: Mon.–Sat. 9–5:30
TYPE OF MERCHANDISE: Clothing,
housewares, furniture
DONATION TAX RECEIPT: Receipt given
upon request

Goodwill Industries Thrift Store
1460 Missouri Ave.
Zephyr Hills, FL 33540
TYPE OF MERCHANDISE: Clothing,
housewares, furniture
DONATION TAX RECEIPT: Receipt given
upon request

Goodwill Industries Thrift Store
6739 Gall Blvd.
Zephyr Hills, FL 33541
TYPE OF MERCHANDISE: Clothing,
housewares, furniture
DONATION TAX RECEIPT: Receipt given
upon request

Georgia

Goodwill Industries Thrift Store
226 W. Broad St.
Albany, GA 31701
PHONE: 912-436-7330
HOURS: Mon.–Sat. 9–6
TYPE OF MERCHANDISE: Clothing,
housewares, furniture
DONATION TAX RECEIPT: Receipt given
upon request

Salvation Army Thrift Store
393 N. Finley St.
Athens, GA 30601
TYPE OF MERCHANDISE: Clothing,
housewares, furniture
DONATION TAX RECEIPT: Receipt given
upon request

Salvation Army Thrift Store
470 Oconee St.
Athens, GA 30601
TYPE OF MERCHANDISE: Clothing,
housewares, furniture
DONATION TAX RECEIPT: Receipt given
upon request

Salvation Army Thrift Store
1424 Northeast Expwy.
Atlanta, GA 30329
TYPE OF MERCHANDISE: Clothing,
housewares, furniture
DONATION TAX RECEIPT: Receipt given
upon request

Junior League Nearly New Shop
2581 Piedmont Rd NE
Atlanta, GA 30324
TYPE OF MERCHANDISE: Clothing for men,
women, and children
DONATION TAX RECEIPT: Receipt given
upon request

Salvation Army Thrift Store
746 Marietta St. NW
Atlanta, GA 30318
TYPE OF MERCHANDISE: Clothing,
housewares, furniture
DONATION TAX RECEIPT: Receipt given
upon request

Salvation Army Thrift Store
838 Cascade Ave. SW
Atlanta, GA 30311
TYPE OF MERCHANDISE: Clothing,
housewares, furniture
DONATION TAX RECEIPT: Receipt given
upon request

Salvation Army Thrift Store
883 Dill Ave. SW
Atlanta, GA 30310
TYPE OF MERCHANDISE: Clothing,
housewares, furniture
DONATION TAX RECEIPT: Receipt given
upon request

Goodwill Industries Thrift Store
888 Gordon St. SW
Atlanta, GA 30310
TYPE OF MERCHANDISE: Clothing,
housewares, furniture
DONATION TAX RECEIPT: Receipt given
upon request

Salvation Army Thrift Store
2517 Deans Bridge Rd.
Augusta, GA 30906
TYPE OF MERCHANDISE: Clothing,
housewares, furniture
DONATION TAX RECEIPT: Receipt given
upon request

Goodwill Industries Thrift Store
1632 E. Shotwell St.
Bainbridge, GA 31717
TYPE OF MERCHANDISE: Clothing,
housewares, furniture
DONATION TAX RECEIPT: Receipt given
upon request

Saint Vincent De Paul Thrift Store
1217 Newcastle St.
Brunswick, GA 31520
TYPE OF MERCHANDISE: Clothing,
housewares, furniture
DONATION TAX RECEIPT: Receipt given
upon request
COMMENTS: Monthly markdowns

Saint Vincent De Paul Thrift Store
3660 Clairmont Rd. NE
Chamblee, GA 30341
TYPE OF MERCHANDISE: Clothing,
housewares, furniture
DONATION TAX RECEIPT: Receipt given
upon request
COMMENTS: Monthly markdowns

Goodwill Industries Thrift Store
1036 Broadway
Columbus, GA 31901
TYPE OF MERCHANDISE: Clothing,
housewares, furniture
DONATION TAX RECEIPT: Receipt given
upon request

Rescue Mission Valley
1815 27th St.
Columbus, GA 31901
TYPE OF MERCHANDISE: Clothing,
housewares,
DONATION TAX RECEIPT: Receipt given
upon request

Goodwill Industries Thrift Store
316 Brown Ave.
Columbus, GA 31903
TYPE OF MERCHANDISE: Clothing,
housewares, furniture

DONATION TAX RECEIPT: Receipt given upon request

Goodwill Industries Thrift Store
210 N. Hamilton St.
Dalton, GA 30720
TYPE OF MERCHANDISE: Clothing, housewares, furniture
DONATION TAX RECEIPT: Receipt given upon request

Goodwill Industries Thrift Store
North Hill Shopping Center
Dalton, GA 30720
PHONE: 706-259-8599
HOURS: Mon.–Sat. 9–7, Sun. 1–7
TYPE OF MERCHANDISE: Clothing, housewares, furniture
DONATION TAX RECEIPT: Receipt given upon request

Salvation Army Thrift Store
2857 E. College Ave.
Decatur, GA 30030
TYPE OF MERCHANDISE: Clothing, housewares, furniture
DONATION TAX RECEIPT: Receipt given upon request

Salvation Army Thrift Store
72 Battlefield Pkwy.
Ft. Oglethorpe, GA 37407
PHONE: 706-861-4770
HOURS: Mon.–Sat. 9–7, Sun. 1–7
TYPE OF MERCHANDISE: Clothing, housewares, furniture
DONATION TAX RECEIPT: Receipt given upon request

Salvation Army Thrift Store
1713a Atlanta Rd.
Gainesville, GA 30504
TYPE OF MERCHANDISE: Clothing, housewares, furniture
DONATION TAX RECEIPT: Receipt given upon request

Salvation Army Thrift Store
331 Northside Dr.
Gainesville, GA 30501
TYPE OF MERCHANDISE: Clothing, housewares, furniture
DONATION TAX RECEIPT: Receipt given upon request

Goodwill Industries Thrift Store
132 Main St.
La Grange, GA 30240
TYPE OF MERCHANDISE: Clothing, housewares, furniture
DONATION TAX RECEIPT: Receipt given upon request

Saint Vincent De Paul Thrift Store
243 Scenic Hwy.
Lawrenceville, GA 30245
TYPE OF MERCHANDISE: Clothing, housewares, furniture
DONATION TAX RECEIPT: Receipt given upon request
COMMENTS: Monthly markdowns

Saint Vincent De Paul Thrift Store
4974 Lawrenceville Hwy.
Lilburn, GA 30247
TYPE OF MERCHANDISE: Clothing, housewares, furniture
DONATION TAX RECEIPT: Receipt given upon request
COMMENTS: Monthly markdowns

Salvation Army Thrift Store
317 E. First Ave.
Rome, GA 30161
TYPE OF MERCHANDISE: Clothing, housewares, furniture
DONATION TAX RECEIPT: Receipt given upon request

Goodwill Industries Thrift Store
18 Simmons Shopping Ctr.
Statesboro, GA 30458
TYPE OF MERCHANDISE: Clothing, housewares, furniture
DONATION TAX RECEIPT: Receipt given upon request

Saint Vincent De Paul Thrift Store
4687 Rockbridge Rd.
Stone Mountain, GA 30083
TYPE OF MERCHANDISE: Clothing, housewares, furniture
DONATION TAX RECEIPT: Receipt given upon request
COMMENTS: Monthly markdowns

Goodwill Industries Thrift Store
359 Commerce Way
Tifton, GA 31763

PHONE: 912-382-0093
HOURS: Mon.–Sat. 9–6
TYPE OF MERCHANDISE: Clothing,
housewares, furniture
DONATION TAX RECEIPT: Receipt given
upon request
Salvation Army Thrift Store
504 N. Oak St.
Valdosta, GA 31601
TYPE OF MERCHANDISE: Clothing,
housewares, furniture
DONATION TAX RECEIPT: Receipt given
upon request

Idaho

Saint Vincent de Paul Store
206 S. Spruce St.
Blackfoot, ID 83221
TYPE OF MERCHANDISE: Clothing,
housewares, furniture
DONATION TAX RECEIPT: Receipt given
upon request
COMMENTS: Monthly markdowns
TVI Savers Thrift Store
10475 Fairview Ave.
Boise, ID 83704
CONTACT: Joe Van Dam
PHONE: 208-377-2001
HOURS: Mon.–Sat. 9–9, Sun. 10–6
TYPE OF MERCHANDISE: Clothing,
housewares, furniture
DONATION TAX RECEIPT: Receipt given
upon request
Saint Vincent De Paul Thrift Store
201 W. Boise Ave.
Boise, ID 83705
TYPE OF MERCHANDISE: Clothing,
housewares, furniture
DONATION TAX RECEIPT: Receipt given
upon request
COMMENTS: Monthly markdowns
Salvation Army Thrift Store
3209 Overland Rd.
Boise, ID 83705
TYPE OF MERCHANDISE: Clothing,
housewares, furniture

DONATION TAX RECEIPT: Receipt given
upon request
Salvation Army Thrift Store
4306 W. State St.
Boise, ID 83703
TYPE OF MERCHANDISE: Clothing,
housewares, furniture
DONATION TAX RECEIPT: Receipt given
upon request
Junior League Second Time Round
5266 Franklin Rd.
Boise, ID 83705
CONTACT: Pam Frei
PHONE: 208-344-0760
HOURS: Mon.–Sat. 10–5, Wed. 10–8
TYPE OF MERCHANDISE: Clothing,
housewares, toys
DONATION TAX RECEIPT: Receipt given
upon request
COMMENTS: Quarterly clearance sales
National Assistance League Thrift Shop
5825 Glenwood
Boise, ID 83703
PHONE: 208-377-4327
TYPE OF MERCHANDISE: Clothing,
housewares, furniture
DONATION TAX RECEIPT: Receipt given
upon request
COMMENTS: Monthly markdowns
Saint Vincent De Paul Thrift Store
6464 W. State St.
Boise, ID 83703
TYPE OF MERCHANDISE: Clothing,
housewares, furniture
DONATION TAX RECEIPT: Receipt given
upon request
COMMENTS: Monthly markdowns
Salvation Army Thrift Store
8727 Fairview Ave.
Boise, ID 83704
TYPE OF MERCHANDISE: Clothing,
housewares, furniture
DONATION TAX RECEIPT: Receipt given
upon request
Saint Vincent De Paul Thrift Store
3719 E. Cleveland Blvd.
Caldwell, ID 83605
TYPE OF MERCHANDISE: Clothing,
housewares, furniture

DONATION TAX RECEIPT: Receipt given upon request
COMMENTS: Monthly markdowns
Salvation Army Thrift Store
606 Main St.
Caldwell, ID 83605
TYPE OF MERCHANDISE: Clothing, housewares, furniture
DONATION TAX RECEIPT: Receipt given upon request
Saint Vincent De Paul Thrift Store
108 E. Walnut
Coeur d'Alene, ID 83814
TYPE OF MERCHANDISE: Clothing, housewares, furniture
DONATION TAX RECEIPT: Receipt given upon request
COMMENTS: Monthly markdowns
Saint Vincent De Paul Thrift Store
104 E. Riverside
Kellogg, ID 83837
TYPE OF MERCHANDISE: Clothing, housewares, furniture
DONATION TAX RECEIPT: Receipt given upon request
COMMENTS: Monthly markdowns
Goodwill Industries Thrift Store
3134 Fifth St.
Lewiston, ID 83501
TYPE OF MERCHANDISE: Clothing, housewares, furniture
DONATION TAX RECEIPT: Receipt given upon request
Saint Vincent De Paul Thrift Store
3138 Fifth St.
Lewiston, ID 83501
TYPE OF MERCHANDISE: Clothing, housewares, furniture
DONATION TAX RECEIPT: Receipt given upon request
COMMENTS: Monthly markdowns
Saint Vincent De Paul Thrift Store
213 E. First St.
Meridian, ID 83642
TYPE OF MERCHANDISE: Clothing, housewares, furniture
DONATION TAX RECEIPT: Receipt given upon request
COMMENTS: Monthly markdowns

MCC More for Less
1211A First St. S
Nampa, ID 83651
PHONE: 208-467-5980
TYPE OF MERCHANDISE: Clothing, housewares, furniture
DONATION TAX RECEIPT: Receipt given upon request
Salvation Army Thrift Store
1324 First St. S
Nampa, ID 83651
TYPE OF MERCHANDISE: Clothing, housewares, furniture
DONATION TAX RECEIPT: Receipt given upon request
Saint Vincent De Paul Thrift Store
244 Main Ave. S
Twin Falls, ID 83301
TYPE OF MERCHANDISE: Clothing, housewares, furniture
DONATION TAX RECEIPT: Receipt given upon request
COMMENTS: Monthly markdowns
Salvation Army Thrift Store
561 Main Ave. E
Twin Falls, ID 83301-7113
TYPE OF MERCHANDISE: Clothing, housewares, furniture
DONATION TAX RECEIPT: Receipt given upon request

Illinois

Goodwill Industries Thrift Store
1234 Milton Rd.
Alton, IL 62002
TYPE OF MERCHANDISE: Clothing, housewares, furniture
DONATION TAX RECEIPT: Receipt given upon request
Salvation Army Thrift Store
24 Eastgate Plaza
Alton, IL 62024
PHONE: 618-254-4575
HOURS: Mon.–Sat. 10–6
TYPE OF MERCHANDISE: Clothing, housewares, furniture
DONATION TAX RECEIPT: Receipt given upon request

COMMENTS: 50% off and manager's
sales etc.
Salvation Army Thrift Store
218 N. Illinois
Belleville, IL 62220
PHONE: 618-233-7617
HOURS: Mon.–Sat. 10–6
TYPE OF MERCHANDISE: Clothing,
housewares, furniture
DONATION TAX RECEIPT: Receipt given
upon request
COMMENTS: 50% off manager's sales etc.
Goodwill Industries Thrift Store
24 N. High St.
Belleville, IL 62220
TYPE OF MERCHANDISE: Clothing,
housewares, furniture
DONATION TAX RECEIPT: Receipt given
upon request
Salvation Army Thrift Store
407 W. Washington St.
Bloomington, IL 61701
TYPE OF MERCHANDISE: Clothing,
housewares, furniture
DONATION TAX RECEIPT: Receipt given
upon request
Goodwill Industries Thrift Store
428 N. Main St.
Bloomington, IL 61701
TYPE OF MERCHANDISE: Clothing,
housewares, furniture
DONATION TAX RECEIPT: Receipt given
upon request
Goodwill Industries Thrift Store
219 N. Neil St.
Champaign, IL 61820
TYPE OF MERCHANDISE: Clothing,
housewares, furniture
DONATION TAX RECEIPT: Receipt given
upon request
Goodwill Industries Thrift Store
1283 N. Milwaukee Ave.
Chicago, IL 60622
TYPE OF MERCHANDISE: Clothing,
housewares, furniture
DONATION TAX RECEIPT: Receipt given
upon request

Salvation Army Thrift Store
1515 N. Milwaukee Ave.
Chicago, IL 60622
TYPE OF MERCHANDISE: Clothing,
housewares, furniture
DONATION TAX RECEIPT: Receipt given
upon request
NCJW Thrift Shop
1524 Howard St.
CROSS STREET: Bosworth
Chicago, IL 60626
CONTACT: Carmen Lara
PHONE: 312-764-2364
HOURS: Mon.–Sat. 10–6, Wed. 10–2
TYPE OF MERCHANDISE: Clothing,
housewares, furniture
DONATION TAX RECEIPT: Receipt given
upon request
COMMENTS: Seasonal and holiday sales
Disabled American Vets Thrift Store
1541 N. Milwaukee Ave.
Chicago, IL 60622
TYPE OF MERCHANDISE: Clothing,
housewares
DONATION TAX RECEIPT: Receipt given
upon request
Disabled American Vets Thrift Store
1718 W. Chicago Ave.
Chicago, IL 60622
TYPE OF MERCHANDISE: Clothing,
housewares
DONATION TAX RECEIPT: Receipt given
upon request
Salvation Army Thrift Store
1826 S. Halsted St.
Chicago, IL 60608
TYPE OF MERCHANDISE: Clothing,
housewares, furniture
DONATION TAX RECEIPT: Receipt given
upon request
Disabled American Vets Thrift Store
212 E. 43rd St.
Chicago, IL 60653
TYPE OF MERCHANDISE: Clothing,
housewares
DONATION TAX RECEIPT: Receipt given
upon request

Salvation Army Thrift Store
2260 N. Clybourn Ave.
Chicago, IL 60614
CONTACT: Vanessa Tubbs
PHONE: 312-404-2946
HOURS: Mon.–Sat. 9–6
TYPE OF MERCHANDISE: Clothing,
housewares, furniture
DONATION TAX RECEIPT: Receipt given
upon request
Salvation Army Thrift Store
2501 N. Harlem
Chicago, IL 60635
CONTACT: Ellis Winfrey
PHONE: 312-745-0738
HOURS: Mon.–Fri. 10–6, Sat. 9–5
TYPE OF MERCHANDISE: Clothing,
housewares, furniture
DONATION TAX RECEIPT: Receipt given
upon request
Disabled American Vets Thrift Store
2854 N. Milwaukee Ave.
Chicago, IL 60618
TYPE OF MERCHANDISE: Clothing,
housewares
DONATION TAX RECEIPT: Receipt given
upon request
Salvation Army Thrift Store
2941 N. Central
Chicago, IL 60634
CONTACT: Carolyn Woodley
PHONE: 312-283-1315
HOURS: Mon.–Fri. 9–6, Sat. 9–5
TYPE OF MERCHANDISE: Clothing,
housewares, furniture
DONATION TAX RECEIPT: Receipt given
upon request
Goodwill Industries Thrift Store
3039 N. Pulaski Rd.
Chicago, IL 60641
TYPE OF MERCHANDISE: Clothing,
housewares, furniture
DONATION TAX RECEIPT: Receipt given
upon request
Salvation Army Thrift Store
3055 W. 63rd St.
Chicago, IL 60629
TYPE OF MERCHANDISE: Clothing,
housewares, furniture

DONATION TAX RECEIPT: Receipt given
upon request
Disabled American Vets Thrift Store
3243 W. North Ave.
Chicago, IL 60647
TYPE OF MERCHANDISE: Clothing,
housewares
DONATION TAX RECEIPT: Receipt given
upon request
Salvation Army Thrift Store
3301 W. Montrose
Chicago, IL 60618
CONTACT: Clariebel Nava
PHONE: 312-588-7343
HOURS: Mon.–Fri. 10–6, Sat. 9–5
TYPE OF MERCHANDISE: Clothing,
housewares, furniture
DONATION TAX RECEIPT: Receipt given
upon request
Goodwill Industries Thrift Store
3315 N. Marshfield Ave.
Chicago, IL 60657
TYPE OF MERCHANDISE: Clothing,
housewares, furniture
DONATION TAX RECEIPT: Receipt given
upon request
Disabled American Vets Thrift Store
3318 N. Milwaukee Ave.
Chicago, IL 60641
TYPE OF MERCHANDISE: Clothing,
housewares, furniture
DONATION TAX RECEIPT: Receipt given
upon request
Disabled American Vets Thrift Store
3430 W. Diversey Ave.
Chicago, IL 60647
TYPE OF MERCHANDISE: Clothing,
housewares, furniture
DONATION TAX RECEIPT: Receipt given
upon request
Disabled American Vets Thrift Store
3514 S. Michigan Ave.
Chicago, IL 60653
TYPE OF MERCHANDISE: Clothing,
housewares, furniture
DONATION TAX RECEIPT: Receipt given
upon request

Salvation Army Thrift Store
3837 W. Fullerton
Chicago, IL 60647
CONTACT: Harold Koop
PHONE: 312-276-1955
HOURS: Mon.–Fri. 10–6, Sat. 9–5
TYPE OF MERCHANDISE: Clothing,
housewares, furniture
DONATION TAX RECEIPT: Receipt given
upon request

Salvation Army Thrift Store
3868 N. Lincoln
Chicago, IL 60613
CONTACT: Yasmeen Ali
PHONE: 312-528-8893
HOURS: Mon.–Fri. 10–6, Sat. 9–5
TYPE OF MERCHANDISE: Clothing,
housewares, furniture
DONATION TAX RECEIPT: Receipt given
upon request

Salvation Army Thrift Store
4315 N. Broadway
Chicago, IL 60613
CONTACT: Jeanette Ingram
PHONE: 312-348-1401
HOURS: Mon.–Fri. 10–6, Sat. 9–5
TYPE OF MERCHANDISE: Clothing,
housewares, furniture
DONATION TAX RECEIPT: Receipt given
upon request

Goodwill Industries Thrift Store
4850 S. Kilbourn Ave.
Chicago, IL 60632
TYPE OF MERCHANDISE: Clothing,
housewares, furniture
DONATION TAX RECEIPT: Receipt given
upon request

Salvation Army Thrift Store
5050 N. Sheridan
Chicago, IL 60648
CONTACT: Nasreen Wahidi
PHONE: 312-784-7330
HOURS: Mon.–Fri. 10–6, Sat. 9–5
TYPE OF MERCHANDISE: Clothing,
housewares, furniture
DONATION TAX RECEIPT: Receipt given
upon request

Salvation Army Thrift Store
5110 S. Ashland Ave.
Chicago, IL 60609-4930
TYPE OF MERCHANDISE: Clothing,
housewares, furniture
DONATION TAX RECEIPT: Receipt given
upon request

Saint Vincent De Paul Thrift Store
5413 S. Kedzie Ave.
Chicago, IL 60623
TYPE OF MERCHANDISE: Clothing,
housewares, furniture
DONATION TAX RECEIPT: Receipt given
upon request
COMMENTS: Monthly markdowns

Salvation Army Thrift Store
5556 N. Clark
Chicago, IL 60640
CONTACT: Scottie Williams
PHONE: 312-728-8079
HOURS: Mon.–Fri. 10–6, Sat. 9–5
TYPE OF MERCHANDISE: Clothing,
housewares, furniture
DONATION TAX RECEIPT: Receipt given
upon request

Salvation Army Thrift Store
5713 W. Chicago Ave.
Chicago, IL 60651
TYPE OF MERCHANDISE: Clothing,
housewares, furniture
DONATION TAX RECEIPT: Receipt given
upon request

Disabled American Vets Thrift Store
5900 W. Roosevelt Rd.
Chicago, IL 60650
TYPE OF MERCHANDISE: Clothing,
housewares, furniture
DONATION TAX RECEIPT: Receipt given
upon request

Goodwill Industries Thrift Store
6840 S. Stony Island Ave.
Chicago, IL 60649
TYPE OF MERCHANDISE: Clothing,
housewares, furniture
DONATION TAX RECEIPT: Receipt given
upon request

Goodwill Industries Thrift Store
7010 W. Grand Ave.
Chicago, IL 60635
TYPE OF MERCHANDISE: Clothing,
housewares, furniture
DONATION TAX RECEIPT: Receipt given
upon request

Saint Vincent De Paul Thrift Store
9321 S. Western Ave.
Chicago, IL 60620
TYPE OF MERCHANDISE: Clothing,
housewares, furniture
DONATION TAX RECEIPT: Receipt given
upon request
COMMENTS: Monthly markdowns

Salvation Army Thrift Store
1802 Sycamore Rd.
De Kalb, IL 60115
TYPE OF MERCHANDISE: Clothing,
housewares, furniture
DONATION TAX RECEIPT: Receipt given
upon request

Salvation Army Thrift Store
251 E. Lincoln Hwy.
De Kalb, IL 60115
TYPE OF MERCHANDISE: Clothing,
housewares, furniture
DONATION TAX RECEIPT: Receipt given
upon request

Salvation Army Thrift Store
1032 E. Sibley Blvd.
Dolton, IL 60419
PHONE: 708-201-1146
HOURS: Mon.–Sat. 10–6
TYPE OF MERCHANDISE: Clothing,
housewares, furniture
DONATION TAX RECEIPT: Receipt given
upon request
COMMENTS: Weekly 50% discount on
selected items

Saint Vincent De Paul Thrift Store
104 S. Franklin
Dwight, IL 60420
TYPE OF MERCHANDISE: Clothing,
housewares, furniture
DONATION TAX RECEIPT: Receipt given
upon request
COMMENTS: Monthly markdowns

Salvation Army Thrift Store
23a E. Gate Plaza
East Alton, IL 62024
TYPE OF MERCHANDISE: Clothing,
housewares, furniture
DONATION TAX RECEIPT: Receipt given
upon request

Salvation Army Thrift Store
1145 15th Ave.
East Moline, IL 61244
TYPE OF MERCHANDISE: Clothing,
housewares, furniture
DONATION TAX RECEIPT: Receipt given
upon request

Saint Vincent De Paul Thrift Store
3718 State St.
East St. Louis, IL 62205
TYPE OF MERCHANDISE: Clothing,
housewares, furniture
DONATION TAX RECEIPT: Receipt given
upon request
COMMENTS: Monthly markdowns

Salvation Army Thrift Store
528 Kedzie
Evanston, IL 60202
CONTACT: Guanda Oates
PHONE: 708-869-3033
HOURS: Mon.–Fri. 10–6, Sat. 9–5
TYPE OF MERCHANDISE: Clothing,
housewares, furniture
DONATION TAX RECEIPT: Receipt given
upon request

Junior League Thrift House
920 Chicago Ave.
Evanston, IL 60202
TYPE OF MERCHANDISE: Clothing for men,
women, and children
DONATION TAX RECEIPT: Receipt given
upon request

Salvation Army Thrift Store
105 W. Main St.
Freeport, IL 61032
TYPE OF MERCHANDISE: Clothing,
housewares, furniture
DONATION TAX RECEIPT: Receipt given
upon request

Salvation Army Thrift Store
209 Main St.
Galesburg, IL 61401

PHONE: 309-342-5723
HOURS: Mon.–Sat. 9–5
TYPE OF MERCHANDISE: Clothing,
housewares, furniture
DONATION TAX RECEIPT: Receipt given
upon request
Goodwill Industries Thrift Store
225 S. Main St.
Jacksonville, IL 62650
TYPE OF MERCHANDISE: Clothing,
housewares, furniture
DONATION TAX RECEIPT: Receipt given
upon request
Salvation Army Thrift Store
305 S. Main St.
Jacksonville, IL 62650
TYPE OF MERCHANDISE: Clothing,
housewares, furniture
DONATION TAX RECEIPT: Receipt given
upon request
Saint Vincent De Paul Thrift Store
66 W. Cass St.
Joliet, IL 60432
TYPE OF MERCHANDISE: Clothing,
housewares, furniture
DONATION TAX RECEIPT: Receipt given
upon request
COMMENTS: Monthly markdowns
Salvation Army Thrift Store
737 First St.
La Salle, IL 61301
TYPE OF MERCHANDISE: Clothing,
housewares, furniture
DONATION TAX RECEIPT: Receipt given
upon request
Goodwill Industries Thrift Store
606 13th St.
Lawrenceville, IL 62439
TYPE OF MERCHANDISE: Clothing,
housewares, furniture
DONATION TAX RECEIPT: Receipt given
upon request
Salvation Army Thrift Store
117 S. MacArthur St.
Macomb, IL 61455
TYPE OF MERCHANDISE: Clothing,
housewares, furniture

DONATION TAX RECEIPT: Receipt given
upon request
Saint Vincent De Paul Thrift Store
4644 W. 147th St.
Midlothian, IL 60445
TYPE OF MERCHANDISE: Clothing,
housewares, furniture
DONATION TAX RECEIPT: Receipt given
upon request
COMMENTS: Monthly markdowns
Salvation Army Thrift Store
126 Fourth Ave.
Moline, IL 61265-1132
PHONE: 309-762-8117
HOURS: Mon.–Sat. 9–5
TYPE OF MERCHANDISE: Clothing,
housewares, furniture
DONATION TAX RECEIPT: Receipt given
upon request
Saint Vincent De Paul Thrift Store
107 Wauponsee
Morris, IL 60450
TYPE OF MERCHANDISE: Clothing,
housewares, furniture
DONATION TAX RECEIPT: Receipt given
upon request
COMMENTS: Monthly markdowns
Goodwill Industries Thrift Store
430 W. Third St.
Mount Carmel, IL 62863
TYPE OF MERCHANDISE: Clothing,
housewares, furniture
DONATION TAX RECEIPT: Receipt given
upon request
Disabled American Vets Thrift Store
1013 Garfield St.
Oak Park, IL 60304
TYPE OF MERCHANDISE: Clothing,
housewares, furniture
DONATION TAX RECEIPT: Receipt given
upon request
Salvation Army Thrift Store
6536 Roosevelt Rd.
Oak Park, IL 60304-2142
TYPE OF MERCHANDISE: Clothing,
housewares, furniture
DONATION TAX RECEIPT: Receipt given
upon request

Goodwill Industries Thrift Store
219 N. Main St.
Paris, IL 61944
PHONE: 217-465-2525
HOURS: Mon.–Sat. 9–5
TYPE OF MERCHANDISE: Clothing,
housewares, furniture
DONATION TAX RECEIPT: Receipt given
upon request

Salvation Army Thrift Store
812 Maine St.
Quincy, IL 62301
TYPE OF MERCHANDISE: Clothing,
housewares, furniture
DONATION TAX RECEIPT: Receipt given
upon request

Salvation Army Thrift Store
2125 11th St.
Rock Island, IL 61201
PHONE: 309-794-0220
HOURS: Mon.–Sat. 9–5
TYPE OF MERCHANDISE: Clothing,
housewares, furniture
DONATION TAX RECEIPT: Receipt given
upon request

Goodwill Industries Thrift Store
1625 W. State St.
Rockford, IL 61102
TYPE OF MERCHANDISE: Clothing,
housewares, furniture
DONATION TAX RECEIPT: Receipt given
upon request

Salvation Army Thrift Store
1706 18th Ave.
Rockford, IL 61104
TYPE OF MERCHANDISE: Clothing,
housewares, furniture
DONATION TAX RECEIPT: Receipt given
upon request

Goodwill Industries Thrift Store
1907 Kishwaukee St.
Rockford, IL 61104
TYPE OF MERCHANDISE: Clothing,
housewares, furniture
DONATION TAX RECEIPT: Receipt given
upon request

Salvation Army Thrift Store
5436 N. Second St.
Rockford, IL 61111

TYPE OF MERCHANDISE: Clothing,
housewares, furniture
DONATION TAX RECEIPT: Receipt given
upon request

Goodwill Industries Thrift Store
541 Blackhawk Blvd.
South Beloit, IL 61080
TYPE OF MERCHANDISE: Clothing,
housewares, furniture
DONATION TAX RECEIPT: Receipt given
upon request

Salvation Army Thrift Store
2422 S. MacArthur Blvd.
Springfield, IL 62704
TYPE OF MERCHANDISE: Clothing,
housewares, furniture
DONATION TAX RECEIPT: Receipt given
upon request

Goodwill Industries Thrift Store
815 N. 11th St.
Springfield, IL 62702
TYPE OF MERCHANDISE: Clothing,
housewares, furniture
DONATION TAX RECEIPT: Receipt given
upon request

Saint Vincent De Paul Thrift Store
7 W. Sixth St.
Sterling, IL 61081
TYPE OF MERCHANDISE: Clothing,
housewares, furniture
DONATION TAX RECEIPT: Receipt given
upon request
COMMENTS: Monthly markdowns

Salvation Army Thrift Store
1700 N. Lewis Ave.
Waukegan, IL 60085
TYPE OF MERCHANDISE: Clothing,
housewares, furniture
DONATION TAX RECEIPT: Receipt given
upon request

Saint Vincent De Paul Thrift Store
211 Main St.
West Chicago, IL 60185
TYPE OF MERCHANDISE: Clothing,
housewares, furniture
DONATION TAX RECEIPT: Receipt given
upon request
COMMENTS: Monthly markdowns

NCJW Encore & More
1107 Central
CROSS STREETS: Green Bay and Lake St.
Wilmette, IL 60091
PHONE: 708-853-8888
HOURS: Mon.–Sat. 10–5
TYPE OF MERCHANDISE: Clothing,
housewares, bric-a-brac
DONATION TAX RECEIPT: Receipt given
upon request

Indiana

Goodwill Industries Thrift Store
1410 Jackson St.
Anderson, IN 46016
TYPE OF MERCHANDISE: Clothing,
housewares, furniture
DONATION TAX RECEIPT: Receipt given
upon request
Salvation Army Thrift Store
1520 Meridian Plaza
Anderson, IN 46016
TYPE OF MERCHANDISE: Clothing,
housewares, furniture
DONATION TAX RECEIPT: Receipt given
upon request
Salvation Army Thrift Store
1212 "K" St.
Bedford, IN 47421
TYPE OF MERCHANDISE: Clothing,
housewares, furniture
DONATION TAX RECEIPT: Receipt given
upon request
Saint Vincent De Paul Thrift Store
1711 "I" St.
Bedford, IN 47421
TYPE OF MERCHANDISE: Clothing,
housewares, furniture
DONATION TAX RECEIPT: Receipt given
upon request
COMMENTS: Monthly markdowns
MCC Et Cetera Shop
152 W. Main St.
Berne, IN 46711
TYPE OF MERCHANDISE: Clothing,
housewares
DONATION TAX RECEIPT: Receipt given
upon request

Goodwill Industries Thrift Store
2430 S. Walnut St.
Bloomington, IN 47401
TYPE OF MERCHANDISE: Clothing,
housewares, furniture
DONATION TAX RECEIPT: Receipt given
upon request
Salvation Army Thrift Store
102 E. Sycamore St.
Boonville, IN 47601
PHONE: 812-897-4229
HOURS: Mon.–Sat. 9–5
TYPE OF MERCHANDISE: Clothing,
housewares, furniture
DONATION TAX RECEIPT: Receipt given
upon request
Goodwill Industries Thrift Store
111 W. National St.
Brazil, IN 47834
PHONE: 812-448-1215
HOURS: Mon.–Sat. 9–5
TYPE OF MERCHANDISE: Clothing,
housewares, furniture
DONATION TAX RECEIPT: Receipt given
upon request
Goodwill Industries Thrift Store
15021 Grey Hound Ct.
Carmel, IN 46032
TYPE OF MERCHANDISE: Clothing,
housewares, furniture
DONATION TAX RECEIPT: Receipt given
upon request
Goodwill Industries Thrift Store
1212 Applegate Lane
CROSS STREET: Hwy. 131
Clarksville, IN 47129
CONTACT: Mary Ann Shirely Walsh
PHONE: 812-288-7849
HOURS: Mon.–Sat. 9:30–5:30, Sun. 12–6
TYPE OF MERCHANDISE: Clothing,
housewares, furniture
DONATION TAX RECEIPT: Receipt given
upon request
Goodwill Industries Thrift Store
246 S. Main St.
Clinton, IN 47842
PHONE: 812-832-8450
HOURS: Mon.–Sat. 9–5

TYPE OF MERCHANDISE: Clothing, housewares, furniture
DONATION TAX RECEIPT: Receipt given upon request

Goodwill Industries Thrift Store
25th St.
CROSS STREET: At Central
Columbus, IN 47201
TYPE OF MERCHANDISE: Clothing, housewares, furniture
DONATION TAX RECEIPT: Receipt given upon request

Goodwill Industries Thrift Store
208 Elm St.
Corydon, IN 47112
CONTACT: Margaret Shaflin
PHONE: 812-738-3247
HOURS: Mon.–Sat. 9:30–5:30
TYPE OF MERCHANDISE: Clothing, housewares, furniture
DONATION TAX RECEIPT: Receipt given upon request

Goodwill Industries Thrift Store
1408 Darlington Ave.
Crawfordsville, IN 47933
TYPE OF MERCHANDISE: Clothing, housewares, furniture
DONATION TAX RECEIPT: Receipt given upon request

Goodwill Industries Thrift Store
210A Southway Blvd.
East Kokomo, IN 46902
TYPE OF MERCHANDISE: Clothing, housewares, furniture
DONATION TAX RECEIPT: Receipt given upon request

Salvation Army Thrift Store
2721 Benham Ave.
Elkhart, IN 46516-1953
PHONE: 219-293-7000
HOURS: Mon.–Sat. 9–5
TYPE OF MERCHANDISE: Clothing, housewares, furniture
DONATION TAX RECEIPT: Receipt given upon request
COMMENTS: Sidewalk sales and fashion shows

Salvation Army Thrift Store
1915 Covert Ave.
Evansville, IN 47714
PHONE: 812-473-3886
HOURS: Mon.–Sat. 9–5
TYPE OF MERCHANDISE: Clothing, housewares, furniture
DONATION TAX RECEIPT: Receipt given upon request

Salvation Army Thrift Store
4216 Morgan Ave.
Evansville, IN 47713
PHONE: 812-476-2227
TYPE OF MERCHANDISE: Clothing, housewares, furniture
DONATION TAX RECEIPT: Receipt given upon request

Goodwill Industries Thrift Store
500 S. Green River Rd.
Evansville, IN 47715
TYPE OF MERCHANDISE: Clothing, housewares, furniture
DONATION TAX RECEIPT: Receipt given upon request

Saint Vincent De Paul Thrift Store
767 E. Walnut St.
Evansville, IN 47713
TYPE OF MERCHANDISE: Clothing, housewares, furniture
DONATION TAX RECEIPT: Receipt given upon request
COMMENTS: Monthly markdowns

Salvation Army Thrift Store
801 N.W. Second St.
Evansville, IN 47708
PHONE: 812-424-2235
HOURS: Mon.–Sat. 9–5
TYPE OF MERCHANDISE: Clothing, housewares, furniture
DONATION TAX RECEIPT: Receipt given upon request

Saint Vincent De Paul Thrift Store
1600 S. Calhoun St.
Fort Wayne, IN 46802
TYPE OF MERCHANDISE: Clothing, housewares, furniture
DONATION TAX RECEIPT: Receipt given upon request
COMMENTS: Monthly markdowns

MCC Dove's Nest Gift and Thrift
6746 E. State Blvd.
CROSS STREET: Georgetown Sq.
Fort Wayne, IN 46815
PHONE: 219-493-4774
TYPE OF MERCHANDISE: Clothing,
housewares, furniture
DONATION TAX RECEIPT: Receipt given
upon request
Salvation Army Thrift Store
1351 W. 11th Ave.
Gary, IN 46402
PHONE: 219-882-9377
HOURS: Mon.–Sat. 9–5
TYPE OF MERCHANDISE: Clothing,
housewares, furniture
DONATION TAX RECEIPT: Receipt given
upon request
COMMENTS: Weekly 50% discount on
selected items
Salvation Army Thrift Store
2433 Broadway
Gary, IN 46406
PHONE: 219-882-1730
HOURS: Mon.–Sat. 9–5
TYPE OF MERCHANDISE: Clothing,
housewares, furniture
DONATION TAX RECEIPT: Receipt given
upon request
COMMENTS: Weekly 50% discount on
selected items
Salvation Army Thrift Store
3311 Grant St.
Gary, IN 46408
PHONE: 219-884-7336
HOURS: Mon.–Sat. 10–6
TYPE OF MERCHANDISE: Clothing,
housewares, furniture
DONATION TAX RECEIPT: Receipt given
upon request
COMMENTS: Weekly 50% discount on
selected items
MCC The Whistle Stop
1013 Division St.
Goshen, IN 46526
PHONE: 219-534-1828
TYPE OF MERCHANDISE: Clothing,
housewares

DONATION TAX RECEIPT: Receipt given
upon request
Salvation Army Thrift Store
129 S. Main
Goshen, IN 46526
PHONE: 219-533-9770
HOURS: Mon.–Sat. 9–5
TYPE OF MERCHANDISE: Clothing,
housewares, furniture
DONATION TAX RECEIPT: Receipt given
upon request
COMMENTS: Sidewalk sales and fashion
shows
Goodwill Industries Thrift Store
21 N. Indiana St.
Greencastle, IN 46135
PHONE: 317-653-6587
HOURS: Mon.–Sat. 9–5
TYPE OF MERCHANDISE: Clothing,
housewares, furniture
DONATION TAX RECEIPT: Receipt given
upon request
Goodwill Industries Thrift Store
779 US Hwy. 31 N
Greenwood, IN 46142
TYPE OF MERCHANDISE: Clothing,
housewares, furniture
DONATION TAX RECEIPT: Receipt given
upon request
Salvation Army Thrift Store
6612 Kennedy Ave.
Hessville, IN 46323
PHONE: 219-845-0865
HOURS: Mon.–Sat. 9–5
TYPE OF MERCHANDISE: Clothing,
housewares, furniture
DONATION TAX RECEIPT: Receipt given
upon request
COMMENTS: Weekly 50% discount on
selected items
Salvation Army Thrift Store
1633 E. 27th St.
Hobart, IN 46342
PHONE: 219-947-2877
HOURS: Mon.–Sat. 10–6
TYPE OF MERCHANDISE: Clothing,
housewares, furniture
DONATION TAX RECEIPT: Receipt given
upon request

COMMENTS: Weekly 50% discount on selected items

Saint Vincent De Paul Thrift Store
R.R. 3
Huntingburg, IN 47542
TYPE OF MERCHANDISE: Clothing, housewares, furniture
DONATION TAX RECEIPT: Receipt given upon request
COMMENTS: Monthly markdowns

Saint Vincent De Paul Thrift Store
1111 E. 17th St.
Indianapolis, IN 46202
TYPE OF MERCHANDISE: Clothing, housewares, furniture
DONATION TAX RECEIPT: Receipt given upon request
COMMENTS: Monthly markdowns

Goodwill Industries Thrift Store
1635 W. Michigan St.
Indianapolis, IN 46222
TYPE OF MERCHANDISE: Clothing, housewares, furniture
DONATION TAX RECEIPT: Receipt given upon request

Goodwill Industries Thrift Store
2060 E. 52nd St.
Indianapolis, IN 46205
TYPE OF MERCHANDISE: Clothing, housewares, furniture
DONATION TAX RECEIPT: Receipt given upon request

Salvation Army Thrift Store
2416 W. 16th St.
Indianapolis, IN 46222
TYPE OF MERCHANDISE: Clothing, housewares, furniture
DONATION TAX RECEIPT: Receipt given upon request

Goodwill Industries Thrift Store
2740 Madison Ave.
Indianapolis, IN 46225
TYPE OF MERCHANDISE: Clothing, housewares, furniture
DONATION TAX RECEIPT: Receipt given upon request

Amvets Thrift Store
2794 Lafayette Rd.
Indianapolis, IN 46222

TYPE OF MERCHANDISE: Clothing, housewares, furniture
DONATION TAX RECEIPT: Receipt given upon request

Goodwill Industries Thrift Store
4004 Georgetown Rd.
Indianapolis, IN 46254
TYPE OF MERCHANDISE: Clothing, housewares, furniture
DONATION TAX RECEIPT: Receipt given upon request

Goodwill Industries Thrift Store
5640 W. Washington St.
Indianapolis, IN 46241
TYPE OF MERCHANDISE: Clothing, housewares, furniture
DONATION TAX RECEIPT: Receipt given upon request

Junior League Next-to-New Shop
6180 N. Hillside
Indianapolis, IN 46220
CONTACT: Betty A. Hollin
PHONE: 317-253-6746
HOURS: Mon.–Fri. 10–6, Thurs. 10–8, Sat. 10–4:30
TYPE OF MERCHANDISE: Clothing, housewares, toys
DONATION TAX RECEIPT: Receipt given upon request
COMMENTS: $1.00 sales, back room sales

Goodwill Industries Thrift Store
6366 E. 82nd St.
Indianapolis, IN 46250
TYPE OF MERCHANDISE: Clothing, housewares, furniture
DONATION TAX RECEIPT: Receipt given upon request

Goodwill Industries Thrift Store
8050 N.E. Pendleton Pike
Indianapolis, IN 46226
TYPE OF MERCHANDISE: Clothing, housewares, furniture
DONATION TAX RECEIPT: Receipt given upon request

Goodwill Industries Thrift Store
8456 Michigan Rd.
Indianapolis, IN 46268
TYPE OF MERCHANDISE: Clothing, housewares, furniture

DONATION TAX RECEIPT: Receipt given upon request

Goodwill Industries Thrift Store
9513 E. Washington St.
Indianapolis, IN 46219
TYPE OF MERCHANDISE: Clothing, housewares, furniture
DONATION TAX RECEIPT: Receipt given upon request

Saint Vincent De Paul Thrift Store
1402 Meridian Rd.
Jasper, IN 47546
TYPE OF MERCHANDISE: Clothing, housewares, furniture
DONATION TAX RECEIPT: Receipt given upon request
COMMENTS: Monthly markdowns

Salvation Army Thrift Store
Southgate Plaza Shopping Center
Jasper, IN 47546
PHONE: 812-482-6598
HOURS: Mon.–Sat. 9–5
TYPE OF MERCHANDISE: Clothing, housewares, furniture
DONATION TAX RECEIPT: Receipt given upon request

Goodwill Industries Thrift Store
228 Spring St.
Jeffersonville, IN 47130
TYPE OF MERCHANDISE: Clothing, housewares, furniture
DONATION TAX RECEIPT: Receipt given upon request

Goodwill Industries Thrift Store
2941 S. Washington St.
Kokomo, IN 46902
TYPE OF MERCHANDISE: Clothing, housewares, furniture
DONATION TAX RECEIPT: Receipt given upon request
COMMENTS: Bazaar

Goodwill Industries Thrift Store
360 Brown St.
Lafayette, IN 47906
TYPE OF MERCHANDISE: Clothing, housewares, furniture
DONATION TAX RECEIPT: Receipt given upon request
COMMENTS: Family store

Salvation Army Thrift Store
401 S. Fourth St.
Lafayette, IN 47901
TYPE OF MERCHANDISE: Clothing, housewares, furniture
DONATION TAX RECEIPT: Receipt given upon request

Saint Vincent De Paul Thrift Store
525 Wabash Ave.
Lafayette, IN 47905
TYPE OF MERCHANDISE: Clothing, housewares, furniture
DONATION TAX RECEIPT: Receipt given upon request
COMMENTS: Monthly markdowns

Salvation Army Thrift Store
520 Lincolnway
Laporta, IN 46350
PHONE: 219-326-7555
HOURS: Mon.–Sat. 9–5
TYPE OF MERCHANDISE: Clothing, housewares, furniture
DONATION TAX RECEIPT: Receipt given upon request
COMMENTS: Sidewalk sales and fashion shows

Saint Vincent De Paul Thrift Store
208 Fifth St.
Logansport, IN 46947
TYPE OF MERCHANDISE: Clothing, housewares, furniture
DONATION TAX RECEIPT: Receipt given upon request
COMMENTS: Monthly markdowns

Goodwill Industries Thrift Store
220 Clifty Dr.
Madison, IN 47250
CONTACT: Mary Scroggins
PHONE: 812-944-0771
HOURS: Mon.–Sat. 9:30–5:30
TYPE OF MERCHANDISE: Clothing, housewares, furniture
DONATION TAX RECEIPT: Receipt given upon request

Salvation Army Thrift Store
1804 Franklin St.
Michigan City, IN 46360
PHONE: 219-872-8129
HOURS: Mon.–Sat. 9–5

TYPE OF MERCHANDISE: Clothing, housewares, furniture
DONATION TAX RECEIPT: Receipt given upon request
COMMENTS: Sidewalk sales and fashion shows

Salvation Army Thrift Store
812 E. McKinley Ave.
Mishawaka, IN 46544
PHONE: 219-256-9358
HOURS: Mon.–Sat. 9–5
TYPE OF MERCHANDISE: Clothing, housewares, furniture
DONATION TAX RECEIPT: Receipt given upon request
COMMENTS: Sidewalk sales and fashion shows

Salvation Army Thrift Store
Southwind Shopping Center
Mt. Vernon, IN 47620
PHONE: 812-838-4631
HOURS: Mon.–Sat. 9–5
TYPE OF MERCHANDISE: Clothing, housewares, furniture
DONATION TAX RECEIPT: Receipt given upon request

Goodwill Industries Thrift Store
3310 N. Broadway
Muncie, IN 47303
TYPE OF MERCHANDISE: Clothing, housewares, furniture
DONATION TAX RECEIPT: Receipt given upon request

Saint Vincent De Paul Thrift Store
St. Mary's Church
Muncie, IN 47304
TYPE OF MERCHANDISE: Clothing, housewares, furniture
DONATION TAX RECEIPT: Receipt given upon request
COMMENTS: Monthly markdowns

Goodwill Industries Thrift Store
527 Pearl St.
CROSS STREET: Oak
New Albany, IN 47150-3326
CONTACT: Mary Ann Shirely Walsh
PHONE: 812-944-0771
HOURS: Mon.–Sat. 9–6, Sun. 12–6

TYPE OF MERCHANDISE: Clothing, housewares, furniture
DONATION TAX RECEIPT: Receipt given upon request

Goodwill Industries Thrift Store
3013 S. 14th St.
New Castle, IN 47362
TYPE OF MERCHANDISE: Clothing, housewares, furniture
DONATION TAX RECEIPT: Receipt given upon request

Goodwill Industries Thrift Store
1950 E. Conner St.
Noblesville, IN 46060
TYPE OF MERCHANDISE: Clothing, housewares, furniture
DONATION TAX RECEIPT: Receipt given upon request

Saint Vincent De Paul Thrift Store
62 W. Third St.
Peru, IN 46970
TYPE OF MERCHANDISE: Clothing, housewares, furniture
DONATION TAX RECEIPT: Receipt given upon request
COMMENTS: Monthly markdowns

Salvation Army Thrift Store
113 S. Water
Plymouth, IN 46563
PHONE: 219-936-8822
HOURS: Mon.–Sat. 9–5
TYPE OF MERCHANDISE: Clothing, housewares, furniture
DONATION TAX RECEIPT: Receipt given upon request
COMMENTS: Sidewalk sales and fashion shows

Salvation Army Thrift Store
112 N. Prince St.
Princeton, IN 47670
PHONE: 812-385-2408
HOURS: Mon.–Sat. 9–5
TYPE OF MERCHANDISE: Clothing, housewares, furniture
DONATION TAX RECEIPT: Receipt given upon request

Goodwill Industries Thrift Store
1801 W. National Rd.
Richmond, IN 47374

TYPE OF MERCHANDISE: Clothing, housewares, furniture
DONATION TAX RECEIPT: Receipt given upon request

Salvation Army Thrift Store
413 N. Eighth St.
Richmond, IN 47374
TYPE OF MERCHANDISE: Clothing, housewares, furniture
DONATION TAX RECEIPT: Receipt given upon request

Goodwill Industries Thrift Store
85 Main St.
CROSS STREET: Town Square
Scottsburg, IN 47170
CONTACT: Mary Ann Shirely Walsh
PHONE: 812-752-5200
HOURS: Mon.–Sat. 9:30–5:30
TYPE OF MERCHANDISE: Clothing, housewares, furniture
DONATION TAX RECEIPT: Receipt given upon request

Salvation Army Thrift Store
126 E. Washington St.
Shelbyville, IN 46176
TYPE OF MERCHANDISE: Clothing, housewares, furniture
DONATION TAX RECEIPT: Receipt given upon request

Goodwill Industries Thrift Store
1648 State Rd. 44
Shelbyville, IN 46176
TYPE OF MERCHANDISE: Clothing, housewares, furniture
DONATION TAX RECEIPT: Receipt given upon request

Saint Vincent De Paul Thrift Store
230 E. Sample
South Bend, IN 46601
TYPE OF MERCHANDISE: Clothing, housewares, furniture
DONATION TAX RECEIPT: Receipt given upon request
COMMENTS: Monthly markdowns

Salvation Army Thrift Store
506 S. Main St.
South Bend, IN 46601
PHONE: 219-288-2539

HOURS: Mon.–Sat. 9–5
TYPE OF MERCHANDISE: Clothing, housewares, furniture
DONATION TAX RECEIPT: Receipt given upon request
COMMENTS: Sidewalk sales and fashion shows

Goodwill Industries Thrift Store
921 N. Eddy St.
South Bend, IN 46617
TYPE OF MERCHANDISE: Clothing, housewares, furniture
DONATION TAX RECEIPT: Receipt given upon request

Goodwill Industries Thrift Store
103 S. Main St.
Sullivan, IN 47882
PHONE: 812-268-5820
HOURS: Mon.–Sat. 9–5
TYPE OF MERCHANDISE: Clothing, housewares, furniture
DONATION TAX RECEIPT: Receipt given upon request

Goodwill Industries Thrift Store
2702 South 3rd St.
Terre Haute, IN 47802
PHONE: 812-235-8511
HOURS: Mon.–Sat. 9–8, Sun. 12–6
TYPE OF MERCHANDISE: Clothing, housewares, furniture
DONATION TAX RECEIPT: Receipt given upon request

Goodwill Industries Thrift Store
2000 Lafayette Ave.
Terre Haute, IN 47804
PHONE: 812-466-1625
HOURS: Mon.–Sat. 9–8, Sun. 12–6
TYPE OF MERCHANDISE: Clothing, housewares, furniture
DONATION TAX RECEIPT: Receipt given upon request

Saint Vincent De Paul Thrift Store
1604 Main St.
Vincennes, IN 47591
TYPE OF MERCHANDISE: Clothing, housewares, furniture
DONATION TAX RECEIPT: Receipt given upon request
COMMENTS: Monthly markdowns

Salvation Army Thrift Store
1001 Washington Ave.
Vincennes, IN 47591
PHONE: 812-882-1808
HOURS: Mon.–Sat. 9–5
TYPE OF MERCHANDISE: Clothing,
housewares, furniture
DONATION TAX RECEIPT: Receipt given
upon request

Goodwill Industries Thrift Store
360 Brown St. Levee Plaza
W. Lafayette, IN 47906
TYPE OF MERCHANDISE: Clothing,
housewares, furniture
DONATION TAX RECEIPT: Receipt given
upon request

Saint Vincent De Paul Thrift Store
101 W. Main St.
Washington, IN 47501
TYPE OF MERCHANDISE: Clothing,
housewares, furniture
DONATION TAX RECEIPT: Receipt given
upon request
COMMENTS: Monthly markdowns

Saint Vincent De Paul Thrift Store
1205 State
Washington, IN 47501
TYPE OF MERCHANDISE: Clothing,
housewares, furniture
DONATION TAX RECEIPT: Receipt given
upon request
COMMENTS: Monthly markdowns

Iowa

Salvation Army Thrift Store
411 Kellogg Ave.
Ames, IA 50010
TYPE OF MERCHANDISE: Clothing,
housewares, furniture
DONATION TAX RECEIPT: Receipt given
upon request

American Cancer Society Discovery Shop
2397 Cumberland Sq. Dr.
Bettendorf, IA 52722
CONTACT: Karen McNally
PHONE: 319-355-0824

TYPE OF MERCHANDISE: Clothing, bric-a-
brac
DONATION TAX RECEIPT: Receipt given
upon request
COMMENTS: Monthly markdowns

Salvation Army Thrift Store
708 Arden St.
Boone, IA 50036
TYPE OF MERCHANDISE: Clothing,
housewares, furniture
DONATION TAX RECEIPT: Receipt given
upon request

Salvation Army Thrift Store
831 Harrison Ave.
Burlington, IA 52601
TYPE OF MERCHANDISE: Clothing,
housewares, furniture
DONATION TAX RECEIPT: Receipt given
upon request

Saint Vincent De Paul Thrift Store
203 Main St.
Cedar Falls, IA 50613
TYPE OF MERCHANDISE: Clothing,
housewares, furniture
DONATION TAX RECEIPT: Receipt given
upon request
COMMENTS: Monthly markdowns

Saint Vincent De Paul Thrift Store
2620 Main St.
Cedar Falls, IA 50613
TYPE OF MERCHANDISE: Clothing,
housewares, furniture
DONATION TAX RECEIPT: Receipt given
upon request
COMMENTS: Monthly markdowns

Goodwill Industries Thrift Store
4302C University Ave.
Cedar Falls, IA 50613
TYPE OF MERCHANDISE: Clothing,
housewares, furniture
DONATION TAX RECEIPT: Receipt given
upon request

Goodwill Industries Thrift Store
150 Collins Rd. NE
Cedar Rapids, IA 52402
CONTACT: Kari Pietan
PHONE: 319-373-1244

HOURS: Mon.–Wed. 9–5:30, Thurs.–Fri. 9–9, Sat. 9–5, Sun. 12–5
TYPE OF MERCHANDISE: Clothing, housewares, furniture
DONATION TAX RECEIPT: Receipt given upon request
COMMENTS: Everything half-price once a month

Goodwill Industries Thrift Store
2325 16th Ave. SW
Cedar Rapids, IA 52404
CONTACT: Debbie Sherard
PHONE: 319-365-0935
HOURS: Mon.–Wed. 9–5:30, Thurs.-Fri. 9–9, Sat. 9–5, Sun. 12–5
TYPE OF MERCHANDISE: Clothing, housewares, furniture
DONATION TAX RECEIPT: Receipt given upon request
COMMENTS: Everything half-price once a month

Goodwill Industries Thrift Store
2743 16th Ave. SW
Cedar Rapids, IA 52404
TYPE OF MERCHANDISE: Clothing, housewares, furniture
DONATION TAX RECEIPT: Receipt given upon request

Saint Vincent De Paul Thrift Store
348 23rd St. NW
Cedar Rapids, IA 52405
TYPE OF MERCHANDISE: Clothing, housewares, furniture
DONATION TAX RECEIPT: Receipt given upon request
COMMENTS: Monthly markdowns

American Cancer Society Discovery Shop
3621 Town Country Center
Cedar Rapids, IA 52401
PHONE: 319-362-7845
TYPE OF MERCHANDISE: Clothing, bric-a-brac
DONATION TAX RECEIPT: Receipt given upon request
COMMENTS: Monthly markdowns

Salvation Army Thrift Store
45 16th Ave. SW
Cedar Rapids, IA 52404

PHONE: 319-365-4411
HOURS: Mon.–Sat. 9–7
TYPE OF MERCHANDISE: Clothing, housewares, furniture
DONATION TAX RECEIPT: Receipt given upon request

Salvation Army Thrift Store
717 Third Ave. SE
Cedar Rapids, IA 52403
PHONE: 319-365-9333
HOURS: Mon.–Sat. 9–7
TYPE OF MERCHANDISE: Clothing, housewares, furniture
DONATION TAX RECEIPT: Receipt given upon request

Saint Vincent De Paul Thrift Store
928 Seventh St. SE
Cedar Rapids, IA 52401
TYPE OF MERCHANDISE: Clothing, housewares, furniture
DONATION TAX RECEIPT: Receipt given upon request
COMMENTS: Monthly markdowns

Salvation Army Thrift Store
1010 S. Fourth St.
Clinton, IA 52732
TYPE OF MERCHANDISE: Clothing, housewares, furniture
DONATION TAX RECEIPT: Receipt given upon request

Salvation Army Thrift Store
405 Seventh Ave. S
Clinton, IA 52732
PHONE: 319-242-3211
HOURS: Mon.–Sat. 9–5
TYPE OF MERCHANDISE: Clothing, housewares, furniture
DONATION TAX RECEIPT: Receipt given upon request

Goodwill Industries Thrift Store
1719 Second St.
Coralville, IA 52241
CONTACT: Mary Martha Stoessel
PHONE: 319-338-4184
HOURS: Mon.–Wed. 9–5:30, Thurs.–Fri. 9–9, Sat. 9–5, Sun. 12–5
TYPE OF MERCHANDISE: Clothing, housewares, furniture

DONATION TAX RECEIPT: Receipt given upon request
COMMENTS: Everything half-price once a month

Goodwill Industries Thrift Store
1920 W. Broadway
Council Bluffs, IA 51501
TYPE OF MERCHANDISE: Clothing, housewares, furniture
DONATION TAX RECEIPT: Receipt given upon request

Salvation Army Thrift Store
717 W. Broadway
Council Bluffs, IA 51501
PHONE: 712-325-0684
HOURS: Mon.–Sat. 9–6
TYPE OF MERCHANDISE: Clothing, housewares, furniture
DONATION TAX RECEIPT: Receipt given upon request
COMMENTS: Monthly & seasonal sales

Goodwill Industries Thrift Store
1432 W. Locust St.
Davenport, IA 52804
CONTACT: Linda Ford
PHONE: 319-322-2024
HOURS: Mon.–Wed. 9–5:30, Thurs.–Fri. 9–9, Sat. 9–5, Sun. 12–5
TYPE OF MERCHANDISE: Clothing, housewares, furniture
DONATION TAX RECEIPT: Receipt given upon request
COMMENTS: Everything half-price once a month

Salvation Army Thrift Store
1637 W. Locust St.
Davenport, IA 52804
TYPE OF MERCHANDISE: Clothing, housewares, furniture
DONATION TAX RECEIPT: Receipt given upon request

Salvation Army Thrift Store
2604 W. Locust St.
Davenport, IA 52804
PHONE: 319-388-9953
HOURS: Mon.–Sat. 9–5
TYPE OF MERCHANDISE: Clothing, housewares, furniture

DONATION TAX RECEIPT: Receipt given upon request

Salvation Army Thrift Store
415 W. Second St.
Davenport, IA 52801
PHONE: 319-323-3836
HOURS: Mon.–Sat. 9–5
TYPE OF MERCHANDISE: Clothing, housewares, furniture
DONATION TAX RECEIPT: Receipt given upon request

Salvation Army Thrift Store
420 W. River Dr.
Davenport, IA 52801
TYPE OF MERCHANDISE: Clothing, housewares, furniture
DONATION TAX RECEIPT: Receipt given upon request

American Cancer Society Discovery Shop
902 W. Kimberly
Davenport, IA 58028
CONTACT: Kay Finch
PHONE: 319-286-0721
TYPE OF MERCHANDISE: Clothing, bric-a-brac
DONATION TAX RECEIPT: Receipt given upon request
COMMENTS: Monthly markdowns

Saint Vincent De Paul Thrift Store
1426 Sixth Ave.
Des Moines, IA 50314
TYPE OF MERCHANDISE: Clothing, housewares, furniture
DONATION TAX RECEIPT: Receipt given upon request
COMMENTS: Monthly markdowns

Goodwill Industries Thrift Store
1515 E. Euclid Ave.
Des Moines, IA 50313
TYPE OF MERCHANDISE: Clothing, housewares, furniture
DONATION TAX RECEIPT: Receipt given upon request

Salvation Army Thrift Store
3418 SE. 14th St.
Des Moines, IA 50320
TYPE OF MERCHANDISE: Clothing, housewares, furniture

DONATION TAX RECEIPT: Receipt given upon request

Salvation Army Thrift Store
4807 S.W. Ninth St.
Des Moines, IA 50315
TYPE OF MERCHANDISE: Clothing, housewares, furniture
DONATION TAX RECEIPT: Receipt given upon request

Saint Vincent De Paul Thrift Store
1351 Iowa St.
Dubuque, IA 52001
TYPE OF MERCHANDISE: Clothing, housewares, furniture
DONATION TAX RECEIPT: Receipt given upon request
COMMENTS: Monthly markdowns

Salvation Army Thrift Store
216 First St. E
Independence, IA 50644
PHONE: 319-334-6784
HOURS: Mon.–Sat. 9–7
TYPE OF MERCHANDISE: Clothing, housewares, furniture
DONATION TAX RECEIPT: Receipt given upon request

MCC Crowded Closet
1121 Gilbert Ct.
Iowa City, IA 52240
PHONE: 319-337-5924
TYPE OF MERCHANDISE: Clothing, housewares
DONATION TAX RECEIPT: Receipt given upon request

Salvation Army Thrift Store
1213 Gilbert Ct.
Iowa City, IA 52240
PHONE: 319-338-7945
HOURS: Mon.–Sat. 9–7
TYPE OF MERCHANDISE: Clothing, housewares, furniture
DONATION TAX RECEIPT: Receipt given upon request

Goodwill Industries Thrift Store
1719 Second St.
Iowa City, IA 52241
TYPE OF MERCHANDISE: Clothing, housewares, furniture

DONATION TAX RECEIPT: Receipt given upon request

Goodwill Industries Thrift Store
1835 Boyrum St.
CROSS STREET: Hwy. 6
Iowa City, IA 52245
CONTACT: Andrew Heineman
PHONE: 319-337-3548
HOURS: Mon.–Wed. 9–5:30, Thurs.–Fri. 9–9, Sat. 9–5, Sun. 12–5
TYPE OF MERCHANDISE: Clothing, housewares, furniture
DONATION TAX RECEIPT: Receipt given upon request
COMMENTS: Everything half-price once a month

Salvation Army Thrift Store
1125 Johnson St.
Keokuk, IA 52632
TYPE OF MERCHANDISE: Clothing, housewares, furniture
DONATION TAX RECEIPT: Receipt given upon request

Salvation Army Thrift Store
3335 Seventh Ave.
Marion, IA 52302
PHONE: 319-377-2429
HOURS: Mon.–Sat. 9–7
TYPE OF MERCHANDISE: Clothing, housewares, furniture
DONATION TAX RECEIPT: Receipt given upon request

Salvation Army Thrift Store
116 W. Main St.
Marshalltown, IA 50158
TYPE OF MERCHANDISE: Clothing, housewares, furniture
DONATION TAX RECEIPT: Receipt given upon request

Salvation Army Thrift Store
203 First St. SW
Mason City, IA 50401
TYPE OF MERCHANDISE: Clothing, housewares, furniture
DONATION TAX RECEIPT: Receipt given upon request

American Cancer Society Discovery Shop
Regency Square
Mason City, IA 50401
TYPE OF MERCHANDISE: Clothing, bric-a-brac
DONATION TAX RECEIPT: Receipt given upon request
COMMENTS: Monthly markdowns

Salvation Army Thrift Store
1005 E. Second St.
Muscatine, IA 52761
PHONE: 319-263-8814
HOURS: Mon.–Sat. 9–5
TYPE OF MERCHANDISE: Clothing, housewares, furniture
DONATION TAX RECEIPT: Receipt given upon request

Goodwill Industries Thrift Store
124 Colorado St.
CROSS STREET: Next to Muscatine Mall
Muscatine, IA 52761
CONTACT: Lynn Einfeldt
PHONE: 319-264-1947
HOURS: Mon.–Wed. 9–5:30, Thurs.–Fri. 9–9, Sat. 9–5, Sun. 12–5
TYPE OF MERCHANDISE: Clothing, housewares, furniture
DONATION TAX RECEIPT: Receipt given upon request
COMMENTS: Everything half-price once a month

Salvation Army Thrift Store
522 Mulberry Ave.
Muscatine, IA 52761
TYPE OF MERCHANDISE: Clothing, housewares, furniture
DONATION TAX RECEIPT: Receipt given upon request

Goodwill Industries Thrift Store
13 S. Frederick Ave.
Oelwein, IA 50662
TYPE OF MERCHANDISE: Clothing, housewares, furniture
DONATION TAX RECEIPT: Receipt given upon request

Goodwill Industries Thrift Store
110 S. Iowa Ave.
Washington, IA 52353

CONTACT: Marnie Simmering
PHONE: 319-653-2548
HOURS: Mon.–Wed. 9–5:30, Thurs.–Fri. 9–9, Sat. 9–5, Sun. 12–5
TYPE OF MERCHANDISE: Clothing, housewares, furniture
DONATION TAX RECEIPT: Receipt given upon request
COMMENTS: Everything half-price once a month

Saint Vincent De Paul Thrift Store
320 Broadway
Waterloo, IA 50703
TYPE OF MERCHANDISE: Clothing, housewares, furniture
DONATION TAX RECEIPT: Receipt given upon request
COMMENTS: Monthly markdowns

Salvation Army Thrift Store
820 Sycamore St.
Waterloo, IA 52702
PHONE: 319-233-9119
HOURS: Mon.–Sat. 9–5:30
TYPE OF MERCHANDISE: Clothing, housewares, furniture
DONATION TAX RECEIPT: Receipt given upon request

American Cancer Society Discovery Shop
2900 University Ave. Suite D-5
West Des Moines, IA 50265
TYPE OF MERCHANDISE: Clothing, bric-a-brac
DONATION TAX RECEIPT: Receipt given upon request
COMMENTS: Monthly markdowns

Kansas

Goodwill Industries Thrift Store
224 S. Summit St.
Arkansas City, KS 67005
TYPE OF MERCHANDISE: Clothing, housewares, furniture
DONATION TAX RECEIPT: Receipt given upon request

Salvation Army Thrift Store
213 Scott St.
Fort Scotts, KS 66701

PHONE: 816-421-5434
HOURS: Mon.–Sat. 9–5
TYPE OF MERCHANDISE: Clothing, housewares, furniture
DONATION TAX RECEIPT: Receipt given upon request
COMMENTS: Auctions Mon.–Fri. 9 A.M.

Salvation Army Thrift Store
317 N. Eighth St.
Garden City, KS 67846
TYPE OF MERCHANDISE: Clothing, housewares, furniture
DONATION TAX RECEIPT: Receipt given upon request

ARC Thrift Store
114 E. Fifth Ave.
Garnett, KS 66032
TYPE OF MERCHANDISE: Clothing, housewares
DONATION TAX RECEIPT: Receipt given upon request

Salvation Army Thrift Store
1014 W. 31st St.
Haysville, KS 67060
TYPE OF MERCHANDISE: Clothing, housewares, furniture
DONATION TAX RECEIPT: Receipt given upon request

Salvation Army Thrift Store
2841 S. Hydraulic
Haysville, KS 67060
TYPE OF MERCHANDISE: Clothing, housewares, furniture
DONATION TAX RECEIPT: Receipt given upon request

MCC Et Cetera Shop
119 N. Main St.
Hillsboro, KS 67063
PHONE: 316-947-3817
TYPE OF MERCHANDISE: Clothing, housewares
DONATION TAX RECEIPT: Receipt given upon request

MCC Et Cetera Shop
22 N. Main St.
Hutchinson, KS 67501
PHONE: 316-669-8932
TYPE OF MERCHANDISE: Clothing, housewares

DONATION TAX RECEIPT: Receipt given upon request

Salvation Army Thrift Store
225 W. Main St.
Independence, KS 67301
TYPE OF MERCHANDISE: Clothing, housewares, furniture
DONATION TAX RECEIPT: Receipt given upon request

Salvation Army Thrift Store
117 W. Seventh St.
Junction City, KS 66441
TYPE OF MERCHANDISE: Clothing, housewares, furniture
DONATION TAX RECEIPT: Receipt given upon request

Disabled American Vets Thrift Store
607 N. Washington St.
Junction City, KS 66441
TYPE OF MERCHANDISE: Clothing, housewares
DONATION TAX RECEIPT: Receipt given upon request

Goodwill Industries Thrift Store
6501 State Ave.
Kansas City, KS 66102
PHONE: 913-334-1136
HOURS: Mon.–Sat. 9–9, Sun. 10–6
TYPE OF MERCHANDISE: Clothing, housewares, furniture
DONATION TAX RECEIPT: Receipt given upon request

Saint Vincent De Paul Thrift Store
1001 State Ave.
Kansas City, KS 66102
TYPE OF MERCHANDISE: Clothing, housewares, furniture
DONATION TAX RECEIPT: Receipt given upon request

ARC Thrift Store
3201 State Ave.
Kansas City, KS 66102
TYPE OF MERCHANDISE: Clothing, housewares
DONATION TAX RECEIPT: Receipt given upon request

Goodwill Industries Thrift Store
3744 State Ave.
Kansas City, KS 66102-3831
TYPE OF MERCHANDISE: Clothing,
housewares, furniture
DONATION TAX RECEIPT: Receipt given
upon request

Salvation Army Thrift Store
4933 State Ave.
Kansas City, KS 66102
PHONE: 816-421-5434
HOURS: Mon.–Sat. 10–7
TYPE OF MERCHANDISE: Clothing,
housewares, furniture
DONATION TAX RECEIPT: Receipt given
upon request
COMMENTS: Auctions Mon.–Fri. 9 A.M.

Saint Vincent De Paul Thrift Store
814 Osage Ave.
Kansas City, KS 66105
TYPE OF MERCHANDISE: Clothing,
housewares, furniture
DONATION TAX RECEIPT: Receipt given
upon request
COMMENTS: Monthly markdowns

Salvation Army Thrift Store
1818 Massachusetts
Lawrence, KS 66044
PHONE: 816-421-5434
HOURS: Mon.–Fri. 9–7, Sat. 9–6
TYPE OF MERCHANDISE: Clothing,
housewares, furniture
DONATION TAX RECEIPT: Receipt given
upon request
COMMENTS: Auctions Mon.–Fri. 9 A.M.

ARC Thrift Store
217A Delaware St.
Leavenworth, KS 66048
TYPE OF MERCHANDISE: Clothing,
housewares
DONATION TAX RECEIPT: Receipt given
upon request

Salvation Army Thrift Store
405 S. Fifth St.
Leavenworth, KS 66048
TYPE OF MERCHANDISE: Clothing,
housewares, furniture
DONATION TAX RECEIPT: Receipt given
upon request

MCC Et Cetera Shop
748 S. Kansas
Liberal, KS 67901
PHONE: 316-624-8740
TYPE OF MERCHANDISE: Clothing,
housewares
DONATION TAX RECEIPT: Receipt given
upon request

MCC Et Cetera Shop
619 Main St.
Newton, KS 67114
PHONE: 316-283-9461
TYPE OF MERCHANDISE: Clothing,
housewares, furniture
DONATION TAX RECEIPT: Receipt given
upon request

Salvation Army Thrift Store
703 N. Main
Newton, KS 67114
PHONE: 316-283-4008
HOURS: Mon.–Sat. 10–7
TYPE OF MERCHANDISE: Clothing,
housewares, furniture
DONATION TAX RECEIPT: Receipt given
upon request
COMMENTS: Periodic sales

Salvation Army Thrift Store
207 W. Dennis
Olathe, KS 66061
PHONE: 816-421-5434
HOURS: Mon.–Sat. 9–5
TYPE OF MERCHANDISE: Clothing,
housewares, furniture
DONATION TAX RECEIPT: Receipt given
upon request
COMMENTS: Auctions Mon.–Fri. 9 A.M.

American Cancer Society Discovery Shop
1501 E. 151st St.
CROSS STREET: Indian Trails Plaza
Olathe, KS 66062
TYPE OF MERCHANDISE: Clothing, bric-a-
brac
DONATION TAX RECEIPT: Receipt given
upon request
COMMENTS: Monthly markdowns

ARC Sacks On Santa Fe
8025 Santa Fe
Overland Park, KS 66204
PHONE: 913-642-6061

HOURS: Mon.–Fri. 10–5 (winter 10–4:30)
Sat. 10–4
TYPE OF MERCHANDISE: Clothing,
accessories
DONATION TAX RECEIPT: Receipt given
upon request
COMMENTS: Check out the boutique room
American Cancer Society Discovery Shop
4024 W. 95th St.
Prairie Village, KS 66207
CONTACT: Linda Heller
PHONE: 913-649-1390
TYPE OF MERCHANDISE: Clothing, bric-a-
brac
DONATION TAX RECEIPT: Receipt given
upon request
COMMENTS: Monthly markdowns
Goodwill Industries Thrift Store
158 S. Santa Fe Ave.
Salina, KS 67401
TYPE OF MERCHANDISE: Clothing,
housewares, furniture
DONATION TAX RECEIPT: Receipt given
upon request
Goodwill Industries Thrift Store
6220 Nieman Rd.
Shawnee Mission, KS 66203
PHONE: 913-631-1955
HOURS: Mon.–Fri. 9–9, Sat. 9–8, Sun. 12–5
TYPE OF MERCHANDISE: Clothing,
housewares, furniture
DONATION TAX RECEIPT: Receipt given
upon request
ARC Thrift Store
8025 Santa Fe Dr.
Shawnee Mission, KS 66204
TYPE OF MERCHANDISE: Clothing,
housewares
DONATION TAX RECEIPT: Receipt given
upon request
MCC The Olive Branch
119 S.W. Sixth St.
Topeka, KS 66603
PHONE: 913-233-4811
TYPE OF MERCHANDISE: Clothing,
housewares, furniture
DONATION TAX RECEIPT: Receipt given
upon request

Salvation Army Thrift Store
451 E. 29th St.
Topeka, KS 66617
PHONE: 816-421-5434
HOURS: Mon.–Sat. 9–6
TYPE OF MERCHANDISE: Clothing,
housewares, furniture
DONATION TAX RECEIPT: Receipt given
upon request
COMMENTS: Auctions Mon.–Fri. 9 A.M.
Salvation Army Thrift Store
1014 W. 31st St. S.
Wichita, KS 67217
PHONE: 316-522-1831
HOURS: Mon.–Sat. 10–7
TYPE OF MERCHANDISE: Clothing,
housewares, furniture
DONATION TAX RECEIPT: Receipt given
upon request
COMMENTS: Periodic sales
Salvation Army Thrift Store
1029 W. Douglas
Wichita, KS 67213
PHONE: 316-267-3751
HOURS: Mon.–Sat. 10–7
TYPE OF MERCHANDISE: Clothing,
housewares, furniture
DONATION TAX RECEIPT: Receipt given
upon request
COMMENTS: Periodic sales
Salvation Army Thrift Store
1851 N. Broadway
Wichita, KS 67214
PHONE: 316-264-1615
HOURS: Mon.–Sat. 10–7
TYPE OF MERCHANDISE: Clothing,
housewares, furniture
DONATION TAX RECEIPT: Receipt given
upon request
COMMENTS: Periodic sales
Salvation Army Thrift Store
2201 E. Central
Wichita, KS 67214
PHONE: 316-265-2412
HOURS: Mon.–Sat. 10–7
TYPE OF MERCHANDISE: Clothing,
housewares, furniture

DONATION TAX RECEIPT: Receipt given upon request
COMMENTS: Periodic sales

Junior League Shop
2520 E. Douglas Ave.
Wichita, KS 67214
TYPE OF MERCHANDISE: Clothing for men, women, and children
DONATION TAX RECEIPT: Receipt given upon request

National Assistance League Thrift Shop
2611 E. Douglas
Wichita, KS 67211
PHONE: 316-687-6107
TYPE OF MERCHANDISE: Clothing, housewares, furniture
DONATION TAX RECEIPT: Receipt given upon request
COMMENTS: Monthly markdowns

Junior League Thrift Shop
2734 Boulevard Plaza
Wichita, KS 67211
CONTACT: Denise Lineback
PHONE: 316-686-5854, 683-6328
HOURS: Mon.–Sat. 10–5, Thurs. 10–8
TYPE OF MERCHANDISE: Clothing, housewares, toys
DONATION TAX RECEIPT: Receipt given upon request
COMMENTS: Consignments taken at 50%

Salvation Army Thrift Store
2841 S. Hydraulic St.
Wichita, KS 67216
TYPE OF MERCHANDISE: Clothing, housewares, furniture
DONATION TAX RECEIPT: Receipt given upon request

Salvation Army Thrift Store
4830 E. Lincoln
Wichita, KS 67218
PHONE: 316-686-6541
HOURS: Mon.–Sat. 10–7
TYPE OF MERCHANDISE: Clothing, housewares, furniture
DONATION TAX RECEIPT: Receipt given upon request
COMMENTS: Periodic sales

Salvation Army Thrift Store
501 E. Harry
Wichita, KS 67211
PHONE: 316-262-5650
HOURS: Mon.–Sat. 10–7
TYPE OF MERCHANDISE: Clothing, housewares, furniture
DONATION TAX RECEIPT: Receipt given upon request
COMMENTS: Periodic sales

Disabled American Vets Thrift Store
5455 E. Central Ave.
Wichita, KS 67208
TYPE OF MERCHANDISE: Clothing, housewares
DONATION TAX RECEIPT: Receipt given upon request

Saint Vincent De Paul Thrift Store
722 W. Douglas Ave.
Wichita, KS 67203
TYPE OF MERCHANDISE: Clothing, housewares, furniture
DONATION TAX RECEIPT: Receipt given upon request
COMMENTS: Monthly markdowns

Kentucky

Goodwill Industries Thrift Store
2100 Winchester Ave.
Ashland, KY 41101
PHONE: 606-325-3606
HOURS: Mon. 8–8, Tues.–Thurs. 8–6, Fri. 8–8, Sat. 8–6, Sun. 1–6
TYPE OF MERCHANDISE: Clothing, housewares, furniture
DONATION TAX RECEIPT: Receipt given upon request
COMMENTS: Fall fashion show

Saint Vincent De Paul Thrift Store
342 Church St.
Bowling Green, KY 42101
TYPE OF MERCHANDISE: Clothing, housewares, furniture
DONATION TAX RECEIPT: Receipt given upon request
COMMENTS: Monthly markdowns

Saint Vincent De Paul Thrift Store
233 Pike St.
Covington, KY 41011
TYPE OF MERCHANDISE: Clothing,
housewares, furniture
DONATION TAX RECEIPT: Receipt given
upon request
COMMENTS: Monthly markdowns

Goodwill Industries Thrift Store
25 W. Seventh St.
Covington, KY 41011
PHONE: 513-261-3662
TYPE OF MERCHANDISE: Clothing,
housewares, furniture
DONATION TAX RECEIPT: Receipt given
upon request

Saint Vincent De Paul Thrift Store
712 Sixth Ave.
Dayton, KY 41073
TYPE OF MERCHANDISE: Clothing,
housewares, furniture
DONATION TAX RECEIPT: Receipt given
upon request
COMMENTS: Monthly markdowns

Saint Vincent De Paul Thrift Store
636 Allenville Rd.
Elkton, KY 42220
TYPE OF MERCHANDISE: Clothing,
housewares, furniture
DONATION TAX RECEIPT: Receipt given
upon request
COMMENTS: Monthly markdowns

Saint Vincent De Paul Thrift Store
2655 Crescent Springs Rd.
Erlanger, KY 41018
TYPE OF MERCHANDISE: Clothing,
housewares, furniture
DONATION TAX RECEIPT: Receipt given
upon request
COMMENTS: Monthly markdown

Goodwill Industries Thrift Store
7855 Tanner's Lane
Florence, KY 41042
PHONE: 513-371-1238
TYPE OF MERCHANDISE: Clothing,
housewares, furniture
DONATION TAX RECEIPT: Receipt given
upon request

Saint Vincent De Paul Thrift Store
116 N. Alvasia
Henderson, KY 42420
TYPE OF MERCHANDISE: Clothing,
housewares, furniture
DONATION TAX RECEIPT: Receipt given
upon request
COMMENTS: Monthly markdowns

Goodwill Industries Thrift Store
1441 Leestown Rd.
Lexington, KY 40511
TYPE OF MERCHANDISE: Clothing,
housewares, furniture
DONATION TAX RECEIPT: Receipt given
upon request

Salvation Army Thrift Store
228 New Circle Rd.
Lexington, KY 40505
TYPE OF MERCHANDISE: Clothing,
housewares, furniture
DONATION TAX RECEIPT: Receipt given
upon request

Saint Vincent De Paul Thrift Store
1029 S. Preston St.
Louisville, KY 40203
TYPE OF MERCHANDISE: Clothing,
housewares, furniture
DONATION TAX RECEIPT: Receipt given
upon request
COMMENTS: Monthly markdowns

Disabled American Vets Thrift Store
1701 Berry Blvd.
Louisville, KY 40215
TYPE OF MERCHANDISE: Clothing,
housewares
DONATION TAX RECEIPT: Receipt given
upon request

Salvation Army Thrift Store
1731 Dixie Hwy.
Louisville, KY 40210-2313
TYPE OF MERCHANDISE: Clothing,
housewares, furniture
DONATION TAX RECEIPT: Receipt given
upon request

Saint Vincent De Paul Thrift Store
248 E. Market St.
Louisville, KY 40202

TYPE OF MERCHANDISE: Clothing, housewares, furniture
DONATION TAX RECEIPT: Receipt given upon request
COMMENTS: Monthly markdowns

Amvets Thrift Store
3505 Cane Run Rd.
Louisville, KY 40211
TYPE OF MERCHANDISE: Clothing, housewares, furniture
DONATION TAX RECEIPT: Receipt given upon request

Saint Vincent De Paul Thrift Store
4417 Cane Run Rd.
Louisville, KY 40206
TYPE OF MERCHANDISE: Clothing, housewares, furniture
DONATION TAX RECEIPT: Receipt given upon request
COMMENTS: Monthly markdowns

Salvation Army Thrift Store
4417 S. Third St.
Louisville, KY 40214
TYPE OF MERCHANDISE: Clothing, housewares, furniture
DONATION TAX RECEIPT: Receipt given upon request

Salvation Army Thrift Store
5005 Preston Hwy.
Louisville, KY 40213
PHONE: 502-966-4539
HOURS: Mon.–Sat. 9–5
TYPE OF MERCHANDISE: Clothing, housewares, furniture
DONATION TAX RECEIPT: Receipt given upon request

Salvation Army Thrift Store
7846 Dixie Hwy.
Louisville, KY 40258
PHONE: 502-935-7474
HOURS: Mon.–Thurs. 9–5, Fri.–Sat. 9–6
TYPE OF MERCHANDISE: Clothing, housewares, furniture
DONATION TAX RECEIPT: Receipt given upon request

Goodwill Industries Thrift Store
9615 Milbrook Rd.
Louisville, KY 40242

TYPE OF MERCHANDISE: Clothing, housewares, furniture
DONATION TAX RECEIPT: Receipt given upon request

Saint Vincent De Paul Thrift Store
101 E. Arch St.
Madisonville, KY 42431
TYPE OF MERCHANDISE: Clothing, housewares, furniture
DONATION TAX RECEIPT: Receipt given upon request
COMMENTS: Monthly markdowns

Salvation Army Thrift Store
284 W. Center St.
Madisonville, KY 42431
TYPE OF MERCHANDISE: Clothing, housewares, furniture
DONATION TAX RECEIPT: Receipt given upon request

Saint Vincent De Paul Thrift Store
206 Jim Veatch Rd.
Morganfield, KY 42437
TYPE OF MERCHANDISE: Clothing, housewares, furniture
DONATION TAX RECEIPT: Receipt given upon request
COMMENTS: Monthly markdowns

Saint Vincent De Paul Thrift Store
902 Monmouth St.
Newport, KY 41071
TYPE OF MERCHANDISE: Clothing, housewares, furniture
DONATION TAX RECEIPT: Receipt given upon request
COMMENTS: Monthly markdowns

Saint Vincent De Paul Thrift Store
1001 W. Seventh St.
Owensboro, KY 42301
TYPE OF MERCHANDISE: Clothing, housewares, furniture
DONATION TAX RECEIPT: Receipt given upon request
COMMENTS: Monthly markdowns

Salvation Army Thrift Store
215 S. Ewing Rd.
Owensboro, KY 42301
TYPE OF MERCHANDISE: Clothing, housewares, furniture

DONATION TAX RECEIPT: Receipt given upon request

Saint Vincent De Paul Thrift Store
2014 Cario Rd.
Paducah, KY 42001
TYPE OF MERCHANDISE: Clothing, housewares, furniture
DONATION TAX RECEIPT: Receipt given upon request
COMMENTS: Monthly markdowns

Louisiana

Junior League New to You
1911 Lee St.
Alexandria, LA 71301
CONTACT: Donna Stracenner
PHONE: 318-443-3381
HOURS: Mon.–Fri. 9:30–4:15
TYPE OF MERCHANDISE: Clothing, housewares, toys
DONATION TAX RECEIPT: Receipt given upon request
COMMENTS: Sales, Christmas boutique, back-to-school

Junior League Thrift Shop
1534 N. Foster Dr.
Baton Rouge, LA 70806
TYPE OF MERCHANDISE: Clothing for men, women, and children
DONATION TAX RECEIPT: Receipt given upon request

Goodwill Industries Thrift Store
2545 Choctaw Dr.
Baton Rouge, LA 70805
TYPE OF MERCHANDISE: Clothing, housewares, furniture
DONATION TAX RECEIPT: Receipt given upon request

Saint Vincent De Paul Thrift Store
2655 Plank Rd.
Baton Rouge, LA 70821
TYPE OF MERCHANDISE: Clothing, housewares, furniture
DONATION TAX RECEIPT: Receipt given upon request
COMMENTS: Monthly markdowns

Junior League Nearly Nu
3001 Government St.
CROSS STREET: Acadian Thruway, Exit 157b
Baton Rouge, LA 70806
PHONE: 504-336-4117
HOURS: Tues.–Sat. 10–5
TYPE OF MERCHANDISE: Clothing, housewares
DONATION TAX RECEIPT: Receipt given upon request
COMMENTS: Big sale twice a year, Dec. toy sale

Salvation Army Thrift Store
3898 Plank Rd.
Baton Rouge, LA 70805
TYPE OF MERCHANDISE: Clothing, housewares, furniture
DONATION TAX RECEIPT: Receipt given upon request

Salvation Army Thrift Store
7361 Airline Hwy.
Baton Rouge, LA 70805
TYPE OF MERCHANDISE: Clothing, housewares, furniture
DONATION TAX RECEIPT: Receipt given upon request

Goodwill Industries Thrift Store
2700 E. Texas St.
Bossier City, LA 71111
TYPE OF MERCHANDISE: Clothing, housewares, furniture
DONATION TAX RECEIPT: Receipt given upon request

Goodwill Industries Thrift Store
700 First St.
Gretna, LA 70053
TYPE OF MERCHANDISE: Clothing, housewares, furniture
DONATION TAX RECEIPT: Receipt given upon request
COMMENTS: Rehabilitation center

Goodwill Industries Thrift Store
903 Manhattan Blvd.
Harvey, LA 70058
TYPE OF MERCHANDISE: Clothing, housewares, furniture
DONATION TAX RECEIPT: Receipt given upon request

Saint Vincent De Paul Thrift Store
107 Point St.
Houma, LA 70360
TYPE OF MERCHANDISE: Clothing,
housewares, furniture
DONATION TAX RECEIPT: Receipt given
upon request
COMMENTS: Monthly markdowns

Salvation Army Thrift Store
100 Jefferson Hwy.
Jefferson, LA 70121-2509
TYPE OF MERCHANDISE: Clothing,
housewares, furniture
DONATION TAX RECEIPT: Receipt given
upon request

Goodwill Industries Thrift Store
2525 Williams Blvd.
Kenner, LA 70062
TYPE OF MERCHANDISE: Clothing,
housewares, furniture
DONATION TAX RECEIPT: Receipt given
upon request

Goodwill Industries Thrift Store
113 Pine Park Dr.
Lafayette, LA 70508
TYPE OF MERCHANDISE: Clothing,
housewares, furniture
DONATION TAX RECEIPT: Receipt given
upon request

Salvation Army Thrift Store
117 Lee Ave.
Lafayette, LA 70501
TYPE OF MERCHANDISE: Clothing,
housewares, furniture
DONATION TAX RECEIPT: Receipt given
upon request

Junior League Nearly New Shop
2400 Ryan St.
Lake Charles, LA 70601
PHONE: 318-433-8165
HOURS: Mon.–Sat. 9–4:30
TYPE OF MERCHANDISE: Clothing,
housewares
DONATION TAX RECEIPT: Receipt given
upon request
COMMENTS: Biannual $5 bag sale

Salvation Army Thrift Store
5709 Desiard St.
Monroe, LA 71203
TYPE OF MERCHANDISE: Clothing,
housewares, furniture
DONATION TAX RECEIPT: Receipt given
upon request

Volunteers of America
1523 Constance St.
New Orleans, LA 70130
TYPE OF MERCHANDISE: Clothing,
housewares, furniture
DONATION TAX RECEIPT: Receipt given
upon request

Saint Vincent De Paul Thrift Store
2414 St. Claude St.
New Orleans, LA 70117
TYPE OF MERCHANDISE: Clothing,
housewares, furniture
DONATION TAX RECEIPT: Receipt given
upon request
COMMENTS: Monthly markdowns

Junior League Bloomin' Deals
4645 Freret St.
New Orleans, LA 70115
CONTACT: Virginia Dupont
PHONE: 891-1289, 897-9128
HOURS: Tues.–Weds. 10–5:30, Thurs.
10–7, Sat. 10–5:30, Sun. 12:30–4:30
TYPE OF MERCHANDISE: Clothing,
appliances, furniture
DONATION TAX RECEIPT: Receipt given
upon request
COMMENTS: Annual and monthly toy and
holiday sale

Saint Vincent De Paul Thrift Store
4935 Magazine St.
New Orleans, LA 70115
TYPE OF MERCHANDISE: Clothing,
housewares, furniture
DONATION TAX RECEIPT: Receipt given
upon request
COMMENTS: Monthly markdowns

Volunteers of America
5956 Magazine St.
New Orleans, LA 70115
TYPE OF MERCHANDISE: Clothing,
housewares
DONATION TAX RECEIPT: Receipt given
upon request

Salvation Army Thrift Store
602 Main St.
Pineville, LA 71360
TYPE OF MERCHANDISE: Clothing,
housewares, furniture
DONATION TAX RECEIPT: Receipt given
upon request

Goodwill Industries Thrift Store
2014 Jewella Ave.
Shreveport, LA 71109
TYPE OF MERCHANDISE: Clothing,
housewares, furniture
DONATION TAX RECEIPT: Receipt given
upon request

Salvation Army Thrift Store
3170 Pontchartrain Blvd.
CROSS STREET: Located in Tamany Mall
Slidell, LA 70458
CONTACT: Patti Foil
PHONE: 504-643-5516
HOURS: Mon.–Sat. 9–5
TYPE OF MERCHANDISE: Clothing,
housewares, furniture
DONATION TAX RECEIPT: Receipt given
upon request
COMMENTS: Daily 50% off sale

Salvation Army Thrift Store
145 Reagan St.
West Monroe, LA 71292
TYPE OF MERCHANDISE: Clothing,
housewares, furniture
DONATION TAX RECEIPT: Receipt given
upon request

Salvation Army Thrift Store
2408 Airline Hwy.
Westwego, LA 70094
TYPE OF MERCHANDISE: Clothing,
housewares, furniture
DONATION TAX RECEIPT: Receipt given
upon request

Maine

Goodwill Industries Thrift Store
26 Centre St.
Bath, ME 04530
TYPE OF MERCHANDISE: Clothing,
housewares, furniture

DONATION TAX RECEIPT: Receipt given
upon request

Goodwill Industries Thrift Store
111 Main St.
Biddeford, ME 04005
TYPE OF MERCHANDISE: Clothing,
housewares, furniture
DONATION TAX RECEIPT: Receipt given
upon request

Goodwill Industries Thrift Store
1 School St.
Brunswick, ME 04011
TYPE OF MERCHANDISE: Clothing,
housewares, furniture
DONATION TAX RECEIPT: Receipt given
upon request

Goodwill Industries Thrift Store
188 Lisbon St.
Lewiston, ME 04240
TYPE OF MERCHANDISE: Clothing,
housewares, furniture
DONATION TAX RECEIPT: Receipt given
upon request

Salvation Army Thrift Store
720 Main St.
Lewiston, ME 04240
TYPE OF MERCHANDISE: Clothing,
housewares, furniture
DONATION TAX RECEIPT: Receipt given
upon request

Saint Vincent De Paul Thrift Store
10 Locust St.
Portland, ME 04101
TYPE OF MERCHANDISE: Clothing,
housewares, furniture
DONATION TAX RECEIPT: Receipt given
upon request

Goodwill Industries Thrift Store
353 Cumberland Ave.
Portland, ME 04101
TYPE OF MERCHANDISE: Clothing,
housewares, furniture
DONATION TAX RECEIPT: Receipt given
upon request

Salvation Army Thrift Store
30 Warren Ave.
Portland, ME 04103
TYPE OF MERCHANDISE: Clothing,
housewares, furniture

DONATION TAX RECEIPT: Receipt given
upon request
Salvation Army Thrift Store
49 Alder Ave.
Portland, ME 04101
TYPE OF MERCHANDISE: Clothing,
housewares, furniture
DONATION TAX RECEIPT: Receipt given
upon request
Salvation Army Thrift Store
Route 302 County Corner
Raymond, ME 04071
TYPE OF MERCHANDISE: Clothing,
housewares, furniture
DONATION TAX RECEIPT: Receipt given
upon request

Maryland

Disabled American Vets Thrift Store
1300 E. North Ave.
Baltimore, MD 21213
TYPE OF MERCHANDISE: Clothing,
housewares,
DONATION TAX RECEIPT: Receipt given
upon request
Goodwill Industries Thrift Store
1923 W. Pratt St.
Baltimore, MD 21223
TYPE OF MERCHANDISE: Clothing,
housewares, furniture
DONATION TAX RECEIPT: Receipt given
upon request
Goodwill Industries Thrift Store
200 S. Broadway
Baltimore, MD 21231
TYPE OF MERCHANDISE: Clothing,
housewares, furniture
DONATION TAX RECEIPT: Receipt given
upon request
Disabled American Vets Thrift Store
2008 W. Pratt St.
Baltimore, MD 21223
TYPE OF MERCHANDISE: Clothing,
housewares
DONATION TAX RECEIPT: Receipt given
upon request

Council Thrift Shop
2014 N. Charles St.
Baltimore, MD 21218
TYPE OF MERCHANDISE: Clothing,
housewares, furniture
DONATION TAX RECEIPT: Receipt given
upon request
Goodwill Industries Thrift Store
3101 Greenmount Ave.
Baltimore, MD 21218
TYPE OF MERCHANDISE: Clothing,
housewares, furniture
DONATION TAX RECEIPT: Receipt given
upon request
Goodwill Industries Thrift Store
4001 Southwestern Blvd.
Baltimore, MD 21229
TYPE OF MERCHANDISE: Clothing,
housewares, furniture
DONATION TAX RECEIPT: Receipt given
upon request
Junior League Wise Penny
5902 York Rd.
Baltimore, MD 21212
PHONE: 410-435-3244
HOURS: Mon.–Sat. 9:30–5, Thurs. 9:30–8
TYPE OF MERCHANDISE: Clothing,
housewares, toys
DONATION TAX RECEIPT: Receipt given
upon request
American Cancer Society Discovery Shop
5911 York Rd.
Baltimore, MD 21212
CONTACT: Dorothy Friedman
PHONE: 301-523-9104
TYPE OF MERCHANDISE: Clothing, bric-a-
brac
DONATION TAX RECEIPT: Receipt given
upon request
COMMENTS: Monthly markdowns
Saint Vincent De Paul Thrift Store
6 N. Central Ave.
Baltimore, MD 21201
TYPE OF MERCHANDISE: Clothing,
housewares, furniture
DONATION TAX RECEIPT: Receipt given
upon request
COMMENTS: Monthly markdowns

Goodwill Industries Thrift Store
42 N. Main St.
Bel Air, MD 21014
TYPE OF MERCHANDISE: Clothing,
housewares, furniture
DONATION TAX RECEIPT: Receipt given
upon request
Goodwill Industries Thrift Store
9200 Wisconsin Ave.
Bethesda, MD 20814
TYPE OF MERCHANDISE: Clothing,
housewares, furniture
DONATION TAX RECEIPT: Receipt given
upon request
Goodwill Industries Thrift Store
4813 Annapolis Rd.
Bladensburg, MD 20710
PHONE: 301-864-5145
HOURS: Mon.–Sat.. 10–7, Sun. 12–6
TYPE OF MERCHANDISE: Clothing,
housewares, furniture
DONATION TAX RECEIPT: Receipt given
upon request
American Cancer Society Discovery Shop
6904 Laurel Bowie Rd.
CROSS STREET: Bowie Plaza Shopping
Center
Bowie, MD 20715
TYPE OF MERCHANDISE: Clothing, bric-a-
brac
DONATION TAX RECEIPT: Receipt given
upon request
COMMENTS: Monthly markdowns
American Rescue Workers Thrift Shop
716 Ritchie Rd.
Capitol Heights, MD 20743
PHONE: 301-336-6200
HOURS: Mon.–Sat. 9–5
TYPE OF MERCHANDISE: Clothing,
furniture, and collectibles
DONATION TAX RECEIPT: Receipt given
upon request
American Rescue Workers Thrift Shop
3000 Donnell Dr.
CROSS STREET: Penmar Shopping Center
Forrestville, MD 20747
PHONE: 301-736-6440
HOURS: Mon.-Sat. 9–8:30

TYPE OF MERCHANDISE: Clothing,
housewares, furniture
DONATION TAX RECEIPT: Receipt given
upon request
Goodwill Industries Thrift Store
4 Crain Hwy. NE
Glen Burnie, MD 21061
TYPE OF MERCHANDISE: Clothing,
housewares, furniture
DONATION TAX RECEIPT: Receipt given
upon request
MCC World Treasures
22 W. Franklin St.
Hagerstown, MD 21740
PHONE: 301-797-8624
TYPE OF MERCHANDISE: Clothing,
housewares,
DONATION TAX RECEIPT: Receipt given
upon request
Goodwill Industries Thrift Store
223 N. Prospect St.
Hagerstown, MD 21740
TYPE OF MERCHANDISE: Clothing,
housewares, furniture
DONATION TAX RECEIPT: Receipt given
upon request
Salvation Army Thrift Store
7505 New Hampshire Ave. #205
Langley Park, MD 20783
PHONE: 301-403-1705
HOURS: Mon.–Sat. 10–7
TYPE OF MERCHANDISE: Clothing,
housewares, furniture
DONATION TAX RECEIPT: Receipt given
upon request
Goodwill Industries Thrift Store
8016 New Hampshire Ave.
Langley Park, MD 20783
PHONE: 301-445-5492
HOURS: Mon.–Sat. 10–9, Sun. 12–6
TYPE OF MERCHANDISE: Clothing,
housewares, furniture
DONATION TAX RECEIPT: Receipt given
upon request
Amvets Thrift Store
4800 Indian Head Hwy.
Oxon Hill, MD 20745
PHONE: 301-839-0444

HOURS: Mon.–Sat.. 9–6, Sun. 12–3
TYPE OF MERCHANDISE: Clothing, housewares, furniture
DONATION TAX RECEIPT: Receipt given upon request

American Cancer Society Discovery Shop
392 Hungerford Dr.
Rockville, MD 20852
CONTACT: Peggy Nonemarcher
PHONE: 301-294-9440
TYPE OF MERCHANDISE: Clothing, bric-a-brac
DONATION TAX RECEIPT: Receipt given upon request
COMMENTS: Monthly Markdowns

American Cancer Society Discovery Shop
360 Ritchie Hwy.
Severna Park, MD 21146
TYPE OF MERCHANDISE: Clothing, bric-a-brac
DONATION TAX RECEIPT: Receipt given upon request
COMMENTS: Monthly markdowns

Goodwill Industries Thrift Store
8735 Flower Ave.
Silver Spring, MD 20901
TYPE OF MERCHANDISE: Clothing, housewares, furniture
DONATION TAX RECEIPT: Receipt given upon request

Massachusetts

Salvation Army Thrift Store
159 N. Pleasant St.
Amherst, MA 01002
TYPE OF MERCHANDISE: Clothing, housewares, furniture
DONATION TAX RECEIPT: Receipt given upon request

Salvation Army Thrift Store
413 Main St.
Athol, MA 01331
TYPE OF MERCHANDISE: Clothing, housewares, furniture
DONATION TAX RECEIPT: Receipt given upon request

Saint Vincent De Paul Thrift Store
9 N. Main St.
Bellingham, MA 02019
TYPE OF MERCHANDISE: Clothing, housewares, furniture
DONATION TAX RECEIPT: Receipt given upon request
COMMENTS: Monthly markdowns

Goodwill Industries Thrift Store
1010 Harrison Ave.
Boston, MA 02119
PHONE: 617-541-1270, 541-1492
HOURS: Mon.–Sat. 8:45–5:45, Sun.. 12–5
TYPE OF MERCHANDISE: Clothing, housewares, furniture
DONATION TAX RECEIPT: Receipt given upon request
COMMENTS: Four one-day sales per year

Salvation Army Thrift Store
1253 Hyde Park Ave.
Boston, MA 02136
TYPE OF MERCHANDISE: Clothing, housewares, furniture
DONATION TAX RECEIPT: Receipt given upon request

Saint Vincent De Paul Thrift Store
1280 Washington St.
Boston, MA 02118
TYPE OF MERCHANDISE: Clothing, housewares, furniture
DONATION TAX RECEIPT: Receipt given upon request
COMMENTS: Monthly markdowns

Salvation Army Thrift Store
26 West St.
Boston, MA 02110
TYPE OF MERCHANDISE: Clothing, housewares, furniture
DONATION TAX RECEIPT: Receipt given upon request

Salvation Army Thrift Store
134 Main St.
Bridgewater, MA 03234
TYPE OF MERCHANDISE: Clothing, housewares, furniture
DONATION TAX RECEIPT: Receipt given upon request

Salvation Army Thrift Store
291 Main St.
Brockton, MA 02401
TYPE OF MERCHANDISE: Clothing,
housewares, furniture
DONATION TAX RECEIPT: Receipt given
upon request

Salvation Army Thrift Store
315 N. Main St.
Brockton, MA 02401
TYPE OF MERCHANDISE: Clothing,
housewares, furniture
DONATION TAX RECEIPT: Receipt given
upon request

American Cancer Society Discovery Shop
300 Washington St.
Brookline, MA 02146
CONTACT: Linda Golburgh
PHONE: 617-277-9499
TYPE OF MERCHANDISE: Clothing, bric-a-
brac
DONATION TAX RECEIPT: Receipt given
upon request
COMMENTS: Monthly markdowns

Salvation Army Thrift Store
Rte #6 Cranberry Hwy.
Buzzards Bay, MA 02532
TYPE OF MERCHANDISE: Clothing,
housewares, furniture
DONATION TAX RECEIPT: Receipt given
upon request

Salvation Army Thrift Store
328 Massachusetts Ave.
Cambridge, MA 02139
TYPE OF MERCHANDISE: Clothing,
housewares, furniture
DONATION TAX RECEIPT: Receipt given
upon request

Saint Vincent De Paul Thrift Store
50 Prospect St.
Cambridge, MA 02140
TYPE OF MERCHANDISE: Clothing,
housewares, furniture
DONATION TAX RECEIPT: Receipt given
upon request
COMMENTS: Monthly markdowns

Goodwill Industries Thrift Store
520 Massachusetts Ave.
Cambridge, MA 02139

PHONE: 617-868-6330
HOURS: Mon.–Sat. 10–5:45, Sun. 12–5
TYPE OF MERCHANDISE: Clothing,
housewares, furniture
DONATION TAX RECEIPT: Receipt given
upon request
COMMENTS: Four one-day sales per year

Salvation Army Thrift Store
727 Memorial Dr.
Cambridge, MA 02139
TYPE OF MERCHANDISE: Clothing,
housewares, furniture
DONATION TAX RECEIPT: Receipt given
upon request

Salvation Army Thrift Store
456 Broadway
Chelsea, MA 02150
TYPE OF MERCHANDISE: Clothing,
housewares, furniture
DONATION TAX RECEIPT: Receipt given
upon request

Goodwill Industries Thrift Store
355 Front St.
Chicopee, MA 01013
PHONE: 413-594-5354
HOURS: Mon.–Sat. 9–5
TYPE OF MERCHANDISE: Clothing,
housewares, furniture
DONATION TAX RECEIPT: Receipt given
upon request

Goodwill Industries Thrift Store
66 Newport Ave.
East Providence, MA 02916
PHONE: 401-431-0880
HOURS: Mon.–Fri. 10–8, Sat.–
Sun. 12–5
TYPE OF MERCHANDISE: Clothing,
housewares, furniture
DONATION TAX RECEIPT: Receipt given
upon request
COMMENTS: Four one-day sales per year

Goodwill Industries Thrift Store
186 South Main St.
Fall River, MA 02721
PHONE: 508-675-3665
HOURS: Mon.–Sat. 10–5
TYPE OF MERCHANDISE: Clothing,
housewares, furniture

DONATION TAX RECEIPT: Receipt given upon request
COMMENTS: Four one-day sales per year

Salvation Army Thrift Store
251 S. Main St.
Fall River, MA 02724
TYPE OF MERCHANDISE: Clothing, housewares, furniture
DONATION TAX RECEIPT: Receipt given upon request

Salvation Army Thrift Store
100 Main St.
Fitchburg, MA 01420
TYPE OF MERCHANDISE: Clothing, housewares, furniture
DONATION TAX RECEIPT: Receipt given upon request

Salvation Army Thrift Store
1422 Water St.
Fitchburg, MA 01420
TYPE OF MERCHANDISE: Clothing, housewares, furniture
DONATION TAX RECEIPT: Receipt given upon request

Salvation Army Thrift Store
35–45 Concord St.
Framingham, MA 01701
TYPE OF MERCHANDISE: Clothing, housewares, furniture
DONATION TAX RECEIPT: Receipt given upon request

Salvation Army Thrift Store
8 Union Sq.
Gardner, MA 01440
TYPE OF MERCHANDISE: Clothing, housewares, furniture
DONATION TAX RECEIPT: Receipt given upon request

Salvation Army Thrift Store
178 Main St.
Gloucester, MA 01930
TYPE OF MERCHANDISE: Clothing, housewares, furniture
DONATION TAX RECEIPT: Receipt given upon request

Salvation Army Thrift Store
56 Hope St.
Greenfield, MA 01301

TYPE OF MERCHANDISE: Clothing, housewares, furniture
DONATION TAX RECEIPT: Receipt given upon request

Salvation Army Thrift Store
936 Washington St.
Hanover, MA 02339
TYPE OF MERCHANDISE: Clothing, housewares, furniture
DONATION TAX RECEIPT: Receipt given upon request

Salvation Army Thrift Store
132 Merrimac St.
Haverhill, MA 01830
TYPE OF MERCHANDISE: Clothing, housewares, furniture
DONATION TAX RECEIPT: Receipt given upon request

Salvation Army Thrift Store
274 High St.
Holyoke, MA 01040-6516
TYPE OF MERCHANDISE: Clothing, housewares, furniture
DONATION TAX RECEIPT: Receipt given upon request

Goodwill Industries Thrift Store
354 High St.
Holyoke, MA 01040-6501
TYPE OF MERCHANDISE: Clothing, housewares, furniture
DONATION TAX RECEIPT: Receipt given upon request

Salvation Army Thrift Store
51 Main St.
Hudson, MA 01749
TYPE OF MERCHANDISE: Clothing, housewares, furniture
DONATION TAX RECEIPT: Receipt given upon request

Salvation Army Thrift Store
105 Bassett Ln.
Hyannis, MA 02601
TYPE OF MERCHANDISE: Clothing, housewares, furniture
DONATION TAX RECEIPT: Receipt given upon request

Goodwill Industries Thrift Store
141 Corporation Plaza
Hyannis, MA 02601
PHONE: 508-790-0046
HOURS: Mon.–Tue. 10–5, Wed.–Sat. 10–6
TYPE OF MERCHANDISE: Clothing,
housewares, furniture
DONATION TAX RECEIPT: Receipt given
upon request
COMMENTS: Four one-day sales per year

Salvation Army Thrift Store
1295 River St.
Hyde Park, MA 02136
TYPE OF MERCHANDISE: Clothing,
housewares, furniture
DONATION TAX RECEIPT: Receipt given
upon request

Goodwill Industries Thrift Store
708 Centre St.
Jamaica Plain, MA 02130
PHONE: 617-983-5354
HOURS: Mon.–Sat. 10–5:45, Sun. 12–5
TYPE OF MERCHANDISE: Clothing,
housewares, furniture
DONATION TAX RECEIPT: Receipt given
upon request
COMMENTS: Four one-day sales per year

Goodwill Industries Thrift Store
372 Essex St.
Lawrence, MA 01840
TYPE OF MERCHANDISE: Clothing,
housewares, furniture
DONATION TAX RECEIPT: Receipt given
upon request

Salvation Army Thrift Store
321 Westford Ave.
Lowell, MA 01850
TYPE OF MERCHANDISE: Clothing,
housewares, furniture
DONATION TAX RECEIPT: Receipt given
upon request

Saint Vincent De Paul Thrift Store
701 Merrimack St.
Lowell, MA 01854
TYPE OF MERCHANDISE: Clothing,
housewares, furniture
DONATION TAX RECEIPT: Receipt given
upon request
COMMENTS: Monthly markdowns

Salvation Army Thrift Store
10–16 Munroe St.
Lynn, MA 01901
TYPE OF MERCHANDISE: Clothing,
housewares, furniture
DONATION TAX RECEIPT: Receipt given
upon request

Saint Vincent De Paul Thrift Store
11–13 Market Sq.
Lynn, MA 01902
TYPE OF MERCHANDISE: Clothing,
housewares, furniture
DONATION TAX RECEIPT: Receipt given
upon request
COMMENTS: Monthly markdowns

Salvation Army Thrift Store
771 Boston Post Rd.
Marlboro, MA 01752
TYPE OF MERCHANDISE: Clothing,
housewares, furniture
DONATION TAX RECEIPT: Receipt given
upon request

Salvation Army Thrift Store
51 County St.
Mattapoisett, MA 02739
TYPE OF MERCHANDISE: Clothing,
housewares, furniture
DONATION TAX RECEIPT: Receipt given
upon request

Goodwill Industries Thrift Store
461 Salem St.
Medford, MA 02155
PHONE: 617-391-7867
HOURS: Mon.–Sat. 10–6, Sun. 12–5
TYPE OF MERCHANDISE: Clothing,
housewares, furniture
DONATION TAX RECEIPT: Receipt given
upon request
COMMENTS: Four one-day sales per year

Salvation Army Thrift Store
1145 Acushnet Ave.
New Bedford, MA 02746
TYPE OF MERCHANDISE: Clothing,
housewares, furniture
DONATION TAX RECEIPT: Receipt given
upon request

Goodwill Industries Thrift Store
37 Main St.
Northampton, MA 01060
PHONE: 413-586-4173
HOURS: Mon.–Sat. 9–5
TYPE OF MERCHANDISE: Clothing,
housewares, furniture
DONATION TAX RECEIPT: Receipt given
upon request

Salvation Army Thrift Store
59 Service Center Rd.
Northampton, MA 01060
TYPE OF MERCHANDISE: Clothing,
housewares, furniture
DONATION TAX RECEIPT: Receipt given
upon request

Salvation Army Thrift Store
9 Market St.
Northampton, MA 01060
TYPE OF MERCHANDISE: Clothing,
housewares, furniture
DONATION TAX RECEIPT: Receipt given
upon request

Salvation Army Thrift Store
385 Main St.
Oxford, MA 01540
TYPE OF MERCHANDISE: Clothing,
housewares, furniture
DONATION TAX RECEIPT: Receipt given
upon request

Salvation Army Thrift Store
426 Main St.
Palmer, MA 01069
TYPE OF MERCHANDISE: Clothing,
housewares, furniture
DONATION TAX RECEIPT: Receipt given
upon request

Salvation Army Thrift Store
440–444 Main St.
Palmer, MA 01069
TYPE OF MERCHANDISE: Clothing,
housewares, furniture
DONATION TAX RECEIPT: Receipt given
upon request

Goodwill Industries Thrift Store
51 Thorndike St.
Palmer, MA 01069
PHONE: 413-283-5785

HOURS: Mon.–Sat. 9–6, Thurs. 9–8,
Sun. 12–5
TYPE OF MERCHANDISE: Clothing,
housewares, furniture
DONATION TAX RECEIPT: Receipt given
upon request

Goodwill Industries Thrift Store
13 Peabody Sq.
Peabody, MA 01960
PHONE: 508-532-2953
HOURS: Mon.–Sat. 9–5
TYPE OF MERCHANDISE: Clothing,
housewares, furniture
DONATION TAX RECEIPT: Receipt given
upon request
COMMENTS: Four one-day sales per year

Goodwill Industries Thrift Store
369 North St.
Pittsfield, MA 01201
TYPE OF MERCHANDISE: Clothing,
housewares, furniture
DONATION TAX RECEIPT: Receipt given
upon request

Junior League Thrift Shop
379 North St.
Pittsfield, MA 01201
CONTACT: Patricia Clark
PHONE: 413-448-8189
HOURS: Mon.–Fri. 10–4, Sat. 10–2
TYPE OF MERCHANDISE: Clothing, gifts,
housewares
DONATION TAX RECEIPT: Receipt given
upon request
COMMENTS: Boutique "Fashion Finds,"
designer wear

Salvation Army Thrift Store
440 W. Housatonic St./Rte. 20
Pittsfield, MA 01201
TYPE OF MERCHANDISE: Clothing,
housewares, furniture
DONATION TAX RECEIPT: Receipt given
upon request

Goodwill Industries Thrift Store
179 Parking Way
Quincy, MA 02169
PHONE: 617-479-8853
HOURS: Mon.–Wed., 9:30–6, Thur.–Fri.
9:30–8, Sat. 9:30–6, Sun. 12–5

TYPE OF MERCHANDISE: Clothing, housewares, furniture
DONATION TAX RECEIPT: Receipt given upon request
COMMENTS: Four one-day sales per year
Salvation Army Thrift Store
209 Broadway (Rte. 1)
Saugus, MA 01906
TYPE OF MERCHANDISE: Clothing, housewares, furniture
DONATION TAX RECEIPT: Receipt given upon request
Salvation Army Thrift Store
1135 GAR Hwy./Rte. 6
Somerset, MA 02725
TYPE OF MERCHANDISE: Clothing, housewares, furniture
DONATION TAX RECEIPT: Receipt given upon request
Goodwill Industries Thrift Store
230 Elm St.
Somerville, MA 02144
PHONE: 617-628-3618
HOURS: Mon.–Sat. 10–6, Sun. 12–5
TYPE OF MERCHANDISE: Clothing, housewares, furniture
DONATION TAX RECEIPT: Receipt given upon request
COMMENTS: Four one-day sales per year
Salvation Army Thrift Store
486 Broadway
Somerville, MA 02143
TYPE OF MERCHANDISE: Clothing, housewares, furniture
DONATION TAX RECEIPT: Receipt given upon request
Goodwill Industries Thrift Store
315 West Broadway
South Boston, MA 02127
PHONE: 617-268-7960
HOURS: Mon.–Sat. 10–6
TYPE OF MERCHANDISE: Clothing, housewares, furniture
DONATION TAX RECEIPT: Receipt given upon request
COMMENTS: Four one-day sales per year

Salvation Army Thrift Store
22 Mill St.
Southbridge, MA 01550
TYPE OF MERCHANDISE: Clothing, housewares, furniture
DONATION TAX RECEIPT: Receipt given upon request
Saint Vincent De Paul Thrift Store
136 Main St.
Spencer, MA 01562
TYPE OF MERCHANDISE: Clothing, housewares, furniture
DONATION TAX RECEIPT: Receipt given upon request
COMMENTS: Monthly markdowns
Salvation Army Thrift Store
1340 Boston Post Rd.
Springfield, MA 01129
TYPE OF MERCHANDISE: Clothing, housewares, furniture
DONATION TAX RECEIPT: Receipt given upon request
Salvation Army Thrift Store
176 Main St.
Springfield, MA 01151
TYPE OF MERCHANDISE: Clothing, housewares, furniture
DONATION TAX RECEIPT: Receipt given upon request
Salvation Army Thrift Store
204 Dickinson St.
Springfield, MA 01108
TYPE OF MERCHANDISE: Clothing, housewares, furniture
DONATION TAX RECEIPT: Receipt given upon request
Junior League
254 Worthington St.
Springfield, MA 01103
TYPE OF MERCHANDISE: Clothing for men, women, and children
DONATION TAX RECEIPT: Receipt given upon request
Goodwill Industries Thrift Store
285 Dorset St.
Springfield, MA 01108
PHONE: 413-788-6981
HOURS: Mon.–Sat. 8:30–4

TYPE OF MERCHANDISE: Clothing, housewares, furniture
DONATION TAX RECEIPT: Receipt given upon request
Goodwill Industries Thrift Store
611 Main St.
Springfield, MA 01105
PHONE: 413-739-4556
HOURS: Mon.–Sat. 9–5
TYPE OF MERCHANDISE: Clothing, housewares, furniture
DONATION TAX RECEIPT: Receipt given upon request
Salvation Army Thrift Store
984 W. Columbus Ave.
Springfield, MA 01105-2513
TYPE OF MERCHANDISE: Clothing, housewares, furniture
DONATION TAX RECEIPT: Receipt given upon request
Salvation Army Thrift Store
42–52 Main St.
Taunton, MA 02780
TYPE OF MERCHANDISE: Clothing, housewares, furniture
DONATION TAX RECEIPT: Receipt given upon request
Goodwill Industries Thrift Store
436 Moody St.
Waltham, MA 02154
TYPE OF MERCHANDISE: Clothing, housewares, furniture
DONATION TAX RECEIPT: Receipt given upon request
Goodwill Industries Thrift Store
91 Main St.
Ware, MA 01082
PHONE: 413-967-6045
HOURS: Mon.–Sat. 9–5
TYPE OF MERCHANDISE: Clothing, housewares, furniture
DONATION TAX RECEIPT: Receipt given upon request
Salvation Army Thrift Store
625 Main St.
Wilmington, MA 01887
TYPE OF MERCHANDISE: Clothing, housewares, furniture

DONATION TAX RECEIPT: Receipt given upon request
Salvation Army Thrift Store
17 Blackstone Ave.
Worcester, MA 01604
TYPE OF MERCHANDISE: Clothing, housewares, furniture
DONATION TAX RECEIPT: Receipt given upon request
Salvation Army Thrift Store
29 Charles St.
Worcester, MA 01604
TYPE OF MERCHANDISE: Clothing, housewares, furniture
DONATION TAX RECEIPT: Receipt given upon request
Council Thrift Shop
322 Pleasant St.
Worcester, MA 01609
TYPE OF MERCHANDISE: Clothing, housewares, furniture
DONATION TAX RECEIPT: Receipt given upon request
Junior League Second Impression
71 Pleasant St.
Worcester, MA 01609
CONTACT: Beatric C. Baroussa
PHONE: 508-752-2073
HOURS: Mon.–Fri.10–2:30, Sat. 10–2
TYPE OF MERCHANDISE: Clothing, accessories, housewares
DONATION TAX RECEIPT: Receipt given upon request
COMMENTS: Christmas boutique sale and tag sales
Salvation Army Thrift Store
72 Cambridge St.
Worcester, MA 01603
TYPE OF MERCHANDISE: Clothing, housewares, furniture
DONATION TAX RECEIPT: Receipt given upon request

Michigan

Goodwill Industries Thrift Store
137 S. Main St.
Adrian, MI 49221

CONTACT: Leslie Massengill
PHONE: 517-263-1665, 265-9740
HOURS: Mon.–Sat. 9–5:30
TYPE OF MERCHANDISE: Clothing,
housewares, furniture
DONATION TAX RECEIPT: Receipt given
upon request
COMMENTS: Holiday sales
Salvation Army Thrift Store
309 College Ave.
Adrian, MI 49221
TYPE OF MERCHANDISE: Clothing,
housewares, furniture
DONATION TAX RECEIPT: Receipt given
upon request
Goodwill Industries Thrift Store
119 N. Superior St.
Albion, MI 49224
TYPE OF MERCHANDISE: Clothing,
housewares, furniture
DONATION TAX RECEIPT: Receipt given
upon request
Saint Vincent De Paul Thrift Store
19310 Ecorse Rd.
Allen Park, MI 48101
TYPE OF MERCHANDISE: Clothing,
housewares, furniture
DONATION TAX RECEIPT: Receipt given
upon request
COMMENTS: Monthly markdowns
Salvation Army Thrift Store
5600 Allen Rd.
CROSS STREET: Southfield Rd.
Allen Park, MI 48101
CONTACT: Deborah Glenn
PHONE: 313-383-6711
HOURS: Mon.–Sat. 10–6
TYPE OF MERCHANDISE: Clothing,
housewares, furniture
DONATION TAX RECEIPT: Receipt given
upon request
COMMENTS: Weekly sales
Salvation Army Thrift Store
418 N. Second Ave.
Alpena, MI 49707
TYPE OF MERCHANDISE: Clothing,
housewares, furniture
DONATION TAX RECEIPT: Receipt given
upon request

Saint Vincent De Paul Thrift Store
805 W. Chisholm St.
Alpena, MI 49707
TYPE OF MERCHANDISE: Clothing,
housewares, furniture
DONATION TAX RECEIPT: Receipt given
upon request
COMMENTS: Monthly markdowns
Saint Vincent De Paul Thrift Store
913 W. Chisholm St.
Alpena, MI 49707
TYPE OF MERCHANDISE: Clothing,
housewares, furniture
DONATION TAX RECEIPT: Receipt given
upon request
COMMENTS: Monthly markdowns
Salvation Army Thrift Store
105 E. Ann St.
Ann Arbor, MI 48104
TYPE OF MERCHANDISE: Clothing,
housewares, furniture
DONATION TAX RECEIPT: Receipt given
upon request
Goodwill Industries Thrift Store
15383 Helmer Rd. S
Battle Creek, MI 49017
TYPE OF MERCHANDISE: Clothing,
housewares, furniture
DONATION TAX RECEIPT: Receipt given
upon request
Salvation Army Thrift Store
265 Fountain St. E
Battle Creek, MI 49017
TYPE OF MERCHANDISE: Clothing,
housewares, furniture
DONATION TAX RECEIPT: Receipt given
upon request
Salvation Army Thrift Store
44–46 S. 20th St., Columbia Plaza
Battle Creek, MI 49015
PHONE: 616-964-4151
HOURS: Mon.–Sat. 9:30–6
TYPE OF MERCHANDISE: Clothing,
housewares, furniture
DONATION TAX RECEIPT: Receipt given
upon request
COMMENTS: Weekly half-price sales

Salvation Army Thrift Store
405 Sixth St.
Bay City, MI 48708
TYPE OF MERCHANDISE: Clothing,
housewares, furniture
DONATION TAX RECEIPT: Receipt given
upon request

Saint Vincent De Paul Thrift Store
523 Michigan Ave.
Bay City, MI 48708
TYPE OF MERCHANDISE: Clothing,
housewares, furniture
DONATION TAX RECEIPT: Receipt given
upon request
COMMENTS: Monthly markdowns

Salvation Army Thrift Store
514 Main St.
Belleville, MI 48111
CONTACT: Pam Cooke
PHONE: 313-696-2505
HOURS: Mon.–Sat. 10–6
TYPE OF MERCHANDISE: Clothing,
housewares, furniture
DONATION TAX RECEIPT: Receipt given
upon request
COMMENTS: Weekly sales

NCJW Thrift Shop
3297 W. 12 Mile Rd.
Berkley, MI 48072
PHONE: 810-548-6664
TYPE OF MERCHANDISE: Clothing,
housewares, furniture
DONATION TAX RECEIPT: Receipt given
upon request
COMMENTS: Annual sale (Nov.) in
separate store

Saint Vincent De Paul Thrift Store
103 N. Case St.
Bessemer, MI 49911
TYPE OF MERCHANDISE: Clothing,
housewares, furniture
DONATION TAX RECEIPT: Receipt given
upon request
COMMENTS: Monthly markdowns

Salvation Army Thrift Store
924 S. Mitchell St.
Cadillac, MI 49601

TYPE OF MERCHANDISE: Clothing,
housewares, furniture
DONATION TAX RECEIPT: Receipt given
upon request

Saint Vincent De Paul thrift Store
24021 Van Dyke
Centerline, MI 48015
TYPE OF MERCHANDISE: Clothing,
housewares, furniture
DONATION TAX RECEIPT: Receipt given
upon request
COMMENTS: Monthly markdowns

Salvation Army Thrift Store
35891 Gratiot Ave.
Clinton Township, MI 48043
CONTACT: Tina Johnson
PHONE: 313-790-9058
HOURS: Mon.–Sat. 10–9
TYPE OF MERCHANDISE: Clothing,
housewares, furniture
DONATION TAX RECEIPT: Receipt given
upon request
COMMENTS: Daily clothing sales

Saint Vincent De Paul Thrift Store
136 Superior Ave.
Crystal Falls, MI 49920
TYPE OF MERCHANDISE: Clothing,
housewares, furniture
DONATION TAX RECEIPT: Receipt given
upon request
COMMENTS: Monthly markdowns

Saint Vincent De Paul Thrift Store
14074 E. Seven Mile Rd.
Detroit, MI 48205
TYPE OF MERCHANDISE: Clothing,
housewares, furniture
DONATION TAX RECEIPT: Receipt given
upon request
COMMENTS: Monthly markdowns

Saint Vincent De Paul Thrift Store
14922 Kercheval
Detroit, MI 48214
TYPE OF MERCHANDISE: Clothing,
housewares, furniture
DONATION TAX RECEIPT: Receipt given
upon request
COMMENTS: Monthly markdowns

Salvation Army Thrift Store
15530 W. Warren Ave.
CROSS STREET: Greenfield
Detroit, MI 48228
CONTACT: Pat Parrish
PHONE: 313-584-8151
HOURS: Mon.–Sat. 9–9
TYPE OF MERCHANDISE: Clothing,
housewares, furniture
DONATION TAX RECEIPT: Receipt given
upon request
COMMENTS: Daily clothing sales

Saint Vincent De Paul Thrift Store
15725 Grand River
Detroit, MI 48227
TYPE OF MERCHANDISE: Clothing,
housewares, furniture
DONATION TAX RECEIPT: Receipt given
upon request
COMMENTS: Monthly markdowns

Salvation Army Thrift Store
1627 W. Fort St.
CROSS STREET: Trumbull
Detroit, MI 48216
CONTACT: Dorothy Avakian
PHONE: 313-961-3521, 965-7803
HOURS: Mon.–Sat. 9–5
TYPE OF MERCHANDISE: Clothing,
housewares, furniture
DONATION TAX RECEIPT: Receipt given
upon request
COMMENTS: Daily clothing sales

Saint Vincent De Paul Warehouse
2929 E. Grand Blvd.
Detroit, MI 48202
TYPE OF MERCHANDISE: Clothing,
housewares, furniture
DONATION TAX RECEIPT: Receipt given
upon request
COMMENTS: Monthly markdowns

Saint Vincent De Paul Thrift Store
2950 Gratiot Ave.
Detroit, MI 48207
TYPE OF MERCHANDISE: Clothing,
housewares, furniture
DONATION TAX RECEIPT: Receipt given
upon request
COMMENTS: Monthly markdowns

NCJW Council Thrift Shop
3403 Puritan St.
Detroit, MI 48238
TYPE OF MERCHANDISE: Clothing,
housewares, furniture
DONATION TAX RECEIPT: Receipt given
upon request

Saint Vincent De Paul Thrift Store
5200 E. McNichols
Detroit, MI 48234
TYPE OF MERCHANDISE: Clothing,
housewares, furniture
DONATION TAX RECEIPT: Receipt given
upon request
COMMENTS: Monthly markdowns

Salvation Army Thrift Store
5560 Chene
Detroit, MI 48211
CONTACT: Kathy Moore
PHONE: 313-924-5166
HOURS: Mon.–Sat. 9–5
TYPE OF MERCHANDISE: Clothing,
housewares, furniture
DONATION TAX RECEIPT: Receipt given
upon request
COMMENTS: Daily clothing sales

Salvation Army Thrift Store
5600 E. Eight Mile Rd.
Detroit, MI 49234
CONTACT: Nancy Stohecker
PHONE: 313-891-6644
HOURS: Mon.–Sat. 9–9
TYPE OF MERCHANDISE: Clothing,
housewares, furniture
DONATION TAX RECEIPT: Receipt given
upon request
COMMENTS: Daily clothing sales

Saint Vincent De Paul Thrift Store
5840 W. Fort St.
Detroit, MI 48209
TYPE OF MERCHANDISE: Clothing,
housewares, furniture
DONATION TAX RECEIPT: Receipt given
upon request
COMMENTS: Monthly markdowns

Salvation Army Thrift Store
5848–50 Fort St.
CROSS STREET: Junction
Detroit, MI 48209

CONTACT: Mary Kondakor
PHONE: 313-841-2720
HOURS: Mon.–Sat. 9–5
TYPE OF MERCHANDISE: Clothing, housewares, furniture
DONATION TAX RECEIPT: Receipt given upon request
COMMENTS: Daily clothing sales

Salvation Army Thrift Store
7640 Michigan Ave.
CROSS STREET: Central
Detroit, MI 48210
CONTACT: Ola Joiner
PHONE: 313-849-4177
HOURS: Mon.–Sat. 9–9
TYPE OF MERCHANDISE: Clothing, housewares, furniture
DONATION TAX RECEIPT: Receipt given upon request
COMMENTS: Daily clothing sales

Salvation Army Thrift Store
22522 Gratiot Ave.
East Detroit, MI 48021
TYPE OF MERCHANDISE: Clothing, housewares, furniture
DONATION TAX RECEIPT: Receipt given upon request

Saint Vincent De Paul Thrift Store
1014 Ludington
Escanaba, MI 49829
TYPE OF MERCHANDISE: Clothing, housewares, furniture
DONATION TAX RECEIPT: Receipt given upon request
COMMENTS: Monthly markdowns

American Cancer Society Discovery Shop
23330 Farmington Rd.
Farmington, MI 48336
CONTACT: Marni Kiefer
PHONE: 313-477-1081
TYPE OF MERCHANDISE: Clothing, bric-a-brac
DONATION TAX RECEIPT: Receipt given upon request
COMMENTS: Monthly markdowns

Saint Vincent De Paul Thrift Store
28417 Detroit St.
Flat Rock, MI 48134

TYPE OF MERCHANDISE: Clothing, housewares, furniture
DONATION TAX RECEIPT: Receipt given upon request
COMMENTS: Monthly markdowns

Saint Vincent De Paul thrift Store
1912 N. Franklin
Flint, MI 48506
TYPE OF MERCHANDISE: Clothing, housewares, furniture
DONATION TAX RECEIPT: Receipt given upon request
COMMENTS: Monthly markdowns

Goodwill Industries Thrift Store
2188 Center Rd.
Flint, MI 48519
TYPE OF MERCHANDISE: Clothing, housewares, furniture
DONATION TAX RECEIPT: Receipt given upon request

Salvation army thrift Store
2309 Fenton Rd.
Flint, MI 48507
TYPE OF MERCHANDISE: Clothing, housewares, furniture
DONATION TAX RECEIPT: Receipt given upon request

Goodwill Industries Thrift Store
2320 W. Pierson Rd.
Flint, MI 48504
TYPE OF MERCHANDISE: Clothing, housewares, furniture
DONATION TAX RECEIPT: Receipt given upon request

Goodwill Industries Thrift Store
3375 S. Saginaw St.
Flint, MI 48529
TYPE OF MERCHANDISE: Clothing, housewares, furniture
DONATION TAX RECEIPT: Receipt given upon request

Goodwill Industries Thrift Store
3825 Corunna Rd.
Flint, MI 48532
TYPE OF MERCHANDISE: Clothing, housewares, furniture
DONATION TAX RECEIPT: Receipt given upon request

Amvets Thrift Store
  4122 Clio Rd.
  Flint, MI 48504
  TYPE OF MERCHANDISE: Clothing,
  housewares,
  DONATION TAX RECEIPT: Receipt given
  upon request
Salvation Army Thrift Store
  4423 Richfield Rd.
  Flint, MI 48506
  TYPE OF MERCHANDISE: Clothing,
  housewares, furniture
  DONATION TAX RECEIPT: Receipt given
  upon request
Saint Vincent De Paul Thrift Store
  422 Sleepy Hollow Dr.
  Flushing, MI 48433
  TYPE OF MERCHANDISE: Clothing,
  housewares, furniture
  DONATION TAX RECEIPT: Receipt given
  upon request
  COMMENTS: Monthly markdowns
Salvation Army Thrift Store
  28982 Ford Rd.
  CROSS STREET: Middlebelt
  Garden City, MI 48135
  CONTACT: Diann Dudonis
  PHONE: 313-261-7175
  HOURS: Mon.–Sat. 10–6
  TYPE OF MERCHANDISE: Clothing,
  housewares, furniture
  DONATION TAX RECEIPT: Receipt given
  upon request
  COMMENTS: Weekly sales
Saint Vincent De Paul Thrift Store
  816 Delta Ave.
  Gladstone, MI 49837
  TYPE OF MERCHANDISE: Clothing,
  housewares, furniture
  DONATION TAX RECEIPT: Receipt given
  upon request
  COMMENTS: Monthly markdowns
Salvation Army Thrift Store
  1491 S. Division
  Grand Rapids, MI 49507
  PHONE: 616-452-3133
  HOURS: Mon.–Sat. 9:30–6
  TYPE OF MERCHANDISE: Clothing,
  housewares, furniture

DONATION TAX RECEIPT: Receipt given
  upon request
  COMMENTS: Weekly half-price sales
Saint Vincent De Paul Thrift Store
  1737 S. Division
  Grand Rapids, MI 49507
  TYPE OF MERCHANDISE: Clothing,
  housewares, furniture
  DONATION TAX RECEIPT: Receipt given
  upon request
  COMMENTS: Monthly markdowns
American Cancer Society Discovery Shop
  3539 Alpine Ave. NE
  Grand Rapids, MI 49504
  CONTACT: Sally Hitchcock
  PHONE: 616-784-7381
  TYPE OF MERCHANDISE: Clothing, bric-a-brac
  DONATION TAX RECEIPT: Receipt given
  upon request
  COMMENTS: Monthly markdowns
Goodwill Industries Thrift Store
  3630 Plainfield Ave. NE
  Grand Rapids, MI 49505
  TYPE OF MERCHANDISE: Clothing,
  housewares, furniture
  DONATION TAX RECEIPT: Receipt given
  upon request
Goodwill Industries Thrift Store
  705 28th St. SW
  Grand Rapids, MI 49509
  TYPE OF MERCHANDISE: Clothing,
  housewares, furniture
  DONATION TAX RECEIPT: Receipt given
  upon request
Goodwill Industries Thrift Store
  3035 Prairie St. SW
  Grandville, MI 49418
  TYPE OF MERCHANDISE: Clothing,
  housewares, furniture
  DONATION TAX RECEIPT: Receipt given
  upon request
Saint Vincent De Paul Thrift Store
  46 N. Johnson Lake Rd.
  Gwinn, MI 49841
  TYPE OF MERCHANDISE: Clothing,
  housewares, furniture
  DONATION TAX RECEIPT: Receipt given
  upon request
  COMMENTS: Monthly markdowns

Saint Vincent De Paul ThriftStore
3290 N. M-65
Hale, MI 48739
TYPE OF MERCHANDISE: Clothing,
housewares, furniture
DONATION TAX RECEIPT: Receipt given
upon request
COMMENTS: Monthly markdowns

Saint Vincent De Paul Thrift Store
204 Quincy St.
Hancock, MI 49930
TYPE OF MERCHANDISE: Clothing,
housewares, furniture
DONATION TAX RECEIPT: Receipt given
upon request
COMMENTS: Monthly markdowns

Salvation Army Thrift Store
21810 John R.
Hazel Park, MI 48030
PHONE: 810-546-9094
TYPE OF MERCHANDISE: Clothing,
housewares, furniture
DONATION TAX RECEIPT: Receipt given
upon request

Salvation Army Thrift Store
135 W. Eighth
Holland, MI 49423
PHONE: 616-396-4264
HOURS: Mon.–Sat. 9:30–6
TYPE OF MERCHANDISE: Clothing,
housewares, furniture
DONATION TAX RECEIPT: Receipt given
upon request
COMMENTS: Weekly half-price sales

Saint Vincent De Paul Thrift Store
220 Sheldon
Houghton, MI 49931
TYPE OF MERCHANDISE: Clothing,
housewares, furniture
DONATION TAX RECEIPT: Receipt given
upon request
COMMENTS: Monthly markdowns

Saint Vincent De Paul Thrift Store
27114 Michigan Ave.
Inkster, MI 48141
TYPE OF MERCHANDISE: Clothing,
housewares, furniture
DONATION TAX RECEIPT: Receipt given
upon request

COMMENTS: Monthly markdowns

Salvation Army Thrift Store
200 W. Main St.
Ionia, MI 48846
TYPE OF MERCHANDISE: Clothing,
housewares, furniture
DONATION TAX RECEIPT: Receipt given
upon request

Saint Vincent De Paul Thrift Store
207 E. Hughitt
Iron Mountain, MI 49801
TYPE OF MERCHANDISE: Clothing,
housewares, furniture
DONATION TAX RECEIPT: Receipt given
upon request
COMMENTS: Monthly markdowns

Saint Vincent De Paul Thrift Store
211 W. Maple
Iron River, MI 49935
TYPE OF MERCHANDISE: Clothing,
housewares, furniture
DONATION TAX RECEIPT: Receipt given
upon request
COMMENTS: Monthly markdowns

Saint Vincent De Paul Thrift Store
212 E. McLeod
Ironwood, MI 49938
TYPE OF MERCHANDISE: Clothing,
housewares, furniture
DONATION TAX RECEIPT: Receipt given
upon request
COMMENTS: Monthly markdowns

Saint Vincent De Paul Thrift Store
322 Cleveland Ave.
Ishpeming, MI 49849
TYPE OF MERCHANDISE: Clothing,
housewares, furniture
DONATION TAX RECEIPT: Receipt given
upon request
COMMENTS: Monthly markdowns

Saint Vincent De Paul thrift Store
1509 E. Michigan Ave.
Jackson, MI 49202
TYPE OF MERCHANDISE: Clothing,
housewares, furniture
DONATION TAX RECEIPT: Receipt given
upon request
COMMENTS: Monthly markdowns

Goodwill Industries Thrift Store
617 N. Mechanic St.
Jackson, MI 49202
TYPE OF MERCHANDISE: Clothing,
housewares, furniture
DONATION TAX RECEIPT: Receipt given
upon request
Salvation Army Thrift Store
909 E. Michigan Ave.
Jackson, MI 49201
TYPE OF MERCHANDISE: Clothing,
housewares, furniture
DONATION TAX RECEIPT: Receipt given
upon request
Salvation Army Thrift Store
1005 Portage
Kalamazoo, MI 49001
PHONE: 616-381-4148
HOURS: Mon.–Sat. 9:30–6
TYPE OF MERCHANDISE: Clothing,
housewares, furniture
DONATION TAX RECEIPT: Receipt given
upon request
COMMENTS: Weekly half-price sales
American Cancer Society Discovery Shop
4426 W. Main
Kalamazoo, MI 49007
CONTACT: Mary Bachleda
PHONE: 616-345-0661
TYPE OF MERCHANDISE: Clothing, bric-a-
brac
DONATION TAX RECEIPT: Receipt given
upon request
COMMENTS: Monthly markdowns
Saint Vincent De Paul Thrift Store
513 Eleanor St.
Kalamazoo, MI 49007
TYPE OF MERCHANDISE: Clothing,
housewares, furniture
DONATION TAX RECEIPT: Receipt given
upon request
COMMENTS: Monthly markdowns
Junior League Clothes Encounters
607 S. Burdick
Kalamazoo, MI 49007
PHONE: 616-342-9075
HOURS: Tue.–Fri. 10–4, Sat. 10–2

TYPE OF MERCHANDISE: Clothing,
housewares
DONATION TAX RECEIPT: Receipt given
upon request
COMMENTS: Nov./Dec., toy sale, May
Attic sale
American Cancer Society Discovery Shop
4443-B Brenton Rd.
Kentwood, MI 49508
CONTACT: Sally Hitchcock
PHONE: 616-281-4988
TYPE OF MERCHANDISE: Clothing, bric-a-
brac
DONATION TAX RECEIPT: Receipt given
upon request
COMMENTS: Monthly markdowns
Saint Vincent De Paul Thrift Store
14 S. Main St.
L'Anse, MI 49946
TYPE OF MERCHANDISE: Clothing,
housewares, furniture
DONATION TAX RECEIPT: Receipt given
upon request
COMMENTS: Monthly markdowns
Saint Vincent De Paul Thrift Store
1020 S. Washington Ave.
Lansing, MI 48910
TYPE OF MERCHANDISE: Clothing,
housewares, furniture
DONATION TAX RECEIPT: Receipt given
upon request
COMMENTS: Monthly markdowns
Salvation Army Thrift Store
2019 E. Michigan Ave.
Lansing, MI 48912
TYPE OF MERCHANDISE: Clothing,
housewares, furniture
DONATION TAX RECEIPT: Receipt given
upon request
Junior League Cedar Chest
221 Washington Sq. S
Lansing, MI 48933
TYPE OF MERCHANDISE: Clothing for men,
women, and children
DONATION TAX RECEIPT: Receipt given
upon request

Salvation Army Thrift Store
317 E. North St.
Lansing, MI 48906
TYPE OF MERCHANDISE: Clothing,
housewares, furniture
DONATION TAX RECEIPT: Receipt given
upon request

Salvation army Thrift Store
1456 Fort St.
Lincoln Park, MI 48146
TYPE OF MERCHANDISE: Clothing,
housewares, furniture
DONATION TAX RECEIPT: Receipt given
upon request

Salvation Army Thrift Store
27476 Schoolcraft
CROSS STREET: Inkster Rd.
Livonia, MI 48150
CONTACT: Teresa Williams
PHONE: 313-422-3560
HOURS: Mon.–Sat. 10–6
TYPE OF MERCHANDISE: Clothing,
housewares, furniture
DONATION TAX RECEIPT: Receipt given
upon request
COMMENTS: Weekly sales

Salvation Army Thrift Store
33600 Plymouth Rd.
CROSS STREET West and Farmington Rd.
Livonia, MI 48150
CONTACT: Lyle Dechert
PHONE: 313-425-7573
HOURS: Mon.–Sat. 10–6
TYPE OF MERCHANDISE: Clothing,
housewares, furniture
DONATION TAX RECEIPT: Receipt given
upon request
COMMENTS: Weekly sales

Salvation Army Thrift Store
513 S. James St.
Ludington, MI 49431
TYPE OF MERCHANDISE: Clothing,
housewares, furniture
DONATION TAX RECEIPT: Receipt given
upon request

Saint Vincent De Paul Thrift Store
333 Oak St.
Manistique, MI 49854

TYPE OF MERCHANDISE: Clothing,
housewares, furniture
DONATION TAX RECEIPT: Receipt given
upon request
COMMENTS: Monthly markdowns

Saint Vincent De Paul Thrift Store
2118 Fitch Ave.
Marquette, MI 49855
TYPE OF MERCHANDISE: Clothing,
housewares, furniture
DONATION TAX RECEIPT: Receipt given
upon request
COMMENTS: Monthly markdowns

Saint Vincent De Paul Thrift Store
501 Gratiot Blvd.
Maryville, MI 48040
TYPE OF MERCHANDISE: Clothing,
housewares, furniture
DONATION TAX RECEIPT: Receipt given
upon request
COMMENTS: Monthly markdowns

Saint Vincent De Paul Thrift Store
2227 F 41
Mikado, MI 48745
TYPE OF MERCHANDISE: Clothing,
housewares, furniture
DONATION TAX RECEIPT: Receipt given
upon request
COMMENTS: Monthly markdowns

Salvation Army Thrift Store
36646 S. Gratiot Ave.
Mt. Clemens, MI 48035
TYPE OF MERCHANDISE: Clothing,
housewares, furniture
DONATION TAX RECEIPT: Receipt given
upon request

American Cancer Society Discovery Shop
36690 Garfield Rd.
Mt. Clemens, MI 48043
CONTACT: Becky Hilborn
PHONE: 313-790-8805
TYPE OF MERCHANDISE: Clothing, bric-a-
brac
DONATION TAX RECEIPT: Receipt given
upon request
COMMENTS: Monthly markdowns

Saint Vincent De Paul Thrift Store
107 Elm Street
Munising, MI 49862
TYPE OF MERCHANDISE: Clothing,
housewares, furniture
DONATION TAX RECEIPT: Receipt given
upon request
COMMENTS: Monthly markdowns

Salvation Army Thrift Store
2905 Peck St.
Muskegon Heights, MI 49444
PHONE: 616-737-0241
HOURS: Mon.–Sat. 9:30–6
TYPE OF MERCHANDISE: Clothing,
housewares, furniture
DONATION TAX RECEIPT: Receipt given
upon request
COMMENTS: Weekly half-price sales

Salvation Army Thrift Store
35765 Green
New Baltimore, MI 48047
TYPE OF MERCHANDISE: Clothing,
housewares, furniture
DONATION TAX RECEIPT: Receipt given
upon request
COMMENTS: Daily clothing sales

Goodwill Industries Thrift Store
109 E. Main St.
Niles, MI 49120
TYPE OF MERCHANDISE: Clothing,
housewares, furniture
DONATION TAX RECEIPT: Receipt given
upon request

Salvation Army Thrift Store
1919 Oak St.
Niles, MI 49120
TYPE OF MERCHANDISE: Clothing,
housewares, furniture
DONATION TAX RECEIPT: Receipt given
upon request

Saint Vincent De Paul Thrift Store
728 Main St.
Norway, MI 49870
TYPE OF MERCHANDISE: Clothing,
housewares, furniture
DONATION TAX RECEIPT: Receipt given
upon request
COMMENTS: Monthly markdowns

Saint Vincent De Paul Thrift Store
8138 W. Nine Mile Rd.
Oak Park, MI 48237
TYPE OF MERCHANDISE: Clothing,
housewares, furniture
DONATION TAX RECEIPT: Receipt given
upon request
COMMENTS: Monthly markdowns

Saint Vincent De Paul Thrift Store
317 River St.
Ontonagon, MI 49953
TYPE OF MERCHANDISE: Clothing,
housewares, furniture
DONATION TAX RECEIPT: Receipt given
upon request
COMMENTS: Monthly markdowns

Salvation Army Thrift Store
812 W. Main St.
Owosso, MI 48867
TYPE OF MERCHANDISE: Clothing,
housewares, furniture
DONATION TAX RECEIPT: Receipt given
upon request

Salvation Army Thrift Store
1224 Krusel St.
Petoskey, MI 49770
TYPE OF MERCHANDISE: Clothing,
housewares, furniture
DONATION TAX RECEIPT: Receipt given
upon request

Salvation Army Thrift Store
4318 Plainfield Ave.
Plainfield Township, MI
PHONE: 616-364-5736
HOURS: Mon.–Sat. 9:30–6
TYPE OF MERCHANDISE: Clothing,
housewares, furniture
DONATION TAX RECEIPT: Receipt given
upon request
COMMENTS: Weekly half-price sales

Salvation Army Thrift Store
118 W. Lawrence
Pontiac, MI 48341
PHONE: 810-338-9601
HOURS: Mon.–Sat. 9:30–5
TYPE OF MERCHANDISE: Clothing,
housewares, furniture
DONATION TAX RECEIPT: Receipt given
upon request

Salvation Army Thrift Store
1185 N. Perry St.
Pontiac, MI 48340
PHONE: 810-334-4666
HOURS: Mon.–Sat. 9:30–5
TYPE OF MERCHANDISE: Clothing,
housewares, furniture
DONATION TAX RECEIPT: Receipt given
upon request

Goodwill Industries Thrift Store
1013 26th St.
Port Huron, MI 48060
TYPE OF MERCHANDISE: Clothing,
housewares, furniture
DONATION TAX RECEIPT: Receipt given
upon request

Saint Vincent De Paul Thrift Store
1337 24th St.
Port Huron, MI 48060
TYPE OF MERCHANDISE: Clothing,
housewares, furniture
DONATION TAX RECEIPT: Receipt given
upon request
COMMENTS: Monthly markdowns

Salvation Army Thrift Store
1602 Griswold St.
Port Huron, MI 48060-5658
TYPE OF MERCHANDISE: Clothing,
housewares, furniture
DONATION TAX RECEIPT: Receipt given
upon request

Saint Vincent De Paul Thrift Store
5290 Henderson Lake Rd.
Prescott, MI 48756
TYPE OF MERCHANDISE: Clothing,
housewares, furniture
DONATION TAX RECEIPT: Receipt given
upon request
COMMENTS: Monthly markdowns

Saint Vincent De Paul Thrift Store
805 W. Houghton Lake
Prudenville, MI 48651
TYPE OF MERCHANDISE: Clothing,
housewares, furniture
DONATION TAX RECEIPT: Receipt given
upon request
COMMENTS: Monthly markdowns

Salvation Army Thrift Store
27170 Grand River Ave.
CROSS STREET: Inkster
Redford, MI 48240
CONTACT: Tina Smith
PHONE: 313-255-0777
HOURS: Mon.–Sat. 10–9
TYPE OF MERCHANDISE: Clothing,
housewares, furniture
DONATION TAX RECEIPT: Receipt given
upon request
COMMENTS: Daily clothing sales

Saint Vincent De Paul Thrift Store
Kloman Ave.
Republic, MI 49879
TYPE OF MERCHANDISE: Clothing,
housewares, furniture
DONATION TAX RECEIPT: Receipt given
upon request
COMMENTS: Monthly markdowns

Salvation Army Thrift Store
33800 Goddard Rd.
Romulus, MI 48174
CONTACT: George Zilba
PHONE: 313-941-5100
HOURS: Mon.–Sat. 10–6
TYPE OF MERCHANDISE: Clothing,
housewares, furniture
DONATION TAX RECEIPT: Receipt given
upon request
COMMENTS: Weekly sales

Goodwill Industries Thrift Store
26510 Gratiot Ave.
Roseville, MI 48066
TYPE OF MERCHANDISE: Clothing,
housewares, furniture
DONATION TAX RECEIPT: Receipt given
upon request

Salvation Army Thrift Store
122 E. Fourth St.
Royal Oak, MI 48067
PHONE: 810-542-6661
HOURS: Mon.–Sat. 9:30–5
TYPE OF MERCHANDISE: Clothing,
housewares, furniture
DONATION TAX RECEIPT: Receipt given
upon request

NCJW Thrift Shop
1221 E. Lincoln
Royal Oak, MI 48067
TYPE OF MERCHANDISE: Clothing,
housewares, furniture
DONATION TAX RECEIPT: Receipt given
upon request
COMMENTS: Annual sale (Nov.) in a
separate store

Junior League Thrift Shop
114 S. Hamilton
Saginaw, MI 48602
PHONE: 810-793-0394
HOURS: Mon.–Fri. 10–5, Sat. 10–1
TYPE OF MERCHANDISE: Clothing,
housewares, toys
DONATION TAX RECEIPT: Receipt given
upon request

Goodwill Industries Thrift Store
3417 E. Genesee Ave.
Saginaw, MI 48601
TYPE OF MERCHANDISE: Clothing,
housewares, furniture
DONATION TAX RECEIPT: Receipt given
upon request

Salvation Army Thrift Store
722 E. Genesee Ave.
Saginaw, MI 48607
TYPE OF MERCHANDISE: Clothing,
housewares, furniture
DONATION TAX RECEIPT: Receipt given
upon request

Salvation Army Thrift Store
132 W. Spruce St.
Sault Sainte Marie, MI 49783
TYPE OF MERCHANDISE: Clothing,
housewares, furniture
DONATION TAX RECEIPT: Receipt given
upon request

American Cancer Society Discovery Shop
19791 W. Twelve Mile
Southfield, MI 48076
CONTACT: Marni Kiefer
PHONE: 313-477-1081
TYPE OF MERCHANDISE: Clothing, bric-a-brac
DONATION TAX RECEIPT: Receipt given
upon request
COMMENTS: Monthly markdowns

Saint Vincent De Paul Thrift Store
12354 Fort St.
Southgate, MI 48195
TYPE OF MERCHANDISE: Clothing,
housewares, furniture
DONATION TAX RECEIPT: Receipt given
upon request
COMMENTS: Monthly markdowns

Saint Vincent De Paul Thrift Store
23746 Greater Mack St.
St. Clair Shores, MI 48080
TYPE OF MERCHANDISE: Clothing,
housewares, furniture
DONATION TAX RECEIPT: Receipt given
upon request
COMMENTS: Monthly markdowns

Salvation Army Thrift Store
24301 Harper Ave.
CROSS STREET: 9½ Mile
St. Clair Shores, MI 48080
CONTACT: Kathleen Krim
PHONE: 313-777-6045
HOURS: Mon.–Sat. 10–9
TYPE OF MERCHANDISE: Clothing,
housewares, furniture
DONATION TAX RECEIPT: Receipt given
upon request
COMMENTS: Daily clothing sales

Saint Vincent De Paul Thrift Store
1008 Arcade St.
St. Paul, MN 55106
TYPE OF MERCHANDISE: Clothing,
housewares, furniture
DONATION TAX RECEIPT: Receipt given
upon request
COMMENTS: Monthly markdowns

Saint Vincent De Paul Thrift Store
115 First St.
Tawas City, MI 48763
TYPE OF MERCHANDISE: Clothing,
housewares, furniture
DONATION TAX RECEIPT: Receipt given
upon request
COMMENTS: Monthly markdowns

Salvation Army Thrift Store
22557 Ecorse Rd.
Taylor, MI 48180
TYPE OF MERCHANDISE: Clothing,
housewares, furniture

DONATION TAX RECEIPT: Receipt given upon request

Saint Vincent De Paul Thrift Store
1028 Hannah St.
Traverse City, MI 49684
TYPE OF MERCHANDISE: Clothing, housewares, furniture
DONATION TAX RECEIPT: Receipt given upon request
COMMENTS: Monthly markdowns

Goodwill Industries Thrift Store
1151 S. Airport Rd. W
Traverse City, MI 49684
TYPE OF MERCHANDISE: Clothing, housewares, furniture
DONATION TAX RECEIPT: Receipt given upon request

Salvation Army Thrift Store
545 W. 11th St.
Traverse City, MI 49684
TYPE OF MERCHANDISE: Clothing, housewares, furniture
DONATION TAX RECEIPT: Receipt given upon request

Saint Vincent De Paul Thrift Store
14040 E. Nine Mile Rd.
Warren, MI 48089
TYPE OF MERCHANDISE: Clothing, housewares, furniture
DONATION TAX RECEIPT: Receipt given upon request
COMMENTS: Monthly markdowns

Salvation Army Thrift Store
23524 Van Dyke Ave.
Warren, MI 48089-1646
TYPE OF MERCHANDISE: Clothing, housewares, furniture
DONATION TAX RECEIPT: Receipt given upon request

Salvation Army Thrift Store
3518 Wayne Rd.
CROSS STREET: Michigan Ave.
Wayne, MI 48184
CONTACT: Mary Vallely
PHONE: 313-941-5100
HOURS: Mon.–Sat. 10–6
TYPE OF MERCHANDISE: Clothing, housewares, furniture

DONATION TAX RECEIPT: Receipt given upon request
COMMENTS: Weekly sales

Salvation Army Thrift Store
9633 Highland Rd.
White Lake, MI 48386
PHONE: 810-698-4449
HOURS: Mon.–Sat. 9:30–5
TYPE OF MERCHANDISE: Clothing, housewares, furniture
DONATION TAX RECEIPT: Receipt given upon request

Saint Vincent De Paul Thrift Store
2717 Tenth St.
Wyandotte, MI 48192
TYPE OF MERCHANDISE: Clothing, housewares, furniture
DONATION TAX RECEIPT: Receipt given upon request
COMMENTS: Monthly markdowns

Salvation Army Thrift Store
2740 Hague St.
Wyoming, MI 49509
PHONE: 616-530-8020
HOURS: Mon.–Sat. 9:30–5:45, Fri. 9:30–7
TYPE OF MERCHANDISE: Clothing, housewares, furniture
DONATION TAX RECEIPT: Receipt given upon request
COMMENTS: Weekly half-price sales

Salvation Army Thrift Store
1960 E. Michigan
Ypsilanti, MI 48197
CONTACT: Fannie Fonville
PHONE: 313-941-5100
HOURS: Mon.–Sat. 9–5
TYPE OF MERCHANDISE: Clothing, housewares, furniture
DONATION TAX RECEIPT: Receipt given upon request
COMMENTS: Weekly sales

Minnesota

Salvation Army Thrift Store
214 S. Washington Ave.
Albert Lea, MN 56007
TYPE OF MERCHANDISE: Clothing, housewares, furniture

DONATION TAX RECEIPT: Receipt given
upon request
Salvation Army Thrift Store
511 "L" St. NE
Brainerd, MN 56401
TYPE OF MERCHANDISE: Clothing,
housewares, furniture
DONATION TAX RECEIPT: Receipt given
upon request
Goodwill Industries Thrift Store
716 Brainerd Mall
Brainerd, MN 56401
TYPE OF MERCHANDISE: Clothing,
housewares, furniture
DONATION TAX RECEIPT: Receipt given
upon request
TVI Savers Thrift Store
4849 Central Ave. NE
Columbia Hts., MN 55421
CONTACT: Peter Boes
PHONE: 612-571-1319
HOURS: Mon.–Sat. 9–9, Sun. 12–7
TYPE OF MERCHANDISE: Clothing,
housewares, furniture
DONATION TAX RECEIPT: No
Salvation Army Thrift Store
1326 Coon Rapids Blvd.
Coon Rapids, MN 55433
PHONE: 612-757-6740
TYPE OF MERCHANDISE: Clothing,
housewares, furniture
DONATION TAX RECEIPT: Receipt given
upon request
Saint Vincent De Paul Thrift Store
109 W. Fourth St.
Duluth, MN 55806
TYPE OF MERCHANDISE: Clothing,
housewares, furniture
DONATION TAX RECEIPT: Receipt given
upon request
COMMENTS: Monthly markdowns
Salvation Army Thrift Store
1814 W. Superior St.
Duluth, MN 55806
TYPE OF MERCHANDISE: Clothing,
housewares, furniture
DONATION TAX RECEIPT: Receipt given
upon request

Saint Vincent De Paul Thrift Store
1923 W. Superior St.
Duluth, MN 55806
TYPE OF MERCHANDISE: Clothing,
housewares, furniture
DONATION TAX RECEIPT: Receipt given
upon request
COMMENTS: Monthly markdowns
Saint Vincent De Paul Thrift Store
321 N. Central Ave.
Duluth, MN 55808
TYPE OF MERCHANDISE: Clothing,
housewares, furniture
DONATION TAX RECEIPT: Receipt given
upon request
COMMENTS: Monthly markdowns
Salvation Army Thrift Store
1404 Mainstreet
Hopkins, MN 55343
PHONE: 612-932-0814
TYPE OF MERCHANDISE: Clothing,
housewares, furniture
DONATION TAX RECEIPT: Receipt given
upon request
Goodwill Industries Thrift Store
2116 E. Lake St.
Minneapolis, MN 55407
TYPE OF MERCHANDISE: Clothing,
housewares, furniture
DONATION TAX RECEIPT: Receipt given
upon request
Salvation Army Thrift Store
2121 E. Lake St.
Minneapolis, MN 55407
TYPE OF MERCHANDISE: Clothing,
housewares, furniture
DONATION TAX RECEIPT: Receipt given
upon request
Salvation Army Thrift Store
2750 Nicollet Ave.
Minneapolis, MN 55408
PHONE: 612-871-4414
TYPE OF MERCHANDISE: Clothing,
housewares, furniture
DONATION TAX RECEIPT: Receipt given
upon request

Salvation Army Thrift Store
2822 Washington Ave. N
Minneapolis, MN 55411
PHONE: 612-529-4077
TYPE OF MERCHANDISE: Clothing,
housewares, furniture
DONATION TAX RECEIPT: Receipt given
upon request

Salvation Army Thrift Store
3740 Nicollet Ave.
Minneapolis, MN 55409
PHONE: 612-822-1200
TYPE OF MERCHANDISE: Clothing,
housewares, furniture
DONATION TAX RECEIPT: Receipt given
upon request

Salvation Army Thrift Store
900 N. Fourth St.
Minneapolis, MN 55401
PHONE: 612-332-5855
TYPE OF MERCHANDISE: Clothing,
housewares, furniture
DONATION TAX RECEIPT: Receipt given
upon request

TVI Savers Thrift Store
Hi-Lake Shopping Center, 2124 E. Lake St.
Minneapolis, MN 55407
CONTACT: Jerry Larsen
PHONE: 612-729-9271
HOURS: Mon.–Sat. 9–9, Sun. 12–7
TYPE OF MERCHANDISE: Clothing,
housewares, furniture
DONATION TAX RECEIPT: No

MCC Care & Share Thrift Shop
208 Tenth St.
Mountain Lake, MN 56159
PHONE: 507-427-3468
TYPE OF MERCHANDISE: Clothing,
housewares
DONATION TAX RECEIPT: Receipt given
upon request

Salvation Army Thrift Store
325 Plum St.
Red Wing, MN 55066
TYPE OF MERCHANDISE: Clothing,
housewares, furniture
DONATION TAX RECEIPT: Receipt given
upon request

Salvation Army Thrift Store
104 Fourth St. SE
Rochester, MN 55904
TYPE OF MERCHANDISE: Clothing,
housewares, furniture
DONATION TAX RECEIPTS: Receipt given
upon request

Salvation Army Thrift Store
Hwy. 88 & St. Anthony Pkwy.
St. Anthony, MN
PHONE: 612-782-9440
TYPE OF MERCHANDISE: Clothing,
housewares, furniture
DONATION TAX RECEIPT: Receipt given
upon request

Salvation Army Thrift Store
631 Lincoln Ave. NE
St. Cloud, MN 56304
TYPE OF MERCHANDISE: Clothing,
housewares, furniture
DONATION TAX RECEIPT: Receipt given
upon request

Disabled American Vets Thrift Store
572 University Ave. W
St. Paul, MN 55103
TYPE OF MERCHANDISE: Clothing,
housewares
DONATION TAX RECEIPT: Receipt given
upon request

Goodwill Industries Thrift Store
946 Payne Ave.
St. Paul, MN 55101
TYPE OF MERCHANDISE: Clothing,
housewares, furniture
DONATION TAX RECEIPT: Receipt given
upon request

Salvation Army Thrift Store
1411 E. Magnolia
St. Paul, MN 55106
PHONE: 612-771-1047
TYPE OF MERCHANDISE: Clothing,
housewares, furniture
DONATION TAX RECEIPT: Receipt given
upon request

Salvation Army Thrift Store
149 E. Thompson Ave.
St. Paul, MN 55118
PHONE: 612-451-7146

TYPE OF MERCHANDISE: Clothing, housewares, furniture
DONATION TAX RECEIPT: Receipt given upon request

TVI Savers Thrift Store
235 E. Maryland Ave.
St. Paul, MN 55117
CONTACT: Jerry Larsen
PHONE: 612-488-6293
HOURS: Mon.–Sat. 9–9, Sun. 10–6
TYPE OF MERCHANDISE: Clothing, housewares, furniture
DONATION TAX RECEIPT: No

Saint Vincent De Paul Thrift Store
461 W. Seventh St.
St. Paul, MN 55102
TYPE OF MERCHANDISE: Clothing, housewares, furniture
DONATION TAX RECEIPT: Receipt given upon request
COMMENTS: Monthly markdowns

Salvation Army Thrift Store
927 Payne Ave.
St. Paul, MN 55101
PHONE: 612-776-3585
TYPE OF MERCHANDISE: Clothing, housewares, furniture
DONATION TAX RECEIPT: Receipt given upon request

Goodwill Industries Thrift Store
1270 Frontage Rd. W
Stillwater, MN 55082
TYPE OF MERCHANDISE: Clothing, housewares, furniture
DONATION TAX RECEIPT: Receipt given upon request

Goodwill Industries Thrift Store
522 Chestnut St.
Virginia, MN 55792
TYPE OF MERCHANDISE: Clothing, housewares, furniture
DONATION TAX RECEIPT: Receipt given upon request

Goodwill Industries Thrift Store
28 Second Ave.
Waite Park, MN 56387
TYPE OF MERCHANDISE: Clothing, housewares, furniture

DONATION TAX RECEIPT: Receipt given upon request

Salvation Army Thrift Store
307 Third St. SW
Willmar, MN 56201
TYPE OF MERCHANDISE: Clothing, housewares, furniture
DONATION TAX RECEIPT: Receipt given upon request

Mississippi

Salvation Army Thrift Store
1887 Pass Rd.
Biloxi, MS 39531
TYPE OF MERCHANDISE: Clothing, housewares, furniture
DONATION TAX RECEIPT: Receipt given upon request

Saint Vincent De Paul Thrift Store
870 Nativity Dr.
Biloxi, MS 39530
TYPE OF MERCHANDISE: Clothing, housewares, furniture
DONATION TAX RECEIPT: Receipt given upon request
COMMENTS: Monthly markdowns

Salvation Army Thrift Store
304 Washington Ave.
Greenville, MS 38701
TYPE OF MERCHANDISE: Clothing, housewares, furniture
DONATION TAX RECEIPT: Receipt given upon request

Goodwill Industries Thrift Store
124 E. Front St.
Hattiesburg, MS 39401
TYPE OF MERCHANDISE: Clothing, housewares, furniture
DONATION TAX RECEIPT: Receipt given upon request

Salvation Army Thrift Store
105 N. Gallatin St.
Jackson, MS 39203
TYPE OF MERCHANDISE: Clothing, housewares, furniture
DONATION TAX RECEIPT: Receipt given upon request

Salvation Army Thrift Store
  2509 Old Brandon Rd.
  Jackson, MS 39208
  TYPE OF MERCHANDISE: Clothing,
  housewares, furniture
  DONATION TAX RECEIPT: Receipt given
  upon request
Salvation Army Thrift Store
  2400 "A" St.
  Meridian, MS 39301
  TYPE OF MERCHANDISE: Clothing,
  housewares, furniture
  DONATION TAX RECEIPT: Receipt given
  upon request
Salvation Army Thrift Store
  1210 Government St.
  Ocean Springs, MS 39564
  TYPE OF MERCHANDISE: Clothing,
  housewares, furniture
  DONATION TAX RECEIPT: Receipt given
  upon request
Saint Vincent De Paul Thrift Store
  307-D Coleman Ave.
  Waveland, MS 39576
  TYPE OF MERCHANDISE: Clothing,
  housewares, furniture
  DONATION TAX RECEIPT: Receipt given
  upon request
  COMMENTS: Monthly markdowns

Missouri

Salvation Army Thrift Store
  402 S. Sprigg St.
  Cape Girardeau, MO 63701
  TYPE OF MERCHANDISE: Clothing,
  housewares, furniture
  DONATION TAX RECEIPT: Receipt given
  upon request
Salvation Army Thrift Store
  1304 Parkade Blvd.
  Columbia, MO 65203
  TYPE OF MERCHANDISE: Clothing,
  housewares, furniture
  DONATION TAX RECEIPT: Receipt given
  upon request

Salvation Army Thrift Store
  11220 E. 23rd St.
  CROSS STREET: Sterling
  Independence, MO 64052
  PHONE: 816-421-5434
  FAX: 816-471-3946
  HOURS: Mon.–Sat. 10–7
  TYPE OF MERCHANDISE: Clothing,
  housewares, furniture
  DONATION TAX RECEIPT: Receipt given
  upon request
  COMMENTS: Auctions Mon.–Fri. 9 A.M.
Goodwill Industries Thrift Store
  651 E. Hwy. 24
  Independence, MO 64052
  PHONE: 816-461-5511
  HOURS: Mon.–Sat. 9–9, Sun. 12–5
  TYPE OF MERCHANDISE: Clothing,
  housewares, furniture
  DONATION TAX RECEIPT: Receipt given
  upon request
Salvation Army Thrift Store
  825 Broadway
  Joplin, MO 64801
  TYPE OF MERCHANDISE: Clothing,
  housewares, furniture
  DONATION TAX RECEIPT: Receipt given
  upon request
Goodwill Industries Thrift Store
  11138 Blue Ridge Parkway
  Kansas City, MO 64134
  PHONE: 816-765-8546
  HOURS: Mon.–Sat. 9–9, Sun. 12–5
  TYPE OF MERCHANDISE: Clothing,
  housewares, furniture
  DONATION TAX RECEIPT: Receipt given
  upon request
Salvation Army Thrift Store
  1320 E. Tenth St.
  CROSS STREET: Tracy
  Kansas City, MO 64106
  PHONE: 812-421-5434,
  HOURS: Mon.–Sat. 9–5
  TYPE OF MERCHANDISE: Clothing,
  housewares, furniture
  DONATION TAX RECEIPT: Receipt given
  upon request
  COMMENTS: Auctions Mon.–Fri. 9 A.M.

Goodwill Industries Thrift Store
1817 Campbell St.
Kansas City, MO 64108
TYPE OF MERCHANDISE: Clothing,
housewares, furniture
DONATION TAX RECEIPT: Receipt given
upon request

Goodwill Industries Thrift Store
319 N.E. Vivion Rd.
CROSS STREET: N. Oak
Kansas City, MO 64118
PHONE: 816-459-7169
HOURS: Mon.–Sat. 9–9, Sun. 12–5
TYPE OF MERCHANDISE: Clothing,
housewares, furniture
DONATION TAX RECEIPT: Receipt given
upon request

Salvation Army Thrift Store
4027 N. Oak Traffic Way
Kansas City, MO 64118
PHONE: 816-452-1418
HOURS: Mon.–Sat. 10–7
TYPE OF MERCHANDISE: Clothing,
housewares, furniture
DONATION TAX RECEIPT: Receipt given
upon request
COMMENTS: Auctions Mon.–Fri. 9 A.M.

Junior League KCMO Thrift Shop
4509 Troost Ave.
Kansas City, MO 64110
TYPE OF MERCHANDISE: Clothing for men,
women, and children
DONATION TAX RECEIPT: Receipt given
upon request

Council Thrift Shop
4626 Troost Ave.
Kansas City, MO 64110
TYPE OF MERCHANDISE: Clothing,
housewares, furniture
DONATION TAX RECEIPT: Receipt given
upon request

American Cancer Society Discovery Shop
512 W. 103rd St.
Kansas City, MO 64114
TYPE OF MERCHANDISE: Clothing, bric-a-
brac
DONATION TAX RECEIPT: Receipt given
upon request
COMMENTS: Monthly markdowns

Junior League Thrift Shop
6398 Troost Ave.
Kansas City, MO 64131-1226
CONTACT: Dot Dixon
PHONE: 816-523-7467
HOURS: Mon. 10:30–8, Tues. 10:30–5,
Wed.–Thurs. 10:30–8, Fri. 10:30–5, Sat.
10:30–6
TYPE OF MERCHANDISE: Clothing,
housewares, toys
DONATION TAX RECEIPT: Receipt given
upon request
COMMENTS: Quarterly clearance sales

Goodwill Industries Thrift Store
7740 Wornall Rd.
Kansas City, MO 64114
PHONE: 816-333-9622
HOURS: Mon.–Sat. 9–8, Sun. 12–5
TYPE OF MERCHANDISE: Clothing,
housewares, furniture
DONATION TAX RECEIPT: Receipt given
upon request

Salvation Army Thrift Store
8710 E. 63rd St.
CROSS STREET: Brywood Center
Kansas City, MO 64133
PHONE: 816-421-5434
HOURS: Mon.–Sat. 10–8
TYPE OF MERCHANDISE: Clothing,
housewares, furniture
DONATION TAX RECEIPT: Receipt given
upon request
COMMENTS: Auctions Mon.–Fri. 9 A.M.

Salvation Army Thrift Store
901 Tracy
CROSS STREET: Ninth
Kansas City, MO 64106
PHONE: 816-421-5434
FAX: 816-471-3946
HOURS: Mon.–Sat. 9–12
TYPE OF MERCHANDISE: Clothing,
housewares, furniture
DONATION TAX RECEIPT: Receipt given
upon request
COMMENTS: Auctions Mon.–Fri. 9 A.M.

Junior League Plaid Door Shop
1135 E. Commercial St.
Springfield, MO 65803

TYPE OF MERCHANDISE: Clothing for men, women, and children
DONATION TAX RECEIPT: Receipt given upon request

Salvation Army Thrift Store
431 W. Walnut St.
Springfield, MO 65806
TYPE OF MERCHANDISE: Clothing, housewares, furniture
DONATION TAX RECEIPT: Receipt given upon request

Salvation Army Thrift Store
2700 Droste Rd.
St. Charles, MO 63301
PHONE: 314-947-8489
HOURS: Mon.–Sat. 10–6
TYPE OF MERCHANDISE: Clothing, housewares, furniture
DONATION TAX RECEIPT: Receipt given upon request
COMMENTS: 50% off and manager's sales

Saint Vincent De Paul Thrift Store
1722 Commercial St.
St. Joseph, MO 64503
TYPE OF MERCHANDISE: Clothing, housewares, furniture
DONATION TAX RECEIPT: Receipt given upon request
COMMENTS: Monthly markdowns

Salvation Army Thrift Store
5940 King Hill Ave.
St. Joseph, MO 64504
TYPE OF MERCHANDISE: Clothing, housewares, furniture
DONATION TAX RECEIPT: Receipt given upon request

Amvets Thrift Store
2212 Chambers Rd.
St. Louis, MO 63136
TYPE OF MERCHANDISE: Clothing, housewares
DONATION TAX RECEIPT: Receipt given upon request

Amvets Thrift Store
3722 S. Grand Blvd.
St. Louis MO 63118
TYPE OF MERCHANDISE: Clothing, housewares

DONATION TAX RECEIPT: Receipt given upon request

Amvets Thrift Store
3733 Bell Ave.
St. Louis, MO 63108
TYPE OF MERCHANDISE: Clothing, housewares,
DONATION TAX RECEIPT: Receipt given upon request

Amvets Thrift Store
4231 N. Grand Blvd.
St. Louis, MO 63107
TYPE OF MERCHANDISE: Clothing, housewares,
DONATION TAX RECEIPT: Receipt given upon request

Salvation Army Thrift Store
6150 Natural Bridge Ave.
St. Louis, MO 63120
TYPE OF MERCHANDISE: Clothing, housewares, furniture
DONATION TAX RECEIPT: Receipt given upon request

Salvation Army Thrift Store
1040 Lemay Ferry Rd.
St. Louis, MO 63125
PHONE: 314-631-3233
HOURS: Mon.–Sat. 10–6
TYPE OF MERCHANDISE: Clothing, housewares, furniture
DONATION TAX RECEIPT: Receipt given upon request
COMMENTS: 50% off and manager's sales

Salvation Army Thrift Store
2832 Cherokee
St. Louis, MO 63118
PHONE: 314-771-2684
HOURS: Mon.–Sat. 10–6
TYPE OF MERCHANDISE: Clothing, housewares, furniture
DONATION TAX RECEIPT: Receipt given upon request
COMMENTS: 50% off and manager's sales

Salvation Army Thrift Store
3949 Forrest Park Blvd.
St. Louis, MO 63108
PHONE: 314-535-0057
HOURS: Mon.–Sat. 10–6

TYPE OF MERCHANDISE: Clothing, housewares, furniture
DONATION TAX RECEIPT: Receipt given upon request
COMMENTS: 50% off and manager's sales

Saint Vincent De Paul Thrift Store
4141 Forest Park Blvd.
St. Louis, MO 63108
TYPE OF MERCHANDISE: Clothing, housewares, furniture
DONATION TAX RECEIPT: Receipt given upon request
COMMENTS: Monthly markdowns

Salvation Army Thrift Store
6150 Natural Bridge Rd.
CROSS STREET: Pine Lawn
St. Louis, MO 63121
PHONE: 314-385-0092
HOURS: Mon.–Sat. 10–6
TYPE OF MERCHANDISE: Clothing, housewares, furniture
DONATION TAX RECEIPT: Receipt given upon request
COMMENTS: 50% off and manager's sales

Salvation Army Thrift Store
8913 Natural Bridge Rd.
St. Louis, MO 63121
PHONE: 314-426-6410
HOURS: Mon.–Sat. 10–6
TYPE OF MERCHANDISE: Clothing, housewares, furniture
DONATION TAX RECEIPT: Receipt given upon request
COMMENTS: 50% off and manager's sales

Montana

Goodwill Industries Thrift Store
1041 Main St.
Billings, MT 59105
TYPE OF MERCHANDISE: Clothing, housewares, furniture
DONATION TAX RECEIPT: Receipt given upon request

Goodwill Industries Thrift Store
1945 Grand Ave.
Billings, MT 59102

TYPE OF MERCHANDISE: Clothing, housewares, furniture
DONATION TAX RECEIPT: Receipt given upon request

Junior League Wise Penny
2103 Grand Ave.
Billings, MT 59102
CONTACT: Sue Evans, Marie Pippin
PHONE: 406-652-0012
HOURS: Mon.–Sat. 10–5
TYPE OF MERCHANDISE: Clothing, housewares, toys
DONATION TAX RECEIPT: Receipt given upon request
COMMENTS: Christmas and collectibles spring sales

Goodwill Industries Thrift Store
2135 Grand Ave.
Billings, MT 59102
PHONE: 406-656-4020, 656-3750
HOURS: Mon.–Sat. 9–6, Sun. 12–5
TYPE OF MERCHANDISE: Clothing, housewares, furniture
DONATION TAX RECEIPT: Receipt given upon request

Saint Vincent De Paul Thrift Store
2610 Montana Ave.
Billings, MT 59101
TYPE OF MERCHANDISE: Clothing, housewares, furniture
DONATION TAX RECEIPT: Receipt given upon request
COMMENTS: Monthly markdowns

Salvation Army Thrift Store
2910 Minnesota Ave.
Billings, MT 59101
TYPE OF MERCHANDISE: Clothing, housewares, furniture
DONATION TAX RECEIPT: Receipt given upon request

Saint Vincent De Paul Thrift Store
123 E. Park St.
Butte, MT 59701
TYPE OF MERCHANDISE: Clothing, housewares, furniture
DONATION TAX RECEIPT: Receipt given upon request
COMMENTS: Monthly markdowns

Goodwill Industries Thrift Store
507 Centennial
Butte, MT 59701
PHONE: 406-723-5858, 723-9595
HOURS: Mon.–Sat. 9–6
TYPE OF MERCHANDISE: Clothing,
housewares, furniture
DONATION TAX RECEIPT: Receipt given
upon request
Salvation Army Thrift Store
53 E. Park St.
Butte, MT 59701
TYPE OF MERCHANDISE: Clothing,
housewares, furniture
DONATION TAX RECEIPT: Receipt given
upon request
Goodwill Industries Thrift Store
1525 Tenth Ave. S.
Great Falls, MT 59405
PHONE: 406-453-0311, 761-5110
HOURS: Mon.–Sat. 9–6, Sun. 12–5
TYPE OF MERCHANDISE: Clothing,
housewares, furniture
DONATION TAX RECEIPT: Receipt given
upon request
COMMENTS: Holiday sales
Saint Vincent De Paul Thrift Store
500 Central Ave. W
Great Falls, MT 59404
TYPE OF MERCHANDISE: Clothing,
housewares, furniture
DONATION TAX RECEIPT: Receipt given
upon request
COMMENTS: Monthly markdowns
Salvation Army Thrift Store
2481 Hwy. 93 S
Kalispell, MT 59901
TYPE OF MERCHANDISE: Clothing,
housewares, furniture
DONATION TAX RECEIPT: Receipt given
upon request
Goodwill Industries Thrift Store
1020 North Ave. W
Missoula, MT 59801
PHONE: 406-549-6997, 549-2166
HOURS: Mon.–Sat. 9–6, Sun. 12–5
TYPE OF MERCHANDISE: Clothing,
housewares, furniture

DONATION TAX RECEIPT: Receipt given
upon request

Nebraska

Goodwill Industries Thrift Store
2409 13th St.
Columbus, NE 68601
CONTACT: Brenda Staley
PHONE: 402-563-1194
HOURS: Mon.–Sat. 9–9, Sun. 12–6
TYPE OF MERCHANDISE: Clothing,
housewares, furniture
DONATION TAX RECEIPT: Receipt given
upon request
Goodwill Industries Thrift Store
2415 E. 23rd St.
Fremont, NE 68025
TYPE OF MERCHANDISE: Clothing,
housewares, furniture
DONATION TAX RECEIPT: Receipt given
upon request
Salvation Army Thrift Store
507 N. Broad St.
Fremont, NE 68025
PHONE: 402-721-3823
HOURS: Mon.–Sat. 9–5
TYPE OF MERCHANDISE: Clothing,
housewares, furniture
DONATION TAX RECEIPT: Receipt given
upon request
COMMENTS: Monthly and seasonal sales
Salvation Army Thrift Store
201 E. Second St.
Grand Island, NE 68801
TYPE OF MERCHANDISE: Clothing,
housewares, furniture
DONATION TAX RECEIPT: Receipt given
upon request
Goodwill Industries Thrift Store
2223 Webb Rd.
Grand Island, NE 68803
CONTACT: Shari Johnson
PHONE: 308-384-7010
HOURS: Mon.–Sat. 9–9, Sun. 12–6
TYPE OF MERCHANDISE: Clothing,
housewares, furniture
DONATION TAX RECEIPT: Receipt given
upon request

Goodwill Industries Thrift Store
385 N. Pine St.
Grand Island, NE 68801
TYPE OF MERCHANDISE: Clothing,
housewares, furniture
DONATION TAX RECEIPT: Receipt given
upon request

Goodwill Industries Thrift Store
2416 W. Second St.
Hastings, NE 68901
CONTACT: Ron Augustin
PHONE: 402-463-5869
HOURS: Mon.–Sat. 9–9, Sun. 12–6
TYPE OF MERCHANDISE: Clothing,
housewares, furniture
DONATION TAX RECEIPT: Receipt given
upon request

Goodwill Industries Thrift Store
3906 Fourth Ave.
CROSS STREET: 39th St.
Kearney, NE 68847
CONTACT: Jane Fellows
PHONE: 308-237-7047
HOURS: Mon.–Sat. 9–9, Sun. 12–6
TYPE OF MERCHANDISE: Clothing,
housewares, furniture
DONATION TAX RECEIPT: Receipt given
upon request

Junior League Thrift Shop
2201 "O" St.
Lincoln, NE 68510
CONTACT: Gwen Gies
PHONE: 402-435-7506
HOURS: Mon.–Sat. 10–5
TYPE OF MERCHANDISE: Clothing,
housewares
DONATION TAX RECEIPT: Receipt given
upon request
COMMENTS: Consignments accepted

Saint Vincent De Paul Thrift Store
530 N.W. 27
Lincoln, NE 68528
TYPE OF MERCHANDISE: Clothing,
housewares, furniture
DONATION TAX RECEIPT: Receipt given
upon request
COMMENTS: Monthly markdowns

Salvation Army Thrift Store
115 N. Dewey St.
North Platte, NE 69101
TYPE OF MERCHANDISE: Clothing,
housewares, furniture
DONATION TAX RECEIPT: Receipt given
upon request

Goodwill Industries Thrift Store
1111 S. 41st St.
Omaha, NE 68105
TYPE OF MERCHANDISE: Clothing,
housewares, furniture
DONATION TAX RECEIPT: Receipt given
upon request

Saint Vincent De Paul Thrift Store
2101 Leavenworth
Omaha, NE 68102
TYPE OF MERCHANDISE: Clothing,
housewares, furniture
DONATION TAX RECEIPT: Receipt given
upon request
COMMENTS: Monthly markdowns

Salvation Army Thrift Store
2410 Center St. (Sleepy Hollow Shop)
Omaha, NE 68105
PHONE: 402-342-4135
HOURS: Mon.–Sat. 9–5
TYPE OF MERCHANDISE: Clothing,
housewares, furniture
DONATION TAX RECEIPT: Receipt given
upon request
COMMENTS: Collectibles and Uniques
Shop

Salvation Army Thrift Store
2913 N. 108th St. (Maple 108 Plaza)
Omaha, NE 68164
PHONE: 402-496-7663
HOURS: Mon.–Fri. 9–9, Sat. 9–8
TYPE OF MERCHANDISE: Clothing,
housewares, furniture
DONATION TAX RECEIPT: Receipt given
upon request
COMMENTS: Monthly and seasonal sales

Goodwill Industries Thrift Store
3017 S. 84th St.
Omaha, NE 68124
TYPE OF MERCHANDISE: Clothing,
housewares, furniture

DONATION TAX RECEIPT: Receipt given upon request

Junior League Jumble Shop
3038 N. 90th St.
Omaha, NE 68134
CONTACT: Diane Blum
PHONE: 402-573-7119
HOURS: Mon.–Fri. 10–4, Thur. 10–8
TYPE OF MERCHANDISE: New and used clothing
DONATION TAX RECEIPT: Receipt given upon request

Salvation Army Thrift Store
4814 S. 24th St.
Omaha, NE 68107
PHONE: 402-733-4039
HOURS: Mon.–Sat. 9–6
TYPE OF MERCHANDISE: Clothing, housewares, furniture
DONATION TAX RECEIPT: Receipt given upon request
COMMENTS: Monthly and seasonal sales

Salvation Army Thrift Store
4857 S. 137th St.
Omaha, NE 68137
TYPE OF MERCHANDISE: Clothing, housewares, furniture
DONATION TAX RECEIPT: Receipt given upon request

Saint Vincent De Paul Thrift Store
5022 Center St.
Omaha, NE 68107
TYPE OF MERCHANDISE: Clothing, housewares, furniture
DONATION TAX RECEIPT: Receipt given upon request
COMMENTS: Monthly markdowns

Saint Vincent De Paul Thrift Store
5037 S. 24th St.
Omaha, NE 68107
TYPE OF MERCHANDISE: Clothing, housewares, furniture
DONATION TAX RECEIPT: Receipt given upon request
COMMENTS: Monthly markdowns

Saint Vincent De Paul Thrift Store
5102 S. 24th St.
Omaha, NE 68107

TYPE OF MERCHANDISE: Clothing, housewares, furniture
DONATION TAX RECEIPT: Receipt given upon request
COMMENTS: Monthly markdowns

Disabled American Vets Thrift Store
5124 S. 24th St.
Omaha, NE 68107
TYPE OF MERCHANDISE: Clothing, housewares,
DONATION TAX RECEIPT: Receipt given upon request

Saint Vincent De Paul Thrift Store
5920 Maple St.
Omaha, NE 68104
TYPE OF MERCHANDISE: Clothing, housewares, furniture
DONATION TAX RECEIPT: Receipt given upon request
COMMENTS: Monthly markdowns

NCJW Thrift Shop
6005 Maple St.
Omaha, NE 68104
PHONE: 402-551-7176
HOURS: Mon.–Sat. 10–4
TYPE OF MERCHANDISE: Clothing, housewares, furniture
DONATION TAX RECEIPT: Receipt given upon request
COMMENTS: Gift, toy, and sidewalk sales

Salvation Army Thrift Store
6022 Maple St.
Omaha, NE 68104
PHONE: 402-556-5079
HOURS: Mon.–Sat. 9–5
TYPE OF MERCHANDISE: Clothing, housewares, furniture
DONATION TAX RECEIPT: Receipt given upon request
COMMENTS: Monthly and seasonal sales

Junior League Jumble Shop
6104 Maple St.
Omaha, NE 68104
TYPE OF MERCHANDISE: Clothing for men, women, and children
DONATION TAX RECEIPT: Receipt given upon request

Salvation Army Thrift Store
7266 N. 30th St.
Omaha, NE 68112
PHONE: 402-455-3222
HOURS: Mon.–Sat. 9–6
TYPE OF MERCHANDISE: Clothing,
housewares, furniture
DONATION TAX RECEIPT: Receipt given
upon request
COMMENTS: Monthly and seasonal sales

MCC Et Cetera Shop
504 Seward St.
Seward, NE 68434
PHONE: 402-643-4767
TYPE OF MERCHANDISE: Clothing,
housewares
DONATION TAX RECEIPT: Receipt given
upon request

Nevada

TVI Savers Thrift Store
1100 E. Charleston Blvd.
Las Vegas, NV 89104
CONTACT: Renee Larson
PHONE: 702-474-4773
HOURS: Mon.–Sat. 9–9, Sun. 10–6
TYPE OF MERCHANDISE: Clothing,
housewares, furniture
DONATION TAX RECEIPT: Receipt given
upon request

Humane Society Thrift Shop
1430 E. Charleston Blvd.
Las Vegas, NV 89104
TYPE OF MERCHANDISE: Clothing,
housewares
DONATION TAX RECEIPT: Receipt given
upon request

Salvation Army Thrift Store
1625 Fremont St.
Las Vegas, NV 89101
TYPE OF MERCHANDISE: Clothing,
housewares, furniture
DONATION TAX RECEIPT: Receipt given
upon request

American Cancer Society Discovery Shop
1768 E. Charleston Blvd. Suite F-3
Las Vegas, NV 89104

PHONE: 702-598-4077
TYPE OF MERCHANDISE: Clothing, bric-a-
brac
DONATION TAX RECEIPT: Receipt given
upon request
COMMENTS: Monthly markdowns

Junior League Boutique
300 E. Mesquite Ave.
Las Vegas, NV 89101
TYPE OF MERCHANDISE: Clothing for men,
women, and children
DONATION TAX RECEIPT: Receipt given
upon request

Salvation Army Thrift Store
4001 W. Charleston Blvd.
Las Vegas, NV 89102
TYPE OF MERCHANDISE: Clothing,
housewares, furniture
DONATION TAX RECEIPT: Receipt given
upon request

Salvation Army Thrift Store
429 N. Main St.
Las Vegas, NV 89101
TYPE OF MERCHANDISE: Clothing,
housewares, furniture
DONATION TAX RECEIPT: Receipt given
upon request

Saint Vincent De Paul Thrift Store
4921 Vegas Dr.
Las Vegas, NV 89108
TYPE OF MERCHANDISE: Clothing,
housewares, furniture
DONATION TAX RECEIPT: Receipt given
upon request
COMMENTS: Monthly markdowns

National Assistance League Thrift Shop
570 S. Decatur Blvd.
Las Vegas, NV 89107
PHONE: 702-878-2558
TYPE OF MERCHANDISE: Clothing,
housewares, furniture
DONATION TAX RECEIPT: Receipt given
upon request
COMMENTS: Monthly markdowns

Saint Vincent De Paul Thrift Store
808 S. Main St.
Las Vegas, NV 89101

TYPE OF MERCHANDISE: Clothing, housewares, furniture
DONATION TAX RECEIPT: Receipt given upon request
COMMENTS: Monthly markdowns

Goodwill Industries Thrift Store
820 Las Vegas Blvd S.
Las Vegas, NV 89101
TYPE OF MERCHANDISE: Clothing, housewares, furniture
DONATION TAX RECEIPT: Receipt given upon request

Saint Vincent De Paul Thrift Store
275 E. Fourth St.
Reno, NV 89501
TYPE OF MERCHANDISE: Clothing, housewares, furniture
DONATION TAX RECEIPT: Receipt given upon request
COMMENTS: Monthly markdowns

Salvation Army Thrift Store
560 Gentry Way
Reno, NV 89502
TYPE OF MERCHANDISE: Clothing, housewares, furniture
DONATION TAX RECEIPT: Receipt given upon request

Salvation Army Thrift Store
642 E. 14th
Reno, NV 89503
TYPE OF MERCHANDISE: Clothing, housewares, furniture
DONATION TAX RECEIPT: Receipt given upon request

TVI Savers Thrift Store
2350 Oddie Blvd.
Sparks, NV 89431
CONTACT: Ron Smith
PHONE: 702-359-4244
HOURS: Mon.–Sat. 9–9, Sun. 10–6
TYPE OF MERCHANDISE: Clothing, housewares, furniture
DONATION TAX RECEIPT: No

New Hampshire

Saint Vincent De Paul Thrift Store
153 Graftons
Berlin, NH 03570
TYPE OF MERCHANDISE: Clothing, housewares, furniture
DONATION TAX RECEIPT: Receipt given upon request
COMMENTS: Monthly markdowns

Goodwill Industries Thrift Store
168 S. Main St.
Manchester, NH 03102
TYPE OF MERCHANDISE: Clothing, housewares, furniture
DONATION TAX RECEIPT: Receipt given upon request

Goodwill Industries Thrift Store
268 Mammoth Rd.
Manchester, NH 03109
TYPE OF MERCHANDISE: Clothing, housewares, furniture
DONATION TAX RECEIPT: Receipt given upon request

Saint Vincent De Paul Thrift Store
530 Cartier St.
Manchester, NH 03102
TYPE OF MERCHANDISE: Clothing, housewares, furniture
DONATION TAX RECEIPT: Receipt given upon request
COMMENTS: Monthly markdowns

Salvation Army Thrift Store
913 Elm St.
Manchester, NH 03103
TYPE OF MERCHANDISE: Clothing, housewares, furniture
DONATION TAX RECEIPT: Receipt given upon request

Goodwill Industries Thrift Store
121 W. Pearl St.
Nashua, NH 03060
TYPE OF MERCHANDISE: Clothing, housewares, furniture
DONATION TAX RECEIPT: Receipt given upon request

Salvation Army Thrift Store
28 Signal St.
Rochester, NH 03867

TYPE OF MERCHANDISE: Clothing,
housewares, furniture
DONATION TAX RECEIPT: Receipt given
upon request
Salvation Army Thrift Store
183 Main St.
Salem, NH 03079
TYPE OF MERCHANDISE: Clothing,
housewares, furniture
DONATION TAX RECEIPT: Receipt given
upon request

New Jersey

Saint Vincent De Paul Thrift Store
1412 Lake Ave.
Asbury Park, NJ 07712
TYPE OF MERCHANDISE: Clothing,
housewares, furniture
DONATION TAX RECEIPT: Receipt given
upon request
COMMENTS: Monthly markdowns
Salvation Army Thrift Store
821 Main St.
Asbury Park, NJ 07712
TYPE OF MERCHANDISE: Clothing,
housewares, furniture
DONATION TAX RECEIPT: Receipt given
upon request
Goodwill Industries Thrift Store
3005 Atlantic Ave.
Atlantic City, NJ 08401
PHONE: 609-348-8401
TYPE OF MERCHANDISE: Clothing,
housewares, furniture
DONATION TAX RECEIPT: Receipt given
upon request
Salvation Army Thrift Store
340 N. Albany Ave.
Atlantic City, NJ 08401
TYPE OF MERCHANDISE: Clothing,
housewares, furniture
DONATION TAX RECEIPT: Receipt given
upon request
Salvation Army Thrift Store
650 N. Albany Ave.
Atlantic City, NJ 08401
TYPE OF MERCHANDISE: Clothing,
housewares, furniture

DONATION TAX RECEIPT: Receipt given
upon request
Salvation Army Thrift Store
482 Avenue C
Bayonne, NJ 07002
TYPE OF MERCHANDISE: Clothing,
housewares, furniture
DONATION TAX RECEIPT: Receipt given
upon request
Goodwill Industries Thrift Store
48 E. Main St.
Bergenfield, NJ 07621
TYPE OF MERCHANDISE: Clothing,
housewares, furniture
DONATION TAX RECEIPT: Receipt given
upon request
Saint Vincent De Paul Thrift Store
120 S. White Horse Pike
Berlin, NJ 08009
TYPE OF MERCHANDISE: Clothing,
housewares, furniture
DONATION TAX RECEIPT: Receipt given
upon request
COMMENTS: Monthly markdowns
Goodwill Industries Thrift Store
594 Route 206
Bordertown, NJ 08620
PHONE: 609-291-1850
HOURS: Mon.–Sat. 8–9, Sun. 10–6
TYPE OF MERCHANDISE: Clothing,
housewares, furniture
DONATION TAX RECEIPT: Receipt given
upon request
Goodwill Industries Thrift Store
32 E. Commerce St.
Bridgeton, NJ 08302
TYPE OF MERCHANDISE: Clothing,
housewares, furniture
DONATION TAX RECEIPT: Receipt given
upon request
Goodwill Industries Thrift Store
100 S. 17th St.
Camden, NJ 08105
TYPE OF MERCHANDISE: Clothing,
housewares, furniture
DONATION TAX RECEIPT: Receipt given
upon request

Goodwill Industries Thrift Store
2501 Federal St.
Camden, NJ 08105
TYPE OF MERCHANDISE: Clothing,
housewares, furniture
DONATION TAX RECEIPT: Receipt given
upon request

Goodwill Industries Thrift Store
546 Federal St.
Camden, NJ 08103
TYPE OF MERCHANDISE: Clothing,
housewares, furniture
DONATION TAX RECEIPT: Receipt given
upon request

Salvation Army Thrift Store
1221 Main Ave.
Clifton, NJ 07011
TYPE OF MERCHANDISE: Clothing,
housewares, furniture
DONATION TAX RECEIPT: Receipt given
upon request

Salvation Army Thrift Store
24 Basett Highway
Dover, NJ 07801
TYPE OF MERCHANDISE: Clothing,
housewares, furniture
DONATION TAX RECEIPT: Receipt given
upon request

Salvation Army Thrift Store
520 Martin Luther King Blvd.
E. Orange, NJ 07018
TYPE OF MERCHANDISE: Clothing,
housewares, furniture
DONATION TAX RECEIPT: Receipt given
upon request

Salvation Army Thrift Store
1155–57 Elizabeth Ave.
Elizabeth, NJ 07201
TYPE OF MERCHANDISE: Clothing,
housewares, furniture
DONATION TAX RECEIPT: Receipt given
upon request

Salvation Army Thrift Store
185 Englewood Ave.
Englewood, NJ 07631
TYPE OF MERCHANDISE: Clothing,
housewares, furniture
DONATION TAX RECEIPT: Receipt given
upon request

Salvation Army Thrift Store
2607 S. Broad St.
Hamilton Township, NJ 08610
TYPE OF MERCHANDISE: Clothing,
housewares, furniture
DONATION TAX RECEIPT: Receipt given
upon request

Goodwill Industries Thrift Store
109 Bellevue Ave.
Hammonton, NJ 08037
PHONE: 609-561-9620
HOURS: Mon.–Fri. 9–7, Sat. 9–6, Sun. 1–6
TYPE OF MERCHANDISE: Clothing,
housewares, furniture
DONATION TAX RECEIPT: Receipt given
upon request

Salvation Army Thrift Store
1057 Springfield Ave.
Irvington, NJ 07111
TYPE OF MERCHANDISE: Clothing,
housewares, furniture
DONATION TAX RECEIPT: Receipt given
upon request

Salvation Army Thrift Store
242 Martin Luther King Dr.
Jersey City, NJ 07305
TYPE OF MERCHANDISE: Clothing,
housewares, furniture
DONATION TAX RECEIPT: Receipt given
upon request

Salvation Army Thrift Store
248 Erie St.
Jersey City, NJ 07310
TYPE OF MERCHANDISE: Clothing,
housewares, furniture
DONATION TAX RECEIPT: Receipt given
upon request

Salvation Army Thrift Store
15 State Hwy. #33
Mercerville/Hamilton Township, NJ
08619
TYPE OF MERCHANDISE: Clothing,
housewares, furniture
DONATION TAX RECEIPT: Receipt given
upon request

NCJW Thrift Shop
220 Bloomfield Ave.
Montclair, NJ 07042
HOURS: Mon.–Sat. 8:30–4

TYPE OF MERCHANDISE: Clothing, housewares, furniture
DONATION TAX RECEIPT: Receipt given upon request

Junior League Nearly New Thrift Shop
7 King Place
Morristown, NJ 07960
CONTACT: Florence (Flo) Rice
PHONE: 201-539-4274
HOURS: Mon.–Tues. 10–4, Wed. 10–7, Thurs.–Fri. 10–4, Sat. 10–3
TYPE OF MERCHANDISE: Clothing, housewares
DONATION TAX RECEIPT: Receipt given upon request
COMMENTS: Thrift and consignment special sales

Salvation Army Thrift Store
526 Broadway
Newark, NJ 07104
TYPE OF MERCHANDISE: Clothing, housewares, furniture
DONATION TAX RECEIPT: Receipt given upon request

Salvation Army Thrift Store
74–78 Pennington St.
Newark, NJ 07105
TYPE OF MERCHANDISE: Clothing, housewares, furniture
DONATION TAX RECEIPT: Receipt given upon request

Junior League of Summit Costume Shop
340 Central Ave.
New Providence, NJ 07974
PHONE: 908-464-1992
HOURS: Tues. 9:30–5 Sept.–June; October 9:30–8
TYPE OF MERCHANDISE: Costumes
DONATION TAX RECEIPT: Receipt given upon request
COMMENTS: Low-cost nonprofit theater rental

Salvation Army Thrift Store
7425 Bergenline Ave.
N. Bergen, NJ 07047
TYPE OF MERCHANDISE: Clothing, housewares, furniture
DONATION TAX RECEIPT: Receipt given upon request

Salvation Army Thrift Store
417 Broadway
Passaic, NJ 07055
TYPE OF MERCHANDISE: Clothing, housewares, furniture
DONATION TAX RECEIPT: Receipt given upon request

Salvation Army Thrift Store
31 Van Houten St.
Paterson, NJ 07505
TYPE OF MERCHANDISE: Clothing, housewares, furniture
DONATION TAX RECEIPT: Receipt given upon request

Goodwill Industries Thrift Store
5461 Route 70
Pennsauken, NJ 08109
PHONE: 609-486-0300
HOURS: Mon.–Sat. 8–9, Sun. 10–6
TYPE OF MERCHANDISE: Clothing, housewares, furniture
DONATION TAX RECEIPT: Receipt given upon request

Saint Vincent De Paul Thrift Store
286 Smith St.
Perth Amboy, NJ 08861
TYPE OF MERCHANDISE: Clothing, housewares, furniture
DONATION TAX RECEIPT: Receipt given upon request
COMMENTS: Monthly markdowns

Salvation Army Thrift Store
326 Park Ave.
CROSS STREET: W 4th
Plainfield, NJ 07060
PHONE: 908-456-9509
TYPE OF MERCHANDISE: Clothing, housewares, furniture
DONATION TAX RECEIPT: Receipt given upon request

Salvation Army Thrift Store
43 Colfax Ave.
Pompton Lake, NJ 07442
TYPE OF MERCHANDISE: Clothing, housewares, furniture
DONATION TAX RECEIPT: Receipt given upon request

Salvation Army Thrift Store
193 E. Broadway
Salem, NJ 08079
TYPE OF MERCHANDISE: Clothing,
housewares, furniture
DONATION TAX RECEIPT: Receipt given
upon request

Salvation Army Thrift Store
223 E. Broadway
Salem, NJ 08079
TYPE OF MERCHANDISE: Clothing,
housewares, furniture
DONATION TAX RECEIPT: Receipt given
upon request

NCJW Thrift Shop
51 Academy St.
S. Orange, NJ
HOURS: Mon.–Sat. 8:30–4
TYPE OF MERCHANDISE: Clothing,
housewares, furniture
DONATION TAX RECEIPT: Receipt given
upon request

Junior League of Summit Inc.
37 Deforest Ave.
Summit, NJ 07901
PHONE: 908-273-7349, 522-4553
HOURS: Mon.–Tues. 9:30–2:30, Thurs.
9:30–8:30, Fri. 9:30–2:30; Sat. 9:30–12:30
TYPE OF MERCHANDISE: Clothing,
housewares
DONATION TAX RECEIPT: Receipt given
upon request
COMMENTS: Some consignments and
boutique sales

American Cancer Society Discovery Shop
Routes 166 and 37 W (Dover Mall)
Toms River, NJ 08753
TYPE OF MERCHANDISE: Clothing, bric-a-
brac
DONATION TAX RECEIPT: Receipt given
upon request
COMMENTS: Monthly markdowns

Salvation Army Thrift Store
436 Mulberry St.
Trenton, NJ 08638
TYPE OF MERCHANDISE: Clothing,
housewares, furniture
DONATION TAX RECEIPT: Receipt given
upon request

Salvation Army Thrift Store
800 S. Broad St.
Trenton, NJ 08611
TYPE OF MERCHANDISE: Clothing,
housewares, furniture
DONATION TAX RECEIPT: Receipt given
upon request

Salvation Army Thrift Store
900 Kennedy Blvd.
Union City, NJ 07087
TYPE OF MERCHANDISE: Clothing,
housewares, furniture
DONATION TAX RECEIPT: Receipt given
upon request

Salvation Army Thrift Store
2279 S. Delsea Dr.
Vineland, NJ 08360
TYPE OF MERCHANDISE: Clothing,
housewares, furniture
DONATION TAX RECEIPT: Receipt given
upon request

Goodwill Industries Thrift Store
618 Landis Ave.
Vineland, NJ 08360
PHONE: 609-696-9824
HOURS: Mon.–Sat. 9–8, Sun. 10–6
TYPE OF MERCHANDISE: Clothing,
housewares, furniture
DONATION TAX RECEIPT: Receipt given
upon request

American Cancer Society Discovery Shop
311 South Ave.
Westfield, NJ 07090
PHONE: 908-232-3332
TYPE OF MERCHANDISE: Clothing, bric-a-
brac
DONATION TAX RECEIPT: Receipt given
upon request
COMMENTS: Monthly markdowns

NCJW Thrift Shop
20 Central Ave.
W. Orange, NJ
HOURS: Mon.–Sat. 8:30–4
TYPE OF MERCHANDISE: Clothing,
housewares, furniture
DONATION TAX RECEIPT: Receipt given
upon request

Goodwill Industries Thrift Store
117 S. Broad St.
Woodbury, NJ 08096
PHONE: 609-848-9834
HOURS: Mon.–Sat. 9–9, Sun. 10–6
TYPE OF MERCHANDISE: Clothing,
housewares, furniture
DONATION TAX RECEIPT: Receipt given
upon request
Goodwill Industries Thrift Store
339 S. Broad St.
Woodbury, NJ 08096
TYPE OF MERCHANDISE: Clothing,
housewares, furniture
DONATION TAX RECEIPT: Receipt given
upon request

New Mexico

National Assistance League Bargain Box
529 Chama NE
Albuquerque, NM 87108
PHONE: 505-255-8213
TYPE OF MERCHANDISE: Clothing,
housewares, furniture
DONATION TAX RECEIPT: Receipt given
upon request
COMMENTS: Monthly markdowns
TVI Savers Thrift Store
111 Coors Blvd. NW
Albuquerque, NM 87121
CONTACT: Blaine Jimenez
PHONE: 505-836-3393
HOURS: Mon.–Sat. 9–9, Sun. 10–6
TYPE OF MERCHANDISE: Clothing,
housewares, furniture
DONATION TAX RECEIPT: No
Saint Vincent De Paul Thrift Store
1596 Five Points Rd. SW
Albuquerque, NM 87105
TYPE OF MERCHANDISE: Clothing,
housewares, furniture
DONATION TAX RECEIPT: Receipt given
upon request
COMMENTS: Monthly markdowns
Disabled American Vets Thrift Store
200 San Mateo Blvd. SE
Albuquerque, NM 87108

TYPE OF MERCHANDISE: Clothing,
housewares
DONATION TAX RECEIPT: Receipt given
upon request
Goodwill Industries Thrift Store
2209 Central Ave. W
Albuquerque, NM 87104
TYPE OF MERCHANDISE: Clothing,
housewares, furniture
DONATION TAX RECEIPT: Receipt given
upon request
Goodwill Industries Thrift Store
3100 Juan Tabo Blvd. NE
Albuquerque, NM 87111
TYPE OF MERCHANDISE: Clothing,
housewares, furniture
DONATION TAX RECEIPT: Receipt given
upon request
TVI Savers Thrift Store
3300 San Mateo Blvd. NE
Albuquerque, NM 87110
CONTACT: Vern Dunn
PHONE: 505-888-0116
HOURS: Mon.–Sat. 9–9, Sun. 10–6
TYPE OF MERCHANDISE: Clothing,
housewares, furniture
DONATION TAX RECEIPT: No
Goodwill Industries Thrift Store
5000 San Mateo Blvd. NE
Albuquerque, NM 87109
TYPE OF MERCHANDISE: Clothing,
housewares, furniture
DONATION TAX RECEIPT: Receipt given
upon request
Salvation Army Thrift Store
501 Broadway Blvd. SE
Albuquerque, NM 87102
TYPE OF MERCHANDISE: Clothing,
housewares, furniture
DONATION TAX RECEIPT: Receipt given
upon request
Goodwill Industries Thrift Store
506 Central Ave. SW
Albuquerque, NM 87102
TYPE OF MERCHANDISE: Clothing,
housewares, furniture
DONATION TAX RECEIPT: Receipt given
upon request

Saint Vincent De Paul Thrift Store
714 Fourth St. SW
Albuquerque, NM 87102
TYPE OF MERCHANDISE: Clothing,
housewares, furniture
DONATION TAX RECEIPT: Receipt given
upon request
COMMENTS: Monthly markdowns

National Assistance League Clothes Close
710 N. Canyon
Carlsbad, NM 88220
PHONE: 505-885-3333
TYPE OF MERCHANDISE: Clothing,
housewares, furniture
DONATION TAX RECEIPT: Receipt given
upon request
COMMENTS: Monthly markdowns

Goodwill Industries Thrift Store
200 S. Gold Ave.
Deming, NM 88030
TYPE OF MERCHANDISE: Clothing,
housewares, furniture
DONATION TAX RECEIPT: Receipt given
upon request

Goodwill Industries Thrift Store
2305 Nevada Ave.
Las Cruces, NM 88001
TYPE OF MERCHANDISE: Clothing,
housewares, furniture
DONATION TAX RECEIPT: Receipt given
upon request

National Assistance League Thrift Shop
100 N. Union
Roswell, NM 88201
PHONE: 505-624-1185
TYPE OF MERCHANDISE: Clothing,
housewares, furniture
DONATION TAX RECEIPT: Receipt given
upon request
COMMENTS: Monthly markdowns

Saint Vincent De Paul Thrift Store
1088 Early St.
Santa Fe, NM 87502
TYPE OF MERCHANDISE: Clothing,
housewares, furniture
DONATION TAX RECEIPT: Receipt given
upon request
COMMENTS: Monthly markdowns

Goodwill Industries Thrift Store
927 Baca St.
Santa Fe, NM 87501
TYPE OF MERCHANDISE: Clothing,
housewares, furniture
DONATION TAX RECEIPT: Receipt given
upon request

Saint Vincent De Paul Thrift Store
225 Sixth St.
Santa Rosa, NM 88435
TYPE OF MERCHANDISE: Clothing,
housewares, furniture
DONATION TAX RECEIPT: Receipt given
upon request
COMMENTS: Monthly markdowns

New York

Junior League Next-to-New-Shop
419 Madison Ave.
Albany, NY 12210
TYPE OF MERCHANDISE: Clothing for men,
women, and children
DONATION TAX RECEIPT: Receipt given
upon request

Salvation Army Thrift Store
452 Clinton Ave.
Albany, NY 12206
TYPE OF MERCHANDISE: Clothing,
housewares, furniture
DONATION TAX RECEIPT: Receipt given
upon request

Salvation Army Thrift Store
139 Grant Ave.
Auburn, NY 13021
TYPE OF MERCHANDISE: Clothing,
housewares, furniture
DONATION TAX RECEIPT: Receipt given
upon request

Salvation Army Thrift Store
227 Little E. Neck Rd.
Babylon, NY 11702
TYPE OF MERCHANDISE: Clothing,
housewares, furniture
DONATION TAX RECEIPT: Receipt given
upon request

Salvation Army Thrift Store
98 Jackson St.
Batavia, NY 14020
TYPE OF MERCHANDISE: Clothing,
housewares, furniture
DONATION TAX RECEIPT: Receipt given
upon request
Salvation Army Thrift Store
121 Liberty St.
Bath, NY 14810
TYPE OF MERCHANDISE: Clothing,
housewares, furniture
DONATION TAX RECEIPT: Receipt given
upon request
Salvation Army Thrift Store
355 W. Morris St.
Bath, NY 14810
TYPE OF MERCHANDISE: Clothing,
housewares, furniture
DONATION TAX RECEIPT: Receipt given
upon request
Salvation Army Thrift Store
348 Main St.
Beacon, NY 12508
TYPE OF MERCHANDISE: Clothing,
housewares, furniture
DONATION TAX RECEIPT: Receipt given
upon request
American Cancer Society Discovery Shop
419-A Beach 129th
Belle Harbor, NY 11694
TYPE OF MERCHANDISE: Clothing, bric-a-
brac
DONATION TAX RECEIPT: Receipt given
upon request
COMMENTS: Monthly markdowns
Saint Vincent De Paul Thrift Store
259 Broadway
Bethpage, NY 11714
TYPE OF MERCHANDISE: Clothing,
housewares, furniture
DONATION TAX RECEIPT: Receipt given
upon request
COMMENTS: Monthly markdowns
Salvation Army Thrift Store
5–9 Griswold
Binghamton, NY 13904

TYPE OF MERCHANDISE: Clothing,
housewares, furniture
DONATION TAX RECEIPT: Receipt given
upon request
Salvation Army Thrift Store
Griswold St.
Binghamton, NY 13904
TYPE OF MERCHANDISE: Clothing,
housewares, furniture
DONATION TAX RECEIPT: Receipt given
upon request
Salvation Army Thrift Store
1294 Southern Blvd.
Bronx, NY 10459
TYPE OF MERCHANDISE: Clothing,
housewares, furniture
DONATION TAX RECEIPT: Receipt given
upon request
Goodwill Industries Thrift Store
1638 Bruckner Blvd.
Bronx, NY 10473
PHONE: 212-328-9808
TYPE OF MERCHANDISE: Clothing,
housewares, furniture
DONATION TAX RECEIPT: Receipt given
upon request
Salvation Army Thrift Store
2359 Jerome Ave.
Bronx, NY 10468
TYPE OF MERCHANDISE: Clothing,
housewares, furniture
DONATION TAX RECEIPT: Receipt given
upon request
Salvation Army Thrift Store
2582 Third Ave.
Bronx, NY 10454
TYPE OF MERCHANDISE: Clothing,
housewares, furniture
DONATION TAX RECEIPT: Receipt given
upon request
Salvation Army Thrift Store
3400 Boston Rd.
Bronx, NY 10469
TYPE OF MERCHANDISE: Clothing,
housewares, furniture
DONATION TAX RECEIPT: Receipt given
upon request

Saint Vincent De Paul Thrift Store
402 E. 152nd St.
Bronx, NY 10455
TYPE OF MERCHANDISE: Clothing,
housewares, furniture
DONATION TAX RECEIPT: Receipt given
upon request
COMMENTS: Monthly markdowns

Salvation Army Thrift Store
4109 Park Ave.
Bronx, NY 10457
TYPE OF MERCHANDISE: Clothing,
housewares, furniture
DONATION TAX RECEIPT: Receipt given
upon request

Salvation Army Thrift Store
413–15 E. 152nd St.
Bronx, NY 10455
TYPE OF MERCHANDISE: Clothing,
housewares, furniture
DONATION TAX RECEIPT: Receipt given
upon request

Salvation Army Thrift Store
4761 White Plains Rd.
Bronx, NY 10466
TYPE OF MERCHANDISE: Clothing,
housewares, furniture
DONATION TAX RECEIPT: Receipt given
upon request

Goodwill Industries Thrift Store
52 W. Fordham Rd.
Bronx, NY 10468
PHONE: 718-733-2453, 733-2320
HOURS: Mon.–Sat. 11–7
TYPE OF MERCHANDISE: Clothing,
housewares, furniture
DONATION TAX RECEIPT: Receipt given
upon request

Salvation Army Thrift Store
5622 Broadway
Bronx, NY 10463
TYPE OF MERCHANDISE: Clothing,
housewares, furniture
DONATION TAX RECEIPT: Receipt given
upon request

Salvation Army Thrift Store
860 Longwood Ave.
Bronx, NY 10459

TYPE OF MERCHANDISE: Clothing,
housewares, furniture
DONATION TAX RECEIPT: Receipt given
upon request

Salvation Army Thrift Store
11 Downing St.
Brooklyn, NY 11238
TYPE OF MERCHANDISE: Clothing,
housewares, furniture
DONATION TAX RECEIPT: Receipt given
upon request

Saint Vincent De Paul Thrift Store
111 Franklin St.
Brooklyn, NY 11222
TYPE OF MERCHANDISE: Clothing,
housewares, furniture
DONATION TAX RECEIPT: Receipt given
upon request
COMMENTS: Monthly markdowns

Salvation Army Thrift Store
176 Bedford Ave.
Brooklyn, NY 11211
TYPE OF MERCHANDISE: Clothing,
housewares, furniture
DONATION TAX RECEIPT: Receipt given
upon request

Saint Vincent De Paul Thrift Store
191 Joralemon St.
Brooklyn, NY 11201
TYPE OF MERCHANDISE: Clothing,
housewares, furniture
DONATION TAX RECEIPT: Receipt given
upon request
COMMENTS: Monthly markdowns

Salvation Army Thrift Store
239 Flatbush Ave.
Brooklyn, NY 11217
TYPE OF MERCHANDISE: Clothing,
housewares, furniture
DONATION TAX RECEIPT: Receipt given
upon request

NCJW Thrift Shop
255 Flatbush Ave.
Brooklyn, NY 11217
CONTACT: Natalie Kuflik
PHONE: 718-622-2422
HOURS: Mon.–Sat. 9–5
TYPE OF MERCHANDISE: Clothing,
housewares, furniture

DONATION TAX RECEIPT: Receipt given upon request

Salvation Army Thrift Store
268 Knickerbocker Ave.
Brooklyn, NY 11237
TYPE OF MERCHANDISE: Clothing, housewares, furniture
DONATION TAX RECEIPT: Receipt given upon request

Goodwill Industries Thrift Store
269 Columbia St.
Brooklyn, NY 11231
PHONE: 718-624-0322
TYPE OF MERCHANDISE: Clothing, housewares, furniture
DONATION TAX RECEIPT: Receipt given upon request

Salvation Army Thrift Store
282 Broadway
Brooklyn, NY 11211
TYPE OF MERCHANDISE: Clothing, housewares, furniture
DONATION TAX RECEIPT: Receipt given upon request

Salvation Army Thrift Store
3522 Nostrand Ave.
Brooklyn, NY 11229
TYPE OF MERCHANDISE: Clothing, housewares, furniture
DONATION TAX RECEIPT: Receipt given upon request

Salvation Army Thrift Store
436 Atlantic Ave.
Brooklyn, NY 11217
TYPE OF MERCHANDISE: Clothing, housewares, furniture
DONATION TAX RECEIPT: Receipt given upon request

Salvation Army Thrift Store
576 Fifth Ave.
Brooklyn, NY 11215
TYPE OF MERCHANDISE: Clothing, housewares, furniture
DONATION TAX RECEIPT: Receipt given upon request

Saint Vincent De Paul Thrift Store
6202 Fifth Ave.
Brooklyn, NY 11220

TYPE OF MERCHANDISE: Clothing, housewares, furniture
DONATION TAX RECEIPT: Receipt given upon request
COMMENTS: Monthly markdowns

Salvation Army Thrift Store
6822 Third Ave.
Brooklyn, NY 11220
TYPE OF MERCHANDISE: Clothing, housewares, furniture
DONATION TAX RECEIPT: Receipt given upon request

Salvation Army Thrift Store
829 Broadway
Brooklyn, NY 11206
TYPE OF MERCHANDISE: Clothing, housewares, furniture
DONATION TAX RECEIPT: Receipt given upon request

Salvation Army Thrift Store
963 Coney Island Ave.
Brooklyn, NY 11230
TYPE OF MERCHANDISE: Clothing, housewares, furniture
DONATION TAX RECEIPT: Receipt given upon request

Salvation Army Thrift Store
981 Manhattan Ave.
Brooklyn, NY 11222
TYPE OF MERCHANDISE: Clothing, housewares, furniture
DONATION TAX RECEIPT: Receipt given upon request

Saint Vincent De Paul Thrift Store
1294 Hertel Ave.
Buffalo, NY 14216
TYPE OF MERCHANDISE: Clothing, housewares, furniture
DONATION TAX RECEIPT: Receipt given upon request
COMMENTS: Monthly markdowns

Junior League of Buffalo Thrift Shop
168 Allen St.
Buffalo, NY 14201-1516
CONTACT: Anne Fiden
PHONE: 716-884-4933
HOURS: Mon. 10–2, Tues.–Sat. 10–5
TYPE OF MERCHANDISE: Clothing, gifts, housewares

DONATION TAX RECEIPT: Receipt given
upon request
COMMENTS: Annual toy sales
Salvation Army Thrift Store
2196 Seneca St.
Buffalo, NY 14210
TYPE OF MERCHANDISE: Clothing,
housewares, furniture
DONATION TAX RECEIPT: Receipt given
upon request
Salvation Army Thrift Store
278 W. Ferry St.
Buffalo, NY 14213
TYPE OF MERCHANDISE: Clothing,
housewares, furniture
DONATION TAX RECEIPT: Receipt given
upon request
Salvation Army Thrift Store
3139 Bailey Ave.
Buffalo, NY 14215
TYPE OF MERCHANDISE: Clothing,
housewares, furniture
DONATION TAX RECEIPT: Receipt given
upon request
Goodwill Industries Thrift Store
3230 Main St.
Buffalo, NY 14214
TYPE OF MERCHANDISE: Clothing,
housewares, furniture
DONATION TAX RECEIPT: Receipt given
upon request
Salvation Army Thrift Store
7000 Transit Rd.
Buffalo, NY 14221
TYPE OF MERCHANDISE: Clothing,
housewares, furniture
DONATION TAX RECEIPT: Receipt given
upon request
Saint Vincent De Paul Thrift Store
72 E. Huron St.
Buffalo, NY 14203
TYPE OF MERCHANDISE: Clothing,
housewares, furniture
DONATION TAX RECEIPT: Receipt given
upon request
COMMENTS: Monthly markdowns
Goodwill Industries Thrift Store
892 Genesee St.
Buffalo, NY 14211

TYPE OF MERCHANDISE: Clothing,
housewares, furniture
DONATION TAX RECEIPT: Receipt given
upon request
Amvets Thrift Store
Central Park Plaza
Buffalo, NY 14214
TYPE OF MERCHANDISE: Clothing,
housewares
DONATION TAX RECEIPT: Receipt given
upon request
Salvation Army Thrift Store
136 S. Main St.
Canandaigua, NY 14424
TYPE OF MERCHANDISE: Clothing,
housewares, furniture
DONATION TAX RECEIPT: Receipt given
upon request
Salvation Army Thrift Store
450 Rockaway Turnpike
Cedarhurst, NY 11516
PHONE: 516-371-2729
HOURS: Mon.–Sat. 9–5:15
TYPE OF MERCHANDISE: Clothing,
housewares, furniture
DONATION TAX RECEIPT: Receipt given
upon request
Goodwill Industries Thrift Store
1500 Middle Country Rd.
Centereach, NY 11720
PHONE: 516-698-0860, 698-0808
HOURS: Seven days, 10–7
TYPE OF MERCHANDISE: Clothing,
housewares, furniture
DONATION TAX RECEIPT: Receipt given
upon request
Salvation Army Thrift Store
93 Carlton Ave.
Central Islip, NY 11722
TYPE OF MERCHANDISE: Clothing,
housewares, furniture
DONATION TAX RECEIPT: Receipt given
upon request
American Cancer Society Discovery Shop
400 King St.
Chappaqua, NY 10514
CONTACT: Betty Tisne
PHONE: 914-238-4900

TYPE OF MERCHANDISE: Clothing, bric-a-brac
DONATION TAX RECEIPT: Receipt given upon request
COMMENTS: Monthly markdowns

Salvation Army Thrift Store
205 Tuscarora
Chittenango, NY 13037
TYPE OF MERCHANDISE: Clothing, housewares, furniture
DONATION TAX RECEIPT: Receipt given upon request

Salvation Army Thrift Store
7365 Church St.
Cicero, NY 13039
TYPE OF MERCHANDISE: Clothing, housewares, furniture
DONATION TAX RECEIPT: Receipt given upon request

Salvation Army Thrift Store
2145 Central Ave.
Colonie, NY 12205
TYPE OF MERCHANDISE: Clothing, housewares, furniture
DONATION TAX RECEIPT: Receipt given upon request

Saint Vincent De Paul Thrift Store
430 Mill Rd.
Coram, NY 11727
TYPE OF MERCHANDISE: Clothing, housewares, furniture
DONATION TAX RECEIPT: Receipt given upon request
COMMENTS: Monthly markdowns

Salvation Army Thrift Store
209 W. Pultney St.
Corning, NY 14830
TYPE OF MERCHANDISE: Clothing, housewares, furniture
DONATION TAX RECEIPT: Receipt given upon request

Salvation Army Thrift Store
3975 West Rd.
Cortland, NY 13045
TYPE OF MERCHANDISE: Clothing, housewares, furniture
DONATION TAX RECEIPT: Receipt given upon request

Rescue Mission Thrifty Shopper
40 Owego St.
Cortland, NY 13045
TYPE OF MERCHANDISE: Clothing, housewares
DONATION TAX RECEIPT: Receipt given upon request

Salvation Army Thrift Store
6 Chestnut St.
Dansville, NY 14437
TYPE OF MERCHANDISE: Clothing, housewares, furniture
DONATION TAX RECEIPT: Receipt given upon request

Salvation Army Thrift Store
29 Lakeshore Dr. W
Dunkirk, NY 14048
TYPE OF MERCHANDISE: Clothing, housewares, furniture
DONATION TAX RECEIPT: Receipt given upon request

Salvation Army Thrift Store
110 Bellerose Ave.
E. Northport, NY 11731
TYPE OF MERCHANDISE: Clothing, housewares, furniture
DONATION TAX RECEIPT: Receipt given upon request

Salvation Army Thrift Store
364 Corning Rd.
Elmira, NY 14901
TYPE OF MERCHANDISE: Clothing, housewares, furniture
DONATION TAX RECEIPT: Receipt given upon request

Salvation Army Thrift Store
462 Hempstead Turnpike
Elmont, NY 11003
TYPE OF MERCHANDISE: Clothing, housewares, furniture
DONATION TAX RECEIPT: Receipt given upon request

Salvation Army Thrift Store
128 W. Main St.
Endicott, NY 13760
TYPE OF MERCHANDISE: Clothing, housewares, furniture
DONATION TAX RECEIPT: Receipt given upon request

Salvation Army Thrift Store
711 E. Main St.
Endicott, NY 13760
TYPE OF MERCHANDISE: Clothing,
housewares, furniture
DONATION TAX RECEIPT: Receipt given
upon request

Salvation Army Thrift Store
204 Canal St.
Ft. Plain, NY 13339
TYPE OF MERCHANDISE: Clothing,
housewares, furniture
DONATION TAX RECEIPT: Receipt given
upon request

NCJW Thrift Shop
25-A W. Merrick Rd.
Freeport, NY 11520
CONTACT: Elizabeth Weber
PHONE: 516-546-2117
HOURS: Mon.–Sat. 10:30–3:30
TYPE OF MERCHANDISE: Clothing,
housewares, furniture
DONATION TAX RECEIPT: Receipt given
upon request

Salvation Army Thrift Store
N. Second & Ontario St.
Fulton, NY 13069
TYPE OF MERCHANDISE: Clothing,
housewares, furniture
DONATION TAX RECEIPT: Receipt given
upon request

Saint Vincent De Paul Thrift Store
2160 Jericho Turnpike
Garden City Park, NY 11040
PHONE: 516-746-8250
HOURS: Mon.–Sat. 10–6
TYPE OF MERCHANDISE: Clothing,
housewares, furniture
DONATION TAX RECEIPT: Receipt given
upon request
COMMENTS: Monthly markdowns

Salvation Army Thrift Store
430 Exchange Ave.
Geneva, NY 14456
TYPE OF MERCHANDISE: Clothing,
housewares, furniture
DONATION TAX RECEIPT: Receipt given
upon request

Salvation Army Thrift Store
Quaker Rd.
Glens Falls, NY 12801
TYPE OF MERCHANDISE: Clothing,
housewares, furniture
DONATION TAX RECEIPT: Receipt given
upon request

Salvation Army Thrift Store
282 Saratoga Rd.
Glenville, NY 12325
TYPE OF MERCHANDISE: Clothing,
housewares, furniture
DONATION TAX RECEIPT: Receipt given
upon request

Salvation Army Thrift Store
37–43 W. Fulton St.
Gloversville, NY 12078
TYPE OF MERCHANDISE: Clothing,
housewares, furniture
DONATION TAX RECEIPT: Receipt given
upon request

NCJW Thrift Shop
581 Middle Rock Rd.
Great Neck, NY 11021
CONTACT: Bea Nash
PHONE: 516-482-9246
HOURS: Mon.–Fri. & every
2nd Sun. 10–4
TYPE OF MERCHANDISE: Clothing,
housewares, furniture
DONATION TAX RECEIPT: Receipt given
upon request
COMMENTS: "Buy a bag" sales

Salvation Army Thrift Store
194 Front St.
Hempstead, NY 11550
TYPE OF MERCHANDISE: Clothing,
housewares, furniture
DONATION TAX RECEIPT: Receipt given
upon request

Salvation Army Thrift Store
76 Seneca St.
Hornell, NY 14843
TYPE OF MERCHANDISE: Clothing,
housewares, furniture
DONATION TAX RECEIPT: Receipt given
upon request

Salvation Army Thrift Store
  Greenport Shopping Center
  300 Fairview Ave.
  Greenport, NY 12534
  PHONE: 518-828-0420
  HOURS: Mon.–Sat. 9–9
  TYPE OF MERCHANDISE: Clothing,
  housewares, furniture
  DONATION TAX RECEIPT: Receipt given
  upon request
Goodwill Industries Thrift Store
  1900 Jericho Turnpike
  Huntington, NY 11731
  PHONE: 516-462-4219, 462-9413
  HOURS: Seven days, 10:30–8
  TYPE OF MERCHANDISE: Clothing,
  housewares, furniture
  DONATION TAX RECEIPT: Receipt given
  upon request
Saint Vincent De Paul Thrift Store
  1433 New York Ave.
  Huntington Station, NY 11746
  TYPE OF MERCHANDISE: Clothing,
  housewares, furniture
  DONATION TAX RECEIPT: Receipt given
  upon request
  COMMENTS: Monthly markdowns
Salvation Army Thrift Store
  164 W. Main St.
  Ilion, NY 13357
  TYPE OF MERCHANDISE: Clothing,
  housewares, furniture
  DONATION TAX RECEIPT: Receipt given
  upon request
Saint Vincent De Paul Thrift Store
  2775 Sunrise Highway
  Islip Terrace, NY 11752
  TYPE OF MERCHANDISE: Clothing,
  housewares, furniture
  DONATION TAX RECEIPT: Receipt given
  upon request
  COMMENTS: Monthly markdowns
Salvation Army Thrift Store
  339 Elmira Rd.
  Ithaca, NY 14850
  TYPE OF MERCHANDISE: Clothing,
  housewares, furniture
  DONATION TAX RECEIPT: Receipt given
  upon request

Salvation Army Thrift Store
  585 Fairmont Ave. W
  Jamestown, NY 14701
  TYPE OF MERCHANDISE: Clothing,
  housewares, furniture
  DONATION TAX RECEIPT: Receipt given
  upon request
Salvation Army Thrift Store
  1080 Military Rd.
  Kenmore, NY 14217
  TYPE OF MERCHANDISE: Clothing,
  housewares, furniture
  DONATION TAX RECEIPT: Receipt given
  upon request
Saint Vincent De Paul Thrift Store
  56 Main St.
  Kings Park, NY 11754
  TYPE OF MERCHANDISE: Clothing,
  housewares, furniture
  DONATION TAX RECEIPT: Receipt given
  upon request
  COMMENTS: Monthly markdowns
Salvation Army Thrift Store
  884 Albany Ave.
  Kingston, NY 12401
  TYPE OF MERCHANDISE: Clothing,
  housewares, furniture
  DONATION TAX RECEIPT: Receipt given
  upon request
American Cancer Society Discovery Shop
  139 Larchmont Ave.
  Larchmont, NY 10538
  CONTACT: Pina Hemment
  PHONE: 914-834-4242
  TYPE OF MERCHANDISE: Clothing, bric-a-
  brac
  DONATION TAX RECEIPT: Receipt given
  upon request
  COMMENTS: Monthly markdowns
Junior League, The Golden Shoestring
  149 Larchmont Ave.
  CROSS STREETS: Btw. Boston Post Rd. &
  Addison St.
  Larchmont, NY 10538
  CONTACT: Ms. Lolly Panarello
  PHONE: 914-834-8383
  HOURS: Mon.–Sat. 9:30–4
  TYPE OF MERCHANDISE: Clothing,
  housewares, furniture

DONATION TAX RECEIPT: Receipt given upon request
COMMENTS: Some collectibles, jewelry, and paintings

Salvation Army Thrift Store
350 Troy-Schenectady Rd.
Latham, NY 12110
TYPE OF MERCHANDISE: Clothing, housewares, furniture
DONATION TAX RECEIPT: Receipt given upon request

Council Thrift Shop
340 Central Ave.
Lawrence, NY 11559
TYPE OF MERCHANDISE: Clothing, housewares, furniture
DONATION TAX RECEIPT: Receipt given upon request

NCJW Thrift Shop
342 Central Ave.
CROSS STREETS: Near Rockaway Turnpike
Lawrence, NY 11559
PHONE: 516-569-0510
FAX: 516-569-3634
HOURS: Mon.–Wed. 9:30–4, Thurs. 9:30–8, Fri. 9:30–3, Sun. 10–3
TYPE OF MERCHANDISE: Clothing, housewares, furniture
DONATION TAX RECEIPT: Receipt given upon request
COMMENTS: Special sales throughout the year

Salvation Army Thrift Store
148 Gardners Ave.
Levittown, NY 11756
TYPE OF MERCHANDISE: Clothing, housewares, furniture
DONATION TAX RECEIPT: Receipt given upon request

American Cancer Society Discovery Shop
253–15 Northern Blvd.
Little Neck, NY 11363
TYPE OF MERCHANDISE: Clothing, bric-a-brac
DONATION TAX RECEIPT: Receipt given upon request
COMMENTS: Monthly markdowns

Salvation Army Thrift Store
Route 57/7595 Oswego Rd.

Liverpool, NY 13090
TYPE OF MERCHANDISE: Clothing, housewares, furniture
DONATION TAX RECEIPT: Receipt given upon request

Goodwill Industries Thrift Store
215 Walnut St.
Lockport, NY 14094
TYPE OF MERCHANDISE: Clothing, housewares, furniture
DONATION TAX RECEIPT: Receipt given upon request

Salvation Army Thrift Store
58 West Ave.
Lockport, NY 14094
TYPE OF MERCHANDISE: Clothing, housewares, furniture
DONATION TAX RECEIPT: Receipt given upon request

Goodwill Industries Thrift Store
330 S. Transit Rd.
Lyndonville, NY 14098
TYPE OF MERCHANDISE: Clothing, housewares, furniture
DONATION TAX RECEIPT: Receipt given upon request

Saint Vincent De Paul Thrift Store
128 Main St.
Massena, NY 13662
TYPE OF MERCHANDISE: Clothing, housewares, furniture
DONATION TAX RECEIPT: Receipt given upon request
COMMENTS: Monthly markdowns

Salvation Army Thrift Store
Route 211
Middletown, NY 10940
TYPE OF MERCHANDISE: Clothing, housewares, furniture
DONATION TAX RECEIPT: Receipt given upon request

Salvation Army Thrift Store
745 S. Third Ave.
Mt. Vernon, NY 10550
TYPE OF MERCHANDISE: Clothing, housewares, furniture
DONATION TAX RECEIPT: Receipt given upon request

Salvation Army Thrift Store
61 N. Chestnut St.
New Paltz, NY 12561
TYPE OF MERCHANDISE: Clothing,
housewares, furniture
DONATION TAX RECEIPT: Receipt given
upon request

Goodwill Industries Thrift Store
248 North Ave.
New Rochelle, NY 10805
PHONE: 914-235-1663
TYPE OF MERCHANDISE: Clothing,
housewares, furniture
DONATION TAX RECEIPT: Receipt given
upon request

Humane Society Thrift Shop
364 North Ave.
New Rochelle, NY 10801
TYPE OF MERCHANDISE: Clothing,
housewares
DONATION TAX RECEIPT: Receipt given
upon request

Salvation Army Thrift Store
562 North Ave.
New Rochelle, NY 10801
TYPE OF MERCHANDISE: Clothing,
housewares, furniture
DONATION TAX RECEIPT: Receipt given
upon request

Goodwill Industries Thrift Store
130 W. Third St.
CROSS STREET: Sixth Ave.
New York, NY 10012
PHONE: 212-673-0231, 979-9642
HOURS: 12–8
TYPE OF MERCHANDISE: Clothing,
housewares, furniture
DONATION TAX RECEIPT: Receipt given
upon request
COMMENTS: Good finds, very low pricing

Goodwill Industries Thrift Store
1704 Second Ave.
CROSS STREETS: Btw. 88th & 89th St.
New York, NY 10128
PHONE: 212-831-1830
HOURS: Mon.–Sat. 11–6:45, Sun. 11–5
TYPE OF MERCHANDISE: Clothing,
housewares, furniture

DONATION TAX RECEIPT: Receipt given
upon request
COMMENTS: Large, lots of goodies, great
prices

Goodwill Industries Thrift Store
186 Second Ave.
CROSS STREETS: Btw. 11th & 12th St.
New York, NY 10003
PHONE: 212-533-2768
HOURS: Mon.–Fri. 11–7, Sat. 10–6,
Sun. 11–6
TYPE OF MERCHANDISE: Clothing,
housewares, furniture
DONATION TAX RECEIPT: Receipt given
upon request
COMMENTS: Smaller store, some good
finds

Goodwill Industries Thrift Store
201 8th Ave.
CROSS STREETS: Btw. 20th & 21st Sts.
New York, NY 10011
PHONE: 212-675-1520, 633-6579
HOURS: Mon.–Sat. 10–6
TYPE OF MERCHANDISE: Clothing,
housewares, furniture
DONATION TAX RECEIPT: Receipt given
upon request

Goodwill Industries Thrift Store
217 W. 79th St.
CROSS STREETS: Btw. Broadway &
Amsterdam
New York, NY 10021
PHONE: 212-874-5050, 874-5333
HOURS: Mon.–Sat. 10–5:45; Wed., Fri.
11:30–5:30
TYPE OF MERCHANDISE: Clothing,
housewares, furniture
DONATION TAX RECEIPT: Receipt given
upon request
COMMENTS: Great prices, average to good
finds

Goodwill Industries Thrift Store
2196 Fifth Ave.
CROSS STREET: 135th St.
New York, NY 10037
PHONE: 212-926-3985, 862-0020
HOURS: Mon.–Sat. 10–6
TYPE OF MERCHANDISE: Clothing,
housewares, furniture

DONATION TAX RECEIPT: Receipt given
upon request

Goodwill Industries Thrift Store
402 Third Ave.
CROSS STREET: 29th St.
New York, NY 10016
PHONE: 212-679-0786, 689-8230
HOURS: Mon.–Sat. 11–7
TYPE OF MERCHANDISE: Clothing,
housewares, furniture
DONATION TAX RECEIPT: Receipt given
upon request

Goodwill Industries Thrift Store
730 Amsterdam Ave.
CROSS STREET: 96th St.
New York, NY 10025
PHONE: 212-666-3655
TYPE OF MERCHANDISE: Clothing,
housewares, furniture
DONATION TAX RECEIPT: Receipt given
upon request

Salvation Army Thrift Store
112 Fourth Ave.
New York, NY 10003
TYPE OF MERCHANDISE: Clothing,
housewares, furniture
DONATION TAX RECEIPT: Receipt given
upon request

Salvation Army Thrift Store
115 Allen St.
New York, NY 10002
TYPE OF MERCHANDISE: Clothing,
housewares, furniture
DONATION TAX RECEIPT: Receipt given
upon request

Housing Works Thrift Shop
143 W. 17th St.
CROSS STREETS: Btw. Sixth & Seventh Aves.
New York, NY 10011
PHONE: 212-366-0820
FAX: 212-691-8892
HOURS: Mon.–Sat. 10–6
TYPE OF MERCHANDISE: Clothing,
housewares, furniture
DONATION TAX RECEIPT: Receipt given
upon request
COMMENTS: Supports services for people
with HIV and AIDS

Goodwill Industries Thrift Store
176 Second Ave.
New York, NY 10003
TYPE OF MERCHANDISE: Clothing,
housewares, furniture
DONATION TAX RECEIPT: Receipt given
upon request

Housing Works Thrift Shop
202 E. 77th St.
CROSS STREETS: Btw. Second & Third Aves.
New York, NY 10021
PHONE: 212-772-8461
FAX: 212-772-8592
HOURS: Mon.–Sat. 10–6
TYPE OF MERCHANDISE: Clothing,
housewares, furniture
DONATION TAX RECEIPT: Receipt given
upon request
COMMENTS: Supports services for people
with HIV and AIDS

Salvation Army Thrift Store
208 Eighth Ave.
New York, NY 10011
TYPE OF MERCHANDISE: Clothing,
housewares, furniture
DONATION TAX RECEIPT: Receipt given
upon request

Salvation Army Thrift Store
220 E. 23rd St.
New York, NY 10010
TYPE OF MERCHANDISE: Clothing,
housewares, furniture
DONATION TAX RECEIPT: Receipt given
upon request

Salvation Army Thrift Store
26 E. 125th St.
New York, NY 10035
TYPE OF MERCHANDISE: Clothing,
housewares, furniture
DONATION TAX RECEIPT: Receipt given
upon request

Salvation Army Thrift Store
268 W. 96th St.
New York, NY 10025
TYPE OF MERCHANDISE: Clothing,
housewares, furniture
DONATION TAX RECEIPT: Receipt given
upon request

Salvation Army Thrift Store
536 W. 46th St.
New York, NY 10036
TYPE OF MERCHANDISE: Clothing,
housewares, furniture
DONATION TAX RECEIPT: Receipt given
upon request
NCJW Council Thrift Shop
767 Ninth Ave.
New York, NY 10019
TYPE OF MERCHANDISE: Clothing,
housewares, furniture
DONATION TAX RECEIPT: Receipt given
upon request
NCJW Council Thrift Shop
9 E. 69th St.
CROSS STREETS: W. 51st & W. 52nd St.
New York, NY 10021
CONTACT: Debbie Loman
PHONE: 212-457-6132
HOURS: Mon.–Fri. 9:30–5, Sat.–Sun. 11–4
TYPE OF MERCHANDISE: Clothing,
housewares, furniture
DONATION TAX RECEIPT: Receipt given
upon request
COMMENTS: Fashion and end-of-season
sales
Salvation Army Thrift Store
235 Murray St.
Newark, NY 14513
TYPE OF MERCHANDISE: Clothing,
housewares, furniture
DONATION TAX RECEIPT: Receipt given
upon request
Salvation Army Thrift Store
315 Broadway
Newburgh, NY 12550
TYPE OF MERCHANDISE: Clothing,
housewares, furniture
DONATION TAX RECEIPT: Receipt given
upon request
Goodwill Industries Thrift Store
1901 Main St.
Niagara Falls, NY 14305
TYPE OF MERCHANDISE: Clothing,
housewares, furniture
DONATION TAX RECEIPT: Receipt given
upon request

Salvation Army Thrift Store
939 Ontario Ave.
Niagara Falls, NY 14305
TYPE OF MERCHANDISE: Clothing,
housewares, furniture
DONATION TAX RECEIPT: Receipt given
upon request
Salvation Army Thrift Store
9491 Niagara Falls Blvd.
Niagara Falls, NY 14304
TYPE OF MERCHANDISE: Clothing,
housewares, furniture
DONATION TAX RECEIPT: Receipt given
upon request
Salvation Army Thrift Store
401 N. Main St.
N. Syracuse, NY 13212
TYPE OF MERCHANDISE: Clothing,
housewares, furniture
DONATION TAX RECEIPT: Receipt given
upon request
Salvation Army Thrift Store
895 Payne Ave.
North Tonawanda, NY 14120
TYPE OF MERCHANDISE: Clothing,
housewares, furniture
DONATION TAX RECEIPT: Receipt given
upon request
Salvation Army Thrift Store
17–19 S. Broad St.
Norwich, NY 13815
TYPE OF MERCHANDISE: Clothing,
housewares, furniture
DONATION TAX RECEIPT: Receipt given
upon request
NCJW Thrift Shop
145 Main St.
Nyack, NY 10960
CONTACT: Addy Frankel
PHONE: 914-358-8521
HOURS: Mon.–Fri. 10–4, Sat. 10:30–4:30,
Sun. 11–5
TYPE OF MERCHANDISE: Clothing,
housewares, furniture
DONATION TAX RECEIPT: Receipt given
upon request
Saint Vincent De Paul Thrift Store
415 Hamilton St.

Ogdensburg, NY 13669
TYPE OF MERCHANDISE: Clothing,
housewares, furniture
DONATION TAX RECEIPT: Receipt given
upon request
COMMENTS: Monthly markdowns
Saint Vincent De Paul Thrift Store
441 N. Union St.
Olean, NY 14760
TYPE OF MERCHANDISE: Clothing,
housewares, furniture
DONATION TAX RECEIPT: Receipt given
upon request
COMMENTS: Monthly markdowns
Salvation Army Thrift Store
169 Main St.
Oneida, NY 13421
TYPE OF MERCHANDISE: Clothing,
housewares, furniture
DONATION TAX RECEIPT: Receipt given
upon request
Salvation Army Thrift Store
105 Main St.
Oneonta, NY 13820
TYPE OF MERCHANDISE: Clothing,
housewares, furniture
DONATION TAX RECEIPT: Receipt given
upon request
Salvation Army Thrift Store
119 E. Bridge St.
Oswego, NY 13126
TYPE OF MERCHANDISE: Clothing,
housewares, furniture
DONATION TAX RECEIPT: Receipt given
upon request
Salvation Army Thrift Store
87 W. First St.
Oswego, NY 13021
TYPE OF MERCHANDISE: Clothing,
housewares, furniture
DONATION TAX RECEIPT: Receipt given
upon request
Saint Vincent De Paul Thrift Store
202 E. Main St.
Patchogue, NY 11772
TYPE OF MERCHANDISE: Clothing,
housewares, furniture
DONATION TAX RECEIPT: Receipt given
upon request

COMMENTS: Monthly markdowns
Salvation Army Thrift Store
414 E. Main St.
Patchogue, NY 11772
TYPE OF MERCHANDISE: Clothing,
housewares, furniture
DONATION TAX RECEIPT: Receipt given
upon request
Salvation Army Thrift Store
1022 Main St.
Peekskill, NY 10566
TYPE OF MERCHANDISE: Clothing,
housewares, furniture
DONATION TAX RECEIPT: Receipt given
upon request
Salvation Army Thrift Store
110 N. Main St.
Port Chester, NY 10573
TYPE OF MERCHANDISE: Clothing,
housewares, furniture
DONATION TAX RECEIPT: Receipt given
upon request
Salvation Army Thrift Store
36 N. Main St.
Port Chester, NY 10573
TYPE OF MERCHANDISE: Clothing,
housewares, furniture
DONATION TAX RECEIPT: Receipt given
upon request
Salvation Army Thrift Store
1011 Port Washington Blvd.
Port Washington, NY 11050
TYPE OF MERCHANDISE: Clothing,
housewares, furniture
DONATION TAX RECEIPT: Receipt given
upon request
Junior League Bargain Box
794 Main St.
Poughkeepsie, NY 12603
CONTACT: Ann-Margret Parker
PHONE: 914-471-3530
HOURS: Tues.–Sat. 10–4
TYPE OF MERCHANDISE: Clothing, jewelry,
housewares
DONATION TAX RECEIPT: Receipt given
upon request
COMMENTS: Some consignments taken,
and toy sales

Salvation Army Thrift Store
574 Main St.
Poughkeepsie, NY 12601
TYPE OF MERCHANDISE: Clothing,
housewares, furniture
DONATION TAX RECEIPT: Receipt given
upon request

Council Thrift Shop
10718 Corona Ave.
Queens, NY 11368
TYPE OF MERCHANDISE: Clothing,
housewares, furniture
DONATION TAX RECEIPT: Receipt given
upon request

Goodwill Industries Thrift Store
31–20 Ditmars Blvd.
CROSS STREETS: Between 32nd and 33rd St.
Queens, NY 11105
PHONE: 718-545-8875, 545-8879
HOURS: Mon.–Sat. 11–6:45, Sun. 10–6
TYPE OF MERCHANDISE: Clothing,
housewares, toys
DONATION TAX RECEIPT: Receipt given
upon request
COMMENTS: Great toy selection

Goodwill Industries Thrift Store
(Main Plant)
4–21 27th Ave.
CROSS STREET: 4th Ave.
Queens, NY 11102
CONTACT: R. Borsari
PHONE: 718-728-5400 ext. 229, 721-1739
TYPE OF MERCHANDISE: Clothing,
housewares, furniture
DONATION TAX RECEIPT: Receipt given
upon request
COMMENTS: Senior discounts and 50%
discount sales

Goodwill Industries Thrift Store
32–36 Steinway St.
Queens, NY 11103
PHONE: 718-932-0418
HOURS: Mon. 10–7, Wed.–Thurs.
11:30–7, Fri.–Sat. 10–7, Sun. 10–6
TYPE OF MERCHANDISE: Clothing,
housewares, furniture
DONATION TAX RECEIPT: Receipt given
upon request
COMMENTS: Low pricing

Goodwill Industries Thrift Store
30–15 30th Ave.
Queens, NY 11102
PHONE: 718-932-2476, 956-8626
HOURS: Mon.–Fri. 10:30–6:30, Sat.–Sun.
10–6
TYPE OF MERCHANDISE: Clothing,
housewares, furniture
DONATION TAX RECEIPT: Receipt given
upon request

Goodwill Industries Thrift Store
40–04 Junction Blvd.
Queens, NY 11368
PHONE: 718-478-9881, 478-9882
HOURS: Mon.-Sat. 11–7, Sun. 10–6
TYPE OF MERCHANDISE: Clothing,
housewares, furniture
DONATION TAX RECEIPT: Receipt given
upon request

Goodwill Industries Thrift Store
4625 Greenpoint Ave.
CROSS STREET: Queens Blvd.
Queens, NY 11104
PHONE: 718-937-2598
HOURS: Mon.-Sat. 11–7, Sun. 10–6
TYPE OF MERCHANDISE: Clothing,
housewares, furniture
DONATION TAX RECEIPT: Receipt given
upon request

Salvation Army Thrift Store
34–02 Steinway St.
Queens, NY 11102
PHONE: 718-472-2414
HOURS: Mon.–Fri. 10–7:30, Sat. 10–5:45
TYPE OF MERCHANDISE: Clothing,
housewares, furniture
DONATION TAX RECEIPT: Receipt given
upon request

Salvation Army Thrift Store
39–11 61st St.
Queens, NY 11277
PHONE: 718-426-9222
TYPE OF MERCHANDISE: Clothing,
housewares, furniture
DONATION TAX RECEIPT: Receipt given
upon request

Saint Vincent De Paul Thrift Store
124–01 Liberty Ave.
Queens, NY 11419

TYPE OF MERCHANDISE: Clothing,
housewares, furniture
DONATION TAX RECEIPT: Receipt given
upon request
COMMENTS: Monthly markdowns
Salvation Army Thrift Store
17–15 Myrtle Ave.
Queens, NY 11418
PHONE: 718-846-4670
HOURS: Mon.–Sat. 9–5:30
TYPE OF MERCHANDISE: Clothing,
housewares, furniture
DONATION TAX RECEIPT: Receipt given
upon request
Salvation Army Thrift Store
148–15 Archer Ave.
Queens, NY 11435
PHONE: 718-523-4648
HOURS: Mon.–Sat. 9–5:15
TYPE OF MERCHANDISE: Clothing,
housewares, furniture
DONATION TAX RECEIPT: Receipt given
upon request
Salvation Army Thrift Store
220–01 Linden Blvd.
Queens, NY 11412
PHONE: 718-525-1219
HOURS: Mon.–Sat. 9–5:30
TYPE OF MERCHANDISE: Clothing,
housewares, furniture
DONATION TAX RECEIPT: Receipt given
upon request
Salvation Army Thrift Store
815 Seneca Ave.
Queens, NY 11385
PHONE: 718-381-6687
TYPE OF MERCHANDISE: Clothing,
housewares, furniture
DONATION TAX RECEIPT: Receipt given
upon request
Salvation Army Thrift Store
319 E. Main St.
Riverhead, NY 11901
TYPE OF MERCHANDISE: Clothing,
housewares, furniture
DONATION TAX RECEIPT: Receipt given
upon request
Volunteers of America Thrift

1221 Main St. E
Rochester, NY 14609
TYPE OF MERCHANDISE: Clothing,
housewares,
DONATION TAX RECEIPT: Receipt given
upon request
Salvation Army Thrift Store
458–62 Monroe Ave.
Rochester, NY 14607
TYPE OF MERCHANDISE: Clothing,
housewares, furniture
DONATION TAX RECEIPT: Receipt given
upon request
Salvation Army Thrift Store
571 Stone Rd.
Rochester, NY 14616
TYPE OF MERCHANDISE: Clothing,
housewares, furniture
DONATION TAX RECEIPT: Receipt given
upon request
Salvation Army Thrift Store
745 West Ave.
Rochester, NY 14611
TYPE OF MERCHANDISE: Clothing,
housewares, furniture
DONATION TAX RECEIPT: Receipt given
upon request
Salvation Army Thrift Store
1186 Erie Blvd. W
Rome, NY 13440
TYPE OF MERCHANDISE: Clothing,
housewares, furniture
DONATION TAX RECEIPT: Receipt given
upon request
Junior League Thrift Shop
1395 Old Northern Blvd.
Roslyn, NY 11576
TYPE OF MERCHANDISE: Clothing for men,
women, and children
DONATION TAX RECEIPT: Receipt given
upon request
Salvation Army Thrift Store
1442 Castleton Ave.
Staten Island, NY 13202
TYPE OF MERCHANDISE: Clothing,
housewares, furniture
DONATION TAX RECEIPT: Receipt given
upon request

Salvation Army Thrift Store
2053 Clove Rd.
Staten Island, NY 10304
TYPE OF MERCHANDISE: Clothing,
housewares, furniture
DONATION TAX RECEIPT: Receipt given
upon request

Salvation Army Thrift Store
1105 S. State St.
Syracuse, NY 13202
TYPE OF MERCHANDISE: Clothing,
housewares, furniture
DONATION TAX RECEIPT: Receipt given
upon request

Salvation Army Thrift Store
2221 Erie Blvd. W
Syracuse, NY 13224
TYPE OF MERCHANDISE: Clothing,
housewares, furniture
DONATION TAX RECEIPT: Receipt given
upon request

Rescue Mission Thrifty Shopper
3501 James St.
Syracuse, NY 13206
TYPE OF MERCHANDISE: Clothing,
housewares
DONATION TAX RECEIPT: Receipt given
upon request

Salvation Army Thrift Store
400 N. Midler Ave.
Syracuse, NY 13206
TYPE OF MERCHANDISE: Clothing,
housewares, furniture
DONATION TAX RECEIPT: Receipt given
upon request

NCJW Council Thrift Shop
541 N. Salina St.
Syracuse, NY 13208
TYPE OF MERCHANDISE: Clothing,
housewares, furniture
DONATION TAX RECEIPT: Receipt given
upon request

Salvation Army Thrift Store
720 S. Geddes St.
Syracuse, NY 13204
TYPE OF MERCHANDISE: Clothing,
housewares, furniture
DONATION TAX RECEIPT: Receipt given
upon request

Goodwill Industries Thrift Store
83 Broad St.
Tonawanda, NY 14150
TYPE OF MERCHANDISE: Clothing,
housewares, furniture
DONATION TAX RECEIPT: Receipt given
upon request

NCJW Council Thrift Shop
16 Columbus Ave.
Tuckahoe, NY 10707
CONTACT: Helen Gemunder
PHONE: 914-337-8280
HOURS: Mon.–Fri. 10–4
TYPE OF MERCHANDISE: Clothing,
housewares, furniture
DONATION TAX RECEIPT: Receipt given
upon request

Junior League, The Pennypincher
4 Depot Sq.
Tuckahoe, NY 10707
CONTACT: Erika Bauer
PHONE: 914-961-3145
HOURS: Mon.–Sat. 10–6
TYPE OF MERCHANDISE: Clothing,
housewares, bric-a-brac
DONATION TAX RECEIPT: Receipt given
upon request
COMMENTS: Seasonal sales and monthly
discounts

Salvation Army Thrift Store
400 Columbia St.
Utica, NY 13502
TYPE OF MERCHANDISE: Clothing,
housewares, furniture
DONATION TAX RECEIPT: Receipt given
upon request

Salvation Army Thrift Store
122 E. Main St.
Wappingers Falls, NY 12590
TYPE OF MERCHANDISE: Clothing,
housewares, furniture
DONATION TAX RECEIPT: Receipt given
upon request

MCC Agape Shoppe
136 Court St.
Watertown, NY 13601
PHONE: 315-788-7470
TYPE OF MERCHANDISE: Clothing,
housewares

DONATION TAX RECEIPT: Receipt given upon request

Salvation Army Thrift Store
780 W. Main St.
Watertown, NY 13601
TYPE OF MERCHANDISE: Clothing, housewares, furniture
DONATION TAX RECEIPT: Receipt given upon request

Salvation Army Thrift Store
913 Arsenal St.
Watertown, NY 13601
TYPE OF MERCHANDISE: Clothing, housewares, furniture
DONATION TAX RECEIPT: Receipt given upon request

Salvation Army Thrift Store
581 Broad St.
Waverly, NY 14892
TYPE OF MERCHANDISE: Clothing, housewares, furniture
DONATION TAX RECEIPT: Receipt given upon request

Salvation Army Thrift Store
93 E. Main St.
Westfield, NY 14787
TYPE OF MERCHANDISE: Clothing, housewares, furniture
DONATION TAX RECEIPT: Receipt given upon request

Salvation Army Thrift Store
440 W. Nyack Rd. W
W. Nyack, NY 10994
CONTACT: Timothy Rains
TYPE OF MERCHANDISE: Clothing, housewares, furniture
DONATION TAX RECEIPT: Receipt given upon request

Salvation Army Thrift Store
84 E. Post Rd.
White Plains, NY 10601
TYPE OF MERCHANDISE: Clothing, housewares, furniture
DONATION TAX RECEIPT: Receipt given upon request

Salvation Army Thrift Store
6998–7000 Transit Rd.
Williamsville, NY 14221

TYPE OF MERCHANDISE: Clothing, housewares, furniture
DONATION TAX RECEIPT: Receipt given upon request

Salvation Army Thrift Store
29 Palisades Ave.
Yonkers, NY 10701
TYPE OF MERCHANDISE: Clothing, housewares, furniture
DONATION TAX RECEIPT: Receipt given upon request

North Carolina

Salvation Army Thrift Store
24 N. Lexington Ave.
Asheville, NC 28801
TYPE OF MERCHANDISE: Clothing, housewares, furniture
DONATION TAX RECEIPT: Receipt given upon request

Junior League Nearly New
29 Biltmore Ave.
Asheville, NC 28801
PHONE: 704-253-8051
HOURS: Mon.–Fri. 9:30–4:30, Sat. 10–2:30
TYPE OF MERCHANDISE: Clothing, housewares, bric-a-brac
DONATION TAX RECEIPT: Receipt given upon request

Salvation Army Thrift Store
1011 Central Ave.
Charlotte, NC 28204
TYPE OF MERCHANDISE: Clothing, housewares, furniture
DONATION TAX RECEIPT: Receipt given upon request

Salvation Army Thrift Store
2412 Freedom Dr.
Charlotte, NC 28208
TYPE OF MERCHANDISE: Clothing, housewares, furniture
DONATION TAX RECEIPT: Receipt given upon request

Salvation Army Thrift Store
6301 South Blvd.
Charlotte, NC 28217

TYPE OF MERCHANDISE: Clothing, housewares, furniture
DONATION TAX RECEIPT: Receipt given upon request

Goodwill Industries Thrift Store
321 W. Harnett
Durham, NC 27703
TYPE OF MERCHANDISE: Clothing, housewares, furniture
DONATION TAX RECEIPT: Receipt given upon request

Salvation Army Thrift Store
1124 W. Main St.
Elizabeth City, NC 27909
TYPE OF MERCHANDISE: Clothing, housewares, furniture
DONATION TAX RECEIPT: Receipt given upon request

Salvation Army Thrift Store
3102 Murchison Rd.
Fayetteville, NC 28301
TYPE OF MERCHANDISE: Clothing, housewares, furniture
DONATION TAX RECEIPT: Receipt given upon request

Goodwill Industries Thrift Store
2549 Kings Mountain Highway
Gastonia, NC 28052
CONTACT: Marcia Atkinson
PHONE: 704-864-2225, 864-2049
HOURS: Mon.–Sat. 9–7, Sun. 1–5:30
TYPE OF MERCHANDISE: Clothing, housewares, furniture
DONATION TAX RECEIPT: Receipt given upon request
COMMENTS: Special price sales

Salvation Army Thrift Store
1017 W. Lee St.
Greensboro, NC 27403
TYPE OF MERCHANDISE: Clothing, housewares, furniture
DONATION TAX RECEIPT: Receipt given upon request

Goodwill Industries Thrift Store
1235 S. Eugene St.
Greensboro, NC 27406
TYPE OF MERCHANDISE: Clothing, housewares, furniture

DONATION TAX RECEIPT: Receipt given upon request

Salvation Army Thrift Store
239 Third Ave. E
Hendersonville, NC 28792
TYPE OF MERCHANDISE: Clothing, housewares, furniture
DONATION TAX RECEIPT: Receipt given upon request

Salvation Army Thrift Store
312 First Ave. SE
Hickory, NC 28602
TYPE OF MERCHANDISE: Clothing, housewares, furniture
DONATION TAX RECEIPT: Receipt given upon request

Junior League Bargain Boutique
128 S. Main St.
High Point, NC 27260
TYPE OF MERCHANDISE: Clothing for men, women, and children
DONATION TAX RECEIPT: Receipt given upon request

Salvation Army Thrift Store
1418 English Rd.
High Point, NC 27262
TYPE OF MERCHANDISE: Clothing, housewares, furniture
DONATION TAX RECEIPT: Receipt given upon request

Junior League Bargain Boutique
308 W. Broad St.
High Point, NC 27262
CONTACTS: Ms. Sharon Shore, Ms. Lina Riggs
PHONE: 910-884-1793
HOURS: Mon.–Sat. 10–4:30
TYPE OF MERCHANDISE: Clothing, housewares, toys
DONATION TAX RECEIPT: Sent out in late January
COMMENTS: "$2 bag" sales

Goodwill Industries Thrift Store
511 N. Cannon Blvd.
Kannapolis, NC 28083
TYPE OF MERCHANDISE: Clothing, housewares, furniture
DONATION TAX RECEIPT: Receipt given upon request

Goodwill Industries Thrift Store
113 N. Main St.
Kernersville, NC 27284
TYPE OF MERCHANDISE: Clothing,
housewares, furniture
DONATION TAX RECEIPT: Receipt given
upon request

Junior League Bargain Box
2104½ Smallwood Dr.
Raleigh, NC 27605
CONTACT: Judy Adams
PHONE: 919-833-7587
HOURS: Mon.–Sat. 9–3
TYPE OF MERCHANDISE: Clothing,
housewares, furniture
DONATION TAX RECEIPT: Receipt given
upon request

Salvation Army Thrift Store
215 S. Person St.
Raleigh, NC 27601
TYPE OF MERCHANDISE: Clothing,
housewares, furniture
DONATION TAX RECEIPT: Receipt given
upon request

Goodwill Industries Thrift Store
321 W. Hargett St.
Raleigh, NC 27601
TYPE OF MERCHANDISE: Clothing,
housewares, furniture
DONATION TAX RECEIPT: Receipt given
upon request

Goodwill Industries Thrift Store
1109 US 301 Bypass
Rocky Mount, NC 27801
TYPE OF MERCHANDISE: Clothing,
housewares, furniture
DONATION TAX RECEIPT: Receipt given
upon request

Salvation Army Thrift Store
1711 S. Church St.
Rocky Mount, NC 27803
TYPE OF MERCHANDISE: Clothing,
housewares, furniture
DONATION TAX RECEIPT: Receipt given
upon request

Salvation Army Thrift Store
820 N. Third St.
Wilmington, NC 28401

TYPE OF MERCHANDISE: Clothing,
housewares, furniture
DONATION TAX RECEIPT: Receipt given
upon request

North Dakota

Saint Vincent De Paul Thrift Store
1425 First Ave. S
Fargo, ND 58102
TYPE OF MERCHANDISE: Clothing,
housewares, furniture
DONATION TAX RECEIPT: Receipt given
upon request
COMMENTS: Monthly markdowns

Salvation Army Thrift Store
915 N. Third St.
Grand Forks, ND 58203
TYPE OF MERCHANDISE: Clothing,
housewares, furniture
DONATION TAX RECEIPT: Receipt given
upon request

Ohio

Salvation Army Thrift Store
1033 Bellows St.
Akron, OH 44311
TYPE OF MERCHANDISE: Clothing,
housewares, furniture
DONATION TAX RECEIPT: Receipt given
upon request

Salvation Army Thrift Store
1356 S. Arlington St.
Akron, OH 44306
TYPE OF MERCHANDISE: Clothing,
housewares, furniture
DONATION TAX RECEIPT: Receipt given
upon request

Salvation Army Thrift Store
1400 Arlington Plaza
Akron, OH 44309
TYPE OF MERCHANDISE: Clothing,
housewares, furniture
DONATION TAX RECEIPT: Receipt given
upon request

Salvation Army Thrift Store
3333 Manchester Rd.
Akron, OH 44319

TYPE OF MERCHANDISE: Clothing, housewares, furniture
DONATION TAX RECEIPT: Receipt given upon request

Salvation Army Thrift Store
522 E. Cuyahoga Falls Ave.
Akron, OH 44310
TYPE OF MERCHANDISE: Clothing, housewares, furniture
DONATION TAX RECEIPT: Receipt given upon request

Salvation Army Thrift Store
137 S. Arch Ave.
Alliance, OH 44601
TYPE OF MERCHANDISE: Clothing, housewares, furniture
DONATION TAX RECEIPT: Receipt given upon request

Goodwill Industries Thrift Store
2445 W. State St.
Alliance, OH 44601
CONTACT: Joe Arnal
PHONE: 216-821-4880
HOURS: Mon. 9–8, Tues.–Wed. 9–6, Thurs.–Sat. 9–8, Sun. 9–1
TYPE OF MERCHANDISE: Clothing, housewares, furniture
DONATION TAX RECEIPT: Receipt given upon request

Salvation Army Thrift Store
430 S. Union Ave.
Alliance, OH 44601
TYPE OF MERCHANDISE: Clothing, housewares, furniture
DONATION TAX RECEIPT: Receipt given upon request

MCC Care & Share Center
1201 S. Defiance St.
Archbold, OH 43502
PHONE: 419-445-1926
TYPE OF MERCHANDISE: Clothing, housewares
DONATION TAX RECEIPT: Receipt given upon request

Goodwill Industries Thrift Store
1215 Claremont Ave.
Ashland, OH 44805

TYPE OF MERCHANDISE: Clothing, housewares, furniture
DONATION TAX RECEIPT: Receipt given upon request

Salvation Army Thrift Store
4631 Main Ave.
Ashtabula, OH 44004
TYPE OF MERCHANDISE: Clothing, housewares, furniture
DONATION TAX RECEIPT: Receipt given upon request

Salvation Army Thrift Store
125 Wooster Rd. N
Barberton, OH 44203
TYPE OF MERCHANDISE: Clothing, housewares, furniture
DONATION TAX RECEIPT: Receipt given upon request

Salvation Army Thrift Store
210 Second St. NW
Barberton, OH 44203
TYPE OF MERCHANDISE: Clothing, housewares, furniture
DONATION TAX RECEIPT: Receipt given upon request

MCC Et Cetera Shop
111 S. Main St.
Bluffton, OH 45817
PHONE: 419-358-4201
TYPE OF MERCHANDISE: Clothing, housewares, furniture
DONATION TAX RECEIPT: Receipt given upon request

Volunteers of America
1053 N. Main St.
Bowling Green, OH 43402
TYPE OF MERCHANDISE: Clothing, housewares, furniture
DONATION TAX RECEIPT: Receipt given upon request

Salvation Army Thrift Store
309 S. Main St.
Bowling Green, OH 43402
TYPE OF MERCHANDISE: Clothing, housewares, furniture
DONATION TAX RECEIPT: Receipt given upon request

American Cancer Society Discovery Shop
2729 B. Fulton Rd. NW
Canton, OH 44718
TYPE OF MERCHANDISE: Clothing, bric-a-brac
DONATION TAX RECEIPT: Receipt given upon request
COMMENTS: Monthly markdowns

Goodwill Industries Thrift Store
2819 Whipple Ave. NW
CROSS STREETS: Hillsdale Shopping Center
Canton, OH 44708
CONTACT: Catherine Shahan
PHONE: 216-478-8500
HOURS: Mon.–Sat. 9–8, Sun. 12–6
TYPE OF MERCHANDISE: Clothing, housewares, furniture
DONATION TAX RECEIPT: Receipt given upon request

Salvation Army Thrift Store
315 Market Ave. N
Canton, OH 44702
TYPE OF MERCHANDISE: Clothing, housewares, furniture
DONATION TAX RECEIPT: Receipt given upon request

Salvation Army Thrift Store
3522 Lesh St. NE
Canton, OH 44705
TYPE OF MERCHANDISE: Clothing, housewares, furniture
DONATION TAX RECEIPT: Receipt given upon request

Goodwill Industries Thrift Store
408 Ninth St. SW
Canton, OH 44707
CONTACT: Betsy Shumaker
PHONE: 216-454-9462, 454-9465 Ext 508
HOURS: Mon. 9–8, Tues.–Wed. 9–6, Thurs.–Sat. 9–8, Sun. 12–6
TYPE OF MERCHANDISE: Clothing, housewares, furniture
DONATION TAX RECEIPT: Receipt given upon request

Salvation Army Thrift Store
4561 W. Tuscarawas St.
Canton, OH 44708
TYPE OF MERCHANDISE: Clothing, housewares, furniture
DONATION TAX RECEIPT: Receipt given upon request

Goodwill Industries Thrift Store
10600 Springfield Pike
Cincinnati, OH 45215
PHONE: 513-771-4804
TYPE OF MERCHANDISE: Clothing, housewares, furniture
DONATION TAX RECEIPT: Receipt given upon request

Saint Vincent De Paul Thrift Store
10800 Reading Rd.
Cincinnati, OH 45241
TYPE OF MERCHANDISE: Clothing, housewares, furniture
DONATION TAX RECEIPT: Receipt given upon request
COMMENTS: Monthly markdowns

Salvation Army Thrift Store
110 Mill St.
Cincinnati, OH 45215
TYPE OF MERCHANDISE: Clothing, housewares, furniture
DONATION TAX RECEIPT: Receipt given upon request

Saint Vincent De Paul Thrift Store
1125 Bank St.
Cincinnati, OH 45214
TYPE OF MERCHANDISE: Clothing, housewares, furniture
DONATION TAX RECEIPT: Receipt given upon request
COMMENTS: Monthly markdowns

Salvation Army Thrift Store
1826 Race St.
Cincinnati, OH 45210
TYPE OF MERCHANDISE: Clothing, housewares, furniture
DONATION TAX RECEIPT: Receipt given upon request

Salvation Army Thrift Store
2250 Park Ave.
Cincinnati, OH 45212
TYPE OF MERCHANDISE: Clothing, housewares, furniture
DONATION TAX RECEIPT: Receipt given upon request

Saint Vincent De Paul Thrift Store
2622 Vine St.
Cincinnati, OH 45219
TYPE OF MERCHANDISE: Clothing,
housewares, furniture
DONATION TAX RECEIPT: Receipt given
upon request
COMMENTS: Monthly markdowns

Saint Vincent De Paul Thrift Store
3198 Spring Grove Ave.
Cincinnati, OH 45225
TYPE OF MERCHANDISE: Clothing,
housewares, furniture
DONATION TAX RECEIPT: Receipt given
upon request
COMMENTS: Monthly markdowns

Saint Vincent De Paul Thrift Store
3717–19 St. Lawrence Ave.
Cincinnati, OH 45205
TYPE OF MERCHANDISE: Clothing,
housewares, furniture
DONATION TAX RECEIPT: Receipt given
upon request
COMMENTS: Monthly markdowns

Goodwill Industries Thrift Store
3980 N. Bend Rd.
Cincinnati, OH 45211
PHONE: 513-662-7080
TYPE OF MERCHANDISE: Clothing,
housewares, furniture
DONATION TAX RECEIPT: Receipt given
upon request

Amvets Thrift Store
4619 Montgomery Rd.
Cincinnati, OH 45212
TYPE OF MERCHANDISE: Clothing,
housewares
DONATION TAX RECEIPT: Receipt given
upon request
COMMENTS: Donation pickup service

Goodwill Industries Thrift Store
606 Mt. Moriah Dr.
Cincinnati, OH 45245
PHONE: 513-752-0067
TYPE OF MERCHANDISE: Clothing,
housewares, furniture
DONATION TAX RECEIPT: Receipt given
upon request

NCJW Thrift Shop
6200 Montgomery Rd.
Cincinnati, OH 45213
PHONE: 513-631-5545
HOURS: Mon.–Sat. 10–4
TYPE OF MERCHANDISE: Clothing,
housewares, furniture
DONATION TAX RECEIPT: Receipt given
upon request
COMMENTS: Semiannual 50% off and
$5 bag sale

Goodwill Industries Thrift Store
8340 Colerain Ave.
Cincinnati, OH 45239
PHONE: 513-245-0304
TYPE OF MERCHANDISE: Clothing,
housewares, furniture
DONATION TAX RECEIPT: Receipt given
upon request

Salvation Army Thrift Store
939 McMillian St.
Cincinnati, OH 45206
TYPE OF MERCHANDISE: Clothing,
housewares, furniture
DONATION TAX RECEIPT: Receipt given
upon request

Saint Vincent De Paul Thrift Store
10322 Lorain Ave.
Cleveland, OH 44111
TYPE OF MERCHANDISE: Clothing,
housewares, furniture
DONATION TAX RECEIPT: Receipt given
upon request
COMMENTS: Monthly markdowns

Salvation Army Thrift Store
11624 Lorain Ave.
Cleveland, OH 44111
TYPE OF MERCHANDISE: Clothing,
housewares, furniture
DONATION TAX RECEIPT: Receipt given
upon request

NCJW Thrift Shop
12611 Larchmere Blvd.
CROSS STREET: 1 block north of Shaker
Square
Cleveland, OH 44120
PHONE: 216-231-6060
HOURS: Mon.–Sat. 11–5

TYPE OF MERCHANDISE: Clothing, housewares, furniture
DONATION TAX RECEIPT: Receipt given upon request
COMMENTS: Annual designer dress days sale

American Cancer Society Discovery Shop
13130 Shaker Blvd.
Cleveland, OH 44120
CONTACT: Donna Jackson
PHONE: 216-295-0017
TYPE OF MERCHANDISE: Clothing, bric-a-brac
DONATION TAX RECEIPT: Receipt given upon request
COMMENTS: Monthly markdowns

Amvets Thrift Store
14805 St. Clair Ave.
Cleveland, OH 44110
TYPE OF MERCHANDISE: Clothing, housewares
DONATION TAX RECEIPT: Receipt given upon request

Goodwill Industries Thrift Store
16122 Lake Shore Blvd.
Cleveland, OH 44110
PHONE: 216-481-5152
HOURS: Mon.–Sat. 9–9, Sun. 9:30–6
TYPE OF MERCHANDISE: Clothing, housewares, furniture
DONATION TAX RECEIPT: Receipt given upon request

Saint Vincent De Paul Thrift Store
16730 Lorain Ave.
Cleveland, OH 44111
TYPE OF MERCHANDISE: Clothing, housewares, furniture
DONATION TAX RECEIPT: Receipt given upon request
COMMENTS: Monthly markdowns

Goodwill Industries Thrift Store
16940 Lorain Ave.
Cleveland, OH 44111
PHONE: 216-476-8330
HOURS: Mon.–Sat. 9–9, Sun. 9:30–6
TYPE OF MERCHANDISE: Clothing, housewares, furniture

DONATION TAX RECEIPT: Receipt given upon request

Salvation Army Thrift Store
1871 W. 25th St.
Cleveland, OH 44113
TYPE OF MERCHANDISE: Clothing, housewares, furniture
DONATION TAX RECEIPT: Receipt given upon request

Goodwill Industries Thrift Store
2295 E. 55th St.
CROSS STREET: Central
Cleveland, OH 44103
PHONE: 216-431-8309
HOURS: Mon.–Sat. 8:30–5
TYPE OF MERCHANDISE: Clothing, housewares, furniture
DONATION TAX RECEIPT: Receipt given upon request

Saint Vincent De Paul Thrift Store
3074 W. 25th St.
Cleveland, OH 44113
TYPE OF MERCHANDISE: Clothing, housewares, furniture
DONATION TAX RECEIPT: Receipt given upon request
COMMENTS: Monthly markdowns

Amvets Thrift Store
3201 W. 25th St.
Cleveland, OH 44109
TYPE OF MERCHANDISE: Clothing, housewares, furniture
DONATION TAX RECEIPT: Receipt given upon request

Salvation Army Thrift Store
4100 E. 71st St.
Cleveland, OH 44105
TYPE OF MERCHANDISE: Clothing, housewares, furniture
DONATION TAX RECEIPT: Receipt given upon request

Salvation Army Thrift Store
4125 Lee Rd.
Cleveland, OH 44128
TYPE OF MERCHANDISE: Clothing, housewares, furniture
DONATION TAX RECEIPT: Receipt given upon request

Salvation Army Thrift Store
5005 Euclid Ave.
Cleveland, OH 44103
TYPE OF MERCHANDISE: Clothing,
housewares, furniture
DONATION TAX RECEIPT: Receipt given
upon request

Saint Vincent De Paul Thrift Store
5309 Superior Ave.
Cleveland, OH 44103
TYPE OF MERCHANDISE: Clothing,
housewares, furniture
DONATION TAX RECEIPT: Receipt given
upon request
COMMENTS: Monthly markdowns

Saint Vincent De Paul Thrift Store
5462 Broadway
Cleveland, OH 44127
TYPE OF MERCHANDISE: Clothing,
housewares, furniture
DONATION TAX RECEIPT: Receipt given
upon request
COMMENTS: Monthly markdowns

Salvation Army Thrift Store
6107 Broadway
Cleveland, OH 44127
TYPE OF MERCHANDISE: Clothing,
housewares, furniture
DONATION TAX RECEIPT: Receipt given
upon request

Salvation Army Thrift Store
700 E. 185th St.
Cleveland, OH 44119
TYPE OF MERCHANDISE: Clothing,
housewares, furniture
DONATION TAX RECEIPT: Receipt given
upon request

Salvation Army Thrift Store
7503 Brookpark Rd.
Cleveland, OH 44129
TYPE OF MERCHANDISE: Clothing,
housewares, furniture
DONATION TAX RECEIPT: Receipt given
upon request

MCC Selfhelp Gift & Thrift Shop
35 S. Main St.
Columbiana, OH 44408
PHONE: 216-482-3667

TYPE OF MERCHANDISE: Clothing,
housewares
DONATION TAX RECEIPT: Receipt given
upon request

Junior League Nearly New Shop
3667 E. Broad St.
Columbus, OH 43213
CONTACT: Linda Pressman
PHONE: 614-231-7861
HOURS: Tues.–Sat. 10–5
TYPE OF MERCHANDISE: Clothing,
housewares, furniture
DONATION TAX RECEIPT: Receipt given
upon request
COMMENTS: Biannual "Bag sales"

Salvation Army Thrift Store
1936 N. Fourth St.
Columbus, OH 43201
PHONE: 614-294-1819
TYPE OF MERCHANDISE: Clothing,
housewares, furniture
DONATION TAX RECEIPT: Receipt given
upon request

Salvation Army Thrift Store
1957 Parsons Ave.
Columbus, OH 43207
TYPE OF MERCHANDISE: Clothing,
housewares, furniture
DONATION TAX RECEIPT: Receipt given
upon request

Salvation Army Thrift Store
24242 Macsway Rd.
Columbus, OH 43232
TYPE OF MERCHANDISE: Clothing,
housewares, furniture
DONATION TAX RECEIPT: Receipt given
upon request

Salvation Army Thrift Store
2632 Morse Rd.
Columbus, OH 43231
PHONE: 614-471-5080
TYPE OF MERCHANDISE: Clothing,
housewares, furniture
DONATION TAX RECEIPT: Receipt given
upon request

Salvation Army Thrift Store
2872 W. Broad St.
Columbus, OH 43204

PHONE: 614-272-8198
TYPE OF MERCHANDISE: Clothing,
housewares, furniture
DONATION TAX RECEIPT: Receipt given
upon request

Volunteers of America Thrift
3300 S. High St.
Columbus, OH 43207
TYPE OF MERCHANDISE: Clothing,
housewares, furniture
DONATION TAX RECEIPT: Receipt given
upon request

Saint Vincent De Paul Thrift Store
367 W. State St.
Columbus, OH 43215
TYPE OF MERCHANDISE: Clothing,
housewares, furniture
DONATION TAX RECEIPT: Receipt given
upon request
COMMENTS: Monthly markdowns

Salvation Army Thrift Store
420 Georgesville Rd.
Columbus, OH 43228
PHONE: 614-274-4550
HOURS: Mon.–Sat. 9–9
TYPE OF MERCHANDISE: Clothing,
housewares, furniture
DONATION TAX RECEIPT: Receipt given
upon request

Salvation Army Thrift Store
570 S. Front St.
Columbus, OH 43215
PHONE: 614-225-9608
TYPE OF MERCHANDISE: Clothing,
housewares, furniture
DONATION TAX RECEIPT: Receipt given
upon request

Saint Vincent De Paul Thrift Store
987 N. High St.
Columbus, OH 43201
TYPE OF MERCHANDISE: Clothing,
housewares, furniture
DONATION TAX RECEIPT: Receipt given
upon request
COMMENTS: Monthly markdowns

Goodwill Industries Thrift Store
360 W. Main Rd.
Conneaut, OH 44030
TYPE OF MERCHANDISE: Clothing,
housewares, furniture
DONATION TAX RECEIPT: Receipt given
upon request

Goodwill Industries Thrift Store
301 Main St.
Coshocton, OH 43812
TYPE OF MERCHANDISE: Clothing,
housewares, furniture
DONATION TAX RECEIPT: Receipt given
upon request

Salvation Army Thrift Store
2131 State Rd.
Cuyahoga Falls, OH 44223
TYPE OF MERCHANDISE: Clothing,
housewares, furniture
DONATION TAX RECEIPT: Receipt given
upon request

Saint Vincent De Paul Thrift Store
13 S Saint Clair St.
Dayton, OH
TYPE OF MERCHANDISE: Clothing,
housewares, furniture
DONATION TAX RECEIPT: Receipt given
upon request
COMMENTS: Monthly markdowns

Saint Vincent De Paul Thrift Store
141 Ringgold St.
Dayton, OH 45403
TYPE OF MERCHANDISE: Clothing,
housewares, furniture
DONATION TAX RECEIPT: Receipt given
upon request
COMMENTS: Monthly markdowns

Saint Vincent De Paul Thrift Store
18 W. Fifth St.
Dayton, OH 45402
TYPE OF MERCHANDISE: Clothing,
housewares, furniture
DONATION TAX RECEIPT: Receipt given
upon request
COMMENTS: Monthly markdowns

Salvation Army Thrift Store
3122 N. Main St.
Dayton, OH 45405
TYPE OF MERCHANDISE: Clothing,
housewares, furniture

DONATION TAX RECEIPT: Receipt given upon request

Saint Vincent De Paul Thrift Store
3968 Linden Ave.
Dayton, OH 45410
TYPE OF MERCHANDISE: Clothing, housewares, furniture
DONATION TAX RECEIPT: Receipt given upon request
COMMENTS: Monthly markdowns

Salvation Army Thrift Store
4143 Salem Ave.
Dayton, OH 45408
TYPE OF MERCHANDISE: Clothing, housewares, furniture
DONATION TAX RECEIPT: Receipt given upon request

Salvation Army Thrift Store
4287 W. Third St.
Dayton, OH 45417
TYPE OF MERCHANDISE: Clothing, housewares, furniture
DONATION TAX RECEIPT: Receipt given upon request

Goodwill Industries Thrift Store
501 E. Fifth St.
Dayton, OH 45402
TYPE OF MERCHANDISE: Clothing, housewares, furniture
DONATION TAX RECEIPT: Receipt given upon request

Salvation Army Thrift Store
5322 N. Dixie Highway
Dayton, OH 45414
TYPE OF MERCHANDISE: Clothing, housewares, furniture
DONATION TAX RECEIPT: Receipt given upon request

Saint Vincent De Paul Thrift Store
542 Xenia Ave.
Dayton, OH 45410
TYPE OF MERCHANDISE: Clothing, housewares, furniture
DONATION TAX RECEIPT: Receipt given upon request
COMMENTS: Monthly markdowns

Salvation Army Thrift Store
913 S. Patterson Blvd.
Dayton, OH 45402
TYPE OF MERCHANDISE: Clothing, housewares, furniture
DONATION TAX RECEIPT: Receipt given upon request

Salvation Army Thrift Store
554 W. Central Ave.
Delaware, OH 43015
TYPE OF MERCHANDISE: Clothing, housewares, furniture
DONATION TAX RECEIPT: Receipt given upon request

Goodwill Industries Thrift Store
515 Union Ave.
CROSS STREET: Heritage Square
Dover, OH 44622
CONTACT: Sally Moncman
PHONE: 216-364-4310
HOURS: Mon.–Sat. 9–8, Sun. 12–6
TYPE OF MERCHANDISE: Clothing, housewares, furniture
DONATION TAX RECEIPT: Receipt given upon request

American Cancer Society Discovery Shop
637 S. Abbe Rd.
Elyria, OH 44035
TYPE OF MERCHANDISE: Clothing, bric-a-brac
DONATION TAX RECEIPT: Receipt given upon request
COMMENTS: Monthly markdowns

Salvation Army Thrift Store
165 Cleveland St.
Elyria, OH 44035
TYPE OF MERCHANDISE: Clothing, housewares, furniture
DONATION TAX RECEIPT: Receipt given upon request

Salvation Army Thrift Store
57 S. Main St.
Englewood, OH 45322
TYPE OF MERCHANDISE: Clothing, housewares, furniture
DONATION TAX RECEIPT: Receipt given upon request

Salvation Army Thrift Store
22530 Lake Shore Blvd.
Euclid, OH 44123
TYPE OF MERCHANDISE: Clothing,
housewares, furniture
DONATION TAX RECEIPT: Receipt given
upon request
Saint Vincent De Paul Thrift Store
403 E. Spring St.
Fayette, OH 43521
TYPE OF MERCHANDISE: Clothing,
housewares, furniture
DONATION TAX RECEIPT: Receipt given
upon request
COMMENTS: Monthly markdowns
Salvation Army Thrift Store
461 E. Main St.
Findlay, OH 45840
TYPE OF MERCHANDISE: Clothing,
housewares, furniture
DONATION TAX RECEIPT: Receipt given
upon request
Salvation Army Thrift Store
509 N. Main St.
Findlay, OH 45830
TYPE OF MERCHANDISE: Clothing,
housewares, furniture
DONATION TAX RECEIPT: Receipt given
upon request
Saint Vincent De Paul Thrift Store
305 S. Main St.
Fostoria, OH 44830
TYPE OF MERCHANDISE: Clothing,
housewares, furniture
DONATION TAX RECEIPT: Receipt given
upon request
COMMENTS: Monthly markdowns
Goodwill Industries Thrift Store
311 S. Broadway
Greenville, OH 45331
TYPE OF MERCHANDISE: Clothing,
housewares, furniture
DONATION TAX RECEIPT: Receipt given
upon request
Saint Vincent De Paul Thrift Store
126 Pershing Ave.
Hamilton, OH 45011

TYPE OF MERCHANDISE: Clothing,
housewares, furniture
DONATION TAX RECEIPT: Receipt given
upon request
COMMENTS: Monthly markdowns
Salvation Army Thrift Store
1990–1996 S. Erie Highway
Hamilton, OH 45011
TYPE OF MERCHANDISE: Clothing,
housewares, furniture
DONATION TAX RECEIPT: Receipt given
upon request
Goodwill Industries Thrift Store
451 W. Second
Hamilton, OH 45011
TYPE OF MERCHANDISE: Clothing,
housewares, furniture
DONATION TAX RECEIPT: Receipt given
upon request
Goodwill Industries Thrift Store
1110 Harrison Ave.
Harrison, OH 45030
PHONE: 513-367-2495
TYPE OF MERCHANDISE: Clothing,
housewares, furniture
DONATION TAX RECEIPT: Receipt given
upon request
MCC Gift & Thrift Shoppe
1295 Edison St. NE
Hartville, OH 44632
PHONE: 216-877-2769
TYPE OF MERCHANDISE: Clothing,
housewares
DONATION TAX RECEIPT: Receipt given
upon request
Salvation Army Thrift Store
115 E. Hubert Ave.
Lancaster, OH 43130
TYPE OF MERCHANDISE: Clothing,
housewares, furniture
DONATION TAX RECEIPT: Receipt given
upon request
Salvation Army Thrift Store
123 E. Hubert St.
Lancaster, OH 43130
TYPE OF MERCHANDISE: Clothing,
housewares, furniture

DONATION TAX RECEIPT: Receipt given upon request

Goodwill Industries Thrift Store
10 S. Mechanic
Lebanon, OH 45036
PHONE: 513-932-6856
TYPE OF MERCHANDISE: Clothing, housewares, furniture
DONATION TAX RECEIPT: Receipt given upon request

Salvation Army Thrift Store
509 W. High St.
Lima, OH 45801
TYPE OF MERCHANDISE: Clothing, housewares, furniture
DONATION TAX RECEIPT: Receipt given upon request

Goodwill Industries Thrift Store
949 S. Main St.
Lima, OH 45804
TYPE OF MERCHANDISE: Clothing, housewares, furniture
DONATION TAX RECEIPT: Receipt given upon request

Salvation Army Thrift Store
110 Mills St.
Lockland, OH 45215
TYPE OF MERCHANDISE: Clothing, housewares, furniture
DONATION TAX RECEIPT: Receipt given upon request

Goodwill Industries Thrift Store
1600 Broadway
Lorain, OH 44052
TYPE OF MERCHANDISE: Clothing, housewares, furniture
DONATION TAX RECEIPT: Receipt given upon request

Salvation Army Thrift Store
2601 Broadway
Lorain, OH 44052
TYPE OF MERCHANDISE: Clothing, housewares, furniture
DONATION TAX RECEIPT: Receipt given upon request

Amvets Thrift Store
3020 Pearl Ave.
Lorain, OH 44055
TYPE OF MERCHANDISE: Clothing, housewares
DONATION TAX RECEIPT: Receipt given upon request

Goodwill Industries Thrift Store
920 Loveland-Madeira Rd.
Loveland, OH 45140
PHONE: 513-683-1151
TYPE OF MERCHANDISE: Clothing, housewares, furniture
DONATION TAX RECEIPT: Receipt given upon request

Salvation Army Thrift Store
Route 42/Ashland Rd.
Mansfield, OH 44903
TYPE OF MERCHANDISE: Clothing, housewares, furniture
DONATION TAX RECEIPT: Receipt given upon request

Goodwill Industries Thrift Store
5300 Northfield Rd.
CROSS STREET: Southgate Shopping Center
Maple Heights, OH 44137
PHONE: 216-662-5563
HOURS: Mon.–Sat. 9–9, Sun. 9:30–6
TYPE OF MERCHANDISE: Clothing, housewares, furniture
DONATION TAX RECEIPT: Receipt given upon request

Salvation Army Thrift Store
1101 Mt. Vernon Ave.
Marion, OH 43302
TYPE OF MERCHANDISE: Clothing, housewares, furniture
DONATION TAX RECEIPT: Receipt given upon request

Goodwill Industries Thrift Store
2424 Lincolnway E
CROSS STREET: Massillon Village Center
Massillon, OH 44646
CONTACT: Joyce Lewis
PHONE: 216-833-4700
HOURS: Mon.–Sat. 9–8, Sun. 12–6
TYPE OF MERCHANDISE: Clothing, housewares, furniture
DONATION TAX RECEIPT: Receipt given upon request

Goodwill Industries Thrift Store
125 Erie St. N
Massillon, OH 44646
TYPE OF MERCHANDISE: Clothing,
housewares, furniture
DONATION TAX RECEIPT: Receipt given
upon request

Goodwill Industries Thrift Store
110 W. Liberty St.
Medina, OH 44256
TYPE OF MERCHANDISE: Clothing,
housewares, furniture
DONATION TAX RECEIPT: Receipt given
upon request

Salvation Army Thrift Store
57–59 S. Main St.
Miamisburg, OH 45342
TYPE OF MERCHANDISE: Clothing,
housewares, furniture
DONATION TAX RECEIPT: Receipt given
upon request

Salvation Army Thrift Store
8065 Southwind Dr.
Miamisburg, OH 45459
TYPE OF MERCHANDISE: Clothing,
housewares, furniture
DONATION TAX RECEIPT: Receipt given
upon request

Salvation Army Thrift Store
712 S. Breiel Blvd.
Middletown, OH 45042
TYPE OF MERCHANDISE: Clothing,
housewares, furniture
DONATION TAX RECEIPT: Receipt given
upon request

Goodwill Industries Thrift Store
733 Hwy. 28
Milford, OH 45150
TYPE OF MERCHANDISE: Clothing,
housewares, furniture
DONATION TAX RECEIPT: Receipt given
upon request

Saint Vincent De Paul Thrift Store
813 Main St.
Milford, OH 45150
TYPE OF MERCHANDISE: Clothing,
housewares, furniture

DONATION TAX RECEIPT: Receipt given
upon request
COMMENTS: Monthly markdowns

MCC Save'n Serve Shop
South Mad Anthony St.
Millersburg, OH 44654
PHONE: 216-674-1323
TYPE OF MERCHANDISE: Clothing,
housewares
DONATION TAX RECEIPT: Receipt given
upon request

Salvation Army Thrift Store
8061 Hamilton Ave.
Mt. Healthy, OH 45231
TYPE OF MERCHANDISE: Clothing,
housewares, furniture
DONATION TAX RECEIPT: Receipt given
upon request

Goodwill Industries Thrift Store
14 E. Ohio Ave.
Mt. Vernon, OH 43050
TYPE OF MERCHANDISE: Clothing,
housewares, furniture
DONATION TAX RECEIPT: Receipt given
upon request

Salvation Army Thrift Store
14 E. Gambier St.
Mt. Vernon, OH 43050
TYPE OF MERCHANDISE: Clothing,
housewares, furniture
DONATION TAX RECEIPT: Receipt given
upon request

Salvation Army Thrift Store
1409 N. Scott St.
Napoleon, OH 43545
TYPE OF MERCHANDISE: Clothing,
housewares, furniture
DONATION TAX RECEIPT: Receipt given
upon request

Salvation Army Thrift Store
34 S. Fifth Ave.
Newark, OH 43055
TYPE OF MERCHANDISE: Clothing,
housewares, furniture
DONATION TAX RECEIPT: Receipt given
upon request

Goodwill Industries Thrift Store
23359 Lorain Ave.
N. Olmsted, OH 44070
PHONE: 216-777-4422
HOURS: Mon.–Sat. 9–9, Sun. 9:30–6
TYPE OF MERCHANDISE: Clothing,
housewares, furniture
DONATION TAX RECEIPT: Receipt given
upon request

Salvation Army Thrift Store
4633 Northfield Rd.
N. Randall, OH 44128
TYPE OF MERCHANDISE: Clothing,
housewares, furniture
DONATION TAX RECEIPT: Receipt given
upon request

Salvation Army Thrift Store
4211 N. Woodville Rd.
Northwood, OH 43616
TYPE OF MERCHANDISE: Clothing,
housewares, furniture
DONATION TAX RECEIPT: Receipt given
upon request

Salvation Army Thrift Store
3200 Greenwich Rd.
Norton, OH 44203
TYPE OF MERCHANDISE: Clothing,
housewares, furniture
DONATION TAX RECEIPT: Receipt given
upon request

Saint Vincent De Paul Thrift Store
4607 Montgomery Rd.
Norwood, OH 45212
TYPE OF MERCHANDISE: Clothing,
housewares, furniture
DONATION TAX RECEIPT: Receipt given
upon request
COMMENTS: Monthly markdowns

Salvation Army Thrift Store
2250 Park Ave.
Norwood, OH 45212
TYPE OF MERCHANDISE: Clothing,
housewares, furniture
DONATION TAX RECEIPT: Receipt given
upon request

MCC Global Treasures
116 N. Main St.
Orrville, OH 44667
PHONE: 216-683-6143

TYPE OF MERCHANDISE: Clothing,
housewares, furniture
DONATION TAX RECEIPT: Receipt given
upon request

Goodwill Industries Thrift Store
137 Richmond St.
Painesville, OH 44077
TYPE OF MERCHANDISE: Clothing,
housewares, furniture
DONATION TAX RECEIPT: Receipt given
upon request

Goodwill Industries Thrift Store
6339 Olde York Rd.
Parma Heights, OH 44130
PHONE: 216-842-2228
HOURS: Mon.–Sat. 9–9, Sun. 9:30–6
TYPE OF MERCHANDISE: Clothing,
housewares, furniture
DONATION TAX RECEIPT: Receipt given
upon request

Goodwill Industries Thrift Store
8252 N. Miami County Rd.
Piqua, OH 45356
TYPE OF MERCHANDISE: Clothing,
housewares, furniture
DONATION TAX RECEIPT: Receipt given
upon request

Goodwill Industries Thrift Store
1036 W. Main St.
Ravenna, OH 44266
TYPE OF MERCHANDISE: Clothing,
housewares, furniture
DONATION TAX RECEIPT: Receipt given
upon request

Salvation Army Thrift Store
1130 Cleveland Ave.
Sandusky, OH 44870
TYPE OF MERCHANDISE: Clothing,
housewares, furniture
DONATION TAX RECEIPT: Receipt given
upon request

Goodwill Industries Thrift Store
419 W. Market St.
Sandusky, OH 44870
TYPE OF MERCHANDISE: Clothing,
housewares, furniture
DONATION TAX RECEIPT: Receipt given
upon request

Goodwill Industries Thrift Store
291 E. Leffel Ln.
Springfield, OH 45505
TYPE OF MERCHANDISE: Clothing,
housewares, furniture
DONATION TAX RECEIPT: Receipt given
upon request

Salvation Army Thrift Store
403 E. Main St.
Springfield, OH 45503
TYPE OF MERCHANDISE: Clothing,
housewares, furniture
DONATION TAX RECEIPT: Receipt given
upon request

Saint Vincent De Paul Thrift Store
6633 New Carlisle Pike
Springfield, OH 45505
TYPE OF MERCHANDISE: Clothing,
housewares, furniture
DONATION TAX RECEIPT: Receipt given
upon request
COMMENTS: Monthly markdowns

Salvation Army Thrift Store
810 Bechtle Ave.
Springfield, OH 45502
TYPE OF MERCHANDISE: Clothing,
housewares, furniture
DONATION TAX RECEIPT: Receipt given
upon request

Saint Vincent De Paul Thrift Store
184 S. Washington
Tiffin, OH 44883
TYPE OF MERCHANDISE: Clothing,
housewares, furniture
DONATION TAX RECEIPT: Receipt given
upon request
COMMENTS: Monthly markdowns

Saint Vincent De Paul Thrift Store
1001 Washington St.
Toledo, OH 43624
TYPE OF MERCHANDISE: Clothing,
housewares, furniture
DONATION TAX RECEIPT: Receipt given
upon request
COMMENTS: Monthly markdowns

Salvation Army Thrift Store
1123–27 Reynolds Rd.
Toledo, OH 43615

TYPE OF MERCHANDISE: Clothing,
housewares, furniture
DONATION TAX RECEIPT: Receipt given
upon request

Salvation Army Thrift Store
1341 N. Reynolds Rd.
Toledo, OH 43615
TYPE OF MERCHANDISE: Clothing,
housewares, furniture
DONATION TAX RECEIPT: Receipt given
upon request

Goodwill Industries Thrift Store
1625 Broadway
Toledo, OH 43609
TYPE OF MERCHANDISE: Clothing,
housewares, furniture
DONATION TAX RECEIPT: Receipt given
upon request

Salvation Army Thrift Store
1856 Sylvania Ave.
Toledo, OH 43613
TYPE OF MERCHANDISE: Clothing,
housewares, furniture
DONATION TAX RECEIPT: Receipt given
upon request

Goodwill Industries Thrift Store
1939 W. Laskey Rd.
Toledo, OH 43613
TYPE OF MERCHANDISE: Clothing,
housewares, furniture
DONATION TAX RECEIPT: Receipt given
upon request

Salvation Army Thrift Store
27 Moorish Ave.
Toledo, OH 43602
TYPE OF MERCHANDISE: Clothing,
housewares, furniture
DONATION TAX RECEIPT: Receipt given
upon request

Goodwill Industries Thrift Store
3024 Monroe St.
Toledo, OH 43606
TYPE OF MERCHANDISE: Clothing,
housewares, furniture
DONATION TAX RECEIPT: Receipt given
upon request

Salvation Army Thrift Store
3535 Stickney Ave.
Toledo, OH 43608
TYPE OF MERCHANDISE: Clothing,
housewares, furniture
DONATION TAX RECEIPT: Receipt given
upon request

Salvation Army Thrift Store
4211 Woodville Rd.
Toledo, OH 43619
TYPE OF MERCHANDISE: Clothing,
housewares, furniture
DONATION TAX RECEIPT: Receipt given
upon request

Goodwill Industries Thrift Store
525 Cherry St.
Toledo, OH 43604
TYPE OF MERCHANDISE: Clothing,
housewares, furniture
DONATION TAX RECEIPT: Receipt given
upon request

Goodwill Industries Thrift Store
530 S. Saint Clair St.
Toledo, OH 43602
TYPE OF MERCHANDISE: Clothing,
housewares, furniture
DONATION TAX RECEIPT: Receipt given
upon request

Salvation Army Thrift Store
223 E. Main St.
Troy, OH 45373
TYPE OF MERCHANDISE: Clothing,
housewares, furniture
DONATION TAX RECEIPT: Receipt given
upon request

Goodwill Industries Thrift Store
275 McCauley Dr.
CROSS STREET: Claymont Center
Uhrichsville, OH 44683
PHONE: 614-922-6330
HOURS: Mon. 9–8, Tues.–Wed. 9–6,
Thurs.–Sat. 9–8, Sun. 12–6
TYPE OF MERCHANDISE: Clothing,
housewares, furniture
DONATION TAX RECEIPT: Receipt given
upon request

Salvation Army Thrift Store
Route 32
Union Township, OH 45245

TYPE OF MERCHANDISE: Clothing,
housewares, furniture
DONATION TAX RECEIPT: Receipt given
upon request

Salvation Army Thrift Store
2680 Youngstown Rd.
Warren, OH 44481
TYPE OF MERCHANDISE: Clothing,
housewares, furniture
DONATION TAX RECEIPT: Receipt given
upon request

Salvation Army Thrift Store
2720 Mahoning Ave.
Warren, OH 44483
TYPE OF MERCHANDISE: Clothing,
housewares, furniture
DONATION TAX RECEIPT: Receipt given
upon request

MCC Global Crafts
106 N. Detroit St.
West Liberty, OH 43357
PHONE: 513-465-3077
TYPE OF MERCHANDISE: Clothing,
housewares
DONATION TAX RECEIPT: Receipt given
upon request

Goodwill Industries Thrift Store
30800 Lake Shore Blvd.
Willoughby, OH 44095
TYPE OF MERCHANDISE: Clothing,
housewares, furniture
DONATION TAX RECEIPT: Receipt given
upon request

Salvation Army Thrift Store
29429 Lakeshore Blvd.
Willowick, OH 44095
TYPE OF MERCHANDISE: Clothing,
housewares, furniture
DONATION TAX RECEIPT: Receipt given
upon request

Goodwill Industries Thrift Store
30604 Lake Shore Blvd.
Willowick, OH 44095
PHONE: 216-944-9201
HOURS: Mon.–Sat. 9–9, Sun. 9:30–6
TYPE OF MERCHANDISE: Clothing,
housewares, furniture
DONATION TAX RECEIPT: Receipt given
upon request

Goodwill Industries Thrift Store
904 Cadiz Rd.
Wintersville, OH 43952
CONTACT: John Foley
PHONE: 614-264-6000
HOURS: Mon.–Sat. 9–8, Sun. 12–6
TYPE OF MERCHANDISE: Clothing,
housewares, furniture
DONATION TAX RECEIPT: Receipt given
upon request

Saint Vincent De Paul Thrift Store
B7-534 Bantam Ridge R.R. 2
Wintersville, OH 43952
TYPE OF MERCHANDISE: Clothing,
housewares, furniture
DONATION TAX RECEIPT: Receipt given
upon request
COMMENTS: Monthly markdowns

Goodwill Industries Thrift Store
87 E. Main St.
Xenia, OH 45385-3201
TYPE OF MERCHANDISE: Clothing,
housewares, furniture
DONATION TAX RECEIPT: Receipt given
upon request

Salvation Army Thrift Store
2942 Mccartney Rd.
Youngstown, OH 44505
TYPE OF MERCHANDISE: Clothing,
housewares, furniture
DONATION TAX RECEIPT: Receipt given
upon request

American Cancer Society Discovery Shop
143 Boardman Canfield Rd.
Youngstown, OH 44512
TYPE OF MERCHANDISE: Clothing, bric-a-
brac
DONATION TAX RECEIPT: Receipt given
upon request
COMMENTS: Monthly markdowns

Saint Vincent De Paul Thrift Store
235 Wick Ave.
Youngstown, OH 44503
TYPE OF MERCHANDISE: Clothing,
housewares, furniture
DONATION TAX RECEIPT: Receipt given
upon request
COMMENTS: Monthly markdowns

Salvation Army Thrift Store
574 Mahoning Ave.
Youngstown, OH 44502
TYPE OF MERCHANDISE: Clothing,
housewares, furniture
DONATION TAX RECEIPT: Receipt given
upon request

Oklahoma

Salvation Army Thrift Store
115 N. Oak Ave.
Ada, OK 74820
TYPE OF MERCHANDISE: Clothing,
housewares, furniture
DONATION TAX RECEIPT: Receipt given
upon request

Goodwill Industries Thrift Store
214 N. Main
Altus, OK 73521
PHONE: 405-482-8294
HOURS: Mon.–Sat. 9–6
TYPE OF MERCHANDISE: Clothing,
housewares, furniture
DONATION TAX RECEIPT: Receipt given
upon request
COMMENTS: Tag sales daily, weekly senior
discount

Salvation Army Thrift Store
1 W. Broadway
Ardmore, OK 73401
TYPE OF MERCHANDISE: Clothing,
housewares, furniture
DONATION TAX RECEIPT: Receipt given
upon request

Goodwill Industries Thrift Store
3816 E. Frank Phillips Blvd.
Bartlesville, OK 74006
TYPE OF MERCHANDISE: Clothing,
housewares, furniture
DONATION TAX RECEIPT: Receipt given
upon request

Salvation Army Thrift Store
122 N. Fifth St.
Chickasha, OK 73018
TYPE OF MERCHANDISE: Clothing,
housewares, furniture
DONATION TAX RECEIPT: Receipt given
upon request

Goodwill Industries Thrift Store
419 Chickasha Ave.
CROSS STREET: Fourth
Chickasha, OK 73018
PHONE: 405-224-2970
HOURS: Mon.–Sat. 9–6
TYPE OF MERCHANDISE: Clothing,
housewares, furniture
DONATION TAX RECEIPT: Receipt given
upon request
COMMENTS: Tag sales daily, weekly senior
discount

Salvation Army Thrift Store
420 W. Chickasha Ave.
Chickasha, OK 73018
TYPE OF MERCHANDISE: Clothing,
housewares, furniture
DONATION TAX RECEIPT: Receipt given
upon request

Goodwill Industries Thrift Store
1204 Lynn Riggs Blvd.
Claremore, OK 74017
TYPE OF MERCHANDISE: Clothing,
housewares, furniture
DONATION TAX RECEIPT: Receipt given
upon request

Goodwill Industries Thrift Store
605 W. Main St.
Duncan, OK 73533
PHONE: 405-252-0921
HOURS: Mon.–Sat. 9–6
TYPE OF MERCHANDISE: Clothing,
housewares, furniture
DONATION TAX RECEIPT: Receipt given
upon request
COMMENTS: Tag sales daily, weekly senior
discount

Goodwill Industries Thrift Store
606 Main St.
Duncan, OK 73533
TYPE OF MERCHANDISE: Clothing,
housewares, furniture
DONATION TAX RECEIPT: Receipt given
upon request

Salvation Army Thrift Store
516 N. Independence St.
Enid, OK 73701
TYPE OF MERCHANDISE: Clothing,
housewares, furniture

DONATION TAX RECEIPT: Receipt given
upon request

Goodwill Industries Thrift Store
1203 W. Lee Blvd.
CROSS STREET: 11th
Lawton, OK 73501
PHONE: 405-353-9503
HOURS: Mon.–Sat. 9–6
TYPE OF MERCHANDISE: Clothing,
housewares, furniture
DONATION TAX RECEIPT: Receipt given
upon request
COMMENTS: Tag sales daily, weekly senior
discount

Salvation Army Thrift Store
1742 W. Lindsey
CROSS STREET: McGee
Norman, OK 73071
PHONE: 405-364-0126
HOURS: Mon.–Sat. 9:30–5:30
TYPE OF MERCHANDISE: Clothing,
housewares, furniture
DONATION TAX RECEIPT: Receipt given
upon request
COMMENTS: Half-price sales

Junior League Remarkable Shop
1010 N. Virginia Ave.
Oklahoma City, OK 73106-2445
CONTACT: Kraid Fuller
PHONE: 405-236-5078
HOURS: Mon.–Sat. 10–5:30,
Tues., Thurs. 10–7
TYPE OF MERCHANDISE: Clothing,
housewares, vintage collectibles
DONATION TAX RECEIPT: Receipt given
upon request
COMMENTS: Promotional sales
throughout the year

Salvation Army Thrift Store
1740 N.E. 23rd St.
Oklahoma City, OK 73111
TYPE OF MERCHANDISE: Clothing,
housewares, furniture
DONATION TAX RECEIPT: Receipt given
upon request

Goodwill Industries Thrift Store
1821 N.E. 23rd St.
Oklahoma City, OK 73111

TYPE OF MERCHANDISE: Clothing, housewares, furniture
DONATION TAX RECEIPT: Receipt given upon request
Goodwill Industries Thrift Store
2409 N. Janeway Ave.
Oklahoma City, OK 73160
TYPE OF MERCHANDISE: Clothing, housewares, furniture
DONATION TAX RECEIPT: Receipt given upon request
Junior League Designer Consignor
2636 W. Britton Rd.
Oklahoma City, OK 73120
CONTACT: Nita Ebert
PHONE: 405-749-5171
HOURS: Mon.–Sat. 10–5:30
TYPE OF MERCHANDISE: Women's and children's clothing
DONATION TAX RECEIPT: Receipt given upon request
COMMENTS: Some consignments taken at 50%
Salvation Army Thrift Store
2700 S. Robinson
CROSS STREET: S.W. 27th St.
Oklahoma City, OK 73109
PHONE: 405-235-6892
HOURS: Mon.–Sat. 9:30–5:30
TYPE OF MERCHANDISE: Clothing, furniture, appliances
DONATION TAX RECEIPT: Receipt given upon request
Disabled American Vets Thrift Store
3436 S.W. 29th St.
Oklahoma City, OK 73119
TYPE OF MERCHANDISE: Clothing, housewares
DONATION TAX RECEIPT: Receipt given upon request
Disabled American Vets Thrift Store
3633 N.W. 39th St.
Oklahoma City, OK 73112-6309
TYPE OF MERCHANDISE: Clothing, housewares
DONATION TAX RECEIPT: Receipt given upon request

Goodwill Industries Thrift Store
400 S. Walker Ave.
Oklahoma City, OK 73109
TYPE OF MERCHANDISE: Clothing, housewares, furniture
DONATION TAX RECEIPT: Receipt given upon request
Goodwill Industries Thrift Store
4024 N.W. Tenth St.
Oklahoma City, OK 73107-6064
TYPE OF MERCHANDISE: Clothing, housewares, furniture
DONATION TAX RECEIPT: Receipt given upon request
Goodwill Industries Thrift Store
410 S.W. Third St.
Oklahoma City, OK 73109
TYPE OF MERCHANDISE: Clothing, housewares, furniture
DONATION TAX RECEIPT: Receipt given upon request
Salvation Army Thrift Store
4513 S. May
CROSS STREET: S.W. 44th St.
Oklahoma City, OK 73119-4601
PHONE: 405-685-7023
HOURS: Mon.–Sat. 9:30–5:30
TYPE OF MERCHANDISE: Furniture, clothing, collectibles
DONATION TAX RECEIPT: Receipt given upon request
Salvation Army Thrift Store
6469 N. Macarthur
CROSS STREET: N.W. 63rd St.
Oklahoma City, OK 73132
PHONE: 405-721-5422
HOURS: Mon.–Sat. 9:30–5:30
TYPE OF MERCHANDISE: Furniture, clothing, collectibles
DONATION TAX RECEIPT: Receipt given upon request
COMMENTS: Half-price sales
Salvation Army Thrift Store
824 N. Pennsylvania Ave.
CROSS STREETS: Btw. N.W. Seventh and N.W. Eighth St.
Oklahoma City, OK 73107
PHONE: 405-286-3060

FAX: 405-232-5841
HOURS: Mon.–Sat. 9:30–5:30
TYPE OF MERCHANDISE: Clothing,
furniture, appliances
DONATION TAX RECEIPT: Receipt given
upon request
COMMENTS: "As Is" auction 9 A.M. Mon.,
Wed., Fri.
Salvation Army Thrift Store
200 E. Ninth St.
Shawnee, OK 74801
TYPE OF MERCHANDISE: Clothing,
housewares, furniture
DONATION TAX RECEIPT: Receipt given
upon request
Goodwill Industries Thrift Store
102 S. Garnett Rd.
Tulsa, OK 74128
TYPE OF MERCHANDISE: Clothing,
housewares, furniture
DONATION TAX RECEIPT: Receipt given
upon request
Goodwill Industries Thrift Store
1447 N. Yale Ave.
Tulsa, OK 74115
TYPE OF MERCHANDISE: Clothing,
housewares, furniture
DONATION TAX RECEIPT: Receipt given
upon request
Goodwill Industries Thrift Store
1920 S. Garnett Rd.
Tulsa, OK 74128
TYPE OF MERCHANDISE: Clothing,
housewares, furniture
DONATION TAX RECEIPT: Receipt given
upon request
Salvation Army Thrift Store
2132 S. Sheridan
CROSS STREET: 21st
Tulsa, OK 74129
HOURS: Mon.–Sat. 10–6
TYPE OF MERCHANDISE: Clothing,
housewares, furniture
DONATION TAX RECEIPT: Receipt given
upon request
COMMENTS: Monthly sales
Goodwill Industries Thrift Store
2800 Southwest Blvd.
Tulsa, OK 74107

TYPE OF MERCHANDISE: Clothing,
housewares, furniture
DONATION TAX RECEIPT: Receipt given
upon request
Salvation Army Thrift Store
4404 S. Peoria
CROSS STREET: 44th
Tulsa, OK 74105
CONTACT: Jon Wright
PHONE: 918-747-5272
HOURS: Mon.–Sat. 10–6
TYPE OF MERCHANDISE: Clothing,
housewares, furniture
DONATION TAX RECEIPT: Receipt given
upon request
COMMENTS: Monthly sales
National Assistance League Bargain A.L.
501 S. Lewis
Tulsa, OK 74104
PHONE: 918-587-5144
TYPE OF MERCHANDISE: Clothing,
housewares, furniture
DONATION TAX RECEIPT: Receipt given
upon request
COMMENTS: Monthly markdowns
Salvation Army Thrift Store
601 N. Main St.
Tulsa, OK 74106
COMMENTS: Guy K. Nickum
TYPE OF MERCHANDISE: Clothing,
housewares, furniture
DONATION TAX RECEIPT: Receipt given
upon request
Disabled American Vets Thrift Store
6336 E. Fourth Pl.
Tulsa, OK 74112
TYPE OF MERCHANDISE: Clothing,
housewares
DONATION TAX RECEIPT: Receipt given
upon request
MCC Et Cetera Shop
121 N. State St.
Weatherford, OK 73096
PHONE: 405-772-7531
TYPE OF MERCHANDISE: Clothing,
housewares
DONATION TAX RECEIPT: Receipt given
upon request

Oregon

Salvation Army Thrift Store
  1224 Santiam Hwy. SE
  Albany, OR 97321
  TYPE OF MERCHANDISE: Clothing,
  housewares, furniture
  DONATION TAX RECEIPT: Receipt given
  upon request

Salvation Army Thrift Store
  223 Second Ave. SW
  Albany, OR 97321
  TYPE OF MERCHANDISE: Clothing,
  housewares, furniture
  DONATION TAX RECEIPT: Receipt given
  upon request

Saint Vincent De Paul Thrift Store
  1465 Grand Ave.
  Astoria, OR 97103
  TYPE OF MERCHANDISE: Clothing,
  housewares, furniture
  DONATION TAX RECEIPT: Receipt given
  upon request
  COMMENTS: Monthly markdowns

Goodwill Industries Thrift Store
  4700 S.W. Griffith Dr.
  Beaverton, OR 97005
  TYPE OF MERCHANDISE: Clothing,
  housewares, furniture
  DONATION TAX RECEIPT: Receipt given
  upon request

Saint Vincent De Paul Thrift Store
  401 N.E. Second St.
  Bend, OR 97709
  TYPE OF MERCHANDISE: Clothing,
  housewares, furniture
  DONATION TAX RECEIPT: Receipt given
  upon request
  COMMENTS: Monthly markdowns

Saint Vincent De Paul Thrift Store
  950 S.E. Third St.
  Bend, OR 97709
  TYPE OF MERCHANDISE: Clothing,
  housewares, furniture
  DONATION TAX RECEIPT: Receipt given
  upon request
  COMMENTS: Monthly markdowns

Salvation Army Thrift Store
  957 N.E. First St.
  Bend, OR 97701
  TYPE OF MERCHANDISE: Clothing,
  housewares, furniture
  DONATION TAX RECEIPT: Receipt given
  upon request

Goodwill Industries Thrift Store
  922 N.W. Kings Blvd.
  Corvallis, OR 97330
  TYPE OF MERCHANDISE: Clothing,
  housewares, furniture
  DONATION TAX RECEIPT: Receipt given
  upon request

Goodwill Industries Thrift Store
  501 E. Main St.
  Cottage Grove, OR 97424
  TYPE OF MERCHANDISE: Clothing,
  housewares, furniture
  DONATION TAX RECEIPT: Receipt given
  upon request

Saint Vincent De Paul Thrift Store
  110 E. 11th Ave.
  Eugene, OR 97401-3537
  TYPE OF MERCHANDISE: Clothing,
  housewares, furniture
  DONATION TAX RECEIPT: Receipt given
  upon request
  COMMENTS: Monthly markdowns

National Assistance League Thrift Shop
  1149 Williamette St.
  Eugene, OR 97401
  PHONE: 503-485-3721
  TYPE OF MERCHANDISE: Clothing,
  housewares, furniture
  DONATION TAX RECEIPT: Receipt given
  upon request
  COMMENTS: Monthly markdowns

American Cancer Society Discovery Shop
  1412 Pearl
  Eugene, OR 97401
  PHONE: 503-484-2843
  TYPE OF MERCHANDISE: Clothing, bric-a-
  brac
  DONATION TAX RECEIPT: Receipt given
  upon request
  COMMENTS: Monthly markdowns

Junior League Thrift of Eugene
2839 Williamette St.
Eugene, OR 97405
TYPE OF MERCHANDISE: Clothing for men, women, and children
DONATION TAX RECEIPT: Receipt given upon request

Salvation Army Thrift Store
451 W. 111th Ave.
Eugene, OR 97401
TYPE OF MERCHANDISE: Clothing, housewares, furniture
DONATION TAX RECEIPT: Receipt given upon request

Saint Vincent De Paul Thrift Store
705 S. Seneca St.
Eugene, OR, 97402
TYPE OF MERCHANDISE: Clothing, housewares, furniture
DONATION TAX RECEIPT: Receipt given upon request
COMMENTS: Monthly markdowns

Salvation Army Thrift Store
143 N.W. "E" St.
Grants Pass, OR 97526
TYPE OF MERCHANDISE: Clothing, housewares, furniture
DONATION TAX RECEIPT: Receipt given upon request

Saint Vincent De Paul Thrift Store
220 S.W. "H" St.
Grants Pass, OR 97526
TYPE OF MERCHANDISE: Clothing, housewares, furniture
DONATION TAX RECEIPT: Receipt given upon request
COMMENTS: Monthly markdowns

Salvation Army Thrift Store
1311 E. Powell
Gresham, OR 97030
TYPE OF MERCHANDISE: Clothing, housewares, furniture
DONATION TAX RECEIPT: Receipt given upon request

American Cancer Society Discovery Shop
200 N.E Second St.
Gresham, OR 97030
CONTACT: Reva Ortez

PHONE: 503-669-0431
TYPE OF MERCHANDISE: clothing, bric-a-brac
DONATION TAX RECEIPT: Receipt given upon request
COMMENTS: Monthly markdowns

Goodwill Industries Thrift Store
200 N.E. Second St.
Gresham, OR 97030
TYPE OF MERCHANDISE: Clothing, housewares, furniture
DONATION TAX RECEIPT: Receipt given upon request

Goodwill Industries Thrift Store
S. Hwy. 395
Hermiston, OR 97838
TYPE OF MERCHANDISE: Clothing, housewares, furniture
DONATION TAX RECEIPT: Receipt given upon request

Salvation Army Thrift Store
2055 Tualatin Valley
Hillsboro, OR 97123
TYPE OF MERCHANDISE: Clothing, housewares, furniture
DONATION TAX RECEIPT: Receipt given upon request

Saint Vincent De Paul Thrift Store
646 S.W. Oak
Hillsboro, OR 97123
TYPE OF MERCHANDISE: Clothing, housewares, furniture
DONATION TAX RECEIPT: Receipt given upon request
COMMENTS: Monthly markdowns

Goodwill Industries Thrift Store
757 Ivy St.
Junction City, OR 97448
TYPE OF MERCHANDISE: Clothing, housewares, furniture
DONATION TAX RECEIPT: Receipt given upon request

Humane Society Thrift Shop
831 Main St.
Klamath Falls, OR 97601
TYPE OF MERCHANDISE: Clothing, housewares
DONATION TAX RECEIPT: Receipt given upon request

Saint Vincent De Paul Thrift Store
51500 Hwy. 97
La Pine, OR 97739
TYPE OF MERCHANDISE: Clothing,
housewares, furniture
DONATION TAX RECEIPT: Receipt given
upon request
COMMENTS: Monthly markdowns

MCC Et Cetera Shop
836 Main St.
Lebanon, OR 97355
PHONE: 503-258-3938
TYPE OF MERCHANDISE: Clothing,
housewares, furniture
DONATION TAX RECEIPT: Receipt given
upon request

American Cancer Society Discovery Shop
31 W. Sixth St.
Medford, OR 97501
CONTACT: Ann Collins
PHONE: 503-799-6091
TYPE OF MERCHANDISE: Clothing, bric-a-
brac
DONATION TAX RECEIPT: Receipt given
upon request
COMMENTS: Monthly markdowns

Goodwill Industries Thrift Store
7561d Crater Lake Hwy.
Medford, OR 97503
TYPE OF MERCHANDISE: Clothing,
housewares, furniture
DONATION TAX RECEIPT: Receipt given
upon request

Salvation Army Thrift Store
922 N. Central Ave.
Medford,OR 97501
TYPE OF MERCHANDISE: Clothing,
housewares, furniture
DONATION TAX RECEIPT: Receipt given
upon request

Saint Vincent De Paul Thrift Store
10574 S.E. 32nd
Milwaukie, OR 97222
TYPE OF MERCHANDISE: Clothing,
housewares, furniture
DONATION TAX RECEIPT: Receipt given
upon request
COMMENTS: Monthly markdowns

TVI Value Village Thrift Store
18625 S.E. McLoughlin Blvd.
Milwaukie, OR 97222
CONTACT: Matt Butler
PHONE: 503-653-7333
HOURS: Mon.–Sat. 9–9, Sun. 10–6
TYPE OF MERCHANDISE: Clothing,
housewares, furniture
DONATION TAX RECEIPT: No

Saint Vincent De Paul Thrift Store
126 N. Main St.
Myrtle Creek, OR 97457
TYPE OF MERCHANDISE: Clothing,
housewares, furniture
DONATION TAX RECEIPT: Receipt given
upon request
COMMENTS: Monthly markdowns

Salvation Army Thrift Store
226 S. Main St.
Myrtle Creek, OR 97457
TYPE OF MERCHANDISE: Clothing,
housewares, furniture
DONATION TAX RECEIPT: Receipt given
upon request

Salvation Army Thrift Store
424 N. Oregon St.
Ontario, OR 97914
TYPE OF MERCHANDISE: Clothing,
housewares, furniture
DONATION TAX RECEIPT: Receipt given
upon request

Saint Vincent De Paul Thrift Store
700 Mollalla Ave.
Oregon City, OR 97045
TYPE OF MERCHANDISE: Clothing,
housewares, furniture
DONATION TAX RECEIPT: Receipt given
upon request
COMMENTS: Monthly markdowns

Salvation Army Thrift Store
239 S.E. Court Ave.
Pendleton, OR 97801
TYPE OF MERCHANDISE: Clothing,
housewares, furniture
DONATION TAX RECEIPT: Receipt given
upon request

Salvation Army Thrift Store
135 Martin Luther King Blvd.
Portland, OR 97214
TYPE OF MERCHANDISE: Clothing,
housewares, furniture
DONATION TAX RECEIPT: Receipt given
upon request
COMMENTS: "As Is" store

American Cancer Society Discovery Shop
1730 N.E. 40th St.
Portland, OR 97212
PHONE: 503-287-0053
TYPE OF MERCHANDISE: Clothing, bric-a-
brac
DONATION TAX RECEIPT: Receipt given
upon request
COMMENTS: Monthly markdowns

Goodwill Industries Thrift Store
1925 S.E. Sixth Ave.
Portland, OR 97214-4508
TYPE OF MERCHANDISE: Clothing,
housewares, furniture
DONATION TAX RECEIPT: Receipt given
upon request

Salvation Army Thrift Store
11827 N.E. Halsey Ave.
Portland, OR 97220
TYPE OF MERCHANDISE: Clothing,
housewares, furniture
DONATION TAX RECEIPT: Receipt given
upon request

Salvation Army Thrift Store
200 Martin Luther King Blvd.
Portland, OR 97214
TYPE OF MERCHANDISE: Clothing,
housewares, furniture
DONATION TAX RECEIPT: Receipt given
upon request

Saint Vincent De Paul Thrift Store
21935 S.E. Stark
Portland, OR 97030
TYPE OF MERCHANDISE: Clothing,
housewares, furniture
DONATION TAX RECEIPT: Receipt given
upon request
COMMENTS: Monthly markdowns

Saint Vincent De Paul Thrift Store
2740 S.E. Powell
Portland, OR 97202
TYPE OF MERCHANDISE: Clothing,
housewares, furniture
DONATION TAX RECEIPT: Receipt given
upon request
COMMENTS: Monthly markdowns

Saint Vincent De Paul Thrift Store
3600 S.E. 28th St.
Portland, OR 97202
TYPE OF MERCHANDISE: Clothing,
housewares, furniture
DONATION TAX RECEIPT: Receipt given
upon request
COMMENTS: Monthly markdowns

TVI Value Village Thrift Store
5050 S.E. 82nd Ave.
Portland, OR 97266
CONTACT: Kristin Maly
PHONE: 503-771-5472
HOURS: Mon.–Sat. 9–9, Sun. 10–7
TYPE OF MERCHANDISE: Clothing,
housewares, furniture
DONATION TAX RECEIPT: No

National Assistance League Thrift Shop
735 N.W. 23rd Ave.
Portland, OR 97210
PHONE: 503-227-7093
TYPE OF MERCHANDISE: Clothing,
housewares, furniture
DONATION TAX RECEIPT: Receipt given
upon request
COMMENTS: Monthly markdowns

Saint Vincent De Paul Thrift Store
740 N. Killingworth
Portland, OR 97217
TYPE OF MERCHANDISE: Clothing,
housewares, furniture
DONATION TAX RECEIPT: Receipt given
upon request
COMMENTS: Monthly markdowns

Junior League Bargain Tree
837 S.W. Third Ave.
Portland, OR 97204
TYPE OF MERCHANDISE: Clothing for the
family
DONATION TAX RECEIPT: Receipt given
upon request

Salvation Army Thrift Store
8422–26 N. Lombard
Portland, OR 97203
TYPE OF MERCHANDISE: Clothing,
housewares, furniture
DONATION TAX RECEIPT: Receipt given
upon request

Salvation Army Thrift Store
9038 S.E. Foster Rd.
Portland, OR 97266
TYPE OF MERCHANDISE: Clothing,
housewares, furniture
DONATION TAX RECEIPT: Receipt given
upon request

Humane Society Thrift Shop
515 S.W. Cascade Ave.
Redmond, OR 97756
TYPE OF MERCHANDISE: Clothing,
housewares, furniture
DONATION TAX RECEIPT: Receipt given
upon request

Salvation Army Thrift Store
630 S.E. Rose St.
Roseburg, OR 97470
TYPE OF MERCHANDISE: Clothing,
housewares, furniture
DONATION TAX RECEIPT: Receipt given
upon request

Salvation Army Thrift Store
1085 Broadway N.E.
Salem, OR 97361
TYPE OF MERCHANDISE: Clothing,
housewares, furniture
DONATION TAX RECEIPT: Receipt given
upon request

National Assistance League Gift Shop
1085 Saginaw St. S
Salem, OR 97302
PHONE: 503-364-8318
TYPE OF MERCHANDISE: Clothing,
housewares, furniture
DONATION TAX RECEIPT: Receipt given
upon request
COMMENTS: Monthly markdowns

Saint Vincent De Paul Thrift Store
1550 Fairgrounds Rd. NE
Salem, OR 97303

TYPE OF MERCHANDISE: Clothing,
housewares, furniture
DONATION TAX RECEIPT: Receipt given
upon request
COMMENTS: Monthly markdowns

Salvation Army Thrift Store
162/170 Lancaster Dr.
Salem, OR 97301
TYPE OF MERCHANDISE: Clothing,
housewares, furniture
DONATION TAX RECEIPT: Receipt given
upon request

American Cancer Society Discovery Shop
241 Commercial St. NE
Salem, OR 97301
PHONE: 503-581-4577
TYPE OF MERCHANDISE: Clothing, bric-a-
brac
DONATION TAX RECEIPT: Receipt given
upon request
COMMENTS: Monthly markdowns

TVI Savers Thrift Store
2460 Mission SE
Salem, OR 97302
CONTACT: Mike Boyle
PHONE: 503-362-8858
HOURS: Mon.–Sat. 9–9, Sun. 10–6
TYPE OF MERCHANDISE: Clothing,
housewares, furniture
DONATION TAX RECEIPT: No

Goodwill Industries Thrift Store
2655 Portland Rd. NE
Salem, OR 97303
TYPE OF MERCHANDISE: Clothing,
housewares, furniture
DONATION TAX RECEIPT: Receipt given
upon request

Salvation Army Thrift Store
1485 Mohawk Blvd.
Springfield, OR 97477-3353
TYPE OF MERCHANDISE: Clothing,
housewares, furniture
DONATION TAX RECEIPT: Receipt given
upon request

Saint Vincent De Paul Thrift Store
231 S. First
St. Helens, OR 97051

TYPE OF MERCHANDISE: Clothing, housewares, furniture
DONATION TAX RECEIPT: Receipt given upon request
COMMENTS: Monthly markdowns
TVI Value Village Thrift Store
12060 S.W. Main
Tigard, OR 97223
CONTACT: Kris Barnett
PHONE: 503-684-1982
HOURS: Mon.–Sat. 9–9, Sun. 10–6
TYPE OF MERCHANDISE: Clothing, housewares, furniture
DONATION TAX RECEIPT: No
Saint Vincent De Paul Thrift Store
12230 S.W. Main St.
Tigard, OR 97221
TYPE OF MERCHANDISE: Clothing, housewares, furniture
DONATION TAX RECEIPT: Receipt given upon request
COMMENTS: Monthly markdowns
American Cancer Society Discovery Shop
13975 S.W. Pacific Hwy.
Tigard, OR 97223
CONTACT: Jane Frisbie
PHONE: 503-684-9060
TYPE OF MERCHANDISE: Clothing, bric-a-brac
DONATION TAX RECEIPT: Receipt given upon request
COMMENTS: Monthly markdowns
Goodwill Industries Thrift Store
392 N. Pacific Hwy.
Woodburn, OR 97071-5148
TYPE OF MERCHANDISE: Clothing, housewares, furniture
DONATION TAX RECEIPT: Receipt given upon request

Pennsylvania

Goodwill Industries Thrift Store
1015 Airport Rd.
Allentown, PA 18103
TYPE OF MERCHANDISE: Clothing, housewares, furniture
DONATION TAX RECEIPT: Receipt given upon request

LARC Thrift Shop
119 N. Seventh St.
Allentown, PA 18101
TYPE OF MERCHANDISE: Clothing, housewares, toys
DONATION TAX RECEIPT: Receipt given upon request
LARC Thrift Shop
1249 Liberty St.
Allentown, PA 18102
CONTACT: Carla Munsch
PHONE: 610-437-4562
HOURS: Mon.–Sat. 9:30–6
TYPE OF MERCHANDISE: Clothing, housewares, furniture
DONATION TAX RECEIPT: Receipt given upon request
COMMENTS: Designer label sales
LARC Thrift Shop
375 Greenleaf St.
Allentown, PA 18102
HOURS: Mon.–Sat. 9:30–6
TYPE OF MERCHANDISE: Clothing, housewares, furniture
DONATION TAX RECEIPT: Receipt given upon request
COMMENTS: Designer label sales
Salvation Army Thrift Store
200 Seventh Ave.
Altoona, PA 16601
TYPE OF MERCHANDISE: Clothing, housewares, furniture
DONATION TAX RECEIPT: Receipt given upon request
Volunteers of America National Society
653 Merchant St.
Ambridge, PA 15003
TYPE OF MERCHANDISE: Clothing, housewares
DONATION TAX RECEIPT: Receipt given upon request
Salvation Army Thrift Store
945 River Rd.
Apollo, PA 15673
TYPE OF MERCHANDISE: Clothing, housewares, furniture
DONATION TAX RECEIPT: Receipt given upon request

Salvation Army Thrift Store
Rte. 6/Scranton-Carbondale
Archbald, PA 18403
TYPE OF MERCHANDISE: Clothing,
housewares, furniture
DONATION TAX RECEIPT: Receipt given
upon request

Goodwill Industries Thrift Store
1014 Philadelphia Ave.
Barnesboro, PA 15714
PHONE: 814-948-7940
HOURS: Mon.–Sat. 10–5
TYPE OF MERCHANDISE: Clothing,
housewares, furniture
DONATION TAX RECEIPT: Receipt given
upon request
COMMENTS: Frequent sales

Salvation Army Thrift Store
1927 Seventh Ave.
Beaver Falls, PA 15010
TYPE OF MERCHANDISE: Clothing,
housewares, furniture
DONATION TAX RECEIPT: Receipt given
upon request

MCC Thrift & Gift Shop
12 N. Main St.
Belleville, PA 17004
PHONE: 717-935-5233
TYPE OF MERCHANDISE: Clothing,
housewares
DONATION TAX RECEIPT: Receipt given
upon request

LARC Thrift Shop
1401 Broadway
Bethelehem, PA 18015
TYPE OF MERCHANDISE: Clothing,
housewares, toys
DONATION TAX RECEIPT: Receipt given
upon request

Goodwill Industries Thrift Store
30 W. Market St.
Blairsville, PA 15717
PHONE: 412-459-9066
HOURS: Mon.–Sat. 10–4
TYPE OF MERCHANDISE: Clothing,
housewares, furniture
DONATION TAX RECEIPT: Receipt given
upon request
COMMENTS: Frequent sales

Salvation Army Thrift Store
49 W. Main St.
Bloomsburg, PA 17815
TYPE OF MERCHANDISE: Clothing,
housewares, furniture
DONATION TAX RECEIPT: Receipt given
upon request

Salvation Army Thrift Store
Chartiers Valley Mall
Bridgeville, PA
TYPE OF MERCHANDISE: Clothing,
housewares, furniture
DONATION TAX RECEIPT: Receipt given
upon request

Junior League Thrift Shop
1111 Lancaster Ave.
CROSS STREET: Water
Bryn Mawr, PA 19010
CONTACTS: Leslie Marshall, Carol Fisher
PHONE: 610-525-8513
HOURS: Mon.–Tues. 10–9, Wed. 10–9,
Thurs.–Sat. 10–5
TYPE OF MERCHANDISE: Clothing,
housewares, toys
DONATION TAX RECEIPT: Receipt given
upon request
COMMENTS: Christmas and ongoing
monthly sales

Junior League Thrift Shop
604 W. Lancaster Ave.
Bryn Mawr, PA 19010
TYPE OF MERCHANDISE: Clothing for men,
women, and children
DONATION TAX RECEIPT: Receipt given
upon request

Saint Vincent De Paul Thrift Store
157 N. Elm St.
Butler, PA 16001
TYPE OF MERCHANDISE: Clothing,
housewares, furniture
DONATION TAX RECEIPT: Receipt given
upon request
COMMENTS: Monthly markdowns

Salvation Army Thrift Store
1623 N. Main St.
Butler, PA 16001
TYPE OF MERCHANDISE: Clothing,
housewares, furniture

DONATION TAX RECEIPT: Receipt given
upon request
Salvation Army Thrift Store
63 N. Main Ave.
Carbondale, PA 18407
TYPE OF MERCHANDISE: Clothing,
housewares, furniture
DONATION TAX RECEIPT: Receipt given
upon request
Goodwill Industries Thrift Store
203 S. Hanover St.
Carlisle, PA 17013
TYPE OF MERCHANDISE: Clothing,
housewares, furniture
DONATION TAX RECEIPT: Receipt given
upon request
Salvation Army Thrift Store
159 Lincoln Way W
Chambersburg, PA 17201
TYPE OF MERCHANDISE: Clothing,
housewares, furniture
DONATION TAX RECEIPT: Receipt given
upon request
Salvation Army Thrift Store
14 E. Seventh St.
Chester, PA 19013
TYPE OF MERCHANDISE: Clothing,
housewares, furniture
DONATION TAX RECEIPT: Receipt given
upon request
Goodwill Industries Thrift Store
22 N. Third St.
Clearfield, PA 16830
TYPE OF MERCHANDISE: Clothing,
housewares, furniture
DONATION TAX RECEIPT: Receipt given
upon request
MCC Re-Uzit Shop
228 W. Lincoln Highway
Coatesville, PA 19320
PHONE: 717-383-5473
TYPE OF MERCHANDISE: Clothing,
housewares
DONATION TAX RECEIPT: Receipt given
upon request
Salvation Army Thrift Store
66 Chester Pike
Collingdale, PA 19023

TYPE OF MERCHANDISE: Clothing,
housewares, furniture
DONATION TAX RECEIPT: Receipt given
upon request
MCC Re-Uzit Shop
363 Locust St.
Columbia, PA 17512
PHONE: 717-684-7621
TYPE OF MERCHANDISE: Clothing,
housewares
DONATION TAX RECEIPT: Receipt given
upon request
Salvation Army Thrift Store
260 Mill St.
Danville, PA 17821
TYPE OF MERCHANDISE: Clothing,
housewares, furniture
DONATION TAX RECEIPT: Receipt given
upon request
Saint Vincent De Paul Thrift Store
868 Main St.
Darby, PA 19023
TYPE OF MERCHANDISE: Clothing,
housewares, furniture
DONATION TAX RECEIPT: Receipt given
upon request
COMMENTS: Monthly markdowns
Goodwill Industries Thrift Store
122 S. Chestnut St.
Derry, PA 15627
PHONE: 412-694-2203
HOURS: Mon.–Sat. 10–5
TYPE OF MERCHANDISE: Clothing,
housewares, furniture
DONATION TAX RECEIPT: Receipt given
upon request
COMMENTS: Frequent sales
Salvation Army Thrift Store
285 Washington St.
E. Stroudsburg, PA 18301
TYPE OF MERCHANDISE: Clothing,
housewares, furniture
DONATION TAX RECEIPT: Receipt given
upon request
Goodwill Industries Thrift Store
1367 Weaverland Rd.
E. Earl PA 17519
PHONE: 717-445-6016

HOURS: Mon.–Fri. 8–9, Sat. 8–5
TYPE OF MERCHANDISE: Clothing, housewares, furniture
DONATION TAX RECEIPT: Receipt given upon request

Goodwill Industries Thrift Store
85 N. Market
Elizabeth, PA 17023
TYPE OF MERCHANDISE: Clothing, housewares, furniture
DONATION TAX RECEIPT: Receipt given upon request

Salvation Army Thrift Store
520 Lawrence Ave.
Ellwood City, PA 16117
TYPE OF MERCHANDISE: Clothing, housewares, furniture
DONATION TAX RECEIPT: Receipt given upon request

Goodwill Industries Thrift Store
1170 S. State St.
Ephrata, PA 17522
TYPE OF MERCHANDISE: Clothing, housewares, furniture
DONATION TAX RECEIPT: Receipt given upon request

MCC Re-Uzit Home Supply Shop
1755 W. Main St.
Ephrata, PA 17522
PHONE: 717-733-4934
TYPE OF MERCHANDISE: Clothing, housewares, furniture
DONATION TAX RECEIPT: Receipt given upon request

MCC Re-Uzit Shop
20–22 E. Main St.
Ephrata, PA 17522
PHONE: 717-733-4982
TYPE OF MERCHANDISE: Clothing, housewares, furniture
DONATION TAX RECEIPT: Receipt given upon request

Salvation Army Thrift Store
1209 Sassafras St.
Erie, PA 16501-1719
TYPE OF MERCHANDISE: Clothing, housewares, furniture
DONATION TAX RECEIPT: Receipt given upon request

Salvation Army Thrift Store
6853 Peach St.
Erie, PA 16509
TYPE OF MERCHANDISE: Clothing, housewares, furniture
DONATION TAX RECEIPT: Receipt given upon request

Salvation Army Thrift Store
Corner Plaza
Everett, PA 15537
TYPE OF MERCHANDISE: Clothing, housewares, furniture
DONATION TAX RECEIPT: Receipt given upon request

Salvation Army Thrift Store
Rte. 11/Wyoming Ave.
Exeter, PA 18643
TYPE OF MERCHANDISE: Clothing, housewares, furniture
DONATION TAX RECEIPT: Receipt given upon request

LARC Thrift Shop
1401 Broadway
Fountain Hill, PA 18015
HOURS: Mon.–Sat. 9:30–6
TYPE OF MERCHANDISE: Clothing, housewares, furniture
DONATION TAX RECEIPT: Receipt given upon request
COMMENTS: Designer label sales

Salvation Army Thrift Store
Oil City–Franklin Rd., Rte. 8
Franklin, PA 16323
TYPE OF MERCHANDISE: Clothing, housewares, furniture
DONATION TAX RECEIPT: Receipt given upon request

American Cancer Society Discovery Shop
Lancaster Ave., Rte. 30
Frazer, PA 19355
CONTACT: Roslyn Reichert
PHONE: 215-644-8626
TYPE OF MERCHANDISE: Clothing, bric-a-brac
DONATION TAX RECEIPT: Receipt given upon request
COMMENTS: Monthly markdowns

MCC Country Gift and Thrift Shoppe
5602 Old Philadelphia Pike
Gap, PA 17527
PHONE: 717-768-3784
TYPE OF MERCHANDISE: Clothing,
housewares
DONATION TAX RECEIPT: Receipt given
upon request

Saint Vincent De Paul Thrift Store
126 S. Main St.
Greensburg, PA 15601
TYPE OF MERCHANDISE: Clothing,
housewares, furniture
DONATION TAX RECEIPT: Receipt given
upon request
COMMENTS: Monthly markdowns

Salvation Army Thrift Store
211 Main St.
Greenville, PA 16125
TYPE OF MERCHANDISE: Clothing,
housewares, furniture
DONATION TAX RECEIPT: Receipt given
upon request

Salvation Army Thrift Store
236 Blair St.
Grove City, PA 16127
TYPE OF MERCHANDISE: Clothing,
housewares, furniture
DONATION TAX RECEIPT: Receipt given
upon request

Goodwill Industries Thrift Store
234 W. State St.
Hamburg, PA 19526
TYPE OF MERCHANDISE: Clothing,
housewares, furniture
DONATION TAX RECEIPT: Receipt given
upon request

Salvation Army Thrift Store
739 San Souci Parkway
Hanover Township, PA 18702
TYPE OF MERCHANDISE: Clothing,
housewares, furniture
DONATION TAX RECEIPT: Receipt given
upon request

Salvation Army Thrift Store
115 W. Broad St.
Hazleton, PA 18201
TYPE OF MERCHANDISE: Clothing,
housewares, furniture

DONATION TAX RECEIPT: Receipt given
upon request

Saint Vincent De Paul Thrift Store
119 E. Eighth Ave.
Homestead, PA 15120
TYPE OF MERCHANDISE: Clothing,
housewares, furniture
DONATION TAX RECEIPT: Receipt given
upon request
COMMENTS: Monthly markdowns

Goodwill Industries Thrift Store
120 E. Eighth Ave.
Homestead, PA 15120
TYPE OF MERCHANDISE: Clothing,
housewares, furniture
DONATION TAX RECEIPT: Receipt given
upon request

Salvation Army Thrift Store
304–06 E. Eighth Ave.
Homestead, PA 15120
TYPE OF MERCHANDISE: Clothing,
housewares, furniture
DONATION TAX RECEIPT: Receipt given
upon request

Salvation Army Thrift Store
Maple Ave., Rte. #6
Honesdale, PA 18413
TYPE OF MERCHANDISE: Clothing,
housewares, furniture
DONATION TAX RECEIPT: Receipt given
upon request

Goodwill Industries Thrift Store
20 S. Fifth St.
Indiana, PA 15701
PHONE: 412-463-6212
HOURS: Mon.–Sat. 10–5
TYPE OF MERCHANDISE: Clothing,
housewares, furniture
DONATION TAX RECEIPT: Receipt given
upon request
COMMENTS: Frequent sales

Salvation Army Thrift Store
654–656 Philadephia St.
Indiana, PA 15701
TYPE OF MERCHANDISE: Clothing,
housewares, furniture
DONATION TAX RECEIPT: Receipt given
upon request

Saint Vincent De Paul Thrift Store
305 Clay Ave.
Jeannette, PA 15644
TYPE OF MERCHANDISE: Clothing,
housewares, furniture
DONATION TAX RECEIPT: Receipt given
upon request
COMMENTS: Monthly markdowns

Goodwill Industries Thrift Store
2470 Bedford St.
Johnstown, PA 15904
PHONE: 814-266-6143
HOURS: Mon.–Sat. 10–5
TYPE OF MERCHANDISE: Clothing,
housewares, furniture
DONATION TAX RECEIPT: Receipt given
upon request
COMMENTS: Frequent sales

Salvation Army Thrift Store
1025 Eisenhower Blvd.
Johnstown, PA 15906
TYPE OF MERCHANDISE: Clothing,
housewares, furniture
DONATION TAX RECEIPT: Receipt given
upon request

Salvation Army Thrift Store
226 Main St.
Johnstown, PA 15901-1509
TYPE OF MERCHANDISE: Clothing,
housewares, furniture
DONATION TAX RECEIPT: Receipt given
upon request

Salvation Army Thrift Store
542 Main St.
Johnstown, PA 15901
TYPE OF MERCHANDISE: Clothing,
housewares, furniture
DONATION TAX RECEIPT: Receipt given
upon request

American Cancer Society Discovery Shop
121 Town Center Rd.
King of Prussia, PA 19406
PHONE: 215-992-0550
TYPE OF MERCHANDISE: Clothing, bric-a-
brac
DONATION TAX RECEIPT: Receipt given
upon request
COMMENTS: Monthly markdowns

Salvation Army Thrift Store
56 Lincoln Highway
Langhorne, PA 19047
TYPE OF MERCHANDISE: Clothing,
housewares, furniture
DONATION TAX RECEIPT: Receipt given
upon request

Salvation Army Thrift Store
1601 N. Broad St.
Lansdale, PA 19446
TYPE OF MERCHANDISE: Clothing,
housewares, furniture
DONATION TAX RECEIPT: Receipt given
upon request

Saint Vincent De Paul Thrift Store
614 Jefferson St.
Latrobe, PA 15650
TYPE OF MERCHANDISE: Clothing,
housewares, furniture
DONATION TAX RECEIPT: Receipt given
upon request
COMMENTS: Monthly markdowns

Salvation Army Thrift Store
Route 30 W
Latrobe, PA 15650
TYPE OF MERCHANDISE: Clothing,
housewares, furniture
DONATION TAX RECEIPT: Receipt given
upon request

LARC Thrift Store
1249 Liberty St.
Lehigh Valley, PA 18001
CONTACT: Carla Munsch
TYPE OF MERCHANDISE: Clothing,
housewares, furniture
DONATION TAX RECEIPT: Receipt given
upon request

Salvation Army Thrift Store
239 N. First St.
Lehighton, PA 18235
TYPE OF MERCHANDISE: Clothing,
housewares, furniture
DONATION TAX RECEIPT: Receipt given
upon request

Salvation Army Thrift Store
8734 New Falls Road
Levittown, PA 19054
TYPE OF MERCHANDISE: Clothing,
housewares, furniture

DONATION TAX RECEIPT: Receipt given upon request

Salvation Army Thrift Store
2 Lewis Ave.
Lyndora, PA 16045
TYPE OF MERCHANDISE: Clothing, housewares, furniture
DONATION TAX RECEIPT: Receipt given upon request

Salvation Army Thrift Store
22 E. Tenth St.
Marcus Hook, PA 19061
TYPE OF MERCHANDISE: Clothing, housewares, furniture
DONATION TAX RECEIPT: Receipt given upon request

Salvation Army Thrift Store
892 Market St.
Meadville, PA 16335
TYPE OF MERCHANDISE: Clothing, housewares, furniture
DONATION TAX RECEIPT: Receipt given upon request

Goodwill Industries Thrift Store
15 E. Main St.
Mechanicsburg, PA 17055
TYPE OF MERCHANDISE: Clothing, housewares, furniture
DONATION TAX RECEIPT: Receipt given upon request

Salvation Army Thrift Store
4833 Carlisle Pike
Mechanicsburg, PA 17055
TYPE OF MERCHANDISE: Clothing, housewares, furniture
DONATION TAX RECEIPT: Receipt given upon request

Goodwill Industries Thrift Store
233 Center St.
Meyersdale, PA 15552
PHONE: 814-634-8939
HOURS: Mon.–Sat. 10–5
TYPE OF MERCHANDISE: Clothing, housewares, furniture
DONATION TAX RECEIPT: Receipt given upon request
COMMENTS: Frequent sales

Goodwill Industries Thrift Store
600 Pennsylvania Ave.
Monroeville, PA 15146
TYPE OF MERCHANDISE: Clothing, housewares, furniture
DONATION TAX RECEIPT: Receipt given upon request

Goodwill Industries Thrift Store
112 S. Oak St.
Mt. Carmel, PA 17851
TYPE OF MERCHANDISE: Clothing, housewares, furniture
DONATION TAX RECEIPT: Receipt given upon request

MCC International Gift & Thrift
413 W. Main St.
Mt. Joy, PA 17552
PHONE: 717-653-8318
TYPE OF MERCHANDISE: Clothing, housewares
DONATION TAX RECEIPT: Receipt given upon request

Salvation Army Thrift Store
Old Rte. 940
Mr. Pocono, PA 18346
TYPE OF MERCHANDISE: Clothing, housewares, furniture
DONATION TAX RECEIPT: Receipt given upon request

Salvation Army Thrift Store
102 Grove St.
New Castle, PA 16101
TYPE OF MERCHANDISE: Clothing, housewares, furniture
DONATION TAX RECEIPT: Receipt given upon request

Salvation Army Thrift Store
24 Grove St.
New Castle, PA 16101
TYPE OF MERCHANDISE: Clothing, housewares, furniture
DONATION TAX RECEIPT: Receipt given upon request

MCC Re-Uzit Shop
148 E. Main St.
New Holland, PA 17557
PHONE: 717-354-8355

TYPE OF MERCHANDISE: Clothing, housewares, furniture
DONATION TAX RECEIPT: Receipt given upon request

Salvation Army Thrift Store
865 Fifth Ave.
New Kensington, PA 15068
TYPE OF MERCHANDISE: Clothing, housewares, furniture
DONATION TAX RECEIPT: Receipt given upon request

Saint Vincent De Paul Thrift Store
100 E. Main St.
Norristown, PA 19401
TYPE OF MERCHANDISE: Clothing, housewares, furniture
DONATION TAX RECEIPT: Receipt given upon request
COMMENTS: Monthly markdowns

MCC Crossroads Thrift Shop
14–16 E. Main St.
Norristown, PA 19401
PHONE: 215-275-3772
TYPE OF MERCHANDISE: Clothing, housewares, furniture
DONATION TAX RECEIPT: Receipt given upon request

Salvation Army Thrift Store
147 W. Main St.
Norristown, PA 19401
TYPE OF MERCHANDISE: Clothing, housewares, furniture
DONATION TAX RECEIPT: Receipt given upon request

Salvation Army Thrift Store
12751 Route #30 West
N. Huntington, PA 15642
TYPE OF MERCHANDISE: Clothing, housewares, furniture
DONATION TAX RECEIPT: Receipt given upon request

Salvation Army Thrift Store
1532 Sellers St.
Philadelphia, PA 19137
TYPE OF MERCHANDISE: Clothing, housewares, furniture
DONATION TAX RECEIPT: Receipt given upon request

Saint Vincent De Paul Thrift Store
1606 N. 21st St.
Philadelphia, PA 19121
TYPE OF MERCHANDISE: Clothing, housewares, furniture
DONATION TAX RECEIPT: Receipt given upon request
COMMENTS: Monthly markdowns

Salvation Army Thrift Store
2140 Market St.
Philadephia, PA 19103
TYPE OF MERCHANDISE: Clothing, housewares, furniture
DONATION TAX RECEIPT: Receipt given upon request

Salvation Army Thrift Store
3221–25 Kensington Ave.
Philadelphia, PA 19125
TYPE OF MERCHANDISE: Clothing, housewares, furniture
DONATION TAX RECEIPT: Receipt given upon request

Salvation Army Thrift Store
4028 Lancaster Ave.
Philadelphia, PA 19104
TYPE OF MERCHANDISE: Clothing, housewares, furniture
DONATION TAX RECEIPT: Receipt given upon request

Salvation Army Thrift Store
4555 Pechin St.
Philadelphia, PA 19128
TYPE OF MERCHANDISE: Clothing, housewares, furniture
DONATION TAX RECEIPT: Receipt given upon request

Volunteers of America
5440 Lansdowne Ave.
Philadelphia, PA 19131
TYPE OF MERCHANDISE: Clothing, housewares
DONATION TAX RECEIPT: Receipt given upon request

Saint Vincent De Paul Thrift Store
6325 Woodland Ave.
Philadelphia, PA 19142
TYPE OF MERCHANDISE: Clothing, housewares, furniture

DONATION TAX RECEIPT: Receipt given upon request
COMMENTS: Monthly markdowns
Salvation Army Thrift Store
6427 Torresdale Ave.
Philadelphia, PA 19135
TYPE OF MERCHANDISE: Clothing, housewares, furniture
DONATION TAX RECEIPT: Receipt given upon request
Salvation Army Thrift Store
6430 Rising Sun Ave.
Philadephia, PA 19111
TYPE OF MERCHANDISE: Clothing, housewares, furniture
DONATION TAX RECEIPT: Receipt given upon request
Saint Vincent De Paul Thrift Store
7613 Ogontz Ave.
Philadelphia, PA 19150
TYPE OF MERCHANDISE: Clothing, housewares, furniture
DONATION TAX RECEIPT: Receipt given upon request
COMMENTS: Monthly markdowns
Saint Vincent De Paul Thrift Store
1432 Fifth Ave.
Pittsburgh, PA 15219
TYPE OF MERCHANDISE: Clothing, housewares, furniture
DONATION TAX RECEIPT: Receipt given upon request
COMMENTS: Monthly markdowns
Saint Vincent De Paul Thrift Store
1709 E. Carson St.
Pittsburgh, PA 15203
TYPE OF MERCHANDISE: Clothing, housewares, furnture
DONATION TAX RECEIPT: Receipt given upon request
COMMENTS: Monthly markdowns
Saint Vincent De Paul Thrift Store
1917 Brownsville Rd.
Pittsburgh, PA 15210
TYPE OF MERCHANDISE: Clothing, housewares, furniture
DONATION TAX RECEIPT: Receipt given upon request
COMMENTS: Monthly markdowns

Saint Vincent De Paul Thrift Store
202 Brownsville Rd.
Pittsburgh, PA 15210
TYPE OF MERCHANDISE: Clothing, housewares, furniture
DONATION TAX RECEIPT: Receipt given upon request
COMMENTS: Monthly markdowns
Goodwill Industries Thrift Store
224 S. College
Pittsburgh, PA 15232
TYPE OF MERCHANDISE: Clothing, housewares, furniture
DONATION TAX RECEIPT: Receipt given upon request
Goodwill Industries Thrift Store
2600 E. Carson St.
Pittsburgh, PA 15203
TYPE OF MERCHANDISE: Clothing, housewares, furniture
DONATION TAX RECEIPT: Receipt given upon request
NCJW Thrift Shop
3512 Fifth Ave.
Pittsburgh, PA 15213
TYPE OF MERCHANDISE: Clothing, housewares, furniture
DONATION TAX RECEIPT: Receipt given upon request
Goodwill Industries Thrift Store
415 E. Ohio St.
Pittsburgh, PA 15212
TYPE OF MERCHANDISE: Clothing, housewares, furniture
DONATION TAX RECEIPT: Receipt given upon request
Salvation Army Thrift Store
44 S. Ninth St.
Pittsburgh, PA 15203
TYPE OF MERCHANDISE: Clothing, housewares, furniture
DONATION TAX RECEIPT: Receipt given upon request
Junior League Thrift Shop
4707 Liberty Ave.
Pittsburgh, PA 15224
CONTACT: Tina Johnson
PHONE: 412-687-2600

HOURS: Tue.–Fri. 10–4, Sat. 10–2
TYPE OF MERCHANDISE: Clothing,
housewares, toys
DONATION TAX RECEIPT: Receipt given
upon request
COMMENTS: Various sales, toy sale in
December
Salvation Army Thrift Store
6017 Broad St.
Pittsburgh, PA 15206
TYPE OF MERCHANDISE: Clothing,
housewares, furniture
DONATION TAX RECEIPT: Receipt given
upon request
Goodwill Industries Thrift Store
6101 Broad St.
Pittsburgh, PA 15206
TYPE OF MERCHANDISE: Clothing,
housewares, furniture
DONATION TAX RECEIPT: Receipt given
upon request
Saint Vincent De Paul Thrift Store
616 E. Ohio St.
Pittsburgh, PA 15212
TYPE OF MERCHANDISE: Clothing,
housewares, furniture
DONATION TAX RECEIPT: Receipt given
upon request
COMMENTS: Monthly markdowns
Goodwill Industries Thrift Store
641 S. Braddock Ave.
Pittsburgh, PA 15221
TYPE OF MERCHANDISE: Clothing,
housewares, furniture
DONATION TAX RECEIPT: Receipt given
upon request
Saint Vincent De Paul Thrift Store
7233 Frankstown Ave.
Pittsburgh, PA 15208
TYPE OF MERCHANDISE: Clothing,
housewares, furniture
DONATION TAX RECEIPT: Receipt given
upon request
COMMENTS: Monthly markdowns
NCJW Thrift Shop
822 Fifth Ave.
CROSS STREET: Across from Chatham
Center

Pittsburgh, PA 15219
PHONE: 412-281-7467
HOURS: Mon.–Sat. 9–5
TYPE OF MERCHANDISE: Clothing,
housewares, furniture
DONATION TAX RECEIPT: Receipt given
upon request
COMMENTS: Annual toy and Designer
Day sales
Salvation Army Thrift Store
206–08 N. Centre St.
Pottsville, PA 17901
TYPE OF MERCHANDISE: Clothing,
housewares, furniture
DONATION TAX RECEIPT: Receipt given
upon request
Goodwill Industries Thrift Store
5 N. Centre St.
Pottsville, PA 17901
TYPE OF MERCHANDISE: Clothing,
housewares, furniture
DONATION TAX RECEIPT: Receipt given
upon request
Goodwill Industries Thrift Store
310 N. Wyomissing Ave.
Reading, PA 19607
TYPE OF MERCHANDISE: Clothing,
housewares, furniture
DONATION TAX RECEIPT: Receipt given
upon request
Goodwill Industries Thrift Store
600 Penn Ave.
Reading, PA 19611
TYPE OF MERCHANDISE: Clothing,
housewares, furniture
DONATION TAX RECEIPT: Receipt given
upon request
Goodwill Industries Thrift Store
115 E. Penn Ave.
Robesonia, PA 19551
TYPE OF MERCHANDISE: Clothing,
housewares, furniture
DONATION TAX RECEIPT: Receipt given
upon request
Salvation Army Thrift Store
610 S. Washington Ave.
Scranton, PA 18505

TYPE OF MERCHANDISE: Clothing, housewares, furniture
DONATION TAX RECEIPT: Receipt given upon request

Goodwill Industries Thrift Store
103 E. Independence St.
Shamokin, PA 17872
TYPE OF MERCHANDISE: Clothing, housewares, furniture
DONATION TAX RECEIPT: Receipt given upon request

Goodwill Industries Thrift Store
23 Chestnut Ave.
Sharon, PA 16146
TYPE OF MERCHANDISE: Clothing, housewares, furniture
DONATION TAX RECEIPT: Receipt given upon request

Salvation Army Thrift Store
34 Vine St.
Sharon, PA 16146
TYPE OF MERCHANDISE: Clothing, housewares, furniture
DONATION TAX RECEIPT: Receipt given upon request

Salvation Army Thrift Store
80 Shenango Ave.
Sharon, PA 16146
TYPE OF MERCHANDISE: Clothing, housewares, furniture
DONATION TAX RECEIPT: Receipt given upon request

Saint Vincent De Paul Thrift Store
900–902 Main St.
Sharpsburg, PA 15215
TYPE OF MERCHANDISE: Clothing, housewares, furniture
DONATION TAX RECEIPT: Receipt given upon request
COMMENTS: Monthly markdowns

MCC, The World Attic
109 E. Main St.
Somerset, PA 15501
PHONE: 814-445-4886
TYPE OF MERCHANDISE: Clothing, housewares
DONATION TAX RECEIPT: Receipt given upon request

MCC Care & Share Shoppes Inc.
Rtes. 113 and Old 309
Sounderton, PA 18964
PHONE: 214-723-0141, 723-0315
TYPE OF MERCHANDISE: Clothing, housewares
DONATION TAX RECEIPT: Receipt given upon request

Saint Vincent De Paul Thrift Store
214 W. Seventh St.
Tarentum, PA 15084
TYPE OF MERCHANDISE: Clothing, housewares, furniture
DONATION TAX RECEIPT: Receipt given upon request
COMMENTS: Monthly markdowns

Salvation Army Thrift Store
8 W. High St.
Union City, PA 16438
TYPE OF MERCHANDISE: Clothing, housewares, furniture
DONATION TAX RECEIPT: Receipt given upon request

Salvation Army Thrift Store
54 N. Mt. Vernon Ave.
Uniontown, PA 15401
TYPE OF MERCHANDISE: Clothing, housewares, furniture
DONATION TAX RECEIPT: Receipt given upon request

Saint Vincent De Paul Thrift Store
96 Pennsylvania Ave.
Uniontown, PA 15401
TYPE OF MERCHANDISE: Clothing, housewares, furniture
DONATION TAX RECEIPT: Receipt given upon request
COMMENTS: Monthly markdowns

Salvation Army Thrift Store
729 Long Lane
Upper Darby, PA 19082
TYPE OF MERCHANDISE: Clothing, housewares, furniture
DONATION TAX RECEIPT: Receipt given upon request

Goodwill Industries Thrift Store
244 S. College St.
Washington, PA 15301

TYPE OF MERCHANDISE: Clothing,
housewares, furniture
DONATION TAX RECEIPT: Receipt given
upon request

Salvation Army Thrift Store
250 E. Market St.
West Chester, PA 19381
TYPE OF MERCHANDISE: Clothing,
housewares, furniture
DONATION TAX RECEIPT: Receipt given
upon request

Salvation Army Thrift Store
1204 Macarthur Rd.
Whitehall Township, PA 18052
TYPE OF MERCHANDISE: Clothing,
housewares, furniture
DONATION TAX RECEIPT: Receipt given
upon request

Salvation Army Thrift Store
300–4 Wilkes-Barre Township Blvd.
Wilkes-Barre, PA 18702
TYPE OF MERCHANDISE: Clothing,
housewares, furniture
DONATION TAX RECEIPT: Receipt given
upon request

Salvation Army Thrift Store
762 Sans Souci Pkwy.
Wilkes-Barre, PA 18702
TYPE OF MERCHANDISE: Clothing,
housewares, furniture
DONATION TAX RECEIPT: Receipt given
upon request

Salvation Army Thrift Store
163 Hazel St.
Wilkes-Barre, PA 18702
TYPE OF MERCHANDISE: Clothing,
housewares, furniture
DONATION TAX RECEIPT: Receipt given
upon request

Salvation Army Thrift Store
1090 Haines Rd.
York, PA 17402
HOURS: Mon.–Sat. 9–9
PHONE: 717-840-1300
TYPE OF MERCHANDISE: Clothing,
housewares, furniture
DONATION TAX RECEIPT: Receipt given
upon request

Salvation Army Thrift Store
113 S. Duke St.
York, PA 17403
TYPE OF MERCHANDISE: Clothing,
housewares, furniture
DONATION TAX RECEIPT: Receipt given
upon request

Junior League of York Thrift Shop
166 W. Market St.
York, PA 17401
CONTACT: Jodi Attig
PHONE: 717-843-7692
HOURS: Mon.–Sat. 9:30–4
TYPE OF MERCHANDISE: Clothing, jewelry,
housewares
DONATION TAX RECEIPT: Receipt given
upon request
COMMENTS: Christmas, toy, and special
sales

Rhode Island

Salvation Army Thrift Store
91 E. Washington St.
N. Attleboro, RI 02760
TYPE OF MERCHANDISE: Clothing,
housewares, furniture
DONATION TAX RECEIPT: Receipt given
upon request

Salvation Army Thrift Store
6946 Post Rd.
N. Kingston, RI 02852
TYPE OF MERCHANDISE: Clothing,
housewares, furniture
DONATION TAX RECEIPT: Receipt given
upon request

Salvation Army Thrift Store
6835 Post Rd.
N. Kingston, RI 02852
TYPE OF MERCHANDISE: Clothing,
housewares, furniture
DONATION TAX RECEIPT: Receipt given
upon request

Salvation Army Thrift Store
2060 Smith St.
N. Providence, RI 02911
TYPE OF MERCHANDISE: Clothing,
housewares, furniture

DONATION TAX RECEIPT: Receipt given upon request

Salvation Army Thrift Store
504 Central Ave.
Pawtucket, RI 02861
TYPE OF MERCHANDISE: Clothing, housewares, furniture
DONATION TAX RECEIPT: Receipt given upon request

Salvation Army Thrift Store
1955 Westminster St.
Providence, RI 02909
TYPE OF MERCHANDISE: Clothing, housewares, furniture
DONATION TAX RECEIPT: Receipt given upon request

Salvation Army Thrift Store
201 Pitman St.
Providence, RI 02906
TYPE OF MERCHANDISE: Clothing, housewares, furniture
DONATION TAX RECEIPT: Receipt given upon request

Salvation Army Thrift Store
2058 Smith St.
Providence, RI 02911
TYPE OF MERCHANDISE: Clothing, housewares, furniture
DONATION TAX RECEIPT: Receipt given upon request

Salvation Army Thrift Store
650 Metacom Ave.
Warren, RI 02885
TYPE OF MERCHANDISE: Clothing, housewares, furniture
DONATION TAX RECEIPT: Receipt given upon request

Salvation Army Thrift Store
1121 Warwick Ave.
Warwick, RI 02888
TYPE OF MERCHANDISE: Clothing, housewares, furniture
DONATION TAX RECEIPT: Receipt given upon request

Salvation Army Thrift Store
558 Greenwich
Warwick, RI 02886
TYPE OF MERCHANDISE: Clothing, housewares, furniture

DONATION TAX RECEIPT: Receipt given upon request

Salvation Army Thrift Store
269 Washington St.
W. Warwick, RI 02893
TYPE OF MERCHANDISE: Clothing, housewares, furniture
DONATION TAX RECEIPT: Receipt given upon request

Salvation Army Thrift Store
30 N. Main St.
Woonsocket, RI 02895
TYPE OF MERCHANDISE: Clothing, housewares, furniture
DONATION TAX RECEIPT: Receipt given upon request

South Carolina

Salvation Army Thrift Store
1311 Congress St.
Beaufort, SC 29902
TYPE OF MERCHANDISE: Clothing, housewares, furniture
DONATION TAX RECEIPT: Receipt given upon request

Salvation Army Thrift Store
533 Rutledge St.
Camden, SC 29020
TYPE OF MERCHANDISE: Clothing, housewares, furniture
DONATION TAX RECEIPT: Receipt given upon request

Goodwill Industries Thrift Store
325 Folly Rd.
Charleston, SC 29412
PHONE: 803-795-7988
HOURS: Seven days, 9–7
TYPE OF MERCHANDISE: Clothing, housewares, furniture
DONATION TAX RECEIPT: Receipt given upon request

Salvation Army Thrift Store
4248 Dorchester Rd.
Charleston, SC 29405
TYPE OF MERCHANDISE: Clothing, housewares, furniture
DONATION TAX RECEIPT: Receipt given upon request

Goodwill Industries Thrift Store
563 King St.
Charleston, SC 29403
PHONE: 803-722-5917
HOURS: Seven days, 9–5
TYPE OF MERCHANDISE: Clothing,
housewares, furniture
DONATION TAX RECEIPT: Receipt given
upon request

Goodwill Industries Thrift Store
5640 Rivers Ave.
Charleston, SC 29406
PHONE: 803-566-0072
HOURS: Seven days, 9–7
TYPE OF MERCHANDISE: Clothing,
housewares, furniture
DONATION TAX RECEIPT: Receipt given
upon request

Salvation Army Thrift Stores
107 Main St.
Chester, SC 29706
TYPE OF MERCHANDISE: Clothing,
housewares, furniture
DONATION TAX RECEIPT: Receipt given
upon request

Salvation Army Thrift Store
1434 Assembly St.
Columbia, SC 29201
TYPE OF MERCHANDISE: Clothing,
housewares, furniture
DONATION TAX RECEIPT: Receipt given
upon request

Salvation Army Thrift Store
3816 Main St.
Columbia, SC 29203
TYPE OF MERCHANDISE: Clothing,
housewares, furniture
DONATION TAX RECEIPT: Receipt given
upon request

Salvation Army Thrift Store
120 E. Evans St.
Florence, SC 29506
TYPE OF MERCHANDISE: Clothing,
housewares, furniture
DONATION TAX RECEIPT: Receipt given
upon request

Salvation Army Thrift Store
1424 Highmarket St.
Georgetown, SC 29440
TYPE OF MERCHANDISE: Clothing,
housewares, furniture
DONATION TAX RECEIPT: Receipt given
upon request

Salvation Army Thrift Store
1245 Pendleton St.
Greenville, SC 29611
TYPE OF MERCHANDISE: Clothing,
housewares, furniture
DONATION TAX RECEIPT: Receipt given
upon request

Junior League Nearly New Shop
17 W. North St.
Greenville, SC 29601
PHONE: 803-232-1051
HOURS: Mon.–Sat. 10–4
TYPE OF MERCHANDISE: Clothing,
housewares, toys
DONATION TAX RECEIPT: Receipt given
upon request
COMMENTS: Toy sales and bag sales

Saint Vincent De Paul Thrift Store
33 Northwood Pl.
Greenville, SC 29601
TYPE OF MERCHANDISE: Clothing,
housewares, furniture
DONATION TAX RECEIPT: Receipt given
upon request
COMMENTS: Monthly markdowns

Goodwill Industries Thrift Store
3300 Augusta Rd.
Greenville, SC 29605
TYPE OF MERCHANDISE: Clothing,
housewares, furniture
DONATION TAX RECEIPT: Receipt given
upon request

Salvation Army Thrift Store
1120 N. Cherry Rd.
Rock Hill, SC 29732
TYPE OF MERCHANDISE: Clothing,
housewares, furniture
DONATION TAX RECEIPT: Receipt given
upon request

Goodwill Industries Thrift Store
758 E. Heckle Blvd.
Rock Hill, SC 29730
TYPE OF MERCHANDISE: Clothing,
housewares, furniture
DONATION TAX RECEIPT: Receipt given
upon request
Goodwill Industries Thrift Store
167 N. Church St.
Spartanburg, SC 29306
TYPE OF MERCHANDISE: Clothing,
housewares, furniture
DONATION TAX RECEIPT: Receipt given
upon request

South Dakota

MCC Et Cetera Shoppe
308 S. Main St.
Freeman, SD 57029
PHONE: 605-925-7098
TYPE OF MERCHANDISE: Clothing,
housewares, furniture
DONATION TAX RECEIPT: Receipt given
upon request
Salvation Army Thrift Store
237 Illinois Ave. SW
Huron, SD 57350
TYPE OF MERCHANDISE: Clothing,
housewares, furniture
DONATION TAX RECEIPT: Receipt given
upon request
Salvation Army Thrift Store
113 W. Fourth Ave.
Mitchell, SD 57301
TYPE OF MERCHANDISE: Clothing,
housewares, furniture
DONATION TAX RECEIPT: Receipt given
upon request
Salvation Army Thrift Store
230 Main St.
Rapid City, SD 57701
TYPE OF MERCHANDISE: Clothing,
housewares, furniture
DONATION TAX RECEIPT: Receipt given
upon request

Saint Vincent De Paul Thrift Store
300 N. Main Ave.
Sioux Falls, SD 57102
TYPE OF MERCHANDISE: Clothing,
housewares, furniture
DONATION TAX RECEIPT: Receipt given
upon request
COMMENTS: Monthly markdowns
Salvation Army Thrift Store
320 N. Main Ave.
Sioux Falls, SD 57102
TYPE OF MERCHANDISE: Clothing,
housewares, furniture
DONATION TAX RECEIPT: Receipt given
upon request
Disabled American Vets Thrift Store
909 E. Eighth St.
Sioux Falls, SD 57103
TYPE OF MERCHANDISE: Clothing,
housewares
DONATION TAX RECEIPT: Receipt given
upon request
Salvation Army Thrift Store
621 Fourth St. SE
Watertown, SD 57201
TYPE OF MERCHANDISE: Clothing,
housewares, furniture
DONATION TAX RECEIPT: Receipt given
upon request

Tennessee

Goodwill Industries Thrift Store
2037 Antioch Pike
Antioch, TN 37013
TYPE OF MERCHANDISE: Clothing,
housewares, furniture
DONATION TAX RECEIPT: Receipt given
upon request
Goodwill Industries Thrift Store
2103 Dayton Blvd.
Chattanooga, TN
PHONE: 615-875-9349
HOURS: Mon.–Sat. 9–7, Sun. 1–7
TYPE OF MERCHANDISE: Clothing,
housewares, furniture
DONATION TAX RECEIPT: Receipt given
upon request

Goodwill Industries Thrift Store
3500 Dodds Ave.
Chattanooga, TN 37407
PHONE: 615-629-2501
HOURS: Mon.–Sat. 9–7, Sun. 1–7
TYPE OF MERCHANDISE: Clothing,
housewares, furniture
DONATION TAX RECEIPT: Receipt given
upon request

American Cancer Society Discovery Shop
3600 Hixson Pike, Suite I–J
CROSS STREETS: Rivermont Shopping
Center
Chattanooga, TN 37415
TYPE OF MERCHANDISE: Clothing, bric-a-
brac
DONATION TAX RECEIPT: Receipt given
upon request
COMMENTS: Monthly markdowns

Junior League Bargain Mart
702 Market St.
Chattanooga, TN 37402
CONTACT: Michael Woodward
PHONE: 615-266-4457
HOURS: Mon.–Fri. 10–5, Sat. 10–3
TYPE OF MERCHANDISE: Clothing, soft
goods
DONATION TAX RECEIPT: Receipt given
upon request
COMMENTS: Biannual rummage sale
every other spring

Goodwill Industries Thrift Store
212 S. Main St.
Goodlettsville, TN 37072
TYPE OF MERCHANDISE: Clothing,
housewares, furniture
DONATION TAX RECEIPT: Receipt given
upon request

Goodwill Industries Thrift Store
Northgate Crossing Center
CROSS STREET: 200 Old Hixson Pike
Hixson, TN 37343
PHONE: 615-877-9045
HOURS: Mon.–Sat. 9–7, Sun. 1–7
TYPE OF MERCHANDISE: Clothing,
housewares, furniture
DONATION TAX RECEIPT: Receipt given
upon request

Salvation Army Thrift Store
1204 N. Central St.
Knoxville, TN 37917
TYPE OF MERCHANDISE: Clothing,
housewares, furniture
DONATION TAX RECEIPT: Receipt given
upon request

Goodwill Industries Thrift Store
1800 E. Magnolia Ave.
Knoxville, TN 37917
TYPE OF MERCHANDISE: Clothing,
housewares, furniture
DONATION TAX RECEIPT: Receipt given
upon request

Salvation Army Thrift Store
130 N. Danny Thomas Blvd.
Memphis, TN 38103
TYPE OF MERCHANDISE: Clothing,
housewares, furniture
DONATION TAX RECEIPT: Receipt given
upon request

Humane Society Thrift Shop
710 Philadelphia St.
Memphis, TN 38104
TYPE OF MERCHANDISE: Clothing,
housewares
DONATION TAX RECEIPT: Receipt given
upon request

Salvation Army Thrift Store
1014 Mercury Blvd.
Murfreesboro, TN 37130
PHONE: 615-890-2258
HOURS: Mon.–Sat. 9–5
TYPE OF MERCHANDISE: Clothing,
housewares, furniture
DONATION TAX RECEIPT: Receipt given
upon request

Salvation Army Thrift Store
140 N. First St.
Nashville, TN 37213
HOURS: Mon.–Sat. 9–5
TYPE OF MERCHANDISE: Clothing,
housewares, furniture
DONATION TAX RECEIPT: Receipt given
upon request

Goodwill Industries Thrift Store
2606 Nolensville Pike
Nashville, TN 37211-2217

TYPE OF MERCHANDISE: Clothing, housewares, furniture
DONATION TAX RECEIPT: Receipt given upon request

Salvation Army Thrift Store
2612 Nolensville Pike
Nashville, TN 37211
TYPE OF MERCHANDISE: Clothing, housewares, furniture
DONATION TAX RECEIPT: Receipt given upon request

Salvation Army Thrift Store
2700 Nolensville Pike
Nashville, TN 37211
PHONE: 615-259-0735
HOURS: Mon.–Sat. 9–5
TYPE OF MERCHANDISE: Clothing, housewares, furniture
DONATION TAX RECEIPT: Receipt given upon request

Goodwill Industries Thrift Store
3101 Gallatin Rd.
Nashville, TN 37216
TYPE OF MERCHANDISE: Clothing, housewares, furniture
DONATION TAX RECEIPT: Receipt given upon request

Salvation Army Thrift Store
3225 Gallatin Rd.
Nashville, TN 37216
TYPE OF MERCHANDISE: Clothing, housewares, furniture
DONATION TAX RECEIPT: Receipt given upon request

Disabled American Vets Thrift Store
405 Woodland St.
Nashville, TN 37206
TYPE OF MERCHANDISE: Clothing, housewares
DONATION TAX RECEIPT: Receipt given upon request

Goodwill Industries Thrift Store
4507 Charlotte Pike
Nashville, TN 37209
TYPE OF MERCHANDISE: Clothing, housewares, furniture
DONATION TAX RECEIPT: Receipt given upon request

Salvation Army Thrift Store
6214 Charlotte Pike
Nashville, TN 37209
PHONE: 615-352-1154
HOURS: Mon.–Sat. 9–5
TYPE OF MERCHANDISE: Clothing, housewares, furniture
DONATION TAX RECEIPT: Receipt given upon request

Salvation Army Thrift Store
801 Gallatin Rd.
Nashville, TN 37206
TYPE OF MERCHANDISE: Clothing, housewares, furniture
DONATION TAX RECEIPT: Receipt given upon request

Goodwill Industries Thrift Store
203 Elm St.
S. Pittsburg, TN 37380
PHONE: 615-837-8382
HOURS: Mon.–Sat. 8–5
TYPE OF MERCHANDISE: Clothing, housewares, furniture
DONATION TAX RECEIPT: Receipt given upon request

Texas

Saint Vincent De Paul Thrift Store
1241 Walnut
Abilene, TX 79601
TYPE OF MERCHANDISE: Clothing, housewares, furniture
DONATION TAX RECEIPT: Receipt given upon request
COMMENTS: Monthly markdowns

Goodwill Industries Thrift Store
2066 Butternut St.
Abilene, TX 79602
TYPE OF MERCHANDISE: Clothing, housewares, furniture
DONATION TAX RECEIPT: Receipt given upon request

Goodwill Industries Thrift Store
714 E. Tenth Ave.
Amarillo, TX 79101
TYPE OF MERCHANDISE: Clothing, housewares, furniture

DONATION TAX RECEIPT: Receipt given
upon request
Salvation Army Thrift Store
1303 E. Abram St.
CROSS STREET: Hwy. 157
Arlington, TX 76011
CONTACT: Ina Karnatz
PHONE: 817-861-9488
HOURS: Mon.–Sat. 10–6
TYPE OF MERCHANDISE: Clothing,
housewares, furniture
DONATION TAX RECEIPT: Receipt given
upon request
Goodwill Industries Thrift Store
705 N. Palestine St.
Athens, TX 75751
TYPE OF MERCHANDISE: Clothing,
housewares, furniture
DONATION TAX RECEIPT: Receipt given
upon request
Salvation Army Thrift Store
1142 S. Lamar Blvd.
Austin, TX 78704
TYPE OF MERCHANDISE: Clothing,
housewares, furniture
DONATION TAX RECEIPT: Receipt given
upon request
Goodwill Industries Thrift Store
2400 S. First St.
Austin, TX 78704
TYPE OF MERCHANDISE: Clothing,
housewares, furniture
DONATION TAX RECEIPT: Receipt given
upon request
Goodwill Industries Thrift Store
403 Baylor St.
Austin, TX 78703
TYPE OF MERCHANDISE: Clothing,
housewares, furniture
DONATION TAX RECEIPT: Receipt given
upon request
Salvation Army Thrift Store
4201 S. Congress Ave.
Austin, TX 78745
TYPE OF MERCHANDISE: Clothing,
housewares, furniture
DONATION TAX RECEIPT: Receipt given
upon request

Goodwill Industries Thrift Store
4444 N. Lamar Blvd.
Austin, TX 78756
TYPE OF MERCHANDISE: Clothing,
housewares, furniture
DONATION TAX RECEIPT: Receipt given
upon request
Goodwill Industries Thrift Store
5734 Manchaca Rd.
Austin, TX 78745
TYPE OF MERCHANDISE: Clothing,
housewares, furniture
DONATION TAX RECEIPT: Receipt given
upon request
Goodwill Industries Thrift Store
7121 N. Lamar Blvd.
Austin, TX 78752
TYPE OF MERCHANDISE: Clothing,
housewares, furniture
DONATION TAX RECEIPT: Receipt given
upon request
Goodwill Industries Thrift Store
728 W. Stassney Ln.
Austin, TX 78745
TYPE OF MERCHANDISE: Clothing,
housewares, furniture
DONATION TAX RECEIPT: Receipt given
upon request
National Assistance League Thrift House
7951 Burnet Rd.
Austin, TX 78757
PHONE: 512-458-2633
TYPE OF MERCHANDISE: Clothing,
housewares, furniture
DONATION TAX RECEIPT: Receipt given
upon request
COMMENTS: Monthly markdowns
Salvation Army Thrift Store
1407 Pennsylvania St.
Beaumont, TX 77701
TYPE OF MERCHANDISE: Clothing,
housewares, furniture
DONATION TAX RECEIPT: Receipt given
upon request
Goodwill Industries Thrift Store
790 Orleans St.
Beaumont, TX 77701
TYPE OF MERCHANDISE: Clothing,
housewares, furniture

DONATION TAX RECEIPT: Receipt given upon request

Goodwill Industries Thrift Store
301 N. Washington
Beeville, TX 78102
CONTACT: Pamia Arrisola
PHONE: 512-358-8283
HOURS: Mon.–Sat. 9–6, Sun. 12–6
TYPE OF MERCHANDISE: Clothing, housewares, furniture
DONATION TAX RECEIPT: Receipt given upon request

Salvation Army Thrift Store
719 N. Main St.
Borger, TX 79007
TYPE OF MERCHANDISE: Clothing, housewares, furniture
DONATION TAX RECEIPT: Receipt given upon request

Saint Vincent De Paul Thrift Store
2645 Tuipan St.
Brownsville, TX 78521
TYPE OF MERCHANDISE: Clothing, housewares, furniture
DONATION TAX RECEIPT: Receipt given upon request
COMMENTS: Monthly markdowns

Goodwill Industries Thrift Store
1915 S. Texas Ave.
Bryan, TX 77802
PHONE: 409-823-2083
HOURS: Seven days, 9:30–5:30
TYPE OF MERCHANDISE: Clothing, housewares, furniture
DONATION TAX RECEIPT: Receipt given upon request
COMMENTS: Holiday sales

Salvation Army Thrift Store
210 E. Third St.
Burkburnett, TX 76354
TYPE OF MERCHANDISE: Clothing, housewares, furniture
DONATION TAX RECEIPT: Receipt given upon request

Goodwill Industries Thrift Store
445 Sheldon Rd.
CROSS STREET: Near I-10 E
Channelview, TX 77530

PHONE: 713-452-9396
HOURS: Seven days, 9:30–5:30
TYPE OF MERCHANDISE: Clothing, housewares, furniture
DONATION TAX RECEIPT: Receipt given upon request
COMMENTS: Holiday sales

Goodwill Industries Thrift Store
1214-D S. Frazier
Conroe, TX 77301
PHONE: 409-756-2181
HOURS: Seven days, 9:30–5:30
TYPE OF MERCHANDISE: Clothing, housewares, furniture
DONATION TAX RECEIPT: Receipt given upon request
COMMENTS: Holiday sales

Salvation Army Thrift Store
2017 N. Frazier St.
Conroe, TX 77301
TYPE OF MERCHANDISE: Clothing, housewares, furniture
DONATION TAX RECEIPT: Receipt given upon request

National Assistance League Thrift Shop
703 E. Davis
Conroe, TX 77301
PHONE: 409-760-1151
TYPE OF MERCHANDISE: Clothing, housewares, furniture
DONATION TAX RECEIPT: Receipt given upon request
COMMENTS: Monthly markdowns

Saint Vincent De Paul Thrift Store
2302 Laredo St.
Corpus Christi, TX 78405
TYPE OF MERCHANDISE: Clothing, housewares, furniture
DONATION TAX RECEIPT: Receipt given upon request
COMMENTS: Monthly markdowns

Goodwill Industries Thrift Store
2961 S. Port Ave.
Corpus Christi, TX 78405
CONTACT: Neli Lambert
PHONE: 512-884-4068,
FAX: 884-4090
HOURS: Mon.–Sat. 9–7, Sun. 12–6

TYPE OF MERCHANDISE: Clothing,
housewares, furniture
DONATION TAX RECEIPT: Receipt given
upon request
Goodwill Industries Thrift Store
9902 South Padre Island Dr.
Corpus Christi, TX 78418
CONTACT: Chuck Akers
PHONE: 512-937-5705
HOURS: Mon.–Sat. 9–7 Sun. 12–6
TYPE OF MERCHANDISE: Clothing,
housewares, furniture
DONATION TAX RECEIPT: Receipt given
upon request
Goodwill Industries Thrift Store
10522 Leopard
Corpus Christi, TX 78410
CONTACT: Lupe Viera
PHONE: 512-241-6656
HOURS: Mon.–Sat. 9–7, Sun. 12–6
TYPE OF MERCHANDISE: Clothing,
housewares, furniture
DONATION TAX RECEIPT: Receipt given
upon request
Goodwill Industries Thrift Store
107 N. Fourth St.
Crockett, TX 75835
PHONE: 409-544-7870
HOURS: Seven days, 9–6
TYPE OF MERCHANDISE: Clothing,
housewares, furniture
DONATION TAX RECEIPT: Receipt given
upon request
Goodwill Industries Thrift Store
107 S. First St.
Dallas, TX 75231
TYPE OF MERCHANDISE: Clothing,
housewares, furniture
DONATION TAX RECEIPT: Receipt given
upon request
Salvation Army Thrift Store
12895 Josey Lane
CROSS STREET: At Valley View
Dallas, TX 75235
CONTACT: Ken Mackenzie
PHONE: 214-484-5005
HOURS: Mon.–Sat. 10–5:15
TYPE OF MERCHANDISE: Clothing,
furniture, linens, toys

DONATION TAX RECEIPT: Receipt given
upon request
COMMENTS: Two large sidewalk sales per
year
Goodwill Industries Thrift Store
130 Ferguson Village Ctr.
Dallas, TX 75228
TYPE OF MERCHANDISE: Clothing,
housewares, furniture
DONATION TAX RECEIPT: Receipt given
upon request
Goodwill Industries Thrift Store
1606 Greenville Ave.
Dallas, TX 75206
TYPE OF MERCHANDISE: Clothing,
housewares, furniture
DONATION TAX RECEIPT: Receipt given
upon request
Salvation Army Thrift Store
4810 Village Fair Dr.
Dallas, TX
PHONE: 214-372-6965
HOURS: Mon.–Sat. 10–5:30
TYPE OF MERCHANDISE: Clothing,
furniture, linens
DONATION TAX RECEIPT: Receipt given
upon request
Salvation Army Thrift Store
5408 E. Grand
CROSS STREET: I-30
Dallas, TX 75235-1915
CONTACT: Norman Smith
PHONE: 214-821-3976
HOURS: Mon.–Sat. 10–5:45
TYPE OF MERCHANDISE: Clothing,
housewares, furniture
DONATION TAX RECEIPT: Receipt given
upon request
Salvation Army Thrift Store
5554 Harry Hines
CROSS STREET: Inwood
Dallas, TX 75235
CONTACT: Phillip Pfiel
PHONE: 214-630-5611
HOURS: Mon.–Sat. 10–6
TYPE OF MERCHANDISE: Clothing,
furniture, antiques
DONATION TAX RECEIPT: Receipt given
upon request

COMMENTS: Willie's Country Store and Antiques

Disabled American Vets Thrift Store
7303 Ferguson Rd.
Dallas, TX 75228
TYPE OF MERCHANDISE: Clothing, housewares, furniture
DONATION TAX RECEIPT: Receipt given upon request

Salvation Army Thrift Store
7921 Lake June Rd.
Dallas, TX 75217
TYPE OF MERCHANDISE: Clothing, housewares, furniture
DONATION TAX RECEIPT: Receipt given upon request

Disaled American Vets Thrift Store
7925 S. Loop
Dallas, TX 75217
TYPE OF MERCHANDISE: Clothing, housewares
DONATION TAX RECEIPT: Receipt given upon request

Salvation Army Thrift Store
939 W. Jefferson
CROSS STREET: Polk
Dallas, TX 75235
CONTACT: Doug Baker
PHONE: 214-946-5436
HOURS: Mon.–Sat. 10–5:30
TYPE OF MERCHANDISE: Clothing, housewares, furniture
DONATION TAX RECEIPT: Receipt given upon request

Goodwill Industries Thrift Store
2419 Woodlawn Blvd.
Denison, TX 75020
TYPE OF MERCHANDISE: Clothing, housewares, furniture
DONATION TAX RECEIPT: Receipt given upon request

Goodwill Industries Thrift Store
212 N. Temple
Diboll, TX 75941
PHONE: 409-829-3311
HOURS: Mon.–Sun. 9–6
TYPE OF MERCHANDISE: Clothing, housewares, furniture

DONATION TAX RECEIPT: Receipt given upon request

National Assistance League Thrifty House
2200 Montana Ave.
El Paso, TX 79903
PHONE: 915-533-5629
TYPE OF MERCHANDISE: Clothing, housewares, furniture
DONATION TAX RECEIPT: Receipt given upon request
COMMENTS: Monthly markdowns

Goodwill Industries Thrift Store
425a N. Yarbrough Dr.
El Paso, TX 79915
TYPE OF MERCHANDISE: Clothing, housewares, furniture
DONATION TAX RECEIPT: Receipt given upon request

Goodwill Industries Thrift Store
5300 Doniphan Dr.
El Paso, TX 79932
TYPE OF MERCHANDISE: Clothing, housewares, furniture
DONATION TAX RECEIPT: Receipt given upon request

Salvation Army Thrift Store
5421 Montana Ave.
El Paso, TX 79903
TYPE OF MERCHANDISE: Clothing, housewares, furniture
DONATION TAX RECEIPT: Receipt given upon request

Goodwill Industries Thrift Store
7015 Alameda Ave.
El Paso, TX 79915-3403
TYPE OF MERCHANDISE: Clothing, housewares, furniture
DONATION TAX RECEIPT: Receipt given upon request

Salvation Army Thrift Store
2406 Azle Ave.
CROSS STREETS: N.E. 28th St. and Ephriham St.
Fort Worth, TX 76106
CONTACT: Troy Gillespie
PHONE: 817-624-7081
HOURS: Mon.–Sat. 9–5
TYPE OF MERCHANDISE: Clothing, housewares, furniture

DONATION TAX RECEIPT: Receipt given upon request

Saint Vincent De Paul Thrift Store
2712 Seminary Dr. W
Fort Worth, TX 76133
TYPE OF MERCHANDISE: Clothing, housewares, furniture
DONATION TAX RECEIPT: Receipt given upon request
COMMENTS: Monthly markdowns

Salvation Army Thrift Store
2901 N.E. 28th St.
CROSS STREETS: Btw. N. Sylvania and N. Riverside
Fort Worth, TX 76111-2926
CONTACT: Hazel Deville
PHONE: 817-838-8203
HOURS: Mon.-Sat. 10–6
TYPE OF MERCHANDISE: Clothing, housewares, furniture
DONATION TAX RECEIPT: Receipt given upon request
COMMENTS: Boutique inside store

Salvation Army Thrift Store
8133 Hwy. 80 W
Fort Worth, TX 76116
CONTACT: Rachael Gordon
PHONE: 817-560-1563
HOURS: Mon.–Sat. 9–5
TYPE OF MERCHANDISE: Clothing, housewares, furniture
DONATION TAX RECEIPT: Receipt given upon request

Volunteers of America
3530 E. Lancaster Ave.
Fort Worth, TX 76103
TYPE OF MERCHANDISE: Clothing, housewares
DONATION TAX RECEIPT: Receipt given upon request

Disabled American Vets Thrift Store
4117 Denton Hwy.
Fort Worth, TX 76117
TYPE OF MERCHANDISE: Clothing, housewares
DONATION TAX RECEIPT: Receipt given upon request

Junior League Double Exposure
6205 Sunset
Fort Worth, TX 76116
CONTACT: Martha Flynn
PHONE: 817-738-8038
HOURS: Mon.–Sat. 10–5
TYPE OF MERCHANDISE: Clothing, appliances, housewares
DONATION TAX RECEIPT: Receipt given upon request
COMMENTS: Diversity of daily sales and specials

Saint Vincent De Paul Thrift Store
409 E. Main St.
Fredericksburg, TX 78624
TYPE OF MERCHANDISE: Clothing, housewares, furniture
DONATION TAX RECEIPT: Receipt given upon request
COMMENTS: Monthly markdowns

Saint Vincent De Paul Thrift Store
610 W. Live Oak
Fredericksburg, TX 78624
TYPE OF MERCHANDISE: Clothing, housewares, furniture
DONATION TAX RECEIPT: Receipt given upon request
COMMENTS: Monthly markdowns

Goodwill Industries Thrift Store
1010 Gulf Blvd.
Freeport, TX 77541
PHONE: 409-233-9732
HOURS: Seven days, 9:30–5:30
TYPE OF MERCHANDISE: Clothing, housewares, furniture
DONATION TAX RECEIPT: Receipt given upon request
COMMENTS: Holiday sales

Goodwill Industries Thrift Store
E. Highway 82
Gainesville, TX 76240
TYPE OF MERCHANDISE: Clothing, housewares, furniture
DONATION TAX RECEIPT: Receipt given upon request

Goodwill Industries Thrift Store
4525 Avenue "U"
Galveston, TX 77552

PHONE: 409-763-1161
HOURS: Seven days, 9:30–5:30
TYPE OF MERCHANDISE: Clothing,
housewares, furniture
DONATION TAX RECEIPT: Receipt given
upon request
COMMENTS: Holiday sales

Junior League Begin Again Thrift Shop
1456 Betline Rd. Suite 140
CROSS STREET: N. Garland Rd.
Garland, TX 75044
CONTACT: Betty Perkins
PHONE: 213-530-0804
TYPE OF MERCHANDISE: Clothing,
housewares
DONATION TAX RECEIPT: Receipt given
upon request

Salvation Army Thrift Store
1905 Garland Rd.
CROSS STREET: Miller
Garland, TX 75218
CONTACT: Charlene McCall
PHONE: 214-840-1061
HOURS: Mon.–Sat. 10–5:30
TYPE OF MERCHANDISE: Clothing,
furniture, linens
DONATION TAX RECEIPT: Receipt given
upon request

Disabled American Vets Bargain Center
407 Marshall Plaza
Grand Prairie, TX 75051
TYPE OF MERCHANDISE: Clothing,
housewares
DONATION TAX RECEIPT: Receipt given
upon request

Goodwill Industries Thrift Store
2404 Lee St.
Greenville, TX 75401
TYPE OF MERCHANDISE: Clothing,
housewares, furniture
DONATION TAX RECEIPT: Receipt given
upon request

National Assistance League Thrift Shop
1902 Commonwealth
Houston, TX 77006
PHONE: 713-526-5425
TYPE OF MERCHANDISE: Clothing,
housewares, furniture

DONATION TAX RECEIPT: Receipt given
upon request
COMMENTS: Monthly markdowns

Salvation Army Thrift Store
1015 Hemphill St.
Houston, TX 77007
CONTACT: Jack W. Owens
TYPE OF MERCHANDISE: Clothing,
housewares, furniture
DONATION TAX RECEIPT: Receipt given
upon request

Goodwill Industries Thrift Store
1390 Federal Rd.
Houston, TX 77051
PHONE: 713-451-5096
HOURS: Seven days, 9:30–5:30
TYPE OF MERCHANDISE: Clothing,
housewares, furniture
DONATION TAX RECEIPT: Receipt given
upon request
COMMENTS: Holiday sales

Goodwill Industries Thrift Store
1515 Little York
CROSS STREET: Near Hardy Toll Road
Houston, TX 77093
PHONE: 713-442-9520
HOURS: Seven days, 9:30–5:30
TYPE OF MERCHANDISE: Clothing,
housewares, furniture
DONATION TAX RECEIPT: Receipt given
upon request
COMMENTS: Holiday sales

Goodwill Industries Thrift Store
1808 Wirt Rd.
CROSS STREET: Near Long Point
Houston, TX 77055
PHONE: 713-957-9271
HOURS: Seven days, 9:30–5:30
TYPE OF MERCHANDISE: Clothing,
housewares, furniture
DONATION TAX RECEIPT: Receipt given
upon request
COMMENTS: Holiday sales

Salvation Army Thrift Store
2118 Washington Ave.
Houston, TX 77007-6137
TYPE OF MERCHANDISE: Clothing,
housewares, furniture

DONATION TAX RECEIPT: Receipt given
upon request
Saint Vincent De Paul Thrift Store
2403 Holcome Blvd.
Houston, TX 77021
TYPE OF MERCHANDISE: Clothing,
housewares, furniture
DONATION TAX RECEIPT: Receipt given
upon request
COMMENTS: Monthly markdowns
Goodwill Industries Thrift Store
4122 Telephone Rd.
CROSS STREET: Near Griggs
Houston, TX 77087
PHONE: 713-649-9000
HOURS: Seven days, 9:30–5:30
TYPE OF MERCHANDISE: Clothing,
housewares, furniture
DONATION TAX RECEIPT: Receipt given
upon request
COMMENTS: Holiday sales
Goodwill Industries Thrift Store
4535 Harrisburg
Houston, TX 77011
PHONE: 713-926-0041
HOURS: Seven days, 9:30–5:30
TYPE OF MERCHANDISE: Clothing,
housewares, furniture
DONATION TAX RECEIPT: Receipt given
upon request
COMMENTS: Holiday sales
Salvation Army Thrift Store
5105 N. Shepherd Dr.
Houston, TX 77018
TYPE OF MERCHANDISE: Clothing,
housewares, furniture
DONATION TAX RECEIPT: Receipt given
upon request
Goodwill Industries Thrift Store
5200 Jensen Dr.
Houston, TX 77026
PHONE: 713-691-8493, 692-6221
HOURS: Seven days, 9:30–5:30
TYPE OF MERCHANDISE: Clothing,
housewares, furniture
DONATION TAX RECEIPT: Receipt given
upon request
COMMENTS: Holiday sales

Goodwill Industries Thrift Store
5705 Fondren
Houston, TX 77036
PHONE: 713-780-4739
HOURS: Seven days, 9:30–5:30
TYPE OF MERCHANDISE: Clothing,
housewares, furniture
DONATION TAX RECEIPT: Receipt given
upon request
COMMENTS: Holiday sales
Goodwill Industries Thrift Store
6005 N. Sheperd
CROSS STREET: Near Tidwell
Houston, TX 77091
PHONE: 713-691-8103
HOURS: Seven days, 9:30–5:30
TYPE OF MERCHANDISE: Clothing,
housewares, furniture
DONATION TAX RECEIPT: Receipt given
upon request
COMMENTS: Holiday sales
TVI Savers Thrift Store
7645 Dashwood Dr.
Houston, TX 77036
CONTACT: Linda Jackson
PHONE: 713-772-8003
HOURS: Mon.–Sat. 9–9, Sun. 10–6
TYPE OF MERCHANDISE: Clothing,
housewares, furniture
DONATION TAX RECEIPT: No
Goodwill Industries Thrift Store
8525 Mesa Rd.
CROSS STREET: At Lakewood Shopping
Center
Houston, TX 77078
PHONE: 713-633-9480
HOURS: Seven days, 9:30–5:30
TYPE OF MERCHANDISE: Clothing,
housewares, furniture
DONATION TAX RECEIPT: Receipt given
upon request
COMMENTS: Holiday sales
Goodwill Industries Thrift Store
8616 Culen Blvd.
Houston, TX 77051
PHONE: 713-734-9211
HOURS: Seven days, 9:30–5:30
TYPE OF MERCHANDISE: Clothing,
housewares, furniture

DONATION TAX RECEIPT: Receipt given upon request
COMMENTS: Holiday sales
Goodwill Industries Thrift Store
19306-C Hwy. 59
Humble, TX 77338
PHONE: 713-446-4332
HOURS: Seven days, 9:30–5:30
TYPE OF MERCHANDISE: Clothing, housewares, furniture
DONATION TAX RECEIPT: Receipt given upon request
COMMENTS: Holiday sales
Salvation Army Thrift Store
1145 E. Irving Blvd.
CROSS STREET: Nursery
Irving, TX 75060
CONTACT: James Hughes
PHONE: 214-579-1966
HOURS: Mon.–Sat. 10–5:45
TYPE OF MERCHANDISE: Clothing, furniture, linens
DONATION TAX RECEIPT: Receipt given upon request
Disabled American Vets Thrift Store
2310 Rock Island Rd.
Irving, TX 75060
TYPE OF MERCHANDISE: Clothing, housewares
DONATION TAX RECEIPT: Receipt given upon request
Goodwill Industries Thrift Store
808 N. Eighth St.
Killeen, TX 76541
TYPE OF MERCHANDISE: Clothing, housewares, furniture
DONATION TAX RECEIPT: Receipt given upon request
Goodwill Industries Thrift Store
1123 S. 14th St.
CROSS STREET: Carlos Truad Blvd.
Kingsville, TX 78363
CONTACT: Andy Garcia
PHONE: 512-592-2727
HOURS: Mon.–Sat. 9–7, Sun. 12–6
TYPE OF MERCHANDISE: Clothing, housewares, furniture

DONATION TAX RECEIPT: Receipt given upon request
Salvation Army Thrift Store
407 Houston St.
Laredo, TX 78040
TYPE OF MERCHANDISE: Clothing, housewares, furniture
DONATION TAX RECEIPT: Receipt given upon request
Goodwill Industries Thrift Store
808 Austin
Levelland, TX 79336
PHONE: 806-894-6510
HOURS: Mon.–Sat. 9–5:15
TYPE OF MERCHANDISE: Clothing, housewares, furniture
DONATION TAX RECEIPT: Receipt given upon request
Junior League Bargain Box & Repeat
1107 N. Fourth St.
Longview, TX 75606
CONTACT: Jeanie Folzenlogen
PHONE: 903-753-3060
HOURS: Mon.–Sat. 9:30–4:30
TYPE OF MERCHANDISE: Clothing, housewares
DONATION TAX RECEIPT: Mailed out at year's end only
CONTACT: Consignments accepted
Goodwill Industries Thrift Store
1109 Broadway
Lubbock, TX 79401
PHONE: 806-744-1112
HOURS: Mon.–Sat. 8:30–5:30
TYPE OF MERCHANDISE: Clothing, housewares, furniture
DONATION TAX RECEIPT: Receipt given upon request
Goodwill Industries Thrift Store
1940 34th St.
Lubbock, TX 79412
PHONE: 806-747-3733
HOURS: Mon.–Wed. 9–6, Thurs. 9–8, Fri.–Sat. 9–6
TYPE OF MERCHANDISE: Clothing, housewares, furniture
DONATION TAX RECEIPT: Receipt given upon request

Goodwill Industries Thrift Store
715 28th St.
Lubbock, TX 79404
PHONE: 806-744-3348
HOURS: Mon.–Sat. 8:30–5:30
TYPE OF MERCHANDISE: Clothing,
housewares, furniture
DONATION TAX RECEIPT: Receipt given
upon request

Goodwill Industries Thrift Store
1011 W. Frank
Lufkin, TX 75904
PHONE: 409-632-8838
HOURS: Seven days, 9–6
TYPE OF MERCHANDISE: Clothing,
housewares, furniture
DONATION TAX RECEIPT: Receipt given
upon request

Goodwill Industries Thrift Store
802 S. Washington Ave.
Marshall, TX 75670
TYPE OF MERCHANDISE: Clothing,
housewares, furniture
DONATION TAX RECEIPT: Receipt given
upon request

Salvation Army Thrift Store
300 S. Baird St.
Midland, TX 79701
TYPE OF MERCHANDISE: Clothing,
housewares, furniture
DONATION TAX RECEIPT: Receipt given
upon request

Goodwill Industries Thrift Store
503 E. Main
Nacogdoches, TX 75961
PHONE: 409-564-4365
HOURS: Seven days, 9–6
TYPE OF MERCHANDISE: Clothing,
housewares, furniture
DONATION TAX RECEIPT: Receipt given
upon request

Junior League Thrift Shop
418 N. Grant Ave.
Odessa, TX 79761
TYPE OF MERCHANDISE: Clothing for men,
women, and children
DONATION TAX RECEIPT: Receipt given
upon request

Salvation Army Thrift Store
406 S. Cuyler St.
Pampa, TX 79065
TYPE OF MERCHANDISE: Clothing,
housewares, furniture
DONATION TAX RECEIPT: Receipt given
upon request

Goodwill Industries Thrift Store
1161 N.W. Loop
Paris, TX 75460
TYPE OF MERCHANDISE: Clothing,
housewares, furniture
DONATION TAX RECEIPT: Receipt given
upon request

Salvation Army Thrift Store
1401 First St. NE
Paris, TX 75460
TYPE OF MERCHANDISE: Clothing,
housewares, furniture
DONATION TAX RECEIPT: Receipt given
upon request

Salvation Army Thrift Store
7 E. Plaza
Paris, TX 75460
TYPE OF MERCHANDISE: Clothing,
housewares, furniture
DONATION TAX RECEIPT: Receipt given
upon request

Goodwill Industries Thrift Store
1311 Richey
CROSS STREET: Near Southmore
Pasadena, TX 77502
PHONE: 713-472-9233
HOURS: Seven days, 9:30–5:30
TYPE OF MERCHANDISE: Clothing,
housewares, furniture
DONATION TAX RECEIPT: Receipt given
upon request
COMMENTS: Holiday sales

Salvation Army Thrift Store
1818 Strawberry Rd.
Pasadena, TX 77502
TYPE OF MERCHANDISE: Clothing,
housewares, furniture
DONATION TAX RECEIPT: Receipt given
upon request

Goodwill Industries Thrift Store
101-A E. Expwy. 83
CROSS STREET: Expy. 83 & Hwy. 281
Pharr, TX 78577
CONTACT: Jerry Garcia
PHONE: 210-702-4404
HOURS: Mon.–Sat. 9–7, Sun. 12–6
TYPE OF MERCHANDISE: Clothing,
housewares, furniture
DONATION TAX RECEIPT: Receipt given
upon request

Saint Vincent De Paul Thrift Store
122 W. Hawk
Pharr, TX 78577
TYPE OF MERCHANDISE: Clothing,
housewares, furniture
DONATION TAX RECEIPT: Receipt given
upon request
COMMENTS: Monthly markdowns

Goodwill Industries Thrift Store
624 Ash St.
Plainview, TX 79072
TYPE OF MERCHANDISE: Clothing,
housewares, furniture
DONATION TAX RECEIPT: Receipt given
upon request

Goodwill Industries Thrift Store
4448 Gulfway Dr.
Port Arthur, TX 77642
TYPE OF MERCHANDISE: Clothing,
housewares, furniture
DONATION TAX RECEIPT: Receipt given
upon request

Saint Vincent De Paul Thrift Store
1810 S. Irving
San Angelo, TX 76903
TYPE OF MERCHANDISE: Clothing,
housewares, furniture
DONATION TAX RECEIPT: Receipt given
upon request
COMMENTS: Monthly markdowns

Salvation Army Thrift Store
209 Gillis St.
San Angelo, TX 76903
TYPE OF MERCHANDISE: Clothing,
housewares, furniture
DONATION TAX RECEIPT: Receipt given
upon request

Junior League Thrift Shop
7 W. Beauregard Ave.
San Angelo, TX 76903
TYPE OF MERCHANDISE: Clothing for men,
women, and children
DONATION TAX RECEIPT: Receipt given
upon request

Goodwill Industries Thrift Store
1308 Guadalupe St.
San Antonio, TX 78207-5519
TYPE OF MERCHANDISE: Clothing,
housewares, furniture
DONATION TAX RECEIPT: Receipt given
upon request

Goodwill Industries Thrift Store
207 San Pedro Ave.
San Antonio, TX 78205
TYPE OF MERCHANDISE: Clothing,
housewares, furniture
DONATION TAX RECEIPT: Receipt given
upon request

Disabled American Vets Thrift Store
2307 Vance Jackson Rd.
San Antonio, TX 78213
TYPE OF MERCHANDISE: Clothing
housewares
DONATION TAX RECEIPT: Receipt given
upon request

Salvation Army Thrift Store
2541 W. Southcross St.
San Antonio, TX 78211
CONTACT: Ray Mauriciso
PHONE: 210-927-1848
HOURS: Mon.–Sat. 9–6
TYPE OF MERCHANDISE: Clothing,
housewares, furniture
DONATION TAX RECEIPT: Receipt given
upon request
COMMENTS: Monthly sidewalk sale

National Assistance League Thrift House
2611 West Ave.
San Antonio, TX 78201
PHONE: 210-732-1200
TYPE OF MERCHANDISE: Clothing,
housewares, furniture
DONATION TAX RECEIPT: Receipt given
upon request
COMMENTS: Monthly markdowns

Goodwill Industries Thrift Store
2705 W. Southcross Blvd.
San Antonio, TX 78211
TYPE OF MERCHANDISE: Clothing,
housewares, furniture
DONATION TAX RECEIPT: Receipt given
upon request

Salvation Army Thrift Store
2711 West Ave.
San Antonio, TX 78201
CONTACT: Bonnie Crocker
PHONE: 210-342-4131
HOURS: Seven days, 9–6
TYPE OF MERCHANDISE: Clothing,
appliances
DONATION TAX RECEIPT: Receipt given
upon request
COMMENTS: Monthly parking lot sale

Salvation Army Thrift Store
3606 Pleasanton Rd.
San Antonio, TX 78221
TYPE OF MERCHANDISE: Clothing,
housewares, furniture
DONATION TAX RECEIPT: Receipt given
upon request

Disabled American Vets Thrift Store
3610 Nogalitos
San Antonio, TX 78211
TYPE OF MERCHANDISE: Clothing,
housewares
DONATION TAX RECEIPT: Receipt given
upon request

Goodwill Industries Thrift Store
3822 Pleasanton Rd.
San Antonio, TX 78221
TYPE OF MERCHANDISE: Clothing,
housewares, furniture
DONATION TAX RECEIPT: Receipt given
upon request

Salvation Army Thrift Store
301 S.W. Military Dr.
San Antonio, TX 78221
CONTACT: James Shouse
PHONE: 210-977-8220
HOURS: Seven days, 9–6
TYPE OF MERCHANDISE: Specialty—
antique furniture

DONATION TAX RECEIPT: Receipt given
upon request
COMMENTS: Monthly parking lot sale

Goodwill Industries Thrift Store
824 S. Brazos St.
San Antonio, TX 78207
TYPE OF MERCHANDISE: Clothing,
housewares, furniture
DONATION TAX RECEIPT: Receipt given
upon request

Salvation Army Thrift Store
1324 S. Flores St.
San Antonio, TX 78204
CONTACT: Steve Daniels, Al Levering
PHONE: 210-6877
FAX: 223-4448
HOURS: Seven days, 9–6
TYPE OF MERCHANDISE: Clothing,
housewares, furniture
DONATION TAX RECEIPT: Receipt given
upon request
COMMENTS: Specialty country store

Salvation Army Thrift Store
2076 N. Travis St.
Sherman, TX 75090
TYPE OF MERCHANDISE: Clothing,
housewares, furniture
DONATION TAX RECEIPT: Receipt given
upon request

Goodwill Industries Thrift Store
2206 E. Lamar St.
Sherman, TX 75090
TYPE OF MERCHANDISE: Clothing,
housewares, furniture
DONATION TAX RECEIPT: Receipt given
upon request

Salvation Army Thrift Store
402 S. State Line Ave.
Texarkana, TX 75501
TYPE OF MERCHANDISE: Clothing,
housewares, furniture
DONATION TAX RECEIPT: Receipt given
upon request

Goodwill Industries Thrift Store
2312 Palmer Highway
Texas City, TX 77590
PHONE: 409-948-8391
HOURS: Seven days, 9:30–5:30

TYPE OF MERCHANDISE: Clothing, housewares, furniture
DONATION TAX RECEIPT: Receipt given upon request
COMMENTS: Holiday sales

Goodwill Industries Thrift Store
1120 W. Fifth St.
Tyler, TX 75701
TYPE OF MERCHANDISE: Clothing, housewares, furniture
DONATION TAX RECEIPT: Receipt given upon request

Salvation Army Thrift Store
1204 W. Bow St.
Tyler, TX 75702
TYPE OF MERCHANDISE: Clothing, housewares, furniture
DONATION TAX RECEIPT: Receipt given upon request

Goodwill Industries Thrift Store
2200 Loop W
Tyler, TX 75701
TYPE OF MERCHANDISE: Clothing, housewares, furniture
DONATION TAX RECEIPT: Receipt given upon request

Goodwill Industries Thrift Store
409 W. Locust St.
Tyler, TX 75702
TYPE OF MERCHANDISE: Clothing, housewares, furniture
DONATION TAX RECEIPT: Receipt given upon request

Goodwill Industries Thrift Store
1611 N. Laurent St.
Victoria, TX 77901
TYPE OF MERCHANDISE: Clothing, housewares, furniture
DONATION TAX RECEIPT: Receipt given upon request

Goodwill Industries Thrift Store
4102 N. Navarro
Victoria, TX 77901
CONTACT: Robbie Ramos
PHONE: 512-575-6234
HOURS: Mon.–Sat. 9–6, Sun. 12–6
TYPE OF MERCHANDISE: Clothing, housewares, furniture

DONATION TAX RECEIPT: Receipt given upon request

Salvation Army Thrift Store
1911 Park Lake Dr.
Waco, TX 76708
TYPE OF MERCHANDISE: Clothing, housewares, furniture
DONATION TAX RECEIPT: Receipt given upon request

Salvation Army Thrift Store
403 Seventh St.
Wichita Falls, TX 76301
TYPE OF MERCHANDISE: Clothing, housewares, furniture
DONATION TAX RECEIPT: Receipt given upon request

Saint Vincent De Paul Thrift Store
406 Lamar
Wichita Falls, TX 76301
TYPE OF MERCHANDISE: Clothing, housewares, furniture
DONATION TAX RECEIPT: Receipt given upon request
COMMENTS: Monthly markdowns

Disabled American Vets Thrift Store
417 Indiana Ave.
Wichita Falls, TX 76301
TYPE OF MERCHANDISE: Clothing, housewares, furniture
DONATION TAX RECEIPT: Receipt given upon request

Amvets Thrift Store Value Village
717 Indiana Ave.
Wichita Falls, TX 76301
TYPE OF MERCHANDISE: Clothing, housewares, furniture
DONATION TAX RECEIPT: Receipt given upon request

Goodwill Industries Thrift Store
915 Indiana Ave.
Wichita Falls, TX 76301
PHONE: 817-761-2423
HOURS: Mon.–Sat. 9–6
TYPE OF MERCHANDISE: Clothing, housewares, furniture
DONATION TAX RECEIPT: Receipt given upon request
COMMENTS: Tag sales daily, weekly senior discount

Utah

Salvation Army Thrift Store
129 State St.
Clearfield, UT 84015
TYPE OF MERCHANDISE: Clothing,
housewares, furniture
DONATION TAX RECEIPT: Receipt given
upon request

Salvation Army Thrift Store
45 Center Sq.
Midvale, UT 84047
TYPE OF MERCHANDISE: Clothing,
housewares, furniture
DONATION TAX RECEIPT: Receipt given
upon request

Salvation Army Thrift Store
2615 Grant Ave.
Ogden, UT 84401
TYPE OF MERCHANDISE: Clothing,
housewares, furniture
DONATION TAX RECEIPT: Receipt given
upon request

TVI Savers Thrift Store
3833 Washington Blvd.
Ogden, UT 84403
CONTACT: Brennan Bateman
PHONE: 801-399-3919
HOURS: Mon.–Sat. 9–9, Sun. 10–6
TYPE OF MERCHANDISE: Clothing,
housewares, furniture
DONATION TAX RECEIPT: No

TVI Savers Thrift Store
81 N. State St.
Orem, UT 84057
CONTACT: Celeste Vanecko
PHONE: 801-225-9445
HOURS: Mon.–Sat. 9–9, Sun. 10–6
TYPE OF MERCHANDISE: Clothing,
housewares, furniture
DONATION TAX RECEIPT: No

National Assistance League Bargain Box
2060 E. 3300 S.
Salt Lake City, UT 84109
PHONE: 801-484-3401
TYPE OF MERCHANDISE: Clothing,
housewares, furniture
DONATION TAX RECEIPT: Receipt given
upon request
COMMENTS: Monthly markdowns

Salvation Army Thrift Store
4055 W. 5400 South
Salt Lake City, UT 84118
PHONE: 801-967-6134
HOURS: Mon.–Sat. 10–6
TYPE OF MERCHANDISE: Clothing,
housewares, furniture
DONATION TAX RECEIPT: Receipt given
upon request

Salvation Army Thrift Store
427 W. 200 South
Salt Lake City, UT 84101
PHONE: 801-596-1709
HOURS: Mon.–Sat. 10–5
TYPE OF MERCHANDISE: Clothing,
housewares, furniture
DONATION TAX RECEIPT: Receipt given
upon request

TVI Savers Thrift Store
4145 S. Redwood Rd.
Taylorsville, UT 84123
CONTACT: Lee Manwaring
PHONE: 801-262-2150
TYPE OF MERCHANDISE: Clothing,
housewares, furniture
DONATION TAX RECEIPT: No

Vermont

Salvation Army Thrift Store
511–513 South St.
Bennington, VT 05201
TYPE OF MERCHANDISE: Clothing,
housewares, furniture
DONATION TAX RECEIPT: Receipt given
upon request

Virginia

Salvation Army Thrift Store
6528 Little River Turnpike
Alexandria, VA 22312
PHONE: 703-642-9270
HOURS: Seven days, 9–4
TYPE OF MERCHANDISE: Furniture,
clothing, collectibles
DONATION TAX RECEIPT: Receipt given
upon request

COMMENTS: Half-price sales, daily auctions at 9 A.M.

Goodwill Industries Thrift Store
7842 Richmond Hwy.
Alexandria, VA 22306
TYPE OF MERCHANDISE: Clothing, housewares, furniture
DONATION TAX RECEIPT: Receipt given upon request

Goodwill Industries Thrift Store
4714 Columbia Pike
Arlington, VA 22212
PHONE: 702-892-8897
HOURS: Mon.–Sat. 10–6
TYPE OF MERCHANDISE: Clothing, housewares, furniture
DONATION TAX RECEIPT: Receipt given upon request

Junior League of N. Virginia Thrift
5012 Lee Hwy.
Arlington, VA 22207
PHONE: 703-522-1993
HOURS: Tues.–Sat. 10–4 (closed July)
TYPE OF MERCHANDISE: Clothing, housewares, furniture
DONATION TAX RECEIPT: Receipt given upon request

Salvation Army Thrift Store
700 Harris St.
Charlottesville, VA 22903
TYPE OF MERCHANDISE: Clothing, housewares, furniture
DONATION TAX RECEIPT: Receipt given upon request

Goodwill Industries Thrift Store
324 N. Main St.
Chase City, VA 23924
TYPE OF MERCHANDISE: Clothing, housewares, furniture
DONATION TAX RECEIPT: Receipt given upon request

Goodwill Industries Thrift Store
51 W. Main St.
Christiansburg, VA 24073
TYPE OF MERCHANDISE: Clothing, housewares, furniture
DONATION TAX RECEIPT: Receipt given upon request

Salvation Army Thrift Store
502 Main St.
Clifton Forge, VA 24422
TYPE OF MERCHANDISE: Clothing, housewares, furniture
DONATION TAX RECEIPT: Receipt given upon request

Goodwill Industries Thrift Store
1226 W. Main St.
Danville, VA 24541
TYPE OF MERCHANDISE: Clothing, housewares, furniture
DONATION TAX RECEIPT: Receipt given upon request

Salvation Army Thrift Store
101 Possum Point Rd.
Dumfries, VA 22026
TYPE OF MERCHANDISE: Clothing, housewares, furniture
DONATION TAX RECEIPT: Receipt given upon request

Humane Society Orange Crate Thrift Shop
112 West St.
Falls Church, VA 22046
PHONE: 703-533-9268
HOURS: Tues. 10–2, Wed.–Fri. 10–4, Sat. 10–2
TYPE OF MERCHANDISE: Clothing, housewares, furniture
DONATION TAX RECEIPT: Receipt given upon request

Salvation Army Thrift Store
136 Olde Greenwich Dr.
Fredericksburg, VA 22408
TYPE OF MERCHANDISE: Clothing, housewares, furniture
DONATION TAX RECEIPT: Receipt given upon request

Goodwill Industries Thrift Store
1009 W. Stuart Dr.
Galax, VA 24333
PHONE: 703-236-6261
HOURS: Mon.–Sat. 9–9, Sun. 12–8
TYPE OF MERCHANDISE: Clothing, housewares, furniture
DONATION TAX RECEIPT: Receipt given upon request
COMMENTS: Unit pricing, most clothing $2.25 each

Goodwill Industries Thrift Store
65 Main St.
Halifax, VA 24558
TYPE OF MERCHANDISE: Clothing,
housewares, furniture
DONATION TAX RECEIPT: Receipt given
upon request

Salvation Army Thrift Store
1935 E. Pembroke Ave.
Hampton, VA 23663
TYPE OF MERCHANDISE: Clothing,
housewares, furniture
DONATION TAX RECEIPT: Receipt given
upon request

MCC Gift & Thrift Shop
227 N. Main St.
Harrisonburg, VA 22801
PHONE: 703-433-8844
TYPE OF MERCHANDISE: Clothing,
housewares, furniture
DONATION TAX RECEIPT: Receipt given
upon request

Salvation Army Thrift Store
47 Court Sq.
Harrisonburg, VA 22801
TYPE OF MERCHANDISE: Clothing,
housewares, furniture
DONATION TAX RECEIPT: Receipt given
upon request

Salvation Army Thrift Store
2421–A6 Centreville Rd.
Herndon, VA 22071
HOURS: Seven days, 10–7
TYPE OF MERCHANDISE: Clothing,
housewares, furniture
DONATION TAX RECEIPT: Receipt given
upon request
COMMENTS: Half-price sales

Amvets Thrift Store
785 Station St.
Herndon, VA 22070
TYPE OF MERCHANDISE: Clothing,
housewares
DONATION TAX RECEIPT: Receipt given
upon request

Disabled American Vets Thrift Store
5240 Oaklawn Blvd.
Hopewell, VA 23860
TYPE OF MERCHANDISE: Clothing,
housewares, furniture
DONATION TAX RECEIPT: Receipt given
upon request

Disabled American Vets Thrift Store
2211 Florida Ave.
Lynchburg, VA 24501
TYPE OF MERCHANDISE: Clothing,
housewares, furniture
DONATION TAX RECEIPT: Receipt given
upon request

Salvation Army Thrift Store
7440 Sudley Rd.
Manassas, VA 22201
PHONE: 703-361-9904
HOURS: Seven days, 9:30–1:30
TYPE OF MERCHANDISE: Furniture,
clothing, collectibles
DONATION TAX RECEIPT: Receipt given
upon request
COMMENTS: Half-price sales

Goodwill Industries Thrift Store
509 W. Church St.
Martinsville, VA 24112
TYPE OF MERCHANDISE: Clothing,
housewares, furniture
DONATION TAX RECEIPT: Receipt given
upon request

Salvation Army Thrift Store
14863 Warwick Blvd.
Newport News, VA 23602
PHONE: 804-875-1969
HOURS: Seven days, 9–5
TYPE OF MERCHANDISE: Clothing,
furniture, bric-a-brac
DONATION TAX RECEIPT: Receipt given
upon request
COMMENTS: Weekly tag sales

Salvation Army Thrift Store
1401 Monticello Ave.
Norfolk, VA 23510
PHONE: 804-627-2330
HOURS: Seven days, 9–5
TYPE OF MERCHANDISE: Clothing,
furniture, bric-a-brac
DONATION TAX RECEIPT: Receipt given
upon request
COMMENTS: Weekly tag sales

Salvation Army Thrift Store
925 N. Military Hwy.
Norfolk, VA 23502
PHONE: 804-461-7579
HOURS: Seven days, 9–5
TYPE OF MERCHANDISE: Clothing,
furniture, bric-a-brac
DONATION TAX RECEIPT: Receipt given
upon request
COMMENTS: Weekly tag sales
Salvation Army Thrift Store
3102 Airline Blvd.
Portsmouth, VA 23701
TYPE OF MERCHANDISE: Clothing,
housewares, furniture
DONATION TAX RECEIPT: Receipt given
upon request
Goodwill Industries Thrift Store
45 E. Main St.
Pulaski, VA 24301
PHONE: 703-980-9790
HOURS: Mon.–Sat. 9–9, Sun. 12–8
TYPE OF MERCHANDISE: Clothing,
housewares, furniture
DONATION TAX RECEIPT: Receipt given
upon request
COMMENTS: Unit pricing, most clothing
$2.25 each
Salvation Army Thrift Store
2601 Hermitage Rd.
Richmond, VA 23220
CONTACT: Capt. David B. Atkins
TYPE OF MERCHANDISE: Clothing,
housewares, furniture
DONATION TAX RECEIPT: Receipt given
upon request
Salvation Army Thrift Store
3700 Mechanicsville Pike
Richmond, VA 23223
TYPE OF MERCHANDISE: Clothing,
housewares, furniture
DONATION TAX RECEIPT: Receipt given
upon request
Salvation Army Thrift Store
441 E. Belt Blvd.
Richmond, VA 23219
PHONE: 804-230-7140

TYPE OF MERCHANDISE: Clothing,
housewares, furniture
DONATION TAX RECEIPT: Receipt given
upon request
Goodwill Industries Thrift Store
7210 Williamson Rd.
Roanoke, VA 24019
PHONE: 703-366-4765
HOURS: Mon.–Sat. 9–9, Sun. 12–8
TYPE OF MERCHANDISE: Clothing,
housewares, furniture
DONATION TAX RECEIPT: Receipt given
upon request
COMMENTS: Unit pricing, most clothing
$2.25 each
Goodwill Industries Thrift Store
1493 E. Main St.
Salem, VA 24153
PHONE: 703-986-1224
FAX: 986-2067
HOURS: Mon.–Sat. 9–9, Sun. 12–8
TYPE OF MERCHANDISE: Clothing,
housewares, furniture
DONATION TAX RECEIPT: Receipt given
upon request
COMMENTS: Unit pricing, most clothing
$2.25 each
Salvation Army Thrift Store
1722 Plunkett St.
Staunton, VA 24401
TYPE OF MERCHANDISE: Clothing,
housewares, furniture
DONATION TAX RECEIPT: Receipt given
upon request
Goodwill Industries Thrift Store
7 S. Augusta St.
Staunton, VA 24401
TYPE OF MERCHANDISE: Clothing,
housewares, furniture
DONATION TAX RECEIPT: Receipt given
upon request
Goodwill Industries Thrift Store
144 W. Washington St.
Suffolk, VA 23434
TYPE OF MERCHANDISE: Clothing,
housewares, furniture
DONATION TAX RECEIPT: Receipt given
upon request

Salvation Army Thrift Store
5524 Virginia Beach Blvd.
CROSS STREET: Newton Rd.
Virginia Beach, VA 23462
PHONE: 804-499-0032
FAX: 499-1427
HOURS: Seven days, 9–7
TYPE OF MERCHANDISE: Clothing,
housewares, furniture
DONATION TAX RECEIPT: Receipt given
upon request
COMMENTS: Weekly tag sales

Saint Vincent De Paul Thrift Store
13744 Maryos Way
Woodbridge, VA 22191
TYPE OF MERCHANDISE: Clothing,
housewares, furniture
DONATION TAX RECEIPT: Receipt given
upon request
COMMENTS: Monthly markdowns

Salvation Army Thrift Store
14455 Jefferson Davis Highway
Woodbridge, VA 22191-2832
PHONE: 703-494-8140
HOURS: Seven days, 9:30–7
TYPE OF MERCHANDISE: Clothing,
housewares, furniture
DONATION TAX RECEIPT: Receipt given
upon request
COMMENTS: Half-price sales

Washington

Salvation Army Thrift Store
117 E. Heron St.
Aberdeen, WA 98520
TYPE OF MERCHANDISE: Clothing,
housewares, furniture
DONATION TAX RECEIPT: Receipt given
upon request

Saint Vincent De Paul Thrift Store
926 Auburn Way N.
Auburn, WA 98002
TYPE OF MERCHANDISE: Clothing,
housewares, furniture
DONATION TAX RECEIPT: Receipt given
upon request
COMMENTS: Monthly markdowns

TVI Value Village Thrift Store
3990 Meridian St.
Bellingham, WA 98226
CONTACT: Don Pingree
PHONE: 206-733-2333
HOURS: Mon.–Sat. 9–9, Sun. 10–6
TYPE OF MERCHANDISE: Clothing,
housewares, furniture
DONATION TAX RECEIPT: No

Saint Vincent De Paul Thrift Store
1047 Burwell St.
Bremerton, WA 98310
TYPE OF MERCHANDISE: Clothing,
housewares, furniture
DONATION TAX RECEIPT: Receipt given
upon request
COMMENTS: Monthly markdowns

Saint Vincent De Paul Thrift Store
1117 N. Callow Ave.
Bremerton, WA 98312
TYPE OF MERCHANDISE: Clothing,
housewares, furniture
DONATION TAX RECEIPT: Receipt given
upon request
COMMENTS: Monthly markdowns

TVI Value Village Thrift Store
3449 Wheaton Way
Bremerton, WA
CONTACT: Bob Drinkard
PHONE: 206-479-7998
HOURS: Mon.–Sat. 9–9, Sun. 10–6
TYPE OF MERCHANDISE: Clothing,
housewares, furniture
DONATION TAX RECEIPT: No

Salvation Army Thrift Store
606 Park Ave.
Bremerton, WA 98310
TYPE OF MERCHANDISE: Clothing,
housewares, furniture
DONATION TAX RECEIPT: Receipt given
upon request

American Cancer Society Discovery Shop
714 Lebo Blvd.
Bremerton, WA 98310
PHONE: 206-373-1025
TYPE OF MERCHANDISE: Clothing, bric-a-
brac

DONATION TAX RECEIPT: Receipt given upon request
COMMENTS: Monthly markdowns
TVI Value Village Thrift Store
131 S.W. 157th St.
Burien, WA 98166
CONTACT: Larry Crone
PHONE: 206-246-6237
HOURS: Mon.–Sat. 9–9, Sun. 10–6
TYPE OF MERCHANDISE: Clothing, housewares, furniture
DONATION TAX RECEIPT: No
Goodwill Industries Thrift Store
1405 S. Gold St.
Centralia, WA 98531
PHONE: 360-736-3828
TYPE OF MERCHANDISE: Clothing, housewares, furniture
DONATION TAX RECEIPT: YES
Salvation Army Thrift Store
608 W. Main
Centralia, WA 98531
TYPE OF MERCHANDISE: Clothing, housewares, furniture
DONATION TAX RECEIPT: Receipt given upon request
Saint Vincent De Paul Thrift Store
317 First St.
Cheney, WA 99004
TYPE OF MERCHANDISE: Clothing, housewares, furniture
DONATION TAX RECEIPT: Receipt given upon request
COMMENTS: Monthly markdowns
Saint Vincent De Paul Thrift Store
609 Third St.
Clarkston, WA 99403
TYPE OF MERCHANDISE: Clothing, housewares, furniture
DONATION TAX RECEIPT: Receipt given upon request
COMMENTS: Monthly markdowns
Saint Vincent De Paul Thrift Store
259 E. Main
Dayton, WA 99328
TYPE OF MERCHANDISE: Clothing, housewares, furniture

DONATION TAX RECEIPT: Receipt given upon request
COMMENTS: Monthly markdowns
National Assistance League Thrift Shop
1916 Hewitt Ave.
Everett, WA 98201
PHONE: 206-252-3011
TYPE OF MERCHANDISE: Clothing, housewares, furniture
DONATION TAX RECEIPT: Receipt given upon request
COMMENTS: Monthly markdowns
American Cancer Society Discovery Shop
2817 Rockefeller Ave.
Everett, WA 98201
PHONE: 206-339-4141
TYPE OF MERCHANDISE: Clothing, bric-a-brac
DONATION TAX RECEIPT: Receipt given upon request
COMMENTS: Monthly markdowns
TVI Value Village Thrift Store
5209 Evergreen Way
Everett, WA 98203
CONTACT: Mike Allred
PHONE: 206-355-8320
HOURS: Mon.–Sat. 9–9, Sun. 10–6
TYPE OF MERCHANDISE: Clothing, housewares, furniture
DONATION TAX RECEIPT: No
Saint Vincent De Paul Thrift Store
5303 Evergreen Way
Everett, WA 98203
TYPE OF MERCHANDISE: Clothing, housewares, furniture
DONATION TAX RECEIPT: Receipt given upon request
COMMENTS: Monthly markdowns
Salvation Army Thrift Store
5313 Evergreen Way
Everett, WA 98203
TYPE OF MERCHANDISE: Clothing, housewares, furniture
DONATION TAX RECEIPT: Receipt given upon request
Saint Vincent De Paul Thrift Store
6430 Broadway
Everett, WA 98203

TYPE OF MERCHANDISE: Clothing, housewares, furniture
DONATION TAX RECEIPT: Receipt given upon request
COMMENTS: Monthly markdowns
Saint Vincent De Paul Thrift Store
6500 Evergreen Way
Everett, WA 98203
TYPE OF MERCHANDISE: Clothing, housewares, furniture
DONATION TAX RECEIPT: Receipt given upon request
COMMENTS: Monthly markdowns
TVI Value Village Thrift Store
32945 Pacific Hwy. S
Federal Way, WA 98003
CONTACT: Margaret Pettit
PHONE: 206-874-3966
HOURS: Mon.–Sat. 9–9, Sun. 10–6
TYPE OF MERCHANDISE: Clothing, housewares, furniture
DONATION TAX RECEIPT: No
Salvation Army Thrift Store
412 S. Vancouver St.
Kennewick, WA 99336
TYPE OF MERCHANDISE: Clothing, housewares, furniture
DONATION TAX RECEIPT: Receipt given upon request
American Cancer Society Discovery Shop
225 First Ave. S
Kent, WA 98032
PHONE: 206-852-9692
TYPE OF MERCHANDISE: Clothing, bric-a-brac
DONATION TAX RECEIPT: Receipt given upon request
COMMENTS: Monthly markdowns
Salvation Army Thrift Store
26401 Pacific Hwy. S
Kent, WA 98032
TYPE OF MERCHANDISE: Clothing, housewares, furniture
DONATION TAX RECEIPT: Receipt given upon request
TVI Value Village Thrift Store
27241 132nd Ave. SE
Kent, WA 98042

CONTACT: Julianne Eugley
PHONE: 206-630-9885
HOURS: Mon.–Sat. 9–9, Sun. 10–6
TYPE OF MERCHANDISE: Clothing, housewares, furniture
DONATION TAX RECEIPT: No
American Cancer Society Discovery Shop
137 Park Lane
Kirkland, WA 98033
PHONE: 206-827-3785
TYPE OF MERCHANDISE: Clothing, bric-a-brac
DONATION TAX RECEIPT: Receipt given upon request
COMMENTS: Monthly markdowns
Salvation Army Thrift Store
1209 Commerce Ave.
Longview, WA 98632
PHONE: 306-423-3920
TYPE OF MERCHANDISE: Clothing, housewares, furniture
DONATION TAX RECEIPT: Receipt given upon request
TVI Value Village Thrift Store
17216 Highway 99
Lynnwood, WA 98036
CONTACT: Joan Allred
PHONE: 206-745-6603
HOURS: Mon.–Sat. 9–9, Sun. 10–6
TYPE OF MERCHANDISE: Clothing, housewares, furniture
DONATION TAX RECEIPT: No
Saint Vincent De Paul Thrift Store
6501 196th St. SW
Lynnwood, WA 98036
TYPE OF MERCHANDISE: Clothing, housewares, furniture
DONATION TAX RECEIPT: Receipt given upon request
COMMENTS: Monthly markdowns
Salvation Army Thrift Store
16530 Hwy. 99 N
Lynnwood, WA 98037
TYPE OF MERCHANDISE: Clothing, housewares, furniture
DONATION TAX RECEIPT: Receipt given upon request

Saint Vincent De Paul Thrift Store
Highway 3 (rear red barn)
Mason, WA 98528
TYPE OF MERCHANDISE: Clothing,
housewares, furniture
DONATION TAX RECEIPT: Receipt given
upon request
COMMENTS: Monthly markdowns

Goodwill Industries Thrift Store
723 W. Third Ave.
Moses Lake, WA 98837
TYPE OF MERCHANDISE: Clothing,
housewares, furniture
DONATION TAX RECEIPT: Receipt given
upon request

Salvation Army Thrift Store
1101 E. College Way
Mt. Vernon, WA 98273
TYPE OF MERCHANDISE: Clothing,
housewares, furniture
DONATION TAX RECEIPT: Receipt given
upon request

Salvation Army Thrift Store
2020 Harrison Ave.
Olympia, WA 98501
TYPE OF MERCHANDISE: Clothing,
housewares, furniture
DONATION TAX RECEIPT: Receipt given
upon request

TVI Value Village Thrift Store
2100 W. Harrison
Olympia, WA 98501
CONTACT: Mike Blomquist
PHONE: 206-786-5630
HOURS: Mon.–Sat. 9–9, Sun. 10–6
TYPE OF MERCHANDISE: Clothing,
housewares, furniture
DONATION TAX RECEIPT: No

Goodwill Industries Thrift Store
4512b Lacey Blvd. SE
Olympia, WA 98503
TYPE OF MERCHANDISE: Clothing,
housewares, furniture
DONATION TAX RECEIPT: Receipt given
upon request

Saint Vincent De Paul Thrift Store
1120 W. Sylvester
Pasco, WA 99301
TYPE OF MERCHANDISE: Clothing,
housewares, furniture
DONATION TAX RECEIPT: Receipt given
upon request
COMMENTS: Monthly markdowns

Salvation Army Thrift Store
310 N. Fourth Ave.
Pasco, WA 99301
TYPE OF MERCHANDISE: Clothing,
housewares, furniture
DONATION TAX RECEIPT: Receipt given
upon request

Salvation Army Thrift Store
112 E. Eighth St.
Port Angeles, WA 98362
TYPE OF MERCHANDISE: Clothing,
housewares, furniture
DONATION TAX RECEIPT: Receipt given
upon request

Saint Vincent De Paul Thrift Store
116 W. Eighth
Port Angeles, WA 98362
TYPE OF MERCHANDISE: Clothing,
housewares, furniture
DONATION TAX RECEIPT: Receipt given
upon request
COMMENTS: Monthly markdowns

Saint Vincent De Paul Thrift Store
1209 Bay St.
Port Orchard, WA 98366
TYPE OF MERCHANDISE: Clothing,
housewares, furniture
DONATION TAX RECEIPT: Receipt given
upon request
COMMENTS: Monthly markdowns

TVI Value Village Thrift Store
1124 River Rd.
Puyallup, WA 98371
CONTACT: Sue Barr
PHONE: 206-848-1582
HOURS: Mon.–Sat. 9–9, Sun. 10–7
TYPE OF MERCHANDISE: Clothing
housewares, furniture
DONATION TAX RECEIPT: No

Saint Vincent De Paul Thrift Store
113 Meeker St.
Puyallup, WA 98371

TYPE OF MERCHANDISE: Clothing,
housewares, furniture
DONATION TAX RECEIPT: Receipt given
upon request
COMMENTS: Monthly markdowns

Goodwill Industries Thrift Store
12007 Meridian E
Puyallup, WA 98373
TYPE OF MERCHANDISE: Clothing,
housewares, furniture
DONATION TAX RECEIPT: Receipt given
upon request

Salvation Army Thrift Store
12904 Meridian St.
Puyallup, WA 98373
TYPE OF MERCHANDISE: Clothing,
housewares, furniture
DONATION TAX RECEIPT: Receipt given
upon request

TVI Value Village Thrift Store
16771 Redmond Way
Redmond, WA 98052
CONTACT: Tony Di Maina
PHONE: 206-883-2049
HOURS: Mon.–Sat. 9–9, Sun. 10–6
TYPE OF MERCHANDISE: Clothing,
housewares, furniture
DONATION TAX RECEIPT: No

TVI Value Village Thrift Store
1222 Bronson Way N
Renton, WA 98055
CONTACT: Nellie Peppel
PHONE: 206-255-5637
HOURS: Mon.–Sat. 9–9, Sun. 10–6
TYPE OF MERCHANDISE: Clothing,
housewares, furniture
DONATION TAX RECEIPT: No

Saint Vincent De Paul Thrift Store
2825 Sunset Blvd. NE
Renton, WA 98056
TYPE OF MERCHANDISE: Clothing,
housewares, furniture
DONATION TAX RECEIPT: Receipt given
upon request
COMMENTS: Monthly markdowns

Salvation Army Thrift Store
1000 Fourth Ave. S
Seattle, WA 98134

TYPE OF MERCHANDISE: Clothing,
housewares, furniture
DONATION TAX RECEIPT: Receipt given
upon request

Salvation Army Thrift Store
1020 Fourth Ave.
Seattle, WA 98134
TYPE OF MERCHANDISE: Clothing,
housewares, furniture
DONATION TAX RECEIPT: Receipt given
upon request

Salvation Army Thrift Store
12526 33rd Ave. NE
Seattle, WA 98134
TYPE OF MERCHANDISE: Clothing,
housewares, furniture
DONATION TAX RECEIPT: Receipt given
upon request

TVI Value Village Thrift Store
12548 Lake City Way NE
Seattle, WA 98125
CONTACT: Margaret Squair
PHONE: 206-365-8232
HOURS: Mon.–Sat. 9–9, Sun. 10–6
TYPE OF MERCHANDISE: Clothing,
housewares, furniture
DONATION TAX RECEIPT: No

Saint Vincent De Paul Thrift Store
13445 First Ave. S
Seattle, WA 98166
TYPE OF MERCHANDISE: Clothing,
housewares, furniture
DONATION TAX RECEIPT: Receipt given
upon request
COMMENTS: Monthly markdowns

National Assistance League Bargain Fair
1419 N. 45th St.
Seattle, WA 98103
PHONE: 206-547-4680
TYPE OF MERCHANDISE: Clothing,
housewares, furniture
DONATION TAX RECEIPT: Receipt given
upon request
COMMENTS: Monthly markdowns

Saint Vincent De Paul Thrift Store
17712 15th Ave NE
Seattle, WA 98155
TYPE OF MERCHANDISE: Clothing,
housewares, furniture

DONATION TAX RECEIPT: Receipt given upon request
COMMENTS: Monthly markdowns
TVI Value Village Thrift Store
2929 27th Ave. S
Seattle, WA 98144
CONTACT: Donna Crone
PHONE: 206-723-5000
HOURS: Mon.–Sat. 9–9, Sun. 10–6
TYPE OF MERCHANDISE: Clothing, housewares, furniture
DONATION TAX RECEIPT: No
American Cancer Society Discovery Shop
4535 California Ave. SW
Seattle, WA 98116
TYPE OF MERCHANDISE: Clothing, bric-a-brac
DONATION TAX RECEIPT: Receipt given upon request
COMMENTS: Monthly markdowns
City of Hope Thrift Shop
6412 32nd Ave., NW
Seattle, WA 98107
TYPE OF MERCHANDISE: Clothing, housewares
DONATION TAX RECEIPT: Receipt given upon request
American Cancer Society Discovery Shop
6814 Roosevelt Way NE
Seattle, WA 98115
PHONE: 206-524-3399
TYPE OF MERCHANDISE: Clothing, bric-a-brac
DONATION TAX RECEIPT: Receipt given upon request
COMMENTS: Monthly markdowns
TVI Value Village Thrift Store
8700 15th Ave. NW
Seattle, WA 98117
CONTACT: Eloise Akau
PHONE: 206-783-4648
HOURS: Mon.–Sat. 9–9, Sun. 10–6
TYPE OF MERCHANDISE: Clothing, housewares, furniture
DONATION TAX RECEIPT: No
Saint Vincent De Paul Thrift Store
9835 16th St. SW
Seattle, WA 98106

TYPE OF MERCHANDISE: Clothing, housewares, furniture
DONATION TAX RECEIPT: Receipt given upon request
COMMENTS: Monthly markdowns
Goodwill Industries Thrift Store
135 E. Naches Ave.
Selah, WA 98942
TYPE OF MERCHANDISE: Clothing, housewares, furniture
DONATION TAX RECEIPT: Receipt given upon request
Goodwill Industries Thrift Store
130 E. Third Ave.
Spokane, WA 99202
TYPE OF MERCHANDISE: Clothing, housewares, furniture
DONATION TAX RECEIPT: Receipt given upon request
TVI Value Village Thrift Store
13112 E. Sprague
Spokane, WA 99216
CONTACT: Dorothy Geyer
PHONE: 509-921-7889
HOURS: Mon.–Sat. 9–9, Sun. 10–6
TYPE OF MERCHANDISE: Clothing, housewares, furniture
DONATION TAX RECEIPT: No
Saint Vincent De Paul Thrift Store
2625 N.W. Boulevard
Spokane, WA 99205
TYPE OF MERCHANDISE: Clothing, housewares, furniture
DONATION TAX RECEIPT: Receipt given upon request
COMMENTS: Monthly markdowns
Saint Vincent De Paul Thrift Store
2901 E. Trent Ave.
Spokane, WA 99202
TYPE OF MERCHANDISE: Clothing, housewares, furniture
DONATION TAX RECEIPT: Receipt given upon request
COMMENTS: Monthly markdowns
Saint Vincent De Paul Thrift Store
3019 E. Diamond Ave.
Spokane, WA 99207
TYPE OF MERCHANDISE: Clothing, housewares, furniture

DONATION TAX RECEIPT: Receipt given upon request
COMMENTS: Monthly markdowns

Goodwill Industries Thrift Store
5114 S. Dartmouth Rd.
Spokane, WA 99206
TYPE OF MERCHANDISE: Clothing, housewares, furniture
DONATION TAX RECEIPT: Receipt given upon request

American Cancer Society Discovery Shop
W. 909 Indiana Ave.
Spokane, WA 99205
PHONE: 509-328-9373
TYPE OF MERCHANDISE: Clothing, bric-a-brac
DONATION TAX RECEIPT: Receipt given upon request
COMMENTS: Monthly markdowns

TVI Value Village Thrift Store
708 West Boone
Spokane, WA 99201
CONTACT: Brenda Binder
PHONE: 509-325-2569
HOURS: Mon.–Sat. 9–9, Sun. 10–6
TYPE OF MERCHANDISE: Clothing, housewares, furniture
DONATION TAX RECEIPT: No

Salvation Army Thrift Store
1201 Main St.
Sumner, WA 98390
TYPE OF MERCHANDISE: Clothing, housewares, furniture
DONATION TAX RECEIPT: Receipt given upon request

Goodwill Industries Thrift Store
771 S. Eighth St.
Sunnyside, WA 98944
TYPE OF MERCHANDISE: Clothing, housewares, furniture
DONATION TAX RECEIPT: Receipt given upon request

Salvation Army Thrift Store
2805 Sixth Ave.
Tacoma, WA 98406
TYPE OF MERCHANDISE: Clothing, housewares, furniture
DONATION TAX RECEIPT: Receipt given upon request

Salvation Army Thrift Store
309 Puyallup Ave.
Tacoma, WA 98421
TYPE OF MERCHANDISE: Clothing, housewares, furniture
DONATION TAX RECEIPT: Receipt given upon request

Saint Vincent De Paul Thrift Store
3805–07 S. Yakima
Tacoma, WA 98408
TYPE OF MERCHANDISE: Clothing, housewares, furniture
DONATION TAX RECEIPT: Receipt given upon request
COMMENTS: Monthly markdowns

Saint Vincent De Paul Thrift Store
4009 S. 56th St.
Tacoma, WA 98409
TYPE OF MERCHANDISE: Clothing, housewares, furniture
DONATION TAX RECEIPT: Receipt given upon request
COMMENTS: Monthly markdowns

American Cancer Society Discovery Shop
5412 S. Tacoma Way
Tacoma, WA 98409
PHONE: 506-473-3378
TYPE OF MERCHANDISE: Clothing, bric-a-brac
DONATION TAX RECEIPT: Receipt given upon request
COMMENTS: Monthly markdowns

Junior League Second Closet
7 Tacoma Ave. N
Tacoma, WA 98403
PHONE: 206-383-9269
TYPE OF MERCHANDISE: Clothing, housewares, toys
DONATION TAX RECEIPT: Receipt given upon request
COMMENTS: Annual toy sale in December, "bag" sales

Goodwill Industries Thrift Store
714 S. 27th St.
Tacoma, WA 98409
TYPE OF MERCHANDISE: Clothing, housewares, furniture
DONATION TAX RECEIPT: Receipt given upon request

Salvation Army Thrift Store
7241 S. Tacoma Way
Tacoma, WA 98409
TYPE OF MERCHANDISE: Clothing,
housewares, furniture
DONATION TAX RECEIPT: Receipt given
upon request
TVI Value Village Thrift Store
8025 S. Hosmer St.
Tacoma, WA 98408
CONTACT: Robert Eugley
PHONE: 206-539-0886
HOURS: Mon.–Sat. 9–9, Sun. 10–6
TYPE OF MERCHANDISE: Clothing,
housewares, furniture
DONATION TAX RECEIPT: No
TVI Value Village Thrift Store
2503 Main St.
Union Gap, WA 96903
CONTACT: Bill Collins
PHONE: 509-454-4061
HOURS: Mon.–Sat. 9–9, Sun. 10–6
TYPE OF MERCHANDISE: Clothing,
housewares, furniture
DONATION TAX RECEIPT: No
American Cancer Society Discovery Shop
2011 Main St.
Vancouver, WA 98660-2636
PHONE: 206-695-2278
TYPE OF MERCHANDISE: Clothing, bric-a-
brac
DONATION TAX RECEIPT: Receipt given
upon request
COMMENTS: Monthly markdowns
TVI Value Village Thrift Store
7110 NE Fourth Plain Rd.
Vancouver, WA 98661
CONTACT: Brent Barnett
PHONE: 206-944-5225
HOURS: Mon.–Sat. 9–9, Sun. 10–6
TYPE OF MERCHANDISE: Clothing,
housewares, furniture
DONATION TAX RECEIPT: No
Salvation Army Thrift Store
801 Grand Blvd.
Vancouver, WA 98660
TYPE OF MERCHANDISE: Clothing,
housewares, furniture

DONATION TAX RECEIPT: Receipt given
upon request
Goodwill Industries Thrift Store
217 E. Alder St.
Walla Walla, WA 99362-1908
PHONE: 509-525-5992
HOURS: Mon.–Fri. 9–5:30, Sat. 9–5
TYPE OF MERCHANDISE: Clothing,
housewares, furniture
DONATION TAX RECEIPT: Receipt given
upon request
Saint Vincent De Paul Thrift Store
308 W. Main St.
Walla Walla, WA 99362
TYPE OF MERCHANDISE: Clothing,
housewares, furniture
DONATION TAX RECEIPT: Receipt given
upon request
COMMENTS: Monthly markdowns
Goodwill Industries Thrift Store
222 S. Third St.
Yakima, WA 98901
TYPE OF MERCHANDISE: Clothing,
housewares, furniture
DONATION TAX RECEIPT: Receipt given
upon request
Saint Vincent De Paul Thrift Store
3629 S. First St.
Yakima, WA 98903
TYPE OF MERCHANDISE: Clothing,
housewares, furniture
DONATION TAX RECEIPT: Receipt given
upon request
COMMENTS: Monthly markdowns
American Cancer Society Discovery Shop
513 W. Yakima Ave.
Yakima, WA 98902
TYPE OF MERCHANDISE: Clothing, bric-a-
brac
DONATION TAX RECEIPT: Receipt given
upon request
COMMENTS: Monthly markdowns
Salvation Army Thrift Store
9 S. Sixth Ave.
Yakima, WA 98902
TYPE OF MERCHANDISE: Clothing,
housewares, furniture
DONATION TAX RECEIPT: Receipt given
upon request

West Virginia

Goodwill Industries Thrift Store
6424 Rte. 60 E
Barboursville, WV 25570
PHONE: 304-736-8624
HOURS: Mon. 8–8, Tues.–Thurs. 8–6,
Fri. 8–8, Sat. 8–6, Sun. 1–6
TYPE OF MERCHANDISE: Clothing,
housewares, furniture
DONATION TAX RECEIPT: Receipt given
upon request
COMMENTS: Fall fashion show

Salvation Army Thrift Store
302 S. Fayette St.
Beckley, WV 25801
TYPE OF MERCHANDISE: Clothing,
housewares, furniture
DONATION TAX RECEIPT: Receipt given
upon request

Goodwill Industries Thrift Store
230 Seventh Ave. SW
Charleston, WV 25303
TYPE OF MERCHANDISE: Clothing,
housewares, furniture
DONATION TAX RECEIPT: Receipt given
upon request

Goodwill Industries Thrift Store
403 Washington St. W
Charleston, WV 25302
TYPE OF MERCHANDISE: Clothing,
housewares, furniture
DONATION TAX RECEIPT: Receipt given
upon request

Goodwill Industries Thrift Store
1005 Virginia Ave.
Huntington, WV 25776
PHONE: 304-523-7461
HOURS: Mon. 8–8, Tues.–Thurs. 8–6,
Fri. 8–8, Sat. 8–6, Sun. 1–6
TYPE OF MERCHANDISE: Clothing,
housewares, furniture
DONATION TAX RECEIPT: Receipt given
upon request
COMMENTS: Fall fashion show

Salvation Army Thrift Store
1317 Fourth Ave.
Huntington, WV 25701

TYPE OF MERCHANDISE: Clothing,
housewares, furniture
DONATION TAX RECEIPT: Receipt given
upon request

Goodwill Industries Thrift Store
2626 Fifth Ave.
Huntington, WV 25705
PHONE: 304-529-1841
HOURS: Mon. 8–8, Tues.–Thurs. 8–6,
Fri. 8–8, Sat. 8–6, Sun. 1–6
TYPE OF MERCHANDISE: Clothing,
housewares, furniture
DONATION TAX RECEIPT: Receipt given
upon request
COMMENTS: Fall fashion show

Salvation Army Thrift Store
550 Fifth St.
Parkersburg, WV 26101
TYPE OF MERCHANDISE: Clothing,
housewares, furniture
DONATION TAX RECEIPT: Receipt given
upon request

Junior League Shop
717 Market St.
Parkersburg, WV 26101
TYPE OF MERCHANDISE: Clothing for men,
women, and children
DONATION TAX RECEIPT: Receipt given
upon request

Goodwill Industries Thrift Store
2416 Jackson Ave.
Point Pleasant, WV 25550
PHONE: 304-675-4460
HOURS: Mon. 8–8, Tues.–Thurs. 8–6,
Fri. 8–8, Sat. 8–6, Sun. 1–6
TYPE OF MERCHANDISE: Clothing,
housewares, furniture
DONATION TAX RECEIPT: Receipt given
upon request
COMMENTS: Fall fashion show

Wisconsin

Saint Vincent De Paul Thrift Store
303 Third St.
Algoma, WI 54201
TYPE OF MERCHANDISE: Clothing,
housewares, furniture

DONATION TAX RECEIPT: Receipt given upon request

COMMENTS: Monthly markdowns

Saint Vincent De Paul Thrift Store
720 W. Linbergh
Appleton, WI 54914
TYPE OF MERCHANDISE: Clothing, housewares, furniture
DONATION TAX RECEIPT: Receipt given upon request
COMMENTS: Monthly markdowns

Saint Vincent De Paul Thrift Store
316 S. Spring St.
Beaver Dam, WI 53916
TYPE OF MERCHANDISE: Clothing, housewares, furniture
DONATION TAX RECEIPT: Receipt given upon request
COMMENTS: Monthly markdowns

Saint Vincent De Paul Thrift Store
610 Fourth St.
Beloit, WI 53511
TYPE OF MERCHANDISE: Clothing, housewares, furniture
DONATION TAX RECEIPT: Receipt given upon request
COMMENTS: Monthly markdowns

Salvation Army Thrift Store
809 Broad St.
Beloit, WI 53511-6348
TYPE OF MERCHANDISE: Clothing, housewares, furniture
DONATION TAX RECEIPT: Receipt given upon request

Salvation Army Thrift Store
4747 W. Bradley Rd.
Brown Deer, WI 53223
CONTACT: Georgianna Sattler
PHONE: 414-357-6277
HOURS: Mon.–Fri. 10–5, Sat. 9–5
TYPE OF MERCHANDISE: Clothing, housewares, furniture
DONATION TAX RECEIPT: Receipt given upon request

Saint Vincent De Paul Thrift Store
135 W. Chestnut St.
Burlington, WI 53105
TYPE OF MERCHANDISE: Clothing, housewares, furniture

DONATION TAX RECEIPT: Receipt given upon request

COMMENTS: Monthly markdowns

Salvation Army Thrift Store
1610 Bellinger St.
Eau Claire, WI 54703
TYPE OF MERCHANDISE: Clothing, housewares, furniture
DONATION TAX RECEIPT: Receipt given upon request

Salvation Army Thrift Store
206 Emery St.
Eau Claire, WI 54701
TYPE OF MERCHANDISE: Clothing, housewares, furniture
DONATION TAX RECEIPT: Receipt given upon request

Goodwill Industries Thrift Store
2819 E. Hamilton Ave.
Eau Claire, WI 54701
TYPE OF MERCHANDISE: Clothing, housewares, furniture
DONATION TAX RECEIPT: Receipt given upon request

Saint Vincent De Paul Thrift Store
204 W. Fulton St.
Edgerton, WI 53534
TYPE OF MERCHANDISE: Clothing, housewares, furniture
DONATION TAX RECEIPT: Receipt given upon request
COMMENTS: Monthly markdowns

Saint Vincent De Paul Thrift Store
401 N. Hickory St.
Fond Du Lac, WI 54935
TYPE OF MERCHANDISE: Clothing, housewares, furniture
DONATION TAX RECEIPT: Receipt given upon request
COMMENTS: Monthly markdowns

Goodwill Industries Thrift Store
610 Fond Du Lac Ave.
Fond Du Lac, WI 54935
TYPE OF MERCHANDISE: Clothing, housewares, furniture
DONATION TAX RECEIPT: Receipt given upon request

Goodwill Industries Thrift Store
3319 Roberts St.
Franksville, WI 53126
TYPE OF MERCHANDISE: Clothing,
housewares, furniture
DONATION TAX RECEIPT: Receipt given
upon request

Salvation Army Thrift Store
121 N. Broadway
Green Bay, WI 54303
TYPE OF MERCHANDISE: Clothing,
housewares, furniture
DONATION TAX RECEIPT: Receipt given
upon request

Saint Vincent De Paul Thrift Store
1529 Webster Ct.
Green Bay, WI 54302
TYPE OF MERCHANDISE: Clothing,
housewares, furniture
DONATION TAX RECEIPT: Receipt given
upon request
COMMENTS: Monthly markdowns

Goodwill Industries Thrift Store
2814 S. Oneida St.
Green Bay, WI 54304
TYPE OF MERCHANDISE: Clothing,
housewares, furniture
DONATION TAX RECEIPT: Receipt given
upon request

Saint Vincent De Paul Thrift Store
31 N. Main St.
Hartford, WI 53027
TYPE OF MERCHANDISE: Clothing,
housewares, furniture
DONATION TAX RECEIPT: Receipt given
upon request
COMMENTS: Monthly markdowns

Goodwill Industries Thrift Store
1224 Woodman Rd.
Janesville, WI 53545
TYPE OF MERCHANDISE: Clothing,
housewares, furniture
DONATION TAX RECEIPT: Receipt given
upon request

Salvation Army Thrift Store
1819 Center Ave.
Janesville, WI 53546
TYPE OF MERCHANDISE: Clothing,
housewares, furniture

DONATION TAX RECEIPT: Receipt given
upon request

Salvation Army Thrift Store
415 W. Milwaukee St.
Janesville, WI 53545
TYPE OF MERCHANDISE: Clothing,
housewares, furniture
DONATION TAX RECEIPT: Receipt given
upon request

Saint Vincent De Paul Thrift Store
1438 S. Ryan Ave.
Jefferson, WI 53549
TYPE OF MERCHANDISE: Clothing,
housewares, furniture
DONATION TAX RECEIPT: Receipt given
upon request
COMMENTS: Monthly markdowns

Saint Vincent De Paul Thrift Store
217 E. Second St.
Kaukauna, WI 54130
TYPE OF MERCHANDISE: Clothing,
housewares, furniture
DONATION TAX RECEIPT: Receipt given
upon request
COMMENTS: Monthly markdowns

Goodwill Industries Thrift Store
5109 52nd St.
Kenosha, WI 53144
TYPE OF MERCHANDISE: Clothing,
housewares, furniture
DONATION TAX RECEIPT: Receipt given
upon request

Salvation Army Thrift Store
6114 22nd Ave.
Kenosha, WI 53143
TYPE OF MERCHANDISE: Clothing,
housewares, furniture
DONATION TAX RECEIPT: Receipt given
upon request

Saint Vincent De Paul Thrift Store
6201 14th Ave.
Kenosha, WI 53143
TYPE OF MERCHANDISE: Clothing,
housewares, furniture
DONATION TAX RECEIPT: Receipt given
upon request
COMMENTS: Monthly markdowns

Salvation Army Thrift Store
8005 Sheridan Rd.
Kenosha, WI 53143
TYPE OF MERCHANDISE: Clothing,
housewares, furniture
DONATION TAX RECEIPT: Receipt given
upon request

Goodwill Industries Thrift Store
1024 19th St. S
La Crosse, WI 54601
TYPE OF MERCHANDISE: Clothing,
housewares, furniture
DONATION TAX RECEIPT: Receipt given
upon request

Saint Vincent De Paul Thrift Store
720 E. Lake St.
Lake Mills, WI 53551
TYPE OF MERCHANDISE: Clothing,
housewares, furniture
DONATION TAX RECEIPT: Receipt given
upon request
COMMENTS: Monthly markdowns

Goodwill Industries Thrift Store
1302 Mendota St.
Madison, WI 53714
TYPE OF MERCHANDISE: Clothing,
housewares, furniture
DONATION TAX RECEIPT: Receipt given
upon request

Saint Vincent De Paul Thrift Store
1309 Williamson St.
Madison, WI 53703
TYPE OF MERCHANDISE: Clothing,
housewares, furniture
DONATION TAX RECEIPT: Receipt given
upon request
COMMENTS: Monthly markdowns

Goodwill Industries Thrift Store
4595 W. Beltline Hwy.
Madison, WI 53713
PHONE: 608-271-4687
TYPE OF MERCHANDISE: Clothing,
housewares, furniture
DONATION TAX RECEIPT: Receipt given
upon request

Saint Vincent De Paul Thrift Store
4293 W. Beltline Hwy.
Madison, WI 53711

TYPE OF MERCHANDISE: Clothing,
housewares, furniture
DONATION TAX RECEIPT: Receipt given
upon request
COMMENTS: Monthly markdowns

Salvation Army Thrift Store
65 S. Baldwin St.
Madison, WI 53703
TYPE OF MERCHANDISE: Clothing,
housewares, furniture
DONATION TAX RECEIPT: Receipt given
upon request

Goodwill Industries Thrift Store
664 State St.
Madison, WI 53703
PHONE: 608-527-2040
TYPE OF MERCHANDISE: Clothing,
housewares, furniture
DONATION TAX RECEIPT: Receipt given
upon request

Goodwill Industries Thrift Store
3720 Calumet Ave.
Manitowoc, WI 54220
TYPE OF MERCHANDISE: Clothing,
housewares, furniture
DONATION TAX RECEIPT: Receipt given
upon request

Salvation Army Thrift Store
401 N. Ninth St.
Manitowoc, WI 54220
TYPE OF MERCHANDISE: Clothing,
housewares, furniture
DONATION TAX RECEIPT: Receipt given
upon request

Saint Vincent De Paul Thrift Store
916 Buffalo St.
Manitowoc, WI 54220
TYPE OF MERCHANDISE: Clothing,
housewares, furniture
DONATION TAX RECEIPT: Receipt given
upon request
COMMENTS: Monthly markdowns

Saint Vincent De Paul Thrift Store
1619 Main St.
Marinette, WI 54143
TYPE OF MERCHANDISE: Clothing,
housewares, furniture

DONATION TAX RECEIPT: Receipt given
upon request
COMMENTS: Monthly markdowns

Saint Vincent De Paul Thrift Store
169 N. Central Ave.
Marshfield, WI 54449
TYPE OF MERCHANDISE: Clothing,
housewares, furniture
DONATION TAX RECEIPT: Receipt given
upon request
COMMENTS: Monthly markdowns

Saint Vincent De Paul Thrift Store
144-C S. Main St.
Medford, WI 54451
TYPE OF MERCHANDISE: Clothing,
housewares, furniture
DONATION TAX RECEIPT: Receipt given
upon request

Goodwill Industries Thrift Store
2405 Allen Blvd.
Middleton, WI 53562
TYPE OF MERCHANDISE: Clothing,
housewares, furniture
DONATION TAX RECEIPT: Receipt given
upon request

Salvation Army Thrift Store
1305 W. Forest Home Ave.
Milwaukee, WI 53204
CONTACT: Glenda Lovit
PHONE: 414-384-9992
HOURS: Mon.–Sat. 10–8
TYPE OF MERCHANDISE: Clothing,
housewares, furniture
DONATION TAX RECEIPT: Receipt given
upon request

Salvation Army Thrift Store
2264 S. Kinnickinnic
CROSS STREET: Lincoln
Milwaukee, WI 53207
CONTACT: Dennis Higgins
PHONE: 414-744-3355
HOURS: Mon.–Sat. 9–5:30
TYPE OF MERCHANDISE: Clothing,
housewares, furniture
DONATION TAX RECEIPT: Receipt given
upon request

Salvation Army Thrift Store
332 W. Broadway
Milwaukee, WI 53166
CONTACT: Corinne Dorbriz
PHONE: 414-547-8536
HOURS: Mon.–Fri. 9–6, Sat. 9–5
TYPE OF MERCHANDISE: Clothing,
housewares, furniture
DONATION TAX RECEIPT: Receipt given
upon request

Salvation Army Thrift Store
1015 W. Lincoln Ave.
Milwaukee, WI 53215
TYPE OF MERCHANDISE: Clothing,
housewares, furniture
DONATION TAX RECEIPT: Receipt given
upon request

Disabled American Vets Thrift Store
1730 S. 13th St.
Milwaukee, WI 53204
TYPE OF MERCHANDISE: Clothing,
housewares
DONATION TAX RECEIPT: Receipt given
upon request

Salvation Army Thrift Store
1824 W. North Ave.
CROSS STREET: 18th
Milwaukee, WI 53205
CONTACT: Odessa Grundy
PHONE: 414-263-4576
HOURS: Mon.–Sat. 9–5
TYPE OF MERCHANDISE: Clothing,
housewares, furniture
DONATION TAX RECEIPT: Receipt given
upon request

Saint Vincent De Paul Thrift Store
1862 W. Fond Du Lac Ave.
Milwaukee, WI 53205
TYPE OF MERCHANDISE: Clothing,
housewares, furniture
DONATION TAX RECEIPT: Receipt given
upon request
COMMENTS: Monthly markdowns

Salvation Army Thrift Store
2170 N. Prospect Ave.
Milwaukee, WI 53202
CONTACT: Pat Neely
PHONE: 414-291-6909

HOURS: Mon.–Sat. 10–6
TYPE OF MERCHANDISE: Clothing, housewares, furniture
DONATION TAX RECEIPT: Receipt given upon request

Saint Vincent De Paul Thrift Store
2320 W. Lincoln Ave.
Milwaukee, WI 53215
TYPE OF MERCHANDISE: Clothing, housewares, furniture
DONATION TAX RECEIPT: Receipt given upon request
COMMENTS: Monthly markdowns

Disabled American Vets Thrift Store
2430 N. Murray Ave.
Milwaukee, WI 53211
TYPE OF MERCHANDISE: Clothing, housewares
DONATION TAX RECEIPT: Receipt given upon request

Goodwill Industries Thrift Store
3305 W. Forest Home Ave.
Milwaukee, WI 53215
TYPE OF MERCHANDISE: Clothing, housewares, furniture
DONATION TAX RECEIPT: Receipt given upon request

Salvation Army Thrift Store
3385 N. Martin Luther King Dr.
Milwaukee, WI 53212
TYPE OF MERCHANDISE: Clothing, housewares, furniture
DONATION TAX RECEIPT: Receipt given upon request

Salvation Army Thrift Store
3500 W. Villard Ave.
Milwaukee, WI 53209
CONTACT: Carmen Banks
PHONE: 414-535-0855
HOURS: Mon.–Sat. 9–5
TYPE OF MERCHANDISE: Clothing, housewares, furniture
DONATION TAX RECEIPT: Receipt given upon request

Salvation Army Thrift Store
7713 W. Greenfield Ave.
Milwaukee, WI 53214
CONTACT: Ethel Rozenski

PHONE: 414-453-1267
HOURS: Mon.–Sat. 9–5
TYPE OF MERCHANDISE: Clothing, housewares, furniture
DONATION TAX RECEIPT: Receipt given upon request

Saint Vincent De Paul Thrift Store
2837 Bowen St.
Oshkosh, WI 54901
TYPE OF MERCHANDISE: Clothing, housewares, furniture
DONATION TAX RECEIPT: Receipt given upon request
COMMENTS: Monthly markdowns

Salvation Army Thrift Store
586 N. Main St.
Oshkosh, WI 54901
TYPE OF MERCHANDISE: Clothing, housewares, furniture
DONATION TAX RECEIPT: Receipt given upon request

Salvation Army Thrift Store
115 Division St.
Plymouth, WI 53073
TYPE OF MERCHANDISE: Clothing, housewares, furniture
DONATION TAX RECEIPT: Receipt given upon request

Saint Vincent De Paul Thrift Store
120 Lake Shore Rd.
Port Washington, WI 53074
TYPE OF MERCHANDISE: Clothing, housewares, furniture
DONATION TAX RECEIPT: Receipt given upon request
COMMENTS: Monthly markdowns

Saint Vincent De Paul Thrift Store
1016 State St.
Racine, WI 53404
TYPE OF MERCHANDISE: Clothing, housewares, furniture
DONATION TAX RECEIPT: Receipt given upon request
COMMENTS: Monthly markdowns

Salvation Army Thrift Store
1129 Washington Ave.
Racine, WI 53403
TYPE OF MERCHANDISE: Clothing, housewares, furniture

DONATION TAX RECEIPT: Receipt given
upon request

Goodwill Industries Thrift Store
2300 Rapids Dr.
Racine, WI 53404
TYPE OF MERCHANDISE: Clothing,
housewares, furniture
DONATION TAX RECEIPT: Receipt given
upon request

Saint Vincent De Paul Thrift Store
926 Lasalle St.
Racine, WI 53404
TYPE OF MERCHANDISE: Clothing,
housewares, furniture
DONATION TAX RECEIPT: Receipt given
upon request
COMMENTS: Monthly markdowns

Goodwill Industries Thrift Store
5607 S. Business Hwy. 51
Schofield, WI 54476
TYPE OF MERCHANDISE: Clothing,
housewares, furniture
DONATION TAX RECEIPT: Receipt given
upon request

Salvation Army Thrift Store
1124 N. Eighth St.
Sheboygan, WI 53081
TYPE OF MERCHANDISE: Clothing,
housewares, furniture
DONATION TAX RECEIPT: Receipt given
upon request

Saint Vincent De Paul Thrift Store
522 S. Eighth St.
Sheboygan, WI 53081
TYPE OF MERCHANDISE: Clothing,
housewares, furniture
DONATION TAX RECEIPT: Receipt given
upon request
COMMENTS: Monthly markdowns

Saint Vincent De Paul Thrift Store
1306 Post Rd.
Stevens Point, WI 54481
TYPE OF MERCHANDISE: Clothing,
housewares, furniture
DONATION TAX RECEIPT: Receipt given
upon request
COMMENTS: Monthly markdowns

Saint Vincent De Paul Thrift Store
111 W. Jefferson St.
Stoughton, WI 53589
TYPE OF MERCHANDISE: Clothing,
housewares, furniture
DONATION TAX RECEIPT: Receipt given
upon request
COMMENTS: Monthly markdowns

Saint Vincent De Paul Thrift Store
1217 Ogden Ave.
Superior, WI 54880
TYPE OF MERCHANDISE: Clothing,
housewares, furniture
DONATION TAX RECEIPT: Receipt given
upon request
COMMENTS: Monthly markdowns

Goodwill Industries Thrift Store
1717 Belknap St.
Superior, WI 54880
TYPE OF MERCHANDISE: Clothing,
housewares, furniture
DONATION TAX RECEIPT: Receipt given
upon request

Saint Vincent De Paul Thrift Store
1181 N. Fourth St.
Watertown, WI 53094
TYPE OF MERCHANDISE: Clothing,
housewares, furniture
DONATION TAX RECEIPT: Receipt given
upon request
COMMENTS: Monthly markdowns

Saint Vincent De Paul Thrift Store
305 E. Main St.
Waukesha, WI 53186
TYPE OF MERCHANDISE: Clothing,
housewares, furniture
DONATION TAX RECEIPT: Receipt given
upon request
COMMENTS: Monthly markdowns

Salvation Army Thrift Store
351 W. Main St.
Waukesha, WI 53186
TYPE OF MERCHANDISE: Clothing,
housewares, furniture
DONATION TAX RECEIPT: Receipt given
upon request

Salvation Army Thrift Store
1002 S. Third Ave.
Wausau, WI 54401
TYPE OF MERCHANDISE: Clothing,
housewares, furniture
DONATION TAX RECEIPT: Receipt given
upon request

Salvation Army Thrift Store
7711 W. Greenfield Ave.
West Allis, WI 53201
CONTACT: Ethel Rozanski
PHONE: 414-453-1267
HOURS: Mon.–Sat. 9–5
TYPE OF MERCHANDISE: Clothing,
housewares, furniture
DONATION TAX RECEIPT: Receipt given
upon request

Saint Vincent De Paul Thrift Store
7125 W. Greenfield Ave.
West Allis, WI 53215
TYPE OF MERCHANDISE: Clothing,
housewares, furniture
DONATION TAX RECEIPT: Receipt given
upon request
COMMENTS: Monthly markdowns

Saint Vincent De Paul Thrift Store
420 N. River Rd.
West Bend, WI 53095
TYPE OF MERCHANDISE: Clothing,
housewares, furniture
DONATION TAX RECEIPT: Receipt given
upon request
COMMENTS: Monthly markdowns

11

Canadian Thrift Stores, by Province

Alberta

TVI Value Village Thrift Store
104 58th Ave. SE
Calgary, Alberta T2H 0N7
CONTACT: Lorie Gantz
PHONE: 403-255-5501
HOURS: Mon.–Fri. 9–9, Sat. 9–6
TYPE OF MERCHANDISE: Clothing,
housewares, furniture
DONATION TAX RECEIPT: No

MCC Variety Store
1314 Ninth Ave. SE
Calgary, Alberta T2G 0T3
TYPE OF MERCHANDISE: Clothing,
housewares

TVI Value Village Thrift Store
3405 34th St. NE
Calgary, Alberta T1Y 6J6
CONTACT: Stan Siudy
PHONE: 403-291-3323
HOURS: Mon.–Fri. 9–9, Sat. 9–6
TYPE OF MERCHANDISE: Clothing,
housewares, furniture
DONATION TAX RECEIPT: No

Goodwill Industries Thrift Store G-Mart
10572 101st St.
Edmonton, Alberta T5H 2R9
PHONE: 403-424-0080
HOURS: Mon.–Fri. 10–9, Sat. 10–6, Sun. 12–5
TYPE OF MERCHANDISE: Clothing,
housewares, furniture
DONATION TAX RECEIPT: On furniture only
COMMENTS: 44 years in business

TVI Value Village Thrift Store
11850 103rd Ave.
Edmonton, Alberta T5G 2J2
CONTACT: Joan MacKenzie
PHONE: 403-477-0025
HOURS: Mon.–Fri. 9–9, Sat. 9–6
TYPE OF MERCHANDISE: Clothing,
housewares, furniture
DONATION TAX RECEIPT: No

Goodwill Industries Thrift Store G-Mart
12510 132nd Ave.
Edmonton, Alberta T5L 4X5
CONTACT: Karen Quinn
PHONE: 403-455-4818
HOURS: Mon.–Fri. 10–9, Sat. 10–6,
Sun. 12–5

TYPE OF MERCHANDISE: Clothing, housewares, furniture
DONATION TAX RECEIPT: On furniture only
COMMENTS: 44 years in business

Goodwill Industries Thrift Store G-Mart
5008 50th Ave.
Edmonton, Alberta T6E 5H1
PHONE: 403-352-6461
HOURS: Mon.–Fri. 10–9, Sat. 10–6
TYPE OF MERCHANDISE: Clothing, housewares, furniture
DONATION TAX RECEIPT: On furniture only
COMMENTS: 44 years in business

Goodwill Industries Thrift Store G-Mart
8759 51st Ave.
Edmonton, Alberta T6E 5H1
CONTACT: Darren Rossander
PHONE: 403-462-1333
HOURS: Mon.–Fri. 10–9, Sat. 10–6, Sun. 12–5
TYPE OF MERCHANDISE: Clothing, housewares, furniture
DONATION TAX RECEIPT: On furniture only
COMMENTS: 44 years in business

TVI Value Village Thrift Store
8930 82nd Ave.
Edmonton, Alberta T6C 0Z3
CONTACT: Martina Nopper
PHONE: 403-468-1259
HOURS: Mon.–Fri. 9–9, Sat. 9–6
TYPE OF MERCHANDISE: Clothing, housewares, furniture
DONATION TAX RECEIPT: No

TVI Value Village Thrift Store
9540–41 63rd St.
Edmonton, Alberta T5P 3M7
CONTACT: Henry Lau
PHONE: 403-484-4177
HOURS: Mon.–Fri. 9–9, Sat. 9–6
TYPE OF MERCHANDISE: Clothing, housewares, furniture
DONATION TAX RECEIPT: No

MCC Variety & Selfhelp Store
1211 Second Ave. S
Lethbridge, Alberta T1J 0E4
TYPE OF MERCHANDISE: Clothing, housewares
DONATION TAX RECEIPT: Check store policy

TVI Value Village Thrift Store
2235 50th Ave.
Red Deer, Alberta T4R 1L2
CONTACT: Robert Leggo
PHONE: 403-343-3000
HOURS: Mon.–Fri. 9–9, Sat. 9–6
TYPE OF MERCHANDISE: Clothing, housewares, furniture
DONATION TAX RECEIPT: No

British Columbia

Salvation Army Thrift Store
7301 Edmonds St.
Burnaby, B.C. V3N 1A7
TYPE OF MERCHANDISE: Clothing, housewares, furniture
DONATION TAX RECEIPT: Check store policy

Salvation Army Thrift Store
3451 Wayburne Dr.
Burnaby, B.C. V5G 3L1
TYPE OF MERCHANDISE: Clothing, housewares, furniture
DONATION TAX RECEIPT: Check store policy

TVI Value Village Thrift Store
7350 Edmonds St.
Burnaby, B.C. V3N 1A8
CONTACT: Brenda Beecroft
PHONE: 604-540-4066
HOURS: Mon.–Fri. 9–9, Sat. 9–6, Sun. 10–6
TYPE OF MERCHANDISE: Clothing, housewares, furniture
DONATION TAX RECEIPT: No

MCC Selfhelp Warehouse
31414 Marshall Rd.
Clearbrook, B.C. V2T 3T8
TYPE OF MERCHANDISE: Clothing, housewares
DONATION TAX RECEIPT: Check store policy

MCC Sales & Selfhelp
31872 S. Frazer Way
Clearbrook, B.C. V2T 1V7
TYPE OF MERCHANDISE: Clothing, housewares
DONATION TAX RECEIPT: Check store policy

TVI Value Village Thrift Store
31970 S. Fraser Way
Clearbrook, B.C. V2T 1W6
CONTACT: Richard Farley
PHONE: 604-850-3712
HOURS: Mon.–Fri. 9–9, Sat. 9–6, Sun. 10–6
TYPE OF MERCHANDISE: Clothing,
housewares, furniture
DONATION TAX RECEIPT: No

TVI Value Village Thrift Store
540 Clarke Rd.
Coquitlam, B.C. V3J 3X5
CONTACT: Lindsey Williams
PHONE: 604-937-7087
HOURS: Mon.–Fri. 9–9, Sat. 9–6, Sun. 10–6
TYPE OF MERCHANDISE: Clothing,
housewares, furniture
DONATION TAX RECEIPT: No

Salvation Army Thrift Store
22537 Loughheed Hwy.
Haney, B.C. V2X 2V2
TYPE OF MERCHANDISE: Clothing,
housewares, furniture
DONATION TAX RECEIPT: Check store
policy

TVI Value Village Thrift Store
190 Aurora Crescent
Kelowna, B.C. V1X 7M3
CONTACT: Maxine Dorninelli
PHONE: 604-491-1356
HOURS: Mon.–Fri. 9–9, Sat. 9–6, Sun. 10–6
TYPE OF MERCHANDISE: Clothing,
housewares, furniture
DONATION TAX RECEIPT: No

MCC Sales
575 Bernard Ave.
Kelowna, B.C. V1Y 6N9
TYPE OF MERCHANDISE: Clothing,
housewares, furniture
DONATION TAX RECEIPT: Check store
policy

Salvation Army Thrift Store
20179 56th St.
Langley, B.C. V3A 3Y5
TYPE OF MERCHANDISE: Clothing,
housewares, furniture
DONATION TAX RECEIPT: Check store
policy

MCC Mennonite Sales
20514 Fraser Highway
Langley, B.C. V3A 4G3
TYPE OF MERCHANDISE: Clothing,
housewares, furniture
DONATION TAX RECEIPT: Check store
policy

TVI Value Village Thrift Store
5666 Glover Rd.
Langley, B.C. V3A 4H8
CONTACT: Ed Burtnyk
PHONE: 604-533-1663
HOURS: Mon.–Fri. 9–9, Sat. 9–6, Sun. 10–6
TYPE OF MERCHANDISE: Clothing,
housewares, furniture
DONATION TAX RECEIPT: No

TVI Value Village Thrift Store
110–22255 Dewdney Trunk Rd.
Maple Ridge, B.C. V2X 3J1
CONTACT: Chris Richards
PHONE: 604-467-5585
HOURS: Mon.–Tues. 9–6, Wed.–
Fri. 9–9, Sat. 9–6, Sun. 10–6
TYPE OF MERCHANDISE: Clothing,
housewares, furniture
DONATION TAX RECEIPT: No

Salvation Army Thrift Store
2275 Elgin Ave.
Port Coquitlam, B.C. V3C 2B3
TYPE OF MERCHANDISE: Clothing,
housewares, furniture
DONATION TAX RECEIPT: Check store
policy

Salvation Army Thrift Store
5491#3 Rd.
Richmond, B.C. V6X 2C7
TYPE OF MERCHANDISE: Clothing,
housewares, furniture
DONATION TAX RECEIPT: Check store
policy

Saint Vincent De Paul Thrift Store
9788B Second St.
Sidney, B.C. V8L 3Y8
TYPE OF MERCHANDISE: Clothing,
housewares, furniture
DONATION TAX RECEIPT: Check store
policy

Salvation Army Thrift Store
9775 Second St.
Sidney, B.C. V8L 4P9
TYPE OF MERCHANDISE: Clothing,
housewares, furniture
DONATION TAX RECEIPT: Check store
policy

TVI Value Village Thrift Store
10642 King George Hwy.
Surrey, B.C. V3T 2X3
CONTACT: John Woolner
PHONE: 604-588-5225
HOURS: Mon.–Fri. 9–9, Sat. 9–6, Sun. 10–6
TYPE OF MERCHANDISE: Clothing,
housewares, furniture
DONATION TAX RECEIPT: No

Salvation Army Thrift Store
13530 76th Ave.
Surrey, B.C. V3W 7P8
TYPE OF MERCHANDISE: Clothing,
housewares, furniture
DONATION TAX RECEIPT: Check store
policy

Salvation Army Thrift Store
5658 176th St.
Surrey, B.C. V3S 4C6
TYPE OF MERCHANDISE: Clothing,
housewares, furniture
DONATION TAX RECEIPT: Check store
policy

TVI Value Village Thrift Store
1820 E. Hastings St.
Vancouver, B.C. V5L 1T2
CONTACT: Ray Pratt
PHONE: 604-254-4282
HOURS: Mon.–Fri. 9–9, Sat. 9–6, Sun. 10–6
TYPE OF MERCHANDISE: Clothing,
housewares, furniture
DONATION TAX RECEIPT: No

Salvation Army Thrift Store
241 Lonsdale Ave.
Vancouver, B.C. V7M 2E9
TYPE OF MERCHANDISE: Clothing,
housewares, furniture
DONATION TAX RECEIPT: Check store
policy

Salvation Army Thrift Store
2438 E. Hastings St.
Vancouver, B.C. V5K 1Z1
TYPE OF MERCHANDISE: Clothing,
housewares, furniture
DONATION TAX RECEIPT: Check store
policy

Salvation Army Thrift Store
2714–2718 W. Broadway
Vancouver, B.C. V6K 2G4
TYPE OF MERCHANDISE: Clothing,
housewares, furniture
DONATION TAX RECEIPT: Check store
policy

Salvation Army Thrift Store
2775 Sophia St.
Vancouver, B.C. V5T 3L1
TYPE OF MERCHANDISE: Clothing,
housewares, furniture
DONATION TAX RECEIPT: Check store
policy

MCC Sales
5920 Fraser St.
Vancouver, B.C. V5W 2Z7
TYPE OF MERCHANDISE: Clothing,
housewares
DONATION TAX RECEIPT: Check store
policy

TVI Value Village Thrift Store
6415 Victoria Dr.
Vancouver, B.C. V5P 3X5
CONTACT: Tracie Soyka
PHONE: 604-327-4434
HOURS: Mon.–Fri. 9–9, Sat. 9–6, Sun 10–6
TYPE OF MERCHANDISE: Clothing,
housewares, furniture
DONATION TAX RECEIPT: No

Salvation Army Thrift Store
811 Columbia St.
Vancouver, B.C. V3M 1B9
TYPE OF MERCHANDISE: Clothing,
housewares, furniture
DONATION TAX RECEIPT: Check store
policy

TVI Value Village Thrift Store
1810 Store St.
Victoria, B.C. V8T 4R4
CONTACT: Kris Novak

PHONE: 604-380-9422
HOURS: Mon.–Tues. 9–6, Wed.–Fri. 9–9,
Sat. 9–6, Sun. 10–6
TYPE OF MERCHANDISE: Clothing,
housewares, furniture
DONATION TAX RECEIPT: No

Saint Vincent De Paul Thrift Store
2784 Claude Rd.
Victoria, B.C. V9B 3T6
TYPE OF MERCHANDISE: Clothing,
housewares, furniture
DONATION TAX RECEIPT: Check store
policy

Saint Vincent De Paul Thrift Store
340 View St.
Victoria, B.C. V8W 1K2
TYPE OF MERCHANDISE: Clothing,
housewares, furniture
DONATION TAX RECEIPT: Check store
policy

Salvation Army Thrift Store
3948 Quadra St.
Victoria, B.C. V8X 1J6
TYPE OF MERCHANDISE: Clothing,
housewares, furniture
DONATION TAX RECEIPT: Check store
policy

Salvation Army Thrift Store
525 Johnson St.
Victoria, B.C. V8W 1M2
TYPE OF MERCHANDISE: Clothing,
housewares, furniture
DONATION TAX RECEIPT: Check store
policy

Salvation Army Thrift Store
6686-C Sooke Rd.
Victoria, B.C. V9B 5B4
TYPE OF MERCHANDISE: Clothing,
housewares, furniture
DONATION TAX RECEIPT: Check store
policy

Salvation Army Thrift Store
7177 West Saanich Rd.
Victoria, B.C. V8X 4M6
TYPE OF MERCHANDISE: Clothing,
housewares, furniture
DONATION TAX RECEIPT: Check store
policy

Salvation Army Thrift Store
777 Goldstream Ave.
Victoria, B.C. V9B 2X4
TYPE OF MERCHANDISE: Clothing,
housewares, furniture
DONATION TAX RECEIPT: Check store
policy

Salvation Army Thrift Store
855 Shawnigan Rd.
Victoria, B.C. V0R 2P0
TYPE OF MERCHANDISE: Clothing,
housewares, furniture
DONATION TAX RECEIPT: Check store
policy

MCC Sales
42232 Central Rd.
Yarrow, B.C. V0X 2A0
TYPE OF MERCHANDISE: Clothing,
housewares
DONATION TAX RECEIPT: Check store
policy

Manitoba

MCC Community Selfhelp Center
414 Pacific Ave.
Brandon, Manitoba R7A 0H5
TYPE OF MERCHANDISE: Clothing,
housewares
DONATION TAX RECEIPT: Check store
policy

MCC Carman Community Selfhelp Center
20 First Ave. SW
Carman, Manitoba R0G 0J0
TYPE OF MERCHANDISE: Clothing,
housewares
DONATION TAX RECEIPT: Check store
policy

MCC Grunthal Community Thrift Shop
185 Main St.
Grunthal, Manitoba R0A 0R0
TYPE OF MERCHANDISE: Clothing,
housewares
DONATION TAX RECEIPT: Check store
policy

MCC Morris Community Selfhelp Center
162 Charles St. W
Morris, Manitoba R0G 1K0

TYPE OF MERCHANDISE: Clothing,
housewares

DONATION TAX RECEIPT: Check store
policy

MCC Niverville Community Selfhelp Center
226 Main St.
Niverville, Manitoba R0A 1E0
TYPE OF MERCHANDISE: Clothing,
housewares
DONATION TAX RECEIPT: Check store
policy

MCC Portage Gift & Thrift Store
206 Saskatchewan Ave. E
Portage la Prairie, Manitoba R1N 0K9
TYPE OF MERCHANDISE: Clothing,
housewares
DONATION TAX RECEIPT: Check store
policy

MCC Riverton Thrift Store
18 Riverton Ave.
Riverton, Manitoba R0C 2R0
TYPE OF MERCHANDISE: Clothing,
housewares
DONATION TAX RECEIPT: Check store
policy

MCC Steinbach Community Selfhelp Center
410 Elmdale Dr.
Steinbach, Manitoba R0A 2A0
TYPE OF MERCHANDISE: Clothing,
housewares
DONATION TAX RECEIPT: Check store
policy

MCC Winkler Community Selfhelp Center
325 Fourth St.
Winkler, Manitoba R6W 4B6
TYPE OF MERCHANDISE: Clothing,
housewares
DONATION TAX RECEIPT: Check store
policy

TVI Value Village Thrift Store
1560 Regent Ave.
Winnipeg, Manitoba R2C 3D4
CONTACT: Jeff Smail
PHONE: 204-661-9045
HOURS: Mon.–Fri. 9–9, Sat. 9–6, Sun. 10–5
TYPE OF MERCHANDISE: Clothing,
housewares, furniture
DONATION TAX RECEIPT: No

Salvation Army Thrift Store
1686 Pembina Hwy.
Winnipeg, Manitoba R3T 2G2
TYPE OF MERCHANDISE: Clothing,
housewares, furniture
DONATION TAX RECEIPT: Check store
policy

TVI Value Village Thrift Store
1729 Pembina Hwy.
Winnipeg, Manitoba R3T 2G6
CONTACT: Phil Martens
PHONE: 204-261-8719
HOURS: Mon.–Fri. 9–9, Sat. 9–6, Sun. 10–5
TYPE OF MERCHANDISE: Clothing,
housewares, furniture
DONATION TAX RECEIPT: No

MCC Community Gift & Thrift Shop
499 Jamison Ave.
Winnipeg, Manitoba R2K 1N3
TYPE OF MERCHANDISE: Clothing,
housewares
DONATION TAX RECEIPT: Check store
policy

MCC West End Community Selfhelp Center
859 Sargent Ave.
Winnipeg, Manitoba R3E 0C5
TYPE OF MERCHANDISE: Clothing,
housewares
DONATION TAX RECEIPT: Check store
policy

Junior League Thriftique
894 Croydon Ave.
Winnipeg, Manitoba R3M 0Y4
CONTACT: Jane Todd
PHONE: 204-474-2224
HOURS: Tues.–Sat. 10–5
TYPE OF MERCHANDISE: Clothing,
footwear, housewares
DONATION TAX RECEIPT: Check store
policy
COMMENTS: Spring, fall, garage sales,
Christmas sales

TVI Value Village Thrift Store
942 Jefferson Ave.
Winnipeg, Manitoba R2P 1W1
CONTACT: Blair Grabski
PHONE: 204-694-6844
HOURS: Mon.–Fri. 9–9, Sat. 9–6, Sun. 10–5

TYPE OF MERCHANDISE: Clothing, housewares, furniture
DONATION TAX RECEIPT: No

New Brunswick

Salvation Army Thrift Store
102 Norwood Dr.
Moncton, N.B. E1C 6L9
TYPE OF MERCHANDISE: Clothing, housewares, furniture
DONATION TAX RECEIPT: Check store policy

Salvation Army Thrift Store
16 Church St.
Moncton, N.B. E1C 4Y9
TYPE OF MERCHANDISE: Clothing, housewares, furniture
DONATION TAX RECEIPT: Check store policy

Salvation Army Thrift Store
16 Bridge St.
Sackville, N.B. E0A 3C0
TYPE OF MERCHANDISE: Clothing, housewares, furniture
DONATION TAX RECEIPT: Check store policy

Salvation Army Thrift Store
160 Main St.
Saint John, N.B. E2K 1H4
TYPE OF MERCHANDISE: Clothing, housewares, furniture
DONATION TAX RECEIPT: Check store policy

Newfoundland

Salvation Army Thrift Store
11 Waldegrave St.
St. John's, Nfld. A1C 4M5
TYPE OF MERCHANDISE: Clothing, housewares, furniture
DONATION TAX RECEIPT: Check store policy

Saint Vincent De Paul Thrift Store
120 Mundy Pond Rd.
St. John's, Nfld. A1E 1V1

TYPE OF MERCHANDISE: Clothing, housewares, furniture
DONATION TAX RECEIPT: Check store policy

Nova Scotia

Salvation Army Thrift Store
106 Portland St.
Dartmouth, N.S. B2Y 1H8
TYPE OF MERCHANDISE: Clothing, housewares, furniture
DONATION TAX RECEIPT: Check store policy

Salvation Army Thrift Store
1 Hartlen Ave.
Halifax, N.S. B3R 1R5
TYPE OF MERCHANDISE: Clothing, housewares, furniture
DONATION TAX RECEIPT: Check store policy

Salvation Army Thrift Store
2044 Gottingen St.
Halifax, N.S. B3K 3A9
TYPE OF MERCHANDISE: Clothing, housewares, furniture
DONATION TAX RECEIPT: Check store policy

Salvation Army Thrift Store
320 Commercial St.
North Sydney, N.S. B2A 1C2
TYPE OF MERCHANDISE: Clothing, housewares, furniture
DONATION TAX RECEIPT: Check store policy

Ontario

Goodwill Industries Thrift Store
76 Harwood Ave. S
Ajax, Ontario
PHONE: 416-683-0782
TYPE OF MERCHANDISE: Clothing, housewares, furniture
DONATION TAX RECEIPT: Check store policy

Saint Vincent De Paul Thrift Store
61 Murray
Amherstburg, Ontario N9B 1H6

TYPE OF MERCHANDISE: Clothing, housewares, furniture
DONATION TAX RECEIPT: Check store policy

MCC Aylmer Community Store
20 Talbot St. E
Aylmer, Ontario N5H 1H4
TYPE OF MERCHANDISE: Clothing, housewares
DONATION TAX RECEIPT: Check store policy

Saint Vincent De Paul Thrift Store
106 Dunlop St. E
Barrie, Ontario L4M 1A4
TYPE OF MERCHANDISE: Clothing, housewares, furniture
DONATION TAX RECEIPT: Check store policy

Goodwill Industries Thrift Store
44 Cedar Pointe Drive, Unite 1104B
Barrie, Ontario L4N 5R7
CONTACT: Georgine Olmstead
PHONE: 705-737-9213
TYPE OF MERCHANDISE: Clothing, housewares, furniture
DONATION TAX RECEIPT: Check store policy

Goodwill Industries Thrift Store
534 Bayfield St.
Barrie, Ontario
PHONE: 705-737-1286
TYPE OF MERCHANDISE: Clothing, housewares, furniture
DONATION TAX RECEIPT: Check store policy

Saint Vincent De Paul Thrift Store
506 Notre-Dame
Belle River, Ontario N0R 1A0
TYPE OF MERCHANDISE: Clothing, housewares, furniture
DONATION TAX RECEIPT: Check store policy

Saint Vincent De Paul Thrift Store
12 Talbot
Blenheim, Ontario N0P 1A0
TYPE OF MERCHANDISE: Clothing, housewares, furniture
DONATION TAX RECEIPT: Check store policy

Saint Vincent De Paul Thrift Store
106 Main St. N
Brampton, Ontario
PHONE: 416-453-8480
TYPE OF MERCHANDISE: Clothing, housewares, furniture
DONATION TAX RECEIPT: Check store policy

Salvation Army Thrift Store
147 Queen St. W
Brampton, Ontario
PHONE: 416-454-4909
TYPE OF MERCHANDISE: Clothing, housewares, furniture
DONATION TAX RECEIPT: Check store policy

TVI Value Village Thrift Store
150 West Dr.
Brampton, Ontario L6T 4P9
CONTACT: Chris Paabo
PHONE: 905-451-7975
HOURS: Mon.–Fri. 9–9, Sat. 9–6, Sun. 10–6
TYPE OF MERCHANDISE: Clothing, housewares, furniture
DONATION TAX RECEIPT: No

Saint Vincent De Paul Thrift Store
16 Queen St. W
Brampton, Ontario
TYPE OF MERCHANDISE: Clothing, housewares, furniture
DONATION TAX RECEIPT: Check store policy

Goodwill Industries Thrift Store
200 Clarence St.
Brampton, Ontario
PHONE: 416-451-7845
TYPE OF MERCHANDISE: Clothing, housewares, furniture
DONATION TAX RECEIPT: Check store policy

Salvation Army Thrift Store
187 Dalhousie St.
Brantford, Ontario N3T 2J6
TYPE OF MERCHANDISE: Clothing, housewares, furniture
DONATION TAX RECEIPT: Check store policy

Goodwill Industries Thrift Store Amity
2014 Victoria St.
CROSS STREET: Brant
Burlington, Ontario
HOURS: Mon.–Sat. 9–5:30, Fri. 9–9
TYPE OF MERCHANDISE: Clothing,
housewares, appliances
DONATION TAX RECEIPT: Receipt given
upon request

Goodwill Industries Thrift Store Amity
4051 New St.
CROSS STREET: Walker's Line
Burlington, Ontario
HOURS: Mon.–Sat. 9:30–5:30, Thurs.–Fri.
9:30–9
TYPE OF MERCHANDISE: Clothing,
housewares, appliances
DONATION TAX RECEIPT: Receipt given
upon request

Salvation Army Thrift Store
495 Brant St.
Burlington, Ontario L7R 2G5
TYPE OF MERCHANDISE: Clothing,
housewares, furniture
DONATION TAX RECEIPT: Check store
policy

Salvation Army Thrift Store
62–64 Argyle St. N
Caledonia, Ontario N0A 1A0
TYPE OF MERCHANDISE: Clothing,
housewares, furniture
DONATION TAX RECEIPT: Check store
policy

TVI Value Village Thrift Store
480 Hespeler Rd.
Cambridge, Ontario N1R 7R9
CONTACT: Marshall King
PHONE: 519-624-1812
HOURS: Mon.–Fri. 9–9, Sat. 9–6, Sun. 10–6
TYPE OF MERCHANDISE: Clothing,
housewares, furniture
DONATION TAX RECEIPT: No

Salvation Army Thrift Store
525 Hespeler Rd.
Cambridge, Ontario N1R 6J2
TYPE OF MERCHANDISE: Clothing,
housewares, furniture
DONATION TAX RECEIPT: Check store
policy

Salvation Army Thrift Store
706 King St.
Cambridge, Ontario N3H 3N9
TYPE OF MERCHANDISE: Clothing,
housewares, furniture
DONATION TAX RECEIPT: Check store
policy

Salvation Army Thrift Store
55 King St. W
Chatham, Ontario N7M 1C7
TYPE OF MERCHANDISE: Clothing,
housewares, furniture
DONATION TAX RECEIPT: Check store
policy

Saint Vincent De Paul Thrift Store
80 King St. E
Chatham, Ontario N7M 3M8
TYPE OF MERCHANDISE: Clothing,
housewares, furniture
DONATION TAX RECEIPT: Check store
policy

Saint Vincent De Paul Thrift Store
159 Brown St.
Dresden, Ontario N0P 1M0
TYPE OF MERCHANDISE: Clothing,
housewares, furniture
DONATION TAX RECEIPT: Check store
policy

Salvation Army Thrift Store
36 King St. E
Dundas, Ontario L9H 1B8
TYPE OF MERCHANDISE: Clothing,
housewares, furniture
DONATION TAX RECEIPT: Check store
policy

Saint Vincent De Paul Thrift Store
208 Alder St. W
Dunnville, Ontario N1A 1R4
TYPE OF MERCHANDISE: Clothing,
housewares, furniture
DONATION TAX RECEIPT: Check store
policy

Goodwill Industries Thrift Store
60 Overlea Blvd. Unit 4
East York, Ontario M4H 1B6
CONTACT: Mike Holm
PHONE: 416-422-0998
TYPE OF MERCHANDISE: Clothing,
housewares, furniture

DONATION TAX RECEIPT: Check store
policy

MCC Thrift & Gift
2 Samuel St.
Elmira, Ontario N3B 1N5
TYPE OF MERCHANDISE: Clothing,
housewares
DONATION TAX RECEIPT: Check store
policy

Saint Vincent De Paul Thrift Store
37 Wilson St.
Essex, Ontario N8M 2L8
TYPE OF MERCHANDISE: Clothing,
housewares, furniture
DONATION TAX RECEIPT: Check store policy

Saint Vincent De Paul Thrift Store
3 King St.
Forest, Ontario N0N 1J0
TYPE OF MERCHANDISE: Clothing,
housewares, furniture
DONATION TAX RECEIPT: Check store
policy

Saint Vincent De Paul Thrift Store
143 Gilmore
Fort Erie, Ontario L2A 2L9
TYPE OF MERCHANDISE: Clothing,
housewares, furniture
DONATION TAX RECEIPT: Check store
policy

Salvation Army Thrift Store
50–52 Jarvis St.
Fort Erie, Ontario L2A 2S4
TYPE OF MERCHANDISE: Clothing,
housewares, furniture
DONATION TAX RECEIPT: Check store
policy

Saint Vincent De Paul Thrift Store
7 James St.
Georgetown, Ontario L7E 2H2
TYPE OF MERCHANDISE: Clothing,
housewares, furniture
DONATION TAX RECEIPT: Check store
policy

Salvation Army Thrift Store
78 Mill St.
Georgetown, Ontario L7G 2C9
TYPE OF MERCHANDISE: Clothing,
housewares, furniture

DONATION TAX RECEIPT: Check store
policy

Salvation Army Thrift Store
80 Mill St.
Georgetown, Ontario
PHONE: 416-877-8522
TYPE OF MERCHANDISE: Clothing,
housewares, furniture
DONATION TAX RECEIPT: Check store
policy

Saint Vincent De Paul Thrift Store
209 Main St.
Glencoe, Ontario N0L 1N0
TYPE OF MERCHANDISE: Clothing,
housewares, furniture
DONATION TAX RECEIPT: Check store
policy

Saint Vincent De Paul Thrift Store
RR #2
Goderich, Ontario N7A 3X8
TYPE OF MERCHANDISE: Clothing,
housewares, furniture
DONATION TAX RECEIPT: Check store
policy

Salvation Army Thrift Store
3 Mountain St.
Grimsby, Ontario L3M 3J5
TYPE OF MERCHANDISE: Clothing,
housewares, furniture
DONATION TAX RECEIPT: Check store
policy

TVI Value Village Thrift Store
214 Silvercreek Pkwy. N
Guelph, Ontario N1H 7P8
CONTACT: Rob Van Dolder
PHONE: 519-821-9994
HOURS: Mon.–Fri. 9–9, Sat. 9–6, Sun. 10–6
TYPE OF MERCHANDISE: Clothing,
housewares, furniture
DONATION TAX RECEIPT: No

Saint Vincent De Paul Thrift Store
46 Quebec
Guelph, Ontario N1H 2T4
TYPE OF MERCHANDISE: Clothing,
housewares, furniture
DONATION TAX RECEIPT: Check store
policy

Goodwill Industries Thrift Store Amity
  1366 Main St. E
  Hamilton, Ontario
  HOURS: Mon.–Sat. 9–5:30, Fri. 9–9
  TYPE OF MERCHANDISE: Clothing,
  housewares, appliances
  DONATION TAX RECEIPT: Receipt given
  upon request
Goodwill Industries Thrift Store Amity
  225 King William St.
  CROSS STREET: Wellington
  Hamilton, Ontario
  PHONE: 905-526-8481
  HOURS: Mon.–Sat. 9–5:30, Fri. 9–9
  TYPE OF MERCHANDISE: Clothing,
  housewares, appliances
  DONATION TAX RECEIPT: Receipt given
  upon request
Goodwill Industries Thrift Store Amity
  423 Barton St. E
  CROSS STREET: Victoria
  Hamilton, Ontario
  HOURS: Mon.–Sat. 9–5:30, Fri. 9–9
  TYPE OF MERCHANDISE: Clothing,
  housewares, appliances
  DONATION TAX RECEIPT: Receipt given
  upon request
Saint Vincent De Paul Thrift Store
  461 Cumberland Ave.
  Hamilton, Ontario L3M 2A8
  TYPE OF MERCHANDISE: Clothing,
  housewares, furniture
  DONATION TAX RECEIPT: Check store
  policy
MCC New Horizons
  510 James St. N
  Hamilton, Ontario L8L 1J3
  TYPE OF MERCHANDISE: Clothing,
  housewares
  DONATION TAX RECEIPT: Check store
  policy
Salvation Army Thrift Store
  529 Concession St.
  Hamilton, Ontario L8V 1A7
  TYPE OF MERCHANDISE: Clothing,
  housewares, furniture
  DONATION TAX RECEIPT: Check store
  policy

Goodwill Industries Thrift Store Amity
  604 Concession St.
  Hamilton, Ontario
  HOURS: Mon.–Sat. 9–5:30, Fri. 9–9
  TYPE OF MERCHANDISE: Clothing,
  furniture, appliances
  DONATION TAX RECEIPT: Receipt given
  upon request
Salvation Army Thrift Store
  654 Barton St. E
  Hamilton, Ontario L8L 3A2
  TYPE OF MERCHANDISE: Clothing,
  housewares, furniture
  DONATION TAX RECEIPT: Check store
  policy
Saint Vincent De Paul Thrift Store
  715 Barton St. E
  Hamilton, Ontario
  TYPE OF MERCHANDISE: Clothing,
  housewares, furniture
  DONATION TAX RECEIPT: Check store
  policy
Salvation Army Thrift Store
  94 York Blvd.
  Hamilton, Ontario L8R 1R6
  TYPE OF MERCHANDISE: Clothing,
  housewares, furniture
  DONATION TAX RECEIPT: Check store
  policy
Saint Vincent De Paul Thrift Store
  45 Centre St.
  Harrow, Ontario N0R 1G0
  TYPE OF MERCHANDISE: Clothing,
  housewares, furniture
  DONATION TAX RECEIPT: Check store
  policy
Goodwill Industries Thrift Store
  1316 Princess St.
  Kingston, Ontario K7M 3E2
  CONTACT: Darren Nelles
  PHONE: 613-545-3643
  TYPE OF MERCHANDISE: Clothing,
  housewares, furniture
  DONATION TAX RECEIPT: Check store
  policy
TVI Value Village Thrift Store
  412 Bath Rd.
  Kingston, Ontario K7M 4X6

CONTACT: Stacey Scher
PHONE: 613-544-4849
HOURS: Mon.–Fri. 9–9, Sat. 9–6, Sun. 10–6
TYPE OF MERCHANDISE: Clothing,
housewares, furniture
DONATION TAX RECEIPT: No
Salvation Army Thrift Store
1436 Victoria St. N
Kitchener, Ontario N2B 3E2
TYPE OF MERCHANDISE: Clothing,
housewares, furniture
DONATION TAX RECEIPT: Check store
policy
MCC Benefit Shop
315A Lancaster St. W
Kitchener, Ontario N2H 4V4
TYPE OF MERCHANDISE: Clothing,
housewares
DONATION TAX RECEIPT: Check store
policy
Saint Vincent De Paul Thrift Store
97 Victoria St. N
Kitchener, Ontario N2H 5C1
TYPE OF MERCHANDISE: Clothing,
housewares, furniture
DONATION TAX RECEIPT: Check store
policy
Saint Vincent De Paul Thrift Store
111 Erie St. N
Leamington, Ontario N8H 2O9
TYPE OF MERCHANDISE: Clothing,
housewares, furniture
DONATION TAX RECEIPT: Check store
policy
MCC Et Cetera Shoppe
19 Erie St. N
Leamington, Ontario N8H 2Z2
TYPE OF MERCHANDISE: Clothing,
housewares
DONATION TAX RECEIPT: Check store
policy
Salvation Army Thrift Store
1700 Dundas St.
London, Ontario N5W 3C9
TYPE OF MERCHANDISE: Clothing,
housewares, furniture
DONATION TAX RECEIPT: Check store
policy

Salvation Army Thrift Store
185 Horton St.
London, Ontario N6B 1K7
TYPE OF MERCHANDISE: Clothing,
housewares, furniture
DONATION TAX RECEIPT: Check store
policy
TVI Value Village Thrift Store
4465 Wellington Rd.
London, Ontario N6E 2Z8
CONTACT: Frank Roperti
PHONE: 519-680-3711
HOURS: Mon.–Fri. 9–9, Sat. 9–6, Sun 10–6
TYPE OF MERCHANDISE: Clothing,
housewares, furniture
DONATION TAX RECEIPT: No
Saint Vincent De Paul Thrift Store
585 York St.
London, Ontario N6B 1R6
TYPE OF MERCHANDISE: Clothing,
housewares, furniture
DONATION TAX RECEIPT: Check store
policy
Salvation Army Thrift Store
632 Dundas St. E
London, Ontario N5W 2Y8
TYPE OF MERCHANDISE: Clothing,
housewares, furniture
DONATION TAX RECEIPT: Check store
policy
Salvation Army Thrift Store
360 Main St. E
Milton, Ontario L9T 1P1
TYPE OF MERCHANDISE: Clothing,
housewares, furniture
DONATION TAX RECEIPT: Check store
policy
Salvation Army Thrift Store
363 Main St. E
Milton, Ontario
PHONE: 416-876-4831
TYPE OF MERCHANDISE: Clothing,
housewares, furniture
DONATION TAX RECEIPT: Check store
policy
Salvation Army Thrift Store
256 Lakeshore Rd.
Mississauga, Ontario L5H 1G6

TYPE OF MERCHANDISE: Clothing, housewares, furniture
DONATION TAX RECEIPT: Check store policy

TVI Value Village Thrift Store
3130 Dixie Rd.
Mississauga, Ontario L4Y 1Z
CONTACT: Bruce Bell
PHONE: 905-949-4440
HOURS: Mon.–Fri. 9–9, Sat. 9–6, Sun. 10–6
TYPE OF MERCHANDISE: Clothing, housewares, furniture
DONATION TAX RECEIPT: No

MCC New Hamburg Thrift & Selfhelp
Heritage Dr.
New Hamburg, Ontario N0B 2G0
TYPE OF MERCHANDISE: Clothing, housewares
DONATION TAX RECEIPT: Check store policy

Goodwill Industries Thrift Store
1111 Davis Dr.
Newmarket, Ontario L3Y 1N7
PHONE: 905-898-5911
TYPE OF MERCHANDISE: Clothing, housewares
DONATION TAX RECEIPT: Check store policy

Salvation Army Thrift Store
1166 Gorham St.
Newmarket, Ontario L3Y 5G9
TYPE OF MERCHANDISE: Clothing, housewares, furniture
DONATION TAX RECEIPT: Check store policy

Salvation Army Thrift Store
36 Wilstead Dr.
Newmarket, Ontario L3Y 4T9
TYPE OF MERCHANDISE: Clothing, housewares, furniture
DONATION TAX RECEIPT: Check store policy

Salvation Army Thrift Store
464 Timothy
Newmarket, Ontario
PHONE: 905-895-5572
TYPE OF MERCHANDISE: Clothing, housewares, furniture

DONATION TAX RECEIPT: Check store policy

Saint Vincent De Paul Thrift Store
4693 Victoria St.
Niagara Falls, Ontario L2E 4B8
TYPE OF MERCHANDISE: Clothing, housewares, furniture
DONATION TAX RECEIPT: Check store policy

Goodwill Industries Thrift Store Amity
6758 Lundy's Lane
CROSS STREET: Next to Flying Saucer Restaurant
Niagara Falls, Ontario
PHONE: 905-641-0366
HOURS: Mon.–Sat. 9–5:30, Fri. 9–9
TYPE OF MERCHANDISE: Clothing, housewares, accessories
DONATION TAX RECEIPT: Receipt given upon request
COMMENTS: 10 years in business

Goodwill Industries Thrift Store
1 Cross Rd. Place
CROSS STREET: 401 & Weston Rd.
North York, Ontario
PHONE: 416-241-2020
HOURS: Mon.–Fri. 9–9, Sat. 9–6, Sun. 10–5
TYPE OF MERCHANDISE: Clothing, housewares, furniture
DONATION TAX RECEIPT: Check store policy

Goodwill Industries Thrift Store
3905 Keel St.
North York, Ontario M3J 1N6
PHONE: 416-398-6416
TYPE OF MERCHANDISE: Clothing, housewares, furniture
DONATION TAX RECEIPT: Check store policy

Goodwill Industries Thrift Store Amity
407 Speers Rd.
CROSS STREET: Dorval exit
Oakville, Ontario
HOURS: Mon.–Sat. 9:30–5:30, Thurs.–Fri. 9:30–9
TYPE OF MERCHANDISE: Clothing, housewares, appliances

DONATION TAX RECEIPT: Receipt given upon request

Salvation Army Thrift Store
2284 Speers Rd.
Oakville, Ontario
PHONE: 416-825-2828
TYPE OF MERCHANDISE: Clothing, housewares, furniture
DONATION TAX RECEIPT: Check store policy

Salvation Army Thrift Store
2300 Lakeshore Blvd. W
Oakville, Ontario
PHONE: 416-825-3758
TYPE OF MERCHANDISE: Clothing, housewares, furniture
DONATION TAX RECEIPT: Check store policy

Salvation Army Thrift Store
366 Kerr St.
Oakville, Ontario L6K 3B8
TYPE OF MERCHANDISE: Clothing, housewares, furniture
DONATION TAX RECEIPT: Check store policy

Goodwill Industries Thrift Store
1300 King St.
Oshawa, Ontario L1H 8J4
PHONE: 416-434-8202
TYPE OF MERCHANDISE: Clothing, housewares, furniture
DONATION TAX RECEIPT: Check store policy

Saint Vincent De Paul Thrift Store
27 Celina St.
Oshawa, Ontario L1H 4M9
TYPE OF MERCHANDISE: Clothing, housewares, furniture
DONATION TAX RECEIPT: Check store policy

TVI Value Village Thrift Store
1162 Cyrville Rd.
Ottawa, Ontario K1J 7S9
CONTACT: Brad Langner
PHONE: 613-749-4977
HOURS: Mon.–Fri. 9–9, Sat. 9–6, Sun. 10–6
TYPE OF MERCHANDISE: Clothing, housewares, furniture
DONATION TAX RECEIPT: No

Salvation Army Thrift Store
1250–60 Old Innes Rd.
Ottawa, Ontario K1B 5L3
TYPE OF MERCHANDISE: Clothing, housewares, furniture
DONATION TAX RECEIPT: Check store policy

Saint Vincent De Paul Thrift Store
1313 Wellington St.
Ottawa, Ontario K1Y 3B1
TYPE OF MERCHANDISE: Clothing, housewares, furniture
DONATION TAX RECEIPT: Check store policy

Salvation Army Thrift Store
1320 Carling Ave.
Ottawa, Ontario K1Z 7K9
TYPE OF MERCHANDISE: Clothing, housewares, furniture
DONATION TAX RECEIPT: Check store policy

Salvation Army Thrift Store
1560 Triole St.
Ottawa, Ontario K1B 3Z2
TYPE OF MERCHANDISE: Clothing, housewares, furniture
DONATION TAX RECEIPT: Check store policy

Salvation Army Thrift Store
1706 Bank St.
Ottawa, Ontario K1V 7Y6
TYPE OF MERCHANDISE: Clothing, housewares, furniture
DONATION TAX RECEIPT: Check store policy

Salvation Army Thrift Store
175 George St.
Ottawa, Ontario K1N 5W5
TYPE OF MERCHANDISE: Clothing, housewares, furniture
DONATION TAX RECEIPT: Check store policy

Salvation Army Thrift Store
2405 St. Laurent Blvd.
Ottawa, Ontario K1G 5B4
TYPE OF MERCHANDISE: Clothing, housewares, furniture
DONATION TAX RECEIPT: Check store policy

Salvation Army Thrift Store
3030 Conroy Rd.
Ottawa, Ontario K1G 5H8
TYPE OF MERCHANDISE: Clothing,
housewares, furniture
DONATION TAX RECEIPT: Check store
policy

Salvation Army Thrift Store
310 Moodie Dr.
Ottawa, Ontario K2H 8G3
TYPE OF MERCHANDISE: Clothing,
housewares, furniture
DONATION TAX RECEIPT: Check store
policy

Salvation Army Thrift Store
4025 Innes Rd.
Ottawa, Ontario
TYPE OF MERCHANDISE: Clothing,
housewares, furniture
DONATION TAX RECEIPT: Check store
policy

Salvation Army Thrift Store
60 Waller St.
Ottawa, Ontario K1N 7G5
TYPE OF MERCHANDISE: Clothing,
housewares, furniture
DONATION TAX RECEIPT: Check store
policy

Salvation Army Thrift Store
14 Mechanic St.
Paris, Ontario N3L 1J9
TYPE OF MERCHANDISE: Clothing,
housewares, furniture
DONATION TAX RECEIPT: Check store
policy

Saint Vincent De Paul Thrift Store
256 Murray St.
Peterborough, Ontario K9H 2S9
TYPE OF MERCHANDISE: Clothing,
housewares, furniture
DONATION TAX RECEIPT: Check store
policy

Saint Vincent De Paul Thrift Store
41B7 Petrolla St.
Petrolla, Ontario N0N 1R0
TYPE OF MERCHANDISE: Clothing,
housewares, furniture

DONATION TAX RECEIPT: Check store
policy

MCC Port Gift 'n Thrift Shop
12 Charlotte St.
Port Colborne, Ontario L3K 3C6
TYPE OF MERCHANDISE: Clothing,
housewares
DONATION TAX RECEIPT: Check store policy

Salvation Army Thrift Store
645 King St.
Port Colborne, Ontario L3K 4H5
TYPE OF MERCHANDISE: Clothing,
housewares, furniture
DONATION TAX RECEIPT: Check store
policy

Salvation Army Thrift Store
256 Lakeshore Blvd.
Port Credit, Ontario
PHONE: 416-278-6928
TYPE OF MERCHANDISE: Clothing,
housewares, furniture
DONATION TAX RECEIPT: Check store
policy

Saint Vincent De Paul Thrift Store
271 Lakeshore Rd. E
Port Credit, Ontario
PHONE: 416-278-0437
TYPE OF MERCHANDISE: Clothing,
housewares, furniture
DONATION TAX RECEIPT: Check store
policy

MCC Nifty Gift 'n Thrift
Main St.
Port Rowan, Ontario
TYPE OF MERCHANDISE: Clothing,
housewares, furniture
DONATION TAX RECEIPT: Check store
policy

TVI Value Village Thrift Store
45 Woodbine Downs Blvd.
CROSS STREETS: Hwy. 27 & Finch Ave.
Rexdale, Ontario
PHONE: 416-675-7450
TYPE OF MERCHANDISE: Clothing,
housewares, furniture
DONATION TAX RECEIPT: Check store
policy
COMMENTS: Opened January 1995

Salvation Army Thrift Store
10620 Yonge St.
Richmond Hill, Ontario L4C 3C8
TYPE OF MERCHANDISE: Clothing,
housewares, furniture
DONATION TAX RECEIPT: Check store
policy

Goodwill Industries Thrift Store
9625 Yonge St.
Richmond Hill, Ontario L4C 8J4
PHONE: 416-737-6460
TYPE OF MERCHANDISE: Clothing,
housewares, furniture
DONATION TAX RECEIPT: Check store
policy

Salvation Army Thrift Store
203 Church St.
St. Catharines, Ontario L2R 3E8
TYPE OF MERCHANDISE: Clothing,
housewares, furniture
DONATION TAX RECEIPT: Check store
policy

Salvation Army Thrift Store
210 Bunting Rd.
St. Catharines, Ontario L2M 3Y1
TYPE OF MERCHANDISE: Clothing,
housewares, furniture
DONATION TAX RECEIPT: Check store
policy

MCC Christian Benefit Shop
114–116 Chetwood Ave.
St. Catharines, Ontario L2S 2A8
TYPE OF MERCHANDISE: Clothing,
housewares
DONATION TAX RECEIPT: Check store
policy

MCC Christian Benefit Shop
172–174 Eastchester Ave.
St. Catharines, Ontario L2P 2Z7
TYPE OF MERCHANDISE: Clothing,
housewares, furniture
DONATION TAX RECEIPT: Check store
policy

Goodwill Industries Thrift Store Amity
185 Bunting Rd.
CROSS STREET: Skyway
St. Catharines, Ontario L2M 3Y2

CONTACT: Marilyn Barr
PHONE: 905-641-5237
HOURS: Mon.–Sat. 9–5:30, Fri. 9–9
TYPE OF MERCHANDISE: Clothing,
housewares, accessories
DONATION TAX RECEIPT: Receipt given
upon request
COMMENTS: 10 years in business

Saint Vincent De Paul Thrift Store
67 Queston St.
St. Catharines, Ontario L2R 2Z1
TYPE OF MERCHANDISE: Clothing,
housewares, furniture
DONATION TAX RECEIPT: Check store
policy

Saint Vincent De Paul Thrift Store
106 East St. S
Sarnia, Ontario N7T 7H9
TYPE OF MERCHANDISE: Clothing,
housewares, furniture
DONATION TAX RECEIPT: Check store
policy

Goodwill Industries Thrift Store
106 N. Christina St.
CROSS STREET: Davis
Sarnia, Ontario N7T 3P4
CONTACT: Betty Hollingsworth
PHONE: 519-336-1750
HOURS: Mon.–Fri. 9–5:30, Sat. 9–5
TYPE OF MERCHANDISE: Clothing,
housewares, appliances
DONATION TAX RECEIPT: Receipt given
upon request
COMMENTS: 61 years in business

TVI Value Village Thrift Store
248 Northern Ave. E
Sault Ste. Marie, Ontario
PHONE: 705-256-1801
TYPE OF MERCHANDISE: Clothing,
housewares
DONATION TAX RECEIPT: No
COMMENTS: Opened March 1955

TVI Value Village Thrift Store
3701 Lawrence Ave. E #1
Scarborough, Ontario M1G 1P7
CONTACT: Darin Schweder
PHONE: 416-439-4464
HOURS: Mon.–Fri. 9–9, Sat. 9–6, Sun. 10–6

TYPE OF MERCHANDISE: Clothing,
housewares, furniture
DONATION TAX RECEIPT: No
Salvation Army Thrift Store
1399 Kennedy Rd.
Scarborough, Ontario
CONTACT: Art Frank
PHONE: 416-751-8050
HOURS: Mon.–Sat. 10–6
TYPE OF MERCHANDISE: Clothing,
housewares, furniture
DONATION TAX RECEIPT: Check store
policy
COMMENTS: New metro Toronto
recycling center
Goodwill Industries Thrift Store
2075 Lawrence Ave. E
Scarborough, Ontario
PHONE: 416-755-1248
TYPE OF MERCHANDISE: Clothing,
housewares, furniture
DONATION TAX RECEIPT: Check store
policy
Goodwill Industries Thrift Store
2800 Eglington Ave. E (Elaine Plaza)
Scarborough, Ontario M1J 2C9
PHONE: 416-261-7610
TYPE OF MERCHANDISE: Clothing,
housewares, furniture
DONATION TAX RECEIPT: Check store
policy
TVI Value Village Thrift Store
840 Queenston Rd.
Stoney Creek, Ontario L8G 4A8
CONTACT: Craig Rasmussen
PHONE: 905-664-8884
HOURS: Mon.–Fri. 9–9, Sat. 9–6, Sun. 10–6
TYPE OF MERCHANDISE: Clothing,
housewares, furniture
DONATION TAX RECEIPT: No
MCC Care and Share Shoppe
6280 Main St.
Stouffville, Ontario L4A 1G7
TYPE OF MERCHANDISE: Clothing,
housewares, furniture
DONATION TAX RECEIPT: Check store
policy

Saint Vincent De Paul Thrift Store
322 Oak Ave.
Strathroy, Ontario N7G 3T2
TYPE OF MERCHANDISE: Clothing,
housewares, furniture
DONATION TAX RECEIPT: Check store
policy
Salvation Army Thrift Store
154 Queen St. E
Streetsville, Ontario L5M 2P5
TYPE OF MERCHANDISE: Clothing,
housewares, furniture
DONATION TAX RECEIPT: Check store
policy
Salvation Army Thrift Store
134 Larch St.
Sudbury, Ontario P3E 1C2
TYPE OF MERCHANDISE: Clothing,
housewares, furniture
DONATION TAX RECEIPT: Check store
policy
Salvation Army Thrift Store
1855 LaSalle Blvd.
Sudbury, Ontario P3A 2A3
TYPE OF MERCHANDISE: Clothing,
housewares, furniture
DONATION TAX RECEIPT: Check store
policy
Salvation Army Thrift Store
19 Albert St.
Thorold, Ontario L2V 2G2
TYPE OF MERCHANDISE: Clothing,
housewares, furniture
DONATION TAX RECEIPT: Check store
policy
Salvation Army Thrift Store
545 N. Cumberland St.
Thunder Bay, Ontario P7A 4S2
TYPE OF MERCHANDISE: Clothing,
housewares, furniture
DONATION TAX RECEIPT: Check store
policy
Saint Vincent De Paul Thrift Store
41 Queen St. N
Tilbury, Ontario N0P 2L0
TYPE OF MERCHANDISE: Clothing,
housewares, furniture
DONATION TAX RECEIPT: Check store
policy

Salvation Army Thrift Store
1179 Weston Ave.
Toronto, Ontario M6M 4P5
PHONE: 416-243-0848
TYPE OF MERCHANDISE: Clothing,
housewares, furniture
DONATION TAX RECEIPT: Check store
policy

TVI Value Village Thrift Store
1319 Bloor St. W
Toronto, Ontario M6H 1P3
CONTACT: Don McIntyre
PHONE: 416-539-0585
HOURS: Mon.–Fri. 9–9, Sat. 9–6, Sun. 10–6
TYPE OF MERCHANDISE: Clothing,
housewares, furniture
DONATION TAX RECEIPT: No

Saint Vincent De Paul Thrift Store
1395 Queen St. W
Toronto, Ontario
PHONE: 416-537-5678
TYPE OF MERCHANDISE: Clothing,
housewares, furniture
DONATION TAX RECEIPT: Check store
policy

Saint Vincent De Paul Thrift Store
1440 Queen St. W
CROSS STREET: Lansdowne
Toronto, Ontario
PHONE: 416-537-5678
HOURS: Mon.–Thurs. 7–4, Fri. 7–3
TYPE OF MERCHANDISE: Clothing,
housewares
DONATION TAX RECEIPT: Check store
policy

Salvation Army Thrift Store
1447 Queen St. W
Toronto, Ontario M6R 1A1
PHONE: 416-536-3361
TYPE OF MERCHANDISE: Clothing,
housewares, furniture
DONATION TAX RECEIPT: Check store
policy

Salvation Army Thrift Store
1490 Dundas St. W
Toronto, Ontario M6K 1T5
PHONE: 416-537-1993
TYPE OF MERCHANDISE: Clothing,
housewares, furniture

DONATION TAX RECEIPT: Check store
policy

Saint Vincent De Paul Thrift Store
Warehouse
175 Toryork Dr., Units 42 and 43
Toronto, Ontario
TYPE OF MERCHANDISE: Clothing,
housewares, furniture
DONATION TAX RECEIPT: Check store
policy

TVI Value Village Thrift Store
2119 Danforth Ave.
Toronto, Ontario M4C 1J9
CONTACT: Rob Brown
PHONE: 416-698-0621
HOURS: Mon.–Fri. 9–9, Sat. 9–6, Sun. 10–6
TYPE OF MERCHANDISE: Clothing,
housewares, furniture
DONATION TAX RECEIPT: No

Salvation Army Thrift Store
219 Queen St. E
Toronto, Ontario M5A 1S2
PHONE: 416-366-9871
TYPE OF MERCHANDISE: Clothing,
housewares, furniture
DONATION TAX RECEIPT: Check store
policy

Salvation Army Thrift Store
2300 Lakeshore Rd. W
Toronto, Ontario M8V 1B4
TYPE OF MERCHANDISE: Clothing,
housewares, furniture
DONATION TAX RECEIPT: Check store
policy

Goodwill Industries Thrift Store
234 Adelaide Ave.
CROSS STREET: Jarvis
Toronto, Ontario M5A 1M9
PHONE: 416-366-2083
TYPE OF MERCHANDISE: Clothing,
housewares, furniture
DONATION TAX RECEIPT: Check store
policy

Goodwill Industries By the Pound
234 Adelaide Ave. E
Toronto, Ontario M5A 1M9
PHONE: 416-362-4710
TYPE OF MERCHANDISE: Clothing sold by
the pound—cheap!

DONATION TAX RECEIPT: Check store
policy

Saint Vincent De Paul Thrift Store
253 Broadview Ave.
Toronto, Ontario
TYPE OF MERCHANDISE: Clothing,
housewares, furniture
DONATION TAX RECEIPT: Check store
policy

Saint Vincent De Paul Thrift Store
271 Lakeshore Rd. E
Toronto, Ontario
TYPE OF MERCHANDISE: Clothing,
housewares, furniture
DONATION TAX RECEIPT: Check store
policy

Goodwill Industries Thrift Store
28 Roncesvalles
Toronto, Ontario
PHONE: 416-534-1686
TYPE OF MERCHANDISE: Clothing,
housewares, furniture
DONATION TAX RECEIPT: Check store
policy

Goodwill Industries Thrift Store
2985 Lakeshore Blvd. W
Toronto, Ontario
PHONE: 416-255-3211
TYPE OF MERCHANDISE: Clothing,
housewares, furniture
DONATION TAX RECEIPT: Check store
policy

Salvation Army Thrift Store
306 Rutherford S
Toronto, Ontario
PHONE: 416-451-8840
TYPE OF MERCHANDISE: Clothing,
housewares, furniture
DONATION TAX RECEIPT: Check store
policy

Saint Vincent De Paul Thrift Store
3194 Danforth Ave.
CROSS STREET: Pharmacy
Toronto, Ontario
PHONE: 416-699-5105
TYPE OF MERCHANDISE: Clothing,
housewares, furniture
DONATION TAX RECEIPT: Check store
policy

Saint Vincent De Paul Thrift Store
3437 Lakeshore Blvd. W
CROSS STREET: Kipling
Toronto, Ontario
PHONE: 416-252-1057
TYPE OF MERCHANDISE: Clothing,
housewares, furniture
DONATION TAX RECEIPT: Check store
policy

Saint Vincent De Paul Thrift Store
391 Driftwood Ave.
CROSS STREET: Jane
Toronto, Ontario
PHONE: 416-661-3126
TYPE OF MERCHANDISE: Clothing,
housewares, furniture
DONATION TAX RECEIPT: Check store
policy

Goodwill Industries Thrift Store
4566–4568 Kingston Rd.
Toronto, Ontario
PHONE: 416-284-4776, 284-0146
TYPE OF MERCHANDISE: Clothing,
housewares, furniture
DONATION TAX RECEIPT: Check store
policy

Goodwill Industries Thrift Store
465 Parliament St.
Toronto, Ontario
PHONE: 416-921-6648
TYPE OF MERCHANDISE: Clothing,
housewares, furniture
DONATION TAX RECEIPT: Check store
policy

Salvation Army Thrift Store
496 Richmond St. W
CROSS STREETS: Btw. Spadina and Bathurst
Toronto, Ontario
PHONE: 416-366-4680
TYPE OF MERCHANDISE: Clothing,
housewares, furniture
DONATION TAX RECEIPT: Check store policy
COMMENTS: Three floors, as-is, appliances

Junior League of Toronto Opportunity Shop
539 Mt. Pleasant Rd.
CROSS STREET: South of Eglinton Ave.
Toronto, Ontario M5S 2M5
CONTACT: Gayle Leitch

PHONE: 416-488-7127
HOURS: Tues.–Sat. 10–5
TYPE OF MERCHANDISE: Clothing, bric-a-brac
DONATION TAX RECEIPT: No
COMMENTS: Consignments taken

Goodwill Industries Thrift Store
548 College St.
Toronto, Ontario M6C 1B1
PHONE: 416-967-0364
TYPE OF MERCHANDISE: Clothing, housewares, furniture
DONATION TAX RECEIPT: Check store policy

Saint Vincent De Paul Thrift Store
793 Dundas St. W
CROSS STREET: Bathurst
Toronto, Ontario
PHONE: 416-364-2780
TYPE OF MERCHANDISE: Clothing, housewares, furniture
DONATION TAX RECEIPT: Check store policy

Salvation Army Thrift Store
892 Queen St. E
Toronto, Ontario
PHONE: 416-461-9721
TYPE OF MERCHANDISE: Clothing, housewares, furniture
DONATION TAX RECEIPT: Check store policy

Salvation Army Thrift Store
943 St. Clair Ave. W
Toronto, Ontario
PHONE: 416-651-2825
TYPE OF MERCHANDISE: Clothing, housewares, furniture
DONATION TAX RECEIPT: Check store policy

Salvation Army Thrift Store
974 Pape Ave.
Toronto, Ontario M4K 3V7
PHONE: 416-425-9625
TYPE OF MERCHANDISE: Clothing, housewares, furniture
DONATION TAX RECEIPT: Check store policy

Salvation Army Thrift Store
38–42 King St. N
Waterloo, Ontario N2J 2W8
TYPE OF MERCHANDISE: Clothing, housewares, furniture
DONATION TAX RECEIPT: Check store policy

Salvation Army Thrift Store
3 Main St. E
Welland, Ontario L3B 3W4
TYPE OF MERCHANDISE: Clothing, housewares, furniture
DONATION TAX RECEIPT: Check store policy

MCC Welland Christian Benefit Shop
53 Southworth St. N
Welland, Ontario L3B 1Y3
TYPE OF MERCHANDISE: Clothing, housewares
DONATION TAX RECEIPT: Check store policy

Salvation Army Thrift Store
1725–35 College
Windsor, Ontario N9B 1M4
TYPE OF MERCHANDISE: Clothing, housewares, furniture
DONATION TAX RECEIPT: Check store policy

Salvation Army Thrift Store
19 Cenke St.
Windsor, Ontario N8M 1N8
TYPE OF MERCHANDISE: Clothing, housewares, furniture
DONATION TAX RECEIPT: Check store policy

TVI Value Village Thrift Store
2411 Dougall Ave.
Windsor, Ontario N8X 1T3
CONTACT: Wendy Seifried
PHONE: 519-250-8818
HOURS: Mon.–Fri. 9–9, Sat. 9–6, Sun. 10–6
TYPE OF MERCHANDISE: Clothing, housewares, furniture
DONATION TAX RECEIPT: No

Saint Vincent De Paul Thrift Store
3177 Sandwich St.
Windsor, Ontario N9C 1A4

TYPE OF MERCHANDISE: Clothing,
housewares, furniture
DONATION TAX RECEIPT: Check store policy
Salvation Army Thrift Store
341 Chatham St. E
Windsor, Ontario N9A 2W7
TYPE OF MERCHANDISE: Clothing,
housewares, furniture
DONATION TAX RECEIPT: Check store policy
Salvation Army Thrift Store
342 University Ave. E
Windsor, Ontario N9A 2Z1
TYPE OF MERCHANDISE: Clothing,
housewares, furniture
DONATION TAX RECEIPT: Check store policy
Saint Vincent De Paul Thrift Store
357 Pitt St. E
Windsor, Ontario N9A 2Y7
TYPE OF MERCHANDISE: Clothing,
housewares, furniture
DONATION TAX RECEIPT: Check store policy
Saint Vincent De Paul Thrift Store
812 Pillette Ave.
Windsor, Ontario M8Y 3B5
TYPE OF MERCHANDISE: Clothing,
housewares, furniture
DONATION TAX RECEIPT: Check store policy
Goodwill Industries Thrift Store
1121 Dundas St. E
Witby, Ontario
PHONE: 416-430-6093
TYPE OF MERCHANDISE: Clothing,
housewares, furniture
DONATION TAX RECEIPT: Check store policy

Saskatchewan

MCC Mennonite Community Closet
1022 102nd St. N
Battleford, Sask. S9A 0Z3
TYPE OF MERCHANDISE: Clothing,
housewares
DONATION TAX RECEIPT: Check store policy
MCC Mennonite Central Committe
612 Herbert Ave.
Herbert, Sask. S0H 2A0

TYPE OF MERCHANDISE: Clothing,
housewares
DONATION TAX RECEIPT: Check store policy
TVI Value Village Thrift Store
1230 Broad St.
Regina, Sask. S4R 1Y3
CONTACT: Steve Tod
PHONE: 306-522-1228
HOURS: Mon.–Fri. 9–9, Sat. 9–6
TYPE OF MERCHANDISE: Clothing,
housewares, furniture
DONATION TAX RECEIPT: No
Salvation Army Thrift Store
1733 Dewdney Ave. E
Regina, Sask. S4R 1G5
TYPE OF MERCHANDISE: Clothing,
housewares, furniture
DONATION TAX RECEIPT: Check store policy
Salvation Army Thrift Store
3524 13th Ave.
Regina, Sask. S4T 1P7
TYPE OF MERCHANDISE: Clothing,
housewares, furniture
DONATION TAX RECEIPT: Check store policy
Salvation Army Thrift Store
455 Broad St. N
Regina, Sask. S4R 1X4
TYPE OF MERCHANDISE: Clothing,
housewares, furniture
DONATION TAX RECEIPT: Check store policy
Salvation Army Thrift Store
5052 Fourth Ave.
Regina, Sask. S4T 0J6
TYPE OF MERCHANDISE: Clothing,
housewares, furniture
DONATION TAX RECEIPT: Check store policy
MCC The Clothes Basket
1008 Seventh St.
Rosthern, Sask. S0K 3R0
TYPE OF MERCHANDISE: Clothing,
housewares
DONATION TAX RECEIPT: Check store policy
MCC Clothes Closet & Global Village Crafts
127 20th St. W
Saskatoon, Sask. S7M 0W7
TYPE OF MERCHANDISE: Clothing,
housewares
DONATION TAX RECEIPT: Check store policy

Salvation Army Thrift Store
  1501 Eighth St. E
  Saskatoon, Sask. S7H 5J6
  TYPE OF MERCHANDISE: Clothing,
  housewares, furniture
  DONATION TAX RECEIPT: Check store
  policy

Salvation Army Thrift Store
  1619 29th St. W
  Saskatoon, Sask. S7L 0N6
  TYPE OF MERCHANDISE: Clothing,
  housewares, furniture
  DONATION TAX RECEIPT: Check store
  policy

TVI Value Village Thrift Store
  2115 Faithfull Ave.
  Saskatoon, Sask. S7K 1T8
  CONTACT: Martie La Pointe
  PHONE: 306-668-6161
  HOURS: Mon.–Fri. 9–9, Sat. 9–6
  TYPE OF MERCHANDISE: Clothing,
  housewares, furniture
  DONATION TAX RECEIPT: No

Salvation Army Thrift Store
  248 Edson St.
  Saskatoon, Sask. S7J 0P9
  TYPE OF MERCHANDISE: Clothing,
  housewares, furniture
  DONATION TAX RECEIPT: Check store
  policy

Salvation Army Thrift Store
  511 33rd St.
  Saskatoon, Sask. S7L 0V7
  TYPE OF MERCHANDISE: Clothing,
  housewares, furniture
  DONATION TAX RECEIPT: Check store
  policy

Salvation Army Thrift Store
  705 Central Ave. #7
  Saskatoon, Sask. S7N 3A4
  TYPE OF MERCHANDISE: Clothing,
  housewares, furniture
  DONATION TAX RECEIPT: Check store
  policy

Salvation Army Thrift Store
  720 Broadway
  Saskatoon, Sask. S7N 1B4
  TYPE OF MERCHANDISE: Clothing,
  housewares, furniture
  DONATION TAX RECEIPT: Check store
  policy

MCC Gift and Thrift
  50 Central Ave. N
  Swift Current Sask. S9H 0K7
  TYPE OF MERCHANDISE: Clothing,
  housewares
  DONATION TAX RECEIPT: Check store
  policy

Appendix A

Glossary of Terms and Buzzwords

Antique: No matter how you slice it, the items must be at least *one hundred years old* or older.

Art Deco: 1920–1930.

Art Nouveau: 1880–1914.

Arts and Crafts: 1890–1914.

Be-backs: The people who proclaim as they walk away from a dealer's table, "We'll think about it and be back."

Cherry: Perfect condition.

Circa (ca.): This means dated about the year indicated, usually within ten years earlier or later.

Collectible: Anything that is presently desirable to consumers; not necessarily an antique (the two can be mutually exclusive). It usually refers to items of fashion or furnishing that were made between the 1940s and 1960s.

Consignment: A way of selling merchandise whereby the proceeds from a sale are shared between the seller (consignee or store) and the consignor. Note that the consignment store (owner/operator) does not take title to merchandise—it only facilitates the transaction between the seller and the end user.

Dustible: This is an item that someone may try to pass off as a collectible, but it is usually only about eight to fifteen years old and presently doesn't have any value except for collecting dust.

Early bird shopper: Those who pester you by arriving too early with flashlights waiting for you to set up your treasures for sale; what *you* should aspire to be when you are out there shopping.

Edwardian: 1901–1910.

Fair market value: What other dealers are offering an item for, coupled with what the public will pay. IRS definition: The price at which property would change hands between a willing buyer and a willing seller, neither being required to buy or sell, and both having reasonable knowledge of all the relevant facts.

Game, the: The business of buying and selling merchandise for profit. Also, how much or how little you or the dealer will really take for an item.

Garage saler: Those who shop at garage sales.

Georgian: 1714–1837.

Haggler: Someone who knows how to wheel and deal in order to get their best possible price from the person selling. A good haggler is someone you should aspire to be, and someone you need to be savvy to deal with.

High-end dealers: People who deal in higher-priced merchandise of superior quality.

Industry: Anyone who works in the antique or collectible resale market.

Lookie-looker: People who come to your sales really just to window-shop; they seldom buy.

Members of the trade: Art directors, interior designers, antique dealers.

Mint condition: (*Primo, Cherry* or *like new*) The best possible condition an item can be in, in order to demand the highest possible price. This means no damage or repair. Usually, the condition it was in when it came off the rack or out of the box.

Museum day: When everyone who comes to your sale seems to think you're running a museum, and all they do is look and touch but never buy.

Outdated: This refers to fashion that has had its time, usually about five to twenty years. The item is still not old enough to be considered retro, vintage, collectible or antique; however, in a few years it's sure to resurface as fashionable again.

Picker: Someone who buys things at flea markets or thrift stores and sells them to other dealers or stores for a profit.

Player: Those who are in "the game"; a dealer or member of the trade or industry.

Price, best possible: Using every trick in *this* book, what you attempt to negotiate for.

Price, final selling: The amount an item sells for after all discounts and markdowns.

Price, floor: This price may be higher than the list price on your consignment contract, to incorporate the store's costs.

Price, honest: The true value and date of the item (based on the recognized sale markdown and depreciation factors).

Price, list: Per your consignment contract, the price that your garment will sell for and for which you will receive a percentage.

Price, original purchase: The original retail price paid, that is, the first price the item sold for.

Retro: This refers to fashion and furnishings dating from about 1935 to 1950.

Stingy cheapskate: No one *you* ever want to be or do business with!

Thrifter: Anyone who shops alternatively in thrift shops and flea markets, etc.

Underground economy: A system in which the participants make their living in a cash-only or barter-only business and do not report their income to the IRS.

Victorian, early to late: 1837–1901.

Vintage: A broad term used by the industry. It can refer to fashions and furnishings dated anywhere from the 1920s to the 1970s.

Wily huckster: Shrewd, disingenuous, crafty, cagey, canny, sly, tricky, clever seller whom you need to be on guard against.

Ãppendix B

Selected Reading and References

BOOKS

Berthold-Bond, Annie. *Clean and Green.* Woodstock, N.Y.: Ceres Press, 1990.

Collector Books. *Wanted to Buy: A Listing of Serious Buyers Paying CASH for Everything Collectible!* 4th ed. Paducah, Ky.: Collector Books, 1993.

Ensko, Stephen, G. C. *American Silversmiths and Their Marks: The Definitive (1948) Edition with 226 Illustrations.* New York: Dover, 1983.

Kovel, Ralph and Terry. *Kovel's New Dictionary of Marks: Pottery and Porcelain 1850 to the Present.* New York: Crown, 1986.

LaFarge, Albert. *Flea Market Directory: Over 850 of the Best Flea Markets from Coast to Coast.* New York: The Confident Collector, Avon Books, 1993.

Levine, Michael. *Guerrilla P.R.; How You Can Wage an Effective Publicity Campaign . . . Without Going Broke.* New York: HarperBusiness, 1993.

Miller, Anna M. *The Buyer's Guide to Affordable Antique Jewelry: How to Find, Buy and Care for Fabulous Antique Jewelry.* New York: Carol Publishing, 1993.

Pickford, Ian. *Jackson's Hallmarks: Pocket Edition, English, Scottish, Irish Silver & Gold Marks from 1300 to the Present Day.* Woodbridge, Suffolk, England: Antique Collectors' Club, 1991.

NEWSLETTERS

Recycling Times, The Newspaper of Recycling Markets. Recycling Times, P.O. Box 420168, Palm Coast, FL 32142-0168.

The Resale Connection. P.O. Box 562, Palm Harbor, FL 34682-0562.

Second Hand News. 3120 Forty-first St., San Diego, CA 92105-4133.

Society of Decorative Plastics. P.O. Box 199, Guerneville, CA 95446.

Thrift Score, A Zine About Thriftin'. P.O. Box 90282, Pittsburgh, PA 15224 (E-mail: hoffo@drycas.club.cc.cmu.edu).

Too Good to Be Threw. Kate Holmes, Katydid Press, 1521 W. Fifth Ave., Columbus, OH 43212.

The Upscale Downscale Times. BargainWave Publications, P.O. Box 511, Healdsburg, CA 95448.

Vintage Clothing Newsletter. P.O. Box 1422, Corvallis, OR 97339.

Vintage Fashion & Costume Jewelry Club Newsletter. P.O. Box 265, Glen Oaks, NY 11004.

ASSOCIATIONS

Canadian Conservation Institute. 1030 Innes Rd., Ottawa, Ontario, Canada K1A 0C8. (613) 998-3721.

NARTS, National Association of Resale and Thrift Shops. 153 Halsted, Chicago Heights, IL 60411.

National Costume Society of America. 55 Edgewater Dr., P.O. Box 73, Earleville, MD 21919. (410) 275-2329.

National Recycling Coalition Inc. 1101 Thirtieth St. NW, Suite 305, Washington, DC 20007.

TALK RADIO SHOW

"Your Money's Worth," a talk radio program about thrift and consignment shopping. Sunday, 1:00 P.M. to 2:00 P.M. WCEM 680 AM radio. Toll free: 1-800-922-6680. Write to: "Your Money's Worth," 68 Radio Plaza, Owings Mills, MD 21117; Attention: Lois Madow.

Barbie Dolls and The Rag Street Recycling Program

The Rag Street Recycling Program is a program designed to recycle Barbie, her friends, and accessories by giving them to less fortunate little girls across the country.

Vanity Fair, in the May 1994 issue, announced Barbie's (and family members') thirty-fifth anniversary and boasted a population growth worldwide at 800 million.

According to one of Mattel's press releases, if all the eleven-and-one-half inch Barbie dolls sold since 1959 were laid head to high-heeled foot, "The doll would circle the Earth more than six times. . . . In 1993, on average, over one million Barbie dolls were sold per week. . . . Two Barbie dolls are sold every second somewhere in the world."

In a recent press release, Mattel stated that "more than 100 million yards of fabric have gone into making Barbie's and her friends' fashions, and that over 900 million fashions have been produced since 1959 as well as more than a billion pairs of shoes."

Discarded garments account for 4 percent of the trash dumped in our landfills each year. Textiles are a higher fraction of the residential solid waste stream than corrugated cardboard or magazines.

In 1993, America used 921 million pounds of plastic to make toys. Statistically, substantially less than 1 percent of all plastic toys are recycled every year. Industry sources say that 97 percent to 98 percent of *all* plastics end up in landfills or are incinerated.

I bought a doll at a garage sale for my four-year-old niece and to this day it is her *most* loved treasure. Little girls love Barbie and always will. However, this particular one came with no fancy boxes or wrapping. *Packaging accounts for 30 percent of the nation's solid waste.*

I think many of us are aware of Barbie as a collectible commodity. I am not suggesting anyone recycle their original Bob Mackie "Empress Bride" Barbie doll (valued at between $300 and $500, according to Dunning's Auction Service in Elgin, Illinois). She should take her rightful place and sit high on a shelf out of Fido's reach.

What I'm suggesting is that we recycle *all* those contemporary items that will have to hang around for years before they are recognized collectibles, *if ever.* I am referring to the dolls, clothing, and accessories that will get stashed in the back of the garage—all the stuff that doesn't get sold in your Last Chance Garage Sales and is destined for our landfills.

It is those items that I am calling to you to pack up and ship to The Rag Street Recycling Program, where Barbie, her friends, garments, and accessories will find their way into the loving arms of little girls. It is there that Barbie and her friends will escape our overflowing landfills and begin a whole new existence in The Circle of Life.

Please send your Barbie recyclables to:

> Elizabeth M. Mason
> The Rag Street Recycling Program
> P.O. Box 69A116
> Los Angeles, CA 90069

Note: If you include a self-addressed stamped envelope with your package, I will send you an update on your doll's new home and a certificate inscribed to you as an Honorary Member of The Rag Street Recycling Program.

The Rag Street Journal
Wants Your Best Stories!

I would love you to share your best thrifting stories with me. What was the craziest, wackiest thing you ever bought, where did you buy it, and how much did you pay for it? What is the most expensive thing you ever found for the least amount of money? Don't forget that every picture tells a story, so if you have a picture of that item, send it along too. Please don't be shy—include a picture of yourself so I can put a face to your name.

What is that one elusive item that you would do anything to find? Perhaps it was a favorite toy or doll, your monster model, Frosty's Snow Cone Machine, or Pitiful Polly doll. What is it you long for and why?

Perhaps there is a possession you once held dear, and could have died when you discovered Mom had shipped it off to the Salvation Army. Tell me your worst nightmare . . . the day *they* (usually a well-intentioned parent on a cleaning spree) gave that steamer trunk with all your worldly possessions (well, at least your entire baseball card collection, some old soccer shoes, and a broken tennis racket) to that nice man with the big truck. There you were, carefree and away at college, dreaming of the day you would return and sell your Barbie doll collection and buy that dream house with the profits!

Additional Listings

I have attempted to make the listings in this book as up to date as possible; however, it is conceivable that new treasure troves have popped up since its publication. It is likewise conceivable that some shops may unfortunately no longer be in business. If you would like to see your favorite shop included in upcoming editions, or if you know of a shop that should be removed from the listings, please send your information and comments to:

>*The Rag Street Journal*
>**Your Best**
>**P.O. Box 69A116**
>**Los Angeles, CA 90069**

If you wish to subscribe to the *Rag Street Journal Newsletter,* please send a self-addressed stamped envelope to:

>*The RAG STREET JOURNAL*
>Newsletter
>P.O. Box 69A116
>Los Angeles, CA 90069